Francis A. Drexel
LIBRARY

Books for College Libraries
Third Edition

Core Collection

PITT LATIN AMERICAN SERIES

Social Security in Latin America

Social Security in Latin America

Social
Security

in Latin America

Pressure Groups, Stratification, and Inequality

Carmelo Mesa-Lago

UNIVERSITY OF PITTSBURGH PRESS

Published by the University of Pittsburgh Press, Pittsburgh, Pa. 15260
Copyright © 1978, University of Pittsburgh Press
All rights reserved
Feffer and Simons, Inc., London
Manufactured in the United States of America

Library of Congress Cataloging in Publication Data

Mesa Lago, Carmelo.
  Social security in Latin America.

  (Pitt Latin American series)
  Includes index.
  1. Social security—Latin America—Case studies.
I. Title.
HD7130.5.M47   368.4′0098   77–15732
ISBN 0-8229-3368-3

This book is devoted to the millions of workers and peasants in Latin America who suffer from lack of coverage or poor protection against social risks. It is intended as a modest contribution to the long quest for a universal, unified, uniform, and equitable social security system in the region.

Contents

Figures

Tables

Degree of Social Security Protection of the Economically Active Population by State/
Province

Social Security Contributions from Employees, Employers, and State by Occupational Group

Percentage Distribution of Social Security Fund Revenues by Financing Source and
Occupational Group

Revenue of Social Security Funds per Insured by Occupational Group

Transfer of Social Security Costs Among Occupational Groups

Cost of Social Security

Social Security Benefits by Occupational Group

Average Yearly Pensions [and Family Allowances*] by Occupational Group

Health Facilities and Expenditures by Occupational Group/Sector

Preface

This book is the end product of two decades of study; compilation of legislation, statistics, and technical reports; discussion, analysis, and writing on the subject of social security. It began in 1957 when I was studying for a doctorate in law at the Universidad de Madrid and pursuing at the same time special training at the Organización Iberoamericana de Seguridad Social (OISS). My dissertation dealt with the legal, administrative, and social problems generated by the multiplicity and heterogeneity of social security systems around the world, and especially in Cuba, and prescribed unification and standardization as ideal solutions. It was eventually published in Madrid by the OISS (*Planificación de la seguridad social: Análisis especial de la problemática cubana,* 1959) with a second edition in Havana (1960). As a brand new graduate, at the beginning of 1959 I had the precious opportunity of immediately implementing my thesis recommendations in Cuba when the newly installed revolutionary government entrusted me with the challenging task of social security reform. With the aid of the International Labor Organization (ILO) and Cuban experts, I founded the Banco de Seguros Sociales de Cuba which, without delay, began the gradual unification and standardization of fifty-four social security funds, a goal completed in 1963 after I had left the island. Coming to the United States in 1962, I was able to continue the study of social security, but under a new perspective, as a research associate and graduate student in economics at the University of Miami. While there, I co-authored a comprehensive analysis of Cuba's social security which contrasted the pre-revolutionary situation with the revolutionary reform (*Social Security in Cuba,* 1964). In the School of Labor and Industrial Relations at Cornell University, studying for a Ph.D. in labor economics and social security (1965–1968), I expanded my comparative vision of social security by doing research on the systems of Chile, Yugoslavia, China, and the USSR.

Field work for this book began in Argentina and Chile, in the spring and summer of 1969, under a faculty research grant from the Center for Latin American Studies of the University of Pittsburgh. It continued in the winter and spring of 1971, with research in Mexico, Peru, and Uruguay financed by a Fulbright-Hays faculty research grant. The computations and most of the writing of the book were done in 1972–1974 with the generous support of two postdoctoral research grants from the Foreign Area Fellowship Program of the Social Science Research Council (SSRC) and the American Council of Learned Societies (ACLS). In 1975, a new grant from SSRC-ACLS enabled me to organize an Inter-American Research Training Seminar on the subject of this book at the Centro Interamericano de Seguridad Social, Mexico

City. The seminar, co-directed by James M. Malloy and me, provided a forum in which eighteen doctoral students and professionals, in various disciplines, coming from the United States and Latin America, systematically compared and analyzed eight Latin American social security systems from a social-sciences perspective. This book was greatly enriched by that seminar which also stimulated a dozen participants to do further research in seven Latin American countries. Finally, the editing and indexing of the book were financed by the Center for International Studies of the University of Pittsburgh.

Several graduate students from the University of Pittsburgh, who were my research assistants either at the Center for Latin American Studies or under SSRC grants, gave substantial aid in the preparation of this book: Ernesto Quintanilla, now professor of economics at the Universidad de Nuevo León, assisted in the collection of data on Mexico and in the initial computations; Arturo Porzecanski, now economist at the Morgan Guaranty Trust Company, New York, prepared the chapter on Uruguay; David Hoelscher, now visiting professor at the Universidad Ténica Federico Santamaría, Valparaíso, helped in a second stage of the computations; Mitchell A. Seligson, now assistant professor of political science at the University of Arizona, computed the factor analysis and KYST discussed in appendix H, as well as the standardized scores and means used in the conclusions; and Steven Reed, my current assistant, provided invaluable aid in the final revision of all computations and in the refining of the comparative tables in the conclusions. Useful criticism and suggestions were made by participants in the SSRC-ACLS seminar in Mexico: Mark Rosenberg, now assistant professor of political science at Florida International University; Richard Wilson, Ph.D. candidate in sociology at Yale University; Ariel Gianola, magistrate in the administrative-labor court of Montevideo; Aldo Isuani, professor of political science at the Universidad de Cuyo, Mendoza, and currently Mellon Fellow at the University of Pittsburgh; Rose Spalding, Ph.D. candidate in government at the University of North Carolina; Eduardo Viñuela, professor of sociology at the Universidad Católica de Chile, and currently Tinker Research Fellow at the University of Pittsburgh; and Elizabeth Beardsley, Ph.D. candidate in political science at Stanford University.

In the field research for the book I obtained information on legislation, statistics, technical reports, academic works, and advice from hundreds of scholars, officials from social security and government institutions, and leaders from labor unions and management associations. It is obviously impossible to list all of them here but I am obliged to show my gratitude at least to those who were most helpful: Guillermo Cabanellas, Juan J. Etala, Humberto Podetti, Alfredo Ruprecht, Mario Deveali, and Héctor Genoud (Argentina); Luis Orlandini, Eduardo Miranda, Mercedes Ezquerra, Francisco Walker Linares, Jorge Tapia Videla, and Luis Santibáñez (Chile); Lucila Leal de Araujo, Gastón Novelo, Mario de la Cueva, Juan Bernaldo de Quirós, Jaime González, and Ricardo Orozco (Mexico); José Gómez Sánchez, Julio Chávez Ferrer, Luis Aparicio Valdez, Jorge García la Puerta, César San Román, and Martín Fajardo C. (Peru); and Ariel Gianola, Américo Pla Rodríguez, Francisco de Ferrari, Oscar Monserrat, Rafael Gelós, and Ofelia Belistri (Uruguay).

In reciprocity for the generous aid given by Latin Americans I have made a special effort to publish the results of my research in various countries of the region: *Modelos de seguridad social en América Latina: Estudio comparado* (Buenos Aires: Ediciones SIAP, 1977); "Social Security Stratification and Inequality in Mexico," in *Contemporary Mexico: Papers of the IV International Congress of Mexican History,*

J. W. Wilkie, M. C. Mayer and E. M. Wilkie, eds. (Berkeley-México: University of California Press-El Colegio de México, 1976), pp. 228–255; *La seguridad social* (Santiago: CEPLAN, no. 50, 1975)—publication cancelled for political reasons; and "La estratificación de la seguridad social y el efecto de desigualdad en América Latina: El caso peruano," *Estudios Andinos,* 3:2 (1973), pp. 17–47. Publication of the Uruguayan case study is under negotiation with the Biblioteca de Derecho Laboral Montevideo. I have also lectured on or presented papers on the subject at: Universidad de Buenos Aires; Seminario Latinoamericano de Previdência Social, Universidade de Brasília; Pontificia Universidad Javeriana, Bogotá; Programa Regional de Empleo para América Latina y el Caribe, and Universidad Católica de Chile, Santiago; Centro Interamericano de Estudios Seguridad Social, Mexico City, and Universidad de Nuevo León, Monterrey; Seguro Social del Perú and Universidad del Pacífico, Lima; Universidad del Uruguay, Montevideo; and Universidad de Trabajadores de América Latina, Caracas.

The following specialists commented on chapters or parts of the book: Robert J. Alexander, professor of economics, Rutgers University; Rainer C. Baum, associate professor of sociology, University of Pittsburgh; Héctor Diéguez, senior economist, Instituto Torcuato Di Tella; Paul Fisher, chief International Staff, Office of External Affairs, Social Security Administration; Beryl Frank, chief Department of Social and Institutional Development, Organization of American States; Duncan MacIntyre, and James O. Morris, professors of industrial and labor relations, Cornell University; James M. Malloy, professor of political science, and Magnus Mörner, Mellon professor of history, both at the University of Pittsburgh; Alejandro Portes, professor of sociology, Duke University; Aldo Solari, senior sociologist at the Instituto Latinoamericano de Planificación Económica y Social; Peter Thullen, former chief of the social security division of the International Labour Office; and Marshall Wolfe, chief of the Division of Social Development of the Economic Commission for Latin America.

The staff of the Center for Latin American Studies of the University of Pittsburgh provided pivotal help in the physical completion of this book: my assistant director Shirley Kregar edited and proofread several drafts; my administrative assistant Carolyn Wilson and secretaries Erma MacPherson and Lori Stuart typed the manuscript several times. The final editing was done by Eleanor Walker.

The previous long list of acknowledgments makes it evident that this book is not the work of an individual alone but truly the result of a collective undertaking. While assuming full responsibility for all that is said here, I express my deep appreciation for the invaluable cooperation received by all those listed above and many others who remain unnamed. Finally a special recognition to my wife Elena and my daughters Elizabeth, Ingrid, and Helena, who for seven interminable years were coparticipants in the agony involved in the completion of this enterprise, giving me crucial support with their patience and love.

Social Security in Latin America

1 Introduction

Significance, Objectives, Organization, and Methodology

Social security is one of the most important social services in Latin America today.[1] In some countries of Latin America, social security expenditures take as much as 15 percent of the Gross National Product (GNP), substantially more than what those countries spend on public health and close to what they spend on education. If health services are considered a component of social security, the latter becomes the most costly social service in the region and one of the most onerous in the world. Social security annual revenues are equivalent in some Latin American countries to total government revenue. Despite the scarcity of capital in the region, social security funds are seldom invested efficiently. The generosity of social security benefits and magnitude of their cost, combined with the poor handling of financial resources, have contributed to runaway inflation, financial crises, economic stagnation, and the decline of living standards in some Latin American countries.

In addition to its economic importance, social security has obvious social and political significance. If its theoretical principle of solidarity is adequately pursued, social security can become an efficient means to achieve a better income redistribution by taxing the wealthy to help the needy. In real life, however, social security in Latin America has often been manipulated to gain the electoral support of a particular clientele, to legitimate a spurious political regime, and to satisfy the needs and coopt powerful pressure groups which threaten the status quo.

In spite of its pivotal economic, social, and political prominence in Latin America, social security has rarely been included in national planning and has received scant attention in social science literature. Most published scholarly works and technical reports from international and regional organizations on the subject have focused on the historical and juridical aspects of social security or on the technical aspects of its administration, such as actuarial and financial, medical and rehabilitative, bureaucratic and informational. More surprising, social security has seldom been used as a social or economic indicator in Latin America or elsewhere. In a recent study by the Economic Commission for Latin America (ECLA), in which forty-three socioeconomic indicators were computed to measure and classify the level of development of the countries in the region, none was based on any aspect of social security.[2] Furthermore, the United Nations has pointed out that social security is one of the areas in which it is not possible to find suitable indicators for international comparison.[3]

In a few instances, selective Latin American social security programs have been included in cross-national, aggregate, quantitative studies aimed at establishing classificatory schemes by which to evaluate the countries in the comparison. These studies, nevertheless, have normally relied on the deficient information available, without generating new data, and have arrived at gross generalizations since they did not involve an in-depth study of the countries in question.[4] Calling attention to the technical problems arising from international comparisons of social security (compounded in Latin America by the poor availability and reliability of data), Vladimir Rys has recommended that substantial work first be done in individual countries:

> A start should be made with national case studies concerning two or three countries and permitting sociological analysis in depth. A research worker must obligatorily pass through this stage if he is to appreciate the difficulty involved in large-scale studies and if he wishes to fabricate reasonably reliable tools for international analysis. The basic work has to be done and the methods must be tested in this field before any real progress can be achieved on a world scale.[5]

This book constitutes the first attempt to apply social science approaches and methodolgies in a multidisciplinary manner to the comparative study of social security in various Latin American countries. For that purpose I have relied essentially on my formal training in law, economics, and industrial relations and on my rudimentary knowledge of political science and sociology. The reader should logically expect a divergent degree of sophistication in the use of social science techniques relative to the various disciplines involved in this study. The overall goal of the book is to analyze the principal inputs and outputs of the social security system, that is, the major forces which determine its inception and evolution and its outcome in terms of the distribution of its services. It is my contention that both aspects are closely interrelated: a variety of pressure groups with divergent powers constitute the predominant factor in the historical inception of a "stratified" social security system in Latin America, and that system generates significant inequalities in the distribution of its services.[6]

The book has three concrete objectives: first, to describe in a comparative manner the role of pressure groups and subgroups in the gradual development of a stratified social security system in five Latin American countries since colonial times; second, to analyze the current inequalities generated by this stratified system in the coverage of the population, manner of financing, and benefits available to those insured; third, to develop a set of standardized indicators of these inequalities and integrate them in order to compare the five countries and rank them according to their degree of social security inequality.

In order to implement these objectives, the book is divided into three major parts: an introduction, five case studies, and the conclusions. The introduction reviews the various forces that shape the inception of social security and selects the force that, in my opinion, is most significant: pressure groups. A typology of pressure groups is developed and a model (which integrates a set of hypotheses) is proposed to explain the inequality effects of social security stratification. The current stratification of social security is shown to have its antecedents in colonial practices.

The core of the study is composed of chapters 2 to 6, where the ideal typology and hypotheses are tested in five Latin American countries: Chile, Uruguay, Peru, Argentina, and Mexico. These countries were selected because they represent a spectrum in terms of the time of inception of social security, the scope of their systems, and the socio-politico-economic regimes existing in them.[7]

Field research was conducted in 1969 and 1971 in the five countries selected and, as a result, fairly complete collections of social security legislation, statistics, and technical and background literature were gathered. More than 200 informal interviews were held with government officials, social security administrators, trade union leaders, managers, and university specialists. The objectives of these interviews were to fill gaps in the information, grasp the reality of the situation aside from law and statistics, and detect whether and how the problem of stratification was understood by these sectors of the population.

Each country study is divided into three sections: (1) a chronology of the evolution of social security from independence until the early 1970s, in which the main pressure groups are identified and their role in stratification is analyzed; (2) a description of the current structure and organization of the stratified social security system circa 1970; and (3) a statistical analysis of social security inequalities during the 1960s. Findings in the first and third sections are summarized at the end of each. In the statistical analysis, a set of fifteen standardized tables contrasts the various pressure groups in terms of: (a) time of inception of various coverages; (b) their degree of coverage; (c) the financing mechanisms of the groups' funds and overall cost of the social security system; and (d) the inequalities of the system of benefits. To facilitate comparisons and final integration, each of the fifteen standardized tables is denoted in the case studies with the same number, preceded by the number of the corresponding chapter. When a table could not be included in a case study because of lack of adequate data, the corresponding number is skipped.

In the concluding chapter of the study, the five countries are compared to show similarities and differences of the pressure groups' role in gaining social security protection. In addition, nineteen indicators of inequality are computed from the fifteen standardized tables of the case studies and used for comparison, analysis, and testing of the hypotheses. Finally, the indicators are integrated to rank the countries in terms of their overall social security inequality.

The analysis of the case studies in this book is lengthy and complex. For those readers who want to skip historical details and statistical analyses, I have provided three summaries in each of chapters 2 through 6: the concluding paragraph of "The Historical Evolution of Social Security Since Independence," "The Role of Pressure Groups in Social Security Stratification," and "The Inequality Effect of Social Security Stratification." A shortcut to reading this book consists of the introduction, the summaries in each of the five case studies, and the conclusions.

Forces Shaping the Inception and Stratification of Social Security

Social security has evolved through five centuries in Latin America in a piecemeal fashion. Its antecedents can be traced to pre-Columbian cultures and Iberian colonial governments (see "The Stratification of Social Protection in the Colonial Period" below), although modern institutions gradually appeared in the republican period and have flourished especially since the 1920s. As new institutions were juxtaposed to those already in existence, a mosaic of divergent forms of protection evolved. Within one country and among several countries, marked differences in coverage and degree and quality of protection of the population against various social risks or contingencies exist. In some countries with a relatively new social security system (e.g., most of Central America), coverage is limited to part of the salaried labor force living in the capital city or most populated areas. In a few countries with old social security systems (e.g., Chile, Uruguay), coverage extends to almost the whole labor force and the majority of the population, but there are different degrees and quality of protection. There are countries (e.g., Mexico, Peru) in which the social security system has begun to expand to rural areas but still has remarkable differences in protection among segments of the labor force and geographical regions.[8] Social security in Latin America has become a mirror that reflects the overall societal stratification.

The pattern of the general evolution of social security in the world can be explained in various ways. The traditional position rather superficially relies on altruistic or humanistic reasons: society introduces social security to help the worker who— affected by a social risk, e.g., occupational accident—has lost or suffered a reduction in his source of income. In this position social security is also seen as a mechanism for income redistribution—to help the needy in society by taxing the wealthy.[9] Another explanation points to "diffusion" as the main cause of social security inception; that is, the demonstrative effect of nations with active social security programs or the influence of international organizations that support such programs (e.g., the International Labor Organization, ILO).[10] A third position points to idiosyncratic forces: a president or high government official, hoping to build his personal or national prestige and power, may paternalistically introduce social security to help the needy, or in response to programs in other nations (due to the demonstrative effect explained above), or to avoid social strife.[11] Although these interpretations may be correct in some countries and at given points in history, they do not explain systematically the underlying forces behind the universal inception of social security through history.

A more refined position explicates the phenomenon in question as a product of the socio-politico-economic structure. Thus it is argued that social security is the result of the process of industrialization, urbanization, and modernization which erodes the traditional private means of social protection (the extended family, the guild) and necessitates the introduction of public means of protection to reduce social turmoil. Environmental or administrative factors can also be crucial in the decision of whom to grant protection first: it is easier and cheaper to protect urban wage-earners than peasants or the self-employed. (The former are concentrated, they are more easily identified, and they earn salaries which are taxable and have employers capable of paying, while the opposite is true of peasants and self-employed.) Economic reasons affecting the inception of social security are: increases in labor productivity, incentives to generate certain skills needed in the labor market, provision of minimum income to the unemployed to help break a recession or avoid a depression by guaranteeing a stable level of demand and consumption. Politically, social security is seen as the result of the power that pressure groups have to extract concessions from the state or as a state instrument to neutralize and coopt such groups, avoid grave conflicts, and maintain the status quo and political stability.[12] Rather than being mutually exclusive, this second set of explanations appears as coadjutant to me. The process of industrialization constitutes the foundation of a modern economy in which the market and cycles play the above-mentioned roles. Industrialization also goes hand in hand with a modern state and the generation of social ferment and conflict among interest groups. Notice also that some of the economic reasons are tied to the political ones; for instance, the creation of unemployment relief can be justified as an anticyclical device but also as an instrument for avoiding a source of popular discontent, social strife, and political instability.

If we take the socio-politico-economic structure as the force behind the inception of social security, we see an intimate relation between structure, societal stratification, and pressure groups. Based on my own experience and observation, I perceive social security stratification as a reflection of overall societal stratification and pressure groups as the link between the two. (It is not my aim to prove here the relationship between these factors but simply to identify potential sources of social security stratification.) Some sources of social stratification identified by sociologists are: occupation, income, status, place of residence, race, education, and access to weapons. Although all these sources of societal stratification seem to be pertinent also in social security stratification, the occupational structure appears as the predominant one.

The role of the occupational structure has been pivotal in determining rewards and inequalities in both modern (or developed) and traditional (or developing) societies. In industrialized, market-economy societies, a typical hierarchy of occupations appears as follows: (1) professional, managerial, and top administrative; (2) semi-professional, lower administrative, and top white-collar; (3) average white-collar and skilled blue-collar; (4) semiskilled blue-collar; and (5) unskilled blue-collar. The higher the occupation in the hierarchy, the larger the "reward" (salary, wages, fringe benefits, etc.) that it receives from society. Some sociologists assert that power is the key to the relationship between occupation and reward but have failed to explain the source of such power. The functionalist school maintains that both the occupational structure and the corresponding rewards are functions of the system's needs in a society. To define such "needs," some point vaguely to the maintenance of the social order.[13] An eclectic and broader interpretation is that the possession of skills which are scarce and have a high value in an industrialized-market economy conveys "market power," the most important single determinant of occupational reward and the dominant source of inequality. This theory admits that other "social influences" (e.g., status, trade union organization) may play some part in societal stratification but reduce such nonmarket factors to "secondary determinants." In nonindustrialized and less market-oriented economies, a greater variety in the sources of reward is found—such as military control over arms or the prestige of certain careers.[14] In this interpretation, social security is considered part of the "reward" that a society gives to its members according to established criteria based on occupation, job skills (education), status, military power, and so forth. Place of residence (urban versus rural) as well as race (white versus Indian) also appear as additional, interlocking sources of social security stratification.

Earlier we saw social security stratification as resulting from force brought by pressure groups or by the state cooptation of such groups. Stressing the first force, ECLA has suggested that the piecemeal growth of the social security system in Latin America is the result of pressures brought to bear by the better-educated and more influential urban minorities, the middle-income strata with organizational strength and electoral power, and that the system is manipulated for the benefit of that minority at the expense of the whole population.[15] Tapia and Parrish, from their study of the Chilean case, also find interest groups, operating in a milieu of political pluralism, as the key to explaining social security stratification and inequalities. Social security privileges are a function of the degree of "bargaining power" (in political terms) that groups in high and middle levels in society (mainly white-collars) have to articulate their interests, influence implementation of policies in their favor, and defend their acquired rights vis-a-vis other less powerful groups in the low levels (mainly blue-collars).[16] This explanation can be presented graphically with the following model:

$$PG \rightarrow S \rightarrow SS$$

Interest or pressure groups (PG) exert their power over the state (S) to obtain social security protection (SS).[17] The main actors or initiators in this model are the pressure groups (represented by a solid arrow), and this operation occurs in a pluralistic-democratic society.

The second explanation—the state as the major force in social security stratification—has been developed by Cotler and Astiz based on their analyses of the Peruvian power elite. They maintain that the status quo is preserved in Peru by state cooptation of relatively small pressure groups predominantly of urban and middle-class extraction (e.g., civil servants, professionals, white-collars, and blue-collars in strategic trades) who have education and skills and/or union and·political strength. In order to neutralize these "occupational enclaves," the elite in power have granted benefits (such as social security). This action, however, widens the gap between these middle and upper groups and the marginal sectors, the majority of the population in the lower class (the illiterate, unorganized, devoid-of-vote masses of peasants—essentially Indians in Peru—and the urban, unskilled, underemployed masses of workers). The coopted groups constantly push to improve their standards under the established order and often oppose a massive redistribution program that would incorporate the marginal sectors since this would jeopardize their advantages. Recently, the increased power of the marginal sectors (through political mobilization and unionization) has opened the door for their entrance into the system of privileges, but the size of such sectors presents a threat to the viability of such cooptation and the stability of the system.[18] This explanation can be presented graphically with the following model:

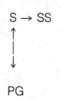

The state coopts the pressure groups by granting them social security protection. The main actor in this model is the state; there is a mutual influence between the state and pressure groups (represented by the dotted arrow) but the state, not the pressure groups, is the initiator of social security. This model functions better in an autocratic society, but it can also operate in a pluralistic one under certain circumstances.

Variations of the above two models can be developed by adding two other forces: political parties and the social security bureaucracy. Political parties may be instrumental in sponsoring social security measures in order to gain, maintain, or expand a political clientele. The social security bureaucracy may act, with relative independence, when making decisions such as expanding coverage to new groups, either as a response to its vested interests (survival, prestige, power, income) or to administrative-financial factors.[19] Various forces may operate in the same country at different historical periods (e.g., first pressure groups, then the state) or may intertwine at the same time (e.g., groups may exert pressure on the political parties or the social security bureaucracy and these in turn upon the state).

Without denying the importance that the state, political parties, and the bureaucracy may have had in certain countries and historical periods, I consider pressure groups as the most significant force, the one that can systematically and best explain the inception and stratification of social security throughout Latin American history. The other three forces often operate in response to, or in anticipation of, or as mediators of the demands of pressure groups. For instance, in the second model the presence of pressure groups is vital to allow the coopting action of the state. The same may be said of political parties serving an electoral clientele, that is, that clientele has to be there first and be important. The social security bureaucracy can only acquire power of its own and become a force in granting coverage after a segment of the population has already been covered.

If pressure groups are the force behind the inception and stratification of social security, it is necessary to identify those groups, their source of power, and their hierarchy. Roemer was probably the first to develop a hierarchy of these groups (which he called "social classes") in Latin America, in relation to the kind and quality of health care that they receive: (1) the elite (landowners, large merchants, industrialists, and upper-level professionals); (2) militarymen, policemen, and civil servants; (3) white-collar workers and small entrepreneurs; (4) manual industrial workers; (5) peasants, peons, and urban underemployed; and (6) the Indians. Roemer suggests the source of power of each group, but he does not elaborate on this significant subject.[20]

Wolfe's more sophisticated analysis of pressure groups in terms of social security in general proposes the following tentative hierarchy: (1) law-makers and law-enforcers; (2) civil servants (professionals and white-collars); (3) middle-class strata, urban salaried employees (mostly white-collars); (4) urban wage-earners (mostly blue-collars) in the better organized activities such as large-scale manufacturing, mining, and basic services such as transportation; and (5) the urban (e.g., domestic servants and other unskilled occupations) and rural low-income strata which constitute the majority of the population.[21] There are several significant aspects in this categorization. Groups whose power is political rather than market-based are at the top of the hierarchy. Civil servants occupy more or less the same position as in the occupational structure of developed economies but with a substantially larger share in social security expenditures.[22] Employees of social security funds (in the second group) appear as privileged as the professionals and well above the mass of the insured. The difference between white- and blue-collar workers does not seem exclusively determined by their respective skills, but also by geographical factors. The managerial group is excluded because, although at the top of the occupational structure, it does not use its "market power" to obtain social security protection but protects itself through property, savings, and private insurance and hospitals.

From this review of the various forces behind the inception of social security, that is, altruistic, diffusional, idiosyncratic, and structural, we have selected structural force as the most significant force influenced by economic, political, and social factors, especially pressure groups and the state. Pressure groups appear as the connecting link between societal stratification and social security stratification. The main source of both types of stratification seems to be the occupational structure: social security pressure groups are organized along occupational lines, e.g., militarymen, civil servants, white-collars, blue-collars, peasants. There is an apparent relationship between the occupational structure and other sources of stratification such as skills, income, status, location, and race. A few attempts have been made to develop a hierarchy of pressure groups in terms of the excellence of their social security protection. These hierarchies are synchronic and, hence, although valuable in their descriptive and categorical functions, they fail to adequately and systematically explain the boundary lines of social security stratification, the sources of power of the pressure groups, and the inequality effects of such stratification.

An Ideal Typology of Social Security Pressure Groups

In trying to develop a diachronic categorization, I have constructed four ideal types of social security pressure groups in Latin America according to their dominant source of power: (1) military, (2) politico-administrative, (3) economic or market, and (4) trade union.[23] Some of these groups may have multiple and divergent sources of power in different countries or even in the same country at various stages of evolution. Hence the groups and subgroups are classified in the ideal typology according to their most significant or common source of power, although references are made to other alternative power sources within each type.

Each of the four ideal types presented below includes: an identification of the major group of the labor force that the type embraces and of its potential subdivisions (subgroups); a description of the principal and secondary sources of power of the group; an historical account and analysis of the order of inception of the various forms of social security protection over social risks obtained by the group; and a preliminary evaluation of the excellence of the social security protection received by the group in comparison with the other groups.[24]

Military Pressure Group

The main source of power of the military pressure group (made up of various subgroups, i.e., the army, navy, air force, and police) is its control of weapons and its role in maintaining order. But with its traditional intervention in politics in Latin America, the group often has control of the government, either assuming power directly or behind the facade of a weak civilian regime. Taking advantage of its power, the military pressure group has granted itself or exerted pressure in order to receive the earliest, best, and cheapest social security protection.

Due to the nature of its activities, the group pushed first for disability and survivors' pensions and obtained them during the colonial times or after the wars of independence or wars with border states. In view of the frequent turnover among its ranks, the group next pressed for pensions for dismissal *(cesantía)* and seniority (with a short period of service). Old-age pensions had a low priority because most members of the group did not retire at an old age. Civilian governments, which often had to dismiss a powerful military official who posed a threat to their stability, also contributed to making less rigorous the conditions for retirement. Health coverage for this group came last in most countries because officials usually received special care in public hospitals or could afford private medical attention. With the increasing complexity and cost of modern medicine, and the expansion of coverage to all ranks (as well as opening the armed forces to the lower class in some countries), the need for special hospitals became apparent. Today the most modern and best-equipped hospitals in Latin America serve this group.

Protection of the subgroups has been gradual; it usually began with the army and the navy, was then expanded to the police, and finally to the air force. Often the subgroups compete among themselves for advantages in social security, the air force usually being the one with the best services available.

Politico-Administrative Pressure Group

The politico-administrative pressure group bases its power in handling national affairs, that is, law-making, adjudication, and administration. In those few countries in which political power is solidly held by civilians, the legislative, executive, and judicial branches of government are at the top of the social security hierarchy (or second to the military when these are in command). Congressmen have been quite generous in Chile, for instance, in adopting a privileged social security system for themselves. Judges and court officials have frequently traded their support to the executive for a first-class pension system. Other functionaries with juridical power such as notaries public (a high-status and well-paid profession in Latin America) and registrars of real estate also enjoy special privileges. Diplomats, who commonly are politicians or influential people, have obtained significant concessions. Lawyers are numerous in Latin America and many of them, in a situation of under-employment, turn their energies to politics where their influence wins them good social security protection.

In a hypertrophied civil service system, based more on political patronage than on merit and traditionally paying low salaries, privileged social security programs have become a reward for loyalty from high officials and a supplement to the civil servants' meager remuneration. In arbitration between traditional and new groups with conflicting demands, the government bureaucracy has granted social security benefits to the new groups to prevent revolution or military intervention and has eventually taken advantage of its power and protected itself. Countries with a federal type of government, such as Mexico, have developed a privileged social security system for federal employees vis-a-vis state employees.[¹] The employees of autonomous public agencies or corporations (including social security institutions) with administrative autonomy and autarkic sources of revenue have seldom submitted to central budgetary control and have granted themselves generous social security protection. Civil servants have also formed powerful unions in some countries and resorted to strikes to achieve their goals. In other cases, when their skills have been badly needed to keep the government machinery running, they have achieved protection through market power.

Within this group it is possible to include the news media (journalists, television, radio, and newspaper employees) who have the power to influence public opinion, criticize the government, and exert pressure. Weak governments have often yielded to the blackmail of this subgroup that has promised either silence or support in exchange for a good pension or health-care system.

The politico-administrative group received protection almost at the same time as (and in some countries preceding) the military group. First they obtained pensions for old age, disability, and survivors, then seniority and unemployment pensions, and finally health care and other benefits. The high turnover of civil servants with every change of government also resulted, as with the military, in less rigorous conditions for retirement for this group. It also created (e.g., in Peru, Chile) the unemployment pension which allows a dismissed young servant with a few years of service to "retire" and work in a salaried private job until he can return to the civil service again.

Economic or Market Pressure Group

The economic pressure group derives its strength from the importance that its scarce skills and/or the productive sector in which it works have for the nation's economy. This is the group which has mostly used market power to obtain social security protection. Typical here are professionals whose skills, generally in shortage, are badly needed, such as engineers, public accountants, university professors, teachers, merchant-marine officials, and physicians.[25]

In some Latin American countries there is a clear division between two sectors of the labor force: *empleados* and *obreros*. The former are white-collar, intellectual workers (e.g., office and bank clerks, bookkeepers, insurance agents, salesmen, foremen) of middle-class origin; they are usually paid on a monthly basis *(sueldo)*. *Obreros* are blue-collar workers whose activities are predominantly physical; they commonly come from the lower class and are paid on an hourly or daily basis *(jornal)*. This is analogous to the American salary/wage distinction. The type of occupation, like social class, has more significance for status than income or even skills. Generally, however, the income of *empleados* is substantially higher than that of *obreros*. The distinction between the two groups has been formalized in separate sections of the legislation or labor codes of some countries (e.g., Chile, Peru) with regulations and enforcement favoring *empleados* over *obreros*.[26] Social security echoes this discrimination, with white-collars obtaining better social security protection than blue-collars based partly on their skills but also on their traditionally higher social status. Thus it has been common that powerful blue-collars in strategic sectors (e.g., transportation) or in skilled trades (operators of mechanized equipment) have been assimilated into the white-collar group. In some countries white-collars have also successfully resorted to unions, collective bargaining, and even strikes to gain better social security protection.

Another sector that could be included in the economic pressure group is that of luxury activities linked with entertainment, with good profits and inelastic demands, for example, racetracks and certain artistic activities.

The economic pressure group has usually obtained social security protection long after the other two groups but before the union pressure group. Life insurance was granted first; the group placed higher priority on seniority than on old-age pensions, received health protection late (because originally its members were protected by *cofradías,* or health cooperatives, or could afford private medical attention) and showed little interest in unemployment relief (due to its relatively high job security).

Trade Union Pressure Group

The source of the power of the trade union pressure group (essentially *obreros* or blue-collars) is a combination of their activism through unions, strikes, and collective bargaining and of the strategic importance of their trade. Several subgroups could be distinguished in terms of power: the "labor aristocracy," the bulk of urban blue-collars, rural wage-earners on modern plantations, and the bulk of rural workers and peasants. Both domestic servants and the self-employed can be considered additional subgroups here or part of the noninsured.

The labor aristocracy is made up of a selective subgroup of skilled blue-collars, in strategic sectors of the economy, who are the best organized and most active. The transportation and communication sector (railroad, buses, street cars, "collective taxis," ports, telephone, and wire) and the strategic utilities such as water, gas, oil, and electricity have been the first blue-collar segments to obtain social security protection due to their ability to paralyze the country or the capital city or to stop the flow of imports or exports. In countries where a large portion of the GNP is generated by one product (oil in Venezuela, copper in Chile, sugar in Cuba, bananas in most of Central America), workers in these sectors wield similar power. All these trades became organized early in Latin America, developed strong trade unions, and frequently resorted to strikes. Further, many of the enterprises in which these workers are employed are either monopolies or foreign firms or both and enjoy high profits. Hence they can afford to pay higher social security benefits or easily transfer these costs to the public through price increases.

The bulk of the urban labor force has often won social security protection through political or idiosyncratic factors rather than strict union power. Political strikes and street violence staged by labor to overthrow a government or gain political leverage have sometimes resulted in concessions from weak governments that are afraid of losing office. In other cases, middle-class political parties that have reached power with the workers' support have honored their campaign promises and passed social security legislation for a large segment of the labor force basically made up of this subgroup.[27] Sometimes the bulk of the labor force has obtained social security protection before it has established itself as a powerful pressure group through paternalistic concessions from administration. The latter's objective has been to build up unions as a source of political support (e.g., Alessandri in Chile, Vargas in Brazil, Perón in Argentina) to prevent potential unrest among the underprivileged, or just as a matter of personal conviction of a liberal president, or to enhance national prestige by adhering to international (ILO) agreements.[28] Urban labor, placing a higher priority on the satisfaction of more immediate needs such as minimum wage, did not focus on winning social security protection until these vital needs were satisfied and the subgroup became better organized. Usually short-term risks that present an immediate and direct threat to the workers have received protection prior to long-term risks. For example, at the beginning of the century, the growing number of occupational accidents and professional diseases made coverage against these risks the object of numerous strikes and an explosive situation. The danger of contagious diseases and the lack of resources for medical care made health the next matter of protection. The subgroup has placed higher priority on disability and survivors' pensions than on old-age pensions. The pressure for unemployment compensation has been high, but due to the massive and chronic nature of this phenomenon, it has received protection in only a few Latin American countries.

Social security protection for the remaining subgroups has followed a pattern similar to that of the bulk of urban blue-collars but at a considerably later date. The most concentrated and best-organized rural subgroup (wage-earners on large-scale, modern plantations) were protected first. The bulk of rural workers and peasants followed suit but only in a few countries, in a slow and gradual manner and, frequently, after becoming organized and engaging in violence. Domestic servants and self-employed, probably the weakest subgroup, in most countries remain largely outside of the social security system or are covered only for a few services such as health care.

There are associations of domestic servants, usually poorly organized and weak, in only a few countries. The concentration of domestic servants and self-employed workers (together with other noninsured such as the unemployed and unskilled blue-collar workers) in shantytowns offers another possibility for the subgroup to exert power. However, shantytown communal associations usually place their highest priority on the legalization of their settlements and improvements such as water and electricity, while health care ranks as a lower priority with other communal services (e.g., schools, pavement of streets, public transportation). The scarce social security protection granted to this group has often been the result of government initiative in the pursuit of electoral or political support from the group.[29]

The Noninsured

Those left without social security protection are the wealthy (e.g., large entrepreneurs, financiers, landlords) and the subgroups of the labor force devoid of power because they are unskilled, highly dispersed, unorganized, working in economic sectors which are not strategically important, and without the right to vote because they are illiterate. These subgroups also present complex obstacles for coverage: dispersion, poor capacity to pay contributions, and other administrative problems.

The noninsured includes some urban groups such as domestic servants, home workers, self-employed (e.g., public vendors, shoeshiners, small handicraftsmen, repairmen), and part of the unpaid family workers. But the large mass of the noninsured are concentrated in rural areas: peasants who are either self-employed, live on communal Indian land, or work without salary under one of the many types of agricultural contracts with landowners (e.g., sharecropping), wage-earners in unimportant crops or on small farms (often seasonal workers), and unpaid family workers. The unemployed which often constitute a large segment of the labor force are, of course noninsured.

For the noninsured, practically the only protection is state or public-charity assistance, especially in health. This has been granted in most cases more as a result of public concern over the spread of contagious diseases than as a concession from pressure. The wealthy uninsured have their own means of protection—such as investments, savings, and private medical care.

A Model on the Inequality Effects of Stratification

Each of the pressure groups/subgroups that has been capable of obtaining social security protection usually is covered by a separate fund, public, autonomous, and autarkic, with its own legislation and ad-hoc contingencies covered, conditions for granting benefits, amount of those benefits, and sources of financing. This proliferation and multiplicity of institutions and variety of regulations has created a legislative labyrinth with resultant confusion for the insured, cumbersome procedures for employers (who have to complete several forms for the various funds), difficulties for control resulting in a high rate of evasion and fraud, conflicts of jurisdiction among funds, duplication and waste of human and material resources which increase administrative costs, and lack of continuity in protection for the insured who change occupations.[30] The whole system usually lacks a central agency empowered with policy-making, coordinating, filing, supervising, and auditing. National planning has only recently begun to include social security but with little or no effective strategies and control for implementation.

The more powerful a pressure group/subgroup, the earlier in time it gets social security coverage, the higher its degree of coverage by the system, the less it costs to finance that system (largely because of contributions from the state and from employers), and the more generous its benefits (more benefits available, more flexible requirements to acquire such benefits, and higher amounts granted). The reverse is true when a pressure group is less powerful. In spite of their liberal conditions and generous benefits, the privileged funds rarely go bankrupt for several reasons. First, the group/subgroup is rather small, has a relatively high income, and eliminated the low-income insured. Paying only a small percentage of its income, the group/subgroup generates a large revenue; besides, the contributions of the employer and the state are usually based on a percentage of salary and hence are also substantial. Finally, the number of those who are passive (dependents of the employed) is relatively small in relation to the revenues of the fund. Conversely, the funds covering the least powerful pressure groups embrace a very large number of insured with low incomes. Sometimes these funds expand their scope, rarely upwards (to incorporate higher-income groups) but commonly downwards (incorporating lower-income groups). Even with only minimal benefits to pay, these funds often go bankrupt.

There also seems to be a positive relationship between a pressure group's geographical location and income and the excellence of its social security system. The most powerful groups/subgroups are concentrated in urban areas with relatively high economic development and income and in a few rural areas with mining centers or large plantations, while the least powerful groups and the noninsured are mostly concentrated in rural areas which are less developed and have lower incomes. The most privileged funds cover a relatively small proportion of the labor force in the high-income and upper-middle income categories, the less privileged funds a larger proportion of the labor force in the middle-income category, and the noninsured represent the majority of the labor force in the low-income category. Those with the best protection are the ones with least need, while those with more need are either underprotected or unprotected.[31]

Social security apparently plays either a neutral or a regressive role in income distribution, that is, it either reproduces overall income inequalities or it aggravates them.[32] The contribution of the insured normally has a progressive effect in income distribution, but it generates only a minor part of the total revenue of the system which is mostly financed through employers' and state contributions. Employers' contributions often increase with the group's income; such contributions are normally transferred to the consumers through higher prices for goods and services. State contributions also increase parallel to the group's income; these contributions originate from general taxes (mostly indirect taxes which are paid mainly by the low-income strata of the population) or through special taxes earmarked for financing a privileged fund (e.g., stamps on legal documents for the lawyers' fund, tax on medicines for the physicians' fund).[33] Through higher prices and taxes, the noninsured segment of the population indirectly contributes to the social security funds of those covered and the insured in the underprivileged funds to the privileged funds. In view of the relatively small number of insured in the privileged funds, their indirect contribution to the underprivileged funds with a much larger insured population is smaller than that which they get in return. The regressive nature of social security in Latin America is obvious.[34]

In the most urbanized, industrialized, unionized, and politically aware Latin American countries, where (not by coincidence) the social security system is more developed, a unique phenomenon has been taking place: the "massification of social security privileges." As those insured in the underprivileged funds have become increasingly conscious of their power, aware of the privileges enjoyed by other groups/subgroups, better organized, and more militant, they have exerted sociopolitical pressure upon the government to obtain social security treatment equal to that enjoyed by the most powerful groups. Those noninsured have organized into peasant unions and other associations and exerted pressure for coverage. Politicians have also expanded privilege, even without strong pressure from below, to develop an electoral clientele. Some military regimes devoid of legitimacy have either yielded to pressure or made gracious concessions to provide their government with a more "populistic" face. ·The generous conditions and benefits that are financially viable (although socially unjustifiable) in privileged funds are not found in the underprivileged funds which in many cases are already bankrupt. The financial problems created by the massification of privilege are compounded by the gradual expansion of social security protection to noninsured segments of the population, first in the cities (e.g.,· domestic servants) and later in rural areas. The organization of agrarian leagues and unions has provided rural groups with the necessary pressure. Since these groups have low incomes and many lack employers, the state is forced to subsidize their protection.

In countries such as Uruguay and Chile the gradual extension of social security protection and privileges has resulted in social security costs that reach a proportion of GNP surpassed only by that of some developed Western and Eastern European countries (e.g., Belgium, France, Sweden, USSR).[35] In Uruguay in 1970, for every two active insured persons, there was one passive or on welfare. (This was true of Chile also but was limited to the armed-forces and civil-servant sectors.) Developing countries which require a high rate of investment cannot maintain this situation for long. The stagnation and economic crises of Uruguay and Chile, the pioneer welfare states in the Western Hemisphere, may be partially explained by this phenomenon. In 1966 Chilean President Frei warned his nation that this situation would inevitably lead not only to the bankruptcy of the social security funds but also to the bankruptcy of the country.[36]

The chaotic economic situation of the funds (and even the nations) has induced some Latin American countries to undertake serious studies (usually under ILO's advice) of the problem and its potential solution. These studies have recommended the unification of the multiple social security funds, standardization of the legislation, elimination of privileges, and expansion (universalization) of the system to protect those more in need. These recommendations are difficult to implement, however, because the pressure groups covered by privileged funds also control politics and/or the economy of the country and are reluctant to yield their advantages. Weak governments have hesitated to implement the reform due to their fear of opposition. Expansion of the social security system to the low-income strata of the population cannot be undertaken without a transfer of state support from the wealthier funds or by raising substantial additional revenue through general or special taxes. In a few countries, authoritarian regimes (regardless of ideological coloration, e.g., Cuba, Peru, Argentina) have been able to take steps toward unification. In Argentina and Peru, however, the unification process leaves out the armed forces and civil servants who enjoy the most privileged funds. Social security stratification and inequality are solidly entrenched and resist radical change.[37]

The Stratification of Social Protection in the Colonial Period

The current stratification of social security in Latin American countries is not the exclusive result of their historical evolution since they achieved independence from Spain in the nineteenth century. Most of the governments established in the new republics retained almost unchanged the colonial socioeconomic status quo. They inherited from the colonies several social protective institutions, some of which disappeared or declined, but others persisted throughout the nineteenth century and were transformed in the twentieth century, becoming the backbone of the modern social security system.[38]

The colonial society was very hierarchical and rigidly stratified. Class divisions were closely connected to occupation and race. At the top of the hierarchy were royal functionaries, high military officials, church dignitaries, large landowners, and mine operators. Next came other civil servants, militarymen, priests, and those in the liberal professions (lawyers, physicians, accountants). These two groups were predominantly white. Merchants rose rapidly in income and slowly in status. The artisan group expanded dramatically in the second half of the sixteenth century and throughout the seventeenth century when local manufacturing rose as the threat of piracy reduced trade between Spain and the colonies. However this occupation carried with it a social stigma because it was "manual" not "intellectual." Many mestizos and *libertos* (freed Negro slaves) learned this occupation from Spanish masters. At the bottom of the scale were those working in the mines, agriculture, construction, and domestic service. The bulk of this group was composed of Indians (particularly in Mesoamerica and the Andean region) and imported African slaves (in the Caribbean).

Therefore "intellectual" jobs (in government, the army, the church, management, liberal professions, commerce) were performed by the predominantly white upper classes. "Manual" jobs were performed by the lower classes with some mestizos, mulattoes, and *libertos* engaged in manufacturing and small commerce, and practically all Negro slaves and Indians working in agriculture, mining, construction, and domestic service. The stigma carried by the manual job was compounded by racial discrimination.[39] Until the end of the eighteenth century, those involved in manual jobs could not be appointed to civil-servant posts.

Social protection of each class was undertaken by different institutions: (1) *ayllus* and *calpullis;* (2) *beneficencias;* (3) *Leyes de Indias;* (4) *gracias* or *mercedes;* (5) *cofradías;* and (6) *montepíos.*

Ayllus and Calpullis

Developed by the Inca and Aztec civilizations, the *ayllus* and the *calpullis* were the first social-protection institutions on the American continent. The Inca's basic economic unit was the community called *ayllu* which was a mixture of insurance, public assistance, and agrarian cooperative. The *ayllu's* arable land was divided into portions, one assigned to each family and the others collectively plowed for the Inca, the priests, and the community. The crops raised collectively for the community were put into a communal fund to help the aged, widows, orphans, disabled, and the sick. An annual census of beneficiaries was conducted by local authorities. The system was maintained during the colonial period but showed a declining trend because local governments often seized the *ayllu* funds. At the end of the eighteenth century, the Spanish Crown tried to defend the autonomy of the *ayllu* but with little success since regulations were not enforced in most cases. Currently, in some areas of Bolivia and Peru where Indian communal organization of land has been preserved, the *ayllu* in modified form is still performing its social-protection function.

In Mexico and part of Central America, the Aztecs developed the *calpulli* and the *altepetlali,* also types of communal land worked by the village members to take care of those in need. Under colonial rule some of these indigenous institutions received land grants from the Crown or the local governments and were transformed into savings funds *(cajas)* financed by the community through contributions in cash and kind. The *cajas* helped the old, sick, disabled, widows, and orphans. By the end of the seventeenth century, some *cajas* became very wealthy but, with both the Crown and local governments committing abuses against them, they declined.

Beneficencias

Early in the sixteenth century the Spanish philosopher Juan Luis Vives had a strong influence in changing the system of outdoor relief for the poor *(limosna)* into a system of indoor aid. Vives' ideas were quickly exported to Latin America. In 1521 the first public-charity hospital, Nuestra Señora, was reportedly founded by Hernán Cortez in Mexico. By the end of the seventeenth century all important cities in the colonies had at least one public-charity hospital that provided free medical care for the poor— mostly Indians and Negroes. Orphanages and homes for the elderly were established during the eighteenth century. Many of these institutions *(beneficencias)* were supported by the state and served by religious orders; some were privately supported through donations.

Although conditions in the *beneficencias* were not always exemplary, until the second quarter of the twentieth century, these hospitals were the most important providers of medical care in Latin America.

Leyes de Indias

The abuses committed by the Spaniards against the Indians led to some local regulations which proliferated throughout Hispanic America from the middle of the sixteenth century to the middle of the seventeenth century to protect Indians working in mines against occupational accidents and to make their employers responsible for providing medical care to those injured. In 1680 the Spanish Crown standardized most of these regulations into a legal code (*Recopilación de Leyes de los Reynos de las Indias*). The code made the owners of mines, mills, and plantations responsible for: the prevention of occupational accidents; the provision of medical care to those injured as a result of their work; the payment of cash indemnification in case of temporary disability, of pensions to the worker totally and permanently disabled, and of pensions to survivors in case of death resulting from occupational accidents. The code also prescribed the retirement of an Indian worker at age fifty (an age which very few reached in those days) with his needs met by the *encomendero* or mine owner. Employers of domestic servants were expected to pay for medical care and burial expenses. Although severe penalties against violators were established in the code, it was not enforced in most of Hispanic America. The code was an amazing predecessor to the laws of occupational accidents and diseases enacted in Latin America in the early twentieth century and, in general, of modern social security. But because of its lack of enforcement, it stands as one of the earliest and most dramatic examples of the traditional Latin American divorce between legal theory and practice.

Gracias or Mercedes

At the beginning of the sixteenth century the Spanish Crown began to grant *gracias* or *mercedes* (gratuitous concessions or gifts) on an individual basis to its loyal and most valuable colonial servants (usually in civil service or military careers). These royal concessions were granted both as an incentive to move to the insecure new world and as a reward for meritorious performance or exceptional achievement. The beneficiary did not have a legal hold on the concession and the grantor could therefore withdraw it arbitrarily. In the second quarter of the sixteenth century, gratuitous concessions were extended to protect needy widows and orphans of top civil servants and military officials. In early times these concessions consisted of Indians and land; when such resources became depleted, the Crown turned to monetary payments usually in the form of lump sums and especially pensions. During the seventeenth and eighteenth centuries, wars and economic difficulties forced the Spanish monarchy to reduce or suspend many of the gratuitous concessions. But the institution survived and in a few Latin American countries is still in existence in modified forms.

Cofradías

Cofradías, mutual-aid societies started in the seventeenth century, copied the Spanish model. At the beginning they had both religious and social-protection objectives but, as time passed, the latter increased in importance.

Mutual-aid societies were organized according to different criteria, the most important of which was occupation. Thus there were *cofradías* for the army and navy personnel, for professionals such as physicians, merchants, maritime workers, and for artisans grouped by crafts and often organized into guilds. There were also *cofradías* based on ethnic distinctions (Spaniards, Indians, Negroes) or on locality (by neighborhoods). Most *cofradías* protected their own members against certain adversities, for example, economic aid to widows, orphans, disabled, and the elderly, medical care to the sick, temporary aid to the jobless, and payment of burial expenses. There were also *cofradías* organized as charitable associations to help the poor. The *cofradías'* revenue came from membership dues, gifts, donations, some taxes, and solicitations.

In the second quarter of the seventeenth century, *cofradías* became regulated by the Crown and supervised by the church; and at the end of the eighteenth century, government approval was necessary to establish them in order to prevent activities against state interests. With the development of trade unionism, *montepíos,* and modern social security institutions, the institution had practically disappeared by the mid-twentieth century. (They still exist, but only with religious functions.)

Within the agricultural sector (especially in Nueva España), the *pósitos* replaced the *cofradías.* The former were credit-seed cooperatives also following the Spanish model. The *pósitos* had a grain warehouse that loaned seed to poor farmers and kept a reserve for periods of scarcity; they also granted credit and occasionally helped poor travelers. Their revenue came mainly from farmers' contributions (mostly in kind) in addition to occasional donations. In the second half of the sixteenth century, *pósitos* were regulated by the Crown. After a period of prosperity, they began to decline and were rare in the nineteenth century.

Montepios

The financial difficulties encountered by the gratuitous concessions and the arbitrariness of the system probably contributed to the inception of the *montepíos,* which began to flourish in the second half of the eighteenth century, copying the Spanish model, as public institutions with compulsory membership and dues. They differed from the gratuitous concessions because they protected a group instead of an individual, were financed by their members instead of by the state, and generated a right to benefits.

The first *montepío,* often called *militar,* was established in most of the colonies between 1761 and 1773 and covered viceroys, governors, mayors, army officials, top civil servants, and the administrators of the *montepío.* Another type of *montepío* was also introduced in Mexico, Peru, Cuba, and Nuevo Reino de Granada, covering officials of the ministries of Justice and the Treasury, customs brokers, and bank and postal employees. A third type of *montepío* was added in 1784 in Mexico and Cuba to protect civil servants not covered by previous types. A fourth kind of *montepío* founded in 1785 protected many officials and some crew members of royal fleets and merchant vessels. At the end of the eighteenth century, army physicians and professors of medical schools also got *montepíos.*

The main objective of the *montepío* was to grant pensions for retirements, survivors, and, in some cases, dismissals.[40] The *montepíos'* revenue was generated by monthly contributions proportionate to the members' salaries; pensions were also proportionate to salaries and adjusted to the cost of living. The administration of *montepíos* was local, but cumbersome and highly bureaucratized, with a large number of employees, excessive formality for granting pensions, and long and expensive administrative procedures. Due to improper handling of finances, deficits soon appeared and the state stepped in to subsidize the system and cut the amount of the pensions.

In the early nineteenth century, the system of *montepío* for civil servants was reorganized and standardized in Spain. These regulations were implemented in some of the colonies right before most of them achieved their independence. The republics added new *montepíos,* especially for the military who had fought the wars of independence and for civil servants. In many Latin American countries some of the old *montepíos* still persist in modified form.

On the eve of the fall of the Spanish in Hispanic America, a highly stratified system of social protection had evolved. The most powerful groups, the upper class, such as the military, civil servants, some clerical employees (e.g., those in banking) and a few professions (e.g., medicine, merchant marine), were protected against the risks of old age, disability, and death (and, in some cases, dismissal) through a combined system of gratuitous concessions (totally paid by the state) and *montepíos* (paid by their members with a state subsidy). Some of these groups built their own hospitals or paid their own physicians. A second group composed of artisans, merchants, some professionals, and military personnel of lower rank grouped into mutual-aid societies (financed by their membership) to protect themselves in old age, sickness, and disability and their survivors in case of their death. Indians, originally protected by the *ayllu* and the *calpulli,* found these institutions in rapid decline. Those working in mines, mills, some plantations, and domestic service were theoretically but not practically protected against occupational accidents, sickness, and old age by their own employers. Poor or indigent people, mostly Indians and Negroes, received medical care from public-charity hospitals and other help from orphanages and old-age asylums commonly of very low standards.

The Spanish American society prior to the wars of independence resembled the usual pyramidal model in the matter of social security protection. The vertex consisted of a tiny elite, well protected partly by its own means and partly by the state. The center of the pyramid was composed of a larger segment with a fair system of protection exclusively financed by its members. The base of the pyramid constituted the majority of the population and was the worst protected—by public and private charity. Very few avenues of mobility were open within the pyramid.

The following five chapters recount the historical evolution of social security in Latin America beginning with the independence from Spain and ending circa 1973. (Although the book was completed by mid-1976, the task of keeping data on the ever-changing social security systems up to date in five countries is not within the capabilities of one researcher.) The power of the pressure groups/subgroups is evaluated qualitatively rather than quantitatively in each case study using gross indicators such as: the size of the group, its degree of organization, its control or influence over the state government, the strategic nature of its trade, its levels of activism. In addition, the group's relative income is also utilized as an indirect indicator of its power, that is, the more powerful the group, the higher its income. Pressure groups/subgroups are analyzed in terms of the roles they play (using whatever power they have) in the inception of social security, that is, in the enactment of legislation (or signature of collective contracts) providing legal coverage for the group/subgroup against a given social risk such as occupational accident, illness, or death.[41] The final chapter analyzes the data gleaned from the case studies and proposes conclusions on the role pressure groups have played in social security stratification in Latin America.

2 The Case of Chile

Historical Evolution of Social Security in Chile Since Independence

The evolution of social security in Chile can be summarized into six chronological periods.[1] In each period, some part of the system was established or augmented. (See table 2-1.)

1810–1910

In the first century of the republic (1810–1910), a few minimal programs were instituted, mostly involving pensions for the military and civil servants. The colonial, civil-servant *montepíos* were maintained by the republican government, but financed by sales taxes, paid mainly by the low-income strata of the population. During this early period of the republic, the presidency was held by military men, although the army was actually controlled by civilian aristocrats. Under the paternalistic Supreme Director Bernardo O'Higgins (1817–1823), a new system of state-supported pensions was introduced to protect widows and orphans of the war for independence. In 1855 the first civilian president, conservative Manuel Montt (1851–1861), faced army revolts compounded by an economic crisis. In settling these, he rewarded his loyal military following by improving conditions for their *montepío*. Montt adapted to Chile the Napoleonic civil code, the essence of the laissez-faire, individualistic nineteenth-century liberal ideology. The code, enacted in 1855, did nothing to regulate labor conditions; workers were left at the mercy of employers. (For example, the burden of proof of negligence in occupational accidents lay with the employee.) In 1858 civil servants received a compulsory savings fund, an antecedent to their future pension system. The liberal presidents who ruled from 1861 to 1891 had to yield to the influence of the political parties. The ascendancy of the industrial-commercial class lessened the power formerly held by the aristocratic landowners. The government was still controlled, however, by the upper class with no influence from the middle and lower classes. The only social legislation passed was for the protection of sailors (1866)—a powerful guild at the time—and for veterans of the War of the Pacific (1881). President José Manuel Balmaceda (1886–1891), a liberal nationalist, passed a system of retirement pensions for civil servants paid out of government funds and enacted a progressive mining code (1888) which regulated safety measures and minimum labor conditions in the mines.

Throughout this period the already poor labor conditions were worsened by inflation and economic decline. Workers' organizations gradually changed from mutual-aid societies of workers in one trade (typographers, sailors, railroad engineers, dock

Table 2-1
Significant Social Security Legislation in Chile: 1810–1972

Year	President	Type of Coverage	Group Protected
1810s	O'Higgins (m)	Pensions (old age, death)	Military (veterans)
1855	Montt (c)	Pensions	Military
1888	Balmaceda (c)	Pensions[a]	Civil servants
1911	Barros (c)	Pensions (old age)	Railroad
1915	Barros (c)	Pensions, health	Military[b]
1916	Sanfuentes (c)	Occupational accidents	Blue-collars
1916–1918	Sanfuentes (c)	Pensions (expanded)	Railroad
1924	Alessandri (c)	Occupational diseases	Blue-collars
1924	Alessandri (c)	Pensions (except death), health-maternity (for worker)	Blue-collars
1924	Alessandri (c)	Pensions (old age), life insurance[c]	White-collars
1925	Alessandri (c)	Pensions, health[d]	Civil servants, journalists
1925	Figueroa (c)	Pensions (old age)	Merchant marine
1925–1927	Figueroa (c) Ibáñez (m)	Pensions	Police[e]
1933	Alessandri (c)	Lump sum (retirement)	Petroleum
1936	Alessandri (c)	Pensions	Racetracks
1937	Alessandri (c)	Family allowances, unemployment lump sum (retirement)	White-collars
1937	Alessandri (c)	Pensions (disability)	White-collars, merchant marine
1938	Alessandri (c)	Preventive medicine	All
1938	Alessandri (c)	Health-maternity (for family)	Blue-collars
1940	Aguirre Cerda (c)	Unemployment	Railroad
1941	Aguirre Cerda (c)	Pensions	Racetracks
1942	Ríos (c)	Health[d]	White-collars
1943	Ríos (c)	Unemployment	Municipalities
1946	Duhalde (c)	Pensions, life insurance, funeral aid, occupational accidents, health-maternity	Banks
1952	González Videla (c)	Family allowances	Civil servants, military, police
1952	González Videla (c)	Pensions (death), funeral aid, health-maternity[f]	Blue-collars
1952	González Videla (c)	Pensions (seniority), funeral aid	White-collars
1952	González Videla (c)	Pensions	Municipalities, merchant marine (sailors)
1953	Ibáñez (c)	Family allowances, unemployment, lump sum (retirement)	Blue-collars
1953	Ibáñez (c)	Health-maternity	White-collars, civil servants, merchant marine, municipalities[g]
1954	Ibáñez (c)	Health, occupational accidents	Police
1954	Ibáñez (c)	Funeral aid, unemployment	Military
1957	Ibáñez (c)	Pensions	State bank
1961	Alessandri (c)	Pensions (disability)[h]	Air Force
1968	Frei (c)	Occupational accidents and diseases	All, except armed forces
1968	Frei (c)	Health-maternity[i]	White-collars and others
1968	Frei (c)	Pensions, occupational accidents,[j] health, etc.	Military
1972	Allende (c)	Pensions, health	Small merchants, artisans and other self-employed

SOURCE: Legislative information compiled by the author.
NOTE: (m) = military; (c) = civilian.
a. This was preceded by a savings fund in 1858 (Montt).
b. Navy was included.
c. Plus voluntary programs for enterprises with capital of more than 2 million E°.
(Notes continued on page 24)

workers) into more militant and aggressive organizations. The first strikes took place in the 1880s, initially in the larger cities (Santiago and Valparaíso) among skilled or semiskilled workers (dock, railroad, and construction workers) and later in the mining areas. Poor labor conditions, job safety, and enforcement of the few labor regulations led to increasing labor grievances, strikes, riots, and even civil war (1890). The government, through the army, repressed the rebellious workers who, in turn, became more radical, better organized, and integrated more strongly with political parties. In 1909, the first workers' federation, mostly a grouping of railroad unions, was founded (Gran Federación Obrera, GFO). One year later, the first federation of white-collar workers (Unión de Empleados de Chile) was established. In 1917 the GFO merged with coal and copper unions and founded the first labor confederation (Federación Obrera de Chile, FOCh). At this point the workers had almost no representation in Congress.

1911–1923

In this time period, in response to growing labor tension and worker demands, more pensions were passed and some protection against occupational accidents for blue-collar workers was provided. In this era of parliamentary government, the power center shifted from the central government to the Congress. Political parties proliferated and the old order grew unstable. An economic coalition of conservatives and liberals gained control and protected its own interests. The powerful railroad workers union won retirement pensions in 1911. In 1915, new legislation enlarged the *montepío* or pensions for retirement, disability, and survivors, and added medical care for the army and the navy. Under President Luis Sanfuentes (1915–1920), a new law (1916) protected blue-collars against accidents, shifting the burden of proof of responsibility to the employer. This was an improvement over the civil code (1855), but workers were not protected against occupational diseases, and enforcement of the law was very poor. Other laws improved social protection of railroad workers. These were only palliatives that did not solve the worsening labor situation.

In the international arena the Mexican Revolution led to the 1917 Constitution of Mexico, the first Latin American document to include a long section on labor and social security rights, which soon became a model for sister republics. The Bolshevik Revolution of 1917 produced a labor code establishing in the USSR the principle of total social insurance. Finally, the establishment of the International Labor Organization (ILO) in 1919 resulted in the approval of international conventions on labor and social security matters.

The 1920 presidential campaign brought all these issues to the fore; for the first time both the middle class and the workers actively participated. The Liberal alliance supported Arturo Alessandri Palma (1920–1924) and his program for workers: recognition of unions, the creation of the Ministry of Labor and Social Security, and the establishment of social insurance for old age, sickness, and occupational accidents.

---

d. The implementation of the health program was postponed.

e. Separated from the military.

f. Unification and expansion of several services; indigents were included in health.

g. Protection was granted in some cases only for statutory diseases and for the insured, in others medical care in general for the insured, and in others including the family of the insured.

h. Special system.

i. Medical care granted to insured and his family unprotected in 1953.

j. Reorganization and coordination of the system.

Alessandri's victory opened an era of social reform and put an end to the parliamentary system.

1924–1938

In the third phase of Chilean social legislation history, reformist president Alessandri, facing strong opposition in the Senate, was unable to pass his program of social reform for four years. In September of 1924, in the midst of popular discontent, military conspiracy, and congressional inaction, a group of young army officers exerted pressure and Alessandri appointed a general as head of his cabinet. The Congress then rapidly approved the pending social legislation. Unions were legally recognized and a Ministry of Labor, Hygiene, Assistance, and Social Welfare was created. Three laws in particular established a basis for the modern social security system of Chile. The employer's responsibility for occupational accidents was reiterated and protection against occupational diseases was added. Compulsory social insurance (Caja de Seguro Obligatorio, CSO) was founded, stipulating medical and dental care, hospitalization and medicines, pensions for old age and disability, and burial expenses for blue-collar workers (originally including some peasants, self-employed with low incomes, and domestic servants). Another law established a compulsory savings program to pay retirement pensions and life insurance for white-collar workers and encouraged enterprises with more than two million escudos (E°) to grant additional benefits voluntarily (e.g., medical care through contracts with private clinics).

Alessandri also regulated occupational hazards, granted protection during pregnancy to blue-collar workers, and created a fund (Caja Nacional de Empleados Públicos y Periodistas, CNEPP) granting pensions for old age, disability, and survivors, as well as medical assistance, to civil servants and journalists. Alessandri's successor, Emiliano Figueroa Larraín (1925–1927), passed legislation regulating social insurance of journalists (within the CNEPP), granting pensions to white-collar employees in the merchant marine, separating pensions for policemen from the montepío of the armed forces, and elevating the white-collar social insurance to the category of a public fund (Caja de Previsión de Empleados Particulares, CPEP).

Figueroa's successor, Colonel Carlos Ibáñez (1927–1931), ruled as a dictator for four years, repressing some labor unions, domesticating political parties, and reestablishing a strong presidential system. In the field of social security Ibáñez implemented and enforced the new legislation which had been opposed by many employers and by the extreme-left unions. He also decided that health protection should be granted mainly through the existing system of state, public-charity, and private hospitals supplemented with outpatient clinics, first constructed during his tenure in office. The police had been instrumental in restoring order and Ibáñez took special care to put their separate pension fund in operation. He also enacted regulations for protection against occupational diseases and enabled a public agency (Caja Nacional de Ahorros) to insure workers in competition with employer's mutual insurance companies and commercial insurance. He created the Department of Social Security in the Ministry of Labor to supervise the other social insurances. Ibáñez also enacted regulations for the civil-servant fund (CNEPP), including in it the white-collars employed in associations of employers, such as industrialists and land and mine owners, and excluding the armed forces and the police. Finally, he also approved two ILO conventions dealing with health insurance for industrial and commercial employees and domestic servants.

Ibáñez compiled all the labor legislation of this period into a labor code, the first in Latin America. This code unified labor legislation, but because it excluded social security legislation except workmen's compensation, safety regulations, and protection of pregnant workers, it contributed to the proliferation of institutions in the field. The code also ratified the different treatment of white- and blue-collar workers both in labor and—indirectly—in social security.

A grave economic crisis and a series of violent strikes induced the resignation of Ibáñez which was followed by one of the most chaotic periods in Chilean history. Eight presidents occupied the office in less than one-and-a-half years, including Colonel Marmaduke Grove (1932) who proclaimed a Socialist republic in Chile. It lasted only two weeks but had time, however, to make public a program which included total social insurance.

The reelection of Arturo Alessandri in 1932 brought a few new social measures. In his second term Alessandri was less the representative of the worker and more that of the middle and the new upper class. He established a lump sum paid on the retirement of the powerful petroleum workers (1933); granted pensions for the retirement of some racetrack employees (1936); and separated the Ministry of Labor and the Ministry of Health, Social Security, and Assistance (1936). In the midst of the Great Depression, Alessandri did not take any significant steps to help the workers in their desperate situation. But in the last two years of his term, responding to mounting pressure from organized labor (including the foundation of the Confederation of Workers of Chile, CTCh, in 1936), he passed some important legislation. In 1937 three laws were enacted: granting family allowances, unemployment relief, and retirement lump sum for white-collars under the CPEP; expanding pensions for old age and disability to merchant-marine officials; and incorporating teachers with a state degree employed by private schools into the CNEPP. In 1938 preventive medical care was introduced for all insured workers; this consisted of an annual medical checkup to detect tuberculosis, venereal disease, and heart disease (diseases covered by government statute since they were the causes of 60 percent of deaths in Chile at that time) and paid rest and medical care if these illnesses were discovered. Maternity care was extended to the wife of the worker and medical care in general to the wife and children of the insured.

1938–1952

In the fourth phase of Chile's social legislation, the Radical governments, representing the middle class, made deals and compromises with the upper class and enjoyed in part the support of the workers through the CTCh, the Socialists, and the Communists. The Radicals raised popular expectations as evidenced in the increase in voter turnout (from 6 percent in 1920 to 10 percent in 1941) and in union membership (80,000 in 1938 to 210,000 in 1941). The strength of organized labor was weakened, however, by internal struggles (between Socialists and Communists) and by Conservative forces in the Congress. The Radicals worked to fill important holes in the system to extend coverage to special subgroups.

Alessandri's successor, Pedro Aguirre Cerda (1938–1941), passed only three social security laws, all of secondary importance. Under the pressure of the powerful Federation of Railroad Workers of Chile (founded in 1938), lump sums for layoff were granted to railroad workers; and under the pressure of the Maritime Confederation of Chile and the powerful mining unions, special safety regulations for longshoremen and miners were introduced. Finally, racetrack employees received survivor's pensions.

After Aguirre Cerda's death, social security legislation, although prolific, was of secondary importance, granted to a specific group of workers, benefitting mostly white-collars. Health insurance for white-collar workers was instituted in 1942, including preventive and curative medicine in the case of the three statutory diseases as well as limited medical care in certain cases. In the same year the *sueldo vital* ("basic salary" used, among other things, for computing social security benefits) was established for the benefit of white-collar workers. In addition, lump sums for dismissal were granted to blue-collar workers at the Santiago sewage system and municipalities. Between 1942 and 1945 several small groups of influential professionals and workers were *equiparados* (made equal with respect to status and rights) with white-collars and incorporated into the CPEP: salaried lawyers, notaries public, registrars of real estate, officials in charge of public archives, insurance agents, salaried professionals, and drivers employed by commercial and industrial enterprises and in public transportation. In 1946 provisional president Alfredo Duhalde passed a law establishing an independent fund for employees of banks and credit institutions granting pensions, health-maternity care, funeral aid, and other benefits.

With a deteriorating economy and increasing inflation, strikes doubled in frequency between 1947 and 1952 and involved four times as many workers. This included a general strike in 1950. In the first five years of his term, President Gabriel González Videla (1946–1952) tried to repress the illegal strikes threatening his government and enacted only two laws, both of minor importance, incorporating into the CPEP traveling salesmen, hairdressers, and barbers. By contrast, in 1952, courting support of union workers, he passed six laws, some of them of great significance. Most important, he reorganized the blue-collar social insurance system, dividing it into two main branches, one dealing with health (Servicio Nacional de Salud, SNS) and the other with pensions and cash benefits (formerly the CSO, now renamed Servicio de Seguro Social, SSS). The SNS integrated numerous services previously dispersed: preventive medicine and medical, maternity, and dental attention for the insured and his family. It also unified all the facilities of public-charity hospitals, former CSO outpatient clinics, and state and municipal health services. The SNS protected both the insured blue-collar workers and the noninsured or indigent. White-collar workers and the armed forces were not integrated into the SNS, in order to avoid conflicts with these groups and with the powerful Medical Association established in 1948. The SSS centralized and unified the payment of pensions for old age and disability and added payment to survivors and funeral aid. A later law reorganized the white-collar system. Additional legislation granted family allowances for civil servants, pensions for blue-collar workers in the merchant marine, a pension fund for municipal employees, and special regulations for mayors and congressmen. Finally the accumulation of years of service and contributions in various occupations covered by different social insurance funds was made possible, thus improving job mobility.

1953–1964

The fifth phase of social security legislation began with the presidential election of General Ibáñez in 1952, and was marked by the addition of benefits for specific

groups. Fearing that Ibáñez might become a dictator again, several labor confederations united to form the Central Unica de Trabajadores de Chile, CUTCh, made up of
Communists, Socialists, Radicals, and the Falange (a progressive offshoot of the
Conservative party). Although CUTCh included only about 15 percent of the labor
force, it became a strong pressure group. Ibáñez responded with important social
security legislation. He created the Superintendency of Social Security within the
Ministry of Public Health and Social Security as a central agency to gather information and supervise all social security institutions. He reorganized and implemented
white-collar health insurance (Servicio Médico Nacional de Empleados, SMNE)
under the Ministry of Public Health. This move integrated preventive and curative
services for many white-collar funds (and a few blue-collar funds) for the three
statutory diseases (tuberculosis, venereal disease, and heart disease). In addition,
three funds received expanded medical care services (civil-servants, merchant-
marine, and municipal employees) and two funds received medical care for their
families (merchant-marine and printing employees). Expanded medical and dental
care for other funds were promised, but not implemented for fifteen years. Other
decrees granted family allowances, unemployment relief, and retirement lump sums
to blue-collars, a benefit that white-collars, civil servants, and special categories of
blue-collars had gained two decades before.

Inflation and a wage freeze led to several strikes especially among miners, and to
a general strike in 1956, and riots in Santiago and other cities in 1957. Ibáñez
repressed these illegal strikes and riots with the aid of the police and the army. (The
police were rewarded for their loyalty with health-care benefits and protection
against occupational accidents; the military received lump sums for funerals and
dismissals.) On the other hand, Ibáñez recognized the Copper Workers' Federation
and gave some concessions to unions in large copper enterprises, as well as granting them a special system in the SSS. Blue-collars in industry, commerce, and
government were granted a "basic wage," a benefit white-collar workers had had
since 1942. Finally, Ibáñez created a special social security fund for state-bank
employees and declared locomotive engineers, butchers, and excavating-machine
operators equal to white-collar workers.

Winning election through a Conservative-Liberal alliance in 1958, industrialist
Jorge Alessandri Rodríguez (1958–1964, son of the former president Alessandri)
made a few changes in the social security system. He raised some groups of blue-
collar workers to the level of white-collars. He also introduced special disability
pensions for airplane pilots. The only important legislation was a result of the workers'
strong opposition to wage ceilings: the introduction of a mechanism to adjust
salaries, wages, and minimum pensions to increases in the cost of living. Alessandri's most significant action was the establishment of a commission to reorganize the
social security system. This exhaustive study compared statistics of benefits of various funds and found the system "one of the most discriminatory in the world" and
regressive in that contributions of the population as a whole were channeled to the
higher income groups ("made possible through the organization of the most powerful
and wealthy groups into privileged funds separated from the common or general
funds").[2] The study recommended reform in the direction of universality of benefits
and away from the cumbersome system of special privileges to specific groups.
Unfortunately the commission's report was not released in its entirety until late 1962.
This was so close to the 1964 presidential election that the weak Alessandri government could not undertake the task of implementing the reforms.

1964-1973

The sixth and most recent phase in the history of Chilean social security legislation saw some reorganization and unification of benefits and the extension of protection to the self-employed and the small employer. Agrarian reform laws were passed rectifying inequities in social insurance available to agricultural workers. (Although protected in theory since 1924, many rural workers were hindered from benefits by *hacendados* and landowners until the late 1930s.) The new laws establishing a minimum wage and legalizing peasant organizations and unions helped enforce social security rights and collective bargaining powers in rural areas. President Eduardo Frei (1964-1970) enacted the new Statute of the Armed Forces which reorganized the social security system of the military. A second law incorporated insurance against occupational accidents and diseases under a state agency, thus eliminating commercial insurance and employer's mutual insurance funds. In 1968 medical care funds were expanded to include passive insured (e.g., retired, pensioners) and some blue-collars previously excluded, as well as the active workers previously covered. The new fund granted medical care, diagnosis, hospitalization, maternity and dental care either through established institutions or free choice (*libre elección*) of hospitals and physicians registered with the SMNE. Frei made several attempts to reorganize and unify the social security system, to reduce its inequalities, and to lighten the intolerable financial burden the ever-increasing new benefits were creating. He felt the situation constituted a "permanent source of instability and unrest [and] a paralyzing obstacle to the plans of economic development and social reform," leading "inevitably to the bankruptcy of the social security funds or to the bankruptcy of the country."[3] But political opposition made reforms impossible.

Coming to office in 1970, Salvador Allende (1970-1973) had to maintain a precarious balance of power between interest groups and made no moves to unify the social security system. Perhaps because of compromises made to secure support from strong labor federations, Allende added to inequities in the system by granting to special funds tax revenues on news and magazine sales and tickets for sports events. A new independent fund was established to cover small merchants and public vendors, owners of small crafts shops, drugstores, and small chemical laboratories, truck and bus owners, and the self-employed. This group was incorporated within the SMNE for health protection but remained autonomous in its other aspects. Minimum pensions were increased but at percentages that favored certain groups. (Military and police were increased by 44 percent, while civil servants and municipal and state employees received an increase of only 35 percent.) Allende's attempts to unify health services were not successful.

By not acting to reform the social security system, Allende gained support from strong labor federations for some of his radical measures. For instance, the nationalization of private banking was achieved, but at the price of keeping the privileged fund covering private-bank workers separate from the less generous fund covering state-bank workers. A similar privilege was granted to copper federations under the nationalization of the copper mines.

In summary, in the first century of the republic (1810-1910), pensions for the military and civil servants were granted. In the next twelve years (1911-1932) protection against occupational accidents in favor of blue-collar workers and pensions for railroad workers were instituted. In the next fourteen years (1924-1938), mostly under Alessandri Palma, the bulk of the system was passed with: protection against occupational diseases for blue-collar workers, pensions for blue- and white-collar workers, policemen, journalists, and merchant-marine and racetrack workers; preventive medicine for all the insured; health-maternity care for the blue-collar workers, civil servants, and journalists; life insurance, family allowances, unemployment relief, and other benefits for white-collars. In the next period (1938–1952), the Radical governments filled important holes in the system with complementary pensions for blue- and white-collar, racetrack, merchant-marine, and municipal workers; health care for white-collar workers; family allowances for civil servants, the military, and policemen; a special system covering all risks for bank employees; and other minor benefits for subgroups. The next decade (1953–1964) saw the granting of pensions for state-bank employees; family allowances and unemployment relief for blue-collar workers; health-maternity care for white-collar workers, civil servants, merchant-marine, and municipal employees; health care and workmen's compensation for policemen; and unemployment relief for the military. In the last decade (1964–1973), Frei reorganized and unified some sectors (all risks covered for the military; health-maternity care for white-collar workers, civil servants, and other groups; and occupational accidents and diseases for all insured under a state agency), but was not successful in obtaining approval for the overall unification of the system; Allende granted protection to the self-employed and small employer but halted the unification process.

The Role of Pressure Groups in Social Security Stratification

Four main pressure groups (each one with various subgroups) have been instrumental in the evolution of social security stratification: (1) the military (including policemen as a subgroup); (2) civil servants (with journalists and municipal and state-bank employees as important subgroups); (3) white-collars (with merchant-marine, racetrack, and private-bank employees as subgroups); and (4) blue-collars (with railroad and racetrack workers and sailors as subgroups). A fifth group could be added, that of the self-employed and small entrepreneurs.

The military in Chile has not been as politically influential as in other Latin American countries (e.g., Argentina, Brazil, and Peru). Presidents with military backgrounds have been in power for fifty years, less than one-third of the republican history, most of that during the first period of the republic. During their periods of control the military passed the first pension system in the republic for the armed forces (a continuation of the colonial *montepío militar*) and pensions for the police between 1925 and 1927. Military subgroups have played important roles in Chilean history; for instance, the navy was instrumental in the Conservative victory of 1891 and in establishing the parliamentary system, while the army and the police were used by Ibáñez to reimpose and consolidate the presidential system in the second half of the 1920s. Other social security measures in favor of the military have been passed by civilian governments, most of which were conservative and weak: the first civilian government of the country reorganized the pension system of the military and passed special regulations for the navy at the peak of its power (1915); Alessandri granted preventive medicine to the military in his second (conservative) term; Ibáñez gave additional benefits to the military and the police also in his second term; and Alessandri Rodríguez enacted special regulations for the air force. Reformist and leftist governments have paid little attention to the military: González Videla approved family allowances for the military when faced with strong opposition (1952); and Frei limited himself to reorganizing the administration of their system. Military governments, in turn, have not passed one single social security measure in favor of nonmilitary pressure groups.

Likewise, civil servants have received the attention of civilian governments, both conservative and reformist, commonly in periods of turbulence in which it was essential to keep the government machinery running. The government bureaucracy has played an important role as arbiter or moderator between conflicting interests, thus becoming the grantor of social security concessions and gaining power to push for its own share of the benefits. The civil-servant pension system was the second introduced in the country, initially as a compulsory savings fund (in 1858 under Montt) and later as a *montepío* (in 1888 under Balmaceda); the civil-servant social security fund (including the second health system in the country) was established by Alessandri when he returned to power briefly in 1925, and preventive medicine benefits were gained under Alessandri in his second term; finally, González Videla granted them the second family-allowance scheme in the country in a difficult period (1952). Special treatment has been received by subgroups such as journalists, municipal workers, state bankers, teachers, judges, congressmen, and mayors. Chilean labor law prohibits unionization by the military and civil servants employed by the central government, municipalities, autonomous agencies, state enterprises, and certain public services. Nevertheless, most civil servants have organized themselves into "associations" which by the 1960s had a large membership: central government employees (30,000 to 50,000), autonomous institutions (10,000), and municipalities (17,000). Teachers unionized early into a public and a private federation which later merged (35,000). Public-health employees also have a strong federation (27,000). The combined membership is more than 100,000 civil servants, making this one of the most powerful groups in Chile.[4] Private teachers were incorporated in the CNEPP in 1937, after the foundation of the CTCh (in which the teacher union was basic); family allowances for civil servants and pensions for municipal employees were passed in 1952 after a wave of strikes; and civil service regulations were enacted in the early 1960s after a general strike.

White-collars did not receive any protection until the Revolt of the Electorate (1920) opened the door to the increasing dominance by the middle class. Reformist governments have initiated most legislation in favor of this group with Conservative governments consolidating, complementing, or expanding previous concessions. Thus white-collars received pensions and life insurance in Alessandri Palma's first term, and family allowances, unemployment relief, additional pensions, and preventive medicine in his second term. Radicals granted this group health-maternity care, although the system (not actually implemented until Ibáñez's second term) was expanded to include the family of the insured by Frei. White-collars received pensions at the same time as blue-collars (long after the military and civil servants); they were the first to get family allowances and unemployment relief, but were the last to obtain health-maternity care. Subgroups in important trades such as merchant marine, water plant, petroleum, and banking or in luxury trades such as racetracks have been able to win special privileges. Multiple blue-collar subgroups with essential skills and bargaining power (in such important trades as industry, insurance, electricity, and transportation) have been declared equal *(equiparado)* to white-collars and integrated into their main fund (CPEP). The first federation of white-collar workers was established in 1910; fifty years later it had 60,000 members. In the 1920s through paternalistic concessions, white-collar subgroups were able to obtain special funds, for example, those granted by gas, beer, and nitrate enterprises. More recently, through collective bargaining, they have gained social security benefits in addition to those granted by legislation.

The first blue-collar workers to receive social security protection were subgroups (miners, railroad workers) organized in strong unions in strategic trades that could paralyze the country or damage its principal source of revenue by calling strikes. The first, although timid, legislation protecting all blue-collars against occupational accidents was not enacted until 1916, after big labor federations became active, strikes increased alarmingly, and the Socialist party was founded. The bulk of social security legislation in favor of blue-collars was passed by Alessandri, but only after intensive political mobilization, coalition of progressive forces, legal drafts prepared even by Conservatives, and a deadlock in the Congress that had to be broken by the military. (Some believe that this was a reformist concession, articulated by intellectuals and pushed by the military without the support of organized labor, to avoid a violent revolution and because the armed forces resented their repressive role against striking workers.) The 1924 law that included coverage of occupational diseases, pensions, and medical care, originated by a Conservative congressman, set the basis for the separation of blue- and white-collar workers and was enforced during the Ibáñez dictatorship. The law that granted preventive medicine to blue-collars during Alessandri Palma's second term was also initiated by a Conservative and was preceded by violent strikes and the establishment of CTCh and the Popular Front in 1936. Radicals who took over in 1938 did little in favor of blue-collars (except for powerful subgroups such as railroad, sewage, and municipal workers). González Videla's reorganization of the blue-collar social security system in 1952 followed increased union activism, and the law finally enacted was mild compared with previous legal drafts for reform. Family allowances and unemployment relief were granted by Ibáñez at the beginning of his second term after the creation of the powerful CUTCh. Special protection for copper workers was also passed by Ibáñez and Frei but only after violent strikes. Frei also enacted legislation protecting agricultural workers after peasant unions organized by his own party launched several strikes. Finally Allende's legislation in favor of marginal groups (e.g., the self-employed) seemed politically strategic in winning this group, previously organized by the Christian Democrats.

In general, the protection of blue-collar workers has been gradually extended in a manner parallel with: (a) the increasing percentage of the population able to vote (from 5 percent in 1915 to 36 percent in 1970); (b) the growing membership in unions and national labor confederations; and (c) the rising number of strikes (a fourfold increase from 1947 to 1967).[5] Although social security coverage in Chile is among the most extensive in Latin America, the earlier organized and more powerful labor groups have been able to obtain better protection: for example, copper miners; nitrate, iron, and coal miners; railroad workers; sailors and longshoremen (each group having from 20,000 to 40,000 members); and metallurgical, textile, construction, and printing workers (from 10,000 to 15,000 members). Many of these groups (copper, steel, large-scale manufacturing) have been able to secure extra social security protection through collective bargaining. Only a small percentage of the labor force is not protected by social security, mostly unorganized, illiterate (hence ineligible to vote) peasants (small farmers, tenants, sharecroppers), and unpaid family workers.

Many technical studies of the Chilean social security system have been conducted over the years; the two most recent and in-depth studies end at the turn of the 1950s and early 1960s. These studies exposed in detail the inequalities of the system and recommended legal, administrative, and financial unification, standardization of requirements to acquire benefits, elimination of privileges, and expansion of coverage to embrace the entire labor force. Conservative presidents Ibáñez and Alessandri Rodríguez did not have power enough to impose the national interest recommended by these studies over that of the pressure groups. The Christian-Democratic government of Frei was able to pass some measures to unify and centralize workmen's compensation and reorganize health protection. But the most important legal drafts unifying the system were blocked in Congress by a coalition of Conservative and extreme-left forces. However, one important step was taken—the elimination of Congress' power to make social security appropriations, thus limiting this to a presidential prerogative. This measure was approved at the end of Frei's term, but he was unable to use his increased power. Allende followed the recommendations in the matter of universalization of the system but failed in moving ahead towards unification, standardization, and eradication of privilege. In fact his government contributed to the expansion of the system in multiplicity of funds and privileges. Due to the grave politico-economic problems that the Popular Unity government faced and Allende's dramatic need to keep all his supporters together, he did not take steps that would have alienated some of the pressure groups that endorsed his regime.

Current Structure and Organization of the System

There is no single legislative body regulating the organization of the social security system in Chile. The labor code includes only certain aspects of protection and is burdened with numerous laws and decrees which add to or modify its text. These sometimes are national in scope, but in other cases apply only to certain sectors, to specific occupations, and even to individuals. The legal labyrinth is even worse outside the code where 1,600 laws, decrees, and regulations remain uncompiled and uncoordinated.[6]

There are more than 160 social security funds in Chile including 31 systems of old-age retirement, 30 of seniority retirement, 30 of disability, 35 of health-maternity, dozens of family allowances and unemployment compensation, and 55 of social welfare. Until 1968 there were one state agency, six commercial insurance companies, several employers' mutual insurance societies, and numerous self-insured employers covering occupational hazards; thereafter, the first two groups merged into a single state agency but the last two remain. There are, in addition, some 1,150 collective agreements which include clauses on social security supplementing the legal system. Most of the funds have their own regulations in terms of administration, financing, benefits, and supervision. Some of them are public (e.g., most pension funds, SMNE, SNS), others are quasi-public (e.g., banking funds), and others private nonprofit corporations. Some funds are independent, others are autonomous but connected to or controlled by other institutions, still others are subordinated or administered by other funds, and there are sectors and subsectors incorporated in funds but having special regulations or separate accounts.

There is no single state agency supervising the planning, policy-making, and coordination of the whole social security system. The Office of Planning (ODEPLAN) includes part of the health sector in its Plan Nacional de Salud Pública which emphasizes more rational organization of the system and expansion of services, sanita-

FIGURE 2-1

Administrative Structure of Social Security in Chile: 1972

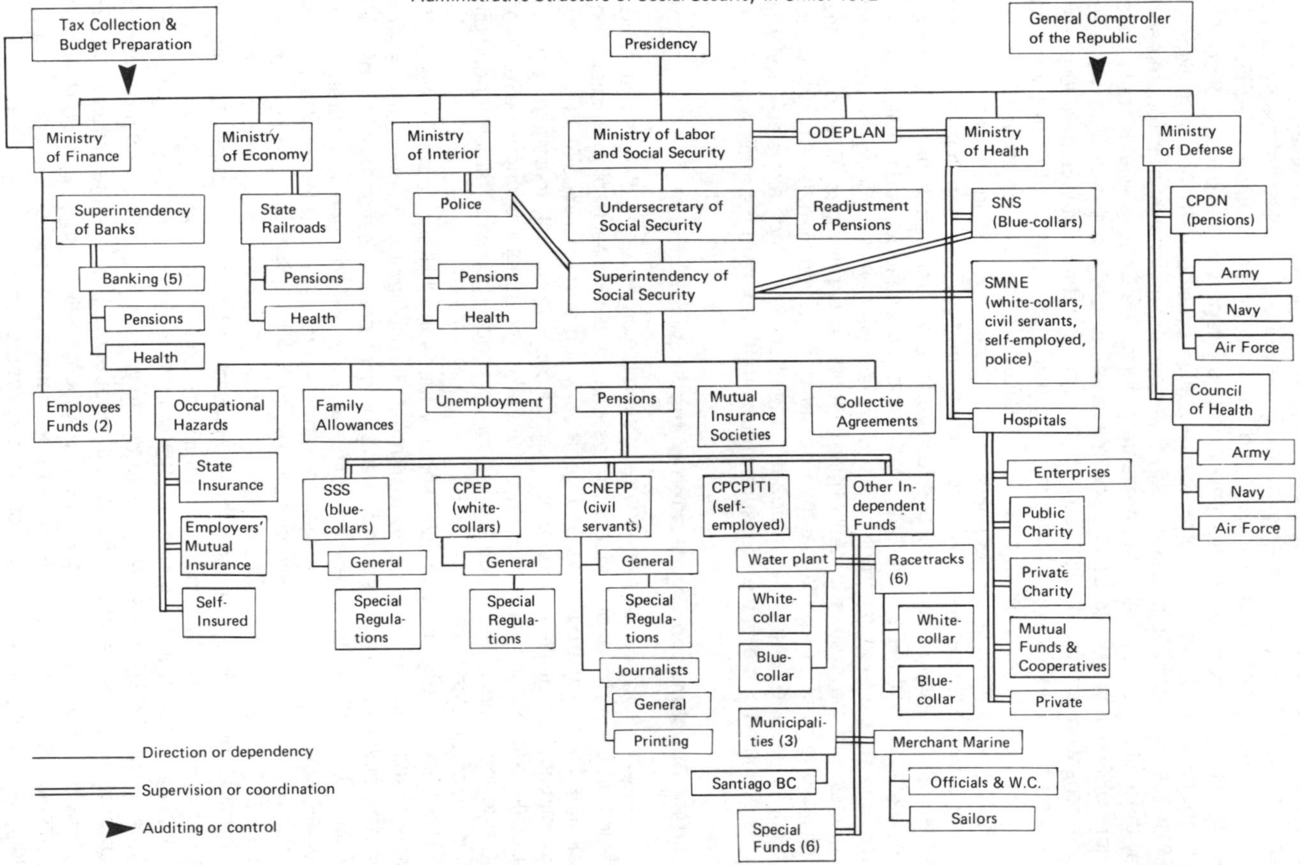

Legend:
— Direction or dependency
═ Supervision or coordination
► Auditing or control

Boxes and labels in the chart:

Tax Collection & Budget Preparation

General Comptroller of the Republic

Presidency

Ministry of Finance — Superintendency of Banks — Banking (5), Pensions, Health

Employees' Funds (2)

Ministry of Economy — State Railroads — Pensions, Health

Occupational Hazards — State Insurance, Employers' Mutual Insurance, Self-Insured

Ministry of Interior — Police — Pensions, Health

Ministry of Labor and Social Security — Undersecretary of Social Security — Superintendency of Social Security

ODEPLAN

Readjustment of Pensions

Ministry of Health — SNS (Blue-collars), SMNE (white-collars, civil servants, self-employed, police), Hospitals

Ministry of Defense — CPDN (pensions) — Army, Navy, Air Force; Council of Health — Army, Navy, Air Force

Family Allowances, Unemployment, Pensions, Mutual Insurance Societies, Collective Agreements

SSS (blue-collars) — General, Special Regulations

CPEP (white-collars) — General, Special Regulations

CNEPP (civil servants) — General, Special Regulations, Journalists — General, Printing

CPCPITI (self-employed)

Other Independent Funds — Racetracks (6), Water plant — White-collar, Blue-collar, Municipalities (3), Santiago B.C., Special Funds (6)

Enterprises, Public Charity, Private Charity, Mutual Funds & Cooperatives, Private

Merchant Marine — Officials & W.C., Sailors; White-collar, Blue-collar

tion and vaccination. The presidency has the power to appoint the directors, to propose laws to Congress and enact regulatory decrees, to make budgetary appropriations, and to supervise most public and quasi-public funds. The Ministry of Labor and Social Security is entrusted with legal studies, preparation of legal drafts for the executive, and enactment of minor regulations. The Ministry's Commission of Readjustment of Pensions adjusts these benefits to the cost of living. The Superintendency of Social Security, also part of the Ministry of Labor, supervises the operation, administration, and policies of most pension funds, and gathers statistics, provides technical advice, and trains employees. The state agency and mutual insurance funds cover occupational accidents and diseases, the two main health-maternity funds (SNS and SMNE), and more than 500 mutual insurance societies. The Ministry of Labor controls thousands of collective agreements which also include social security clauses. The General Comptroller of the republic audits the whole system (including the armed forces and other sectors excluded from the superintendency's scope), checking especially the legality of resolutions, expenditures and granting of benefits, as well as personnel matters. (Due to the similarity in the supervisory functions of the superintendency and the comptroller, conflicts often result necessitating an agreement between the two agencies.) The Ministry of Finance collects taxes and transfers them to the funds, prepares the public-fund budgets (including those of the armed forces), and grants pensions in all cases where the insured has contributed to various funds or when the state has made a financial contribution to the benefit (except in the armed forces and the police). The Ministry of Public Health participates in health planning and supervises the health-maternity funds and the various types of hospitals (e.g., social security, enterprise, public-charity, private-charity, mutual-fund, and private). The Ministry of Interior inspects the police fund, and the Ministry of Mines supervises safety measures in mines. Finally, the Labor Courts have jurisdiction over violation of social security laws. (See figure 2–1.)

The Chilean social security system may be divided into five occupational groups (each with subgroups) closely following the pressure groups already identified: (1) armed forces, (2) civil servants, (3) white-collar workers, (4) blue-collar workers, and (5) self-employed and small entrepreneurs.

Armed Forces

There are two main subgroups of the armed forces, the military (army, navy, and air force) and the police. The first subgroup includes: a pension fund (Caja de Previsión de la Defensa Nacional, CPDN) with sections for the three main branches; the Council of Health which supervises three health services (each provides preventive and curative care through three hospitals and contract services with other hospitals); family allowances; unemployment compensation fund; and special regulations on occupational hazards. The police subgroup is covered by: a pension fund (Caja de Previsión de Carabineros, CPC); health services which provide preventive and limited curative care; family allowances; indemnification for dismissal paid by the employer; and special regulations on occupational hazards.

Civil Servants

Civil servants receive pensions either through CNEPP (which includes a general pension fund and the special fund for journalists) or through one of the independent funds (state bank, central bank, National Debt Agency, the state railroad, or the municipalities).[7]

Health and maternity care is provided to civil servants by the SMNE, except for those in the state railroads (which have their own hospitals and outpatient clinics supported by the employer), the National Health Service (provided by the SNS), and the state and central banks (each one with its own medical services). Since 1968 most civil servants under SMNE are covered for maternity (both the insured and the insured's wife) and at least partially for preventive and curative medicine. SMNE has five hospitals and a dozen clinics; a large part of its services are granted, however, through the system of *libre elección* through contracts with hospitals and physicians.

There are various systems for family allowances besides the general one which covers most civil servants under CNEPP. Coverage of unemployment is organized through special funds that grant pensions and indemnification paid by the employer. Civil servants covered by the state agency protecting occupational hazards receive pensions through CNEPP (or the corresponding pension fund) and medical care and subsidies through SMNE; the rest are mostly under employers' mutual insurance funds and self-insurance.

White-Collar Workers

Most white-collar workers receive pensions through the CPEP. Numerous subgroups have been incorporated into the CPEP general system, for example, employees of notaries and archives; insurance carriers and traveling salesmen; public bus and locomotive drivers; bulldozer and crane operators; lathe and milling-machine operators and patternmakers; mechanics; electrical employees; meat-shop and drugstore clerks. (Obviously many of those incorporated are blue-collar workers.) In addition to the CPEP, there are several independent pension funds: the five funds created by private corporations in the 1920s (nitrate, brewery, Gildemeister, Hochschilds, and Gas of Santiago companies); the six racetrack funds; two private-bank funds; the Santiago water-plant fund; and, finally, two sections of the merchant-marine fund.

Health and maternity care is granted to this group by SMNE (as it is for civil servants) except for the employees of private banks and the Bank of Chile. Most insured under SMNE (including the spouse of the insured) are covered for preventive medicine and maternity care. Curative services for the insured and his family were originally available only under the merchant-marine fund but currently are available from SMNE, at least for partial payment.

There are several family-allowance systems, a general one for those under CPEP and special ones for those under private-bank, merchant-marine, and racetrack funds. In addition supplementary allowances are paid through employers' association funds and collective agreements. Unemployment pensions are available for those under private-bank, merchant-marine, and racetrack funds, but only unemployment subsidies for those under CPEP. Protection against occupational hazards is undertaken by the state insurance agency for most white-collars, with the rest under employers' mutual insurance companies and self-insurance.

Blue-Collar Workers

Pensions for most blue-collar workers in agriculture, mining, industry, and commerce are paid by the SSS. Some independent workers have been incorporated into this fund, particularly agricultural workers and newspaper vendors usually under special regulations. In addition to the SSS there are several independent pension funds or accounts for blue-collars: racetrack funds, the water-plant fund, the sailors' separate section of the merchant-marine fund, and the blue-collar fund of the municipality of Santiago.

Preventive medicine, maternity care (for both the insured and the wife of the insured), and curative medicine (for the insured and his family) are granted through the SNS. These services apply not only to those under SSS but also to those under the independent pension funds. In the 1960s the SNS had about 100 urban outpatient hospitals, 76 small rural outpatient hospitals, 20 polyclinics, 42 stations for maternity and child care, 461 rural and suburban medical posts, and 16 emergency stations. In the late 1960s the SNS had 13 health zones and 55 hospital areas, each served by a main hospital. Some 15 company hospitals provide additional coverage to blue-collars in isolated mining communities (e.g., copper, nitrates), in electrical plants, and in other large enterprises.

There are various family-allowance systems. The basic allowance is granted by SSS (which covered 77 percent of the insured in 1969), but supplementary payments are made either by five employers' compensation funds or through collective agreements. Blue-collars do not have unemployment pensions or subsidies but a forced-savings system under SSS which allows them to withdraw any accumulated sum when dismissed. Most blue-collar workers (including domestic servants) are protected against occupational accidents and diseases by the state insurance agency (pensions are paid by the SSS and medical services and subsidies by the SNS) and the rest by employers' mutual insurance companies and self-insurance.

Self-Employed and Small Entrepreneurs

Those self-employed and small merchants (including public vendors), artisans, and transporters are covered by Caja de Previsión de los Comerciantes, Pequeños Industriales, Transportistas e Independientes (CPCPITI). This pension fund may incorporate small and middle-sized farm owners in the future. Health-maternity care is granted under the SMNE general system. Protection against occupational hazards through the state agency is optional.

The Noninsured

The noninsured in Chile represent a minority of the richest and the poorest. The latter are mainly the unemployed, the small farmers (about half of the agricultural labor force), tenants, and sharecroppers, part of the rural wage-earners for which the social security legislation has not been enforced, and unpaid family workers. Medical attention is given at SNS, public-charity, and private-charity hospitals where, in practice, the insured blue-collar workers receive preferential treatment over noninsured indigents. In some hospitals services for the two groups are separated.

The wealthy noninsured are mainly attended at private hospitals, but also at some of the insurance or charity hospitals that have *pensionado* beds.

Inequalities of the System

The inequalities in Chile's social security system are mostly vertical or based on occupation and generated by the pressure groups previously identified. In addition, there are horizontal inequalities among geographical regions which will be described below. Before discussing social security inequalities, it is necessary to present briefly the differences among occupational groups and geographical regions in terms of living standards, particularly as related to income.

There are no complete data on income distribution by occupational groups in Chile (statistics of salaries of militarymen and civil servants are not published), but the information available permits some loose categorization. The high-income stratum of the population, essentially urban, is made up of large industrialists, merchants, businessmen, bankers, landowners, and high-ranking politicians and military. The medium-income stratum, also predominantly urban, consists of most civil servants, professionals (e.g., lawyers, physicians, engineers, university professors, teachers), and white-collars; small industrialists, businessmen and merchants, landlords, and middle landowners; the officers' corps of the armed forces; the police; and skilled blue-collar workers employed in strategic industries (e.g., petroleum, copper, steel, rubber, paper, printing) who have been called "the labor aristocracy." The low-income stratum may be divided into an upper segment composed of urban semi-skilled blue-collars in traditional industries (e.g., wood, furniture, textiles, shoes, clothing, leather, food); a middle segment composed of unskilled manual workers also in urban areas, such as domestic servants, street vendors and peddlers, ditch-diggers; and a bottom segment composed of agricultural workers such as small landholders, wage-earners, tenants and sharecroppers, and fishermen.[8]

The difference between white-collar (empleado) and blue-collar (obrero) workers goes beyond the legal separation formalized in the labor code and additional legislation which grants better benefits (in terms of work schedule, minimum wage, sick leave, paid vacation, job stability) to white- than to blue-collars. Obreros perform manual labor associated with low social status, often have a high proportion of Indian blood, are less stable, with lower mobility and expectations than empleados. The latter, in turn, perform clerical or "intellectual" work in the government bureaucracy or the private sector, enjoy a much higher status than the obreros, imitate the style of living of the upper-income stratum, and have higher stability, mobility, and expectations than the obreros. Some blue-collar groups from the "labor aristocracy" have been equiparados in order to attain the higher social status and better labor and social security protection of the white-collars. The gap between the two groups has been gradually reduced (e.g., in income and labor rights), but the legal distinction and some inequalities still remain.[9] Agricultural work (typically manual labor commonly performed by illiterates with a relatively high percentage of Indian blood) has the lowest status in Chile. Until the mid-1960s, rural workers were largely unprotected by labor and social security legislation, had the right neither to strike nor to form labor federations, and did not enjoy a minimum wage. The few labor laws which did protect them were poorly enforced. Although some of these problems have been corrected, this group still has by far the worst living standards.[10]

A ranking of occupations according to their income in the 1950s showed finance (banking, insurance, real estate), utilities (gas, electricity, water) and government services at the top; transportation, mining, industry, and commerce in the middle; and construction, personal services, fishing, and agriculture at the bottom. In 1960, within the service sector, those employed in commerce, finance, and government received from three to five times what those in personal services made. In the first half of the 1960s, the average salary of white-collars was almost three times that of blue-collars, although the gap was closing.[11]

The following are 1969 ratios of average salaries among white-collars, and of wages among blue-collars, in the private sector, in relation to the lowest-paid occupation (blue-collar agriculture: 1.0). White-collars: mining (8.5), electricity (6.6), industry (6.2), construction (5.2), services (4.5), agriculture (3.7). Blue-collars: mining (4.4), electricity (3.7), industry (2.7), construction (2.1), and services (1.3).[12]

There are three main geographical regions in Chile—North, Center, and South—sharply differentiated in terms of natural resources, climate, population, and socioeconomic development.[13]

The North is characterized by high altitude (Andean range), hot and dry climate, and an abundance of mineral resources. This region is the richest in copper and nitrates, and also has iron, manganese, silver, and salt. In 1970 with 41.6 percent of the territory of the nation, the region only had 12.9 percent of the population. The most important city is Antofagasta, the sixth in population in Chile. Mining workers have developed powerful and radical unions, frequently resorted to strikes (mostly illegal) and, taking advantage of the high profits of foreign corporations, obtained high wages and excellent fringe benefits, particularly in copper. The region as a whole, and particularly the extreme North subregion, had in the early 1960s the highest proportion of the economically active population unionized and the highest percentage of the population registered for voting.

The Center is the most developed region of the country. The altitude is less extreme, there is a good rainfall supplemented by artificial irrigation, the climate is more moderate, and the soil, particularly in the Central Valley, is excellent. The central area contains Chile's main industries (steel, motor vehicles, tires, hydroelectric power), most of the nation's agricultural and livestock output, and important copper mines, as well as iron, coal, and other minerals. The five largest cities are found in the Center and the capital city, Santiago, houses the national government as well as a concentration of finance, commerce, and business. Communication, transportation, educational and recreational facilities are the best in the nation. In 1970, with only 11.9 percent of the territory, the Center had 66.8 percent of the population. Employees in finance, government, and industry have obtained excellent labor conditions. In Santiato, Valparaíso, and Concepción unionization and registration for voting are at a very high level.

The South is the flattest zone, with the highest rainfall, multiple rivers and lakes, abundant vegetation and forests. The region is rich in natural resources (e.g., petroleum and coal), but it is cold and humid, has an irregular topography, and is almost inaccessible in the extreme South during the rainy season. Its main products are wood, livestock, wool, petroleum, coal, fishing, wheat, and potatoes. There is a growing industry in Valdivia, the tenth largest city in Chile, but more than half of the labor force of the region is engaged in agricultural activities. Communications and other facilities are among the worst in the nation. Although the South has the largest territory (46.5 percent), it had only 20.3 percent of the population in 1970. Unionism and registration for voting are the lowest in the country and labor conditions and poorest with the exception of oil-rich Magallanes. The largest concentration of the remaining Araucanian Indians is in the South.

Salaries and wages are highest in mining provinces, in the extreme South (Magallanes), and the extreme North (Antofagasta, Atacama, and Tarapacá). The next highest levels are in the central provinces of Santiago, Valparaíso, and Concepción with their concentration of services and industry. The lowest levels are in the southern provinces which are predominantly agricultural. In the 1960s the ratio between the provinces with the highest and the lowest wage rates was about three to one.[14] The average GDP(Gross Domestic Product) per capita in the extreme North (the provinces of Antofagasta, Atacama, Tarapacá), extreme South (Magallanes), and metropolitan Center (Santiago, Valparaíso) exceeded the national average by 35 to 40 percentage points, while the rest of the provinces in the three regions averaged 35 to 40 percentage points below the national average. The southern provinces of Arauco, Malleco, Cautín, and Bío-Bío made only half the national average GDP per capita, and the province of Chiloé about one-third of that average. The extreme ratio between the highest and lowest GDP per capita in the provinces was five to one.[15]

Inequalities in the Chilean system of social security will be analyzed in three fields: (1) coverage, (2) financing, and (3) benefits. In each field both occupational and geographical sources of inequality will be traced whenever possible.

Coverage

Table 2-2 shows the overall social security coverage in pensions (and usually in preventive medicine and curative medicine for statutory diseases, maternity for the wife of the insured, family allowances, and unemployment compensation). (The proportion covered by these services varied greatly according to the insurance institution; for example, overall coverage of family allowance was about 46 percent above that of pensions but ranged from 35 percent above among blue-collars to 79 percent above among white-collars.) The percentage of the economically active insured population (EAP) increased from 67 percent in 1960 to 70 percent in 1971. This percentage refers to insured active workers; if we add to them both passive insured (pensioners) and dependents with some social security protection, we have the total insured population. This increased from 63 percent of the total population in 1960 to 72 percent in 1971. With the creation in 1972 of the new fund which insures some 200,000 self-employed and small employers (420,000 including their dependents), the proportion of the EAP insured probably increased to 73 percent and that of the total population to 76 percent.[16] These data, however, are somewhat inflated because the active insured holding more than one job and the passive insured who are in the labor market usually are covered at least twice.

The number of those protected against occupational hazards by insurance institutions (i.e., the state fund, six commercial companies, and two employers' mutual insurance funds) increased from 455,981 in 1960 to 540,800 in 1967. (An additional 100,000 workers were personally insured by their employers.) The proportion of the EAP insured in those institutions was stagnant at 18 percent in 1960–1967; therefore, only about one-fifth of those covered by pensions were protected against occupational hazards. In 1968, with the merging of all the institutions (except the mutual insurance funds) into the state fund, the number of insured dramatically increased to 1.7 million or 56 percent of the EAP. Still 430,000 workers insured under pension funds were unprotected against occupational hazards: (a) about 320,000 civil servants under the CNEPP, militarymen, policemen, municipal and state-railroad employees, and workers insured by their employers, and (b) about 110,000 self-employed insured in the SSS. There was a plan to incorporate the first group into the state fund by the end of the 1960s and the second group later.[17]

The most difficult estimate to make is that of the population protected by medical care. In 1961 a team from the Pan American Union gave a low and a high estimate for those covered under the SNS: 3,603,060 and 5,390,785.[18] The number of insured covered by the SMNE was estimated by the author at 609,800. The number covered by the armed-forces, banking, and state-railroad funds was estimated at 166,400. Add-

Table 2-2
Insured Population in Relation to Total and Economically Active Population in Chile: 1960–1971

Year	Total Population (in thousands) (1)	Economically Active Population[a] (in thousands) (2)	Insured Population (in thousands) Active[b] (3)	Passive[c] (4)	Dependents[d] (5)	Total (6)	Percent of EAP Insured (3)/(2)	Percent of Total Population Insured (6)/(1)	Ratio of Active to Passive (3)/(4)
1960	7,689.0	2,521.0	1,691.3	269.4	2,875.0	4,835.7	67.1	63.0	6.3
1961	7,858.0	2,577.0	1,741.8	287.6	2,961.0	4,990.4	67.6	63.5	6.1
1962	8,029.0	2,634.0	1,797.1	311.4	3,055.0	5,163.5	68.2	64.3	5.8
1963	8,217.0	2,695.0	1,835.2	348.7	3,170.0	5,353.9	68.1	65.1	5.3
1964	8,391.0	2,752.0	1,891.8	384.4	3,360.0	5,636.2	68.7	67.1	4.9
1965	8,584.0	2,815.0	1,946.6	441.1	3,584.0	5,971.7	69.1	69.5	4.4
1966	8,850.0	2,903.0	2,026.8	501.1	3,648.0	6,175.9	69.8	69.8	4.0
1967	9,136.6	2,978.0	2,093.2	524.6	3,768.0	6,385.8	70.3	69.9	4.0
1968	9,351.2	3,048.0	2,158.3	552.0	3,885.0	6,595.3	70.8	70.5	3.9
1969	9,555.6	3,107.4	2,143.2	580.7	3,858.0	6,581.9	69.0	68.8	3.7
1970	9,780.1	3,189.2	2,217.3	603.1	3,991.0	6,811.4	69.5	69.6	3.7
1971	10,001.3	3,278.1	2,294.9	643.7	4,253.0	7,191.0	70.0	71.9	3.6

Sources: *Total population,* 1960–1965 from República de Chile, Dirección de Estadística y Censos, *Censos de población 1960: Resumen país* (Santiago: Imprenta de la Dirección de Estadística y Censos, n.d.), p. 16; 1966 author's projection; 1967–1971 from República de Chile Instituto Nacional de Estadística y Censos, *Síntesis Estadística,* 1970–1971 issues, and ODEPLAN, *Informe económico anual, 1971* (Santiago: Editorial Universitaria, 1972), p. 206; *Economically active population* from scattered data published by Superintendency of Social Security and ODEPLAN (1969–1971); author has filled gaps computing the EAP as 32.8 percent of the total population. *Active and passive insured* from República de Chile, ODEPLAN, *Informe económico anual 1971,* p. 211. *Dependents* mostly derived as a residue by subtracting active and passive insured from total insured; in other cases, they were estimated at 1.7–1.8 of the insured. *Total insured,* 1963–1965 from Carlos Briones Olivos et al., "Antecedentes básicos y análisis del estado actual de la seguridad social en Chile," *Seguridad Social,* no. 98 (September 1968), p. 73; 1971 from ODEPLAN, *Informe económico anual,* p. 205; rest by adding active, passive, and dependents.

Note: Coverage is in pension funds; it also includes preventive medicine, maternity, family allowances, and unemployment compensation when the insured and his dependents have such coverage. For coverage of health and occupational accidents and diseases, see text. Estimates are for mid-year.

a. Includes unemployed, unpaid family workers, and employers.

b. Figures are below totals in table 2-3 because the latter are estimates by end of the year.

c. Retired and disabled workers and survivors under pensions.

d. Wives of active insured covered by maternity insurance, and relatives with right to health services under SSS and other funds.

ing the three groups of insured, we come to a low estimate of 4.4 million and a high estimate of 6.2 million or from 56 to 78 percent of the total population. In 1968 with granting of curative services to the insured and their dependents covered by SMNE, the population covered by health care is basically the same as that covered by pensions with the addition of an undisclosed number of indigents that could be as high as one million people.

The division by occupational groups of active workers insured in pension systems is given in table 2-3. The various funds have been classified into the four main groups already identified.[19] The table shows that in 1967 almost 70 percent of all the insured were blue-collars in the SSS, followed by white-collars in the CPEP (12 percent), and civil servants in CNEPP (10 percent). The military represented 2 percent of the total number insured, and the categories merchant marine, state-railroad workers, and policemen each represented a little over 1 percent. The rest of the funds had insured

Table 2-3
Occupational Groups Protected by Social Security in Chile: 1960–1967

Occupational Group	Number Insured								Percentage Distribution in 1967
	1960	1961	1962	1963	1964	1965	1966	1967	
Blue-collars	*1,257,680*	*1,282,550*	*1,312,470*	*1,332,670*	*1,364,710*	*1,412,140*	*1,450,890*	*1,488,439*	*71.0*
General (SSS)	1,240,000	1,264,000	1,291,000	1,310,000	1,340,000	1,375,000	1,410,000	1,450,000	69.2
Merchant marine[a]	12,990	13,700	16,540	17,670	19,750	20,220	22,919	22,124	1.0
Municipal[b]	2,930	2,970	3,020	3,070	3,120	14,500	15,383	13,832	0.7
Racetracks[c]	1,760	1,880	1,910	1,930	1,840	2,420	1,960	1,890	0.1
Water	—	—	—	—	—	—	628	593	0.0
White-collars	*198,660*	*217,950*	*239,600*	*250,020*	*262,880*	*268,920*	*283,203*	*291,009*	*13.9*
General (CPEP)	171,350	189,260	210,000	218,000	225,000	230,000	240,000	248,000	11.8
Merchant marine[d]	5,410	6,010	6,050	7,780	10,640	9,800	13,880	12,465	0.6
Journalists[e]	8,000[i]	8,000[i]	9,000[i]	10,000[i]	11,300	12,150	10,952	12,235	0.6
Banks[f]	7,480	7,900	8,010	8,410	8,710	9,400	10,064	10,166	0.5
Special funds[g]	4,370	4,510	4,470	4,720	5,080	5,520	6,174	6,014	0.3
Racetracks[h]	2,050	2,270	2,070	2,110	2,150	2,050	2,133	2,129	0.1

Civil servants									
General (CNEPP)[i]	140,000	145,000	150,000	155,000	157,132	166,912	188,121	205,509	9.8
	178,150	183,780	189,261	195,310	197,662	207,672	226,887	246,051	11.7
State railroad	27,380	27,800	27,780	27,720	28,000	26,900	24,967	26,512	1.2
Banks[j]	6,320	6,350	6,330	6,550	6,750	7,140	7,361	7,796	0.4
Municipal[k]	3,970	4,140	4,640	5,410	5,210	5,300	5,555	5,394	0.3
Water	400	410	430	490	490	1,340	783	741	0.0
Amortization	80	80	80	80	80	80	100	99	0.0
Armed forces	63,100	64,270	65,730	66,960	72,661	76,050	74,124	70,614	3.4
Military	35,500[l]	36,750	38,280	39,390	44,621	46,950	43,843	41,596	2.0
Police	27,600	27,520	27,450	27,590	28,040	29,100	30,281	29,018	1.4
Totals	1,397,590	1,748,550	1,807,061	1,844,980	1,897,913	1,964,782	2,035,104	2,096,113	100.0

SOURCES: *1960–1965* from Superintendencia de Seguridad Social, *Boletín de Estadísticas de Seguridad Social*, nos. 27–28 (September–December 1965), pp. 6–7. *1966–1967* from Superintendencia de Seguridad Social, *Seguridad Social*, no. 98 (July 1968), p. 35, and appendix, table 1. CNEPP statistics were computed by Carlos Gómez Fuentes, Statistical Department; CNEPP, 1969.

NOTE: Figures are for the end of the year and report only active insured in pension funds which may include family allowances and unemployment compensation. For health-maternity protection and occupational hazards, see text.

a. Section of sailors and blue-collar workers.
b. Fund of municipal blue-collar workers of the republic.
c. Trainers and jockeys of Santiago, Concepción, Antofagasta, and Punta Arenas funds.
d. Sections of officials customs brokers, and white-collar workers.
e. Journalist section of the CNEPP.
f. General banking and Bank of Chile funds.
g. Nitrate, brewery, gas, Gildemeister, and Hochschild funds.
h. White-collars of Chile, Santiago, Valparaíso, Concepción, and Antofagasta funds.
i. Only the general section of civil servants.
j. State Bank and Central Bank funds.
k. Funds of municipal white-collars of the republic, Santiago, and Valparaíso.
l. Estimates.

Table 2-4
Degree of Social Security Protection by Class of Worker
and Occupational Group in Chile: 1964

Class of Worker	Labor Force (in thousands)	Insured (in thousands)	Percent Insured
Salaried	534.8	489.6[b]	91.5[b]
Wage-earners	1,464.4	1,315.8[c]	89.8[c]
Self-employed	655.2	90.0[d]	13.7[d]
Employers	35.0[a]	e	e
Unpaid family workers	40.0[a]	e	e
Not specified	70.6[a]	e	e
Total	2,800.0	1,895.4	67.7

SOURCES: Eduardo Miranda Salas and Juan Gutiérrez Vistozo, "Aspectos del sistema de accidentes del trabajo en Chile," *Boletín de Estadísticas de Seguridad Social,* no. 25 (May–June 1965), pp. 49–51.

a. Disaggregation of a clustered figure of 145,600 for these three categories, based on distribution from the 1960 and 1970 censuses.

b. All insured in white-collar, civil servant, and armed forces funds minus the self-employed.

c. All insured in blue-collar funds (including domestic servants) minus the self-employed.

d. Estimate of self-employed insured in SSS (about 67,000) and in CPEP (about 23,000).

e. A small number of these workers could be insured by other funds.

groups below 1 percent and three of them did not even have enough members to reach a decimal point in the distribution.

The distribution of those insured against occupational hazards in 1968 indicated that the highest concentration was in the blue-collar group insured in SSS (81 percent), followed by white-collars in CPEP (15 percent), and merchant marine (2 percent), the rest being below 1 percent.[20] The distribution of those insured in health-maternity in 1961 showed an even higher concentration in the blue-collar group insured in the SNS (82 to 87 percent), followed by white-collars and civil servants in the SMNE (10 to 14 percent), and the special systems for the armed forces, banking, and state railroad (3 to 4 percent).

Tables 2-4 and 2-5 measure the degree of social security protection of each occupational group. Table 2-4 compares the distribution of the labor force by class of worker with a clustering of insured in pension funds in 1964.[21] According to the table, 92 percent of the salaried employees and 90 percent of wage-earners were insured, but only 14 percent of the self-employed and an insignificant percentage of employers and unpaid family workers. Scattered data published between 1958 and 1971 indicated that from 700,000 to 900,000 members of the labor force did not have social security protection. These were mainly self-employed (about 78 percent), unemployed (9 percent), unpaid family workers (7 percent), and employers (6 percent).[22] Coverage of the self-employed and small employers increased from 8 to 12 percent in the period 1958–1971 to approximately 30 percent in 1972.

Table 2-5 shows the degree of coverage of social security (pension funds) by sectors of economic activity in 1966. The sector having the poorest coverage was

Table 2-5
Degree of Social Security Protection by Sector of Economic Activity in Chile: 1966

Sector of Economic Activity	Labor Force[a] (in thousands)	Insured (in thousands)[b]				Percent of Labor Force Insured
		SSS	CPEP[c]	Others	Total	
Agriculture, fishing	717.7	386.3	6.7	—	393.0	54.8
Mining	93.6	114.2	15.9	4.2[e]	134.3	143.4
Manufacturing	527.7	385.1	43.0	0.5[f]	428.6	81.2
Construction	186.3	181.9	6.9	—	188.8	101.3
Electricity, gas, water	11.9	15.5	9.2	1.9[g]	26.6	223.5
Commerce	351.0	157.9	52.9	17.5[h]	228.3	65.0
Transportation, communications	149.5	18.3	18.0	61.6[i]	97.9	65.4
Services	665.0	114.2[d]	32.9	298.7[j]	445.8	67.0
Not specified	—	36.6	2.4	—	39.0	—
Total	2,702.7	1,410.0	187.9	384.4	1,982.3	73.3

SOURCES: *Labor force* from ODEPLAN, *Informe económico anual, 1971*, p. 23. *SSS* from SSS, *Estadísticas 1966*, p. 24. *CPEP* from CPEP, *Boletín de Estadística 1966*, p. 7. *Others* from Superintendencia de Seguridad Social, *Seguridad Social*, no. 98 (July 1968), p. 35.
 a. Excludes unemployed, some 200,000 in 1966.
 b. Under pension funds.
 c. Based on a sample that included 78 percent of the total number of insured.
 d. Domestic servants.
 e. Nitrate special fund.
 f. Beer special fund.
 g. Gas and water-plant funds.
 h. Bank funds.
 i. Merchant-marine and state-railroad funds.
 j. CNEPP, armed-forces, police, municipal and racetrack funds.

agriculture, with almost half of its workers unprotected. More than one-third of these workers were self-employed (small farmers, agricultural tenants with various types of contracts, fishermen, lumbermen, hunters, and unpaid family workers). In some cases these workers had the option of becoming insured but did not exercise it. There were also some agricultural wage-earners with the right to be insured but who were not protected due to their employers' evasion; nevertheless, this problem was dramatically corrected in the late 1960s.[23] Commerce, transportation, and services were the next most poorly protected sectors although with percentages of coverage very close to the national average. The noninsured were either unpaid family workers or self-employed, such as peddlers, salesmen, performers of personal services, and independent drivers. Nevertheless, salaried workers and wage-earners in commerce, banking, and services, civil servants, armed-forces personnel, maritime and railroad workers, and drivers employed by enterprises and the government or having their own taxis enjoyed almost total coverage. Manufacturing had a degree of coverage substantially higher than the national average; left out of protection were independent craftsmen and artisans and unpaid family workers. Construction workers seemed to be totally covered. Mining and utility workers (either salaried or wage-earners, with an insignificant number of self-employed) were overprotected; this was the result of multiple coverage, duplicate accounting, or a definitional problem.[24] In general, the sectors enjoying the highest income (i.e., mining, utilities) have the best coverage, while those with lowest income (i.e., services, agriculture) have the poorest coverage.

Tables 2-4 and 2-5 are limited to the active insured and do not show the different coverage of dependents. In practically all funds, dependents have a right to survivors' pensions and family allowances, and the wife of the insured to maternity care. Medical care is also granted free to the wife and children of those insured in SNS, merchant-marine, state-railroad, printing, some municipalities, and armed-forces funds and is partially paid for those insured in SMNE and other health institutions. (SMNE and the rest of the health institutions have an optional plan for dependents in which the insured bears part of the cost.)

Since its inception, the Chilean social security system has had, at least in theory, national coverage for each occupational group protected. In practice, developed, urbanized provinces with expanding activities in mining, manufacturing, transportation, finances, commerce, and government services, which also happened to develop strong unions and political activism, received earlier and better social security protection. Conversely those backward, isolated provinces, with a concentration of Indians and illiterates and a labor force engaged in agriculture, controlled by the *hacendados,* poorly unionized and politically passive, were latecomers in social security. Therefore, social security coverage in the central provinces (particularly those close to Santiago, O'Higgins, and Valparaíso) and in the northern provinces (especially in the extreme North where the most important copper mines are located) is much better than in the southern provinces.

Table 2-6 shows the proportion of the total population, clustered by regions, covered by SSS alone and by most funds in 1966. Thus under SSS coverage, the North is 0.2 percentage points above the national average, the Center is 0.9 percentage points above, and the South is 3.2 percentage points below that average. But under coverage of most funds (that is, when most white-collar, all policemen, and a few civil-servant funds are added), the gap between regions expands; thus the North falls 0.3 percentage points below the national average, the Center rises to 1.6 percentage points above, and the South sinks to 4.8 percentage points below the

Table 2-6
Degree of Social Security Protection of the Total Population by Geographic Region in Chile: 1966

			Insured Population					
	Total Population		SSS		Most Funds[a]		Percent of the Total Population Insured by	
Region	Thousands	Percent	Thousands	Percent	Thousands	Percent	SSS	Most Funds
North	1,121.7	12.6	181.2	12.8	204.3	12.4	16.1	18.2
Center	5,911.5	66.5	993.9	70.5	1,183.8	72.1	16.8	20.1
South	1,854.2	29.9	234.9	16.7	254.4	15.5	12.7	13.7
Total	8,887.4	100.0	1,410.0	100.0	1,642.5	100.0	15.9	18.5

Sources: *Population* and *SSS* from SSS, *Estadísticas 1966,* p. 110. *Most funds* from ibid.; CPEP, *Boletín de Estadísticas 1966,* p. 7; Caja de Previsión de Carabineros, *Boletín Estadístico,* no. 1 (December 1966); and Superintendencia de Seguridad Social, *Seguridad Social,* no. 98 (July 1968), p. 35.

a. Includes SSS, CPEP, policemen, racetrack and part of bank, municipal and special funds. Excludes CNEPP, armed-forces, state-railroad, merchant-marine and part of bank, municipal and special funds (about 15 percent of the total number of insured).

average. Data on funds for most civil servants (CNEPP), the armed forces, and transportation are not available, but it is fair to assume that most insured in such funds are concentrated in Santiago and in the most populated cities and important ports mainly located in the Center. If the insured in those funds were added to the distribution by regions, the gap in terms of coverage would be even greater.

Table 2-7 gives an idea of the degree of social security coverage by provinces.

Table 2-7
Degree of Social Security Protection of the Economically Active Population (EAP) by Province in Chile: 1960

			Insured Population					
	EAP[b]		SSS[c]		Others[d]		Total	
Province[a]	Thousands	Urban Percent	Thousands	Percent[e]	Thousands	Percent[e]	Thousands	Percent[e]
Antofagasta (n)	72.3	92.4	51.8	71.6	6.4	8.9	58.2	80.5
Colchagua (c)	48.5	33.0	35.4	73.0	0.9	1.9	36.3	74.8
Atacama (n)	39.3	66.4	25.3	64.4	2.8	7.1	28.1	71.5
O'Higgins (c)	79.9	53.6	53.1	66.5	3.5	4.4	56.6	70.8
Talca (c)	65.2	42.9	43.0	66.0	2.0	3.1	45.0	69.0
Curicó (c)	32.7	40.4	21.5	65.7	0.9	2.7	22.4	68.5
Concepción (c)	164.0	80.8	98.6	60.1	8.7	5.3	107.3	65.4
Aconcagua (n)	45.2	55.1	27.8	61.5	1.5	3.3	29.3	64.8
Tarapacá (n)	42.4	83.3	25.3	59.7	2.1	4.9	27.4	64.6
Santiago (c)	835.4	90.7	434.7	52.0	91.6	10.9	526.3	63.0
Linares (c)	53.9	35.3	32.9	61.0	1.0	1.8	33.9	62.9
Bío-Bío (s)	52.9	36.3	31.6	59.3	1.4	2.6	33.0	62.4
Coquimbo (n)	88.3	52.4	49.3	55.8	2.9	3.3	52.2	59.1
Valparaíso (c)	200.1	88.5	102.4	51.2	14.2	7.1	116.6	58.3
Magallanes (s)	30.6	74.8	15.2	49.7	2.0	6.5	17.2	56.2
Valdivia (s)	81.4	44.7	40.4	49.6	2.2	2.7	42.6	52.3
Malleco (s)	51.5	43.3	25.3	49.1	1.1	2.1	26.4	51.3
Ñuble (c)	89.4	37.9	41.7	46.6	1.6	1.8	43.3	48.4
Osorno (s)	48.6	46.5	21.5	44.2	1.6	3.3	23.1	47.5
Maule (c)	24.4	36.9	10.1	41.4	0.4	1.6	10.5	43.0
Llanquihue (s)	52.6	43.0	20.2	38.4	1.3	2.5	21.5	40.8
Cautín (s)	120.0	38.9	39.2	32.7	3.2	2.7	42.4	35.3
Arauco (s)	26.4	35.6	8.8	33.3	0.5	1.9	9.3	35.2
Aysén (s)	12.7	49.9	3.8	30.0	0.4	3.1	4.2	33.1
Chiloé (s)	30.1	23.9	5.1	16.9	0.4	1.3	5.5	18.3
Total	2,387.8	69.2	1,264.0	52.0	154.6	7.0	1,418.6	59.0

SOURCES: *EAP* from 1960 Census, pp. 320–322. *SSS* from *Estadísticas 1964,* p. 26. *Others* from Superintendencia de Seguridad Social, *Boletín de Estadísticas de Seguridad Social,* no. 24 (March–April 1965), p. 49, and nos. 27–28 (September–December 1965), pp. 6–7; and Caja de Previsión de Carabineros de Chile, *Boletín Estadístico,* no. 1 (December 1966).

NOTE: c = Central; n = North; s = South.

a. Ranked according to degree of coverage (last column).

b. Includes unemployed and unpaid family workers.

c. 1961.

d. Includes CPEP, policemen, racetracks, and part of bank, municipal and special funds. Excludes CNEPP, armed-forces, state-railroad, merchant-marine and part of bank, municipal and special funds (about 15 percent of the total number of insured).

e. Percentage of EAP (first column).

Most recent data available on EAP are from 1960; data on the insured in CNEPP, armed-forces, merchant-marine, state-railroad, some banks, and other funds (about 15 percent of the total number of insured) are not available. Hence coverage in the provinces with a high concentration of government and other services (which tend also to be the most urbanized provinces) is underestimated. Antofagasta, O'Higgins, Colchagua, Talca, Curicó, and Atacama are mining provinces, and the table shows that the highest percentage of SSS coverage was in these provinces, particularly in those with the largest copper mines. Santiago, Antofagasta, Valparaíso, Atacama, Magallanes, and Concepción are provinces with the most populated cities and with an important concentration of services, commerce, port facilities, and mines; and the table shows that the highest percentage of coverage under other funds (mainly CPEP and policemen) was in these provinces.

Data in the table support the proposition that provinces in the North and the Center have a larger coverage than those in the South. Out of the 10 provinces with the highest coverage (63 to 80 percent of the EAP), 6 were in the Center, 4 in the North, and none in the South. Conversely, out of the 15 provinces with the lowest coverage (18 to 63 percent of the EAP), 10 were in the South (that is, all the southern provinces), 4 in the Center, and 1 in the North. A second proposition that can be tested with the data is that the larger the size of the EAP in a province, the better its degree of social security coverage (not only in absolute numbers, of course, but in relative terms). The correlation between these two variables is significant: .99 (N = 25). A third proposition which unfortunately cannot be properly tested with the data available is that the higher the urban vis-a-vis rural proportion of the EAP in each province, the larger its social security coverage. The correlation between the two variables is .24 (N = 25), but this is regrettably misleading because, as previously explained, the number of insured in highly urbanized provinces is underestimated in table 2-7.[25]

Financing

Since the percentage of contributions and taxes are the same throughout Chile, inequalities in the financing of social security are limited to occupational groups. Table 2-8 gives a picture of the complexity of the system and the significant differences in the percentage contributions (deducted from salaries, wages, or income) paid by the occupational groups.

In most occuptional groups, the overall percentage contribution from the insured roughly increases (from 2 to 19 percent) as the income of the group is higher. There is no clear tendency in the employers' percentage contribution which ranges from 2 to 52 percent. The highest is paid by the CPEP and state banks, closely followed by most white-collar funds and then the SSS. In civil-servant and armed-forces funds the employer as such has a small percentage contribution, but the state usually subsidizes or absorbs all costs or deficits resulting from the operation of the system. A good number of funds also enjoy special taxes which cannot be quantified in terms of salary.[26] For these reasons percentage contributions alone are a poor indicator of inequality.

The insurance against occupational hazards is the most homogenous of the various protections in terms of financing. Commonly the employer pays a basic rate from 1 to 4 percent, according to risk. In the armed-forces, state-railroad, and municipal funds, the employer (i.e., state and local government) does not pay a percentage but directly assumes the responsibility for this risk. Family allowances are mostly financed by the employers' contribution of 21.5 to 22.0 percent matched by the insured's contribution of 2 percent. The armed-forces, state-railroad, municipal, and part of the merchant-marine funds do not have fixed percentages, but the employer pays the allowance directly. The health insurance is in most cases paid by a contribution of 1 percent from the insured and of 2.5 percent from the employer with a few funds paying slightly less. In addition, those covered by SMNE have to pay from 30 to 50 percent of their expenses in curative medicine. Those insured under SSS and the state-railroad fund (as well as blue-collars in municipal and racetrack funds) do not pay anything to their health insurance; costs are either paid by the employer or through a state contribution. (However, those insured by SSS—as well as their employers—contribute indirectly to their health insurance through the transfer of 4.5 percent of salaries that SSS makes to SNS.) In the armed forces, all deficits are absorbed by the state. The unemployment insurance is in some cases financed by 1.0–1.5 percent paid by the insured, matched by 0.5–1.0 percent paid by the employer. In the SSS the insured do not pay at all and employers pay 2 percent, while in civil-servant and armed-forces funds, the insured pay 4–6 percent and the state absorbs any resulting deficit from the system. Pensions are the most heterogenous in terms of financing. The insured pays from 5.5 to 11.5 percent with most blue-collars paying the smaller percentage, armed forces and white-collars in between, and civil servants paying the highest percentage. The employers' contribution ranges from 0.5 to 30.5 percent with the armed forces and civil servants paying the smaller percentage, blue-collars in between, and white-collars the highest rate. Taxes are granted to the armed forces, journalists, privileged groups within CNEPP, and state railroad (compensating for the small percentage paid by the employer); to merchant marine, private banks, racetracks, and artists within CPEP (increasing the already high revenue received by these groups mostly by high employer contributions); and to blue-collars in SSS and sailors. The readjustment of pensions according to the cost of living presents a clear case of inequality. In the CNEPP (general) and the armed-forces (and other civil-servants funds), the state finances 100 percent of the adjustment; so, with spiraling inflation, current pensions are almost totally paid by the state. Among blue-collar and white-collar funds there is a 1 percent contribution (divided equally between employer and insured) for the readjustment of pensions although this is usually not enough. The state should make a contribution to the SSS for this purpose, but, as will be seen later, seldom does.

The total percentage contribution for all covered risks and from all contributors ranges from 14 to 67 percent, with civil-servant and armed-forces funds (except state banks) paying the lowest percentage (in addition to being supplemented with state subsidies and taxes) and white-collar funds paying the highest percentage. The percentage paid by SSS is two times higher than that paid by civil servants and three times that paid by the armed forces.

Table 2-9 presents a more accurate picture of what the insured, the employer, and the state actually contribute to each fund because it is based on the revenue received by the fund (which includes most state subsidies and taxes). When the various occupational groups are clustered into the main four groups, it appears that the insured pay less as follows: armed forces (14 percent), blue-collar workers (20 percent), white-collar workers (28 percent), and civil servants (42 percent). Adding the state and employer revenue, the groups receive more as follows: armed forces (84 percent), blue-collar workers (72 percent), white-collar workers (69 percent), and civil servants (50 percent).[27]

Table 2-8
Social Security Contributions from Employees, Employers, and State by Occupational Group in Chile: 1968
(in percentage of wages or income)

Occupational Group	Employee	Employer	State	Total
Blue-collars (SSS)	*8.5*	*37.5*	*5.5*	*51.5*
Pensions[a]	6.5[b]	12.5	[c]	19.0
Health	—	—	5.5[d]	5.5
Unemployment	—	2.0	—	2.0
Family allowances	2.0	22.0	—	24.0
Occupational hazards	—	1.0[e]	—	1.0
White-collars (CPEP)	*13.0*	*52.3*	—	*65.3*
Pensions[a]	8.5	16.8	[i]	25.3
Health	1.0[f]	2.5[g]	—	3.5
Unemployment	1.5	0.5	—	2.0
Family allowances	2.0	21.5	—	23.5
Occupational hazards	—	1.0[e]	—	1.0
Civil servants (CNEPP)[j]	*17.5 or 13.5*	*7.0 or 43.8*	—	*24.5 or 57.3*
Pensions[a]	10.5	4.5 or 18.8	[k]	15.0 or 29.3
Health	1.0[f]	2.5[g]	—	3.5
Unemployment	6.0	—	—	6.0
Family allowances	2.0	21.5	[i]	23.5
Occupational hazards	—	1.0	[i]	1.0
Armed forces[m]	*14.5 & 15.5*	*0 & 2.0*	—	*16.5*
Pensions[a]	8.5	0.5	[i n]	9.0
Health	1.0[f]	1.5[h]	[i]	2.5
Unemployment	6.0	—	[i]	5.0
Family allowances	—	—	[i]	—
Occupational hazards	—	—	[i]	—
Merchant marine[o]	*2.5 to 17.0*	*13.8 to 39.1*	—	*16.7 to 54.0*
Pensions[a]	0 to 11.5	10.5 to 13.8	[p]	10.5 to 25.0
Health	1.0[f]	2.25[g]	—	3.25
Unemployment	1.5	0.5	—	2.0
Family allowances	0 to 3.0	0 to 21.5	—	0 to 23.5
Occupational hazards	—	1.0	—	1.0
State railroad	*8.0 to 10.0*	*6.0*	—	*14.0 to 16.0*
Pensions[a]	6.0	6.0	[q]	12.0
Health	—	—	[i]	—
Unemployment	2.0 to 4.0	—	—	2.0 to 4.0
Family allowances	—	—	[i]	—
Occupational hazards	—	—	[i]	—
Municipal[r]	*12.5 to 19.0*	*15.0 to 43.0*	—	*27.5 to 62.0*
Pensions[a]	8.5 to 11.5	12.0 to 30.5	—	20.5 to 42.0
Health	0 to 2.5[f]	1.0 to 1.5[h]	5.5[d]	1.0 to 4.0
Unemployment	4.0 to 5.0	2.0 to 11.0	—	6.0 to 16.0
Family allowances	—	—	[i]	—
Occupational hazards	—	—	[i]	—
Banks[s]	*14.5 to 16.0*	*43.0 to 49.8*	—	*57.8 to 65.8*
Pensions[a]	10.5 to 11.5	17.5 to 23.8	[t]	—
Health	1.0[f]	2.5[g]	—	—
Unemployment	1.0 to 1.5	0.5 to 1.0	—	—
Family allowances	2.0	21.5	—	—
Occupational hazards	—	1.0	—	—

Occupational Group	Employee	Employer	State	Total
Racetracks	8.5 to 14.5	37.8 to 43.8	5.5	47.3 to 60.3
Pensions[a]	5.5 to 10.5	13.8 to 18.8	u	19.3 to 29.3
Health[v]	0 to 1.0[f]	1.5[g] to 2.5[g]	5.5[d]	3.5 to 5.5
Unemployment	1.0	—	—	1.0
Family allowances	2.0	21.5	—	23.5
Occupational hazards	—	1.0	—	1.0

SOURCES: "Aportes porcentuales por instituciones a los diferentes fondos de seguridad social," *Boletín de Estadísticas*, no. 22 (October–December 1964), pp. 1–48; Carlos Briones et al., "Antecedentes básicos," pp. 61–62, 68; and legislation compiled by the author.

NOTE: The base used for applying the percentage may be the minimum wage or salary, given number of "vital wages," the actual wage, or the wage plus all fringe benefits; in some cases, ceilings are applied to wages or salaries, above which they are exempted for contribution purposes.

a. A discount of 0.5 percent for both employers and employees for readjustment of pensions to the cost of living is included.

b. The self-employed and the voluntarily insured pay 15 percent of its income. The state contributes 10.5 percent of the self-employed income.

c. Taxes: 2 percent on payments from the government and municipalities.

d. In addition, there is a contribution paid directly by SSS of 4.5 percent of salaries. Applies to other funds in which there are blue-collar workers.

e. The rate could be increased to 4 percent; in 1968 the averages were 3.3 for SSS, and 0.6 percent for CPEP. Independents are excluded.

f. Curative medicine only.

g. Preventive and curative medicine.

h. Preventive medicine only.

i. Taxes for the artists fund: 5 percent of cinema and theater tickets.

j. Includes general and journalist funds. Readjustment of pensions is totally financed by the state in the general fund. Contributions for unemployment are only for the general fund, while those for family allowances and occupational hazards are for the journalists (in the general fund the state pays all costs of both services). When two rates are quoted, the first is that of the general fund and the second that of the journalists.

k. Taxes for notaries and registrars (upon public documents), for self-employed lawyers (upon legal paper, stamps, etc.), and for journalists (1–4 percent upon bets in racetracks and 5 percent upon tickets of entertainment). The state also contributes 4 percent of the income of notaries public and judiciary employees, 5 percent of legal clerks and 14 percent of tax collectors. The employee contribution ranges from 0 to 14 percent.

l. The state absorbs all the costs or deficits in this benefit.

m. The insured militarymen pay 1 percent for health while the insured policemen do not pay anything. The state contributes as an employer a total of 2 percent for policemen; the percentage paid by the state for the military is not fixed.

n. Taxes for military (not policemen): 2 percent upon all bills paid by Ministry of Defense. For both the military and the policemen the state pays 75 percent of the readjustment of pensions.

o. Includes sections for (1) custom brokers, (2) officials and white-collars and (3) sailors; employees' rates are lower and employers' rates higher as one moves from the first section to the third.

p. Taxes for custom brokers (upon imports and exports), for officials and white-collars (2 percent upon freight rates and passenger fares) and for sailors (1 percent upon the same).

q. Contribution of 1.5 percent of the enterprise income.

r. The lowest pension contributions for employees and the highest rates for employers are in the Santiago and Valparaíso white-collar funds. The latter is the only one that has a contribution for curative medicine; in the Santiago blue-collar fund the state contributes with 5.5 percent of wages for that purpose; in the other funds the state absorbs all the costs. Unemployment contributions by employers are highest in the Santiago white-collar fund; the blue-collar fund does not have any contribution; apparently it lacks this benefit.

s. The highest pension contributions for employers are those of the State Bank and the Central Bank, with lower for the Bank of Chile and the general bank fund.

t. Contribution of 0.25 percent of the balance of deposits in commercial banks every six months.

u. Tax for white-collar funds: 9.95 percent of tickets for bets.

v. Blue-collar funds belong to the SNS and are financed by the state contribution; white-collar funds belong to SMNE.

Table 2-9
Percentage Distribution of Social Security Fund Revenues by Financing Source and
Occupational Group in Chile: 1965

Occupational Group	Insured[a]	Employer[b]	State[c]	Investment Returns	Others[d]	Total[e]
Blue-collars	*20*	*61*	*11*	*1*	*7*	*100*
General (SSS)	20	64	8	1	7	100
Merchant marine	27	51	21	—	1	100
Municipal[f]	29	69	—	1	1	100
Racetracks[f]	—	—	89	3	8	100
Water	31	62	—	7	—	100
White-collars	*28*	*64*	*5*	*2*	*1*	*100*
General (CPEP)	29	68	—	2	1	100
Merchant marine	20	37	35	2	6	100
Journalists	27	23	46	2	2	100
Banks[g]	25	57	14	1	3	100
Special funds	34	45	1	13	7	100
Racetracks[f]	6	12	56	9	17	100
Civil servants	*42*	*20*	*30*	*3*	*5*	*100*
General (CNEPP)	45	17	32	3	3	100
State railroad	36	26	26	5	7	100
Banks[h]	24	71	5	—	—	100
Municipal	28	40	21	4	7	100
Water	24	48	1	9	18	100
Amortization[f]	14	71	—	11	4	100
Armed forces	*14*	*—*	*84*	*2*	*—*	*100*
Military[h]	16	—	84	—	—	100
Police	13	—	85	2	—	100
Total	26	52	16	2	4	100

SOURCES: Comisión de Estudios de la Seguridad Social, *Informe sobre la reforma de la seguridad social chilena* (Santiago: Editorial Jurídica de Chile, 1965), vol. 2, p. 827; *Boletín de Estadísticas de Seguridad Social,* no. 25 (May–June 1965), pp. 24–27; and *Seguridad Social,* no. 98 (July 1968), appendix.
  a. Active, passive, and self-employed.
  b. Includes the contribution of the state as employer.
  c. Direct contributions, taxes, subsidies.
  d. Payment of debts, devolutions, fines.
  e. Excludes revenue collected for another fund or welfare agency.
  f. Based on 1967 data.
  g. General banking fund only.
  h. Based on 1959 data which excluded revenue from the last two categories.

Table 2-10 relates the total revenue collected by each fund in a given year to the number of insured which that fund covered in the same year. From the data it can be seen that the group with the highest number of insured (general blue-collar workers, 450,000) received the lowest revenue per capita (797 escudos—E°). This observation largely holds true down the scale until the smallest group (amortization, about 100) received the largest revenue per capita (11,276 E°). The three most important factors in a higher revenue per capita seem to be a low number of insured, a large amount of state contributions either directly or through taxes, and a high income of the insured. (The total legal percentage contribution to the fund is largely irrelevant when compared to these other three factors.) The largest revenue per capita is available to those who need it least.

Table 2-10
Revenue of Social Security Funds per Insured by Occupational Group in Chile: 1967

Occupational Group	Revenue (in thousand E°)	Number of Insured (in thousands)	Revenue per Capita (in E°)	Ratio[a]
Blue-collars	*1,258,971.1*	*1,487.7*	*846.2*	*1.1*
General (SSS)	1,156,428.8	1,450.0	797.5	1.0
Merchant marine	60,369.2	22.1	2,731.6	3.4
Municipal	23,992.8	13.8	1,738.6	2.2
Racetracks[b]	18,180.3	1.8	10,100.2	12.7
Water	—	—	—	—
White-collars	*1,299,224.6*	*288.2*	*4,508.1*	*5.6*
General (CPEP)	1,115,064.3	248.0	4,496.2	5.6
Merchant marine	69,032.0	12.4	5,567.1	7.0
Journalist	31,162.6	12.2	2,554.3	3.2
Bank[c]	58,854.9	7.6	7,744.1	9.7
Special funds	17,048.0	6.0	2,841.3	3.6
Racetracks[d]	8,062.8	2.0	4,031.4	5.1
Civil servants	*449,980.1*	*238.2*	*1,889.1*	*2.4*
General (CNEPP)	365,927.6	205.5	1,780.7	2.2
State Railroad	38,998.7	26.5	1,471.6	1.8
Banks	—	—	—	—
Municipal	35,669.8	5.4	6,605.5	8.3
Water	8,256.4	0.7	11,794.9	14.8
Amortization	1,127.6	0.1	11,276.0	14.1
Armed forces	—	—	—	—
Military	—	—	—	—
Police	200,262.0	29.0	6,905.6	8.7

SOURCES: *Seguridad Social*, n° 98 (July 1968), appendix, table IV, and Caja Bancaria de Pensiones, *Memoria y balance al 30 de junio de 1968* (Santiago: 1968).
  a. Ratio of revenue per capita of each fund related to the lowest one—SSS.
  b. Only Santiago and Antofagasta; excludes Concepción and Punta Arenas.
  c. Only general banking fund; excludes Bank of Chile.
  d. All except Concepción.

The financial situation of the SSS badly deteriorated in the 1960s. First, the state debt from unpaid dues to the Fund for Readjustment of Pensions and the Fund of Public Assistance is growing.[28] Second is the problem of the employer's evasion (sometimes in conspiracy with their employees) of payment of contribution. A third problem concerns the contribution of the insured. There is a ceiling placed on the salaries used to compute the contribution to SSS and, in some cases (e.g., industry and commerce for some time and domestic service still), the ceiling is made equal to the minimum wage which commonly is a small fraction of the actual wage received by the insured. An even more serious problem is the increasing drainage from the SSS of highly paid blue-collars who have been able—through special laws—to change their status to white-collars, thus moving into the CPEP or other funds. In such a move the insured carries his accumulated contributions to the new fund. The SSS is therefore being gradually left with the insured who are paid the least. To compound the situation, there have been numerous laws enacted in the 1960s and early 1970s that eliminate or lower some requisites (e.g., age) to obtain benefits, or that allow low-income groups to enter the SSS without providing adequate financial arrangements. In 1971 the required contribution for a large number of those insured was reduced by one-half, resulting in 8,000 new pensions granted that year. Finally there is the fixing of minimum pensions which are above the minimum wage, particularly serious among domestic servants because employers systematically pay their contribution based on the minimum wage. In practice, these concessions and privileges are subsidized by other groups of insured within the SSS. As a result of all these problems, the SSS pension fund began to show a deficit in 1965 which had grown to 827.4 million E° by 1970, an amount almost equal to the revenue of that pension fund in the same year.[29]

Several technical reports written by domestic and foreign technicians have proved that the social security system in Chile has a regressive effect in terms of income redistribution. The pioneer study was conducted by the Klein and Saks Mission in 1956. Three years later, the Prat Commission—sponsored by the Superintendency of Social Security—estimated that 41 percent of the social security cost was paid by the noninsured—through taxes and employers' contributions, most of which were transferred to the consumer through higher prices—and 54 percent by the insured themselves (the remaining 5 percent was the yield of investment). The commission also detected a considerable transfer of costs among groups of insured, with white-collars and civil servants (including the armed forces) profiting at the expense of blue-collars.[30] In 1967 an attempt was made to quantify the real contribution of each broad occupational group to the pension system of the other groups and what each group actually received in return. The results of this study show that the blue-collars' net gain was one-half of that of white-collars and one-fourteenth that of civil servants and armed forces. The gap was even wider when the net gain per capita was contrasted for these three groups.[31] The most sophisticated study on this subject was published in 1968 by a team of the Superintendency of Social Security and embraced the entire social security system.[32] This study estimated that since 1959 there has been a reduction in the amount of the social security revenue paid by the insured himself (from 54 to 52 percent), while that paid by the noninsured (i.e., employers, the self-employed, and landlords) increased from 41 to 44 percent, the rest being generated mostly by investment returns. In 1971 ODEPLAN indicated a new decline in the percentage of social security paid by the insured (then only 46 percent) and a corresponding increase to 50 percent paid by the noninsured.[33]

Table 2-10a
Transfer of Social Security Costs Among Occupational Groups in Chile: 1965

Occupational Group	Paid to Other Groups (in millions of E°)	Received from Other Groups[a] (in millions of E°)	Net Received	Net Received per Capita[b] (in E°)
Blue-collars	227.5	602.3	374.8	265.4
White-collars	111.4	319.4	208.0	563.4
Civil-servants and armed forces	144.4	486.8	342.4	1,205.6

SOURCES: Carlos Briones et al., "Antecedentes básicos y análisis del estado actual de la seguridad social en Chile," *Seguridad Social*, no. 98 (July 1968), p. 98.
   a. Include all that was paid by the noninsured through direct contributions, transfer to prices, and taxes.
   b. *Net received* divided by number of insured in each occupational group in 1965 taken from table 2-3.

Furthermore blue-collar funds, having 70 percent of the total insured and being the lowest income group, received 42 percent of the contribution of the noninsured. Conversely, white-collar, civil-servant, and armed-forces funds, having 30 percent of the total insured and higher income, received 58 percent of the noninsured contribution. The last column of table 2-10a shows that in 1965 blue-collars had a net per-capita gain equal to one-half that of white-collars and about one-fifth that of civil servants and the armed forces. Thus it can be seen that the cost of social security is increasingly being paid by the noninsured; also, among the insured, revenue from the noninsured goes increasingly to those groups which, because of higher income and fewer insured, need it least.

The above mentioned studies have not explored the redistribution effect among subgroups within major occupational groups. One wonders how much the armed forces and those engaged in judicial and legal careers gain from other civil servants; or how much bankers and merchant marines profit from other white-collars; or how much racetrack employees and sailors get from other blue-collars. It would be interesting to study whether underprivileged subgroups such as domestic servants and agricultural workers are really helped—and, if so, to what degree—by other blue-collars in SSS.

The cost of social security in Chile increased steadily in the 1950s. In 1947 social security revenue represented 6 percent of GNP and 17 percent of the compensation of labor, but in 1959 the proportions had increased respectively to 11.9 and 33.5 percent.[34] Table 2-11 shows that the increase continued during the 1960s, reaching in 1970 proportions of 15.8 percent of GNP, 43.1 percent of compensation of labor, and 115.9 percent of government consumption expenditure. These proportions are approximated in Latin American only by Uruguay, in Europe by some industrialized countries with well-developed welfare systems (e.g., Scandinavian and some Eastern European countries), and by Canada and New Zealand. A projection of social security costs from 1947 to 1970, taking into account the factors which tend to increase such costs, suggests that such costs in Chile will probably reach 20 percent of the GNP by the end of the 1970s.

Rising costs of social security are mainly the result of new benefits granted by the law without providing adequate financing (particularly the increase in the number and amount of pensions), rising administrative expenditures,and the expansion of social security coverage to new groups. The total number of pensions in Chile rose from 223,736 in 1957 to 570,000 in 1968.[35] From 1963 to 1966 the labor force increased by 9 percent but the number of passive workers increased by 42 percent.[36] The average ratio of active vis-a-vis passive workers was 6.3 to 1 in 1960 but declined to 3.6 to 1 in 1971 (see table 2-2). While in 1959 about one-third of social security expenditures went to pensions, the proportion increased to about 45 percent in the late 1960s. Thus ever-increasing demands are made for the funds. Family-allowances take the next most important share of social security expenditures, although the proportion declined from about 36 percent of the total expenditures in the late 1950s to about 26 percent in the late 1960s. The cost of health insurance represented about 20 percent of social security expenditures and is increasing; in 1956 total health costs took 1.6 percent of the GNP and in 1965 the proportion had increased to 2.9 percent.[37] About half of the expenditures of the SNS, the most important health institution, go to salaries and administrative costs which showed an increase in the 1950s and 1960s. With the reorganization and expansion

Table 2-11
Cost of Social Security in Chile: 1960–1970
(in billions of current E° and percentages)

Year	GNP	Government Consumption Expenditure	Compensation of Labor	Social Security Revenue				Social Security Expenditure			
				Total	Percent of GNP	Percent of Government Consumption Expenditure	Percent of Compensation of Labor	Total	Percent of GNP	Percent of Government Consumption Expenditure	Percent of Compensation of Labor
1960	4.9	0.5	2.8	0.6	12.2	120.0	21.4	0.4[a]	8.2	80.0	14.3
1963	8.4	0.8	3.1	1.1	13.1	137.5	35.5	0.9	10.7	112.5	29.0
1964	12.7	1.3	4.8	1.7	13.4	130.8	35.4	1.4	11.0	107.7	29.2
1965	18.0	2.0	7.0	2.6	14.4	130.0	37.1	2.3	12.8	115.0	32.9
1966	25.0	3.0	9.2	3.6	14.4	120.0	39.1	3.1	12.4	103.3	33.7
1968	44.3	5.2	15.9	6.5	14.7	125.0	40.9	—	—	—	—
1969	64.5	7.6	22.7	9.3	14.4	122.4	41.0	—	—	—	—
1970	92.2	12.6	33.9	14.6	15.8	115.9	43.1	—	—	—	—

SOURCES: *Social security revenue and expenditure* from ODEPLAN, *Informe económico anual 1971*, pp. 26, 214–216; Briones et al., "Antecedentes básicos y análisis del estado actual de la seguridad social en Chile," p. 74; and Eduardo Miranda Salas, "El sector agrícola en la seguridad social chilena," *Boletín de Estadísticas de Seguridad Social*, nos. 27–28 (September–December 1965), p. 128. *GNP and government consumption expenditure* from IMF *International Financial Statistics* (Washington, D.C.: January 1969 and January 1972). *Compensation of labor* from UN Yearbook of *National Account Statistics 1970* (New York: 1972).

a. 1959.

of health services in 1968, health costs should increase substantially in the 1970s.

The cost of administration of social security is extremely high in Chile. For example, from 1961 to 1969 the average proportion of administrative expenses in relation to total social security expenditures was as high as 48 percent in the SNS.[38] Part of the high administrative costs are derived from the excessive bureaucracy (the reader should again look at figure 2-1) which determines its own share of social security resources without effective central control. At the end of the 1950s the system employed about 26 percent of the total number of civil servants in Chile.[39] (Data on employees for the 1960s are not available.) Administrative costs are not likely to be reduced.

The expansion of social security coverage to include new groups of low income with some state subsidy or taxes has also contributed to the increase in costs. In 1968, with the reorganization and centralization of the insurance against occupational accidents and diseases, the number of insured increased threefold and most entrants were probably hired by small enterprises and had low incomes. Finally, in 1972 some 200,000 small entrepreneurs and self-employed, most of them with low incomes, and their 220,000 dependents entered the social security system.

The cost of social security at a rate of 16 percent of the GNP certainly can be afforded only by highly industrialized countries. The sluggishness of the Chilean economy in the last decade could be partially explained by high social security costs and prospects for the current decade are no better.

Benefits

The regulations on benefits are the same throughout the territory of Chile. There are differences, however, in the quality of hospital and medical services by region which will be discussed later. The most significant inequalities in this field are derived from the occupational structure. Table 2-12 summarizes the benefits that are enjoyed by the main occupational subgroups, which are clustered into four main groups. A simple count of the boxes in the table allows us to rank the main occupational groups (and the subgroups within each) by the number of benefits granted as follows: (1) civil servants (municipal and amortization; general-CNEPP and water; banks; and state railroad) and white-collars (banks; journalists, merchant marine and general-CPEP; and racetracks); (2) armed forces (military and police equal); and (3) blue-collars (racetracks; and municipal, merchant marine and general-SSS). Some subgroups that belong to the same activity but are divided by white- and blue-collar funds usually have more under the former than under the latter (e.g., municipal, merchant marine) with racetracks being the opposite. In any event, the gap shown in the table between the less privileged subgroups (led by the SSS with 26 benefits) and the most privileged (led by private banks with 32 benefits) is a narrow one. This is the result of Chile's long struggle for universalization or massification of privileges.

The most striking difference shown in table 2-12 is that most of the insured, who happen to be blue-collars (SSS, sailors), do not have a right to seniority pensions while all the remaining funds have that right. The same is true of unemployment pensions enjoyed by everybody except most blue-collars and white-collars in the CPEP (which are the majority). Furthermore, the insured in SSS do not have a lump-sum payment for layoff. Rather they only have the right to withdraw savings accumulated in their retirement fund, an action which will eventually reduce their old-age pension if such funds are not redeposited. This lack of blue-collar unemployment pension and indemnification is particularly inequitable because this group is the one

Table 2-12
Social Security Benefits by Occupational Group in Chile: 1970

	Pensions								Other Cash Benefits											Family Allowances								Health-Maternity								Total
Occupational Group	1	2	3	4	5	6^d	7	8	9	10	11	12^a	13	14	15	16	17	18	19	20	21	22	23	24	25	26	27	28^b	29^a	30	31^p	32^a	33^c	34	35^a	
Blue-collars																																				
General (SSS)	x	x	x	x		x	x	x	x	x	x	x	x	x	x^f		x				x		x	x	x	x		x	x	x	x	x	x	x^c	x	25
Merchant marine	x	x	x^j	x		x	x	x	x	x	x	x	x	x^e	x^g		x				x		x	x	x	x		x	x	x	x	x	x	x^c	x	25
Municipal	x	x^j	x^j	x		x	x	x		x	x	x	x	x	x		x				x		x	x	x^o	x		x	x	x	x	x	x		x	25
Racetracks	x	x	x	x	x^j	x	x	x^n	x	x	x	x	x	x	x	x^n	x				x		x	x	x	x		x	x	x	x	x	x	x	x	27
White-collars																																				
General (CPEP)	x	x	x	x	x^f	x	x	x	x	x	x	x	x	x	x	x	x				x		x	x	x	x^s		x	x^r	x	x	x^r	x^r		x^r	28
Merchant marine	x	x	x	x	x^{h,i}	x	x	x	x	x	x	x	x	x^h	x^{g,h}	x^h	x				x		x	x	x	x^s		x^r	x	x	x	x	x		x^r	28
Journalists	x	x	x	x	x	x	x	x	x	x	x	x	x		x	x^h	x				x		x	x	x	x^s		x^r	x^r	x	x	x^r	x^r	x	x^r	28
Banks	x^v	x	x	x	x	x	x	x	x	x	x	x	x	x^i	x	x	x	x			x	x^i	x	x	x	x	x^i	x	x	x	x	x^r	x	x	x	31
Racetracks	x^v	x	x	x^k	x	x	x	x		x	x	x	x	x^i	x	x	x				x		x	x	x	x^s		x	x^r	x	x	x^r	x^r		x^r	25
Civil servants																																				
General (CNEPP)	x	x	x	x	x^f	x	x	x	x	x	x	x	x	x	x	x	x				x		x	x	x	x^s		x^r	x^r	x	x	x^r	x^r	x	x^r	28
State railroad	x	x	x	x	x	x	x	x	x	x	x	x	x	x	x	x	x						x	x	x			x	x	x	x	x	x	x	x	26
Banks	x	x	x	x	x	x	x	x	x	x	x	x	x	x	x^m		x					x^m	x	x	x			x	x	x	x	x	x		x	27
Municipal	x	x	x	x	x	x	x	x	x	x	x	x	x	x^k	x	x^l	x					x^k	x	x	x^o	x^s		x	x^r	x	x	x^r	x^r	x^k	x	30
Water	x	x	x	x	x	x	x	x	x	x	x	x	x	x	x	x	x				x		x	x	x	x^s		x^r	x^r	x	x	x^r	x^r		x^r	28
Amortization	x	x	x	x	x	x	x	x	x	x	x	x	x	x	x	x	x	x			x		x	x	x	x^s		x	x^r	x	x	x^r	x^r		x^r	30
Armed forces																																				
Military	x	x^u	x	x	x	x	x	x	x	x	x	x	x	x	x		x						x	x	x			x	x	x	x	x	x	x	x	27
Police	x	x	x	x	x	x	x	x	x	x	x	x	x	x	x	x	x	x			x		x	x	x^o	x^s		x	x	x	x	x	x	x	x	27

SOURCES: Comisión de Estudios de la Seguridad Social, *Informe sobre la reforma de la seguridad social chilena*, pp. 585–788; Orlandini, "Características básicas de la seguridad social en Chile," pp. 43–63; Briones et al., pp. 39, 48–70; Miguel Requena Criado, "Análisis de la estructura en los Institutos de Previsión Social en Chile," *Memoria* Universidad de Chile, Facultad de Ciencias Económicas, 1968, pp. 26–28; and compilation of recent legislation by the author.

NOTE: See code following table for definition of benefits here signified by numbers 1–35.

a. Includes subsidy for preventive rest in case statutory diseases are discovered in insured.

b. For insured only to check statutory diseases.

c. Only in case of occupational hazards.

d. All funds grant survivors' pension to the widow and/or children. Six funds grant pensions to sisters specifically and all to "other dependents."

e. Unemployment loan.

f. Withdrawal of savings accumulated by the insured.

g. When shipwreck occurs.

h. Officials and white-collar sections only.

i. Only for a period of one to two years.

j. Santiago fund only.

k. Valparaíso fund only.

l. General fund only.

m. State Bank fund only.

n. Antofagasta and Punta Arenas only.

o. Mothers only.

p. For spouse of insured also.

q. For active and passive insured and their dependents who have a right to family allowances (usually spouse and children).

r. The beneficiary has to pay from 30 to 50 percent of the costs according to the insured's income.

s. Available at reduced price.

t. Available for congressmen, councilmen, judges, notaries public, registrars (of real estate, mines, commercial transactions and civil archives), state attorneys, judicial auxiliary personnel and employees of notaries and registrars.

u. For incurable disease only.

v. Only withdrawal of retirement funds but not pension.

(Notes continued on page 60)

Code for Social Security Benefits

Pensions:
1. Old age.
2. Seniority.
3. Permanent disability (total or partial) caused by occupational hazards.
4. Permanent disability (total or partial) caused by nonoccupational hazards.
5. Unemployment/layoff.
6. Survivors'.

Other Cash Benefits:
7. Restitution of contributions.
8. Lump sum at retirement.
9. Bonus added to pension for work-years above the minimum required for retirement.
10. Lump sum for permanent disability (total or partial) caused by occupational hazards.
11. Subsidy for temporary disability caused by occupational hazards.
12. Subsidy for temporary disability caused by nonoccupational hazards.
13. Salary (or percentage thereof) paid for a period before and after childbirth.
14. Unemployment/layoff temporary subsidy.
15. Unemployment/layoff lump sum.
16. Life insurance, lump sum.
17. Funeral aid, lump sum.
18. Lump sum to survivors when no right to pension is granted.
19. Year-end bonus to retired and pensioners.

Family Allowances:
20. Marriage.
21. Pregnancy.
22. Childbirth.
23. Children.
24. Spouse.
25. Parents.
26. Child food (percentage of salary or in kind).
27. School aid (for insured or his/her children).

Health-Maternity Benefits:
28. Preventive medicine.
29. Curative medical care.
30. Rehabilitation and prosthesis in case of occupational hazards.
31. Maternity care.
32. Surgical treatment.
33. Hospitalization.
34. Medicines.
35. Dental care.

which has the least job stability and hence is most affected by unemployment. Conversely blue-collars, protected by the SNS, do well in terms of health care for the insured and dependents which is available free, while many white-collars and civil servants have to pay part of their expenses.

The true inequality among occupational subgroups cannot be evaluated from table 2-12 because, for the sake of comparison, it equates benefits of the same nature which in practice may be significantly different in such matters as: (a) requirements to gain the right (e.g., age, years of service, and degree of disability); (b) basic salary to compute the benefit (e.g., it may be equal to the minimum wage or include all fringe benefits, or it could be computed using an average for the last five years or the salary of the last month); (c) the amount of the benefit (e.g., the percentage of the salary fixed for the pension, the fixed amount of the funeral aid, the length of time in which a subsidy is paid, and ceilings placed on benefits); (d) the adjustment of pensions to the cost of living; and (e) the compatibility of the pension with other pensions or salaried work. What follows are the most relevant differences among occupational subgroups.[40]

Old-age pensions become effective at age 65 for males and 55 for females in SSS, CPEP, and CNEPP (general); at 55 for journalists, merchant marines, and the armed forces; and at 50 for those in the general banking fund. The number of weekly contributions required to gain the benefit is as follows: 1,040 for armed forces, 800 for SSS and merchant marine, 750 for general banking, 520 for CNEPP (including journalists and most civil servants), and 52 for CPEP. The number of years of service for seniority pension are: 35 for males and 30–25 for females in CPEP, 30 and 25 respectively in CNEPP, 25 in racetrack, 24 in general banking (23.5 years in others), 20 in the armed forces and for journalists, and 15 for congressmen. Due to the low number of years required for seniority retirement, some insured can retire at age 28. It has been speculated that this type of pension is a safety valve for middle-class frustrations and keeping the active military out of politics. Those under seniority pensions can be employed in another trade and retired militarymen in politics.[41] The number of years required for unemployment pensions is usually 15 (e.g., CNEPP, armed forces), but in some banking funds only 10–13 years are required. Disability (total or partial) pension requirements are more flexible and broad in the armed-forces, civil-servant, and banking funds than in other funds. Survivors' pensions vary in the generosity of whom they include (all benefit widow, children, and parents; some add sisters and disabled brothers) and the division of benefits. The most generous conditions are those for civil servants, white-collar workers, and the armed forces, while blue-collars have tougher regulations.[42]

The basic remuneration for calculating the pension is usually an average of the *sueldo vital* (roughly the minimum wage, although in some funds, e.g., banking, it is the actual salary including fringe benefits) received in a varying number of months prior to retirement: 60 in SSS and CPEP; 36 in CNEPP, merchant-marine, and banking funds; 12 in railroad and journalist funds; and the last month in the armed forces. Due to spiraling inflation and the usual Chilean practice of increasing the insured's salary at the end of his employemnt, the shorter the period for computing the average and the closer to the time of retirement or death, the higher the pension amount will be. The pension is finally fixed as a percentage of the computed average. Such a percentage varies according to the type of pension and fund; it is usually fixed at 100 percent in seniority pensions; in old age it varies from 50 to 100 percent; in disability, from 40 to 100 percent; and in survivors' pensions, from 20 to 100 percent. (To this basic percentage there is an increment of 1–2 percent for each year of service above a fixed minimum.) Basic and incremental percentages are higher for the armed-forces, banking, and white-collar funds, and lower for blue-collars. There are also special pensions—usually higher than the rest—granted to congressmen, notaries public, and registrars.

Because of galloping inflation in Chile (the cost of living increased by almost 300 percent between 1959 and 1971 and by an additional 134 percent in 1972 alone), the adjustment of pensions is of pivotal importance. Some funds have an automatic adjustment: high-ranking officials of the armed forces receive an adjustment equal to the cost-of-living increase, and about one-fourth of civil servants (among them congressmen, cabinet ministers, supreme court judges, and other high officials) get 75 percent of such an increase. (These adjustments are totally paid by the state.) Furthermore these groups have a special privilege, the *perseguidora,* through which their pensions are also adjusted according to the increases in the salary that they would have been receiving if they were in active service. Until 1963 pensions of the majority of insured (all blue- and white-collars and low-ranked civil servants) were adjusted annually by special laws approved after considerable delay (often causing a loss in the purchasing power of the pension as high as 80 percent). It can be seen that the automatic adjustment renders a pension much more valuable.

Comparison of other benefit requirements also shows substantial inequalities. Funeral aid is fixed as equal to the minimum wage by the SSS, to the last salary by CNEPP, one-and-a-half times the minimum wage for journalists, two for the armed-forces, and three for the CPEP and banking funds. Family allowances are computed upon the minimum wage or the actual salary; at very high rates for banking, merchant-marine, and CPEP and very low rates for SSS. Maternity-leave subsidy is fixed at 85 percent of the insured salary of blue-collars (in SNS) but at 100 percent of those insured by CPEP, CNEPP, and other funds. Subsidies paid for rest periods prescribed for statutory diseases for those under SNS are fixed at 85 percent of the salary for a period of six months, but for those under SMNE at 100 percent of the salary and for one year plus a possible six-month extension. In general, the higher the salary of the insured, the better the benefits. A comparison of the incompatability of a pension with other pensions or salaried work also shows remarkable differences. Multiple pensions may not be accrued by blue-collar workers in the SSS and the merchant marine. Pensions may be accrued in some cases by white-collar workers in the CPEP and the merchant marine and in all cases by the armed forces and journalists. All types of pensions are cumulative for salaried work for policemen, notaries public, registrars, custom brokers, and employees of racetracks, state banks, the amortization agency, and Santiago municipality and water plant. Old-age pensions can be collected while working in a paid job by blue-collars covered by SSS and the merchant-marine fund. Pensions are incompatible with salaried work in the same activity for which the pension is granted for white-collars under CPEP, merchant-marine, and general banking funds. Finally pensions are incompatible with all paid jobs in the public sector for those covered by CNEPP, armed forces (with exceptions), state railroad, and municipalities outside of Santiago and Valparaíso.

The previous information when put together gives a more accurate measurement of the degree of generosity of the benefit system in each occupational group than the simple counting based on table 2-12. In 15 comparisons, the armed forces ranked first in 8, civil servants (CNEPP) in 5, white-collars (CPEP) in 5, and blue-collars (SSS) in none. (Blue-collars were ranked last in more than half of the comparisons.) Bank-

Table 2-13
Average Yearly Pensions and Family Allowances by Occupational Group in Chile: 1967
(in current E° per capita)

Occupational Group	Old-Age	Seniority	Disability	Survivors'	Overall Average[b]	Ratio[c]	Per Capita	Ratio[c]
			Pensions[a]				Family Allowances	
Blue-collars	*2,568*	*3,120*	*2,508*	*828*	*1,980*	*1.1*	*204*	*1.1*
General (SSS)	2,520	d	2,388	792	1,920	1.0	204[h]	1.0
Merchant marine	6,180	d	6,252	1,992	4,656	2.5	420	2.1
Municipal	2,796	3,288	2,916	1,764	2,436	1.3	396	2.0
Racetracks	d	3,000	3,132	2,232	2,880	1.5	360	1.8
Water	—	—	—	—	—	—	—	—
White-collars	*8,568*	*10,944*	*8,424*	*3,144*	*6,025*	*3.2*	*516*	*2.6*
General (CPEP)	9,036	13,392	8,988	3,216	7,464	3.9	492	2.4
Merchant marine	5,760	10,236	5,952	3,612	6,384	3.4	864	4.3
Journalists[e]	—	—	—	—	2,664	1.4	—	—
Banks	3,960	7,104	d	3,396	6,120	3.2	780	3.9
Special funds	4,248	5,916	3,876	1,536	3,558	1.9	492	2.5
Racetracks	d	2,304	2,016	1,248	2,040	1.1	372	1.9
Civil servants	*6,720*	*9,504*	*4,872*	*1,416*	*4,032*	*2.1*	*336*	*1.7*
General (CNEPP)[f]	5,148	7,524	4,044	888	3,840	2.0	288	1.5
State railroad	d	7,164	d	1,536	1,596	0.9	324	1.6
Banks	d	11,208	8,208	6,192	10,152	5.3	864	4.3
Municipal	8,220	21,492	14,172	5,448	10,248	5.4	408	2.0
Water	4,392	9,228	4,824	3,504	7,020	3.7	480	2.4
Amortization	7,704	25,464	d	10,008	16,238	8.5	492	2.5
Armed forces	*5,668*	*8,304*	*6,348*	*4,032*	*6,666*	*3.5*	*300*	*1.5*
Military	d,g	8,868	d	3,432	7,104	3.7	300	1.5
Police	5,688	7,212	6,360	4,728	6,060	3.2	288	1.5
Total	2,808	8,880	2,892	1,596	3,312	1.7	312	1.6

SOURCES: Based on data from República de Chile, Dirección de Estadística y Censo, *Boletín*, 40 (December 1967), pp. 523–30. Journalists from *Seguridad Social*, no. 98 (July 1968), appendix, table 1.

a. Monthly average obtained by dividing the amount of E° paid into the number of beneficiaries in each fund in December 1967.

b. Includes "other pensions" for unemployment and "public utility", and bonuses which are not disaggregated in the table due to its variety.

c. Ratios of average pension per capita (total) and of family allowances in relation to the lowest average per capita, that of SSS.

d. Pension not available in this fund or paid by another institution or enterprise.

e. Disaggregated data not available.

f. Data from December 1966. Due to inflation the figures should be increased by 10–20 percent.

g. The figure for 1966 was 560.

h. Excluded "Compensation Funds" and other family-allowance systems outside of SSS.

ing became clearly a privileged subgroup both among white-collars and civil servants. Congressmen, notaries public, registrars and supreme court judges seem to be a privileged subgroup within the CNEPP.[43]

Table 2-13 presents a comparison of average per-capita yearly benefits in the two most important social security programs: pensions and family allowances. The highest pensions were paid to the armed forces, followed by white-collars, and civil servants, with blue-collars at the bottom. Some small funds such as amortization, banks, and municipal (civil servants) had an average per-capita pension five to eight times higher than that of SSS (mostly blue-collars). The CPEP, merchant marine, and bank (within white-collar funds), the military and policemen, and water plant had an average per capita 3 to 4 times higher than that of SSS. Finally the CNEPP average per capita was twice as high as that of SSS. The lowest family allowance was also paid to those insured under SSS, with merchant marine (white-collar) and banks (both types) receiving 4 times that amount; and the rest of the funds about 2 times the SSS rate. The situation did not improve in 1968 when the extreme differential ratio of family allowances (between SSS and the highest paid subgroup, usually banks) was 1 to 5. (This ratio was stagnant in the period 1965–1969.) Nevertheless, in 1970–1971 the government began a project to reduce the gap in family allowances by increasing the blue-collar rate by 100 percent while reducing that of the civil servants (CNEPP) by 50 percent and that of white-collars (CPEP) by 35 percent. (The armed-forces rate was increased by 112 percent in 1970–1971; however they had a relatively low rate in the 1960s.) Thus in 1971, three of the four main occupational groups (blue-collars, civil servants, and armed forces) had a similar family-allowance rate: 90 E° for the first and 102 E° for the last two. White-collars still had a substantially higher rate (160 E°), but the equalization was clear. The plan called for a total equalization among the fourteen different systems by 1976. Another government legal draft attempting to standardize contributions and requirements for pensions, however, was not successful.[44]

Other comparisons in minor monetary benefits (e.g., funeral aid, unemployment lump sums, life insurance) made in 1965 also show striking differences. The average per-capita funeral aid of the SSS was one-half or less that of any other fund. In life insurance the highest average amount received was by CNEPP (4,366 E°), more than ten times that received by water-plant and municipal (blue-collar) workers. The highest average unemployment lump sum was registered in the water-plant fund (42,946 E°), about 6 times that received by the armed forces and municipal (civil-servant) workers; more than 10 times that received by CNEPP, state-railroad, and bank fund members; and more than 20 times that received by CPEP and merchant marine. (SSS insured do not have these benefits.)[45]

To measure the degree of inequality by occupational groups in the system of benefits, it is also necessary to include a discussion of the availability and quality of health care. See table 2-14. Expenditures in health care exclude administrative expenses and have been estimated (in the two cases) with very poor statistics. Further, uneven quality of data available make it difficult to tabulate relative expenditures in health care. In the first estimate white-collars seem to get the highest per-capita medical benefit, followed by civil servants, blue-collars, and policemen. In the second estimate civil servants and armed forces have been clustered and come up with the highest per-capita medical benefit, followed by blue-collars and white-collars (just the opposite conclusion!).[46] Estimates of the number of indigents receiving health care are highly speculative; in 1965 they ranged from 800,000 to 2 million. The calculations of hospital beds per capita seem to be consistent with my own estimate for expenditures with white-collars and civil servants ranked first, followed by blue-collars and the armed forces. The latter's figures are probably underestimated because a large part of the services are under contract with other hospitals and not included in the table.[47]

A team of Pan American health specialists that visited most Chilean hospital facilities in the early 1960s provided a qualitative judgment which is probably more helpful. According to this team, SNS (blue-collar) hospitals were overcrowded, with

Table 2-14
Health Facilities and Expenditures by Occupational Group in Chile: 1965

	Expenditures[a]				Hospital Beds[b]	
	Estimate 1		Estimate 2			
Occupational Group	Million E°	Per Capita[c]	Million E°	Per Capita[c]	Total	Per 1,000
Blue-collars	103.3	25.9	156.4	39.2	29,150[h]	7.9
White-collars	39.9[d]	75.7	15.6	29.6	7,480[i]	8.4[i]
Civil servants	21.0[e]	49.6	29.4[g]	71.0[g]	1,138[j]	3.2
Armed forces	2.2[f]	13.8				
Indigents	—	—	77.1	—	—	—
Total	166.4	32.7	278.5	32.7	37,668	7.6

SOURCES: *Expenditures,* estimate 1 by the author based on data from *Boletín de Estadísticas de Seguridad Social,* no. 25 (May–June 1965), pp. 21, 28–31, *Seguridad Social,* no. 98 (July 1968), appendices, and scattered data; estimate 2 by Briones et al., pp. 74, 87, 90. *Hospital beds* from Roemer, pp. 232–35, and Roy Penchansky, ed., *Health Services Administration: Policy Cases and the Case Method* (Cambridge, Mass.: Harvard University Press, 1968), pp. 288–331. Estimates of insured population by the author.
  a. Subsidies, preventive and curative medicine, exclude administration costs.
  b. 1963.
  c. Expenditures divided into an estimate of the insured population in that year (active, passive, and dependents) with right to health benefits.
  d. Excludes Bank of Chile.
  e. Excludes state-railroad, bank, water-plant, and some municipal funds.
  f. Policemen only.
  g. Includes civil servants and armed forces.
  h. Includes contracted services with other hospitals.
  i. Includes white-collars and civil servants.
  j. Most services are under contract with other hospitals and not included.

long lines of patients waiting for medical exams, and often had two patients sharing one bed. There were complaints from patients, particularly from agricultural workers, that they did not receive adequate attention. The insured were given preference over indigents when there was a shortage of beds, and in some hospitals there were separate waiting rooms for the two types of patients. Standards of the SMNE (white-collar) hospitals were ranked as "higher" than those of SNS, and bank hospitals in turn "better in quality and attention" than those of SMNE. Hospitals and outpatient clinics supported by large mining, railroad, and industrial enterprises were reported as "well operated" and offered "good service." Finally, private hospitals and clinics (especially in Santiago and other large cities) were evaluated as "excellent" in terms of buildings, equipment, and personnel. These clinics charged high prices for their services, but nevertheless were used by 37 percent of those insured in SNS in Santiago.[48] The Pan American team did not investigate the armed-forces hospitals, but another specialist interviewed a former head of the Air Force Health Service who stated that the care provided by the armed-forces health services was considerably better than that of the SNS in terms of facilities, personnel, and time devoted to patients.[49] In summary, the ranking in terms of facilities, quality, and attention was as follows: private, enterprise, banking, probably armed forces, SMNE, and SNS (within the latter, the insured being better attended than the indigent).

The distribution of hospital and medical services by region is also unequal. There is a large concentration of hospitals, outpatient clinics, and physicians in Santiago,

Table 2-15
Health Facilities by Geographical Region in Chile: 1964

Region	Total Population (in thousands)	Hospital Beds[a]	Beds per 1,000 Inhabitants	Physicians[a]	Physicians per 10,000 Inhabitants	Composite Weighted Index of Beds and Physicians
North	1,041	4,214	4.0	288	2.8	3.6
Center[b]	4,977	22,492	4.5	3,383	6.8	5.7
South[b]	2,474	6,589	2.7	609	2.5	2.6
Total	8,492	33,295	3.9	4,280	5.0	4.4

SOURCES: *Population* from SSS, *Estadísticas 1964*, p. 100. *Hospital bed* and *physician* ratios from Armand Matherlart and Manuel A. Garretón, *Integración nacional y marginalidad: Un ensayo de regionalización social en Chile* (Santiago: Editorial del Pacífico, 1965), pp. 38–39. SNS data from *Boletín de Estadísticas*, no. 24 (March–April 1965), pp. 30, 34, 46.
  a. All of the nation.
  b. Concepcíon province was clustered in the original data into a "health zone" with some southern provinces and the disaggregation was not possible. This has somewhat inflated the per capitas and index of the South and deflated those of the Center.

Valparaíso, and Concepción. In 1959 it was reported that 50 percent of the physicians were concentrated in those three cities, but one year later 63 percent of the physicians were in the province of Santiago alone.[50] Table 2-15 shows the distribution of health facilities by geographical regions in Chile. The Center and the North are very close in number of hospital beds, having twice as many as the South, but physicians are clearly concentrated in the Center which has a ratio almost three times higher than the North and the South. The provinces best serviced by hospital beds and physicians are Santiago, Valparaíso, Magallanes, Antofagasta, and Tarapacá. Conversely, the provinces of Arauco, Llanquihue, Bío-Bío, Malleco, and Cautín (agricultural and with the largest concentration of Indians in the nation), as well as the isolated Chiloé, are the worst in terms of hospital and medical services. In 1970, the province of Santiago had about 6 times the number of physicians per 10,000 inhabitants that Arauco, Llanquihue, and Chiloé had.[51] These differences are reflected in the general and infant mortality indices of the Chilean provinces. In the period 1969–1971, infant mortality in Arauco, Llanquihue, Malleco, Bío-Bío, and Chiloé was from 2 to 3 times higher than in Magallanes, Santiago, Valparaíso, and Tarapacá.[52]

The Inequality Effect of Social Security Stratification

The inequalities of the social security system of Chile can be summarized in terms of: the proportion of the population insured vis-a-vis that noninsured by the system; the different treatment in coverage, financing, and benefits among the occupational groups and subgroups of the insured population; and the different treatment in coverage and benefits among geographical regions. The massification of privilege and its negative consequences must also be considered.

Coverage of the economically active population in Chile is one of the highest in

Latin America and is still increasing, from 67 to 70 percent in the period 1960–1971. Coverage of the whole population expanded even more dramatically from 63 to 72 percent in the same period. With the system's incorporation of a large number of self-employed and small entrepreneurs in the early 1970s, coverage in 1973 was close to four-fifths of both the EAP and total population.

The largest group of insured in Chile (and one of the largest in Latin America) is that of blue-collars in SSS (70 percent of the total number of insured), followed by white-collars in CPEP (12 percent), civil servants in CNEPP (10 percent), and the military (2 percent). Each of the remaining funds has 1 percent or less of the number of insured. In the mid-1960s, the highest degree of protection was registered among the military, civil servants, and white-collars (92 percent), closely followed by blue-collars (90 percent); quite apart were the self-employed (14 percent), and even in a worse situation were small entrepreneurs and unpaid family workers. However, the degree of coverage of self-employed and small entrepreneurs increased to about 30 percent in the early 1970s.

A comparison of the degree of protection by economic sectors resulted in the following ranking: mining and public utilities (above 100 percent, due to duplicate accounting); manufacturing and construction (80 to 100 percent); commerce, transportation, and services (65 to 67 percent); and agriculture (55 percent). Evidence accumulated in this chapter suggests that the segment of the labor force with the most protection is made up of salaried personnel, working in strategic trades, with a high degree of unionization, and with medium to high income. Conversely the segment of the labor force with the least protection is made up mainly of self-employed, unpaid family workers, working in agriculture and personal services, and with low income.

In most occupational groups the overall contribution of the insured roughly increases as the income of the group rises with a progressive effect in income redistribution. And yet, the bulk of social security revenues comes from employers' contributions and state contributions and subsidies. In armed-forces and civil-servant funds (whose insured have relatively high incomes) the employers' contribution is either small or nil, but the state subsidizes or absorbs all resulting deficits. A good number of funds, also covering the workers with relatively high incomes, enjoy the revenues from special taxes paid either directly by the consumers of their product or services or by the general public. In view of this information, the data available on the percentage distribution of social security revenue by source are, in part at least, surprising. According to these data, the major groups can be ranked by the lowest insured contribution (and, consequently, the highest combined employer-state contribution) as follows: armed forces (14 and 84 percent), blue-collars (20 and 72 percent), white-collars (28 and 69 percent), and civil servants (42 and 50 percent). Except for the armed forces, therefore, the financing system appears as progressive instead of regressive. There are, however, groups that fare much better than the general group in which they are clustered, for example, racetrack employees among blue-collars (0 and 89 percent), merchant marines among white-collar (20 and 72 percent), and bank workers among civil servants (24 and 76 percent).

A more accurate picture of the overall effect of social security in income redistribution is provided by the analysis of net transfers among occupational groups. In the mid-1960s, blue-collar funds, having 70 percent of the total insured and being the lowest income group, received 42 percent of the contribution to the social security system from the noninsured. Conversely, white-collar, civil-servant, and armed-forces funds, having 30 percent of the total insured and higher income, received 58 percent of the noninsured contribution. In terms of net transfers, blue-collars had a net per-capita gain equal to one-half that of white-collars and about one-fifth that of both civil servants and the armed forces. The regressive nature of the social security system becomes obvious from these data.

A simple counting of the numerous social security benefits available to each occupational group insured results in the following ranking: (1) civil servants and white-collars receive the most benefits, followed by (2) armed forces, and (3) blue-collars. But this accounting overlooks substantive differences in the conditions to grant benefits among the various groups, benefits that in the simple reckoning are assumed equal. Taking into account such differences, a more accurate ranking shows the armed forces in the first place, followed by civil servants and white-collars, with blue-collars at the end. There are subgroups which either through legislation or collective bargaining enjoy more generous benefits than the major group in which they are classified. This is the case for banking (both among white-collars and civil servants); for congressmen, notaries public, registrars, and supreme court judges among civil servants; and for copper, steel, manufacturing, energy, and construction workers among blue-collars.

A comparison of per-capita pensions among major groups indicates that blue-collars receive one-third the average per-capita pension paid to both the armed forces and white-collars, and one-half that paid to civil servants. In other comparisons of the amount of benefits (e.g., family allowances, funeral aid, maternity leave subsidy) blue-collars consistently receive the lowest per-capita sum. Again subgroups such as merchant-marine, banking, municipal, and water-plant employees receive much better benefits than the major group to which they belong.

Statistics on the availability and quality of health care by occupational groups are contradictory and inconclusive. More useful are qualitative evaluations of hospital facilities and quality of services made by internationally known public health specialists. They indicate that the best services are provided by private and banking clinics, probably followed by those of the armed forces, then those of SMNE which cover civil servants and white-collars and, finally, those of SNS, with the attention given to blue-collars being much better than that to the noninsured.

The various comparisons presented above allow us to rank the four main occupational groups according to the excellence of their social security systems as follows: first the armed forces, clearly separated from the rest; next civil servants, closely followed by white-collars; and finally, at a considerable distance, blue-collars.

Social security inequalities of coverage and health facilities among the three geographic regions of Chile (North, Center, and South) were also detected. The most developed region (and the one with the highest average income) is the Center, in which there is a concentration of government and financial services as well as industry, and in which the largest cities and most important ports are located. The North follows closely with its wealth generated by mining, which in turn has provided the basis for strong unions and militant labor. The South is the least developed region (and the one with the lowest income); it is basically agricultural and its labor force is poorly unionized.

The social security coverage of the population of the regions is 20 percent in the Center, 18 percent in the North, and 14 percent in the South. In terms of the ratio of hospital beds per 1,000 inhabitants, the Center and North are very close, having a ratio twice as high as that of the South. Physicians are clearly concentrated in the Center which has a ratio (of physicians per 10,000 inhabitants) almost three times higher than in the North and the South. Differences of coverage and benefits among the provinces are more remarkable than in the regions. The most populated, industrialized, unionized, and wealthiest provinces have the highest social security coverage of their labor force, for example, Antofagasta (80 percent), Concepción (65 percent), Santiago (63 percent). The most isolated, depopulated, rural, and poorest provinces, with a concentration of Indians and illiterates who are also badly unionized and politically passive, have the lowest social security coverage of their labor force, for example, Chiloé (18 percent), Arauco, and Cautín (both 35 percent). In 1970, the province of Santiago had six times more physicians per 10,000 inhabitants than the southern provinces of Arauco, Llanquihue, and Chiloé.

The massification of social security privileges has taken place in Chile to a larger extent than in any other Latin American country with the exception of Uruguay. Even among blue-collars the group with least power and lowest income, there is a tendency to expand benefits and make them easier to collect. The proportion of social security revenue in relation to GNP increased from 12.2 percent in 1960 to 15.8 percent in 1970. Rising costs of social security are the result of the expansion of coverage, maturation of pension programs for large groups, and granting of new benefits without provision of adequate financing. While in 1960 the ratio of active vis-a-vis passive was 6.3 to 1 (already one of the lowest in Latin America), it declined in 1971 to 3.6 active to 1 passive.

Funds that cover a small group of insured (e.g., armed forces, civil servants, and white-collars), even if they provide a very generous program of benefits, enjoy a stable financial situation because of the high income of their insured and the substantial contributions of the employer and the state. (This is true also of subgroups that have even a smaller population of insured, such as racetracks and banking.) But SSS which covers the largest group of insured, blue-collars (who also happen to have the lowest income and relatively small contributions from employers and the state) cannot afford the luxury of relatively meager benefits. In 1967 per-capita revenue in SSS was one-ninth that of the police fund, one-sixth that of CPEP, and one-half that of CNEPP. The financial situation of SSS has deteriorated even more because of mounting state debts, employers' evasion, and the increasing exodus of the best paid insured to richer funds (thus gradually leaving SSS with the lowest income group). In the mid-1960s the SSS fund showed a deficit that has since been rapidly increasing.

Most experts agree that the prescription for the ills of inequality and excessive costs of the Chilean system of social security is unification and standardization. But successive democratic governments (i.e., Conservative, Christian Democratic, or Socialist) were not capable of implementing the needed reforms. Until the military coup of 1973, the powerful pressure groups had been successful in retaining their privileges. It remains to be seen if the current autocratic, military regime can and will use its power to move towards unification and standardization.

3 The Case of Uruguay
Prepared by Arturo C. Porzecanski

Historical Evolution of Social Security in Uruguay Since Independence

Uruguay's independence efforts, which began around 1810, had been persistently thwarted by the Spanish, the Portuguese, and the British, all of whom took turns in forcibly claiming the sparsely populated piece of land strategically located between two empires.[1] After the signing of a peace treaty in 1828, José Rondeau served as interim governor until the nation's constitution was approved and its first president elected. Understandably concerned with many of the diplomatic and administrative needs of a newborn country, Rondeau also found time to issue directives and sponsor legislation on social affairs. Among these were measures to promote elementary education; to create a Committee on Hygiene to watch over public health and sanitation; and a law (1829) to provide pensions for the relatives of soldiers killed in the struggle for independence, as well as pensions for those disabled in the fighting.[2]

1829-1913

Uruguay's first constitution, approved in 1830, provided for a president to be elected by a General Assembly every four years, but for a period of seventy years Uruguay was torn by internal strife, caused mostly by the unwillingness of various caudillos to surrender their authority peacefully to any one political administration. This clash of personalities slowly gave way to a struggle between differing interest groups and ideological affiliations, leading to the birth of Uruguay's traditional two-party system (the Blancos and the Colorados) in the mid-1830s. The Blancos represent the rural and landed interests, the mangerial elites, the high clergy, and, in general, a traditional, conservative approach to socioeconomic issues. The Colorados, on the other hand, represent the concerns of the capital city (Montevideo), the middle class, the immigrants, and the workers, viewing themselves as the institutional reformers and the carriers of liberalism and modernization.[3]

The early administrators of the nation, busy maintaining political power, made little movement toward institutional reform, economic development, and cultural change,

This chapter was written by Arturo C. Porzecanski under the direction of and with considerable help and input from Carmelo Mesa-Lago, who is responsible for the final editing. The chapter applies the theoretical framework developed by Mesa-Lago and makes use of his collection of primary data and other materials.

as reflected in the lack of social legislation and economic policies until the 1880s and 1890s. During most of the 1830–1880 period, successive governments granted pensions and adopted welfare measures on an *ad hoc* basis, favoring individuals rather than occupational groups. Most pensions were gratuitous concessions, decreed on the basis of "special services rendered" by civil servants and military officers. There were, however, two state-sponsored attempts to provide social security protection to these two groups. In 1835 a pension system for military officers was established, providing for retirement, disability, and survivors' pensions and financed by payroll deductions.[4] In 1838 the machinery was set up to provide pensions for civil servants upon either retirement or the abolition of their posts after ten years of service; this law also required salary deductions.[5] In this period, private charities and religious groups provided some care to the aged, orphans, and other similarly needy people.

During the last quarter of the nineteenth century, political instability continued in Uruguay, but the socioeconomic foundations of the country began to change. A succession of authoritarian presidents drawn mostly from the military ranks (Colonel Lorenzo Latorre, General Máximo Santos, and General Máximo Tajes) governed the country and more firmly established law and order. As the rural areas were tamed, landowners expanded livestock and agricultural output, and were less concerned with their personal struggles for power. In Montevideo, a large European immigration expanded the middle class (merchants, doctors, teachers, craftsmen), thus contributing to the potential for increased stability. As one historian has put it, "these changes had brought neither democracy nor peace, but they had created a substantial body of citizens who thought in national terms."[6] A more orderly political structure allowed for greater administrative control, and legislation was passed which provided a framework for the country's institutional and socioeconomic development. For instance, a reformed rural code and new civil, criminal, commercial, and military codes were enacted during the presidencies of Latorre and Santos. In the field of social security, the coverage offered by the existing military and civil servants' pension funds was temporarily curtailed when in 1876 Dictator Latorre ruled that incoming civil employees and military officers were no longer eligible to enroll in these government-sponsored pension plans.[7] Yet the 1884 military code restored old-age and disability benefits for new military officers, but not survivors' pensions; instead, a *montepio* was created to provide needy survivors with some aid.[8] In addition, disability pensions for policemen and firemen were instituted (1892).

In the political arena, the Colorados managed to stay in office continuously from 1865 until 1958 through the interaction of three factors: first, a series of charismatic leaders appealing to the voters; second, Colorado policies which expanded the bureaucracy and redirected government expenditures to suit the electorate; and third, arrangements with the Blancos to share the political power structure.[9]

Among the most significant changes that took place in Uruguay during the last quarter of the nineteenth century was the reform and expansion of formal education under the leadership of José Pedro Varela, who advocated mandatory, nonreligious, elementary education.[10] In 1877 Dictator Latorre enacted a law launching an extensive, state-sponsored campaign to educate every Uruguayan. This expansion of public education led to the establishment, in 1896, of the Education Pension Fund which awarded pensions to public-school teachers with 25 years of service and to those unfit for further service after 10 years of work. Financed by contributions from the state, deductions from teachers' salaries, and a portion of the yield on inheritance taxes, this fund worked so well that in 1904 the administrative employees of the school system were brought into the plan.[11] This pension fund was probably established as an incentive for private tutors and foreign teachers to join the civil service and as a reward for work in the rural areas of the country.

Between 1875 and 1900 Uruguay's population doubled, from about 450,000 to over 900,000, of which almost one-third lived in Montevideo. Immigrants greatly contributed to this growth, constituting 37 percent of Montevideo's population and 15 percent of the rural population in 1900. This immigration, coupled with economic protection, generated significant industrial activity in the capital city. In rural areas, livestock output continued to grow and hold much influence over the entire economy, supplying a steady flow of exports (meat, wool, and hides) which in turn financed (through tax revenues and foreign-exchange earnings) the expansion of the economic infrastructure.

Montevideo steadily became not only the political but also the economic and cultural nerve center of immigration, exports, and imports. There, financial and other intermediaries, craftsmen, and a variety of skilled and semiskilled workers found their services in demand either for the processing of livestock and agricultural products or for establishing and running small consumer industries. Workers' mutual-aid societies and unions flourished, particularly as the result of the arrival of Europeans with experience in these activities. By 1905 there were 69 unions with a total membership of about 7,000 workers; of these, 32 belonged to the Anarchist labor federation, 25 operated under the aegis of the Socialist labor federation, 8 were grouped into the Christian Democrat labor federation, and 4 others were autonomous.[12] Most came into existence and staged strikes to obtain basic improvements in working conditions. These infant trade unions were energetically repressed by the police and by the early 1900s only about 5 to 7 percent of Montevideo's labor force was at all unionized. There was no social protection of the workers, although it is recorded that in 1899 a group of them founded the Sociedad de Protección Mutua entre Empleados, one purpose of which was to establish an unemployment fund based on contributions of its members.[13]

At this time, José Batlle y Ordóñez (1903–1907, 1911–1915), the son of a former (Colorado) president, General Lorenzo Batlle, became president with the support of Montevideo's masses and insisted on Colorado party reform and an end to existing political arrangements partitioning the country into geographical areas of political control.

During his first administration, Batlle defeated the old political cloak-and-dagger schemes.[14] A liberal, progressive, and nationalistic politician who believed in the expansion of citizens' rights to political and economic participation, he tested the potential strength of Montevideo's middle class and the country's labor force in general. For instance, in cautiously insisting that the police protect both the right to work and the right to strike by acting as mediator rather than repressor of labor disputes, Batlle gained substantial support from the workers, became more popular with the general public, and was increasingly influenced by labor's enthusiastic response.

By the end of his first administration, Batlle abolished the death penalty, instituted divorce, founded research institutes, expanded railway communications, and eliminated subsidies to the church. In 1904 he established a Civil Service Pension Fund which sought to regularize the civil-servant pension system while expanding both coverage and benefits. Financed by contributions from federal and city (Montevideo) governments and through payroll deductions, pensions were paid to invalids and to those who lost their posts after 10 years of service, as well as to those retiring with 30 years of service plus 60 years of age.[15] (Survivors' pensions were not granted until 1940.) Finally, Batlle advanced social welfare by building a military hospital, a senior citizens' home, an orphanage, and a children's hospital.[16]

1914–1920

After a four-year stay in Europe which significantly influenced his thought, Batlle won reelection in 1911 and embarked on the most fruitful administration Uruguay has ever known. His barrage of legislation emphasized four principles: reform of the executive branch (advocating rule by a committee rather than a single individual), separation of church and state, economic nationalism (mainly through the nationalization of key industries and services), and the creation of the welfare state, including vast labor legislation such as the eight-hour day, a mandatory full day of rest per week, the regulation of work conditions (especially those of women and children), and minimum wages.[17]

In the field of social security, there was also some progress. As of 1911 only the military, civil servants, and public-school teachers and administrative personnel were protected by pension plans. (During the interim presidency of Claudio Williman, in 1911, a Military Pension Fund had been created to administer survivors' pensions for all military officers.) Batlle sought to centralize insurance services through a state monopoly to lower rates and increase public confidence. In 1911, the State Insurance Bank (Banco de Seguros del Estado, BSE) was created and granted a monopoly in fire and life insurance as well as in workmen's compensation—the last of which was not mandatory for anyone at this point. Batlle established in 1914 the general principles for the prevention of occupational accidents among blue-collar workers in industry, mining, and construction. The law held business owners and managers legally accountable for its violation and responsible for paying indemnification; but the worker had the burden of proof and hence the application of the law was very limited.

Three other bills on social security were drafted by Batlle but passed by his Colorado successors. Noncontributory pensions were granted to the old and the disabled without means of support in 1919. This unique law established a monthly payment for the indigent financed through a tax paid by employers for each employee in his service, a real-estate surtax, and various indirect taxes on imported and domestic goods (playing cards, alcohol, and liquors). For the old the age minimum was sixty and for the totally incapacitated there was no qualifying age.[18] This system was administered by the BSE until 1933 and by other agencies afterwards. Another landmark in Uruguayan social security was the creation in 1919 of a Public Utilities Pension Fund, a pension fund which covered railway, telegraph, streetcar, telephone, water, and gas-company workers. (Since electrical power plants and part of the railways were state-run, their employees already belonged to the Civil Servants Pension Fund.) The new fund, providing protection against old-age, disability, death, and unemployment, was financed by employers, employees, and a tax on services rendered by the utility companies.[19] The unemployment provision, which awarded a pension to all those dismissed for whatever reason, with the only qualification being ten years' employment in the utilities industry, would soon become one of the worst loopholes in the entire system. According to one economic historian, these two controversial pension plans were passed as "concessions to labour" in a time of growing labor unrest. (Man-days on strike increased from 67,193 in 1916 to 645,864 in 1920.)[20] Finally, in 1920, the first compulsory insurance against occupational accidents was established by law. Government agencies were required to insure their employees (civil servants) against occupational accidents in the BSE. Private employers, though held legally accountable for such accidents occurring to blue- and white-collar workers, were not required to subscribe to this insurance until 1941.

1921–1940

By the beginning of the 1920s labor unrest combined with social concessions by the government had very much awakened the political interests of workers, particularly of the labor aristocracy in Montevideo, resulting in increased pressure from labor on several fronts. First, there were pressures to expand the coverage of existing pension plans. Consequently, the Public Utilities Pension Fund gradually came to include: employees in medical-aid societies and in shipbuilding and repairs (1922); harbor pilots (1926); employees in some corporations and newspaper and printing workers (1928); employees in private hospitals and those engaged in the administration of political parties (1929). Second, there were pressures to create new pension funds, as in the cases of the Jockey Club Pension Fund (1923) and the Banking and Stock-Exchange Pension Fund (1925).[21] Third, there were labor requests for higher pension benefits to be financed by increased indirect taxation instead of by larger employer/employee contributions, thus shifting the burden of social security to consumers in general.

A rather unusual pension program instituted in 1926 (Ley Madre) provided for a lifetime pension to be paid, upon childbirth, to all working women in industry and commerce who wished to leave their jobs in order to raise their children. Designed to encourage women to have children and to raise them personally without sustaining a great loss in family income, the law was financed by a deduction from the take-home pay of all women in industry and commerce. The only qualification was a minimum of ten years' employment, the amount of the pension being a function of average past earnings and the number of years at work. However, the pension was so generous that its benefits accrued irrespective of the woman's return to the labor force or to the age of the children.

The rapidly growing pension system lent itself to political maneuvering and corruption, and the complaint was voiced that the inspectors and administrators of pension funds "were functioning more as electoral agents than as pension officers."[22] Economic efficiency and market incentives were slowly being distorted by the pension system. As a result of higher labor costs, businessmen attempted to maintain profits by hiring fewer workers, passing social security costs on to consumers, and otherwise lobbying for increased protection from foreign competitors.

By 1933 much of the social security system was bankrupt. Important loopholes and generously low age qualifications for benefits drew numerous requests for pensions—particularly unemployment pensions. By the end of 1932, 52.4 percent of pensioners under the Public Utilities Fund had qualified for dismissal: one-half of these men were under fifty years of age, three-fourths had not completed twenty years, and 98.3 percent had not completed thirty years of service. This phenomenon was not really depression-bred; between 1920 and 1933 "employers found more and more men interested in being discharged and frequently performing their duties in a manner that was intended to provoke a dismissal."[23] The reliance upon indirect taxes to produce revenues proved to be cyclical, that is, when economic conditions were bad and aggregate expenditures decreased so did tax revenues. The worldwide 1930s depression only aggravated the situation.

At this time two laws were passed to reorganize and expand social security while incorporating more workers into the pension stream. In 1933, an Institute of Retirement and Survivor Pensions took over the administration of three major pension funds although keeping them separate: Education, Civil Service, and Public Utilities (which administered indigents' old-age and disability pensions). A 1934 law reorganized pensions under four significant provisions. First, all blue- and white-collar workers as well as managers in and owners of manufacturing industry, mining, commerce, construction, transport, profit-making organizations, and sporting and cultural institutions (i.e., all workers except rural workers and professionals) were granted social security pensions, including unemployment. For this purpose, the Public Utilities Pension Fund was reorganized as the Industry, Commerce, and Public Utilities Pension Fund. Second, the qualifications for pensions and particularly for dismissal pensions were considerably toughened with new age requirements, the adoption of the principle that pensioners should not be remuneratively employed, and the restoration of the dismissal pension as an exceptional, short-term, revocable privilege. Third, state-sponsored employment agencies were created to reduce frictional unemployment and related pension claims. Fourth, occupational accident insurance was declared mandatory and covered all blue- and white-collar workers in industry, commerce, services, and rural activities. (Unfortunately this section of the law was suspended in 1935 and was not enforced until 1941.)

During the second half of the 1930s, the reduction in the value of exports combined with a steady flow of immigration resulted in a drop in economic activity and a weakening of the market power of labor unions. This together with the more conservative administration of President Gabriel Terra (1931–1938) placed a temporary brake on the avalanche of social security legislation. However, some minor groups within the labor force were brought into the Industry, Commerce, and Public Utilities Pension Fund: workers in the wine-making industry (1934), musicians (1935), and private-school teachers (1939). Also, the first autonomous unemployment-compensation program was approved (1939) protecting shipwrecked sailors, who could opt for a pension until they found new employment or for a lump-sum payment.

1941–1957

As was the case in other developing countries, World War II and the Korean War generated significant export booms and import shortages in Uruguay. Exports (essentially wool, meat, and hides) were significantly increased—though more in value than in volume—while imports remained rather constant (except for the period between the wars). This relative cutting-off of imports led the government to pursue a more aggressive industrialization program based on protectionist measures: monopoly for the first nine years of operation, high customs duties, and import licensing control. At the same time, Uruguayan manufactured exports were subsidized to be saleable abroad.[24] All this created a strong demand for labor and opened many employment opportunities: manufacturing employment increased by 70 percent in 1936–1948 and by 45 percent in 1948–1955.[25] Since immigration had decreased and the country's rate of population growth was very low (about 1.5 percent), industry was forced to increase wages and grant more generous social security provisions. This situation coincided—not by chance, of course—with a great rise in labor unionization, and the small, narrow, but numerous, trade unions of the

1910s and 1920s gave way to the broad-based, large-scale labor organizations of the 1940s. In March of 1942 the first national labor confederation (the Unión General de Trabajadores, UGT) was founded to represent the largest unionized share of the labor force, especially in obtaining unemployment insurance and a more generous social security coverage.[26] This combination of forces resulted, during the 1940s and early 1950s, in a vigorous expansion of pensions, the introduction of family allowances, and the addition of unemployment-compensation programs.

The Civil Service Pension Fund was expanded to incorporate all the workers in the many state-run industries (e.g., water, telephone, oil-refining) which had previously belonged to the Industry, Commerce, and Public Utilities Pension Fund. This administrative rearrangement was accompanied by the addition of survivors' pensions for all civil servants in 1940. A law providing for mandatory compensation in the event of occupational accidents and diseases and covering all private and public-sector workers was finally enacted in 1941 (implementing the suspended clauses of the 1934 law). In the same year all military personnel (not just officers as earlier) became eligible for pensions. In 1941, the Notaries Public Pension Fund was created; this first fund for professionals organized pensions for retirement, survivors, and disability. In 1942, domestic servants and other household employees were covered by the Industry, Commerce, and Public Utilities Pension Fund. In 1943, a Rural Workers Pension Fund was finally established within the Institute of Retirement and Survivors' Pensions, to administer old-age, disability, and survivors' pensions for farmers, gardeners, and the workers, employees, and managers of agricultural enterprises. In the same year the Banking and Stock-Exchange Pension Fund was restructured into a Banking Pension Fund. In 1948 part-time employees of the Jockey Club who were not covered by the original fund became covered by a separate pension fund. In the same year the Institute of Retirement and Survivor Pensions was disbanded and the three pension funds it supervised were decentralized and regrouped as the Civil Service, Education, and Public Utilities Pension Fund; the Industry and Commerce Pension Fund; and the Rural and Domestic Workers' Pension Fund (domestic workers were transferred to this fund from the Industry and Commerce Fund). A Professionals' Pension Fund was created in 1954 to manage pensions for university-graduated professionals whether self-employed or working for an employer.

A system of family allowances was introduced in 1943, granting payments to blue- and white-collar workers in industry and commerce with dependent minors (whether legitimate or illegitimate) administered by an autonomous public fund, the Central Committee of Family Allowances (Consejo Central de Asignaciones Familiares, CCAF), and financed exclusively by employer contributions.[27] Created as the result of recommendations by a parliamentary committee to improve the economic situation of the poorest members of the labor force and to serve as an incentive to counter the falling rate of population growth, the system was expanded a few years later to cover civil servants and the military (1950) as well as rural workers (1954).[28]

When fears spread that World War II and the export boom it had caused were about to end, lobbying efforts were made to create two very important unemployment compensation funds: one in 1944 for Montevideo-based meat-packing and processing workers and, the other, one year later, for wool- and hides-processing and warehouse workers.

1958–1973

After the Korean War, Uruguay's industrialization and economic growth came to a grinding halt. The sharp decline in foreign demand for and value of the country's exports caused unemployment in the meat and wool-processing industries in particular. The nation's import-substituting industry, burdened by high costs and inefficiency, was unable to compete abroad. Massive rural-to-urban migration in search of jobs and the higher standards of living found in Montevideo led to unemployment and labor unrest. The ruling Colorados, in a final desperate effort to gain the support of labor and the growing ranks of the unemployed for the November 1958 elections, passed three social security laws in October. First, they extended the right of unemployed blue- and white-collar workers in industry and commerce to receive family allowances. Second, they instituted an unemployment-insurance fund to cover all those workers and employees who belonged to the Industry and Commerce Pension Fund. Finally, they approved maternity leave with full pay during six weeks prior to and six weeks after childbirth for all working women. Despite these concessions, the Blanco party won the elections for the first time in ninety-three years.

The traditionally conservative Blanco politicians soon discovered that they could not stop the spiraling growth of the social security system. Labor unions had become quite large and well-organized and even pensioners were being unionized in order to protect and, when feasible, expand their privileges. Labor-union activity rose from an estimated 1¼ million man-days on strike in 1957 to 2½ million in 1963.[29] A confederation of retired pensioners grew militant, and through its own newspaper, mass rallies, and lobbying efforts, sought to advance its cause.[30] Thus, in mid-1960 family-allowance benefits were extended to cover retired rural, domestic, industrial, and commercial workers and employees. A few months later, to placate civil servants and the military the new Blanco administration revamped the whole family-allowance system to make these groups eligible not only for a payment for dependent minors but for a monthly benefit (*hogar constituído*) to help support their families as a whole, as well as for lump-sum payments for marriage and each birth.

During the early and mid-1960s, the ruling Blancos were unable to do much about the stagnating Uruguayan economy. Overall per-capita output either remained constant or fell, while gross investment as well as per-capita agricultural and food production declined drastically.[31] This decline, combined with growing government deficits and overexpansion of the money supply as the government began relying increasingly upon deficit financing to meet its heavy wage and social security bills, caused strong inflationary forces to come into play. Hence, legislators were continuously forced to enact provisions designed to readjust pensions and income-eligibility qualifications (particularly pension floors and ceilings) and thus restore purchasing-power losses. As an example, family-allowance legislation was amended once a year during the 1952–1970 period, except in three years. Increasing urban unemployment and loss of purchasing power further strained socioeconomic relations and an urban guerrilla group (the Tupamaros), organized in the early 1960s, grew to present a serious threat of an armed takeover. Social security legislation under Blanco party administrations became, more than ever, an instrument for buying political stability.

In spite of the remarkable expansion of coverage and benefits of the Uruguayan social security system, by 1960 it still lacked health insurance.[32] Low-cost medical aid was provided by the state through a network of Montevideo hospitals and rural polyclinics, but the quality of such care was steadily deteriorating due to smaller government-budget appropriations and greater demand for such services. Meanwhile, the costs of private-hospital care and of medicines were rapidly increasing— the former due to higher demand and better quality, and the latter as a consequence of costly import substitution in the field of pharmaceuticals. Hence, pressures mounted for the state to intervene in this area too. Workers in transportation and construction were the first two groups to have a health-insurance program (established in 1960), financed by employer and employee contributions. Transport workers were represented by very powerful unions which, by staging a strike, could easily paralyze the Montevideo economy; workers in construction were in a good bargaining position due to a housing boom that developed during the late 1950s as a consequence of inflation. Health-insurance plans soon followed for the wool- and hides-processing and warehouse workers (1961); Montevideo-harbor stevedores (1962); lumber and wood-working industry workers and metallurgical workers (1964); private bank employees, textile and garment-industry workers, and the crews of private merchant and fishing ships (1966). In some cases these special funds were financed by indirect taxes (e.g., wool and hides), by yearly government contributions from its regular tax revenues (e.g., textiles), or by government loans (e.g., merchant-marine and fishing). Until 1964 active and retired members of the military and their dependents were entitled to medical services through the armed forces' own hospitals and clinics. In that year, however, police officers and enlisted men (active and retired) became eligible for these services and the whole health-care program was improved; all this was financed by withholdings from military and police personnel, both active and pensioned.[33]

Additional changes in the social security system took place prior to the 1966 national elections. In late 1965, workers in the tobacco and glass-manufacturing industries (as well as Montevideo-harbor stevedores) were brought into the unemployment fund set up in 1958 for employees in industry and commerce. In addition, the family-allowance system was enlarged to cover retired civil servants and the military. On the eve of the 1966 national elections it became clear that since the ruling Blancos had failed to improve the country's economic condition, voters might well reinstate the Colorados. So, the Blancos, playing the same game the Colorados had played right before the 1958 elections, enacted several key pieces of social security legislation. First, two health-insurance funds were set up for transport and construction workers (see above). Second, meat-packing and processing workers employed outside Montevideo were allowed to establish their own unemployment insurance fund. Third, maternity benefits were granted to rural working women. And fourth, and most important, the family-allowance system (which had been expanded for civil servants and the military in 1960) was dilated to encompass the entire private sector of the economy. Under this system, additional lump-sum payments for births and marriages and an allowance for adult dependents accrued to workers; a scholarship fund was also created. But the Blancos lost the elections anyway.

In 1967 the Colorados came back to power and a new constitution was adopted, providing for the return to a strong, one-man executive branch instead of the unique nine-man Executive Council instituted in 1952. Largely the result of public dissatisfaction with "government by committee," the new constitution sought to re-centralize decision-making and reform the management of the three largest pension funds (Industry and Commerce; Civil Service, Education, and Public Utilities; and Rural and Domestic Workers) by placing them under one common administration: the Social Welfare Bank (Banco de Previsión Social, BPS). The BPS, like its predecessor, the Institute of Retirement and Survivor Pensions, was to achieve economies in administration and to reduce the bureaucratic delays and complexities involved in the management of the three social security funds.[34] This reunification of the bulk of the pension system had been advocated by the author of a 1964 study conducted under the auspices of the International Labor Organization as well as by the authors of the country's first national development plan designed for the period 1965–1974.[35]

The sudden death of Colorado President Oscar D. Gestido left Jorge Pacheco Areco (1967–1972), an obscure and conservative politician who had been chosen for the vice-presidency after an intraparty deal, as president of a country in chaos. While the economic recession continued, inflation was soaring and public discontent and turmoil were evident everywhere. In response, Pacheco adopted a hard-line approach which included a stringent wage and price freeze, closure of opposition newspapers and leftist political parties, and active counterinsurgency operations against Montevideo's urban guerrillas. Seeking to curb inflation induced by labor pressure, he severely restricted labor union activity, banned strikes and demonstrations, and jailed many union leaders who did not comply. During the Pacheco administration little progress in social security legislation was expected and little took place. The family-allowance system was expanded to incorporate newspaper vendors and the rural self-employed (1968), and a health-insurance fund was approved for workers in the alcoholic and nonalcoholic beverage industry (1971). Pacheco was unable to get the economy moving and succeeded only in forcibly quieting popular discontent and social frictions.

National elections were again held in November of 1971 and Pacheco's hand-picked successor, Juan M. Bordaberry, obtained a narrow victory at the polls. Bordaberry, a landowner and former Blanco, also proved to be an unimaginative president concerned more with reestablishing law and order than with finding ways to improve the economic and social situation. He allowed the military to participate increasingly in decision-making and gave them a free hand in restoring order through massive arrests, interrogations, and searches of political dissidents. Faced by a hostile Congress, Bordaberry enacted only three social security measures: health-insurance funds for civil servants, for workers in glass-manufacturing, and leather-processing, and for restaurants and night club workers (1972). Bordaberry initially endorsed but later killed a much-publicized bill setting forth the foundations for comprehensive national health-planning and insurance.

In the end, the military acquired greater power and the nation's institutions proved nonfunctional. In 1973, urged by the more conservative elements within the armed forces, Bordaberry closed down the Parliament and ruled by decree until 1976 when he was, in turn, overthrown by the military. Although the future of social security in Uruguay is uncertain, two trends seem clear. On the one hand the erosion and now absence of democracy has changed the role and greatly diminished the power of several traditional pressure groups (e.g., civil servants and blue- and white-collar workers). On the other hand, a shift in social philosophy away from democratic liberal paternalism and toward autocratic conservatism has taken place within the new breed of high government officials. Both clearly spell the possibility of a considerable reduction in and reform of the role of the state in the provision of social security to parallel the new power structure and the government's ideology.[36]

The evolution of social security in Uruguay can tentatively be broken down into five stages. First, the period 1829–1913 was characterized by pension systems for small groups of the population: the military, civil servants, and public-school teaching and administrative personnel. Second, in the 1914–1920 period, pension plans were established for public-utility and mass-transportation workers as well as for the indigent. In addition, the general principles for the prevention of occupational accidents

Table 3-1
Significant Social Security Legislation in Uruguay: 1829–1972

Year	President	Type of Coverage	Group Protected
1829	Rondeau (m) (Governor)	Pensions (death, disability)	Military (veterans only)
1835	Oribe (m)	Pensions[a]	Military (officers only)
1838	Rivera (m)	Pensions (old age)	Civil servants
1892	Herrera y Obes (c)	Pensions (disability)	Police and firemen
1896	Borda (c)	Pensions (old age, disability)	Schoolteachers[b]
1904	Batlle (c)	Pensions (disability), unemployment[c]	Civil servants
1907	Batlle (c)	Health (hospital)	Military
1914	Batlle (c)	Occupational accidents[d]	Blue-collars
1919	Viera (c)	Noncontributory pensions	Indigents (aged and disabled)
1919	Brum (c)	Pensions, unemployment	Utilities and mass transit
1920	Brum (c)	Occupational accidents	Civil servants
1922	Brum (c)	Pensions, unemployment	Medical workers, shipbuilding
1923	Serrato (c)	Pensions, unemployment	Jockey Club (full-time)
1925–1926	Serrato (c)	Pensions, unemployment	Banking and stock exchange, harbor pilots
1926	Serrato (c)	Special motherhood pension	Female blue- and white-collars in industry and commerce
1928–1929	Campisteguy (c)	Pensions, unemployment	Blue- and white-collars from many corporations; private-hospital and political party employees
1934	Terra (c)	Occupational accidents[e]	All
1934–1938	Terra (c)	Pensions, unemployment	All remaining blue- and white-collars; business owners and managers
1939	Baldomir (c)	Unemployment compensation	Shipwrecked sailors
1940	Baldomir (c)	Pensions (death)	Civil servants
1941	Baldomir (c)	Pensions	Notaries public
1941	Baldomir (c)	Occupational accidents and diseases	All
1941	Baldomir (c)	Pensions	Military (all)
1942–1943	Baldomir (c)	Pensions	Domestic and rural
1943	Amézaga (c)	Family allowances	Blue- and white-collars
1944	Amézaga (c)	Unemployment subsidy	Meat-packing and -processing
1945	Amézaga (c)	Unemployment subsidy	Wool- and hides-processing and warehousing
1948	Batlle (c)	Pensions	Jockey Club (part-time)
1948	Batlle (c)	Health	Congress, state bank
1950	Batlle (c)	Family allowances	Civil servants, military
1954	Trueba (c)	Pensions	Professionals
1954	Trueba (c)	Family allowances	Rural
1958	Fisher (c)	Family allowances	Unemployed blue- and white-collars
1958	Fisher (c)	Unemployment subsidy	Blue- and white-collars in industry and commerce
1958	Fisher (c)	Maternity	All
1960	Nardone (c)	Family allowances	Retired blue- and white-collars; retired rural workers
1960	Nardone (c)	Expanded family allowances	Civil servants, military
1960	Nardone (c)	Health	Transportation, construction
1961	Haedo (c)	Unemployment subsidy	Tobacco, glass
1961	Haedo (c)	Health	Wool- and hides-processing and -warehousing
1962	Harrison (c)	Health	Montevideo longshoremen
1964	Crespo (c)	Health	Lumber- and wood-working
1964	Giannattasio (c)	Health	Metallurgical
1965	Giannattasio (c)	Unemployment subsidy	Montevideo longshoremen
1965	Beltrán (c)	Family allowances	Retired civil servants, retired military

Year	President	Type of Coverage	Group Protected
1966	Heber (c)	Health	Banks, textiles, graphics, garment, sailors
1966	Heber (c)	Unemployment subsidy	Meat-packing and -processing outside Montevideo; and rural workers
1966	Heber (c)	Maternity	Rural working women
1966	Heber (c)	Expanded family allowances	All blue- and white-collars rural
1968	Pacheco (c)	Expanded family allowances	Newspaper vendors, rural self-employed
1971	Pacheco (c)	Health	Beverages
1972	Bordaberry (c)	Health	Civil servants, glass, leather, culinary and restaurant

SOURCE: Information on legislation compiled by the author.

NOTE: (m) = military; (c) = civilian.

a. *Pensions* stands for old age, disability, and survivors' benefits.

b. School administrative employees were added in 1904.

c. *Unemployment* stands for a dismissal pension granted when certain qualifications are met (typically, ten years on the job).

d. The law emphasized prevention of occupational accidents and the worker had the burden of proof, hence its application was very limited.

e. This was suspended in 1935 and its principles were not enforced until 1941.

were introduced and the employers' direct responsibility established for civil servants and blue- and white-collar workers. Third, in the 1920–1940 period, the pension system was greatly expanded to cover the mass of blue- and white-collar workers in industry, commerce, and various trades and services. Fourth, during the 1941–1957 period, the pension system reached almost total coverage by the incorporation of rural workers as well as professionals. Also, the entire working population became protected by mandatory occupational accident and disease insurance. The family-allowance system was introduced and rapidly covered all of the active population: first blue- and white-collars, then civil servants and the military, and ultimately rural workers. Finally, a handful of unemployment insurance funds were set up—particularly for the protection of workers in the export industries. Fifth, in the 1958–1973 period, the family-allowance system was expanded to protect unemployed as well as retired blue- and white-collars, retired civil servants, and the military, and to provide extra payments for births and marriages, scholarships, and an allowance for adult dependents. Also, a number of unemployment funds and close to a dozen health insurance plans were created. Maternity benefits for all working women were enacted as well. (See table 3-1.) The bulk of the system was administratively unified in 1967.

The Role of Pressure Groups in Social Security Stratification

At this point it becomes important to identify the two interacting social forces that have been responsible for the tremendous growth and expansion of social security in Uruguay: government paternalism and the strength of various pressure groups.

Early twentieth-century social security legislation was born out of the social philosophy of several Colorado party statesmen and, in particular, the ideology of President Batlle. Acting on behalf of the rising Montevideo middle and lower classes, Batlle imported social security from Europe at a time when the beneficiaries of such legislation were not very organized, vocal, or powerful. The Uruguayan welfare state started out as a social experiment conceived and put into practice by a progressive and idealistic wing of Montevideo's elite acting in *loco parentis*. On the other hand, the role of various pressure groups becomes increasingly apparent in view of the abnormally large expansion of social security after the 1920s. Most workers seem to have taken social security to be a just reward for their labor services rather than a necessarily costly investment in their own future. Hence, they demanded that employers assume a major portion of the costs of pension benefits and that the public at large, through indirect taxes, also contribute. Social security legislation became an increasingly political issue. One administration after another discovered that a clever maneuvering of the benefits and costs of social security was an easy way to buy political stability. This maneuvering was necessary to appease the demands of workers for a greater share of the national pie and economic security, but at the expense of losing the support of the business and landowning communities and, by increasing the price of labor, hindering the growth of industry. To solve the dilemma, successive Colorado and Blanco administrations placed much of the burden of social security in the laps of consumers in the form of indirect taxation to finance pension benefits and by granting subsidies and economic protection to industry so that it could pass higher labor costs on to consumers. In the end, legislating on social security became an easy way for politicians to earn themselves the vote of labor without alienating the business and landowning elites or paying the bill. Also, an increasingly large bureaucracy was needed to manage the complex social security system, thus providing politicians with a good way to create employment and buy political support.

Specific pressure groups were instrumental in obtaining, spreading, and increasing the benefits of social security. In the first place is the military, a traditionally small and relatively less influential and less powerful group than that found in other Latin American countries. Participating often in government in the nineteenth century, they were the first to receive pension benefits (1828 and 1835), the first to have state-provided medical care and hospital facilities (1907). Less political in this century, still they were the second group to be granted a family allowance (1950), and the first to gain expanded family-allowance benefits (1960).

Civil servants constitute a relatively large and powerful proportion of the labor force. Due to the active involvement of the Uruguayan government in the country's economy, particularly through the ownership of utilities and some basic industries as well as through the comprehensive provision of many services, civil servants were the second group to receive old-age and disability pensions (1838), the first group to have been awarded unemployment pensions (1904), the first group to be mandatorily insured against occupational accidents (1920), the second group to be granted a family allowance (1950, together with the military), and the first to obtain expanded family-allowance benefits (1960, also with the military).

The next pressure group is urban blue- and white-collar workers as well as rural workers. The first law establishing the general principles for occupational accident prevention and indemnification was passed in 1914 and protected blue-collar workers; later on, in 1941, all blue- and white-collar and rural workers became mandatorily insured against occupational accidents and diseases—21 years after civil servants became similarly insured. Between 1919 and 1934, almost all blue- and white-collars became eligible for pensions though, as we examine below, there were priorities within this general category. Blue- and white-collars were the first occupational group to receive family allowances (1943). However, the expanded family-allowance system was approved for blue- and white-collar and rural workers in 1966, six years after civil servants and the military began drawing benefits from it. All nonrural workers and employees have been eligible for unemployment insurance since 1958, although some subgroups obtained unemployment-compensation benefits many years before. There is no general health-insurance system, but about a dozen mostly blue-collar subgroups have their own health insurance fund. Finally, maternity benefits have been available to all female workers and employees since 1958. Women with a minimum of ten years' work in industry or commerce are also eligible to retire upon childbirth.

Yet not all blue- and white-collars have fared alike; some subgroups have apparently been granted priority in social security benefits. The most powerful and, not incidentally, the earliest and best covered subgroups have traditionally been the following four. Workers in utilities and mass transit were the first subgroup to obtain pension benefits (1919); mass-transit workers were the first to have a health insurance fund (1960). Employees in banking and the stock exchange also entered the pension system relatively early and have their own fund (1925). Workers in the Montevideo-based export industries (such as meat-packing and the warehousing and processing of wool and hides) were granted pensions in 1928 and 1934, and were the first subgroup to have an unemployment insurance fund established (1944–1945); in addition, those in wool- and hides-processing were the third subgroup to receive health insurance coverage (1961). Workers in maritime transport and allied activities, particularly Montevideo stevedores, sailors, and those in shipbuilding and repairs have also obtained benefits early.

Within the pressure group composed of blue-collars, white-collars, and rural workers, rural workers are the least and last benefited from social security. Although they became insured against occupational hazards at the same time that other private-sector workers did, those in rural areas became eligible for pensions relatively late, in 1942–1943. Rural workers were the last to obtain family allowance (1954) and unemployment compensation (1966); they are still not eligible for health insurance. Specific provisions on maternity benefits for rural working women were enacted eight years later (1966) than for all other female workers and employees. Finally, rural women are still not eligible for a pension upon childbirth, though other women in industry and commerce are.

The self-employed in Uruguay are, at least nominally, relatively well covered. Since the early 1940s managers, business owners, independent salesmen, and others in commerce and services are eligible for pensions and unemployment insurance; however, they are not covered by a health-insurance plan and must seek medical care through private or mutual insurance hospitals. Independent professionals were the last to become eligible for pensions (1954) although notaries public were eligible since 1941; neither of these two subgroups is eligible for unemployment or health-insurance benefits. Independent rural workers and domestic servants are eligible for pensions but ineligible for unemployment or health insurance. Finally, indigents and those who are totally incapacitated are eligible for very small but noncontributory pensions.

Since its early beginnings Uruguay's social security system, which appears to be quite broad, generous, and complex, has been fractionalized and has made little progress toward unification. The country's three largest pension funds, which were centralized in 1933–1948, have been since 1967 once again under the direct supervision of one agency, the BPS. However, no progress appears to have been made in centralizing the collection and distribution of social security revenues, in establishing uniform and rational standards for the various benefits, or in eliminating the more obvious and politically motivated administrative complexities, duplications, and overall inefficiencies.

Current Structure and Organization of the System

As in most other Latin American countries, the organization of social security in Uruguay is mostly decentralized, heavily bureaucratic, and administratively complex. There is no single entity which regulates the organization or controls the management of social security services. Hundreds of laws and decrees as well as several codes regulate aspects of social security. Since few indexed compilations have been published, knowledge of the maze of social security provisions is handed down orally from one generation of experts (legislators, lawyers, and administrators) to another.

Currently there are nine pension funds, some of which cover hundreds of thousands of people and others which barely benefit a few hundred individuals. The three largest pension funds have been, since 1967, jointly administered by the BPS; they are: Civil Service, Education, and Public Utilities; Industry and Commerce; and Rural and Domestics. The Industry and Commerce Fund, in turn, administers the unemployment insurance program for blue- and white-collar workers. Similarly, the Rural and Domestics' Fund manages the special, noncontributory pension for indigents. The BPS is an autonomous fund; however, its budget is a part of the government's overall budget, prepared by the cabinet-level Planning and Budgeting Office. In addition, the policies of the BPS are influenced by the country's Ministry of Labor and Social Security, which controls the government's labor and social security programs. In other words despite the nominal autonomy of the BPS, the government influences its policies and controls its finances. The only other pension fund over which the government has a similar degree of control is the Military Fund, which is a division of the Ministry of National Defense. (See figure 3-1.)

The remaining five pension funds are also autonomous. They are: Professionals, Notaries-Public, Banking, Jockey Club (full-time employees) and Jockey Club (part-time employees). All of these five funds act independently, although since several of them receive contributions from the government or have part of their revenues collected by government agencies, they are *de facto* under some government financial control.

The complex family allowance system is administered by the CCAF, which takes care of payments for dependent children and adults, births, and marriages. The CCAF also runs a number of low-cost maternity wards and health-care centers for pregnant female workers. In addition, the CCAF manages four health-insurance plans covering workers in the beverage, glass, and leather industries as well as culinary and restaurant employees. As is the case of the BPS, the CCAF's operating budget is an integral part of the government's budget; hence, it has little real autonomy. Furthermore, the CCAF's policies are somewhat dependent upon the attitude of the Ministry of Labor and Social Security.

Aside from the unemployment insurance program managed by the Industry and Commerce Fund, there exist three independent unemployment compensation agencies, responsible for the administration of unemployment benefits for Montevideo-based meat-packing and -processing workers, for meat-packing and -processing workers employed outside Montevideo, and for wool- and hides-processing and warehouse workers. In addition, this last unemployment-insurance fund also man-

FIGURE 3.1

Administrative Structure of Social Security in Uruguay: 1972

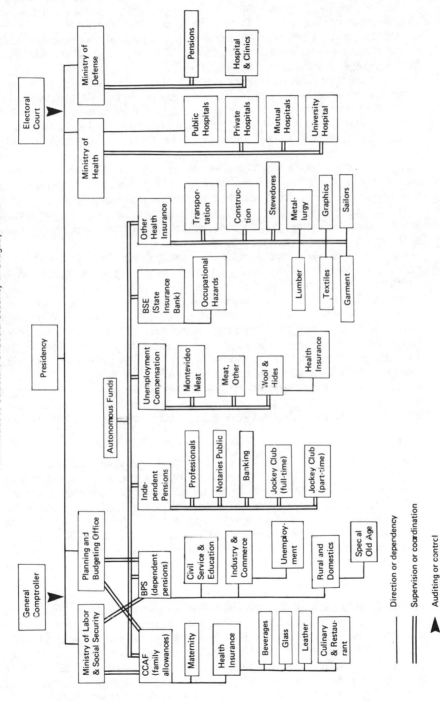

Direction or dependency

Supervision or coordination

Auditing or control

ages the health-insurance program in which wool and hides workers participate.

The State Insurance Bank (BSE) is also an autonomous agency which sells commercial insurance (fire, auto, life, and theft) and has a monopoly on workmen's compensation. Consequently, all claims for occupational accidents and diseases must be filed with BSE. As an added service, BSE runs a hospital and first-aid clinics for the victims of occupational accidents.

Aside from the health-insurance funds managed by the CCAF and the wool and hides unemployment-insurance fund, there are currently nine autonomous health insurance funds. They are for workers in transportation, construction, lumber and wood-working, graphics; metallurgy, textiles, and garment, as well as for Montevideo-harbor stevedores and merchant marines. Neither these nor the other funds have their own hospitals and clinics; rather, they arrange for the delivery of health care through existing private hospitals and mutual insurance hospitals. The public at large is eligible to participate in a number of private health-insurance plans or to seek low-cost (and sometimes low-quality) medical care through the network of public and university hospitals and clinics. However, the military and the police (both active and retired) receive health care through a hospital and several clinics operated by the Ministry of Defense.

Although there is no single government agency which directs, supervises, coordinates, or inspects the provision of social security in Uruguay, there are two ways in which the government can formally intervene in the affairs of the many autonomous agencies. The Electoral Court reviews the election of all fund authorities and the General Comptroller reviews their financial statements. These officials are entitled to appoint a special investigator, although this has only been the case when charges of corruption or gross administrative mismanagement have been levied. In general, then, the government influences the delivery of social security only through indirect means such as budgetary, employment, and inflation policies.

The current structure and administration of social security in Uruguay can be examined in the coverage of each of five groups: the armed forces, civil servants, blue- and white-collar and rural workers, the self-employed, and the noninsured.

Armed Forces

The Military Pension Fund (Caja de Retirados y Pensionistas Militares, hereafter Armed Forces) covers the military personnel of the army, the navy, and the air force as well as certain top civilian employees within the Ministry of Defense and all those of the fund itself. Note that it does not protect the police. The fund is run by a five-man committee of military officers appointed by the president and is a decentralized agency supervised by the Ministry of Defense. Militarymen draw retirement, disability, and survivors' pensions as well as family allowances. Quality health care is available to the military through a network of clinics and a central hospital.

Civil Servants

The Civil Service, Education and Public Utilities Pension Fund (Caja de Jubilaciones y Pensiones Civiles y Escolares, hereafter Civil Service), which operates within the BPS, is divided into two sections: civil service and education. The civil service section covers all elected and appointed civil servants, including those working in ministries, autonomous agencies, state-run industries and public utilities, as well as the police. The education section covers all public, elementary-school teachers and some administrators, physical education teachers, the teachers of one large private school, and the teachers of all state-run schools for the blind, the deaf-mute, and the handicapped. Those covered by this fund are eligible for pensions for retirement, disability, survivors, and unemployment, and for family allowances. The administration of this fund's pensions is quite complicated since many of its members belong to special pension plans which grant higher benefits or reduce the necessary qualifications, as in the case of elected or appointed high government officials, those in the health professions handling patients, animals, or materials which have or transmit contagious diseases, or those working in penal institutions. There is no special health insurance plan for civil servants.

Blue- and White-Collar and Rural Workers

The two largest pension funds covering blue- and white-collars and rural workers operate within the BPS and are the Industry and Commerce Pension Fund (Caja de Jubilaciones y Pensiones de la Industria y el Comercio) and the Rural and Domestic Workers' Pension Fund (Caja de Jubilaciones y Pensiones de los Trabajadores Rurales y Domésticos y de Pensiones a la Vejez). Industry and Commerce protects workers in all industrial and commercial activities, business owners and managers, the independent and self-employed, private-school teachers, and all those who are not included in any other fund. Rural and Domestic covers all those in agriculture and related activities (e.g., gardeners and the employees of agri-businesses). Those insured in both these funds are eligible for old-age, disability, and survivors' pensions, but unemployment insurance is available only to workers in industry and Commerce. There is no health insurance for rural workers; many blue-collar groups, however, are covered by one of the thriteen autonomous health-insurance funds previously described. All blue- and white-collar and rural workers can draw family allowances. Finally, all female blue- and white-collar workers covered by Industry and Commerce are eligible for retirement upon childbirth, given ten years of employment.

There are three other pension funds benefiting blue- and white-collar workers. The Banking Pension Fund (Caja de Jubilaciones Bancarias) protects workers and employees in both government and private banks, the stock exchange, and the various clearinghouses, including bank owners and managers. Pensions are paid upon retirement, death, disability, and dismissal. The two other pension funds cover the Montevideo Jockey Club workers: one is for full-time workers and employees (Caja de Jubilaciones, Pensiones y Subsidios de los Empleados Permanentes del Jockey Club) and the other is for those who work only during the days when the races are actually held (Caja de Jubilaciones, Pensiones y Subsidios de los Empleados por Reunión del Jockey Club de Montevideo). These small funds manage pensions for death, retirement, disability, and dismissal (full-time workers only). The members of all three of the above pension funds can draw family allowances but have no health insurance plan.

Self-Employed

Most independent workers belong either to Industry and Commerce (e.g., salesmen) or to Rural and Domestic (farmers, household workers). The major exception is professionals, who are covered mostly by the Caja de Jubilaciones y Pensiones de los Profesionales Universitarios (hereafter Professionals), a fund serving all university graduates who work by themselves, in association with other professionals or nonprofessionals, or as consultants to industry or business managers. Notaries public have their own pension fund, the Caja Notarial de Jubilaciones y Pensiones (hereafter Notaries Public). Those insured in the last two funds draw pensions for death, disability, and retirement, but neither receive family allowances nor participate in any health insurance or unemployment insurance program.

Noninsured

Uruguay has a unique noncontributory pension system for the indigent, that is, the low-income disabled and the aged. Administered by the Rural and Domestic Fund, it is available without age qualification to all the disabled as well as to those over sixty years of age. Needless to say, these pensions provide nothing but a bare minimum for the survival of indigents. Health facilities for the urban (Montevideo) poor include state and university hospitals which are accessible and quite inexpensive, though long waiting lists are common and the quality of such medical care is many times deficient. In contrast, the rural poor suffer from the lack of rural medical facilities, forcing many to migrate to the cities in search of medical care.

Inequalities of the System

In analyzing Uruguay's social security system, we must consider the extent of the country's occupational and regional income inequalities.

As is the case with many less developed economies, there is no definitive study of income distribution in Uruguay. There are no comprehensive surveys of the personal or occupational distribution of income and there are only scant data on its geographical allotment. Whatever evidence does exist, though, tends to confirm that Uruguay's personal and occupational income distribution is inequitable (although perhaps to a lesser extent than in many other Latin American nations) and that its regional income distribution is also quite inequitable due to the concentration of its economic activity in the capital city.

A partial and preliminary study of personal and occupational income distribution in Uruguay in 1963 showed that, according to varying estimates, the bottom 20 percent of the nation's population drew between 3.0 and 4.6 percent of total income, while the upper 20 percent received between 50.1 and 60.8 percent of total income. Those in the lowest 60 percent income bracket were rural workers in general, domestic servants, unskilled or low-skilled workers in manufacturing or construction industries, craftsmen, and the self-employed, whether engaged in small agriculture or in various commercial activities. Members of the upper 40 percent income bracket included white-collar employees (civil servants and others in the services sector), technicians, professionals, business managers and owners, high military and government officials, and large landowners.[37] A rough ranking of occupations by the proportion of each included in the top 10 percent income bracket was as follows: professionals (71 percent); owners and managers in industry and commerce (45 percent); technicians including bank employees (31 percent); white-collars (15 percent); small merchants and artisans (13 percent); blue-collars (5 percent); and rural wage-earners and domestic servants (3 percent each).[38] Unfortunately, more disaggregated information by occupation or time-series data are unavailable because there have been no other studies on the personal or occupational income distribution.

The problem of regional income inequalities is due to the significant concentration of economic activity (especially secondary and tertiary activities—which include a large share of the nation's GDP and pay high salaries) in the capital city of

Montevideo and surrounding departments (similar to states or provinces). A 1961 study showed that Montevideo, which at that time held about 45 percent of the country's inhabitants, concentrated 71.8 percent of secondary economic activity and 62.1 percent of tertiary activity. At the same time Montevideo was the source of 55.3 percent of total GDP. In terms of GDP per capita, Montevideo received 6,994 pesos versus 4,857 pesos for all other departments combined—a 44 percent GDP per capita differential. Of departments with a GDP per capita of at least 5,000 pesos, all except one were situated in the south and southwest parts of the country, adjacent to or near Montevideo.[39]

This regional income gap between Montevideo and the rest of the country has been both the cause and the consequence of uneven social, political, and economic development. The capital city holds an educated, politicized, and integrated labor force heavily dependent on the civil service as well as on import-substituting and export industries as the source of employment. Meanwhile in much of rural Uruguay, a tradition-bound, relatively apolitical, and nonunionized population has gone on tilling the land and tending its animals without fully participating in the mushrooming of social services and technological developments that have accompanied economic growth in Montevideo.

An examination of the coverage, financing, and benefits of Uruguay's social security system highlights its effects on the country's income inequalities by occupational groups and by geographical regions.

Coverage

Uruguay's population is generously covered by social security both in legislative and actual terms. However, the precise extent of such coverage is relatively more difficult to measure in Uruguay than in other countries because many people concurrently contribute to and draw benefits from several pension funds. The root of the problem lies in the fact that one's social security obligations and rights are a function of one's place of employment; thus, the system has a built-in bias to generate duplications in coverage. This bias has manifested itself quite strongly for at least three reasons. First, successive political administrations have rewarded allegiance at the polls with civil-service jobs. Rather than impose an unbearable burden on the government's budget, appointments have traditionally tended to be fractionalized (maximum of six hours per day), and thus civil-service employment has become synonymous with part-time work. Although a clever way to broaden the incidence of budgetary expenditures, this practice has led to many people holding positions with the private and public sectors simultaneously, resulting in duplications in social security coverage. Second, many of the self-employed, mandatorily insured by one pension fund or another, have found themselves rendering services under short-term contracts with a variety of employers within the private and public sectors, resulting again in multiple enrollments in the social security system. Finally, the Uruguayan society has long had the potential for considerable vertical and horizontal mobility, made a reality by widespread educational opportunities. Hence, it is quite common to find people who have moved from rural to urban occupations, from low-skill jobs with the private sector to employment with the civil service, and from blue- or white-collar appointments to professional activities. This societal mobility, then, has been the source of many social security duplications.

These duplications in coverage must be kept in mind when analyzing many of the figures presented here. Table 3-2 shows the number of actives (i.e., workers insured by some pension fund), passives (individuals drawing old-age, seniority, disability, or survivors' pensions), and dependents (minors receiving payments through the family-allowance system of the private sector) during the years 1960–1969. Coverage of health care is not included in the table because the various social security agencies are not presently involved in the delivery of health care, with the exception of emergency treatment for the victims of occupational accidents and maternity services for low-income groups. The number of actives insured has tended to be greater than the nation's economically active population (due to duplication of coverage). Though declining because of events detailed below, during the 1960s the number of the economically active under the protective umbrella of social security was over 100 percent. When the passive insured as well as the dependents are added, 65 percent of Uruguay's total population appears insured. This latter figure is more reliable than the former one because, although the duplication problem tends to overestimate the proportion of the population which is insured under pensions, our omission of family allowances for the children of civil servants and the military as well as health care and other benefits for which the families of active insured are eligible does underestimate the dependent side.

The final column of table 3-2 presents another striking fact, namely, the rapidly growing proportion of passives to actives. Indeed, while in 1960 there were nearly four actives for every passive (i.e., passives were 25 percent of actives), by 1969 there were 2.3 actives for every passive (i.e., passives were 43 percent of actives).

Table 3-2
Insured Population in Relation to Total and Economically Active Population in Uruguay: 1960–1969

Year	Total Population (in thousands) (1)	Economically Active Population (in thousands) (2)	Insured Population (in thousands)				Percent of EAP Insured (3)/(2)	Percent of Total Population Insured (6)/(1)	Ratio Active Passiv (3)/(4
			Active (3)	Passive (4)	Dependents[b] (5)	Total (6)			
1960	2,540	988[a]	1,077	276	251	1,604	109	63	3.9
1961	2,580	998[a]	1,101	302	288	1,691	110	59	3.6
1962	2,610	1,008[a]	1,109	322	303	1,734	110	66	3.4
1963	2,650	1,016	1,095	337	296	1,728	108	65	3.2
1964	2,680	1,027[a]	1,083	353	284	1,720	106	64	3.1
1965	2,710	1,038[a]	1,230	366	275	1,871	119	69	3.4
1966	2,750	1,050	1,058	394	295	1,747	101	64	2.7
1967	2,780	1,061	1,049	422	305	1,776	99	64	2.5
1968	2,820	1,072	1,042	435	342	1,819	97	65	2.4
1969	2,850	1,084	1,035	451	340	1,826	95	64	2.3

SOURCES: *Total population* from U.N., *Demographic Yearbook: 1970* (New York: United Nations, 1971), pp. 128–12 *Economically active population* from *IV Censo de Población y II de Vivienda: Datos definitivos y cifras principal* (Montevideo: Dirección General de Estadística y Censos, n.d.), pp. 30–31 (for 1963); and from unpublished estimates the Oficina de Planeamiento y Presupuesto (for 1966–69). *Insured population:* Active, from table 3-3; Passive, from infe mation supplied by the various social security funds; 1960–64 data on Passives in the Armed Forces' Fund and 19 datum on Passives in the Professionals' Fund were estimated by the author. Dependents, from information supplied by t Consejo Central de Asignaciones Familiares (for years 1960–69).

a. Interpolated estimates by the author.

b. *Beneficiarios,* which are minors receiving payments through the family allowance system in the private sector: hen only blue- and white-collar and rural beneficiaries are here included.

This phenomenon is caused not only by the expansion of the social security system and the increasing leniency in acquiring benefits (e.g., reduction of age for retirement) but also by the increasing age structure of the population.[40] In any event, the low active/passive ratio of insured has contributed to the nation's economic crisis.

When the aggregates presented in table 3–2 are divided into occupational groups, they reveal some interesting trends in social security coverage. As shown in table 3-3, the three largest pension funds—all managed by the BPS—are the ones which insure workers in industry and commerce, the civil service, and rural and domestic activities. In terms of 1969 actives, they insured 58.0, 19.3, and 18.4 percent of total actives respectively. From 1960 to 1969, these pension funds exhibited the following trends: both Industry and Commerce and Civil-Service grew moderately in terms of the number of actives they insured (540,000 to 600,000 and 173,000 to 200,000, respectively); but Rural and Domestic went through a drastic contraction (317,000 to 190,000). This contraction is probably due to the continuing and rapid rural-to-urban migration as thousands of people flock to Montevideo in search of employment, social services, and other opportunities provided by the capital city.[41] The contraction might also be the result of a probable reduction in the labor force employed in domestic services.[42]

In table 3-3 and in subsequent tables presenting data by occupational groups there is one category which is consistently underestimated: the self-employed, a majority of whom are supposed to be insured by Industry and Commerce. Unfortunately, this fund does not provide disaggregated figures on the number of its actives or passives who are self-employed. Consequently, under "self-employed" the only statistics to appear are those corresponding to Professionals and Notaries Public.

An analysis of the data on passives by occupational groups raises one point: Rural and Domestic, which in 1969 insured less than a fifth of all actives, had a fourth of all passives. (This is not due to the fund's managing the pension for indigents because that pension is excluded from the figures.) During the decade of the 1960s, while the fund's number of actives declined considerably, its passives almost doubled (from 65,000 to 113,000). There are three explanations for this trend; first, a large number of workers retired early taking advantage of a law that retroactively recognized years of service rendered; second, many rural and domestic workers changed their jobs; and third, few youngsters took agricultural and domestic-service jobs. Since all of the pension funds finance themselves, this trend has obviously meant growing indebtedness for Rural and Domestic.[43]

There is difficulty in evaluating the degree of social security protection by sectors of economic activity and occupational groups, since existing social security funds do not disaggregate their data by economic sectors or occupational groups. For example, Industry and Commerce insures workers in manufacturing, construction, commerce, transportation, and many services but does not report how many people actually belong to each of those subgroups. Also, the fund insures salaried workers, wage-earners, employers, and self-employed individuals, but has no data on the actual number of people in each of these subgroups. Likewise, Rural and Domestic fails to distinguish the proportion of actives in agriculture and domestic services or how many of those in agriculture are wage-earners, employers, or self-employed.

Our personal evaluation of the available data, documents, and oral reports on the coverage of social security in Uruguay indicates that such coverage is essentially complete and relatively even. The Uruguayan welfare state has, indeed, reached in

Table 3-3
Occupational Groups Protected by Social Security in Uruguay: 1960–1969

Occupational Group	Number Insured										Percentage Distribution in 1969
	1960	1961	1962	1963	1964	1965	1966	1967	1968	1969	
Blue- and white-collars and rural workers	*874,687*	*896,343*	*897,758*	*882,451*	*867,831*	*853,941*	*840,978*	*829,351*	*818,121*	*807,894*	*78.0*
Industry & commerce	539,590	567,107	574,621	578,126	581,653	585,201	588,771	592,363	595,976	600,000	58.0
Rural & domestic[b]	316,914	310,738	304,562	285,139	266,485	249,051	232,758	217,531	203,300	190,000	18.4
Banking	16,272	16,649	16,870	17,470	18,000	18,120	17,910	17,930	17,344	16,407	1.6
Jockey Club	1,911	1,849	1,705	1,716	1,693	1,569	1,539	1,527	1,501	1,487	0.1
Civil servants[c]	*172,669*	*174,667*	*178,906*	*181,769*	*184,677*	*187,632*	*190,634*	*193,684*	*196,783*	*200,000*	*19.3*
Armed forces	*20,000*	*20,000*	*20,000*	*19,000*	*18,000*	*13,021*	*13,218*	*13,285*	*13,306*	*13,440*	*1.3*
Self-employed	*9,317*	*9,470*	*12,018*	*12,041*	*12,462*	*12,575*	*12,727*	*13,104*	*13,644*	*13,919*	*1.4*
Professionals[d]	7,800	7,887	10,384	10,361	10,697	10,757	10,852	11,189	11,577	11,683	1.1
Notaries public	1,517	1,583	1,634	1,680	1,765	1,818	1,875	1,915	2,067	2,236	0.3
Total	1,076,673	1,100,480	1,108,682	1,095,261	1,082,970	1,230,169	1,057,557	1,049,424	1,041,854	1,035,253	100.0

SOURCES: *Blue- and white-collars and rural workers:* industry & commerce, from Julio E. Kneit, "La Previsión Social en el Uruguay," unpublished thesis submitted to the Facultad de Ciencias Económicas y de Administración, University of Uruguay, 1964, p. 76 (for years 1960–1962), and from *Ley Orgánica del Banco de Previsión Social,* a report presented to the Senate of Uruguay in 1970 and published by the Comisión de Previsión y Asistencia Sociales (carpeta # 1637, distribuído # 301), p. 3 (for 1969); rural & domestic, from Julio E. Kneit (see above) and *Ley Orgánica . . . ,* for 1960–1962 and 1969, respectively; banking, from information supplied by the Caja de Jubilaciones Bancarias (for years 1960–1969); Jockey Club, from information supplied by the Caja de Jubilaciones, Pensiones y Subsidios de los Empleados Permanentes del Jockey Club and by the Caja de Jubilaciones, Pensiones y Subsidios de los Empleados por Reunión del Jockey Club de Montevideo (for years 1960–1969). *Civil servants* from Julio E. Kneit (see above) and *Ley Orgánica . . . ,* for 1960–1962 and 1969, respectively. *Armed forces* from Bureau of Economic Affairs, U.S. Arms Control and Disarmament Agency, *World Military Expenditures: 1971* (Washington, D.C.: USACDA, 1972), p. 35 (for years 1960–1964), and from information supplied by the Caja de Retirados y Pensionistas Militares (for years 1965–1969). *Self-employed:* professionals, from information supplied by the Caja de Jubilaciones y Pensiones de Profesionales Universitarios (for years 1961–1969); notaries public, from information supplied by the Caja Notarial de Jubilaciones y Pensiones (for years 1960–1969).

a. 1963–1968 data are interpolated and correspond to a yearly increase of 0.61 percent.
b. 1963–1968 data are interpolated and correspond to a yearly decline of 7.0 percent.
c. 1963–1968 data are interpolated and correspond to a yearly increase of 1.6 percent.
d. 1960 datum was estimated by the author.

some way or another all income groups and economic sectors. Yet if any one group is comparatively less thoroughly covered it is that of rural workers; although rural workers are formally incorporated into the stream of social security, most experts agree that they are, in practice, inequitably treated and poorly protected. This stems from the fact that, overall, social security and labor laws are poorly enforced, labor unions are virtually nonexistent, employer paternalism and worker loyalty are still important, seasonal work is common, and employment opportunities are scarce enough that compliance with social security provisions is not actively sought by either employers or workers in the agricultural sector. Those agricultural workers who do want to participate fully in the social security system migrate to the cities as the preferred alternative to confrontation with local employers. In fact, as we have already noted, an increasing number of rural workers seem to have exercised that option.

The issue of the relatively poor coverage of rural versus nonrural workers can be better understood when one analyzes the horizontal or geographical inequalities in social security coverage. As pointed out above, Montevideo's political and economic organization is considerably more advanced than that of the rest of the nation. Social services also have long been disproportionately concentrated in the capital city. Although the various pension funds do not collect data by geographical areas, the CCAF does have figures on expenditures in Montevideo and the rest of the country. Such statistics (see table 3-6) indicate the presence of a large gap between expenditures in Montevideo and elsewhere: while from 1961 to 1970 Montevideo had from 45 to 48 percent of the nation's total population, family allowance and related expenditures totaled from 57 to 63 percent in Montevideo versus 38 to 43 percent in all other areas. Note that such concentration cannot be explained by income differentials between the capital city and the rural areas, since most family-allowance payments

Table 3-6
Degree of Social Security Protection of the Total
Population by Geographic Region in Uruguay:
1961–1970

	Percent of Population[a] in		Percent of Expenditures[b] in	
Year	Montevideo	All Other Areas	Montevideo	All Other Areas
1961	45.3	54.7	57.5	42.5
1963	45.9	54.1	59.5	40.5
1964	46.2	53.8	57.9	42.1
1965	46.4	53.5	57.4	42.6
1966	46.8	53.2	57.1	42.9
1969	47.8	52.2	57.7	42.3
1970	48.1	51.9	62.6	38.4

SOURCES: *Population* from Dirección General de Estadística y Censos, *Censos generales de población de 1908 y 1963* (for year 1963) and *Encuesta de hogares* (for the 1968 datum), cited in Luis Vicario, *El crecimiento urbano de Montevideo* (Montevideo: Banda Oriental, 1970), p. 16. *Expenditures* from information supplied by the Consejo Central de Asignaciones Familiares.
    a. Population data are estimated partly by interpolation and partly by extrapolation.
    b. Expenditures on family allowances only.

are equal and not a function of personal earnings. This expenditure gap is aggravated when one realizes that civil servants and the military, who draw family-allowance benefits and are mostly residents of Montevideo, are not included in the above figures because their benefits are paid by the state as salary supplements. The implication here is not that regional inequities are deliberately fostered by bodies such as the CCAF; rather, the lack of pressure from the rural labor force has allowed social security institutions to pursue their objectives without a conscious policy of regional equality, and those institutions have lacked the motivation to reach the rural population effectively and to incorporate it into the stream of social security. Since the major pension funds and this family-allowance body have had to operate under stringent financial constraints, it is perhaps understandable that they have given priority to the more powerful and better-organized labor groups to the detriment of the relatively nonpoliticized rural workers.

Financing

Before examining the statistical evidence on the financing of social security, one must consider the institutional context within which that financing takes place. First, a majority of the pension funds have been faced with lagging revenues due to tax evasion (often by employers in collusion with employees) and delays in the payment of social security contributions (which are profitable in an inflationary economy).[44] These delays were often knowingly tolerated by the various social security funds because of shutdown and layoff threats by many employers.

Secondly, the government has been sluggish in fulfilling its own social security obligations. Many political administrations have found that, when faced by lagging receipts or unanticipated expenditures, tax revenues which are earmarked for the social security agencies and other state contributions can be temporarily impounded. This has become a common practice particularly during the recent inflationary years, when rapidly rising wage demands by civil servants placed a premium on readily available cash. Unfortunately, the practice has proved quite damaging to several social security agencies because the delays have meant not just short-run financial constraints but, due to inflation, a systematic loss in the purchasing power of their revenues.

Table 3-8 presents data, obtained from the current legislation, on the financing of social security by occupational groups. It compares the percentages of wages and salaries contributed by workers and their employers plus the additional revenues generated from taxes and state subsidization. As shown in the table, workers' contributions to pension funds range from 5 to 18 percent of their salaries. If domestic workers are excluded, the percentage contribution of the workers tends to increase as the income of the group falls, as follows: the military (usually 12 percent), civil servants (15 percent), banking employees (16 percent), and the majority of blue- and white-collar workers (17 percent). The professionals' percentage contribution is the highest (18 percent) because, of course, they have no corresponding employer contribution. The contribution of rural workers cannot be appraised in this manner because it is a flat sum fixed annually by the government. As can be observed in table 3-8, employers' contributions to the pension funds fluctuate from 5 to 21 percent of salaries or wages. This contribution tends to increase as the income of the subgroup rises, as follows: domestics (5 percent), part-time Jockey Club (9 percent), full-time Jockey Club (17 percent), part of civil servant (15 to 20 percent), industry and commerce (19 percent), and banking (21 percent). For the armed forces and the civil servants in the central government, there is no direct contribution from the employer, but all deficits are, in fact, covered by the state. Finally, the public at large contributes to most pension funds through various taxes imposed, for instance, on imports, exports, lottery tickets, alcoholic beverages, tobacco products, agricultural goods, property rentals, professional services, and legal documents. Needless to say, the traditional regressiveness of a majority of these indirect taxes serves to introduce yet another mechanism of income redistribution in the direction of further income inequality.

There are other inequities in the financing system, particularly as concerns workers' contributions for family-allowance and unemployment benefits. For example, blue- and white-collar workers (except rural workers) suffer a deduction for family allowances (0.5 percent), while the military and civil servants do not contribute at all. Further, those insured in Industry and Commerce must contribute 1 percent of their earnings toward unemployment benefits, yet those in Civil Service, the Armed Forces, Banking, and Jockey Club (full-time) contribute nothing.

Table 3-9 shows the percentage distribution of aggregate social security revenues by financing sources and occupational groups as reported in 1969 by the pension funds. Here again, certain groups receive preferential treatment. Except civil servants, for whom data are not available, a ranking of the size of workers' contributions as a percentage of total pension fund revenues reveals that members of the military contribute the least (23.1 percent of total armed-forces revenues), followed by professionals (31 percent), rural and domestic workers (40.5 percent), bank employees (40.6 percent), notaries public (47.9 percent), workers in industry and commerce (48.2 percent), and Jockey Club employees (48.9 percent). Furthermore, while Industry and Commerce revenues from taxation constitute less than 1 percent of its total earnings, high-income funds such as those for Notaries Public and Professionals are overwhelmingly funded by the public, receiving 49 and 65 percent of their total incomes from tax revenues. Finally, the state, which is formally pledged to cover all of the operating deficits of the Armed Forces fund, contributed through subsidization 76 percent of its total revenues in 1969.

Table 3-10 presents aggregate data on current revenue per insured by occupational groups for 1969. Comparatively speaking, the wealthiest pension funds are those serving banking employees (average yearly per-capita revenue of 187,879 pesos) and notaries public (161,568 p.), while the poorest funds are those insuring rural and domestic workers (24,328 p.) and those in industry and commerce (36,960 p.). A ranking of the various pension funds parallels, as expected, the existing distribution of income, with white-collar funds having a higher per-capita revenue than blue-collar funds, and with the funds which insure professionals having a higher per-capita revenue than white-collar funds. However, the figures corresponding to two of the pension funds are misleadingly low. The Civil Service fund, which reported per-capita revenues of only 51,755 p. faces two problems mentioned previously: first, many of the insured work part-time (up to thirty hours per week), and, second, government contributions are generally delayed and kept to a bare minimum needed for the fund to meet its monthly obligations. Thus, the figures presented here are underestimates of both the income (in full-time equivalents) of civil servants and of the resources to which the fund is legally entitled. The Professional fund figure is also deceptively low at a per-capita income of just 47,748 p. The problem here is tax evasion since professionals contribute according to a nominal scale of income fixed according to years of service, a figure considerably below the real income. In addi-

Table 3-8
Social Security Contributions from Employees,
Employers, and State by Occupational Group in
Uruguay: 1969
(in percentage of wages or income)

Occupational Group	Employee	Employer	State	Total
Blue- and white-collars and rural workers				
Industry and commerce	19.5–25.5	35.5–39.5	—	55.0–65.0
Pensions	17.0[a]	19.0	[b]	36.0
Health[d]	1.0–7.0[e]	1.0–5.0[e]	[f]	2.0–12.0
Unemployment	1.0	1.0	[c]	2.0
Family allowances	0.5	14.5	—	15.0
Rural				
Pensions	[g]	[h]	[i]	—
Family allowances	—	[h]	—	—
Domestic				
Pensions	5.0	5.0	[j]	10.0
Family allowances	—	—	—	—
Banking	16.5	35.5	—	52.0
Pensions	16.0	21.0	—	37.0
Unemployment	—	[k]	—	—
Family allowances	0.5	14.5	—	15.0
Jockey Club	14.5–17.5	23.5–31.5	—	38.0–49.0
Full-time				
Pensions	14.0	17.0	[l]	31.0
Unemployment	—	[k]	—	—
Family allowances	0.5	14.5	—	15.0
Part-time				
Pensions	17.0	9.0	—	26.0
Family allowances	0.5	14.5	—	15.0
Civil servants	15.0	15.0–20.0	—	30.0–45.0
Pensions	15.0[m]	15.0–20.0[n]	—	30.0–45.0
Unemployment	—	[o]	[o]	—
Family allowances	—	[p]	[p]	—
Armed forces	13.0–16.5	—	—	13.0–16.5
Pensions	12.0–15.0	[q]	[r]	12.0–15.0
Health	1.0–1.5	[q]	—	1.0–1.5
Unemployment	—	[o]	[o]	—
Family allowances	—	[p]	[p]	—
Self-employed				
Professionals	18.0	—	—	18.0
Pensions	18.0	—	[s]	18.0
Notaries public	18.0	—	—	18.0
Pensions[t]	18.0[u]	—	[v]	18.0
Unemployment[w]	—	[o]	[o]	—

SOURCES: *Seguridad Social y Previsión Social en la República Oriental del Uruguay: Tomo 1-Jubilaciones y Pensiones* (Montevideo: Gerencia General Técnica de Seguridad Social, Banco de Previsión Social, 1971); and Jorge L. Lanzaro and María del Rosario Pedemonte, eds., *Recopilación sistematizada de normas de Derecho del Trabajo y Seguridad Social,* vol. 2 (Montevideo: Fundación de Cultura Universitaria, 1970).

a. Female workers pay 18 percent; some other contributions are still higher (e.g., workers exposed to radiation pay 34 percent).

b. Taxes on a variety of imports, domestic livestock sales, and newspaper advertisements.

c. Taxes on lottery tickets, alcoholic beverages, cigars, cigarettes, and other luxury items.

d. This benefit applies to all those workers who have organized a health-insurance fund; they constitute a majority of those in industry and commerce and, specifically, are the following: workers in transportation, construction, metallurgy, graphics, textiles, lumber, garments, beverages, glass, wool, and hides, leather, and restaurants, as well as sailors and Montevideo stevedores.

e. The average worker contribution for most health-insurance funds is 3 percent, while the average employer contribution is 5 percent.

f. Some health-insurance funds obtain the proceeds from various taxes such as on wool, leather, and textile exports; others are eligible for government loans and subsidies.

g. Every year the government fixes the size of this contribution and expresses it as a sum of pesos per working day or month.

h. Every year the government fixes the size of this contribution on the basis of the number of hectares of land which are being worked by the employer, changes in minimum rural wages, and changes in land values.

i. Tax of 8 percent on sales of agricultural products.

j. Variable tax of 1 to 6 percent on all property rentals.

k. Fully funded by employer contributions based on the number of years that a dismissed employee worked in a given business enterprise.

l. Revenues from unclaimed, winning, horse-race tickets as well as a percentage of the sale price of award-winning animals.

m. Policemen and employees of Congress contribute relatively more than do other civil servants.

n. Varies as follows: 15 percent of salaries for the Treasury Department, 17 percent for municipalities, 20 percent for autonomous or decentralized agencies, and unspecified for all others (i.e., the government subsidizes whenever necessary).

o. There is no specific unemployment insurance contribution by any party; rather, the respective pension fund provides for this benefit from its general revenues.

p. Paid in its entirety by the state acting as an employer.

q. Although the government, as their employer, is not responsible for a specific contribution, it is nevertheless pledged to cover all deficits.

r. Tax of 5 percent on the profits of the State National Savings Bank.

s. Taxes on various professional services (e.g., surgery, and medical or other certificates bearing the signature of a professional); on the sale of pharmaceuticals; on farm machinery and parts; on cigarettes, cigars, and tobacco; and on the transfer of automobile ownership.

t. The pension system covers both the notary public and his employees. To support the latter, the notary public contributes 5 percent of their salaries and the employee himself provides an additional 5 percent.

u. This is paid by affixing stamps on legal documents, but it is unclear as to whether the notary public or his clients actually pay for the stamps.

v. Taxes on notarial documents and certificates which the client must pay.

w. Not for the notary public himself but for his employees.

Table 3-9
Percentage Distribution of Social Security Fund Revenues by Financing Source and
Occupational Group in Uruguay: 1969

Occupational Group	Insured	Employer	State	Investment Returns	Others	Total
Blue- and white-collars **and rural workers** Industry and						
commerce[a]	48.2[e]	51.5[e]	0.4	0.2	0.2	100.1[f]
Rural and domestic[b]	40.5	6.2	50.8	1.8	0.7	100.0
Banking[c]	40.6	52.6	0	6.8	0	100.0
Jockey Club[a]	48.9	39.4	8.3	3.4	0	100.0
Civil servants	NA	NA	NA	NA	NA	—
Armed forces[d]	23.1[e]	0.6[e]	76.3	0	0	100.0
Self-employed[a]						
Professionals[a]	31.0	0	65.0	3.0	1.0	100.0
Notaries public[a]	47.9	0	49.0	3.1	0	100.0

SOURCES: From information supplied by the respective social security funds. The information for the estimates comes from Instituto de Economía, *Uruguay: Estadísticas básicas* (Montevideo: Universidad de la República, 1969), p. 149.
a. *State* stands for contributions from tax revenues only.
b. *State* stands for contributions from tax revenues and subsidies; figures are for 1965.
c. The state is the employer.
d. *State* stands for contributions from subsidies only.
e. Estimates based on average contributions during the 1964–1966 period.
f. Due to rounding.

Table 3-10
Revenue of Social Security Funds per Insured by Occupational Group in Uruguay: 1969

Occupational Group	Revenue (in million pesos)	Number of Insured	Revenue per Capita (in pesos)	Ratio[a]
Blue- and white-collars *and rural workers*	*29,954.5*	*807,894*	*37,077*	*1.5*
Industry and commerce	22,176.2	600,000	36,960	1.5
Rural and domestic	4,622.4	190,000	24,328	1.0
Banking	3,082.5	16,407	187,879	7.7
Jockey Club	73.4	1,487	49,369	2.0
Civil servants	*10,351.0*	*200,000*	*51,755*	*2.1*
Armed forces	*835.7*	*13,440*	*62,180*	*2.6*
Self-employed	*919.1*	*13,919*	*66,032*	*2.7*
Professionals	557.8	11,683	47,748	2.0
Notaries public	361.3	2,236	161,568	6.6

SOURCES: *Revenue* from information supplied by the respective social security funds. Number of insured from *Actives insured* from table 3-3.
a. Per-capita revenue for each social security fund divided by the lowest per-capita revenue fund.

tion, the insured has the option of choosing between a minimum and a maximum and normally chooses the minimum.

Table 3-11 shows the overall economic importance of social security in Uruguay. It presents an estimate of the size of social security expenditures during the 1965–1969 period and what proportion these expenditures are of Uruguay's GNP (from 11.8 to 14.5 percent), of government consumption expenditures (87.3 to 98.4 percent), and of total returns to labor (26.0 to 30.6 percent). However, these figures underestimate the significance of social security expenditures in the economy; indeed, due to data unavailability, the expenditures of three unemployment-compensation funds, of over a dozen health-insurance funds, and of the BSE payments for occupational hazards are excluded. Nonetheless, the data in table 3-11 place the cost of social security in Uruguay as the highest in Latin America.

The financial affairs of the various social security agencies are often problematical. Unfortunately, there are no data on revenues raised by private or public institutions for health purposes. Yet when the expenditure and revenue accounts of the individual pension funds for the period 1965–1969 are totaled, three pension funds show a deficit.[45] The largest deficit (in absolute terms) was that of the Armed Forces, due to the small contributions which the military are required to make to social security and to the generosity of their benefits. In any event, the government absorbed the fund's large deficit. The second largest deficit was that of Rural and Domestic, probably due to the falling ratio of its actives to its passives, as noted above. The fund had a deficit in 7 out of 10 years during the 1960–1969 period, ending with a very large overall deficit. Government subsidization of Rural and Domestic, which during the 1960–1963 accounted for 19 percent of total fund revenues, declined to a 1966–1969 average of 13 percent. The Civil Service fund was the third in a deficit position, this attributed to the delays with which the government meets its obligations toward pensioned civil servants. Industry and Commerce, Banking, and Notaries Public funds experienced a relatively strong surplus for the five-year period. As previously noted, Banking and Notaries Public have the highest revenues per insured, thereby explaining their strong financial position.

However, these aggregates and the ones shown in table 3-11 do not really measure the economic costs of social security—only its relative importance within the economy. Generally, the most important costs are microeconomic in nature and center on the distortions introduced by social security legislation on the local labor market. As can be seen in table 3-8, the total employer contribution as a percentage of wages in Uruguay's private sector is usually in the range of 35 to 40 percent. The heavy toll imposed by these contributions has made labor an expensive factor of production, thus influencing the choice of production techniques, the quantity and quality of labor employed, and the types of output produced in the economy. Perhaps this can help explain the disastrous performance of the Uruguayan economy since the early 1950s. For the past two decades, Uruguay has been characterized by, on the one hand, a very traditional, stagnant, and export-dependent livestock sector and, on the other, an urban (Montevideo) economy based on both a similarly stagnant, import-substituting industrial sector and a very large services sector.[46]

Benefits

Table 3-12 presents a concise summary of thirty-five different social security benefits for which the insured occupational groups are eligible. However, two benefits are

Table 3-11
Cost of Social Security in Uruguay: 1965-69
(in millions of current pesos and percentages)

Year	GNP	Government Consumption Expenditure	Compensation of Labor	Social Security Revenue				Social Security Expenditure			
				Total[a]	Percent of GNP	Percent of Government Consumption Expenditure	Percent of Compensation of Labor	Total[b]	Percent of GNP	Percent of Government Consumption Expenditure	Percent of Compensation of Labor
1965	51,780	7,653	24,600	5,224	10.1	68.3	21.2	7,528	14.5	98.4	30.6
1966	98,220	12,972	42,700	9,194	9.4	70.9	21.5	12,732	13.0	98.2	29.8
1967	165,360	23,870	80,100	16,308	9.9	68.3	20.3	22,402	13.6	93.9	28.0
1968	364,220	49,100	164,600	32,860	9.0	66.9	20.0	42,852	11.8	87.3	26.0
1969	494,050	75,400	234,600	47,601	9.6	63.1	20.3	70,350	14.2	93.3	30.0

Sources: *GNP* from International Monetary Fund, *International Financial Statistics*, various issues. *Government consumption expenditures*, ibid. *Compensation of labor* from U.N., *Yearbook of National Accounts Statistics: 1971* (New York: United Nations, 1973), vol. 2, p. 573. *Social security revenues* and *expenditure* from information supplied by the various social security funds and the Consejo Central de Asignaciones Familiares; health expenditure from *Plan Nacional de Desarrollo, 1973–1977* (Montevideo: Presidencia de la República, n.d.), p. XI-38.

a. Includes revenues of the nine social security funds and the family allowance fund; excludes health.

b. Includes expenditures of the nine social security funds and the family allowance fund plus the expenditures on health by the government and mutual insurance organizations. Since the figures on health expenditures during 1965–1966 are not available, an estimate was arrived at by calculating the average of health expenditures as a percentage of gross domestic product during the 1967–1970 period, and then applying it to the 1965–1966 gross domestic product data.

not listed in the table: the pension for indigents, for which anyone who is old or totally incapacitated and without means of support can qualify; and the maternity pension, under which any woman in industry, commerce, or banking can retire after ten years of work to raise her children. A simple quantitative ranking of the number of benefits for which the various groups are eligible shows the following: (1) workers in industry and commerce, with eligibility for 27 different benefits; (2) the armed forces, civil servants, and bank employees, 25; (3) full-time Jockey Club workers, 21; (4) rural and domestic workers, 20; (5) part-time Jockey Club workers, 18; (6) notaries public, 14; and (7) professionals, 12.

An analysis of table 3-12 by category of benefits shows that the various occupational groups are evenly covered in pension benefits (items 1 through 6) with two important exceptions: rural and domestic workers, part-time Jockey Club employees, professionals, and notaries public lack protection from unemployment and are ineligible for seniority pensions. Other cash benefits (items 7 through 19) reveal three major discrepancies: only the Banking fund has provisions for the restitution of contributions; only workers in industry and commerce, rural and domestic activities, and public-school teachers are eligible for a bonus for work-years above the minimum required for retirement; and only workers in industry and commerce, part-time Jockey Club employees, professionals, and notaries public qualify for a subsidy for temporary disability caused by nonoccupational hazards. Professionals and notaries public are ineligible for family-allowance payments (items 20 through 27). Finally, only blue- and white-collar workers and the military receive the full range of health-maternity benefits (items 28 through 35) through the social security system. Nonetheless, all occupational groups are eligible for preventive medicine administered by the Ministry of Public Health (detailed below) as well as for rehabilitation and prosthetics benefits in case of occupational hazards, as provided by law and granted by the BSE. Since the higher-income groups such as professionals, banking employees, and civil servants can be assumed to be able to purchase medical services on their own, the system appears to discriminate most heavily against rural and domestic workers.

A more sophisticated analysis concerns the inequalities of acquiring a benefit available to all or various occupational groups. Inequalities occur in five areas: the age qualification for old-age pensions, the work-years required for seniority pensions, the basic salary used to compute the amount of a pension, the adjustment of pensions to the cost of living, and the existing delays in receiving a pension.[47]

The qualification for old-age pensions in Uruguay varies widely from fund to fund. Several of the funds express this requirement in terms of a sum total (or *coeficiente*), that is, a figure representing the combination of age and work years necessary for retirement. For example, a sum total of 80 means that it is possible to retire at 50 years of age if one has worked for 30 years; alternatively, a 48-year-old person may also retire provided that he has worked for 32 years; and so on with any combination totaling 80. But complications arise because, in many funds, workers 55 years and older have a lower sum-total requirement than younger workers. In addition, several funds have a different sum-total qualification for women than for men, while others have numerous different requirements for specific occupational subgroups. To make a comparison among the funds, it may be more meaningful to assume that all male workers uniformly enter the labor force at age 18 except professionals and notaries public who do so at age 25. Under these assumptions, the military are the most favored because they can retire at age 40 provided that they have been unable to

Table 3-12
Social Security Benefits by Occupational Group in Uruguay: 1971

Occupational Group	Pensions									Other Cash Benefits										Family Allowances								Health-Maternity								Total
	1	2	3	4	5	6[a]	7	8	9	10	11	12	13	14	15	16	17	18	19	20	21	22	23	24	25	26	27	28	29	30	31	32	33	34	35	Total
Blue- and white-collars and rural workers																																				
Industry and commerce																																				
commerce	x	x	x	x	x	x		x	x	x	x	x[b]	x	[c]		x	x			x	x	x	x	x[d]			x	x	x[b]	x	x	x[b]	x[b]	x[b]	x[e]	27
Rural and domestic	x	x	x	x	x	x		x	x	x	x	x	x	[c]			x	x	x	x	x	x	x	x[d]			x	x		x	x	x	x	x	x	20
Banking	x	x	x	x	x	x	x			x	x					x	x			x	x	x	x	x[d]			x	x		x	x	x	x	x	x	25
Jockey Club																																				
Full-time	x	x	x	x	x	x		x		x	x	x	x		x		x		x	x	x	x	x	x[d]			x	x		x	x					21
Part-time	x		x			x					x	x	x			x	x		x	x	x	x	x	x[d]			x	x		x	x					18
Civil servants	x	x	x	x	x	x		x	x[f]	x	x		x				x		x	x	x	x	x	x[d]			x	x		x	x	x	x	x	x	25
Armed forces	x	x	x	x	x	x		x		x	x		x			x	x		x	x	x	x	x	x[d]			x	x		x	x	x	x	x	x[e]	25
Self-employed																																				
Professionals	x		x	x	x	x		x		x	x	x	x			x[h]			x										x	x						12
Notaries public	x		x	x	x[g]	x				x	x	x	x			x		x	x										x	x						14

SOURCE: Information on legislation compiled by the author.

NOTE: See code following table for definition of benefits here signified by numbers 1–35.

a. All funds grant survivors' pensions to widows (including former wives in the majority of cases) and children, as well as parents (in a few cases only if disabled) and sisters (in most cases if single, widowed, or divorced). Jockey Club part-time does not grant pensions to parents and sisters.

b. This benefit applies to all those workers and employees who have organized a health-insurance fund; they constitute a majority of those in industry and commerce and, specifically, are the following ones: workers in hides, leather, and restaurants as well as sailors and Montevideo stevedores.

c. Aside from the unemployment pension for which all workers in industry and commerce are eligible (item #5), there are three unemployment-compensation funds providing a subsidy for workers in wool- and hides-processing as well as for those in meat-packing and -processing, both in Montevideo and elsewhere. In addition, workers in industry, commerce, and rural areas receive compensation.

d. This payment is called hogar constituido (established household).

e. Generally limited to oral surgery.

f. Applies only to schoolteachers.

g. Applies only to the employees of a notary public.

h. Applies only when there are no survivors.

Code for Social Security Benefits

Pensions:
1. Old-age.
2. Seniority.
3. Permanent disability (total or partial) caused by occupational hazards.
4. Permanent disability (total or partial) caused by nonoccupational hazards.
5. Unemployment/layoff.
6. Survivors'.

Other Cash Benefits:
7. Restitution of contributions.
8. Lump sum at retirement.
9. Bonus added to pension for work-years above the minimum required for retirement.
10. Lump sum for permanent disability (total or partial) caused by occupational hazards.
11. Subsidy for temporary disability caused by occupational hazards.
12. Subsidy for temporary disability caused by nonoccupational hazards.
13. Salary (or percentage thereof) paid for a period before and after childbirth.
14. Unemployment/layoff temporary subsidy.
15. Unemployment/layoff lump sum.
16. Life insurance, lump sum.
17. Funeral aid, lump sum.
18. Lump sum to survivors when no right to pension is granted.
19. Year-end bonus to retired and pensioners.

Family Allowances:
20. Marriage.
21. Pregnancy.
22. Childbirth.
23. Children.
24. Spouse.
25. Parents.
26. Child food (percentage of salary or in kind).
27. School aid (for insured or his/her children).

Health-Maternity Benefits:
28. Preventive medicine.
29. Curative medical care.
30. Rehabilitation and prosthesis in case of occupational hazards.
31. Maternity care.
32. Surgical treatment.
33. Hospitalization.
34. Medicines.
35. Dental care.

move to a higher rank (e.g., a sailor who turns 40 may retire); however, the qualifying age is higher for the higher ranks. The second most-favored group is professionals, who can retire at age 48 (assuming that they started practicing at age 25). The third most-favored group is workers in industry and commerce, who can retire at age 49 (given, of course, a 31-year work record). The fourth most-favored group is civil servants, banking employees, notaries public, Jockey Club workers (both full- and part-time), and rural and domestic workers, who can retire at the age of 54 (if they have worked for 36 years). Certainly, it is difficult to estimate what proportion of the population can actually retire so soon, especially since job mobility often implies that the years spent in a given occupation do not count for retirement purposes under a second pension fund.

The qualification for seniority pensions also varies widely but is much easier to compare. Low-ranking members of the armed forces are first, becoming eligible for a pension after 15 years on the job. In second place are high-ranking members of the military, who can retire after 20 years' service. Third are certain workers in industry and commerce (e.g., particularly meat-processing workers, and metallurgical and glass-manufacturing workers) who can retire after 25 years. Fourth, civil servants and banking employees gain the right to a seniority pension after 30 years of work—although for some civil servants in posts with a high incidence of occupational hazards, the requirement is considerably lower. In fifth and last place are full-time Jockey Club workers, who can retire after 36 years.

Although civil servants do not appear to be especially privileged in terms of the qualifications for old-age and seniority pensions, they do enjoy some benefits which no other group does. In Uruguay, a civil-service appointment is a lifetime appointment; indeed, no civil servant can be discharged unless the discharge is specifically approved by the country's Senate. This has traditionally been so unlikely that a number of civil servants never bother to go to work—or to function efficiently when they do go to work. Civil servants can, however, be dismissed in economy moves or when certain government services are discontinued. In these cases they immediately become eligible for a pension which is not suspended even when they find another position elsewhere in the labor force. In conclusion, the age qualification for retirement from the civil service is quite meaningless.

There are additional inequalities in the computation of the so-called "basic salary," that is, an average salary calculated for each individual which serves as the basis for determining the amount of a pension. The basic salary acquires great importance in times of high inflation because, of course, the more past salaries are included in the formula, the smaller the purchasing power of the pension; ideally, the basic salary should be equal to the last salary earned. For the majority of the labor force (male workers in industry and commerce, professionals, and many civil servants), the basic salary is a simple arithmetic average of earnings during the five years prior to retirement. Rural and domestic workers have their basic salary determined by law and expressed in a sum in pesos adjusted every year to the cost of living; thus, their basic salary is not really comparable to that of the rest of the labor force. Most women in the civil service, the professions, and in industry and commerce are favored by basic salaries which are an average of their past three years' earnings. The basic salary for banking employees is an average of their last years' earnings. Most favored of all are members of the armed forces and high government officials, whose basic salary equals their last salary, and some civil servants (e.g., judges, congressmen, presidents and cabinet members, directors of autonomous institutions, rectors and deans of the university), whose basic salary equals the salary currently paid for their previously held post; that is, their retirement income is guaranteed always to remain at par with the income they would be earning had they not retired at all.

There are several techniques for adjusting pensions to the cost of living. Most privileged groups enjoy an automatic adjustment related to the increase in salary for the job that the pensioner used to have. The percentage of adjustment varies as follows: 100 percent for all elective posts (e.g., the president, congressmen, mayors), as well as ministers, judges of the Supreme Court and other high courts, the attorneys general, and heads of autonomous institutions; 80 to 100 percent for the military, according to their rank and years of service; and 70 percent for high officials in the executive and judiciary, all employees of the Congress and the BPS, and teachers. For the remaining groups, the adjustment is not automatic. In the cases of bank employees, public registrars, professionals, and jockeys, the adjustment is made once or twice a year by the directorship of the corresponding fund. The bulk of the insured (in industry, commerce, agriculture, and the rest of the civil service) are left to an annual adjustment by decree of the executive.

Again there are notable inequities in the delays in obtaining a pension. The smaller and better-endowed funds, such as those for the military, professionals, notaries public, and banking employees, rarely impose a very long delay, requiring only a month or so to have one's papers cleared for payment. However, in the three large funds managed by the BPS, because of their precarious financial position as well as their complex bureaucracy, the delays are very much longer and can take several years. As an example, there is one study of 8,666 requests for pensions which were approved by Industry and Commerce during 1962–1963. The figures show that only 30 percent of the requests were less than a year old; that 27 percent of them were at least 5 years old; and that there were some incredible individual delays, for example, 3 requests had been submitted 21 years before and one request had been filed an unbelievable 28 years ago.[48] Yet all this does not mean that everyone who applies for a pension from the three large funds is treated alike. Individuals who have held high posts are able to influence officials of the pension funds and thus have their papers cleared much faster. Known as the *pronto despacho* (literally, quick expedition), this practice probably originated because high pension-fund officials are political appointees who thus feel certain obligations toward fellow civil servants and leading elements of their constituency.

As this discussion suggests, the benefits listed in table 3-12 must be interpreted with caution. In the five comparisons presented above, the armed forces ranked first in 3, civil servants first in 2, and subgroups of the labor aristocracy in 2, while rural workers and domestic servants came out last in all comparisons. In this light, a revised ranking of available benefits by occupational groups shows that: (1) the military has the easiest access to all the benefits it is legally entitled to, namely, low age qualification for old-age pensions, low seniority requirements for seniority pensions, job security, a favorable basic salary, and negligible delays in the processing of applications for social security benefits; (2) civil servants, professionals, notaries public, and banking employees also have a relatively easy and speedy access to social security benefits; (3) workers in industry and commerce are somewhat hindered and relatively less privileged in their enjoyment of social security benefits; and (4) that rural and domestic workers (and Jockey Club workers) find many obstacles in their pursuit of and are least able to actually enjoy whatever social security benefits they are eligible for.

Table 3-13
Average Yearly Pensions and Family Allowances by Occupational Groups in Uruguay: 1969
(in current pesos per capita)

	Pensions				Family Allowances[b]	
Occupational Group	Old-Age	Survivors'	Average	Ratio[a]	Household	Minors
Blue- and white-collar						
and rural workers	*97,431*	*40,872*	*71,731*	*1.7*	*24,000*	*18,000*
Industry and						
commerce	94,881	53,464	79,435	1.8	24,000	18,000
Rural and domestic[c]	79,284	19,850	42,830	1.0	24,000	18,000
Banking	368,829	266,171	334,788	7.8	24,000	18,000
Jockey Club[d]	29,397	10,487	20,413	0.5	24,000	18,000
Civil servants	*169,038*	*57,819*	*102,951*	*2.4*	*84,000*	*36,000*
Armed forces	*159,915*	*95,977*	*125,903*	*2.9*	*84,000*	*36,000*
Self-employed	*174,405*	*72,302*	*125,376*	*2.9*	*0*	*0*
Professionals	158,867	73,989	119,184	2.8	0	0
Notaries public	286,169	63,795	162,512	3.8	0	0

SOURCES: *Pensions* from information supplied by the respective social security funds. *Family allowances* from Ruben Caggiani, "Desarrollo de la Seguridad Social en el Uruguay en el período 1/1/67 al 31/12/69," *Seguridad Social* (Montevideo), 1 (May–June 1970), p. 38.

a. Average per-capita pension benefits for each social security fund and occupational group divided by the fund with the lowest average per-capita pension benefits (Jockey Club).

b. Standard payment for each eligible established household and dependent.

c. The special noncontributory pensions for indigents have been lumped together with survivors' benefits.

d. Part-time employees only; no breakdown was available for full-time Jockey Club employees.

Table 3-13 presents data on average yearly per-capita pensions and family allowances by occupational groups for the year 1969, and makes evident the fact that payments by the pension system closely resemble the existing distribution of income in Uruguay and the ranking of current revenue per insured found in table 3-10. In general, high-income occupational groups receive high revenues from the pension system and low-income occupational groups receive low revenues from the system. In expenditures, the pension funds maintain rather than modify the country's distribution of income. There is a blatant inequity in family-allowance benefits in that civil servants and the military traditionally receive a higher payment for household expenses and dependents than do blue- and white-collar and rural workers. In 1969, while the former received 84,000 p. as an established household benefit and 36,000 p. per eligible dependent, the latter obtained only 24,000 p. and 18,000 p., respectively.

Perhaps the aspect of social security inequality which most defies quantification is the delivery of health care. This is indeed unfortunate because the Uruguayan government has long been involved in providing low-cost medical services specifically geared to the middle- and low-income groups. Since the early twentieth century, numerous hospitals and clinics have been operated by the Ministry of Public Health in a concerted effort to raise the health standards of the community. Many medical services have been provided free of charge for venereal disease, respiratory ailments, and tuberculosis, as well as vaccination services for virtually every communicable disease. A special pass entitles low-income familes to free or low-cost hospitalization, surgery, and medication. Finally, free medical checkups of secondary-school students and many groups of workers (e.g., school teachers, professional drivers, and food service and restaurant employees) have helped Uruguay to achieve one of the highest health standards in Latin America (e.g., low late fetal death ratios, low infant mortality rates, and high life expectancy).

The most popular and widely exercised health-insurance option open to the middle- and upper-income groups is that of enrolling in a mutual insurance (i.e., prepaid, nonprofit) medical plan. Members pay monthly premiums in return for eligibility for all medical services and medication. These health plans attract all those who seek and can afford quality medical care: civil servants, professionals, employers, and employees in banking and commerce. A majority of blue-collar workers, as noted above, have recently succeeded in establishing over a dozen individual health-insurance funds. These funds often subcontract their medical services through already established private health plans; hence, most blue-collar workers now enjoy the kind of medical care previously reserved for white-collar workers and civil servants—the only difference being that the blue-collars receive no employer contribution. The only other group to have a specific health-insurance plan is the military, which is entitled to medical care through a large military hospital financed jointly by personal withholdings and government subsidy. Recently, policemen have joined the military health plan. Finally, for those in the middle- and upper-income groups who do not wish or are not eligible (because of age or health qualifications) to participate in one of the health-insurance programs, private clinics and hospitals are available.

Table 3-14 fails to quantify the delivery of health care during 1968 by occupational categories. Data are unavailable for the various occupational groups previously analyzed except the military, whose health care is centralized under a single medical

Table 3-14
Health Facilities and Expenditures by Sector in Uruguay: 1968

| Sector | Individuals Covered | Expenditures | | Hospital Beds | Beds per 1,000 |
		Million Pesos	Per Capita		
Armed forces	32,864[a]	67.8	2,063	277	8.4
Public[b]	1,839,884	2,873.3	1,562	13,788	7.5
Mutual insurance organizations[c]	647,252	3,161.0	4,884	1,827	2.8
Private[d]	280,000	—	—	1,535	5.5
Total	2,800,000	6,102.1	2,179	17,427	6.2

SOURCES: *Armed Forces,* actives from table 3-3 and passives from Bureau of Economic Affairs, U.S. Arms Control and Disarmament Agency, *World Military Expenditures 1971* respectively; *Military Hospital Beds* and *Expenditures* from Fernando Suescún Caicedo, "Informe sobre la organización de servicios de atención médica, seguridad social y seguros de salud de la República Oriental del Uruguay," the unpublished report of a 1968 misison to Uruguay by the Panamerican Sanitary Bureau, p. 91. *Public,* Suescún Caicedo, pp. 91–92. *Mutual insurance organizations,* Suescún Caicedo, pp. 53–56, 91–92. *Private,* Suescún Caicedo, pp. 91–92.

a. Actives plus passives.

b. Includes the facilities operated by the Ministry of Public Health, the BSE (1965), and the CCAF as well as the Penitentiary Hospital and the University Hospital.

c. Facilities operated by nonprofit medical cooperatives or mutual insurance programs.

d. Profit-making hospitals and clinics.

Table 3-15
Health Facilities by Geographical Region in Uruguay: 1963–1964

Region	Total Population[a] (in thousands)	Hospital Beds[a]	Beds per 1,000 Inhabitants[a]	Physicians[b]	Physicians per 10,000 Inhabitants[b]	Composite Weighted Index of Beds and Physicians
Montevideo	1,228.6	9,244	7.6	2,400	19.5	14.6
All other areas	1,419.4	7,691	5.4	651	4.5	8.2
Total	2,648.0	16,935	6.4	3,051	11.5	8.8

SOURCES: *Total population* from U.N., *Demographic Yearbook: 1970* (New York: United Nations, 1971), p. 109 (for 1963 mid-year estimate). *Hospital beds and physicians: Health Conditions in the Americas: 1961-64* (Washington, D.C.: Pan American Health Organization, 1966), pp. 103 and 122.
a. 1963 figures.
b. 1964 figures.

plan using exclusive facilities. Estimates of the number of individuals serviced by as well as the expenditures of public (government) agencies, mutual insurance funds, and private medical organizations are so aggregated and tentative, though, that they must be taken with great caution—particularly those referring to the population using only public or only private institutions. While the military enjoy the highest ratio of beds per 1,000 insured (8.4), mutual insurance organizations spend the most money per person (4,884 p.); however, there are no expenditure data for private hospitals and clinics which, in all probability, would turn out to be the biggest spenders. The public sector poses a contradiction in that, in terms of beds per 1,000 insured, it ranks second after the military but, in terms of per-capita expenditures, it ranks last. Apparently, the index of available beds provides a poor indicator of the quality and use of medical facilities; indeed, many of the government's hospitals and clinics have no lack of beds but are inadequately staffed, poorly financed, and desperately short of medication and other expensive materials. Thus, the index of per-capita expenditures is more reliable, suggesting that those protected by prepaid medical insurance (e.g., the military, much of Montevideo's unionized labor force, and a considerable proportion of the upper- and middle-income groups) have access to quality medical facilities and enjoy adequate medical care.

Table 3-15 provides some evidence of the disparity between the accessibility of medical services to Montevideo versus non-Montevideo inhabitants during 1963–1964. Not only was there a higher ratio of beds per 1,000 inhabitants in Montevideo than in the rest of the country (7.6 vs. 5.4), but also an acute concentration of physicians in the capital city (19.5 physicians per 10,000 inhabitants in Montevideo, 4.5 elsewhere). A 1966 survey confirmed this gap, estimating about 18.9 physicians per 10,000 population in Montevideo versus only 4.0 in the rural areas.[49] These data suggest that the quality and variety of medical care is considerably higher in the capital city than in the rural areas. As further illustration, a 1963 study showed that infant mortality in Montevideo was 7.8 per 10,000 inhabitants, while, in the rest of the nation, the figure was 12.9 per 10,000 inhabitants, a fact only partly accounted for by birthrate differentials.[50] Beyond doubt, the regional gap in medical benefits has surved as an important incentive for many rural workers to migrate to Montevideo in search of better medical care.

The Inequality Effect of Social Security Stratification

Uruguay lacks an equitable personal or geographical distribution of income, and its social security system, through inequalities in coverage, financing, and benefits, appears to have contributed to that state of affairs. Although the crucial role of pressure groups and the interplay of various political traditions have made it possible for all Uruguayans to count on some social security, the institutional framework delivering the benefits abounds in flagrant inequities.

The available data suggest that about 65 percent of the total population and almost all the economically active population are covered by the social security system, one of the highest coverages in Latin America. These percentages of coverage were not significantly altered during the 1960s.

The largest group of insured in Uruguay consists of a cluster of blue- and white-collar workers: 78 percent of the total number of insured, with industry and commerce workers having the largest subgroup (58 percent) followed by rural and domestic workers (18 percent). It is not possible to disaggregate this group into blue- and white-collars. Next come civil servants, who represent 19 percent of the total number of insured, one of the highest percentages in Latin America. The armed-forces and self-employed groups each embrace about 1 percent of the total number of insured. Since there is no statistical breakdown by occupational groups, class of worker, or economic sectors, one cannot estimate the degree of social security protection by major groups. All indications are, however, that rural workers have the least coverage and that the sociology and traditions of the rural environment as well as the nonunionization of these workers have been responsible for the lag in their effective coverage.

Data on social security coverage by geographic regions and departments are not available either. The only existing statistics refer to the distribution of the population between the capital city (Montevideo) and the rest of the country. During the 1960s, 53 percent of the population lived outside Montevideo; meanwhile, the family-allowance authority, whose payments are only a function of the number of eligible inhabitants and are not dependent on income, spent an average of 42 percent of its total expenditures in areas other than Montevideo. The response of the rural population to these and other cultural, educational, sanitary, and income differentials has been a mass migration to the capital city, currently estimated to hold at least 50 percent of the total population.

In most pension funds (excluding rural and domestic workers and the self-employed), the percentage contribution of the insured roughly increases as the income of the group decreases. Conversely, the employers' percentage contribution tends to increase as the income of the group is higher. The state subsidizes all deficits resulting from pension funds covering the military and civil servants employed by the central government. Revenue is also generated by indirect taxes, most of which have a regressive income distribution effect. In the family-allowance and unemployment programs, the military and civil servants do not contribute (banking employees do not contribute either for their unemployment fund), while the rest of the insured are required to do so.

According to the data on the percentage distribution of total social security revenue by financing sources, the insured groups can be ranked by the lowest contribution paid by the workers (and, consequently, the highest combined employer-state contribution) as follows: the military (23.1 and 76.9 percent), professionals (31 and

65 percent), rural and domestic workers (40.5 and 57 percent), banking employees (40.6 and 52.6 percent), notaries public (47.9 and 49 percent), industry and commerce workers (48.2 and 51.9 percent), and Jockey Club employees (48.9 and 47.7 percent). Disaggregated revenue data for civil servants are not available. An analysis of the revenue generated from taxes alone indicates that, while industry and commerce workers received less than 1 percent from that source, higher-income groups such as notaries public and professionals received 49 and 65 percent from tax revenue, respectively. The state directly subsidized the military, contributing 77 percent of their fund's revenue. Except for rural and domestic workers, therefore, the financing system appears clearly regressive.

A simple quantification of the many social security benefits available to each occupational group results in the following preliminary ranking: (1) industry and commerce; (2) armed forces, civil servants, and banking; (3) full-time Jockey Club; (4) rural and domestic; (5) part-time Jockey Club; (6) notaries public; and (7) professional. It should be noted that the last two groups, being self-employed, are not naturally eligible for certain benefits such as unemployment pension and compensation, and family allowances. Hence, this preliminary ranking shows that, among salaried personnel and wage-earners, rural and domestic workers receive the poorest package of benefits.

A more sophisticated analysis of inequalities in benefit eligibility, taking into account differences in qualifications for pensions, the basic salary used to compute pensions, the adjustment of pensions to the cost of living, and delays in the granting of pensions, allows a more accurate ranking: (1) armed forces; (2) civil servants, professionals, notaries public, and banking; (3) industry and commerce; (4) rural and domestic, and Jockey Club.

A study of average yearly pensions and family allowances by occupational groups indicates that, in expenditures the social security system maintains rather than modifies the nation's distribution of income. High-income pension funds, often financed by regressive revenue-raising techniques, channel their revenues back to high-income occupational groups. The government, which could contribute to a more even distribution of social security payments, appears to do just the contrary. Average pensions received by banking employees are about three times higher than those paid to the military, civil servants, and professionals, and two times higher than those paid to notaries public. In turn, pensions received by the last four groups are 1.5 times higher than those paid to industry and commerce workers and three times higher than those received by rural and domestic workers. Family allowances paid to the military and civil servants are from 2 to 3.5 times higher than those paid to blue- and white-collar workers.

Finally, there are major inequalities in the delivery of health care. All those enrolled in prepaid, nonprofit, group health plans have access to quality medical care at reasonable prices, while the rest must rely either on private physicians and clinics or on government health agencies. The military and many blue- and white-collar groups are legally entitled to such prepaid medical care, and other occupational groups (professionals and civil servants, for instance) can be assumed to be able to afford private health insurance plans or private medical facilities. Rural and domestic workers, however, are deprived of low-cost prepaid, group health plans and cannot afford quality private medical care; therefore they have to resort to government health services. And yet these services are highly concentrated in Montevideo. In 1963–1965, the inhabitants of the capital city had access to an average of 41 percent more hospital beds and 333 percent more physicians than did the residents of the rest of the country. Hence, geographical inequalities aggravate the existing health-care differentials based on the occupational structure.

The various comparisons presented above allow us to rank the four main occupational groups according to the excellency of their social security systems as follows: first, the armed forces, closely followed by banking employees (a subgroup of blue- and white-collars); second, civil servants; third, the self-employed (notaries and professionals in that order); and fourth, blue- and white-collars in this order: industry and commerce, Jockey Club full-time, rural and domestic workers, and Jockey Club part-time.

The massification of social security privileges has taken place in Uruguay to a larger extent than in any other Latin American country. Even the least powerful groups have made significant accomplishments: industrial and commercial workers actually qualify for more benefits than any other group; rural and domestic workers, although at the bottom of the Uruguayan social security ladder, still compare well with their counterparts in the rest of Latin America. In the second half of the 1960s, the proportion of social security expenditures in relation to GNP averaged 13.5 percent, with a Latin American record high of 14.5 percent reached in 1965. (In 1970 Chile established a new record, 15.8 percent, but this was the GNP proportion of social security *revenues,* instead of expenditures, and the latter proportion usually is smaller.) While the 1960 ratio of active vis-a-vis passive was 4 to 1 (already the lowest in Latin America), it declined further in 1969 to a strikingly low ratio of 2.3 actives for each passive.

In 1969, revenue per captia of Banking and Notaries Public funds was from 2 to 3 times higher than the revenue per capita of Civil Service and Armed Forces funds, and 5 to 7 times higher than the revenue per capita of Industry and Commerce and Rural and Domestic funds. Funds like Banking and Notaries Public, cover small groups of insured with relatively high incomes and, in some cases, receive state subsidy; despite their generous program of benefits, though, they amassed a considerable surplus. Other funds, such as Armed Forces and Civil Service, cover high-income groups of varying size. Their system of benefits is quite generous too, while the insured percentage contribution is small (or nil in some programs); therefore they suffer from large deficits, but these are absorbed by the state. The largest group of insured, industry and commerce workers, is a middle-income one, but with a less generous system of benefits and a higher percentage of contributions from the insured. So far this fund has been capable of generating surpluses. Finally, the medium-sized group made up of rural and domestic workers has the worst system of benefits, yet it insures those with lowest incomes. In this instance the insured percentage contribution is the smallest in the system, and there is significant evasion both among employers and employees. In spite of a substantial state contribution, the fund accumulated a deficit during most of the 1960s which, by 1969, reached catastrophic proportions.

The unification of Uruguay's social security system could well contribute to a reduction in the stratification and inequalities currently ingrained in the system. An initial step in this direction was taken in 1967 with the administrative merging of the three largest funds (those covering workers in industry and commerce, the civil service, and rural and domestic activities) under the aegis of a newly created Social Welfare Bank. Yet that unification was largely symbolic, since so far the basic laws relating to social security coverage, financing, or benefits have gone unchanged. It is not known at this point whether, at least in practice, the three pension funds are pooling their revenues into a common account. If so, the surpluses generated by the Industry and Commerce fund might be used to cover the persistent deficits of the Civil Service and Rural and Domestic funds—with a regressive effect in the former case and a progressive effect in the latter instance. But if the Social Welfare Bank is not even conducting a *de facto* financial merger, then that 1967 step toward unification is truly nominal.

The many decades of democracy in Uruguay were unable to produce a nonstratified and equitable social security system. Citizen participation through the activities of pressure groups clearly resulted in a biased system which mirrored the power, influence, or prestige of particular occupational groups at the expense of the collective welfare and the ideals of social security legislation. Now that Uruguay also has a military and autocratic regime, the traditional role of several pressure groups has changed. Whether that change will be taken as an opportunity to reshuffle existing privileges to suit those in positions of power or to introduce unselfish reforms remains to be seen.

4 The Case of Peru

Historical Evolution of Social Security in Peru Since Independence

Social security legislation has evolved in Peru in five distinct chronological stages.[1] (See table 4-1.)

1821-1910

In gaining independence from Spain, Peru suffered destruction to its economy and dislocation of the ruling aristocracy. Military *caudillos* stepped in to rule. In 1820, a few months before the end of Spanish rule, *montepío civil,* pensions for civil servants, had been introduced by the Viceroy.

Under the first constitution of the republic (1822), public assistance was established as an obligation of society, but for thirty years little was added to the *montepío* system. It was supplemented at the top by the arbitrary and privileged *gracias,* an inheritance of the colonial gratuitous concessions, and at the bottom by the *cofradías* and the paternalistic, nongovernmental *sociedades de beneficencia pública* or public-charity boards. In 1826 a General Direction of Public Charities was entrusted with the supervision of charity hospitals and orphanages. These years were characterized by domestic instability and war against border states which considerably reduced the Peruvian territory.

Throughout the first fifty years of the republic, the only powerful group in Peruvian society was the military who had fought in the wars of independence and against border states. But none of them seemed to have force enough to stabilize the country and eighteen governments succeeded until Mariscal Ramón Castilla (1845-1851 and 1855-1862), a benevolent autocrat, managed to impose law and order and some regularity in power succession. With increased production of guano and nitrates, a new class of industrialists and merchants arose. Castilla adapted the Napoleonic Codes of Peru following the Continental trend of laissez faire. He also abolished both negro slavery and the remainder of Indian servitude. In 1850 Castilla's government created the *montepío militar,* establishing pensions for the military who up to that point had relied on the civil-servant legislation and gratuitous concessions for social security protection. Six days later, a new law of pensions for civil servants was passed. Since then, a typical feature of Peruvian social security has been the escalation of benefits granted to the military vis-a-vis civil servants. The Sociedad Benéfica del Callao, one of the most important mutual-aid societies, was organied in 1854.

The first president ever elected by popular vote, civilian Manuel Pardo, enacted a

Table 4-1
Significant Social Security Legislation in Peru: 1820–1972

Year	President	Type of Coverage	Group Protected
1820	De la Pezuela (viceroy)	Pensions (coverage not clear)	Civil servants
1850	Castilla (m)	Pensions (old age, survivors', dismissal)	Military
1850	Castilla (m)	Pensions (old age, survivors', dismissal)	Civil servants
1910	Billinghurst (m)	Pensions	Military
1911	Billinghurst (m)	Occupational accidents	Blue-collars[a]
1923	Leguía (m)	Pensions	Air force
1924	Leguía (m)	Life insurance[b]	White-collars
1934	Benavides (m)	Pensions	Longshoremen
1935	Benavides (m)	Occupational diseases	Blue-collars
1936	Benavides (m)	Health-maternity[c]	Blue-collars
1936	Benavides (m)	Pensions	Civil servants
1941	Prado (c)	Pensions (old age, disability)	Civil servants
1946	Bustamante (c)	Pensions (seniority)	White-collars[d]
1948	Odría (m)	Health-maternity[e]	White-collars and civil servants
1950	Odría (m)	Health-maternity[f]	Military
1950	Odría	Pensions	Civil servants
1960	Prado (c)	Supplement to pensions	Civil servants
1961	Prado (c)	Pensions	Blue-collars
1961–1962	Prado (c)	Pensions	White-collars
1965	Belaúnde (c)	Pensions	Teachers, public registrars, employees of Congress and judiciary
1965	Belaúnde (c)	Unemployment, health	Fishermen
1970	Velasco (m)	Pensions	Domestic servants
1972	Velasco (m)	Pensions	Fishermen
1972	Velasco (m)	Pensions (uniformity)	Military
1973	Velasco (m)	Pensions (uniformity)	Blue- and white-collars and civil servants (new system)

SOURCE: Legislation compiled by the author.

NOTE: (m) = military; (c) = civilian.

a. Only in mechanized activities, manual jobs excluded.

b. Includes subsidy for illness and pension for permanent disability caused by occupational hazards.

c. It covers only nonoccupational hazards; wife of worker is not covered for maternity. Benavides also introduced pensions for blue-collars in 1936, but they were not implemented and then suspended in 1937 until Prado enforced them in 1941.

d. Only in enterprises with capital above two million soles.

e. It covers both occupational and nonoccupational hazards; wife of worker is covered for maternity.

f. This was not a law but a system of hospitals built (or remodeled and expanded) for the four military branches.

law in 1873 timidly limiting gratuitous concessions which, however, remained a common practice in the next century. The war with Chile (the War of the Pacific, 1879–1884) and its calamitous results generated another era of instability. During this period and at the beginning of the twentieth century, there was a significant expansion of mining in the Sierra and production of cotton and sugar in the Coast which resulted in the consolidation of the Peruvian oligarchy.

1911–1935

In the early part of this century, only a few social security laws were enacted. In 1903 a Direction of Public Health was established as part of the Ministry of Development. Two years later, President José Pardo (son of the first civilian president) unsuccessfully sent to Congress several legislative projects regulating industrial safety and compensation for occupational accidents and diseases. At this point, true unions (longshoremen, sugar workers, miners), under the influence of Anarcho-Syndicalist ideas, began to be formed and the first strikes broke out. President Augusto B. Leguía (1908–1911), a nonmilitary *caudillo* who came to power with the support of the armed forces, improved military pensions in 1910. In 1911 he introduced the first significant social security law in Peru, occupational-accident protection limited to workers in mechanized private enterprises with annual salaries below 20,000 soles. In 1918 Pardo, back in the presidency, passed a law protecting pregnant workers. The first Peruvian labor federation was established in 1913: Federación Obrera Regional Peruana, FORP; its Lima local was founded in 1918: Federación Obrera Local, FOL. In 1914, commercial white-collar employees banded together and six years later transformed into a union. The brief post-World War I boom was succeeded by economic recession, social unrest, and violent strikes which in 1919 gained some protective labor legislation but precipitated another military intervention.

Leguía returned to power and ruled for a decade (1919–1930) supported by the armed forces. At the beginning of his administration, Leguía showed moderation toward and had the support of organized labor but soon resorted to repressive techniques, suppressing FORP and FOL although endorsing the union of white-collar employees. A new constitution (1920) sponsored industrial safety, consolidated workmen's compensation, and stipulated that the state introduce social security institutions to help the poor. In practice most of Leguía's legislation was not precisely in favor of the low-income strata of the population. Privileged pensions for air force officials were passed in 1923, surpassing the benefits granted to the military. In 1924 life insurance (including funeral aid and pensions for disability caused by occupational hazards) for *empleados* (white collar workers) was established, initiating the tradition that set this group apart from *obreros* (blue-collar workers). Resolutions passed in 1924 and 1926 imposed the obligation upon enterprises not located near public hospitals to provide free medical assistance to their staff and to establish permanent medical facilities if they had more than 1,000 employees. This legislation particularly favored miners and sugar-plantation workers who had organized themselves into unions with considerable strength.

The first two decades of the century were blessed by an economic boom which pushed modernization forward, transformed the Coast into the financial center of the nation, and supported the rise of the middle class. The Great Depression interrupted these developments and provided the ferment for populist and ideological movements, and new political parties.

The populist party (Alianza Popular Revolucionaria Americana, APRA), founded in 1924 by Víctor Raul Haya de la Torre in Mexico, came to Peru in 1930, becoming the most important party for the next forty years. It appealed mostly to the urban population either of middle-class origins (university students, professionals, teachers, white-collar workers) or from the top of the low class such as blue-collar workers (especially sugar workers and bus and taxi drivers). In general, labor causes prospered in Peru in periods of APRA legality and stagnated when the party was made illegal (mainly by military regimes). But despite its influence, APRA was unable to reach political power due to the staunch opposition of both the armed forces and the oligarchy. APRA's program of 1931 endorsed a social security system, but part of it was established by either anti-APRA governments or by governments with whom APRA reached a compromise. Another important party, the Peruvian Socialist Party (Partido Socialista del Perú), was founded in the 1920s by José Carlos Mariátegui; in 1929 the Comintern condemned it and the party split with a group founding the Communist Party of Peru. In 1929 the Confederación General de Trabajadores Peruanos, CGTP, was founded by the Communists with the Apristas in a minority position which split in 1933–1934 to found the Central Sindical de Trabajadores Peruanos, CSTP.

After Leguía's resignation in 1930, union and political activities dramatically increased. The CGTP called a general strike in 1931, adding heat to the existing tensions. The new president, Colonel Luis Sánchez Cerro (1930–1931), who had stolen the election from APRA, decreed the CGTP and APRA illegal and launched a repressive campaign against the unions.

1936–1959

Marshall Oscar Benavides (1933–1939), appointed president by the Congress, laid the foundations of the modern system of social security in Peru. He gave amnesty to APRA members in prison, legalized the party, and allowed the reorganization and formation of several unions. In 1933, he modified the 1920 constitution, making the state responsible for public sanitation and health and for the protection of the labor force "against the economic effects of old-age, disability, death, and unemployment." Following the recommendations of well-known labor specialist, Edgardo Rebagliati, Benavides initiated many social programs. In 1935 the Ministry of Public Health, Labor, and Social Welfare was created, and occupational diseases were included in workmen's compensation as the employer's direct responsibility. Special regulations were passed in favor of strong pressure groups: a retirement pension fund for Callao longshoremen (1934), safety regulations for miners, and compulsory mutual insurance funds for teachers and judiciary employees (1936). The key legislation in this period was the new civil code, enacted in 1936, which modified the old code's laissez faire tradition, reaffirming the worker's right to workmen's compensation and to compulsory social insurance. The latter (Seguro Social Obligatorio or Caja Nacional de Seguro Social; hereafter SSO), established in 1936, initially granted health and maternity care, pensions for old age and disability, subsidies for temporary incapacity (including pregnancy), and funeral aid. The law covered all blue-collar workers, including the self-employed earning less than 26,000 soles annually, domestic servants, and home workers. The old civil-servant legislation of 1850 was expanded in 1936 to include most employees working for the state, departments, municipalities, public charities, and other public agencies.

In the meantime Benavides had resorted to repressive techniques, making APRA illegal in 1934 and extending his presidential term until 1939. These events had a negative impact upon the new compulsory social insurance. In 1937 SSO coverage was limited to health and maternity care (which did not actually begin until the first hospitals were built in 1941) and excluded domestic servants in private homes, the self-employed, and home workers from its protection.

At the beginning of his mandate, conservative civilian Manuel Prado y Ugarteche (1939–1945) kept tight control over the unions, but liberal currents generated during World War II and domestic pressure changed his attitude. He allowed the formation of a large number of unions in 1943–1944; authorized, in 1944, the establishment of a new labor federation (Confederación de Trabajadores del Perú, CTP) under Communist control; and again legalized APRA shortly before the 1945 elections. The Ministry of Public Health and Social Welfare became independent from the Labor Ministry in 1942 and, within the latter, a Department for Occupational Diseases was created. SSO health-maternity insurance received a big push, as Prado accelerated the construction of SSO hospitals; six of them were opened between 1941 and 1944 in Lima and other important cities. In 1941 Prado enforced pensions for old age and disability and reinstated home workers in SSO coverage. He also granted special concessions to powerful pressure groups: miners suffering from occupational diseases got special medical treatment, construction workers received compensation for seasonal unemployment, and longshoremen and drivers working for the state were incorporated into SSO.

Prado presided over free elections in 1945. APRA was legalized but not allowed to use its name or nominate a candidate for president; hence the party gave its support to José L. Bustamante Rivero, a university professor, who won the election. By 1946 APRA controlled the CTP and had a stronghold in the Congress and several ministries in Bustamante's cabinet. A record number of unions was founded in this year. Through these channels APRA exerted influence to pass social security legislation in favor of white-collar workers, an important group supporting the party. Seniority pensions (paid by the employer) for white-collar employees working in banking, commercial, industrial, mining, and agricultural enterprises with a capital above 2 million soles were established in 1946, favoring a minority of well-paid white-collar employees over the majority of white-collars (in medium and small enterprises) and all blue-collar workers.[2] In 1947 Seguro Social del Empleado, SSE, was formed, providing compulsory social insurance (covering most social risks) for white-collars both in private enterprises (including those under the life-insurance law of 1924) and in the public sector, although it did not function until a later date. For blue-collars, two new SSO hospitals were inaugurated, one of them in a mining town. The SSO was also ordered to initiate insurance for occupational diseases. However, the new SSO and SSE laws did not go into effect because of a government crisis which led to another military takeover.

The new military president, General Manuel Odría Amoretti (1948–1956), impeded the operation of the CTP and imposed tight control over unions. On the other hand, he courted some segments of the labor force by granting them protective labor legislation (supported by high rates of economic growth during this period) and coopted a few union leaders, trying to undermine APRA's influence and to win legitimacy for his regime. In the field of social security, Odría expanded the system of privilege by benefiting the high- and middle-income groups of the population with special health-maternity protection. SSE was put into operation in 1949 but initially limited its functions to medical attention (regardless of whether the illness or accident was or was not caused by occupational hazards), maternity care, and some benefits in case of death. Successive laws incorporated powerful pressure groups into SSE, for example, state teachers in 1953 after a successful strike, and railroad and streetcar workers (obviously blue-collars but *equiparado* as white-collars). For a few years, the two health-maternity funds of blue-collars and white-collars were administered by SSO. In 1952, SSE became independent, although its regulations were not approved until 1958 when the Hospital del Empleado in Lima, the largest and best equipped in Peru, was opened. Odría also built or modernized hospitals for the army, the navy, and the police.

In contrast to the attention received by white-collar workers and the military, health care for blue-collar workers was minimal. Odría completed construction of only three SSO hospitals which had already been under construction in the 1940s. In the SSE, white-collar workers were given medical attention for illness or accident regardless of the cause (occupational or not). Conversely SSO treated blue-collar workers affected by only nonoccupational hazards, leaving the blue-collar worker at the mercy of private insurance companies for occupational-accident protection and of reluctant employers for occupational-disease coverage.[3] In 1952 Odría created a National Fund for Public Health and Social Welfare (Fondo Nacional de Salud y Bienestar Social, FNSBS) allegedly to help prevent contagious diseases, improve sanitation, protect pregnancy, expand coverage of state hospitals, and support public charities among the low-income strata, but little was done by the new agency.[4] In 1950 Odría expanded the pension and subsidy benefits granted to civil servants for old age, seniority, disability, and death; improved military pensions; and increased the subsidies for illness and maternity, and the allowance for funeral aid of blue-collars.

In the 1956 general election Manuel Prado won back the presidency (1956–1962), and through political compromise, APRA was legalized and in return gave political support to Prado. The CTP came back into activity in 1955 and fell under APRA's control in 1956. The number of unions thereafter sharply increased; by 1961 the CTP had a membership equal to three-fourths of total organized labor, and strikes rose twofold between 1957 and 1961. Under pressure from APRA and labor, and taking advantage of the economic growth of those years, Prado introduced several measures in the field of social security. He tried to alleviate the substantial state debt to SSO and SSE, accumulated mostly under Odría's administration. Prado enacted public bonds and raised taxes on tobacco and alcohol to pay the debt and in 1959, for the first time in the SSO history, the state paid all its contributions. Prado also inaugurated another SSO hospital and a polyclinic. But his most notable contribution took place in the last two and a half years of his term with the enactment of three laws related to old age, disability, and survivors' insurance of civil servants and blue- and white-collar workers.

1960–1968

In 1959, the National Association of Civil Servants had been established, concentrating its efforts on social security. Prado's government responded to this pressure by creating in 1960 a new Fund of Retirement of Public Employees (Caja de Retiro del Émpleado Público, CREP). It introduced a system of lump-sum payments for old age, death, disability, and dismissals of civil servants, thus generously supplementing the pension system established in 1820 and successively expanded in 1850, 1936, and 1950.

The new concession to civil servants made even more iniquitous the absence of an adequate pension system for most of the labor force, that is, all blue-collar workers, and white-collar workers in medium and small enterprises. In 1956 blue-collar unions began pressuring for this legislation and in late 1960 made a decisive push. The CTP organized peaceful demonstrations in various cities and carried on a publicity campaign which stressed the notorious legislative gap and its negative effects on social peace. An efficient lobby mounted by a group of APRA congressmen eventually resulted in a rapid approval, in 1961, of the Retirement Fund for Blue-Collar Workers (Fondo de Jubilación Obrera, FJO).[5] The FJO became an autonomous fund administered by SSO separate from the health-maternity fund. It established pensions for old age, nonoccupational disability, and death, plus funeral expenses and other minor benefits. Some groups of the labor force (e.g., the self-employed) were given an opportunity to associate voluntarily with the FJO through special agreements.

The original law of the SSE enacted in 1947 included pensions, but two years later when Odría put the SSE into operation he limited its scope to health care. Several ILO studies, in the 1950s, recommended pensions for white-collar workers.[6] In 1955, a national federation of white-collar workers (Central Sindical de Empleados Particulares del Perú, CSEPP) was founded. Although at the beginning of the 1960s the CSEPP had a membership close to 24,000, it grouped disparate segments of the labor force and lacked sufficient cohesiveness. Additionally, it had remained independent in its first years and thus was not supported by the CTP. In March 1961 the CSEPP endorsed a strike to pressure Congress into approving the legal draft on pensions, but the movement did not generate enough steam to be effective. In November 1961, after long political negotiations, Congress passed a law creating within SSE a pension fund separate from that of health-maternity. Finally, in the midst of rumors of an imminent military coup (and probably under pressure from CTP and CSEPP), Prado put the SSE white-collar pension fund into operation. The fund included pensions for old age, disability, and death, as well as funeral aid and other minor benefits. It covered white-collars, both private and public (civil servants), in four different situations: (a) those employed in the private sector (regardless of the capital of the enterprise), and those in the public sector who had begun to work for a new employer since the inception of the pension fund; (b) those employed in private enterprises with a capital below 2 million soles and therefore not protected by the pension law of 1946; (c) those employed in the public sector (and thus protected by the civil-servant social security system) provided that they had requested entry within a specified deadline; and (d) those dismissed from the public sector, who had previously accumulated seven years of service and, being reemployed as civil servants, opted for affiliation with the SSE. By 1968 only 20 percent of those insured by the SSE pension fund were from the public sector but 38 percent were in the health-maternity fund, suggesting that a good number of civil servants who had an option between the SSE and their privileged pension system wisely decided to stay in the latter.[7] Teachers, supported by their strong Federación Nacional de Educadores del Perú, FENEP (founded in 1960 and which had successfully struck in 1961 for wage increases), managed to stay out of the SSE pension fund. They were protected by the old civil-servant system which had been considerably improved for teachers through special regulations and a mutual insurance fund regulated in 1957.

A military junta then governed the country in 1962–1963 and established the National Institute of Planning (INP). The junta yielded to the pressure exerted by Callao longshoremen who got a special fund for health-maternity care and had their pension fund incorporated into SSO but under a separate account, and to fishermen who received a special fund for assistance and health-maternity. Elected in 1963, Fernando Belaúnde Terry (1963–1968) expanded coverage for part of the noninsured, improved protection for some privileged groups, alleviated financial difficulties of the system, and took the first steps for its needed coordination.

In response to pressure from two new federations of farm workers and peasants (Federación Nacional de Campesinos del Perú, FENCAP, controlled by APRA and the Confederación de Campesinos del Perú, CCP, controlled by Communists), various laws were passed in 1965–1966 incorporating three types of agricultural workers into SSO: peasants associated with the agrarian reform, rural workers in colonization centers built near the new highway through the jungle, and a few selected Indian communities. Other laws enacted in 1964–1968 in response to various pressure groups incorporated various segments of the labor force into some of the existing institutions or granted them independent funds, mutual insurance funds, or special regulations. Employees of Congress, the judiciary, and public registrars as well as teachers were granted special pension regulations which set them apart from the general pension system for civil servants. The influential Lima Bar Association and judiciary secretaries (escribanos) each received a mutual insurance fund and journalists a special fund. Jockeys and employees of the Jockey Club each received an independent fund. Independent taxi drivers who strongly protested an increase in the price of gasoline received an independent fund which later was put under SSO administration but in a separate account. The longshoremen's independent fund for health-maternity came into effect. Trolley workers, who on many occasions paralyzed Lima, were incorporated into SSE. Fishermen, supported by one of the strongest unions in Peru and employed in a booming industry, were granted an independent fund for unemployment compensation.

Under the Ministry of Public Health, an ambitious program to build twelve new state hospitals was launched. These hospitals would serve both the noninsured and the insured living in areas without SSO or SSE hospitals. A substantial number of hospital beds were added when in 1963 most of these hospitals were opened, but later there were complaints about poor maintenance. In 1963 two new hospitals were inaugurated, one for SSE and another for SSO.

In the early 1960s several financial and actuarial studies of the health-maternity and pension funds of the SSO and SSE were conducted by experts from international organizations.[8] The tax increase imposed by Prado in 1958 had produced 200 million soles by 1967, and some 150 million soles in debt had been paid with bonds. But from 1963 to 1967 the state failed to pay its dues to SSO and SSE (mostly as a third contributor to health insurance), and the state debt skyrocketed, reaching in 1967 a record 1 billion soles, 625 million in SSE and 375 million in SSO. At the end of 1968, Belaúnde passed legislation to offset this debt partly through a small cash payment and land transfer but mainly through a new state bond issue. The latter was criticized as inappropriate for the health-maternity fund which needed liquid funds for payment of cash subsidies and construction of facilities.[9]

In the second half of his term, Belaúnde, following the recommendations of experts made in the early 1960s, took the first steps to bring some order to the social security chaos. In 1965 he founded the National Council of Social Security to coordinate and unify social security institutions into a unique agency—the National Institute of Social Security. The budgetary law of 1968 ordered SSO and SSE to standardize their contribution systems, and the council was entrusted with this task, together with the coordination of information, inspection, filing, and mechanized equipment of both institutions, but Belaúnde did not have the power to enforce his recommendations. The unification process required a strong executive capable of imposing himself upon the vested interests of the pressure groups; this was partially to be achieved under the new military government which took power in 1968 through a coup.

1969—

Taking office in a time of political upheaval, the new president General Juan Velasco Alvarado (1968–1975) departed from the traditional status-quo attitude of military regimes in the past by taking a nationalistic, reformist, developmental approach. Laws were passed on agrarian reform, nationalization of mines and industry (including a sort of self-management or *comunidad industrial* which, for the first time, did not discriminate between white- and blue-collar workers), regulation of fishing, and educational reform. The government also curtailed the activities of political parties and began a clever policy of dividing the labor movement, beginning by weakening the powerful CTP, through accusations from rival union groups. The split of the labor movement permitted the government to assume control over social security institutions and initiate radical reforms.

Some of the social security measures taken by Velasco, especially in his first year, were rather conventional: the request for technical assistance from ILO[10] and incorporation of unprotected labor groups into the social security system. But later he took radical steps to unify (even if only partially) the social security system.

In November 1968, the system of pensions founded in 1946, making employers directly responsible for pensions for white-collar workers in large enterprises, was transformed into a special fund administered by SSE (Fondo Especial de Jubilación de Empleados Particulares, FEJEP). FEJEP introduced a new inequality: enterprises established after the SSE pension fund began its operation had to contribute to FEJEP, although their employees did not receive any benefit from it.[11] Velasco also introduced another privilege by retiring obstructionist generals before their required age and paying them 100 percent of their salaries.[12] He also built a hospital for the air force, the best in Peru, and expanded or modernized the army and navy hospitals. In 1969, public vendors of newspapers, magazines, and lottery tickets were incorporated into SSO and in 1970, domestic servants working in private homes. In 1972, an independent pension fund for fishermen was created and artists were incorporated into SSE.

The process of social security unification in Peru began in 1969 with a law reorganizing the Ministry of Labor, entrusting it with policy-making, organization, expansion, and supervision of social security. A new Direction of Social Security within the Ministry was authorized to register and supervise social security institutions, prepare studies for the formulation of policy, and implement decisions made by the government. The SSO and SSE were recognized in their autonomy but connected (*vinculados*) to the Ministry. Administrative councils were organized in both SSO and SSE, presided over by a manager appointed by the government and made up of representatives from the government, the insured, and the employers. (The CTP, being at the time the only recognized labor federation, appointed the blue-collar delegates to SSO—the first to be freely selected since 1939—while the CSEPP selected the white-collar delegates to SSE, continuing the practice established in the 1960s.) SSO and SSE were supervised by the Ministry of Labor, the General Comptroller of the republic, and a new body, the Vigilance Committees, also made up of representatives from the state, employers and workers.

In the first half of 1970, the government moved toward a more radical stand with the nationalization of mining and industry and the expropriation of several newspapers. In the second half of 1970, a mission from the OISS studied the health funds of SSO and SSE, recommending the unification of both institutions under a National Institute of Social Security "to avoid the perpetuation of two separate castes of insured which creates a constant focus of tension." The OISS experts also advised the incorporation of occupational accidents and diseases into the SSO, and the unification of medical attention to blue- and white-collar workers at new decentralized polyclinics.[13]

Also in the second half of 1970, the administration of SSO and SSE became the target of severe criticism, particularly from anti-CTP labor federations. The accusations included lack of accounting and auditing procedures; enormous government and employers' debts to the funds (the latter due to conspiracy of employers and workers' representatives in SSO, and SSE); embezzlement of funds; excessive number of employees and red tape; long delays in the granting of benefits; and blocking of social security reform.[14] This criticism was followed by a wave of resignations and dismissals of top bureaucrats, the weakening of the CTP, and widespread impression that workers were poor social-security administrators. Then the military government replaced the SSO and SSE Administrative Councils (which had representatives of the workers and employers) by Commissions of Reorganization (only integrated by state officials) and entrusted them with the rapid reform of the social security system. At the end of 1970 the Commissions of Reorganization elaborated three legal drafts.[15] The first one stipulated the creation of the Peruvian Institute of Social Security (IPSS) as a superstructure which, in five years, would unify SSO and SSE (omitting social security institutions for civil servants and the military) and would extend social security coverage to the entire country. The second legal draft prescribed the incorporation of occupational accidents and diseases into SSO. This would save 100 million soles annually (which previously went as profit to private insurance companies), eliminate the abuses of these companies and the employers, and permit SSO to provide medical attention for occupationally disabled blue-collar workers. The third legal draft regulated crimes against social security, establishing severe sanctions for administrators, employers, and insured convicted of defalcation, evasion, or fraud.

The Commissions of Reorganization also designed a strategy to gradually eliminate the discrimination in hospital and medical treatment between blue- and white-collar insured. If a locale had an SSO hospital (often working at 60 percent capacity) but not a SSE hospital, the SSO hospital would begin attending white-collar insured. Plans were made for construction or improvement of other hospitals which could treat both groups of workers. Wives of blue-collar workers insured in SSO were to be granted maternity care equivalent to those insured in SSE. Finally the right of the white-collar insured to use SSE hospitals or other facilities of his selection was to be abolished.[16] Most of these recommendations had not yet been implemented by mid-1973.

Labor federations approved these measures but expressed concern that their membership would not be represented in the administration of social security,[17] that once the state controlled the system it could use their reserves for investment in government projects and avoid the payment of its debts,[18] and that the merging of the bankrupt SSO with the financially solvent SSE would result in a loss for the white-collar insured.[19] Most large employers did not oppose the unification and only stipulated that "true employer's representatives" (that is, from private enterprises) should participate in the administration of the system as in 1969–1970. Small employers covered by SSE expressed concern about negative financial results of a merger with SSO.[20]

Social security was not included in national planning in Peru until April of 1971, when sections on social security and health objectives, strategy, and policy became part of the 1971–1975 national plan.[21] The social security section of the plan prescribed: the progressive unification of social security institutions under the IPSS; the establishment of a common directory for SSO and SSE; the incorporation of occupational accidents and diseases into SSO; the coordination of benefits and drastic reduction of inequality in services provided by SSO and SSE; and the gradual expansion of social security protection to low-income groups of the population, especially of agricultural workers and the self-employed, in order to promote a better redistribution of income. This extension would be partially financed by the state. (The plan suggested a shift in state help away from SSE, FNSBS, and, possibly, SSO to help the underprivileged groups.[22]) The plan also prescribed the reorientation of SSO and SSE investment to productive activities, stressing that national development is a precondition for the expansion of social security. Finally the plan made a point of avoiding the creation of new social security funds. Two of the three recommendations by the Commissions of Reorganization were included in the plan: the creation of both the IPSS and the unified directory for SSO and SSE and the incorporation of occupational hazards into SSO.

The health section of the 1971–1975 plan prescribed: the expansion of health care to cover marginal groups such as agricultural workers, the self-employed, and the family of the insured; the decentralization of medical services, away from the capital, through the creation of a network of regional hospitals, city hospitals, suburban health centers, and rural emergency centers; the coordination of SSO and SSE hospitals with the planned hospital network; the reduction in the price of medicines for the poor; the improvement of occupational safety and health in mining, agriculture, and industry; and the establishment of priorities in hospital construction.[23]

As has already been stated, the government enacted in 1972 legislation expanding social security benefits to segments of the labor force (domestic servants, artists, fishermen). This action followed the 1971–1975 plan's policy of extension of the system but violated some of the newly established principles: the priority given to rural workers and the self-employed, the avoidance of creation of new funds, and the caution against expanding coverage without adequate financing. On the other hand, three laws stuck to the plan and agreed with some of the 1970 recommendations of the Commissions of Reorganization.

In 1971 occupational accidents and diseases were incorporated into the SSO, which no longer discriminates in the cause of illness and accidents. (Fishermen were provisionally excluded from the law and continued under the archaic system of employer's responsibility.) In 1972 the Commissions of Reorganization in SSO and SSE were replaced by a unified Directive Council composed of seventeen members: nine from the state, four from the insured (two blue-collars and two white-collars), one from the insured in state enterprises, and three from the employers. Although labor and managerial representation have been reinstituted, the state holds the majority in the Council and has leeway in choosing workers' delegates from a list of ten candidates presented by the various labor federations. In 1973 the Council standardized the SSO, SSE, and FEJEP pension regulations into a unified pension system (Sistema Nacional de Pensiones de Seguridad Social, SNPSS).[24]

The SNPSS covers all blue-collars under SSO-FJO (including subgroups with special regulations such as domestic servants, artists, newspaper vendors, hairdressers, agricultural workers, and "facultative" insured, i.e., those voluntarily covered through special agreements), white-collars under SSE and FEJEP, civil servants under SSE, and future employees of the judicial system, diplomatic corps, and teaching professions. (Nevertheless, the SNPSS does not apply to pensioners or insured who had acquired the right to pensions under the previous regime.) The SNPSS also introduced a new optional insurance for the self-employed. Excluded from the SNPSS are civil servants covered by the old *montepíos* as well as militarymen and policemen, all of which remain under their respective pension systems. It seems that independent pension funds (i.e., for fishermen and racetrack employees) are also excluded from SNPSS. The status of separate pension funds that were formerly under SSO administration (i.e., taxi drivers and longshoremen) is not clear.

The SNPSS regulations slightly improved the conditions to obtain benefits for most blue-collar workers and compensated (through special treatment) a minority affected by the new system. Conditions to obtain benefits for white-collars and civil servants under SSE have not been changed substantially, although their contributions have been increased by 100 percent. Those most negatively affected are white-collars under FEJEP, about 3 percent of the total number of insured, because seniority pensions have been abolished. To placate this segment, a compromise was made: those who met certain conditions were given an opportunity to resign from their jobs and retire under the FEJEP privileged system. Those who did not meet the conditions for a seniority pension in 1973 were given the right to an increment of their old-age pension at the time of retirement.

To administer the SNPSS, the National Pension Fund (Fondo Nacional de Pensiones, FNP) was established. The FNP integrated the administration of the FJO, the SSE, and the FEJEP pension funds, the latter being abolished. The establishment of the IPSS, prescribed both by the Commissions of Reorganization and the 1971–1975 plan, seems to have been postponed indefinitely.

The 1973 regulations did not affect the administration and rules of other benefits such as health-maternity and lump sums, although they announced the unification of health-maternity services provided by SSO and SSE. Towards the end of the year, representatives of these two funds signed an agreement to proceed with the gradual integration of their health facilities, so as to eradicate discrimination in treatment of blue- and white-collars and civil servants.[25]

Public reaction to the unification measures was mixed. Both the CTP and the CGTP praised the unifying and egalitarian features of the new system but criticized the elimination of seniority pensions and the fixed age of retirement as too high. The CTP also requested the participation of workers in the administration of the new FNP.[26] From May to August of 1973, strikes, riots, and public protests of those affected by the new system (among them banking employees, miners, and some professionals) occurred in Lima and Arequipa.[27] An additional irritant for white-collar employees dispossessed of their seniority pensions was the fact that the armed forces were excluded from the unification and (together with civil servants under the old system) managed to keep their privileges.

At the end of 1972, regulations for pensions of the four branches of the armed forces—army, navy, air force, and police—were standardized.[28] The new system still respects the old privileges (e.g., pensions for seniority and dismissals) which are now more obvious than ever. (It seems that the air force lost a few minor advantages, while the police gained a few.) The planned unified pension fund, if implemented, will not cover those already insured by the old system but only future employees. All benefits outside of pensions (e.g., health, family allowances, lump sums) remain unchanged. (We have already seen that the integration of health facilities has so far excluded armed-forces hospitals.) Therefore, if any standardization has taken place, it has been only within the armed forces and without yielding any important privileges.

Summarizing the evolution of social security in Peru, five stages may be distinguished in each of which a significant part of the system was established (see table 4-1): (1) in the first century of the republic (1821–1910), pensions for civil servants and the military; (2) in the next quarter century (1911–1935), protection against occupational accidents and diseases in favor of blue-collar workers and life insurance for white-collar workers; (3) in the next quarter century (1936–1959), medical care for blue-collar workers, white-collar workers, civil servants, and the military, and pensions for blue- and white-collar workers; (4) in the decade of the 1960s, better pensions for blue- and white-collar workers, and supplements to pensions for civil servants; and (5) in the 1970s, unification of the system.

The Role of Pressure Groups in Social Security Stratification

What has been the role of pressure groups in obtaining social security protection in Peru? Obviously the military is the most powerful group. It has controlled the country for more than a century—two-thirds of its republican history—through coups and interventions, dictatorships, congressional appointments, and fraudulent elections. Depending on physical coercion, the military has logically protected its own ranks by enacting four pension laws and establishing an excellent hospital system for its four branches. Within this group, the air force seems to be the most privileged, both in its pension system (at least until 1973) and in the quality of its hospital. Civilian governments have not passed a single measure in favor of the military.

Very close in power to the military are civil servants. The core of their social security system (the oldest in the land) was established by military regimes eager to achieve and maintain stability, operate the administration as efficiently as possible, and protect their nonmilitary collaborators. Thus military governments enacted three pension laws and health-maternity insurance for civil servants. Civilian governments during their fifty years in power granted only one significant law in favor of this group: the 1960 system of pension supplements which followed the establishment of the powerful federation of civil servants in 1959. Stratification within this group is high. Privileged subgroups include elected officials (executive, legislative, judicial), diplomats, teachers (with a federation of 45,000 members which has often struck successfully) and employees of the judiciary, Congress, public registrars, post office, and Ministry of Health who have been able to obtain special regulations and/or mutual insurance funds by exercising pressure.

White-collar workers have received the attention of both civilian and military governments, who have honored their traditionally high status and rewarded their scarce and vital skills. The military has granted them life insurance and health-maternity care. Civilian governments have also catered to white-collar workers. Under influence from APRA and the CSEPP, two pension systems were granted. The government, in general, seems favorably disposed to accede to the "responsible" demands of this group (which has never been very aggressive) and has rarely used repression against it. The strength of CSEPP seems to come more from its market power rather than its capacity to generate violence. Intragroup stratification is high here also because each subgroup supports its own immediate interest and lacks cohesiveness with other subgroups. Three subgroups within the white-collar group, electricity, petroleum, and banking, have been able to obtain the best supplementary social security protection through collective bargaining. The productive activity in which they are employed is of strategic importance to the country, while their enterprises are large, profitable, and, in some cases, monopolies or foreign corporations capable of paying the cost of added social security benefits or of transferring it to the public.

Blue-collar workers as a pressure group come last in the ranking. They first obtained protection against occupational accidents and diseases as well as health care (and pensions for old age and disability, although theses were not implemented until later) from military regimes, especially in the first part of Benavides' administration. In spite of a relative increase in union activities and some influence of APRA in those years, these measures seemed to be the result of a paternalistic concession, perhaps to avoid internal strife (especially after the 1931–1933 violence) and to obtain labor support rather than of direct pressure from the labor movement. In a period of organization of several unions and a labor federation, blue-collars had their pensions for old age and disability implemented. Under President Prado's second term, when trade unions grew stronger and APRA was highly influential with the regime, blue-collar workers obtained an improved and enlarged pension system. Although CTP organized several urban demonstrations in favor of the pension bill, it was passed more as a result of peaceful coercion, connections, and lobbying than through violence. Within the blue-collar segment, there are also some privileged subgroups. Miners, sugar plantation workers, fishermen, longshoremen, and taxi drivers have obtained from the government independent pension funds, mutual insurance, and/or special safety and health provisions. These subgroups are among the largest in union membership in Peru: miners have more than 40,000 members, sugar plantations more than 30,000, and fishermen and taxi drivers around 20,000 each.[29] Mining, sugar, and fishing are crucial sectors in the national economy with large and prosperous enterprises which can be badly hurt by a long strike. Subgroups in these sectors have been able to obtain additional social security protection through collective bargaining. Longshoremen of Callao can stop shipping. Taxi drivers are basic to Lima's transportation system—the bus service is poor and most urban transportation is provided by collective taxis which charge a small amount. Taxi drivers resorted to strike and paralyzed Lima to obtain a special fund. Domestic servants, peasants, and agricultural workers, and newspapers and lottery-ticket vendors are latecomers in social security; only when they organized themselves into unions and federations were they able to obtain total or partial coverage by SSO.

The noninsured population, devoid of power, has received since the nineteenth century only hospital and medical attention through the public-charity system. This system, however, has become increasingly obsolete and since the 1960s the state has been expanding its hospital network to attend the noninsured. In Peru illiterates cannot vote; hence the mass of Indian peasants were not important to political groups such as APRA and Acción Popular. In the 1963 elections, the proportion of qualified voters was 83 percent in Lima but 16 percent in Puno (where Indians are highly concentrated).[30]

Several international experts who have studied the Peruvian social security system have arrived at the same prescription for its cure: curtailment of privileges, unification and standardization, and universalization. Until the 1970s little or nothing was done to implement these recommendations due to the government's lack of interest (with the exception of Belaúnde) and the staunch opposition of the privileged groups. The military regime in power since 1968 has been capable of imposing its will upon the vested interests of the pressure groups. It has assumed control over SSO and SSE, weakened the labor movement through splits and factionalism, and hence has been able to overcome the opposition of white-collars, small employers, and privileged blue-collars to the potential unification of the two main funds. A joint directory for SSO and SSE has been appointed and their pension system unified and standardized, some hospital facilities have been unified, a substantial number of noninsured have been covered, and occupational accidents and diseases have been incorporated into SSO. The unification process has been limited, so far, to blue- and white-collars and those civil servants in the field of health-maternity and under the SSE pension system. The most privileged systems, those of the armed forces and the old one for civil servants, have been left out of the unification process. If the privileges of these two groups are not abolished and the principle of solidarity is not truly embraced by all occupational groups in Peruvian society, the unification process will be perceived by the labor force as a sacrifice imposed upon it while the elite preserves the old stratification and castes inherited from colonial times.

Current Structure and Organization of the System

No single legislative body regulates the organization of the social security system in Peru. Even worse, an official overall legislative compilation does not exist and only partial private compilations for some sectors are available.[31] Due to the gradual creation of the social security system throughout a century and a half, more than 2,000 laws, decrees, and resolutions have been enacted, most of which are still in force. There are dozens of social security funds, each with its own regulations for administration, financing, benefits, and supervision. No logical criteria can be applied to the legal status of these funds; some are completely independent, others are autonomous but connected to or supervised by other institutions, still others are subordinated to or administered by other funds or institutions, and some sectors are incorporated with an existing fund but have special regulations or separate accounts.

There is no state agency entrusted with planning, coordination, or supervision of the whole system. The National Planning Institute has prepared guidelines or sectorial plans for public health (mostly state hospitals) since 1966 and on social security (limited to SSO and SSE) since 1970. The power to enforce these guidelines or plans is relatively small although increasing mainly through budgetary control. The Comptroller in a general way audits most of the system (being more attentive to the private than the public sector) excluding the armed forces. Other central agencies also supervising finances of some sectors are the National Treasury (most of the civil-servant system), the Superintendency of Banking, and the Ministry of Justice (part of the civil-servant system). The Ministry of Labor makes social security policy for the systems which protect blue- and white-collar workers in the private sector. Since 1970 both SSO and SSE have been controlled by this ministry which appoints the manager of both institutions and selects the members of the Directive Council. The ministry also loosely supervises (it has the legal power but not the instruments for enforcement): more than 800 mutual insurance funds, a few of them compulsory, most voluntary; hundreds of social security programs in collective agreements; and four independent social security funds. The Ministry of Public Health administers the network of state hospitals and supervises public-charity, enterprise, and private hospitals as well as the National Fund of Public Health and Welfare. Public-charity hospitals are strongly subsidized by the ministry. The armed forces seem to be

FIGURE 4-1

Administrative Structure of Social Security in Peru: 1973

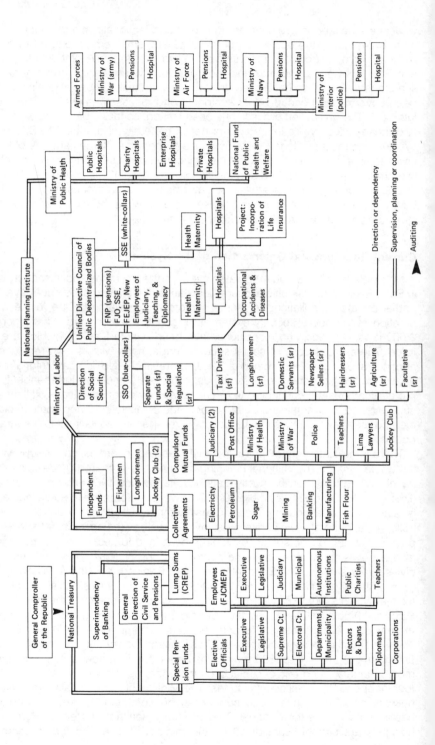

completely free from any central control or supervision except through the National Treasury's budgetary allocations.

In order to explain the structure of this labyrinth, it is convenient to divide it into the various occupational pressure groups that we have identified already: (1) armed forces, (2) civil servants, (3) white-collar workers, and (4) blue-collar workers. The situation of the noninsured will also be described. (See figure 4-1.)

Armed Forces

There are four main subgroups of the armed forces: army, navy, air force, and police. Each has its own organization and regulations (except for pensions which have been standardized since 1973) and is respectively administered by its own ministry. (In 1973 there was a pension fund under study that would unify the administration of the four branches but only for future insured.) Each of the four subgroups has in turn two separate funds with different regulations, one for officials and another for the troops and civilian employees. Each ministry has a department of pensions (for seniority, disability, and survivors, as well as subsidies for occupational hazards and dismissals) and a department of health or sanitation which administers the subgroup's hospital. There are four hospitals in Lima and one in Arequipa. Arrangements are made with local hospitals in other cities and departments to attend the armed forces' insured. Each subgroup pays family allowances for both spouse and children.[32]

Civil Servants

Three main programs of the social security system cover civil servants: pensions (with several systems), lump-sum payments, and health-maternity. The general pension system is the old *montepío civil* (now called Fondo de Jubilación, Cesantía y Montepío de Empleados Públicos, FJCMEP) administered by the National Civil Services' Direction of Pensions. It covers nonelected employees who entered public service in the central government prior to 1962, more than 100 autonomous agencies, public charities, and departments, provinces, and municipalities. (The nation is divided into 23 departments, somewhat like states; these into 145 provinces, or counties; and the provinces into 1,342 municipalities, or cities.) In each central ministry, autonomous agency, charity board, municipality, etc., there is a direction in charge of the pension system. The National Treasury is responsible for payments and the General Comptroller for auditing. Civil servants who entered public administration after mid-1962 (or reentered having previously accumulated the minimum years of service) were covered by the SSE pension fund until 1973 and since then have belonged to the unified FNP. Also under the FNP is a small subgroup of pre-1962 civil servants who decided to join the SSE pension fund in 1962.

There are several civil-servant subgroups separate from both FJCMEP and the SSE-FNP, most of which have independent pension funds each with its own regulations. The largest subgroup is made up of top officials of the executive, legislative, and judiciary: the president of the republic and cabinet ministers; the two congressional chambers: deputies and senators (independent fund); the president and members of the Supreme Court; the president and members of the electoral court (under the Ministry of Justice); and mayors and council members. The educational subgroup is rather complex: the rectors, vicerectors, and deans of state universities and directors of professional schools have their own fund administered by the Ministry of Education; university professors have a special fund also administered by the Ministry of Education; until 1965, secondary and primary school teachers were under the general system of FJCMEP but now have special regulations together with judicial and congressional employees and public registrars. Teachers also have a mutual insurance fund that pays death allowances. The diplomatic corps has special regulations and a fund administered by the Ministry of Justice. Since mid-1973, new employees in the judicial system, the teaching profession, and the diplomatic corps have been under the FNP. Several autonomous agencies which have independent funds include national corporations (National Bank, Economic Development, Public Works, Shipping Line, Housing, Port of Callao, SSE and SSO) and regional corporations (in Cuzco and Arequipa).

Lump-sum payments (which cover all civil servants) are under a special fund (CREP) administered by the General Direction of Civil Service and Pensions and supervised by the National Treasury, the Ministry of Justice, and the Superintendency of Banking. The retirement lump sum is duplicated by additional cash payments *(derramas)* which several civil-servant subgroups (such as teachers, employees of the Ministries of Communication and Public Health, etc.) enjoy. The death lump sum is duplicated by life insurance provided by several compulsory mutual insurance funds covering judges, judicial secretaries, teachers, policemen, and employees of post offices and the Ministries of War and Health.

The health-maternity fund of SSE covers all civil servants without distinction (see below). By 1968, 38 percent of those insured by this fund were civil servants.

White-Collar Workers

SSE is at the core of the white-collar system with two separate funds, each with its own administration: pensions and health-maternity. The pension fund pays pensions for old age, disability (regardless of whether occupational or not), death, and allowances for funeral and (when there is no right to pension) for old age, disability, and death. Since mid-1973 the SSE pension fund has been integrated into the FNP and its regulations standardized by the SNPSS.

Until mid-1973 there was a special seniority pension fund (FEJEP) for employees hired by large enterprises after 1946 and before 1962 (when the SSE pension fund was established). Until the end of 1968, this pension was paid by the employer; from 1968 to 1973 it was administered by SSE as a separate fund; in 1973 FEJEP was abolished, although its pensioners still collect their pensions from SSE-FNP.

Employers are directly responsible for subscribing to life insurance policies for their employees through private insurance companies regulated by the Ministries of Commerce and Labor. (There is a strong probability that this insurance will soon be incorporated into SSE.) The employer is also directly responsible for layoff compensation in certain cases.

The SSE health-maternity fund covers all white-collar workers (both in the private and public sectors) throughout the nation, including medical care for occupational accidents and diseases and maternity care for the wife of the insured. There are three SSE hospitals: two on the Coast, Lima (center) and Chiclayo (north); and one in the Sierra, Arequipa (south). A project to establish a fourth hospital in Iquitos (east, in the Jungle) has not materialized. The insured has the option to receive direct medical, hospital, dental, and pharmaceutical service at SSE facilities (or, if they are too remote, at private hospitals assigned by SSE) or at the hospital of his choice *(libre elección)*; if he chooses the latter, he is reimbursed 50 percent of the cost. About half of the services are through *libre elección*. This fund also pays subsidies for illness, maternity, babies' milk, and funerals.

Blue-Collar Workers

SSO is the core of the blue-collar system with three separate funds, each with its own administration: pensions, health-maternity, and occupational accidents and diseases. The pension fund (FJO, which in 1973 was integrated into the FNP) pays pensions for old age and death as well as an allowance for funerals. Pensions for death and disability resulting from occupational accidents and diseases are also paid by FJO-FNP. The health-maternity fund protects only the insured (not the wife) and through just part of the national territory. (Medical attention is now given for occupational accidents and diseases which was previously given by private hospitals and paid for by insurance companies.) The health-maternity fund also pays subsidies for illness, maternity, babies' milk, and funerals, and for temporary incapacity resulting from occupational accidents. The SSO has 15 hospitals, 11 located on the Coast, 3 in the Sierra, and 1 in the Jungle. These hospitals are supplemented by 4 polyclinics, 29 suburban health centers, 15 rural emergency centers, and 250 first-aid centers or outpatient clinics. SSO has also signed contracts with 65 private hospitals and clinics in those places where it does not have its own facilities; these cover less than 10 percent of the insured. The insured does not have an option to select a private hospital outside of the network. Large enterprises, often foreign corporations which are located far from this network and have a large number of employees (e.g., mines, oil fields, sugar plantations), are required to provide hospital and medical care for their employees (both white- and blue-collars) either through their own hospitals or by means of contractual arrangement with private ones.

Under the SSO administration, there are several blue-collar subgroups which are handled differently. Some have separate funds: taxi drivers who own their cars (those working for a salary are under the general system) and longshoremen (who have a separate fund in FJO and an independent fund for medical care). Others do not have separate funds but are under special regulations: domestic servants working eight hours daily and forty-eight hours weekly in private homes (those working for enterprises are under the general system); vendors of newspapers, magazines, and lottery tickets in the Lima-Callao area; hairdressers; some agricultural projects (e.g., pilot plan of Junín); and facultative insured. It is not yet clear how the integration of the SSO into the FNP will affect these separate funds.

There are also four independent funds which are not connected with SSO. Anchoveta fishermen have the Caja de Beneficios Sociales del Pescador which administers three separate funds: (a) pensions for old age and death and an allowance for funerals; (b) health-maternity for the insured and his family through contracts with hospitals (it is administered by twenty-one port boards under the Ministry of Navy's supervision, but its services have been suspended since 1969); and (c) compensation for seasonal unemployment. Employees of the Jockey Club of Lima have two different independent funds: (a) jockeys and trainers have two funds, one for pensions and another for health-maternity; and (b) other employees (covered by SSO) receive additional benefits for housing, scholarships, etc. Finally, the longshoremen of Callao (covered, at least until 1973, by a special pension fund in FJO) also have a health-maternity fund.

Several occupational subgroups (including both white- and blue-collar workers) covered by SSE or SSO have additional social security protection through hundreds of collective agreements. These fringe benefits, directly paid by the employer, either improve an existing legal provision (in quantity, quality, or extension to family) or grant an additional one. The most important subgroups are electricity, petroleum, sugar, mining, banking, manufacturing, and fish flour.[33]

The Noninsured

The two extremes of the population's income spectrum, the wealthiest and the poorest, are not insured by social security institutions, but that does not mean that they are devoid of protection. The wealthy personally pay for medical attention in private hospitals or as *pensionado* in state, public-charity, or social security hospitals. Through savings, property, and life insurance, they protect themselves for old age and against unforeseeable events.

The poor receive medical attention (besides other minor services such as orphanages) through two main hospital networks: the Ministry of Public Heath and Public Charities. The ministry has divided the country into 20 health regions (roughly congruent with the 23 departments), each with at least one hospital (there are 40 in total). Each region is divided into health units with a health center (totaling 100). The villages and rural areas around the health centers are served by more than 300 medical and emergency centers and first-aid stations.

Public-charity hospitals (some 57 in the mid-1960s) are located in the most important cities. They are autonomous, administered by boards of directors, and financed by private donations, government subsidies, fees paid by private patients, and token fees paid by the poor if they can afford it. The Ministry of Public Health (or rather, the FNSBS) devotes about two-thirds of its budget to subsidizing these hospitals and through this channel has gained increased control over them. A few public-charity hospitals have been transferred to the state, but a project to incorporate all of them into the ministry during the current five-year plan has apparently been postponed.

Inequalities of the System

There are no accurate data on income distribution by occupational groups in Peru, but the scarce information available permits some loose categorization. The high-income stratum of the population is made up of businessmen and landowners in large enterprises, successful professionals, high-ranking military officials, and top civil servants and politicians. The medium-income stratum is made up of most white-collars, civil servants, militarymen, policemen, middle-size landowners, real estate owners, and the rest of the businessmen and professionals. These two strata are predominantly urban, either white, *cholo,* or mestizo. The low-income stratum is divided into an upper segment composed of blue-collars, and a bottom segment including most of the self-employed in the cities, domestic servants, peasants, unpaid family workers, and the unemployed. This stratum is essentially composed of mestizos or *cholos* in the upper segment and Indians in the bottom segment.[34]

Military officials and civil servants with elective posts or working in national corporations or specialized agencies are paid as well or better than the best-paid white-collars, while civil servants working for the central government have average salaries well above those paid in industry and agriculture. White-collar workers are concentrated in well-paid occupations such as public utilities, financing, commerce, professional services, mining, and manufacturing. Blue-collar workers are concentrated in the lowest-paid occupations, such as personal services, agriculture, manufacturing, and mining.[35] In 1965 the annual average per-capita income in the nation was 26,221 soles, the average salary of white-collars and civil servants under SSE was 27,418 soles, and the average wage of blue-collars under SSO was 16,438 soles.[36]

The Andean range divides Peru into three distinct geographical regions: (a) the Coast, a narrow, mostly desert strip, on the west, spotted with isolated valleys irrigated by small rivers (the region where the Spanish colonizers settled and where today the most populated cities are located); (b) the Sierra or Andean highlands, the heart of the country, once the center of Incan civilization and still where most of the Indian population lives; and (c) the Selva or Jungle, on the east, extending from the Andes to the Amazon basin, an enormous territory mostly uninhabited.

The Coast is the region with the highest urbanization, modernization, and economic development, concentrating most industrial, commercial, fishing, and service activities. Lima, the capital, (together with the port of Callao) is the heart of the administrative and economic activity of the nation; it is located at the center of the coastal strip. Some of the most important cities are to the north of Lima on the Coast: Trujillo, Chiclayo, Piura, Chimbote, Ica. This region occupies 11 percent of the national territory and demographically is growing rapidly due to rural-urban migration; in 1876 the Coast had only 23 percent of the population, but by 1961 this had increased to 36 percent and, by 1970, 46 percent.

The Sierra has relatively scarce resources for its large, mainly Indian population. Agriculture, livestock, and mining are the most important economic activities. The region is underdeveloped and peripheral to the Coast. Arequipa, Peru's second most important city, is located in this region but is relatively close to the coast, southeast of Lima. The city of Cuzco, ancient center of the Incan Empire and now the seventh in population, is also in the region. Migration to the Coast and the capital is proportionally reducing the population of the Sierra. With 29 percent of the territory, this region had 73 percent of the population in 1876 but 58 percent in 1961 and 48 percent in 1970.

The Jungle is rich in natural resources but largely uninhabited, with its sparse population confined to the river banks due to the lack of roads. Iquitos is the most important city, the tenth in population in the country. In spite of its large territorial expanse, 60 percent of Peru, the proportion of the Jungle population has increased little—from 4 percent in 1876 to 6 percent in 1970.

Income distribution is very uneven among the three regions. In the mid-1950s, the Coast received 53 percent of the national income (40 percent of the total in Lima alone) and had an average per-capita income 3.4 times higher than that of the Jungle and 2.7 times that of the Sierra.[37] In the early 1960s, the Coast received 61 percent of the national income (42 percent in Lima), the Sierra 35 percent, and the Jungle 4 percent, and per-capita income in the Coast was from 2 to 7 times that of the Sierra. In the mid-1960s per-capita income in the Department of Lima was twice the national average and 3 to 4 times higher than the average of seventeen other departments mostly in the Sierra and in the Jungle.[38]

Inequalities in the Peruvian social security system will be analyzed in three fields: (1) coverage, (2) financing, and (3) benefits. In each field both occupational and geographical sources of inequality will be traced whenever possible.

Coverage

Table 4-2 shows the overall, maximum coverage of the social security system in Peru in the 1960s. The percentage of the economically active insured population increased steadily from 24.8 percent in 1961 (the year before the two most important pension plans began to function) to 35.6 percent in 1969. Adding both passive insured (pensioners) and dependents with social security protection, we have the population with social security protection. This increased from 8.5 percent of the total population in 1961 to 12.3 percent in 1969.

The total number of active workers insured is disaggregated by occupational groups in table 4-3. Some clarifications are necessary. Data on blue-collars are based on the pension system which embraces the highest number of these workers. Coverage under workmen's compensation excludes manual labor and, hence, should be smaller. (Data on this are not available because until 1972 they were protected by numerous private insurance companies and there were no central files.) The health-maternity coverage of blue-collars is only 85 percent that of the pension system. Independent taxi drivers are shown separately because, although under the SSO pension system, they have a separate fund. Longshoremen are also part of the pension system, but it is not clear whether they are included in the blue-collar figures or not. Fishermen had a fund in operation from 1965 to 1969 but

Table 4-2
Insured Population in Relation to Total and Economically Active Population in Peru: 1961–1969

Year	Total Population[a] (in thousands) (1)	Economically Active Population[b] (in thousands) (2)	Insured Population (in thousands)				Percent of EAP Insured (3)/(2)	Percent of Total Population Insured (6)/(1)	Ratio of Active to Passive (3)/(4)
			Active[c] (3)	Passive[d] (4)	Dependents[e] (5)	Total (6)			
1961	10,320.0	3,250.5	807.9	12.6	61.4	881.9	24.8	8.5	64.1
1962	10,630.0	3,344.3	920.3	14.0	67.0	1,001.3	27.5	9.4	65.7
1963	10,960.0	3,442.9	1,023.9	16.4	73.3	1,113.6	29.7	10.1	62.4
1964	11,300.0	3,546.4	1,087.7	19.8	79.2	1,186.7	30.6	10.5	54.9
1965	11,650.0	3,654.7	1,155.7	22.8	85.5	1,264.0	31.6	10.8	50.7
1966	12,011.5	3,767.8	1,216.7	25.5	91.5	1,333.7	32.2	11.1	47.7
1967	12,385.2	3,885.8	1,245.8	29.2	97.8	1,372.8	32.0	11.0	42.7
1968	12,771.8	4,008.6	1,347.3	32.9	104.5	1,484.7	33.6	11.6	40.9
1969	13,171.8	4,136.2	1,474.4	39.5	111.2	1,625.1	35.6	12.3	37.3

SOURCES: *Total population* from U.N. *Demographic Yearbook 1965* and *1970* (New York: 1966 and 1971). *Economically active population* from Sistema Nacional de Planificación (Servicio de Empleos y Recursos Humanos), "Diagnóstico de la situación de los recursos humanos," Lima: 1966, and ibid. "Lineamientos de política de seguridad social para el mediano plazo (Informe de la Comisión Horizontal de Seguridad Social)," Lima: 1970. *Active insured* from table 4-3. *Passive insured and dependents* from data supplied by: José Gómez Sanchez, SSO, Lima, January 14, 1971; Jorge García De la Puerta, SSE, Lima, December 16, 1970; and César San Román Aguirre, FEJEP, Lima, December 1970.

a. Estimate of mid-year. The year 1961 has been adjusted for undernumeration of 1961 census which excluded Indian jungle population.

b. Period not specified. The year 1961 has been adjusted for undernumeration.

c. At the end of the year. Excludes fishermen, jockeys, and possibly longshoremen. See table 4-3.

d. At the end of the year. Retired and disabled workers and survivors under pensions of SSO and SSE in 1961–1968 plus retired from FEJEP in 1969.

e. At the end of the year. Only wives of active insured for maternity care in SSE.

Table 4-3
Occupational Groups Protected by Social Security in Peru: 1961–1969

Occupational Group	Number Insured									Percentage Distribution in 1969
	1961	1962	1963	1964	1965	1966	1967	1968	1969	
Blue-collars[a]	402,802	466,899	531,865	554,865	577,165	595,623	583,556	580,350	583,737	39.60
White-collars[b]	232,791	255,354	279,747	301,448	325,919	350,543	374,550	461,888	542,173	36.77
Civil servants[b]	147,304	158,670	170,134	185,354	203,100	217,970	231,579	246,027	257,109	17.43
Armed forces[c]	25,000	25,400	25,900	26,300	26,800	27,200	27,600	28,000	60,000	4.06
Self-employed taxi drivers		14,002	16,405	19,714	22,720	25,365	28,504	31,067	31,342	2.14
Total	807,897	920,325	1,023,871	1,087,681	1,155,704	1,216,701	1,245,789	1,347,332	1,474,361	100.00

SOURCES: *Blue-collars* from Francisco de Ipiña Gondra. "Estudio de la estructura financiera de la Caja Nacional del Seguro Social Obrero del Perú," Lima: n/d: Caja Naciona de Seguro Social, *Memoria años 1961–1967* (Lima: n/d); Fondo de Jubilación Obrera, *Segunda memoria año 1965* (Lima: n/d); and data given by José Gómez Sánchez, Asesoría Actuarial CNSS, Lima, 1971. *White-collars* and *civil servants* from Seguro Social del Empleado, *Boletín estadístico 1958–1968* (Lima: 1969); and data given by Jorge García La Puerta, Servicio Actuarial Estadístico de SSE, Lima, 1971. *Armed forces* from Dirección General de Planificación Sectorial, Oficina de Programación de la Educación y los Recursos Humanos quoted by Manuel Hubi Campos et al., "Evaluación de la contribución del seguro social del empleado a los programas docentes para la salud en el Perú" Bogotá, Segundo Congreso Americano de Medicina de la Seguridad Social, 1970, and Sistema Nacional de Planificación, "Plan Nacional de Desarrollo para 1971–1975," Lima: 1970. *Taxi drivers* from José Gómez Sánchez (see above).

NOTE: Only active insured (except fishermen, jockeys, and possibly longshoremen); pensioners and dependents excluded. See table 4-2.

a. Only those protected by pension funds; the number of those protected by the health-maternity fund was approximately 100,000 less in 1963–1969.

b. Disaggregation of private white-collars and civil servants under the SSE health-maternity fund; figures for white-collars in 1968–1969 include those under FEJEP (some 40,000). The number of insured (both white-collars and civil servants) is probably overestimated due to double registration (i.e., persons holding two jobs may be reported twice).

c. Figures are grossly underestimated; other sources give the population attended at armed-forces hospitals in 1964 as 670,000. Data on 1961–1965 were given by the INP as for the "military" (perhaps only officials and excluding auxiliary personnel and policemen); data on 1966–1968 are extrapolations; data on 1969 are a sum of the extrapolation for the "military" and the number of policemen as given by INP which did not report on the military for this year.

only for seasonal unemployment compensation (covering some 20,000–25,000), their system of hospital-medical assistance was suspended in this period, and their pension fund was not established until 1972. The number of jockeys, protected by their special fund, should be well below 1,000. Therefore, the figure of insured blue-collars in 1969 is fairly accurate. Some 200,000 domestic servants were incorporated into SSO in 1970, substantially raising the number of blue-collars protected.

The number of white-collar workers and civil servants in table 4-3 is probably overestimated by 10 to 15 percent mainly due to duplicate accounting; this, however, may be partially offset by evasion. Conversely, the number of insured in the armed forces is probably grossly underestimated in the table. Some 50,000 military were reported by other sources for 1960, 45,000 for 1963, and 70,000 for 1965, more than twice the figures of the table.[39] It seems that the series excludes civil employees and troops altogether and policemen except for 1969 in which 30,000 of them are included. An educated guess of the total number of active insured under the armed forces in 1969 is 120,000. The underestimation of the armed forces is counteracted by the overestimation of white-collar and civil servants; thus the total number of active insured in 1969 seems fairly accurate.

Table 4-3 shows the number of insured in each occupational group. In order to measure the degree of social security protection of each group, however, it is necessary to compare the total number of workers within the group with those actually insured. Unfortunately, there are no adequate data of the distribution of the labor force by such occupational groups. A distribution of the labor force by class of worker in 1965, shown in table 4-4, substitutes for the lack of proper data.[40] In 1965 domestic servants were not covered by any of the social security funds and the nonspecified category was probably made up of underemployed or unemployed without specific occupations and, hence, unprotected. A very small number of unpaid workers were facultative insured in SSO. An unknown number of small employees were registered in SSE. The self-employed (two-thirds concentrated in agriculture) were mostly unprotected. Some 20,000 independent drivers had their own fund, a few professional groups had signed special agreements (mainly with SSE), and small segments of self-employed were incorporated into SSO. It seems, therefore, that the comparison between the two columns is a valid one. It shows that one out of two blue-collars was unprotected, while white-collars, civil servants, and the armed forces were overprotected. This overprotection can be explained either by an underestimation of the salaried labor force or by an overestimation of those salaried insured resulting from duplicate accounting. Protection of blue-collars is even worse if coverage by health-maternity instead of pensions is used. In 1965 there were 465,698 blue-collars protected under the former, only 40 percent of the wage-earners. The 2.5 million left unprotected were peasants (mostly Indians in the Sierra and the Jungle) and agricultural workers, unpaid family workers (most of them also in agriculture), domestic servants (protected since 1970), public vendors, and other self-employed in the cities.

Tables 4-3 and 4-4 are limited to the insured and do not show the different coverage of dependents. While most dependents of armed-forces personnel are protected for health-maternity, only the wives of white-collars and civil servants are protected and exclusively for maternity, and blue-collar dependents do not have health-maternity coverage.

The Peruvian social security system grew slowly from west to east; it began in Lima and the coastal cities, next embraced the most populated cities of the Sierra as well

Table 4-4
Degree of Social Security Protection by Class of Worker
and Occupational Group in Peru: 1965

Class of Worker	Labor Force (in thousands)	Insured (in thousands)	Percent Insured
Salaried	403	555[a]	137[a]
Wage-earners	1,358[e]	577[b]	42.5[b]
Self-employed	1,410	23[c]	1.6[c]
Employers	69	[d]	[d]
Unpaid family workers	333	0[f]	0[f]
Not specified	88	0[g]	0[g]
Total	3,661	1,155	31.5

SOURCES: *Labor force* from Sistema Nacional de Planificación, "Diagnóstico de la situación de los recursos humanos." *Insured* from table 4-3.

a. White-collars and civil servants (health-maternity), plus armed forces; overprotection could be the result of either underestimation of the salaried or overestimation of the insured due to duplication.

b. Blue-collars (pensions); if coverage under health-maternity, the degree of protection is reduced to 40 percent.

c. Taxi drivers; if some small groups of self-employed protected by SSO and SSE are added, the degree of protection would be higher.

d. A group of small employers is protected by SSE.

e. Includes domestic servants who became protected in 1970.

f. A small group is protected by SSO.

g. Probably unemployed or underemployed without a specific occupation and largely unprotected.

as important mining centers and sugar plantations, and then began to reach a few cities in the Jungle and some rural areas in the Sierra. Ten of the 11 social security hospitals built between 1941 and 1951 were on the Coast, only 1 in the Sierra (in Arequipa), and none in the Jungle. From 1952 to 1972, 3 more hospitals and 2 polyclinics were built in the Sierra, 2 hospitals and 1 polyclinic on the Coast, and 1 hospital in the Jungle (in Iquitos). At the beginning of the 1970s, the SSO health-maternity system covered one-fourth of the territory of Peru, only 42 provinces (containing the most populated cities), leaving out 103 provinces mainly in the Jungle and the Sierra.[41] An attempt to measure the degree of social security protection in each region faces a severe lack of data on the distribution by region of the total insured population. Table 4-6 compares the region's total population with the number of active insured under SSO and SSE. In 1965, of those insured under the SSO pension system and both the SSE pension and health-maternity systems, 77 percent were on the Coast, 20 percent in the Sierra, and less than 3 percent in the Jungle. Of those insured under the SSO health-maternity system, 87 percent were on the Coast, 13 percent in the Sierra, and none in the Jungle. According to the last two columns of the table, total coverage in the wealthiest coastal region was 4 to 5 times larger than in the poorer Sierra region and 8 to 15 times larger than in the poorest Jungle region.

Table 4-7 gives an idea of the degree of social security coverage by provinces. Most recent data available on EAP are from 1961 and data on insured are limited to health-maternity under SSO and SSE, thus excluding the armed forces, civil servants under the old system, and white-collars under FEJEP. The table shows that in 1961

Table 4-6
Degree of Social Security Protection of the Total Population by Geographic Region in Peru: 1965

	Total Population		Insured Population							Percent of the Total Population Insured by	
			SSE (Both Funds)		SSO						
					Pensions		Health-Maternity[a]				
Region	Thousands	Percent	Thousands	Percent	Thousands	Percent	Thousands	Percent		Pensions[b]	Health[b]
Coast	4,969	42.3	409	77.3	435	77.3	390	87.3		16.9	16.1
Sierra	5,665	48.2	106	20.1	117	20.7	57	12.8		3.9	2.9
Jungle	1,115	9.5	14	2.6	11	2.0	—	—		2.2	1.2
Total	11,750	100.0	529	100.0	563	100.0	447	100.0		9.3	8.3

SOURCES: *Total population* from Oficina Sectorial de Planificación, Ministerio de Agricultura (Lima: 1965). *SSE* from SSE, *Boletín Estadístico 1958–1968*. *SSO* from CNSS, *Segunda memoria del Fondo de Jubilación Obrera: Año 1965* and *Memoria años 1961–1967*.

a. 1964.

b. SSO plus SSE coverage.

SSE covered all provinces in the table, while SSO did not cover half of them. Data in the table support the proposition that coverage of provinces on the Coast is higher than in the Sierra and these, in turn, higher than in the Jungle. Out of the 10 provinces with the highest coverage (40 to 65 percent of the EAP), 7 were in the Coast (70 percent of Coastal provinces), 3 in the Sierra (the important provinces of Arequipa and Cuzco and the mining province of Cerro de Pasco), and none in the Jungle. Conversely out of the 14 provinces with lowest coverage (2 to 26 percent of the EAP), only 3 were in the Coast, 7 were in the Sierra (70 percent of Sierra provinces), and 4 in the Jungle. A second proposition that can also be tested with the data is that the larger the size of the EAP in a province, the better its degree of social security coverage (not only in absolute numbers, of course, but in relative terms). The correlation between these two variables is significant: .98 (N = 24). A third proposition which, unfortunately, cannot be properly tested with the data is that the higher the urban vis-a-vis rural proportion of the EAP in a province, the larger its social security coverage. The correlation between these two variables is .40 (N = 24), but it should be noticed that the number of insured in highly urbanized provinces is underestimated in table 4-7. The table excludes those insured in the armed forces, civil servants in the old system, and white-collars in large enterprises (under FEJEP) who are concentrated in urban centers. Still the correlation in Peru is higher than in Chile (.24) where an even larger number of insured concentrated in urban areas was excluded.

In summary, the best-protected provinces are the most developed and are mainly located in the Coast or close to it. They concentrate most of the government, industry, fishing, mining, and financial services. They also have 8 of the 10 cities above 50,000 inhabitants in the nation. The least-protected provinces are the most underdeveloped, mostly characterized by a pastoral or agricultural economy; they include only two cities above 50,000 inhabitants. The four provinces with poorest social security coverage are in the departments of highest Indian concentration. While coverage in the province of Lima is above 65 percent, in Andahuaylas it is 2 percent.

Financing

Since the percentage of contributions and taxes are the same throughout the territory of Peru covered by social security, inequalities in financing are limited to occupational groups. Table 4-8 gives a picture of the complexity of the system and the significant differences in the contributions by occupational groups and type of risk. In the main four occupational groups, the combined overall percentage contribution from both workers and employers diminishes as the income of the group increases. But, as will be seen later, the social security revenues of the high income groups are larger due to the higher salaries of these groups, and in many cases deficits resulting from insufficient contributions are subsidized by the state.

Differences in percentage contributions to pension funds of SSO and SSE were eliminated in 1973 when the system was standardized. All employers under this system had an equal increase in their contributions, from 2 to 4 percent; white-collars and civil servants under the system had their contributions increased from 1 to 2 percent; and blue-collars' contributions were not increased because they were already set at 2 percent. Civil servants under the old system have the highest percentage contribution in pensions. This is necessary to cover their unique system of lump-sum payments and generous pension system; besides, the state pays any resulting deficit. Those insured under the armed forces pension fund have the lowest

Table 4-7
Degree of Social Security Protection of the Economically Active Population by the Most Populated Province of Each Department in Peru: 1961

| Department | Province[a] | EAP[b] | | Insured Population | | | | | |
| | | | | SSO[c] | | SSE | | Total | |
		Thousands	Urban Percent	Thousands	Percent[d]	Thousands	Percent[d]	Thousands	Percent[d]
Lima (c)	Lima	605.1	96.3	197.0	32.6	196.7	32.5	393.7	65.1
Ica (c)	Ica	34.3	54.6	15.3	44.7	4.8	14.1	20.1	58.6
La Libertad (c)	Trujillo	66.3	67.4	26.4	39.9	11.3	17.0	37.7	56.9
Pasco (s)	Pasco	32.0	40.1	13.2	41.3	3.9	12.2	17.2	53.5
Callao (c)	Callao	75.0	95.3	17.4	23.2	17.1	22.8	34.5	46.0
Tacna (c)	Tacna	20.8	73.5	5.4	26.0	3.9	18.6	9.3	44.6
Arequipa (s)	Arequipa	80.9	78.1	17.5	21.6	16.5	20.4	34.0	42.0
Ancash (s)	Santa (c)	33.3	66.5	10.7[e]	32.2	3.2	9.6	13.9	41.8
Lambayeque (c)	Chiclayo	97.7	64.2	28.6	29.3	10.9	11.2	39.6	40.5
Cuzco (s)	Cuzco	31.2	93.2	5.9	18.9	6.7	21.6	12.6	40.5
Piura (c)	Piura	56.8	57.3	8.8	15.5	6.2	10.9	15.0	26.4
Huánuco (s)	Huanuco	25.9	35.4	2.4[e]	9.2	2.3	8.8	4.6	18.0
Junin (s)	Huancayo	59.6	52.3	4.4	7.5	4.1	6.8	8.5	14.3

Loreto (j)	Maynas	39.5	47.6	0		5.3	13.3	5.3	13.3
Tumbes (c)	Tumbes	12.7	69.0	0.5e	4.2	1.0	7.6	1.5	11.9
Cajamarca (s)	Cajamarca	46.7	19.5	2.7e	5.8	2.1	4.5	4.8	10.2
Moquegua (c)	M. Nieto	12.3	64.5	0		1.1	9.1	1.1	9.1
Madre de Dios (j)	Tambopata	3.4	37.2	0		0.3	8.6	0.3	8.6
Amazonas (j)	Chachapoyas	8.2	51.2	0		0.6	7.7	0.6	7.7
San Martín (j)	San Martín	13.0	69.3	0		0.8	6.2	0.8	6.2
Ayacucho (s)	Huamanga	19.9	41.5	0		1.2	5.8	1.2	5.8
Puno (s)	Puno	39.7	24.6	0		2.2	5.6	2.2	5.6
Huancavelica (s)	Huancavelica	20.9	25.8	0		0.9	4.2	0.9	4.2
Apurímac (s)	Andahuaylas	32.8	13.0	0		0.7	2.2	0.7	2.2
Total		1,468.0		356.2	24.3	303.8	20.7	660.3	45.0

SOURCES: *EAP* from Dirección Nacional de Estadística y Censos, *Sexto Censo nacional de Población levantado el 2 de julio de 1961* (Lima: n/d). *SSO: Memoria: años 1961–1967. SSE: Boletín estadístico 1958–1968.*

NOTE: c = Coast area, j = Jungle area, s = Sierra area.

a. Ranked according to degree of coverage (last column).

b. Includes unemployed and unpaid family workers.

c. SSO zones of coverage do not always coincide with provinces; in Chiclayo and Pasco adjustments were made to match the insured in SSO and SSE with the EAP.

d. Percentage of EAP (first column).

e. In 1964 when coverage began.

Table 4-8
Social Security Contributions from Employees, Employers, and State by
Occupational Group in Peru: 1973
(in percentages of wages or income)

Occupational Group	Employee	Employer	State	Total
Blue-collars	*5.0*	*12.4*	*2.0*	*19.4*
Pensions	2.0[b]	4.0	—	6.0
Health-maternity	3.0[a]	6.0	2.0[c]	11.0
Occupational hazards	—	2.4[d]	—	2.4
White-collars	*5.0*	*11.0*	*0.5*	*16.5*
Pensions (current)[g]	2.0	4.0	—	6.0
Old system[h]	—	2.0	—	2.0
Health-maternity[e]	3.0[f]	3.5	0.5[e]	7.0
Life insurance	—	1.5[d]	—	1.5
Civil servants	*6.5 or 12.5*	*7.0*	*0.5*	*14.0 or 16.00*
Pensions (current)[g]	2.0	4.0	—	6.0
Old system[i]	8.0	[j]	—	8.0
Health-maternity	2.5[f]	3.0	0.5[c]	6.0
Lump sums	2.0	[j]	—	2.0
Armed forces	*1.5*	*3.5*	—	*5.0*
Pensions	1.5	3.5[j]	—	5.0
Health-maternity	—	[k]	—	—
Fishermen	*4.0*	*23.0*	—	*27.0*
Pensions	2.0	2.0	—	4.0
Health-maternity	2.0	3.0	—	5.0
Unemployment, etc.	—	18.0	—	18.0
Self-employed[l]	*8.5*	—	*3.5*	*12.0*
Pensions	4.0	—	1.5	5.5
Health-maternity	4.5	—	2.0	6.5
Taxi drivers	*5.0*	—	*2.0[m]*	*7.0*
Domestic servants	*5.0*	*9.0*	—	*14.0*
Newspaper vendors	*5.0[n]*	—	[o]	*5.0*

SOURCES: Legislation compiled by the author. Estimates on insurance premiums (accidents and life) from Cámara de Comercio de Lima, *Sinopsis y costo de los beneficios sociales en el Perú* (Lima: 1970).

a. Plus voluntary additional contribution of 1–2 percent to protect the wife of the insured.

b. Since 1973 integrated into FNP. Prior to that date the employer paid 2 percent.

c. Plus tax on alcohol and tobacco.

d. Estimate of national average premium in the late 1960s.

e. Includes occupational accidents and diseases whose cost was estimated at 0.6 percent in the late 1950s.

f. Plus additional 2.1 percent above certain salary level.

g. System established in 1962 and integrated in 1973 into FNP. Contributions prior to 1973 were 1 percent from workers and 2 percent from employers.

h. FEJEP from 1968 until 1973 in which it was abolished and merged with FNP.

i. *Montepío civil.*

j. The state pays any resulting deficit.

k. The state pays all costs.

l. Facultative insured in SSO.

m. Plus tax on gasoline.

n. Out of 20 percent commission for sales.

o. Taxes: 2–8 percent on ads and 4 percent on sales of imported printed materials.

percentage contribution in Peru and, in addition, the state covers any resulting deficit. In the old pension system for white-collars working in big enterprises (later FEJEP), the insured did not contribute at all and the system was financed solely by employers until 1973. Even worse, employers who did not have employees under FEJEP had to contribute to this fund as well as to the SSE pension fund. Therefore, employers of medium and small enterprises (and the public, if we assume that some of this contribution was passed on in higher prices) supported a pension system for employees in large enterprises who had high incomes and did not contribute at all to their own pension fund. In 1973 FEJEP and its special contribution were abolished, but its pensioners were absorbed and supported by SSE.

All expenses of the health-maternity system of the armed forces are paid by the state. Civil servants have a lower percentage contribution than white-collars in health-maternity, theoretically because the former do not receive some subsidies. However, it has been argued that the reduction in contribution of civil servants is larger than the cost of the subsidies they lack. If this is correct, civil servants pay less than white-collars for the same benefits, resulting in a transfer of income from the latter to the former. The state percentage contribution for the blue-collar health-maternity fund is four times as high as that for white-collars. Nevertheless, since salaries of white-collars are twice as high as those of blue-collars, the difference in actual contribution is actually reduced by half. Without the state contribution, the SSO health-maternity fund would be in grave financial trouble. By 1961, the expenditures of this fund equalled its revenues and thereafter a deficit resulted. This was in large measure caused by the 375 million soles not paid by the state from 1961 to 1967. On the other hand, the accumulated state debt to SSE had not affected its finances; actually the fund had a surplus.

The separation of SSO and SSE left the former with the group of insured with the lower income. Due to mounting pressures from noninsured subgroups of the labor force (e.g., peasants, self-employed, domestic servants, newspaper vendors), the SSO has gradually expanded its scope to incorporate all or part of these subgroups. The newly covered, however, had even lower income than those already protected and often did not have an employer. In 1961, the average income of agricultural workers, for instance, was half that of miners and manufacturing workers and 40 percent below the average cost per capita of the SSO health-maternity system. In order to provide adequate services to the large number of newly incorporated insured (e.g., 200,000 domestic servants in the early 1970s), SSO should have expanded its hospital facilities, but the current deficit (aggravated by the incorporations) made that impossible. Blue-collars in mining and industry (a group whose income is below that of white-collars, civil servants, and the military) are affected by the expansion of coverage to more deprived groups, while the higher-income groups are free from the negative effects of such expansion because they have separate funds.[42] The principle of solidarity seems to be limited in Peru to the low-income stratum of the labor force. (The incorporation of SSO and SSE into the FNP and the movement toward the unification of health facilities is a proper step to correct this negative situation.)

In view of this, the state contribution to the SSE health-maternity fund appears as highly unfair. Such a contribution is a transfer of state revenue generated by the population as a whole (largely by sales taxes paid by blue-collars, the self-employed, agricultural workers, and other low-income groups poorly protected or unprotected by social security) to a group which is well protected and enjoys high income. An ILO technician has therefore advised the elimination of this state contribution.[43]

The state does not contribute to the pension system of blue-collars or of white-collars but compensates any deficit resulting in the pension systems of the armed forces and the civil servants hired prior to 1962 and in the lump-sum payments for civil servants. The increasing cost of the civil-servant system pushed the state contribution from a little more than one-fourth of the total cost in 1947 to almost one-half in 1962.[44] There are no data on the actual contribution of the state to the armed forces social security system. The total insured-employer contribution in the old civil-servant pension and lump-sum is 10 percent, while that of the armed forces in pension and health-maternity is only 5 percent. If, in spite of the higher contribution, the state had to subsidize half of the civil-servant system by 1962, possibly it was subsidizing more than half the armed forces system at the time. In the 1971–1972 state budget, the combined allocations for the ministries of war, navy, aeronautics, and police represented 27 percent of the total budget.[45] The portion earmarked for social security was not disclosed.

The state contributes to the funds of the self-employed (both for health-maternity and pensions) because this group has a low income and lacks an employer's contribution. But independent taxi drivers who own their cars and have a higher income than most self-employed, have obtained a similar rate of state contribution plus substantial revenue from a gasoline tax, and keep their pension fund separate from the general SSO-FNP pension fund. Fishermen, also with an independent fund, have been able to induce their employers to pay one of the highest percentage contributions in Peru for their unemployment compensation and other benefits.

Table 4-9 compares the percentage distribution of social security revenues by three major occupational groups: blue-collars, white-collars and civil servants under the 1962 system, and white-collars under FEJEP. Unfortunately the two systems in which the state has the higher contribution (civil servants under the *montepío* and armed forces) are not shown due to lack of data. Table 4-10 compares the ratios of revenue per insured in two broad occupational groups: blue-collars on the one hand and most white-collars and civil servants (under the 1962 system) on the other. Data

Table 4-9
Percentage Distribution of Social Security Fund Revenues by Financing Source and Occupational Group in Peru: 1967

Occupational Group	Insured	Employer	State[a]	Investment Returns	Others	Total
Blue-collars	34.6	53.8	4.3	6.0	1.3	100.0
White-collars and civil servants[b]	38.9	50.7	5.2	4.5	0.4	100.0
White-collars (FEJEP)[c]	0	95.0	0	5.0	0	100.0

SOURCES: *Blue-collars* from CSNSS, *Memoria años 1961–1967,* Gómez Sánchez, interview, Lima, 1971, and Antoine Zelenka, "Aspectos financieros de los seguros sociales," Lima, May 12, 1969, table 2. *White-collars and civil servants* from SSE, *Boletín estadístico 1958–1968* and Zelenka, ibid., table 4. *FEJEP* from San Román Aguirre, 1970.

    a. State contributions and taxes.

    b. Current system; excludes civil servants under *montepíos* and FEJEP.

    c. Rough estimate for pension revenue only.

Table 4-10
Revenue of Social Security Funds per Insured by Occupational Group in Peru: 1965

Occupational Group	Revenue[a] (in thousand soles)	Number of Insured	Revenue per Capita (in soles)	Ratio[b]
Blue-collars	1,397,730	1,042,863	1,340	1.0
White-collars and civil servants[c]	1,236,459	719,019	1,719	1.3

SOURCES: *Revenue* from Zelenka, "Aspectos financieros . . . ," tables 1–4. *Number of insured* from Gómez Sánchez, SSO, 1971, and SSE, *Boletín estadístico 1958–1968*.
a. Includes state debt.
b. Revenue per capita of white-collars and civil servants divided by the revenue per capita of blue-collars.
c. Excludes white-collars and civil servants in their old pension systems.

from the armed forces and other groups were not available. According to the table, in 1965 the ratio of revenue for blue-collars was roughly two-thirds that of white-collars and civil servants. The unification of the pension funds of SSO and SSE should help to correct this inequality at least in part.

In addition to the noted inequalities in financing the main social security systems, there are discriminatory regulations in the supplementary systems. In the nine most important compulsory mutual insurance funds, members pay a contribution, but the employer directly contributes only to the mutual funds of teachers and jockeys. Special taxes have been granted to support only the following mutual funds: judiciary secretaries and Lima lawyers (part of the revenues from the compulsory use of "legal papers"), teachers (fees for examinations, transcripts, etc.) and jockeys (percentage of prizes).[46] Social security fringe benefits gained through collective bargaining by seven occupational subgroups are exclusively financed by the employers. The costs of these fringe benefits, as a percentage of salaries, fluctuate widely, for example, 50 percent for sugar plantation workers, 15 to 40 percent for miners, 15 percent for petroleum workers, 5 to 10 percent for fish-flour workers.[47] Some of these costs are undoubtedly transferred to consumers.

The cost of social security including expenditures in health-maternity for all groups and pensions for blue- and white-collars and civil servants under the new system (therefore excluding pensions for the military, FEJEP, civil servants under the old system, and life insurance, workmen's compensation, and other expenditures of minor subgroups) increased from 1.7 billion soles in 1961 to 3.3 billion in 1965. See table 4-11. Until 1961–1962, the major component of these social security costs was the expenditure in health, but the new pension systems for blue-collars and white-collars are costlier than those of health. From 1963 to 1967 expenditures for health-maternity for SSO and SSE increased by 66 percent, while those for pensions rose by 250 percent (and should increase even faster in the 1970s).[48] If all social security expenditures were taken into account including the expanded coverage in the early 1970s, social security costs should probably be above 4 percent of GNP. Table 4-11 also shows that social security revenues (from SSO and SSE alone) as a percentage of GNP increased from 1.8 in 1961 to 2.3 percent in 1965, although they declined to 2 percent in 1968.

Table 4-11
Cost of Social Security in Peru: 1961–1968
(in billions of current soles and percentages)

Year	GNP	Government Consumption Expenditure	Compensation of Labor	Social Security Revenue				Social Security Expenditure			
				Total[a]	Percent of GNP	Percent of Government Consumption Expenditures	Percent of Compensation of Labor	Total[b]	Percent of GNP	Percent of Government Consumption Expenditures	Percent of Compensation of Labor
1961	62.3	5.9	25.3	1.1	1.8	18.6	4.3	1.7	2.7	28.8	6.7
1962	71.7	6.8	28.8	1.6	2.2	23.5	5.5	2.1	2.9	30.9	7.3
1963	78.7	7.7	32.3	1.7	2.2	22.0	5.3	2.5	3.2	32.5	7.7
1964	95.0	10.2	38.7	2.1	2.2	20.6	5.4	3.1	3.3	30.4	8.0
1965	113.0	12.5	46.2	2.6	2.3	20.8	5.6	3.3	2.9	26.4	7.1
1966	134.0	14.8	53.8	2.9	2.2	19.6	5.4	—	—	—	—
1967	153.7	17.7	64.0	3.2	2.1	18.1	5.0	—	—	—	—
1968	181.2	19.4	74.9	3.7	2.0	19.1	4.9	—	—	—	—

SOURCES: GNP, Government consumption expenditure from IMF, *International Financial Statistics* (Washington, D.C.: January 1969 and January 1972). *Compensation of labor* from UN, *Yearbook of National Account Statistics 1970* (New York: 1972). *Social security revenue and expenditure* from CNSS, *Decimaséptima memoria correspondiente al año 1958* (Lima: n/d) and *Memoria años 1961–1967*; FJO, *Segunda memoria año 1965* (Lima: n/d); SSE, *Boletín estadístico 1958–1968* and data provided by Jorge García la Puerta, Lima, 1970; Antoine Zelenka, "Aspectos financieros de los seguros sociales," May 12, 1969; and INP, *Plan de Desarrollo Económico y Social: Salud 1967–1970* (Lima: n/d).

a. Only revenues of the SSO and SSE.
b. Includes all expenditures of SSO and SSE and health expenditures only for the remaining groups.

Rising costs of social security are the result of expanded coverage of the population, protection of risks not previously covered, increase in the amount of benefits and in the costs of medicines and hospital equipment, and the expanded social security bureaucracy and the rapid increase of its salaries. Indeed, an increasing portion of social security revenues is transferred to the social security bureaucracy. From 1961 to 1967 the cost of living rose by 72 percent, the average wage of those insured in SSO by 138 percent, and the number of insured by 16 percent, but salaries of SSO personnel rose by 263 percent. While in 1961 SSO personnel expenditures were equal to 4 percent of the insured salaries, by 1967 they had increased to 5 percent. In SSE, the number of insured increased by 46 percent between 1962 and 1967, the average salary of the insured by 45 percent, and the expenditures in salary paid to SSE personnel by 104 percent.[49]

As has been previously stated, since the 1950s the state has commonly failed to fulfill its social security obligations, both as employer and third party, accumulating a debt above 1 million soles by 1967. Besides emergency taxes and small cash payments, public bonds have been the main device used to offset the debt. The government has also pressured social security funds to invest a substantial part of their resources in other state securities. The future stability of some social security funds, particularly SSO, rests in the state's ability to repay borrowed capital and interest. And yet part of the borrowed funds have been used to compensate state budgetary deficits, the insured in the lessor institution partly helping to maintain the high salaries and juicy pensions of civil servants.[50] Another part of the borrowed funds have been spent in lavish nonproductive investment or lost by embezzlement. The probability that the state will honor its obligations is therefore a poor one and, if it ultimately fails, blue-collars will be the most affected. In the 1971–1975 five-year plan, the military government stressed that social security funds should be placed primarily in state securities but acknowledged the imperious necessity to invest such resources in development. The plan also indicated that to improve income redistribution, the state was going to transfer its contributions from social security funds (without specifying which) and the FNSBS fund to help protect peasants and the self-employed. Such a transfer requires some comment. The abolition of the state contribution to SSE is laudable and it will not affect the group. It is doubtful whether the government will stop its subsidies to the military and civil servants. On the other hand, if the contribution to SSO is also abolished (or the past debts are not paid), the protection of the blue-collars would be jeopardized. Further, FNSBS funds are largely allocated to subsidize public-charity hospitals which protect the noninsured. If this transfer is truly the government's intention, such redistribution would not detract from the well-protected groups but from the less-protected blue collars and the noninsured.

Benefits

The regulations on benefits are the same throughout the territory of Peru; there are differences, however, in the quality of regional hospital and medical services. The most significant inequalities in this field are derived from the occupational structure as summarized in table 4-12. The table is divided into three sections. The top section shows the benefits that each of the main four occupational groups enjoys. The middle section notes benefits of some of the subgroups with independent or special funds, benefits not duplicated by those in the top section. The bottom section identifies benefits gained through collective bargaining by other subgroups (privileged

Table 4-12
Social Security Benefits by Occupational Group in Peru: 1973

Occupational Group	Pensions										Other Cash Benefits								Family Allowances									Health-Maternity[j]								Total
	1	2	3	4	5	6°	7	8	9	10	11	12	13	14	15	16	17	18	19	20	21	22	23	24	25	26	27	28	29	30	31	32	33	34	35	
Main Funds																																				
Blue-collars[a]	x		x^k	x^k	x^k	x			x^r	x	x	x	x	x	u		x	x								x			x		x^v	x	x	x	x	17
White-collars[b]	x	x^n	x^k	x^k	x^k	x			x^r	x	x	x	x	x	u		x	x								x			x		x^v	x	x	x	x	19
Civil-servants[c]	x	x	x^m	x^m	x	x	x^p	x		x^s	x	x	x		x	x	x	x					x							x	x^v	x	x^w	x^w	x^w	24
Armed forces[d]	x^l	x	x^m	x^m	x	x		x^q	x	x		x			x^q	x	x	x					x	x				x	x^w	x	x^v	x^w	x^w	x^w	x^w	24
Minor Funds (independent)																																				
Fishermen[e]	x					x									x^u	x	x	x										x^x	x^x	x	x^x	x^x	x^x	x^x	x	12
Taxi drivers[f]	x		x	x		x			x^r			x	x			x	x	x								x			x^x	x	x	x^w	x^w	x	x	18
Longshoremen[g]	x		x	x		x					x	x	x				x												x^w	x	x^v		x^w	x^w	x	14
Jockeys[h]	x		x	x						x	x	x				x	x												x^w	x	x^v	x^w	x^w	x^w	x	13
Newspaper vendors[i]												x															x									10
Collective Agreements (in addition to main funds)																																				
Electricity	x^y		x^y									x^y				x^y	x^y							x	x				x^w	x	x^y	x^w	x^w	x^w	x	12
Petroleum	x^y											x^y				x^y	x^y												x^w	x	x^y	x^w	x^w	x^w	x	11
Sugar			x^y		x^y					x	x^y									x									x^w	x	x^y	x^w	x^w	x^w	x	11
Mining	x^y											x^y				x^y													x^w	x	x^y	x^w	x^w	x^w	x	10
Banking										x													x	x	x											6

SOURCES: Legislation compiled by the author, data from the Ministry of Labor, and Luis Aparicio Valdez, "Estudio sobre convenios colectivos y seguridad social en el Peru," Lima, n/d.

NOTE: See code following tables for definition of benefits here signified by numbers 1–35.

a. Includes the three funds of SSO: pensions, health-maternity, and occupational accidents and diseases.

b. Includes the two funds of SSE (pensions and health-maternity), life insurance, and seniority pensions under FEJEP.

o. All funds grant survivors' pensions to widow and children and, usually in their absence, to parents. Blue-collars and longshoremen are granted survivors' pensions to parents only in case of occupational hazards.

p. Related to dismissal.

c. Includes the old pension system (for the new see white-collars), lump sums, and health-maternity under SSE.
d. Includes pensions, health-maternity, and mutual insurance funds.
e. Includes independent funds for pensions, health-maternity, and unemployment.
f. Includes special pension fund and health-maternity under SSO.
g. Includes health-maternity independent fund, special pension fund in SSO, and protection for occupational accidents and diseases.
h. Includes independent fund for pensions and health-maternity.
i. Includes independent fund for health-maternity and welfare.
j. Unless otherwise specified only for the worker.
k. Reduction of 2/3 of capacity.
l. Compulsory (not voluntary old-age retirement).
m. Total disability.
n. Only for those under FEJEP that acquired right prior to mid-1973.

q. When the worker has no right to pension.
r. Related to old-age pension.
s. Total disability.
t. Outside of the social security system the employer pays a lump sum in certain cases.
u. Cessation of activities in the off-season.
v. For spouse of worker also.
w. For relatives also.
x. For relatives also but temporarily suspended.
y. Difference is paid to equal 100 percent of salary in disability pensions in sugar and electricity and in all disability subsidies, or to 80 percent in old-age pension in petroleum workers. In mining, old-age and disability pensions are granted if no right under general system. In electricity and petroleum, the disability subsidy is paid for a longer period. Life insurance payment is higher than in the general system. Funeral aid in addition to general; in some cases also granted for relatives.

Code for Social Security Benefits

Pensions:
1. Old-age.
2. Seniority.
3. Permanent disability (total or partial) caused by occupational hazards.
4. Permanent disability (total or partial) caused by nonoccupational hazards.
5. Unemployment/layoff.
6. Survivors.

Other Cash Benefits:
7. Restitution of contributions.
8. Lump sum at retirement.
9. Bonus added to pension for work-years above the minimum required for retirement.
10. Lump sum for permanent disability (total or partial) caused by occupational hazards.
11. Subsidy for temporary disability caused by occupational hazards.
12. Subsidy for temporary disability caused by nonoccupational hazards.
13. Salary (or percentage thereof) paid for a period before and after childbirth.
14. Unemployment/layoff temporary subsidy.
15. Unemployment/layoff lump sum.
16. Life insurance, lump sum.
17. Funeral aid, lump sum.
18. Lump sum to survivors when no right to pension is granted.
19. Year-end bonus to retired and pensioners.

Family Allowances:
20. Marriage.
21. Pregnancy.
22. Childbirth.
23. Children.
24. Spouse.
25. Parents.
26. Child food (percentage of salary or in kind).
27. School aid (for insured or his/her children).

Health-Maternity Benefits:
28. Preventive medicine.
29. Curative medical care.
30. Rehabilitation and prosthesis in case of occupational hazards.
31. Maternity care.
32. Surgical treatment.
33. Hospitalization.
34. Medicines.
35. Dental care.

categories of blue- and white-collar workers) in addition to those listed in the top section. Whenever possible, additional benefits granted by compulsory mutual insurance funds have been included in the top section.

The totals in the table allow us to rank the occupational groups by the number of benefits granted as follows: (a) top section: civil servants (in the old system), armed forces, white-collars (and civil servants in the new system), and blue-collars; (b) middle section: taxi drivers, longshoremen, jockeys, fishermen, and newspaper vendors; and (c) bottom section: workers in electricity, petroleum and sugar, mining, and banking. A detailed study of the table shows remarkable differences among all groups. Only the armed forces, civil servants in the old system, and white-collars in big enterprises (the now-defunct FEJEP) have seniority pensions, and only the first two groups have unemployment pensions. All civil servants have a unique system of lump sums for retirement, disability, and death, in addition to pensions for these risks, a system only partially available to the armed forces, white-collars, and some of the subgroups in the bottom section. Civil servants and fishermen are the only two groups with unemployment compensation, while civil servants, the armed forces, and banking, electricity, and sugar workers have family allowances. Relatives of the military, longshoremen, jockeys, and electricity, petroleum, sugar and mining workers have a right to health-maternity attention; wives of civil servants and white-collars have a right to maternity attention; but most blue-collar relatives are not covered by health-maternity attention at all. (Fishermen's relatives have the right to health-maternity care, but this has been suspended, while newspaper vendors' relatives do not have such a right but apparently receive medical care in practice.) Excluded from the table are other benefits that some of these groups have such as loans with low interest for housing (military, white-collars, blue-collars), car insurance (drivers), vacations (fishermen).

The true magnitude of inequality among groups cannot be evaluated from table 4-12 because, for the sake of comparison, it equates benefits of the same nature which in practice may be significantly different in such matters as: (a) requirements to gain the right; (b) basic salary used to compute the benefit; (c) the amount of the benefit; (d) the adjustment of pensions to the cost of living; and (e) the compatibility of the pension with other pensions or salaried work. What follows are the most relevant differences among principal groups and subgroups.

There are three main types of retirement pensions: compulsory and voluntary based on age plus years of service, and seniority based on years of service alone. The age for compulsory retirement is set at 70 for male civil servants and 60 for females. The military has two age scales, a general one and another lower one for the air force with a range from 35 to 59 years. The higher the rank of the military official, the higher the age limit for retirement, for example, lieutenants, 40 in the general scale and 35 in the air force; generals, 59 and 54 respectively. The exact number of officials who retire at an early age is unknown but is reportedly high; these pensioners constitute a burden on the economy and are strong competitors in the tight labor market because they are allowed to work after retirement.[51] The number of years of service for compulsory retirement is generally set at seven. For voluntary retirement the age is generally set at 60 (for males and often 55 for females) but with divergent minimum years of service, e.g., 5 and 13 or 15 (female or male) for blue- and white-collar workers according to their date of birth, 25 for fishermen, and 25 or 30 (female or male) for civil servants under the old system. (The standardization of 1973 eliminated an old inequality: a shorter period required for retirement of white-collars than blue-collars in spite of the fact that the former usually have a longer life expectancy.) Miners can retire at the established age if they do not have the necessary years of service. Seniority pensions are granted at any age but with divergent minimum years of service, e.g., 15 for militarymen (12½ for females), 25 for male white-collars in the now-abolished FEJEP (20 for females), and 30 for male civil servants in the old system (25 for females).

The basic percentage of salary granted as a pension fluctuates widely; for example, it is equally set at 100 percent in seniority pensions (114 percent for generals in the armed forces), but in voluntary retirement is 80 to 100 percent (fishermen and petroleum workers), and 50 to 80 percent (blue- and white-collars and civil servants in new system). Lump sums at retirement in addition to pensions range from 15,000 to 90,000 soles for civil servants (without further requisites), 15,000 to 65,000 for employees of the Ministry of Health (with some years of service), and an unknown amount to policemen, judiciary secretaries, and lawyers (with certain age and time-of-service requirements). Militarymen can receive a lump sum only when they have accumulated some time of service but not enough to qualify for a pension.

Pensions for permanent total disability distinguish between occupational and nonoccupational causes. Total occupational disability conveys a pension equivalent to a basic rate of 100 percent of salary for the military, civil servants in the old system, electricity and sugar workers, but 80 percent for blue-collars. In the case of total nonoccupational disability, the basic rate is usually 50 percent of the salary, but miners receive 100 percent. Miners can also receive a disability pension paid by the enterprise if they do not fulfill the requirements of the general system. Lump sums from 10,000 to 60,000 soles are paid to civil servants and in unknown amounts to the military, employees of the Ministry of Health, judiciary secretaries, and bank workers. If the insured has not fulfilled all the requisites for a disability pension, miners may receive a pension paid by their enterprise and civil servants in the old system are entitled to an amount equal to one annual salary; other groups do not have any right in this context. Temporary disability, if occupational, is paid at the following percentages of salary and periods of time: 100 percent for indefinite time (military, diplomats, teachers), for 1 year (sugar workers), for 6 months (judiciary), for 2 months (with a third month at 50 percent and a fourth at 33 percent, for civil servants); and 70 percent for 1 year (blue- and white-collar workers). Rates and periods for temporary nonoccupational disability are: 100 percent for 1 year (university professors), from 6 months to 1 year (electricity, petroleum, mining and banking workers), for 2 months (civil servants); 70 percent for 1 year (white-collars), and for 6 months (blue-collars).

Pensions to survivors are fixed at 100 percent of salary in the armed forces (half for widows and half for children) and 50 percent of salary for civil servants in the old system. The following rates are based not on salary but on *pensions:* 50 percent for the widow and 20 percent for each child (blue-collars and white-collars and civil servants in the new system), and 50–80 percent for the widow and 20 percent for each child (fishermen). Lump sums are fixed at: 100,000 soles (judges and employees of Ministry of Health), 30,000 soles (teachers), 10,000 to 36,000 soles (employees of communications), 5,000 to 30,000 soles plus two annual salaries (civil servants), 1.3 annual salaries (white-collars; average in 1968 was about 32,000 soles), 1,200 to 4,000 soles (blue-collars), and unknown amounts to military and judiciary secretaries. Blue- and white-collars in electricity, petroleum, and banking receive additional lump sums. When the insured do not leave a right to pension to their survivors, the latter collect, in terms of annual salaries: three (fishermen), one (civil servants in old system), and one-twelfth (blue- and white-collars and civil servants in new system). Funeral aid is set at two months' salaries for all occupational groups except electricity, petroleum, sugar, and mining which receive higher amounts.

Pensions for early dismissal or abolition of job *(cesantía)* are set at 3.3 percent of salary for each year of service for civil servants in old system and the military, but the latter may accumulate as much as 100 percent of their salary. An additional lump sum of three annual salaries is paid to civil servants, and they are granted one annual salary plus devolution of half of their contributions if they do not fulfill the requisites for a pension. Militarymen and policemen are paid one annual salary for each year of service if they do not qualify for a pension. Fishermen receive an annual lump sum during the off-season which varies according to their accumulated time of service. Outside of the social security system and under certain conditions, dismissed white- and blue-collar workers may be paid by their employers one annual salary for each year of service.

Pregnant workers are granted the following percentages of their salaries for the given periods: 100 percent for 3 months (teachers, white-collars); 100 percent for 2 months, 50 percent for a third month, and 33 percent for a fourth month (civil servants); and 100 percent for 2.5 months (blue-collars; sugar workers receive a higher amount). In addition, an allowance is paid for babies' milk during 8 months to white-collars (set at 50 percent of monthly salary) and blue-collars (30 percent). Family allowances for spouse and children are paid to the military, electricity, and bank workers, and for children only to civil servants.

There are also substantial differences in the manner in which years of work are counted. In the armed forces, if the insured has fifteen years of service, the years spent studying in military or police academies are counted as years of service, and an additional four years in specialized training is countable for qualified officials. (Prior to 1973, pilots and other air force officials with five years of service were granted one extra year of service for every two years actually worked.) Teachers with fifteen years of service can also count their years of study. Civil servants can accumulate the time worked in simultaneous jobs. On the other hand, prior to 1973, the time worked by a blue-collar worker in a white-collar job was not counted and blue-collars working for the state lost their time when they changed their status from public to private.

The basic salary for computing benefits could be only the remuneration received for services performed, such as wage and overtime (blue- and white-collars and civil servants in the new system) or include additional fringe benefits, such as bonuses for seniority and special training (teachers) and also bonuses for cost of living and housing, moving and business expenses, family allowances, and decorations (military). The period of time used to compute the average basic salary varies widely, for example, the last three, four, or five years (blue- and white-collars and civil servants in the new system), the last month (civil servants in the old system and white-collars in the now-defunct FEJEP), the highest salary ever received (diplomats), and the salary of an officer in an activity of equal ranking (or immediately higher ranking in some cases) to that of the insured (militarymen). A former president of the republic's pension is computed as 60 percent of the salary that he had while in office.

A general ceiling for pensions was fixed in 1964 at 25,000 soles per month but did not apply for the president of the republic, judges of the Supreme Court, the armed forces, and civil servants (if they had fifteen years of service at the time). White-collars, then under FEJEP, later had a maximum fixed at 48,000 soles per month. The ceiling therefore is only applicable to blue-collars, white-collars, and civil servants under the new system. With a steady high rate of inflation, the real value of social security benefits rapidly declines in Peru. Some groups (Congress, judiciary, armed forces, registrar's officials, teachers) have solved the problem by automatically adjusting their pensions to the current salary of the job. Civil servants enjoy this privilege only when they have retired at 65 with 35 years of service. Blue- and white-collar benefits can be adjusted to the cost of living only by ministerial resolution (prior to 1973 it was by law), usually a lengthy procedure.

At the end of the nineteenth century, a law prohibited the simultaneous receipt of two or more pensions or a pension and a salary. As successive military and civilian administrations ruled the country in the seventy years of this century, the original law suffered numerous modifications. For instance, militarymen and teachers were alternately exempted from the prohibition and then reincluded. From the legislative entanglement, however, various significant exemptions remain in force. Military pensions can be accumulated with any other pension or salary from the private or teaching sectors. In addition, a survivor's pension can be accumulated with another pension or salary from the public sector, and a pension from the armed forces and another from the public sector can be accumulated. Several autonomous agencies are allowed to accumulate their pensions with another pension or salary even in the public sector. Congressmen and physicians can collect two pensions or one pension and a salary without restriction. Seniority pensions granted by the now-abolished FEJEP can be accumulated with another pension (public or private), but white-collar and blue-collar pensions cannot be simultaneously collected with another pension or subsidy paid by SSO and SSE. Workers who retired under FEJEP regulations can perform salaried work in the private sector (and also in the public sector if they were employed in 1973), but fishermen and those under SSE and SSO funds are prohibited from doing so.

The previous information when put together gives a more accurate measurement of the degree of generosity of the benefit system in each occupational group than the simple account in table 4-12. In the 24 comparisons presented above, the armed forces are ranked first in 16, civil servants in 7, white-collars in 3, and blue-collars in none. The air force was, at least until 1973, a privileged subgroup within the military. Teachers (especially university professors), the executive, the judiciary, Congress, some corporations, and the diplomatic corps are often ranked higher than civil servants. Subgroups such as electricity, petroleum, sugar, mining, banking, and the now-abolished FEJEP when contrasted with white-collars in all those cases that admit comparison are systematically ranked higher. These subgroups and fishing are also above the mass of blue-collar workers. Lack of information precludes an accurate ranking of the benefits of longshoremen, taxi drivers, and newspaper vendors, but the first two seem to be above blue-collars in general while the others are below.

An overall comparison of average pensions by main occupational groups is impossible due to the lack of data from the armed forces, civil servants under the old system, and white-collars who were in FEJEP. Table 4-13 presents the only data available, comparing average pensions among blue-collars under the old (1936–1961) and new (1961 on) systems, civil servants and white-collars under the new system (1962 on), and taxi drivers. The average old-age pension of blue-collars under the old system is one-fourth that under the new system. The average disability pension of blue-collars is that paid under the old system; a pensioner at age 55 can change his disability pension (paid at 40 percent of salary) for an old-age pension

Table 4-13
Average Yearly Pensions by Occupational Group in Peru: 1969
(in current soles per capita)

Occupational Group	Old-age[a]	Old-age[b]	Disability	Widowhood	Orphanhood	Average	Ratio
Blue-collars	4,781	18,103	1,472[a]	8,844	3,578	13,913	1.0
White-collars and civil servants[b]	—	33,149	32,946	13,824	16,061	24,517	1.8
Taxi drivers	—	—	—	—	—	23,159	1.7

SOURCES: *Blue-collars* and *taxi drivers* from José Gómez Sánchez, SSO, 1971. *White-collars* and *civil servants* from Jorge Garcia La Puerta, SSE, 1970.
a. Old system.
b. New system.

under the new system (paid at 80 percent of salary). Thus, since 1966 the number of straight disability pensions has declined steadily. In 1969 the white-collars' average disability pension was 22 times higher than that of blue-collars. Fairer comparisons between old-age and survivors' pensions under the new system of both blue- and white-collars show that the former are twice as high as the latter. The last column of the table indicates that taxi drivers have an overall average pension close to that of white-collars and civil servants, the latter being almost two times higher than that of blue-collars.

To accurately measure the degree of inequality by occupational groups in the system of benefits, it is also necessary to discuss the quality of hospital and medical

Table 4-14
Health Facilities and Expenditures by Occupational Group in Peru: 1964

Occupational Group	Number of Insured (in thousands)	Expenditures (in million soles)[a]	Soles per Insured	Number of Hospital Beds	Beds per 1,000 Insured	Number of Physicians	Physici per 1, Insur
Blue-collars	447	444	993	3,000	6.7	609	1.4
White-collars and civil servants	486	508	1,251	3,300[b]	6.8	780[b]	1.6
Armed forces	670[c]	323	482	1,740[d]	2.6	625	0.9
Enterprises and private	1,200	804	670	2,650[d]	2.2	422	0.4
State and public charity	4,860	1,002	206	12,000[d]	2.5	2,179	0.4
Total/Average	7.723	2,081	482	22,690	2.9	4,615[e]	0.6

SOURCES: Milton I. Roemer, *Medical Care in Latin America* (Washington, D.C.: Pan American Union, 1963); Inst Nacional de Planificación, *Plan de Desarrollo Económico y Social 1967–1970* (Lima: 1966); Carlos Quirós, "Los servi de seguridad social en función de los programas de salud pública en los paises de Latinoamérica," *Anales d Facultad de Medicina*, 2 (June 1966); Manuel Hubi Campos, *op. cit.;* et al., "Evaluación de la contribución del Se Social de Empleado a los programas dolentes para la salud en el Perú," Segundo Congreso Americano de Medi de la Seguridad Social, Bogotá, 1970; SSE, *Boletin estadistico 1958–1968;* and CNSS, *Memoria años 1961–1967*.
a. 1963; excludes pensions and subsidies.
b. Direct services at Lima (1,200 beds) and Arequipa (250 beds) hospitals plus estimate of *libre elección*.
c. Gross overestimation. Compare it with previously estimated 60,000 insured in 1969 in table 4-3; if each ha average of three dependents, the total number of insured would be 240,000.
d. 1960.
e. Overestimation due to double appointments; actual number was about 4,000.

care. Data presented in table 4-14 should be taken cautiously. The number of white-collars is overestimated by the duplication already discussed, but this is partly compensated for because spouses with a right to maternity care are not included. The number of physicians and hospital beds used under the elective system of white-collars and civil servants is unknown and the figure in the table is a rough estimate. The number of those in the armed forces and their relatives is probably grossly overestimated. If we take the estimate of 60,000 active insured from table 4-3 and multiply it by four (the insured and the average three dependents), the total number of insured is 240,000. If the more realistic estimate of 120,000 active insured discussed in relation to table 4-3 is accepted, the total number of insured is 480,000, still considerably below the figure in the table. According to the table, the facilities available to white-collar and civil servants were above that for blue-collars by all three quantitative criteria and were four times better than that of the noninsured population which is cared for at state and public-charity hospitals.

A technician from the Pan American Union who evaluated Peruvian hospitals in 1963 observed that those of the armed forces had larger resources and higher standards than the others.[52] Peruvian physicians estimate that the air force hospital built in 1968 is by far the best-equipped and most modern in the country. In 1971 I visited the SSE and SSO hospitals in Lima and it was evident that the former is far better in terms of physical plant, equipment, and attention than the latter. The Pan American evaluation of 1963 reported that enterprise hospitals were usually excellent and that most private hospitals were small but modern and with first-class service, while state and public-charity hospitals were, for the most part, below the standards of the rest.

The distribution of hospital and medical services by region is also highly unequal. Of 15 SSO hospitals, 11 are on the Coast (with 80 percent of the beds), 3 in the Sierra (15 percent of beds), and only one in the Jungle (5 percent of beds). The hospitals are located in the most populated cities, 3 of them plus 2 polyclinics in the departments of Lima and Callao. Of 3 SSE hospitals, 2 are on the Coast (with 85 percent of the beds, the most important in Lima) and only 1 in the Sierra (in the second largest city, Arequipa). Four of the 5 hospitals of the armed forces are in Lima and the other is in Arequipa. There is also a concentration of state, public-charity, and private hospitals on the Coast particularly in the most populated cities. For an overall comparison among regions, see table 4-15.

Table 4-15
Health Facilities by Geographical Region in Peru: 1970

Region	Total Population (in thousands)	Hospital Beds	Beds per 1,000 Inhabitants	Physicians	Physicians per 10,000 Inhabitants	Composite Weighted Index of Beds and Physicians
Coast	6,250	21,988	3.5	5,366	8.6	6.3
Sierra	6,521	8,539	1.3	1,044	1.6	1.4
Jungle	815	1,226	1.5	135	1.6	1.5
Total	13,586	31,753	2.3	6,545	4.8	3.5

SOURCE: Based on Octavio Mongrut, "Población y salud," *Boletín Informativo Centro de Estudios de Población y Desarrollo*, 4 (June 1970), pp. 2–7.
NOTE: Part of the data are from 1968 and 1969.

In 1970 about 45 percent of hospital beds were in Lima. At that time the national ratio of hospital beds per 1,000 inhabitants was 2.3, but it rose to 5.1 in Lima-Callao; the range of ratios by departments grouped by regions was: Coast (1.2 to 5.4), Sierra (0.5 to 2.9, except Arequipa with 3.7), and Jungle (0.6 to 1.5). Physicians were also concentrated in the capital, the Coast, and the most populated cities. In 1970, 62 percent of the physicians were in Lima-Callao and another 28 percent in other cities with more than 20,000 inhabitants. The national ratio of physicians for 10,000 inhabitants was 4.8, but it rose to 15.9 in Lima; the range of ratios by departments grouped in regions was: Coast (1.8 to 6.2), Sierra (0.3 to 3.8, except Arequipa with 7.2), and Jungle (0.5 to 1.8). While there were 625 inhabitants per physician in Lima, there were 5 departments in the Sierra and 2 in the Jungle with 20,000 to 30,000 inhabitants per physician.[53]

The Inequality Effect of Social Security Stratification

In terms of social security inequalities, differences among occupational groups and geographical regions of Peru must be considered. Social security coverage of the economically active population in Peru is small, although it has increased rapidly from 25 percent in 1961 to 36 percent in 1969. The overall protection of the population is even smaller, 9 percent in 1961 and 12 percent in 1969.

The percentage distribution of the active insured in 1969 by major occupational groups was as follows: 40 percent blue-collars, 37 percent white-collars, 17 percent civil servants, 4 percent armed forces, and 2 percent self-employed (mainly taxi drivers). Although there are three times as many blue-collars as other salaried members of the labor force, the number of blue-collar insured is slightly more than one-third the number of other salaried insured. In 1965, while the military, civil servants, and white-collars were 100 percent protected (actually overprotected—many of them had more than one job), only half of the blue-collars were protected. Self-employed and unpaid family workers (with a combined number larger than the combined number of salaried and wage-earners) were protected by only 2 to 10 percent.

For the most part the unprotected blue-collars, self-employed, and unpaid family workers are concentrated in rural areas, engaged in agricultural work, and have the lowest income of the population. Those protected are mostly working in services (public and private), manufacturing, and mining, and have higher incomes than the noninsured.

In the four main occupational groups, the overall percentage contribution of the insured has been standardized, except for civil servants in the old system (who pay the highest) and the armed forces (who pay the lowest). The impact of this contribution on income distribution is not clear. The overall percentage contribution of the employer diminishes as the income of the group increases with a probable progressive effect in income distribution. Employers, however, pay the total cost for certain social security benefits of subgroups such as white-collars in large enterprises (until 1973), fishermen, and banking, electricity, mining, petroleum, sugar, and fish-flour workers. Part of the employers' contributions are transferred to the public through higher prices. The state pays all the expenditures of the health-maternity system of the armed forces. The state also contributes 2 percent of the salaries of blue-collars and 0.5 percent of the salaries of white-collars and civil servants for their health-maternity system; but in terms of actual revenue this difference is reduced by half, due to income differentials between the two groups. Besides, the state contribution has actually been paid only in exceptional cases. The state absorbs any deficit in the pension system of the armed forces and in both the old pension system and the lump sums for civil servants; it also contributes to the pension fund of taxi drivers the equivalent of 2 percent of their wages or income (many taxi drivers own their cars), but does not contribute at all to the pension system of blue- and white-collars. The state has also granted special taxes to the mutual insurance funds of taxi drivers, lawyers and judiciary secretaries, teachers, and jockeys. All these subgroups have incomes higher than those of the blue-collars and of a good number of white-collars and civil servants.

The noninsured (64 percent of the labor force and 88 percent of the population) contribute indirectly through taxes and higher prices to the social security systems of the small percentage insured. The bulk of the insured population (70 percent, comprised of blue- and white-collars) theoretically should receive a contribution from the state which seldom materializes, while small groups such as civil servants in the old system (about 8 percent), the armed forces (4 percent), taxi drivers (2 percent), lawyers, and teachers actually receive such a contribution. The net transfer of income from the large mass of noninsured and the bulk of the insured in the less privileged funds to the privileged funds is obvious.

In terms of the number of social security benefits available, the generosity of requirements to gain the right to such benefits, the number of the insureds' relatives with some social security protection, the basic salary used to compute the benefit, the amount of the benefit, the adjustment of pensions to the cost of living, and the compatibility of the pension with other pensions or salaried work, the armed forces (and especially the air force) have by far the best social security system in Peru. Next come privileged subgroups of civil servants such as teachers, the judiciary, Congress, diplomatic corps, and autonomous agencies, followed by civil servants under the old system. Subgroups of white-collars such as electricity, petroleum, mining, banking, and FEJEP (until 1973) rank higher than the SSE general system for white-collars and civil servants. Fishermen and taxi drivers seem to rank higher than the mass of blue-collars covered by SSO.

In 1969 the average disability pension under SSE was 22 times higher than that of SSO, while the average old-age and survivors' pensions under SSE and the taxi-driver fund were twice as high as that of SSO. The quality of hospital and medical care follows a similar pattern with the air force hospital at the top, followed by the rest of the armed-forces' facilities, then civil servants and white-collars, far below blue-collars (except those that have enterprise hospitals), and finally, at the bottom, state and public-charity hospitals.

In summary, the armed forces seem to have the best coverage, the most generous benefits, and the cheapest social security system, followed, in order, by civil servants, white-collar workers, and blue-collar workers. The higher the income of the group, the better its social security system seems to be.

Social security inequalities among the three geographic regions of Peru (Coast, Sierra, and Jungle) exist in coverage and in health facilities. The most developed region (and the one with the highest per-capita income) is the Coast, in which there is a high concentration of government, financing, commerce, industry, and fishing activities; most large cities are also located on the Coast. Well behind, both in development and per-capita income, is the Sierra whose main activities are agriculture, livestock, and mining, and where most Indians live. The Jungle, although rich in natural resources, is largely uninhabited; it is the least-developed region and the one with the lowest per-capita income.

The more developed a region, the better its social security coverage. In 1965, coverage of health-maternity and pensions on the Coast was, respectively, 16 and 17 percent; in the Sierra, 3 and 4 percent; and in the Jungle, 1 and 2 percent. In 1970, the ratio of hospital beds per 1,000 inhabitants and of physicians per 10,000 inhabitants was about 2 times higher on the Coast than in the Sierra and about 2 times higher in the Sierra than in the Jungle.

Differences of coverage and facilities among departments/provinces are more remarkable than among regions. The closest to Lima, the most populated and urbanized, and the wealthier department/provinces of the Coast have the highest coverage of their labor force, for example, Lima (65 percent), Ica (59 percent), La Libertad (57 percent), Callao (46 percent). Conversely, the least urbanized, poorest, Indian departments/provinces of the Sierra, and the most isolated and unpopulated departments/provinces of the Jungle have the lowest coverage of their labor force, for example, Amazonas (8 percent), San Martín (6 percent), Huancavelica (4 percent), Apurimac (2 percent). In 1970, Lima had 10 times more hospital beds per 1,000 inhabitants and as much as 50 times more physicians per 10,000 inhabitants than the poorest departments/provinces in the Sierra and the Jungle.

The massification of social security privileges has taken place on a small scale in Peru and only in recent times. In the early 1960s a good pension system, previously reserved for the most privileged funds, was finally passed for most blue- and white-collars. Under the old 1936–1941 legislation, blue-collar workers had pensions for old age and disability but the conditions were rigorous and the amount paid was very small. In 1969 the average old-age pension under the SSO new system was 4 times higher than under the old system. A blue-collar receiving a disability pension under the old system can now change it into an old-age pension under the new system, increasing its amount twofold. The gradual expansion of coverage has also increased social security costs. While the 1961 ratio of active vis-a-vis passive insured was 64 to 1, it declined in 1969 to 37 to 1. Wages of social security personnel in the 1960s rose twice as high as those of the insured in SSO and SSE, increasing social security costs.

The bulk of social security expenditures increased from 2.7 percent of GNP in 1961 to 3.3 percent in 1964 but probably declined somewhat in the rest of the 1960s. Nevertheless, in the 1970s, when the full impact of the new pensions will be felt and with the incorporation of large subgroups (such as domestic servants), the cost of social security will probably increase to well above 4 percent of GNP.

The financial situation of the privileged funds is sound or does not present any serious danger of bankruptcy. The deficits of the armed forces and the old civil servant systems are subsidized by the state. White-collars and civil servants under SSE enjoyed a surplus, at least until 1973. On the other hand, blue-collars under SSO had been left with the lowest income group of insured, because other blue-collars with higher incomes and more power had obtained independent funds or separate accounts or had been incorporated into SSE. Furthermore the SSO had gradually expanded its coverage to include even lower income groups of the population (e.g., domestic servants, newspaper vendors, some peasants) whose meager contributions were smaller than the average cost per insured in SSO. The failure of the state to pay its contributions to and repay its loans from SSO (together with the expansion of SSO coverage) resulted in a growing deficit. The 1973 unification of

SSO and SSE pension funds into the FNP left unclear at the time whether the revenue of these funds would eventually be merged. Initially both institutions were allowed to continue collecting their contributions separately. If such merger finally takes place, it will have a positive effect in terms of income distribution. It will also make more obvious the maintenance of a separate privileged system for the armed forces, the initiators of the process of unification and standardization in Peru.

5 The Case of Argentina

Historical Evolution of Social Security in Argentina Since Independence

Before Argentina proclaimed independence from Spanish rule in 1810, there existed *montepios* and *gracias* for the benefit of some citizens.[1]

1810–1914

Following the independence pronouncement in June 1810, the first pension was granted to a top government official. It reinitiated, in the post-revolutionary period, the *gracias* or gratuitous concession granted by the Argentine state that would continue until the present time. In the same year, all top civil servants became affiliated with the Montepío de Justicia y Real Hacienda (pensions for old age and disability) which until that point had covered only public officials working in the judiciary and the treasury.

In the period 1810–1820, Argentina suffered within the country from the absolute lack of continuity in governmental succession to power and outside from the Wars of Independence of Chile and Peru. Constitutional drafts were discussed in 1813, 1816, and 1819 but none was passed. In 1813 the General Assembly abolished slavery and Indian servitude. A statute enacted in 1815 recognized the obligation of the government to alleviate misery among the citizens, to provide for their education and well-being. The constitutional draft of 1819 stipulated that the state had to provide jobs and assistance to all citizens who requested them. An international agreement, signed with Chile in 1819, granted pensions to disabled veterans of the wars of independence. Three years later a law was enacted which set up the conditions to obtain pensions for veterans' survivors. In 1823 a Public Charity Board was founded which covered a wide range of social services (orphanages, orphans' schools, women's hospitals) to benefit the poor. The government sought to supervise all social service institutions.

After a period of political struggle over federal versus provincial government, a laissez-faire constitution was enacted in 1853, and with amendments made in 1860, 1898, and 1957, is still in force. The constitution stated that Congress would grant gratuitous concessions and the executive would grant old-age and survivors' pensions and sick leave.

The Conservative governments of Bartolomé Mitre (1862–1868) and Domingo Faustino Sarmiento (1868–1874), by emphasizing immigration and foreign investment, territorial expansion and railway construction, technological and industrial development, and increasing literacy and education, laid the foundations of modern Argentina. They granted social security protection to the small segment of the population employed in the central government (civil servants, judges, teachers), but ignored the needs of the masses of workers.

Sarmiento's successor to the presidency, Nicolás Avellaneda (1874–1880), introduced in 1877 the first national pension system supported by government revenue, granting old-age pensions to judges. President General Julio A. Roca (1880–1886 and 1898–1904) extended state financing to old-age pensions for public-school teachers (1885) and disability pensions for civil servants working in the central government (1886). Grave inflation in the late 1880s reduced the real wages of the workers, and, as inequalities in distribution became more acute, the discontent of the lower and middle classes grew.

In 1887 railroad and printing workers organized the first true national unions in Argentina. The railroad union, although it often resorted to strikes, was willing to negotiate with the employers and had, as a major goal, social security protection. Between 1880 and 1890 ten strikes broke out, three of them organized by railroad workers and the others by printers, construction workers, and shoemakers. In 1889 a new party, Unión Cívica (UC), was founded. It sought to end the domination of the country by the landed oligarchy. The party mainly appealed to the growing middle class and did not work seriously with the unions (until the late 1950s). In 1890 the new party led an insurrection which provoked the resignation of the president. UC then split into two factions: Unión Civical Radical (UCR)—headed by Hipólito Yrigoyen—and the old UC led by the aging Conservative Mitre, which soon reached an agreement with the Conservative, former President Roca. The Conservative party then became the National Autonomous party, and elected General Roca president again from 1898 to 1904.

Labor unrest and political activism increased significantly during this period. In 1896 there were 26 strikes by railroad, construction, maritime, and printing workers. The Argentine Socialist party was founded in 1896 by a Radical dissident, Juan B. Justo. The Socialist party got support from European immigrant workers concentrated in Buenos Aires and a small fraction of the middle class, mostly young people from the capital city. In practice, the party did very little work within the unions and failed to provide long-term effective leadership for the working class. (The Communist party, organized in 1918 as a split of the Socialists, never became a populist party either; it was sporadically divided by intraparty struggle and drew an insignificant proportion of votes in national elections.) After several attempts, beginning in 1890, Anarcho-Syndicalists and Socialists joined forces in 1901 to establish the first national workers' federation. Two years later the Socialists branched out and formed their own federation (Unión General de Trabajadores, UGT). In 1904 the Anarcho-Syndicalists changed the name of their organization to Federación Obrera Regional Argentina (FORA). The latter rejected both negotiations with employers and state intervention in labor matters.

Roca reacted against mounting union and political activism by enacting a law to deport all immigrants involved in disturbances, strikes, and union activities. However, some enlightened members of the oligarchy favored a policy of concession rather than repression, and in 1904 proposed an eight-hour work-day, six-day week, and restrictions on night, women's, and children's work; employer's compensation for occupational hazards; and governmental regulation of trade union activity, but this draft never became law. The only social security measure enacted by Roca was the creation, in 1904, of a national social security fund for all civil servants, including not only those working for the central government but also those employed by autonomous institutions and public enterprises. It also expanded the system of benefits providing pensions for old age, disability (total or partial, caused by occupational or nonoccupational hazards), and survivors. The fund was partly financed by employee's contributions. The railroad union requested a similar fund to protect its membership, but business opposition and governmental inertia blocked any progress in this direction.

In the last decade of Conservative rule (1905-1916), union activism continued to increase. Powerful national unions were founded by maritime workers, printers, and commercial employees. In 1909 the Socialist UGT joined a group of Syndicalist unions and organized a new federation (Confederación Obrera Regional Argentina, CORA). In 1914 CORA joined the Anarcho-Syndicalist controlled FORA, but the Syndicalists split a year later and established a second FORA. The Communists began to work within FORA with the goal of eventually controlling it. Roca's successors in the presidency tried to curb the increasing power of the unions through a new National Department of Labor and to placate the workers with palliatives, such as legislation regulating labor by children and women. But they were unsuccessful and the wave of strikes (mostly by railroad, maritime, and printing workers) reached new heights, in 1909 with a general strike, and in 1912 with a paralyzing railroad strike.

1915-1944

The violence of these years presumably convinced the oligarchy that minimal reforms were necessary to avoid a violent revolution. President Roque Saenz Peña (1910-1913) introduced universal suffrage, secret ballot, registration of voters, and compulsory voting and paved the way for the change in government four years later. The last of the Conservative presidents, Victorino de la Plaza (1913-1916), passed in 1915 (less than one year before the elections), the first two social security laws in favor of workers: old age, disability, and survivors' pensions for railroad workers (the blue-collar group that first became organized and launched strikes, and probably the strongest union pressure group at the time and the one most willing to negotiate); and protection against occupational accidents and diseases as well as safety requirements for workers in industry, construction, mining, transportation, and energy (precisely the best-organized and most active workers).

The Radicals (UCR), led by Yrigoyen, mobilized the middle class and part of the workers for the 1916 elections, and increased their proportion of votes from 18 percent in 1912 to 47 percent in 1916 and won a plurality.[2] The Radical Republic, which opened the way to power to the urban middle class, lasted only until 1930. Yrigoyen (1916-1922 and 1928-1930) responded basically to the interests of that class; although he permitted the flourishing of the unions and was generally sympathetic to labor, he resorted to repressive measures against Radical activists when he felt threatened and enforced no significant legislation in favor of the lower class.

Under Radical rule several national unions were organized among municipal blue-collar and streetcar workers, commercial employees, and railroad workers. Until the 1910s the labor movement was dominated by the Anarcho-Syndicalist revolutionary philosophy which rejected any kind of accommodation with the establishment. But in 1910 uncontrolled mobs attacked Anarcho-Syndicalist leaders, their union, and newspaper, and in 1919 the police severely repressed them. Dissatisfied with both the Anarcho-Syndicalist federation (FORA) and the Syndicalist federation (now called Unión Sindical Argentina, USA), the two railroad unions merged in 1926 into a new federation influenced by Socialists (Confederación Obrera Argentina, COA). In 1929 the Communists walked out of USA and founded their own federation (Comité de Unidad Clasista, CUC). Finally, in 1930, USA and COA merged into the largest confederation thus far organized in Argentina (Confederación General del Trabajo, CGT).

Yrigoyen passed social security legislation mainly benefiting those sectors of the middle class (e.g., white-collar employees) from which he received political support. In 1921 he established a fund for old-age, disability, and survivors' pensions for personnel working at various public utilities owned by foreign corporations (such as streetcar, telephone, telegraph, gas, electricity, radiotelegraphy, and buses), as well as for those working in hospitals and clinics. In 1922 he established a pension fund for employees of private and state banks, insurance and savings-and-loan associations. However, a fund proposed for commerce, industry, and merchant-marine workers and printers and journalists in 1928 was abolished before it became effective.

In 1930 the aging Yrigoyen, incapable of facing the grave problems linked with the depression, was overthrown by a military coup and for a decade the nation was governed by a coalition of conservatives and a split of the Radicals, constitutional in format, but with the military in control. Paternalistic General Agustín P. Justo (1932–1938) and liberal Roberto M. Ortiz (1938–1940) tolerated the expansion of the labor movement and passed some social security measures.

In this period two new important national unions were organized, a second one for commercial employees and one of construction workers. The CGT split in 1935 into two rival factions respectively led by Syndicalists and Socialists. One year later the Communist CUC was disbanded and their unions merged with the Socialist CGT which then became the strongest federation in Argentina. The two railroad unions made up about half of the Socialist CGT membership and were very influential. Trade unionism as practiced by the railroad was based on moderation and compromise; it had been successful in obtaining employers' concessions through collective bargaining and social security programs by exerting pressure upon the government. This model was gradually imitated by the majority of the unions. The Syndicalist CGT (USA again since 1939), although not giving up its ultimate goal of revolution, began to accept the idea of collective bargaining. Only the Anarcho-Syndicalist FORA remained faithful to the revolutionary ideal and rejected any type of compromise, but at the cost of losing influence. Another significant factor contributed to the change in philosophy and objectives of the labor movement. By the end of the 1930s, migration had long been halted and the new generation of Argentinians largely rejected Anarcho-Syndicalism (and to some extent Socialism and Communism also) as left-overs of the old generation. The trend away from revolutionary unions did not stop workers' militancy—700 strikes broke out between 1934 and 1943—but such action was more and more oriented to immediate gains.

Three major social security laws were passed in this period. In 1934 a maternity fund was established to pay a subsidy to female employees (in industry, commerce, and other selected activities) on temporary leave due to pregnancy. The fund was financed by employers, employees, and the state. A pension fund for journalists and printers granting old-age, disability, and survivors' pensions was created in 1939, although it was not set in motion until 1944. Finally, merchant-marine and civil airline employees were granted old-age, disability, and survivors' pensions in 1939.

1944–1954

In 1943 the military openly assumed power and established a brief provisional government. Under a situation of political instability, Colonel Juan Domingo Perón developed strong links with the unions and was appointed head of a newly created

Ministry of Labor and Social Security. His support from labor leaders increased as he sided with them in several labor conflicts. In early 1944 Perón became provisional vice-president and head of the important Ministry of War. In late 1945, however, when a military faction forced him to resign and then imprisoned him, a general strike was immediately called by the CGT (by then partly reunited and led by Peronist unions), and a demonstration was held to support Perón's prolabor stand. He was quickly returned to his posts, and in 1946 was elected president with 49 percent of the total vote. (Perón was reelected in 1951 with 62 percent of the vote.)

Perón (1946–1955) recognized labor as a powerful pressure group and designed a clever, successful strategy for using this force to keep his regime in power, adopting the doctrine of *justicialismo*. Allegedly a blend of the best of both capitalism and communism, its main goal was social justice. Perón supported workers' demands, initiated new programs in their favor, and sponsored the unionization of the majority of the labor force. But at the same time, he kept the labor movement almost completely under his own control and channeled its demands through the governmental apparatus. On the eve of Perón's accession to power, the labor movement had been divided into four federations: the Socialist-railroad CGT, the Communist CGT (a split of the former that occurred in 1942), the Syndicalist USA, and the Anarcho-Syndicalist FORA. The Communist federation was outlawed prior to Perón's takeover; he intervened in rebellious Socialist unions, outlawed the Anarcho-Syndicalist FORA, and won over the Syndicalist USA. (Perón deprived opposing union leaders of their posts, often sending them to prison or exile, and rewarded cooperative leaders with positions and payoffs.) By 1944 whatever remained of the four federations had merged into one CGT controlled by the Peronists. The right to strike was restricted, unions were forced to obtain legal recognition from the Ministry of Labor and Social Security, whose decisions were substituted for free collective bargaining. As a result, the labor movement became dependent on the government and the workers attributed their gains to Perón. He transferred the mass base of prolabor parties (Communist and Socialist) to his own Labor (and later Peronist) party.

Perhaps the most successful instrument in Perón's strategy was social security consecrated in the Justicialist constitution as one of the "Ten Rights of the Workers." Until Perón's rise to power, the Argentine social security system had provided pensions for a small segment of the labor force made up of civil servants, the military, some predominantly white-collar subgroups (employed in banking-insurance, public utilities, and news media) and a few powerful blue-collar subgroups (employed in railroads and the merchant marine). The bulk of the labor force was only partially protected against occupational accidents and diseases. Perón changed this situation dramatically in one decade (1944–1954) by expanding the coverage of pensions to most of the labor force: industrial, commercial, and rural workers (the latter organized in 1947 into a national union), policemen, and the self-employed. He also expanded the benefits of those subgroups that had already been protected when he assumed the presidency. Thus he considerably enlarged the pension system of the military, granted life insurance to civil servants, and introduced health care for those employed in the legislature, the judiciary, banking and insurance, railroads, and the merchant marine.

New legislation created a dozen social security funds which provided pensions (old age, disability, and survivors) for a similar number of subgroups. Interestingly, most of the earlier laws were addressed to the armed forces, probably not by mere coincidence: the maritime police, penitentiary police and personnel, and the federal police (1944); the police of national territories (regions dependent on the central government which did not have the status of provinces), the frontier police, and the armed forces (1946). Also covered in this first legislative wave were: commerce employees (1944) and industrial workers (1946). Finally, four additional subgroups were protected in 1954: rural workers (that is, permanent wage-earners in agriculture), self-employed workers, professionals, and entrepreneurs.

Four subgroups received health-care protection through ad-hoc programs supported by employers and employees: railroad workers (1944), maritime workers (1946), banking and insurance employees (1950), and legislators and the judiciary (1952). Perón also completed military hospitals, among the best in the country, which were financed by contributions from the beneficiaries and subsidized by the state. Many unions established mutual insurance funds to provide health care through union clinics and polyclinics, financing them by deductions from the beneficiaries' salaries and small fees. The system was completed with a network of state hospitals that provided free medical care to the whole population, financed mainly by budgetary allocations and partly by small fees paid by patients. Several public-charity hospitals and polyclinics to serve the poor were built by the Eva Perón Foundation, established in 1948 and headed by Mrs. Perón until her death. Civil servants did not receive an ad-hoc health program under Perón, but they were the only group which was granted compulsory life insurance in this period (1947).

Perón tried to cope with the proliferation of social security programs (particularly of pension funds) by creating a national institution in 1944 to eliminate social security inequalities: the Instituto Nacional de Previsión Social (INPS). The six civilian pension funds in existence at the time (civil service, railroad, public utilities, banking and insurance, journalist and printing, and merchant marine) and those civilian pension funds created by Perón immediately became associated with the INPS. In 1953, however, the trend towards unification was reversed: all the pension funds regained independence and autarchy, and the INPS' functions were limited to establishing guidelines, while control and supervision of the system was entrusted to the Ministry of Labor and Social Security. Supervision of the hospital network in turn fell to a newly created Ministry of Public Health.

The prolabor measures taken by Perón during his first term in office resulted in considerable income redistribution in favor of the lower stratum of the population. In his second term, however, the economy deteriorated under declining agricultural output and labor productivity, dwindling reserves, and domestic inflation, forcing Perón to reverse his previous policies and to stress the need for capital accumulation and increased labor productivity. At this point Perón sponsored the organization of a federation of capital and managerial forces, the Confederación General Económica (CGE), as the entrepreneurial counterpart of the CGT. The declining support of the labor movement, rising political opposition and two military revolts eventually ended his rule.

1955–1974

The military has dominated (openly or covertly) the politics of Argentina since Perón's fall, in a period of instability largely caused by the dissolution and proscription of the Peronist parties in 1955 when they still represented a plurality of the population. The military was able to thwart attempts by civilian presidents Frondizi (1958–1962) and Illia (1963–1966) to ease the proscription of Peronists. Throughout this period the government tried to coopt the labor leaders and exert control over the unions often by means of military intervention. The CGT split (in 1957, 1966, and 1968 to become reunited again in 1970), with a major faction remaining loyal to Peronism and other factions occasionally cooperating with the military. The labor movement's loss of independence under Perón and the divisive policy played by the military eroded even more the strength of labor. Nevertheless, labor remained one of the two factors of political power in Argentina, and often launched general strikes in an attempt to overthrow the regime. The policy of using social security concessions to coopt and placate several pressure groups continued. Yet, for the first time in Argentina, the government felt powerful enough to impose a program of social security unification and standardization.

In the period since 1955 there have been four main trends in social security: (1) expansion of coverage, particularly of pensions and workmen's compensation, to incorporate the few main groups which remained uninsured; (2) expansion of coverage in health care and life insurance to the bulk of the labor force; (3) introduction and rapid expansion of family allowances and other minor benefits; and (4) unification and standardization of most of the system.

In 1956, domestic servants were incorporated into the commercial fund and became eligible for old-age, disability, and survivors' pensions. Pension coverage was extended in 1971 to any person who was not covered by a pension fund, who did not have sufficient means of support, or who was either sixty years old or totally disabled.

In 1964 compulsory life insurance was established for rural workers, covering occupational disability and death. In 1971 coverage against occupational hazards was extended to every person working in dependency relationship (i.e., anyone working under the authority of another person for a salary or wage). Health care was expanded to incorporate the following groups: civil servants (1957), policemen and penitentiary personnel (1959), industry and commerce workers (1964), and rural workers and all pensioners (1971).

Family-allowance funds were established for workers in commerce and industry (1957), civil servants (1961), and longshoremen (1965). Furthermore, the commerce fund was expanded to incorporate all transportation workers (1959) and permanent rural workers (1964).[3] The old system of maternity subsidies, set up in 1934 for part of the female labor force, was transformed in 1968 into a universal, paid maternity leave: the insured now receives a salary throughout her ninety-day leave. Two additional benefits introduced in this period were an unemployment fund for construction workers (1967) and funeral aid, paid by employers, for all those insured (1969).

The movement towards unification had been revived in 1957, under General Pedro E. Aramburu (1955–1958), with the reestablishment of the 1853 Constitution with some amendments, one aimed at unification of the social security system. A Social Security Plan was prepared in 1963 by a governmental agency, and a Social Security Program and a Draft for a Social Security Code elaborated in 1966 by a private institution.[4] Not until 1967, during the autocratic government of General Juan Carlos Onganía (1966–1970), was the law passed which put the unification process in motion. As part of the reform, the INPS was dissolved and a new Secretary of Social Security (under the also new Ministry of Social Welfare) was made responsible for the administration and supervision of the social security system outside the armed forces, including pensions, family-allowances, and unemployment, maternity, and occupational hazards. A newly created National Council of Social Security was to advise on the technical problems arising from the unification process.

Twelve pension funds were merged into three decentralized, semiautonomous funds: (1) the blue- and white-collar pension fund (Caja Nacional de Previsión de la Industria, Comercio y Actividades Civiles) unified six funds: industry, commerce, rural, banking-insurance, merchant marine, and journalist-printers; (2) the civil-servant pension fund (Caja Nacional de Previsión para el Personal del Estado y Servicios Públicos) unified three funds: civil servants (including judges and public teachers), public utilities, and railroad workers; (3) the self-employed pension fund (Caja Nacional de Previsión para Trabajadores Autónomos) unified three funds: self-employed workers, professionals, and entrepreneurs. (Funds left out of the unification process were those covering the military and the police: federal, maritime, territorial, frontier, and penitentiary.) Each of the three unified funds is still in charge of affiliation, accounting, archives, and processing of benefits. (Collection of contributions and payment of benefits is done through the central bank.) Upon completion of the unification process, the number of employees of the twelve previous funds had been reduced from 3,700 to 2,500 through transfers, dismissals, and retirement.

Two new laws, enacted in 1968, standardized the legislation of the unified pension funds: one for "personnel in dependency relationship," which is applied equally to the blue- and white-collar fund and to the civil-servant fund, and the other for the self-employed fund. (The uniform regulations for workers in dependency relationship were adopted in 1970–1971 by eight provinces, while the uniform regulations for self-employed workers were adopted in 1970–1972 by two provinces.) The coordination of health and other social services was entrusted to the Public Health Secretariat of the Ministry of Social Welfare and the National Institute of Social Works (INOS) created in 1970. INOS is also linked to the ministry and financed by employers' and workers' contributions. Finally the benefits and employer contributions in the family-allowances system were standardized in 1969 for commerce, industry, and longshoremen. The unification process culminated in the insertion, for the first time in Argentina, of a social security section in a medium-range planning document. The National Development Plan for 1971–1975 set as the ultimate social security goal: "the gradual implementation of an integral system." This means that protection should be expanded to all of the labor force for most risks.[5]

The main flaw of the unification process was that it left out the systems of the military and the police. It is interesting to quote the justifications for this exclusion given by the preliminary technical report that preceded the process of unification. The report started with a quote from the Inter-American Committee of the Alliance for Progress: "Technicians cannot recommend social security reforms that would disturb the political tranquility of the nation." Then the report elaborated on the exclusion: "A practical review of the problem shows that these systems [the armed forces] have peculiar characteristics and a long entrenchment which earns them the right to continue as separate entities from the unified national social security system."[6]

In 1973, in a period of continuously rising inflation, deterioration of real wages, increasing opposition of the labor movement, general discontent of the middle class, political struggle and waves of urban insurrection, the aging Perón returned to the presidency. He launched a social security program aimed at universality (coverage of all the population), integrality (protection against all social risks), unification, and standardization. The program stressed the need for "reviewing those social security funds that involve privileges favoring specific occupational groups," and proposed "the establishment of one social security fund, maintaining separate accounts for the different benefits to be granted." The program also prescribed the organization of a top social security institution with absolute administrative and financial autarchy to coordinate and supervise the various funds. This institution would be administered by representatives from labor, the employers, and the government.[7] Perón's program continued, at least on paper, the trend towards unification of the social security system initiated by the military in 1967. Nonetheless, the change from an autocratic to a relatively democratic system and the problems that Perón faced in maintaining a balance of power (in which labor played a crucial role) prevented the implementation of such a program, thus repeating the Chilean experience under Allende. With Perón's death in 1974 and the brief stay in power of his wife and former vice-president, María Estela Martínez de Perón, the fragmentation of the Argentine society became more acute, making impossible the total unification and standardization of the social security system and generating a new military intervention.

The evolution of the Argentine social security system may be divided into four stages (see table 5-1). In the first century of the republic (1810–1914), pensions were available only for the military, civil servants, and special groups such as the judiciary and public teachers. In the next thirty years (1915–1944) pension coverage was expanded to include strong union pressure groups in railroads, public utilities, banks, insurance, news media, printing, merchant marine, and commercial airlines. In addition, protection against occupational accidents and diseases was introduced to cover workers in industry, construction, mining, transportation, and energy. In the next ten years (1944–1954) under Perón, the foundations of modern social security were laid, expanding the pension system to cover most of the labor force—that is, those employed in commerce, industry and agriculture, various branches of the police (the military improved their system), self-employed workers, professionals, and entrepreneurs. Also in this period a few powerful groups received health care (the military, railroad and maritime workers, banking and insurance employees, legislators, and the judiciary), while civil servants were granted life insurance. Finally, the coordination of social security began with the creation of the INPS in 1944, but in 1953 when Perón's power was already declining, the movement was reversed. In the last twenty years (1955–1974), from the ousting to the return and death of Perón, four different trends may be traced in social security: (1) expansion of coverage of major benefits to the few subgroups left uninsured and protection against occupational hazards to the whole labor force; (2) expansion of health care and life insurance coverage to the bulk of the labor force; (3) granting new minor benefits to powerful subgroups; and (4) the partial unification and standardization of the social security system. The 1973 social security program endorsed by Perón stressed universality, integrality, unification, and standardization. These goals were not achieved due to the political situation faced by Perón and his successor and the need to keep the support of several powerful pressure groups.

The Role of Pressure Groups in Social Security Stratification

Four main pressure groups (each with various subgroups) have been instrumental in the evolution of social security stratification: (1) the military (with policemen as a subgroup); (2) civil servants (with judges and public teachers as subgroups); (3) blue- and white-collars (with the following subgroups: railroad, maritime, banking and insurance, commerce, industry, printing and rural workers, and domestic servants); and (4) self-employed workers, professionals, and entrepreneurs.

For more than one-third of its republican life, Argentina has been ruled by the military, either overtly or covertly, with their power concentrated at the beginning of

the republic and since 1930. Under colonial rule, the military received the first survivor pension program in Argentine history, the *montepío militar* of 1773 which was
expanded in 1775 and 1801. The first social security law passed by the new republic
(1819) granted pensions to disabled veterans of the wars of independence. Then, for
more than a century when civilian governments held power, the military did not
receive any significant addition to their system. It was General Perón, needing the
armed forces to support his regime, who in 1946–1950 resumed the protection of this
group. In the first two years of his rise to power, he introduced pensions for five types
of policemen: federal, local, maritime, territorial, and frontier. As president, he also
enlarged and substantially improved the pension system for the three military
branches and built an excellent hospital network for their use. In 1958–1959 General
Aramburu granted health care to the police, and in 1969 General Onganía completed the protection of the group by including both the police and the military in the
general system of funeral aid. The social security programs of the armed forces have
been excluded from the process of unification and standardization which, paradoxi-
cally, were initiated and consolidated under the military regimes of Generals Onganía and Lanusse from 1967 to 1973. Civilian governments have not given any
significant social security benefits to the armed forces.

The second pressure group is made up of civil servants, judges, and public-
school teachers. This group has received practically all its social security protection
from military governments. In 1803, still under colonial rule, the judiciary and the
treasury became the second subgroup in the nation to be protected by a *montepío*
and the first to get old-age and disability pensions. The *montepío civil* was expanded
in 1810 to include top civil service officials. After 50 years of struggle, the consolidation of the unitarian government led to the development of a strong central administration and this, in turn, to the protection of the public bureaucracy. The first national
pension fund, with financial help from the state, was granted to the judiciary by
Avellaneda in 1877 (the only civilian who enacted a significant social security law in
favor of this group), thus repeating the colonial example. The emphasis both in
education and in the expansion of "civilization" to the southwest probably moved
General Roca, in 1885, to establish another pension fund, this one for teachers. In
1886 Roca created another pension fund for civil servants and in 1904 improved and
expanded it to cover all employees of the central government, autonomous institutions, and state enterprises. The next forty years saw mostly civilian governments,
either of Conservative or Radical affiliation, which did not pass any significant law in
favor of the civil-servant group. The military intervention of 1943 broke the legislative
freeze and generated a wave of social security regulations to protect this group: in
1944 pensions for disability and survivors to the judiciary; in 1947 life insurance (the
first in the country) for civil servants; in 1952, health care for the judiciary and
legislators; in 1957 health care for civil servants; in 1969 improved family allowances;
and in 1970–1971 provincial civil servants were incorporated into the standardized
pension system (almost one century after civil servants employed by the central
government).

In Argentina we do not find the sharp division between blue- and white-collar
workers which is typical of other South American countries such as Chile and Peru.
The division, as in the case of Uruguay, is among three major subgroups: the so-
called "labor aristocracy," the mass of the urban labor force, and rural workers and
domestic servants.

The first subgroup is made up of skilled blue-collars, mostly employed in transpor-

Table 5-1
Significant Social Security Legislation in Argentina: 1801–1972

Year	President	Type of Coverage	Group Protected
1801	Arredondo (viceroy)	Pensions (survivors')	Army (navy since 1785)
1803	Arredondo (viceroy)	Pensions (old age, disability)	Civil servants (originally only for judiciary and treasury, expanded in 1810 to all top officials)
1819–1822	Rondeau (m) (Supreme Director)	Pensions (disability, survivors')	Military (veterans of wars of independence)
1877	Avellaneda (c)	Pensions (old age)	Judiciary
1885	Roca (m)	Pensions (old age, disability)	Public-school teachers
1886	Roca (m)	Pensions (old age, disability)	Civil servants (central government)
1904	Roca (m)	Pensions[a]	Civil servants (central government, autonomous institutions, state enterprises)
1915	de la Plaza (c)	Pensions[a]	Railroad workers
1915	de la Plaza (c)	Occupational accidents and diseases	Industry, mining, energy, construction, and transportation
1921	Yrigoyen (c)	Pensions[a]	Public utilities, hospitals
1922	Yrigoyen (c)	Pensions[a]	Banks, insurance
1934	Justo (m)	Maternity (lump sum)	Women employed in industry, commerce, and home work
1939	Ortiz (c)	Pensions[a]	Journalists, printing workers
1939	Ortiz (c)	Pensions[a]	Merchant marine, commercial airlines
1944	Ramírez (m)	Pensions[a]	All judges
1944	Perón (m)	Pensions[a]	Commercial employees, maritime and federal police, penitentiary personnel
1944–1946	Perón (m)	Health	Railroad workers, maritime personnel
1946	Perón (m)	Pensions[a]	Industrial workers and territorial and frontier police
1946–1950	Perón (m)	Pensions[a], health (hospitals)	Military (army, navy, air force)
1947	Perón (m)	Life insurance	Civil servants (including teachers)
1950–1952	Perón (m)	Health	Banking and insurance, legislators and judiciary

Year	President	Type of Coverage	Group Protected
1954	Perón (m)	Pensions[a]	Rural workers, self-employed, professionals, entrepreneurs
1956	Aramburu (m)	Pensions (old age, disability)	Domestic servants
1957	Aramburu (m)	Family allowances	Commercial employees, industrial workers
1957–1959	Aramburu (m)	Health	Civil servants (including teachers), policemen and penitentiary personnel
1959	Frondizi (c)	Family allowances	Transportation workers, banking-insurance (included in commerce)
1961	Frondizi (c)	Family allowances	Civil servants
1964	Illia (c)	Life insurance	Permanent rural workers
1964	Illia (c)	Health, life insurance	Commerce (including domestic service) and industry (collective bargaining)
1964–1965	Illia (c)	Family allowances	Permanent rural workers (included in commerce), longshoremen
1967	Onganía (m)	Unemployment	Construction
1968	Onganía (m)	Maternity (paid leave of absence)	All working women
1968	Onganía (m)	Pensions[a]	All workers in dependency relationship and self-employed
1969	Onganía (m)	Funeral aid	All workers in dependency relationship
1970–1971	Lanusse (m)	Pensions[a]	Provinces
1971	Lanusse (m)	Pensions (old age, disability)	All noninsured
1971	Lanusse (m)	Occupational hazards	All workers in dependency relationship
1971	Lanusse (m)	Health	Rural workers, pensioners

SOURCE: Legislative information compiled by the author.
NOTE: (m) = military; (c) = civil.
a Old age, disability and survivors' pensions.

tation (railroads, merchant marine, airlines), and white-collars employed in public utilities—electricity, gas, telephone, finance—banking and insurance, and the news media. All these occupations are highly unionized and influential. (In 1964, the highest degree of unionization in Argentina was registered in three occupational groups: public utilities, 79 percent; transportation, 66 percent; and banking and insurance, 65 percent.)[8] Railroad workers organized the first national union of the country, which launched its first strikes in the 1880s, and escalated their activism, reaching a peak in 1912 with a general strike that paralyzed the country. They initiated in Argentina a pattern of negotiation with both employers and the state in order to obtain concessions in social security among other things. (This model was later imitated throughout the labor movement.) Under these pressures railroad workers were granted in 1915 the first pension fund within the private sector. In the same year protection against occupational hazards was granted to segments of the labor force, among them transportation workers. The electoral victory of the Radicals in 1916 opened the door to the middle class. In 1921, Yrigoyen gave a pension fund to employees— predominantly white-collars—in public utilities; these were mostly owned by foreign corporations which earned good profits and were capable of partly financing these pensions. One year later it was the turn of white-collars employed in banking and insurance who probably had the backing of the strong commerce federation established in 1922. Printing workers had become organized and launched their first strikes in the 1890s, while merchant-marine unions became active in the early 1900s. Both obtained pensions funds in 1939 under the liberal government of Ortiz. Railroad workers were the first to receive a health-care program (not only within the private sector but in the nation as a whole), under Perón in 1944; they were rapidly followed by maritime workers (1946) and banking and insurance employees (1950). Bank employees were the first to be granted bonuses for children (1939); they were followed by journalists (1943), railroad workers (1944), and insurance employees (1945); transportation workers were the second in the nation (1959) to obtain a full-fledged system of family allowances.

The second major subgroup embraces the bulk of the urban labor force made up of skilled and semiskilled blue-collars in rising economic activities such as industry (e.g., textiles, metallurgy, construction) and white-collars employed in expanding activities such as commerce. (In 1964 manufacturing and commerce had, respectively, 42 and 31 percent of their workers unionized, ranking fourth and fifth in terms of degree of unionization.) In the 1940s and early 1950s, under the influence of war and post-war economic booms, industrial and commercial activities rapidly expanded and so did the influence of their unions. Perón took advantage of this trend, encouraged the demands of these workers, and made them a strong pillar for his retention of power. In exchange he granted them certain concessions such as pension funds in the mid-1940s. (Before Perón, the only protection received by this subgroup had been, in 1915, insurance against occupational hazards but commerce was excluded.) Industry and commerce workers became, in 1957 under Aramburu, the first to receive family allowances in Argentina. In 1964, under Illia, both subgroups received health care and life insurance through collective agreements.

The third subgroup, made up of rural workers and domestic servants, has little power because of their poor organization, dispersion, and the nonstrategic nature of their trades. Of the two, rural workers are more influential, but their national federation was not organized until 1947. (In 1964, unionization among rural workers was only 5 percent, making this group the next-to-the-least unionized in the nation.) Permanent, salaried workers in agriculture received pensions in 1954, life insurance and family allowances in 1964, and protection against occupational hazards and health care in 1971. Domestic servants were the last to receive pensions (1956) and these were only for old age and disability. Except for limited protection against occupational hazards, they are not eligible for any other benefits.

The last group to be protected by a social security system and whose protection is the poorest is the self-employed—workers, professionals, and entrepreneurs. Their pension program, established in 1954, lacks family allowances, life insurance, funeral aid, and health care. Part of this subgroup (e.g., most professionals and entrepreneurs) have medium or high incomes and therefore can afford to buy protection through commercial insurance and private clinics. However, most insured in the subgroup of self-employed workers have low incomes and are in need of better protection. They are not unionized and are hence unable to exert any pressure to get adequate social security protection. Since insurance coverage for the rural and urban self-employed is difficult to enforce, it is not surprising that this subgroup, particularly those in agriculture, constitutes one of the largest uninsured segments of the labor force. The rest of the noninsured group is made up of unpaid family workers, temporary wage-earners in agriculture, and the unemployed.

A good summary of the different factors behind the inception of social security funds in Argentina is offered by an official publication of the social security administration:

> The creation of the early pension funds [until 1944] was the result of intensive union activism. The economic strength, degree of solidarity and activism of the unions were factors that shaped the fragmentation of the social security system along occupational lines. This explains the autonomy, financial self-sufficiency and unique conditions and benefits of each fund. [More recently] the creation of funds has been not as much the result of union activism but of the government initiative to extend social security coverage to the wide unprotected sectors of the labor force.[9]

Current Structure and Organization of the System

There is no single legislative body regulating the social security system of Argentina, nor is there an overall legislative compilation but only partial compilations for some sectors. (The legislation dealing with the armed forces is not compiled and is difficult to obtain.) There are 10 national social security funds (6 for pensions, 3 for family allowances, and 1 for unemployment compensation), each with its own regulations for administration, financing, and benefits. All of these funds are public, but some are centralized while others are decentralized, and some are autonomous while others are semiautonomous. They embrace one or several occupational subgroups which, in some cases, have, in turn, special regulations. In addition to the funds, there are various state institutions (dealing with health care, occupational hazards, social welfare, life insurance) and numerous mutual insurance funds as well as union programs regulated by collective agreements In practically all provinces (and in many municipalities) there are also funds (a total of about sixty), although these are gradually adopting the standardized regulations applicable to the national funds.[10] In spite of obvious complexity, when we compare the Argentine system with those of other countries (e.g., Chile), it appears that the former, particularly since the late 1960s, has become increasingly standardized and unified.

There is no single state agency entrusted with planning, coordination, and/or supervision of the whole system. The National Development Council (CONADE) prepares guidelines or sectorial plans for public health (mostly state hospitals) and social security. The power to enforce these guidelines or plans is small, although it is increasing mainly through budgetary control. The General Comptroller audits part of the system.

Two main groups may be distinguished in the social security system: the civil sector and the armed forces. The civil sector (National Social Security System) is centered around the Ministry of Social Welfare which has two main executive branches, one dealing with monetary programs (the Social Security Secretariat) and another with health programs (the Public Health Secretariat).[11] See figure 5-1.

The Social Security Secretariat coordinates and supervises five programs:

(a) Pensions, for which there are two standardized (or uniform) sets of regulations, one for salaried employees and wage-earners (personnel in dependency relationship) and another for all the self-employed. The former has two separate funds: the civil-servant fund and the blue- and white-collar pension fund. The self-employed have a single set of regulations and a single fund. The National Bureau for the Collection of Social Security Contributions, a division of the Secretariat, collects social security contributions for the three unified pension funds and supervises their finances; it also coordinates all provincial pension funds. By the end of 1973, eight of the provinces had adopted the standardized national regulations for personnel in dependency relationship and two provinces the standardized regulations for self-employed.

(b) Protection against occupational hazards, through the state insurance agency, commercial insurance companies, or the self-insured employer.

(c) Family allowances, for which there are three funds—for commercial employees (including transportation and rural workers), industrial workers, and longshoremen.

(d) Unemployment compensation, for which there is only one fund, that of construction workers.

(e) Life insurance, for which civil servants, commerce employees, rural workers, and other subgroups are eligible, through the National Savings and Insurance Fund. The National Council for Social Security sets overall guidelines for the whole civil sector, and four bureaus coordinate the system, supervise its finances and administration, and provide technical and legal aid.

The Public Health Secretariat directly administers the state hospital network (there are also provincial and municipal hospitals) whose services are usually free to the population. The Secretariat also supervises private hospitals. A decentralized agency of the Ministry of Social Welfare, the INSSPJP, directly administers the health care program for old-age and survivor pensioners and their dependents. Another decentralized agency, the INOS, is in charge of planning, coordination and control of finances, and administration of all the health programs of the civil sector. This includes the INSSPJP, union clinics, and mutual insurance programs. Some unions have their own clinics and health services financed through deductions from the beneficiaries' salaries, employers' contributions, and small charges to patients. There are numerous mutual insurance funds organized by specific occupations or trades to provide health care at low prices to their affiliates.

The armed-forces group is independent from the National Social Security System (civil sector), has been completely excluded from the process of social security unification and standardization, and is only loosely supervised by the General Comptroller. The Ministry of Interior coordinates the social security programs for the police, and the Ministry of Defense for the military.

The organization of the social security system, clustering it around the various occupational groups can be seen in figure 5-1.

FIGURE 5-1

Administrative Structure of Social Security in Argentina: 1972

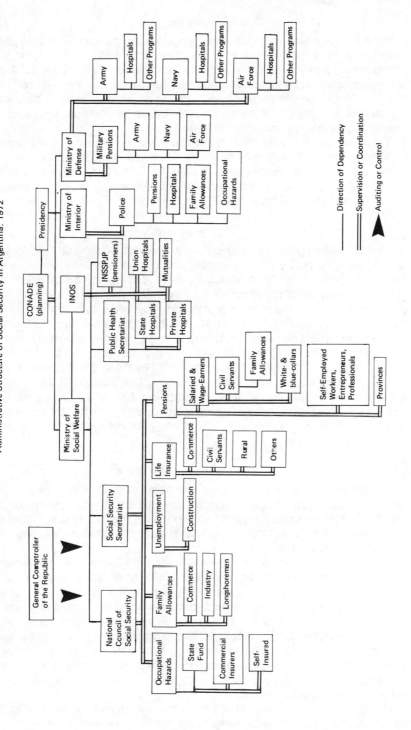

——— Direction of Dependency

═══ Supervision or Coordination

▲ Auditing or Control

Armed Forces

There are two main subgroups of the armed-forces: the military and the police. The military subgroup (made up of three branches: army, navy, and air force) includes: (a) the military pension fund with sections for the three main branches; (b) the system of hospitals of the armed forces (several hospitals for each of the three branches—as many as 96 for the army alone) providing preventive and curative care; (c) family allowances paid by the employer; (d) unemployment compensation fund; and (e) special regulations on occupational hazards.

The police subgroup (embracing federal, maritime, territorial, and frontier police and penitentiary personnel) includes: (a) the police pension fund; (b) health services which provide preventive and curative care; (c) family allowances paid by the employer; (d) indemnification for dismissal paid by the employer; and (e) special regulations for occupational hazards.

Civil Servants

The civil-servant group includes state civil servants, public-utility employees, state railroad workers, public-school teachers, and the judiciary. The last two subgroups as well as elective officials and diplomats enjoy special regulations. Personnel working in the office of the president are excluded from this group and covered by the police pension fund. The group is protected by the following programs: (a) pensions through the civil-servant fund and the standardized regulations for personnel in dependency relationship; (b) health care through their respective mutual insurance funds or union clinics (e.g., for railroad, legislators, judiciary, civil servants); (c) family allowances and maternity leave of absence paid by the employer; (d) indemnification for dismissal, also paid by the employer; and (e) compensation payments for occupational hazards paid by the state insurance agency or directly by the employer. Active and retired state personnel have collective life insurance (through the National Savings and Insurance Fund); it is compulsory for the former and optional for the latter.

Blue- and White-Collar Workers

The pension system for blue- and white-collar workers is also the standaridized one for salaried personnel and wage-earners, but this group is covered by a separate fund which includes all dependent workers in the following activities: industry, commerce, banking, insurance, merchant marine, journalism, printing, domestic service, and agriculture.

Family allowances are administered by three funds: (a) Commerce, which covers mostly white-collars (and some blue-collars) in commerce, banking, insurance, merchant marine, journalism, and printing; (b) Industry, which covers mostly blue-collars in private industry, transportation, and permanent rural workers; and (c) Longshoremen. (In addition, there is a maternity leave of absence, which covers all women working in a dependency relationship with ten months of service, paid by the employer.) Family allowances in Commerce and Industry are paid directly by the employer with their respective funds operating as compensation funds. The Longshoremen's Fund collects the employers' contributions, administers its own resources, and grants benefits.

The group also receives: health care through numerous union hospitals and mutual insurance programs; protection against occupational hazards through commercial insurance or the employer's self-insurance (there is a special reserve fund in case of the employer's insolvency); and indemnification for dismissal paid by the employer. Construction workers are the only ones with an unemployment compensation fund. Commerce employees, rural workers, and other subgroups are eligible for compulsory life insurance through the National Savings and Insurance Fund.

Self-Employed

Self-employed workers (including public vendors), professionals, and entrepreneurs are under the standardized pension regulations for the self-employed pension fund. They are not eligible for family allowances, other than pension cash benefits or health care, although they have access to public hospitals or private clinics.

Noninsured

The noninsured in Argentina include the richest and the poorest. The latter are mainly the unemployed, part of the self-employed farmers, seasonal rural wage-earners, a segment of domestic workers, and most unpaid family workers for whom the social security legislation is either not applicable or has not been enforced. That does not mean that this group is completely devoid of protection. The wealthy noninsured personally pay for medical attention in private hospitals, while the poor receive medical attention provided free (or for a small charge) by the state hospitals.

Inequalities of the System

The inequalities in the social security system in Argentina are mostly vertical or based on occupation, that is, among the pressure groups and subgroups already identified. In addition, there are horizontal inequalities among geographical regions to be described below. Only scarce data is available on income differences among occupational groups and geographical regions which might affect social security inequalities.

The only information available on income distribution is provided by a study of the United Nations Economic Commission for Latin America (ECLA) using 1961 data. Although the income strata in the ECLA study do not match exactly the social security groups and subgroups identified here, we can define the following income groups.[12] The high-income stratum of the population is partly made up of professionals and entrepreneurs (in industry, transportation, commerce, and agriculture). The medium-income stratum consists of salaried employees and wage-earners ranked as follows: banking and insurance, part of industry (salaried, skilled blue- and white-collars), public utilities, mining (part of which is covered by the former industrial fund), transport (most of which is covered by the former railroad and merchant-marine funds), civil servants, small-scale entrepreneurs, commerce, industry (wage-earners), and construction (the latter covered by the former industrial fund). When a weighted average of the average income of all workers in the industrial fund (salaried and waged in industry, mining, and construction) is estimated, the industrial subgroup is ranked at the bottom of the middle-income stratum. The low-income stratum is comprised of those working in "other services" (part self-employed workers and part wage-earners), rural workers (and fishermen, some of whom are covered by the former industrial fund), and domestic servants.

Members of the high-income stratum of the distribution have average incomes which are from 6.2 to 10.7 times the average income of domestic servants (1.0 at the bottom of the scale). In the medium-income stratum, incomes range from 2.5 to 5.0 times those of the bottom income stratum. In the low-income stratum, incomes range from 1.0 to 1.7 times those of the bottom. Although there are no comparable data for the armed forces in 1961, thirteen years later their average income was 3.1 times the minimum income of salaried employees and wage-earners (corresponding to the medium-income stratum of the ECLA study).[13]

The above ranking indicates that:

(1) Two social security subgroups of the self-employed (professionals and entrepreneurs) are in the high-income stratum; one subgroup (small-scale entrepreneurs) in the middle-income stratum; and one subgroup ("other services") in the low-income stratum.

(2) The bulk of the blue- and white-collar group is in the middle-income stratum. Within it, the "labor aristocracy" (banking-insurance, public utilities, transportation) together with salaried industrial workers and probably the armed forces, are at the top; civil servants and commerce are in the middle; and wage-earning industrial and all construction workers are at the bottom.

(3) The subgroups of rural workers and domestic servants are in the low-income stratum.

In 1966 the country was divided into the following eight regions for the purpose of planning and development: (1) Metropolitan (Federal Capital); (2) Pampa (provinces of Buenos Aires, Entre Ríos, and Santa Fé); (3) Center (provinces of La Rioja, Córdoba, and San Luis); (4) Northwest (provinces of Jujuy, Catamarca, Salta, Santiago del Estero, and Tucumán); (5) Cuyo (provinces of Mendoza and San Juan); (6) Patagonia (provinces of Chubut, Santa Cruz, and Tierra del Fuego); (7) Comahue (provinces of Neuquén, La Pampa, and Río Negro); and (8) Northeast (provinces of Chaco, Formosa, Corrientes, and Misiones).[14]

The Metropolitan region covers 0.005 percent of the total national territory and has 14.8 percent of the population which is 100 percent urban. This tiny territory is, however, the center for government administration, financing, commerce, and services, and a good part of industry. In terms of degree of industrialization (industrial contribution to the regional output) and per-capita production, the region ranks second; in terms of contribution to the national GDP, it ranks first. This region includes the city of Buenos Aires (the Federal Capital), the most populated city of the nation.

The Pampa region comprises 9.8 percent of the national territory and has 47.1 percent of the population, 81.9 percent of which is urban. It is the richest region of the country in terms of natural resources; its fertile soil has supported remarkable agricultural development, the fishing industry is also well developed, and the region includes most of the ports of the country (e.g., Rosario, Paraná, Santa Fé). The Pampa has the highest degree of industrialization, ranks second in contribution to the national GDP, and third in per-capita production. It includes five of the ten most populated cities of the nation: Rosario, La Plata, Paraná, Santa Fé, and Bahía Blanca.

The Center region covers 8.9 percent of the national territory and has 10.3 percent of its population, 65.2 of which is urban. It supplies almost half of the national hydroelectric energy, is also rich in livestock, and contains most of the automobile industry in its province of Córdoba. This region ranks third in both degree of industrialization and contribution to the national GDP and sixth in per-capita production. It has one of the ten most populated cities: Córdoba.

The Northwest region represents 12.4 percent of the national territory, with 10.4 percent of its population, 48.5 percent of which is urban. Its main products are sugar, metals, natural gas, and petroleum. It ranks fourth in both degree of industrialization and in contribution to the GDP and the seventh in per-capita production. It has two of the ten most populated cities: Tucumán and Salta.

Cuyo has 6.3 percent of the national territory and 5.9 percent of the population, 61.1 percent of which is urban. The main products of this region are wine, petroleum, and olives. It ranks fifth in degree of industrialization, in contribution to the GDP, and in per-capita production. It has none of the ten most populated cities.

Patagonia embraces 39.1 percent of the national territory, the least populated region (0.9), 55.5 percent of which is urban. It holds 100 percent of the national reserves of coal and almost half of the petroleum; it is a chief producer of wool. It ranks sixth in degree of industrialization and eighth in the contribution to the GDP, but it ranks first in per-capita production due to its enormous energy resources and small population. It has none of the ten most populated cities.

Comahue has 13.9 percent of the national territory, with 2.5 percent of the population, 57.8 percent of which is urban. Its main natural resources are wheat, sheep, natural gas, and petroleum. It is the least industrialized region (eighth), ranks seventh in contribution to the GDP and fourth in per-capita production. It has none of the ten most populated cities.

The Northeast has 9.0 percent of the national territory, with 8.1 percent of the population, being the least urbanized region (38.8 percent). Its main products are fruits, cotton, tobacco, and wood. It ranks seventh in degree of industrialization, sixth in contribution to the national GDP, and eighth (last) in terms of per-capita production. It has one of the ten most populated cities: Corrientes.

An overall ranking of the eight regions, taking into account variables such as degree of industrialization, contribution to the GDP, per-capita production, urban percentage of the population, number of most populated cities, and availability of natural resources gives the following results: the Metropolitan region ranks first, closely followed by La Pampa; next comes the Center, with Northwest and Cuyo lagging behind; finally Patagonia, with Comahue and Northeast at the bottom.

Differences among provinces are significant also. Per-capita production in the Patagonian territory of Tierra del Fuego is 10 times that of the northeastern province of Misiones. La Pampa, the Federal Capital, and Buenos Aires have a per-capita production level nearly 4 times that of Misiones. The provinces of Santa Fé, Mendoza, and Río Negro average 3 times the per-capita production of Misiones. Córdoba, Jujuy, and San Juan have a per-capita production about 2½ times that of Misiones. The remaining half of the provinces have per-capita production levels that average 1½ times that of Misiones.[15]

Data on income distribution by regions and provinces in Argentina are scarce. The 1961 ECLA study includes data on income distribution only in agriculture and its cluster of regions differs from mine. ECLA's ranking of regions according to their income in agriculture places the Metropolitan and Pampa regions (and one province from the Center) at the top, followed by Patagonia, then Northwest and Northeast (with one province from the Center), and, finally, Cuyo and Comahue (with one province from the Pampa region and another from the Center).[16] In the absence of adequate data, we assume that the regions are ranked, in terms of income, in an order similar to that of development.

Coverage

Table 5-2 shows the overall maximum coverage in pensions of the Argentinian social security system in the 1960s. The percentage of the economically active population (EAP) insured may be overestimated due to a probable underestimation of the EAP.[17] According to the table, the percentage of the insured EAP was stagnant at about 55 percent from 1960 to 1965, declined steadily to 48 percent from 1966 to 1969 (with a big drop in 1969), and then jumped to 68 percent in 1970. After Perón's downfall in 1955 (and Aramburu's incorporation of domestic servants in 1956), the government did not expand the coverage of pensions. In 1966 the military took over and the process of unification began. In 1967 all the social security funds (except the military and the police) were merged into three; the standardization of the legal system of pensions into two main branches (workers in dependency relationship and self-employed) was approved in 1968 and implemented in 1969. This process of unification and standardization probably eliminated duplication in the coverage of one person by more than one fund, thus resulting in an apparent decline in the percentage of insured. A program of "rationalization" of public administration, launched in late 1967, contributed to an additional reduction in the number of insured civil servants. On the other hand, in 1970 many of the provinces and municipalities became incorporated into the national standardized system of social security, thus increasing the number of insured, and a moratorium given to employers to pay due

Table 5-2
Insured Population in Relation to Total and Economically Active Population in Argentina: 1960–1970

Year	Total Population[a] (in thousands) (1)	Economically Active Population[a,b] (in thousands) (2)	Insured Population[c] (in thousands) Active[d] (3)	Passive[e] (4)	Dependents (5)	Total (6)	Percent of EAP Insured (3)/(2)	Percent of Total Population Insured (6)/(1)	Ra c Activ Pas (3)/
1960	20,850	7,270	4,011	745	4,412	9,168	55.2	44.0	5
1961	21,203	7,334	4,031	812	4,407	9,250	55.0	43.6	5
1962	21,540	7,447	4,101	889	4,479	9,469	55.1	44.0	4
1963	21,870	7,563	4,137	970	4,520	9,627	54.7	44.0	4
1964	22,202	7,684	4,235	1,013	4,628	9,876	55.1	44.5	4
1965	22,545	7,809	4,322	1,086	4,723	10,131	55.3	44.9	4
1966	22,897	7,939	4,305	1,131	4,698	10,134	54.2	44.3	3
1967	23,255	8,073	4,303	1,150	4,684	10,137	53.3	43.6	3
1968	23,617	8,211	4,297	1,256	4,677	10,230	52.3	43.3	3
1969	23,983	8,353	4,044	1,302	4,414	9,760	48.4	40.7	3
1970	24,350	8,500	5,781	1,389	6,328	13,498	68.0	55.4	4

Sources: *Total population,* 1961–1969 from Organización de Estados Americanos, Instituto Interamericano Estadística, "Situación demográfica: Estado y movimiento de la población," *América en Cifras 1970* (Washington, OEA, 1970); 1960 and 1970 from United Nations, *Demographic Yearbook 1971* (New York: U.N., 1971). *Economic active population* from "Bases para un sistema de seguridad social en la Argentina" (n.p., n.d.). *Active insu* 1960–1965, from data provided by the INPS to the Program for Social Security, Pan American Union, Departme Social Affairs, May 1963, September 1965, and April 1967; 1965–1970 from OEA, Instituto Interamericano de Estadís "Situación social," *América en Cifras 1972* (Washington, D.C.: OEA, 1973); when figures were missing they interpolated and extrapolated by the author. *Passive insured,* 1960–1970, from Ministerio de Bienestar Social, secretaría de Seguridad Social, *Revista de Seguridad Social,* 6 (January–June 1973). *Dependents* based on data the 1960 population census from which a ratio of 1.1 dependents per active insured was estimated by the autho
a. Estimates at mid-year.
b. 18 years and older. Other sources give a higher EAP.
c. Estimates as of December 31.
d. Basically in pension funds. For coverage of other risks, see text.
e. Retired and disabled workers and survivors under pensions.

contributions may have resulted in a reduction of evasion and hence an increase in coverage in that year.

The above figures on coverage refer to active workers insured under pensions. If we add to them both passive insured (pensioners) and dependents (spouse and children) with coverage in terms of family allowances, maternity, and health, then we have the total insured population. The percentage of the total population insured was stagnant, with small variations, at 43–44 percent from 1960 to 1968, declined to 41 percent in 1969, and increased to 55 percent in 1970. The main components here are the active insured and dependents (computed in terms of active insured), thus the pattern can be explained by the same forces as above. The only difference is that the number of passive insured steadily increased throughout the period.

Coverage against occupational hazards is complete for all workers in dependency relationship (3.5 million in 1970), while the self-employed are not covered; hence 41 percent of the EAP is insured. Official estimates of 1964 claim that the whole population had some kind of health-care coverage either through public (state, provincial, municipal, community), mutual, union, or private hospitals (see section on benefits).[18] There are no aggregate data available on the number of those covered by family allowances, but an estimate may be derived from table 5-3 and the information available on legal coverage. By 1970, industry, commerce, transportation, rural, and port workers, as well as all civil servants, were eligible for family allowances and only domestic servants and the self-employed were excluded from this benefit. Thus in 1970 some 3.5 million active insured, or 41 percent of the EAP, had a right to family allowances.

The total number of active workers insured is disaggregated by occupational groups in table 5-3. The aggregate number of insured blue- and white-collar workers has remained stable in the 1960s although when disaggregated, according to available data until 1965, there has been a steady increase in commerce employees, rural workers, journalists and printers, and domestic servants. These increases have probably been compensated for by decreases in the number of insured in industry, banking, and insurance.

The aggregate number of civil servants protected shows two different trends. It increased slightly from 1961 to 1965, decreased sharply from 1966 to 1969, and had a sudden increase in 1970 which left the number of civil servants protected slightly below the 1961 level. The increase from 1961 to 1965 is explained by the steady expansion in both the overall public-administration and public-utilities personnel (electricity, gas, and water) which more than compensated for the decrease in railroad workers. The drop from 1966 to 1969 might have occurred due to the reduction in the staff of the public administration and state enterprises brought about by the policy of rationalization applied by the government. (It may also be the result of the unification of the social security system.) A possible explanation for the rapid increase in 1970 is the incorporation of provinces into the national social security system.

The number of self-employed insured increased steadily from 1960 to 1969, almost tripled in 1970. The latter jump may be due to the moratorium (delayed payment of debt plus interest) offered by the government in that year. Early in 1969, the distribution within this group was as follows: 70 percent self-employed workers, 24 percent entrepreneurs, and 6 percent professionals.

There are no accurate data on the number of insured in the armed forces. Figures

Table 5-3
Occupational Groups Protected by Social Security in Argentina: 1961–1970
(in thousands)

Occupational Group	Number Insured										Percentage Distribution in 1970[b]
	1961	1962	1963	1964	1965	1966	1967	1968	1969	1970	
Blue- and white-collars	2,388	2,388	2,388	2,389	2,389	2,390	2,390	2,390	2,082	2,390	41.3
Industry	975	—	—	—	—	—	—	—	—	—	24.2
Commerce	700	800[c]	915[c]	1,000	1,200	—	—	—	—	—	17.4
Rural workers	450	500	600	700	—	—	—	—	—	—	11.2
Merchant marine	93	95	93	94	94	—	—	—	—	—	2.3
Banking and insurance	78	93	—	—	—	—	—	—	—	—	1.9
Journalists and printers	49	61	61	105	111	—	—	—	—	—	1.2
Domestic servants	43	—	—	—	—	—	—	—	—	—	1.1
Civil servants	1,163	1,182	1,187	1,237	1,269	1,191	1,113	1,035	1,010	1,111	19.2
General	746	797	814	837	828	—	—	—	—	—	18.5
Railroads	225	175	170	180	188	—	—	—	—	—	5.6
Public utilities	192	210	203	220	253	—	—	—	—	—	4.8
Armed forces[a]	127	129	130	130	132	133	144	144	144	144	2.6
Self-employed	353	402	432	479	532	591	656	728	808	2,136	36.9
Workers	199	226	243	197	—	—	—	—	—	—	4.9
Entrepreneurs	150	170	180	—	—	—	—	—	—	—	3.7
Professionals	4	8[c]	12[c]	16	—	—	—	—	—	—	0.1
Total	4,031	4,101	4,137	4,235	4,322	4,305	4,303	4,297	4,044	5,781	100.0

Sources: *1961–1965* from data provided by the INPS to the Program for Social Security, Pan American Union, Department of Social Affairs, May 1963, September 1965, and April 1967. *1965–1970* from OEA, Instituto Interamericano de Estadística, "Situación social," *América en Cifras 1972* (Washington, D.C.: OEA, 1973); when figures were missing they were interpolated and extrapolated by the author. *Armed forces* from Arms Control and Disarmament Agency, *World Military Expenditures 1971* (Washington, D.C.: Bureau of Economic Affairs, 1972), p. 35.

Note: Figures are for the end of the year, and report only active insured in pension funds; pensioners and dependents excluded. See table 5-2.

a. Assuming all military personnel covered.
b. For subgroups in 1961.
c. Estimates.

Table 5-4
Degree of Social Security Protection by Class of
Worker and Occupational Group in Argentina: 1960

Class of Worker	Labor Force (in thousands)	Insured (in thousands)	Percent Insured
Salaried and wage-earners	5,260	3,658[a]	69.5[a]
Self-employed	889	203[b]	22.8[b]
Employers	946	150	15.9
Unpaid family workers	217	c	c
Not specified	287	c	c
Total	7,599	4,011	52.8

SOURCES: *Class of worker* from República Argentina, Poder Ejecutivo Nacional, Secretaría de Estado de Hacienda, Dirección Nacional de Estadísticas y Censos, *Censo nacional de población 1960,* Buenos Aires, November 1963. *Insured* from table 5-3.

a. All insured blue- and white-collar workers, military, civil servants, and domestic servants.

b. Includes self-employed workers and professionals.

c. A small number of these workers may be insured by other funds.

in the table come from the series judged most reliable. Other sources reported only 99,000 militarymen for 1966 and gave a figure of only 300 men in the air force throughout the period 1960-1968 with a sudden rise to 15,000 in 1969.[19] Since all militarymen are covered by social security, we have given those who are on active duty as insured.

Table 5-3 shows the number of insured in each occupational group, but in order to measure the degree of social security protection for each group, it is necessary to compare the total number of workers within the group with those actually insured. Unfortunately there is no exact information on the total number of workers in each occupational group. Tables 5-4 and 5-5 approach the comparison in a different manner.

Table 5-4 compares the distribution of the labor force by "class of worker" with a clustering of insured in pension funds in 1960. It should be stressed, however, that the two columns of the table are not strictly comparable. Salaried workers and wage-earners are roughly congruent with the sum of those in the armed forces, civil servants, and blue- and white-collar workers including domestic servants. Almost 70 percent of them were protected, although the degree of coverage was unequal among them; probably the highest coverage was among militarymen and the lowest among domestic servants. Self-employed, 22.8 percent of which were protected, are mostly concentrated in industry, agriculture, and commerce in that order. (The coverage of self-employed increased dramatically by 1970.) Employers, 15.9 percent of which were protected, are mostly concentrated in commerce, agriculture, and industry in that order. Most of the unpaid family workers are not insured. The nonspecified category includes those uninsured who work in cooperatives, plus those looking for a job for the first time who lack a specific occupation.[20] The 3.5 million left unprotected were probably small farmers, fishermen, seasonal agricultural workers, most unpaid family workers, domestic servants (due to employer's evasion of payments), and part of the urban self-employed.

Table 5-5
Degree of Social Security Protection by Sector of Economic Activity in Argentina: 1960

Sector of Economic Activity	Labor Force (in thousands)	Insured (in thousands)	Percent of Labor Force Insured
Agriculture, forestry, hunting, fishing	826.9	450.0[a]	54.4
Mining, manufacturing, construction	1,802.7	1,024.0[b]	56.8
Public utilities, transportation, communications	526.5	510.0[c]	96.9
Commerce, services, banking, insurance	1,842.0	1,567.0[d]	85.1
Self-employed	1,822.1	353.0[e]	19.4
Not specified	604.3	—	—
Total	7,424.5	3,904.0	52.6

SOURCES: *Labor force* from ILO, *Yearbook of Labor Statistics 1973* (Geneva: ILO, 1973). *Insured* from data provided by the INPS to the Program for Social Security, Pan American Union, Department of Social Affairs, May 1963.
a. Permanent rural workers.
b. Industry workers, journalists, and printers.
c. Public utilities, railroad, and merchant-marine workers.
d. Commerce, banking and insurance employees, civil servants' general fund, and domestic servants.
e. Self-employed workers, entrepreneurs, and professionals.

Table 5-5 shows the degree of social security coverage by sectors of economic activity in 1960. The sector having the poorest coverage was the self-employed with less than 20 percent protected. More than 25 percent of the self-employed are small farmers, agricultural tenants with various types of contracts, loggers, fishermen, and hunters. Another 28.5 percent of the self-employed are in industry (handicrafts) and 23 percent in commerce (a good number of which are probably street vendors). The penultimate sector in terms of protection was agriculture with only slightly more than half of its workers covered. The lack of protection was probably due to the employer's evasion, though a steady increase in the number of insured can be noticed in the years following 1961 (see table 5-3). Mining, quarrying, manufacturing, and construction had a degree of coverage (57 percent) slightly higher than the national average. Commerce, civil servants, banking, and insurance had a degree of protection above 85 percent. The group with the highest social security protection was made up of public utilities, railroads, and merchant marine with almost 97 percent of coverage.

Tables 5-3, 5-4, and 5-5 are limited to the active insured and do not show the different coverage of dependents. In all funds, dependents have a right to survivors' pensions and family allowances, and the wife of the insured to maternity care. Medical care is also granted free to the wife and children of the insured in all funds.

Since its inception, the social security system had, at least in theory, national coverage for each occupational group protected. In practice, developed, urbanized provinces with expanding activities in transportation, public utilities, banking and insurance, commerce, manufacturing, energy, and government services which also had, except for the last group, strong unions and were politically active, received

Table 5-6
Degree of Social Security Protection of the Total
Population by Geographic Region in Argentina: 1960

Region	Total Population		Insured Population[a]	
	Thousands	Percent	Thousands	Percent
Metropolitan	2,966.6	14.8	1,571.9	52.9
Pampa	9,415.3	47.2	1,868.8	19.8
Center	2,056.3	10.3	233.2	11.3
Northwest	2,073.1	10.4	163.4	7.9
Cuyo	1,176.4	5.9	92.9	7.9
Patagonia	206.5	1.0	11.4	5.5
Comahue	461.9	2.3	23.1	4.7
Northeast	1,616.4	8.1	56.5	3.5
Total	20,013.5	100.0	4,021.2	20.1

SOURCES: *Total population* from *Censo Nacional de Población 1960,*
Buenos Aires, November 1963. *Insured* from table 5-7.
a. Estimate by the author; see table 5-7, note c.

earlier and better social security protection. Conversely, those backward, isolated provinces whose labor force was engaged in agriculture, controlled by the *estancieros* (hacienda owners), poorly unionized and politically passive, were latecomes to social security. The social security system began in Buenos Aires, later expanded to the capital cities of the other provinces and large cities, and then to large-scale, mechanized agriculture, agro-industrial, and oil-coal-gas rural areas.[21]

An attempt to measure the degree of social security protection in each region is confounded by the lack of data on the distribution by region of the total insured population. The only data available are the number of pensioners in 1966; those were used to derive the total insured population as explained in table 5-6. The assumption is that the number of pensioners is directly correlated with the total number of insured in each province. According to the last column of table 5-6, social security coverage is higher in the most developed regions and lower in the least developed. Thus, while almost 53 percent of the population in the Metropolitan area is insured, only 3.5 percent is insured in the Northeast.

Table 5-7 gives an idea of coverage by provinces. Most recent data available on EAP are from 1960; data on total insured for the same year was derived from the distribution of beneficiaries as explained in the table.[22] Data on the table support the proposition that the Metropolitan area and the provinces in the Pampa region have (with one exception, Entre Ríos) a higher coverage than provinces in the Center, Northwest, and Cuyo. These in turn (with two exceptions, Salta and Jujuy) have a higher rate of coverage than provinces in Patagonia, Comahue, and Northeast. A second proposition that can be tested with the data in table 5-7 is that the larger the size of the EAP in a province, the better its degree of social security coverage (not only in absolute numbers, of course, but in relative terms). The correlation between these two variables is significant: .82 ($N = 24$). It should be noted that the areas in which the largest cities of the nation are located (Federal Capital, and provinces of Buenos Aires, Santa Fé, and Tucumán) are those with the highest degree of social security coverage. A third proposition that can be tested with the data is that the higher the urban vis-a-vis rural proportion of the EAP in each province, the larger its

Table 5-7
Degree of Social Security Protection of the
Economically Active Population by Province in
Argentina: 1960

Province[a]	EAP[b]		Insured[c]	
	Thousands	Urban Percent	Thousands	Percent
Federal Capital	1,268.5	100.0	1,571.9	123.9
Buenos Aires	2,657.6	87.0	1,429.3	53.8
Sante Fè	702.1	76.2	367.0	52.3
Tucumán	262.9	54.4	88.8	33.8
Còrdoba	658.5	68.2	209.1	31.8
Entre Ríos	279.9	49.5	72.5	25.9
San Luis	61.3	51.8	15.6	25.5
Mendoza	295.8	64.0	68.4	23.1
Catamarca	55.6	41.9	12.4	22.3
La Rioja	40.8	42.6	8.5	20.8
San Juan	120.1	54.3	24.5	20.4
Santiago del Estero	148.4	35.2	27.3	18.4
La Pampa	62.9	57.7	10.2	16.2
Chubut	58.3	54.4	9.2	15.8
Salta	146.1	65.0	22.7	15.5
Corrientes	173.5	46.4	25.5	14.7
Jujuy	90.1	49.1	12.2	13.5
Rio Negro	72.3	63.5	8.6	11.9
Neuquen	38.8	48.0	4.3	11.1
Chaco	180.8	37.8	18.5	10.2
Tierra del Fuego	4.3	88.8	0.3	6.7
Misiones	133.2	31.8	9.0	6.7
Santa Cruz	29.2	53.6	1.9	6.5
Formosa	58.0	33.6	3.5	6.0
Total	7,599.0	73.9	4,021.2	52.9

SOURCES: *EAP* from *Censo nacional de población 1960,* Buenos
Aires, November 1963. *Insured* was calculated using the number of
pensioners from *Censo de beneficiarios de los organismos nacionales
de previsiòn social,* Buenos Aires, 1966.
  a. Ranked according to degree of coverage (last column).
  b. Population 14 years and older.
  c. The only data available were the number of pensioenrs (excluding the military) distributed by province in 1966. These were used
to calculate a percentage distribution which was then applied to the
total number of pensioners in 1960. (For this purpose it was assumed
that the percentage distribution by province between 1960 and 1966
remained unchanged.) Then, the overall ratio of active insured to
pensioners, as in 1960, was applied to the distribution in order to
estimate the number of active insured by province in that year. (Here
it was assumed that the ratio of active insured to pensioners was
equal in all provinces.)

social security coverage. The correlation between the two variables is also significant: .65 (N = 24).[23] Notice that this correlation in Argentina is much higher than in
Chile (.24). One significant difference is that in Argentina those insured in civil service, merchant-marine, banking-insurance, and state railroad funds were included in
the distribution, while they were excluded in Chile. These groups and subgroups are

concentrated in urban centers, thus, the divergent outcome of the correlation. If those insured in the armed forces had been included in the distribution of insured by provinces in Argentina, the correlation would have been even higher.

The best or most fairly protected provinces are the most developed and/or richest in strategic resources. They concentrate most of the industry, government and financial services, port and railroad facilities, energy (oil, coal, natural gas, hydroelectric), cattle and large-scale, relatively modern agriculture (e.g., sugar, wheat, wine). They also have six of the ten most populated cities of the nation. The least protected provinces are the most underdeveloped, characterized by a pastoral (e.g., sheep-raising) or agricultural economy (e.g., fruits, cotton, tobacco, lumber); they include only one of the ten most populated cities in the nation. While coverage in the Federal Capital is above 100 percent (either due to duplication or defects in the derivation of the insured from pensioners), it decreases to 6 percent in Formosa.

Financing

In the national system, the percentage contributions of salaries/wages or income and the taxes are the same throughout the territory of Argentina; hence, differences in social-security financing are limited to occupational groups. (Employees covered by provincial and municipal systems have still another type of financing.) Table 5-8 presents a picture of the national system of financing and the differences among occupational groups and subgroups in the contributions from the insured, employer, and the state, by risk or program.

An analysis of the differences in the overall percentage contribution among all groups is meaningless because in the civil-public and armed-forces groups, family allowances are paid directly by the employer (and hence not shown in the table), while in the civil-private group 12 percent is paid by the employer and shown in the table. In addition, the cost of life insurance and occupational hazards and the revenue from taxes cannot be represented in percentages and hence are excluded from the table too. Therefore it is more meaningful to do a separate analysis by program and, within each, by contributor.

The insurance against occupational hazards is the most homogeneous in terms of financing. Employers pay the whole cost (or a premium to insurance companies) according to the degree of risk. The self-employed group is not covered. Family allowances are financed in most cases by the employer's contribution of 12 percent. In the civil-service and armed-forces groups, there is not a fixed percentage; the employer pays the allowance directly.

The hospital network of unions and mutual insurance funds (the only one shown in the table) is financed by workers' and employers' contributions which fluctuate from 1 to 2 percent paid by the insured (single or married) and 2 percent paid by the employer. Rural workers, however, pay from 2 to 3 percent and their employers 4 percent; this has been justified by the low income of this subgroup. For the military in the army, the employer pays a maximum of only 1.55 percent; in the navy the employer contributes 2.5 percent with an additional state subsidy of 40 percent of budgetary expenditures (the state also subsidizes health services in the army and the air force by an undisclosed percentage). Domestic servants and the self-employed are not insured. The state hopsital network, free to its users who usually are not covered by other social security programs, is financed through the national budget. The private hospital network is financed through direct payment of services or prepayments (e.g., lump sum, monthly contributions) by its users.

Table 5-8
Social Security Contributions from Employees,
Employers, and State by Occupational Group in
Argentina: 1973
(in percentages of wages or income)

Occupational group	Employee	Employer	State	Total
Blue- and white-collars	*6 to 7*	29[a]	—	*35 to 36*
Pensions	5	15	[b]	20
Health	1 to 2[c]	2	—	3 to 4
Family allowances	—	12	—	12
Occupational hazards	—	[d]	—	—
Civil servants	*6 to 7*	17	—	*23 to 24*
Pensions	5	15	—	20
Health	1 to 2[c]	2	—	3 to 4
Family allowances	—	[e]	—	—
Occupational hazards	—	[d]	—	—
Life insurance	—	[f]	—	—
Armed forces (military)	*8 to 9*	29.5 or 38.5	—	*35 or 44*
Pensions	8	27 or 36[g]	—	35 or 44
Health	1 to 2[c,h]	2.5[i]	[j]	—
Family allowances	—	[e]	—	—
Occupational hazards	—	[d]	—	—
Self-employed	*10*	—	—	*10*
Pensions	10	—	—	10
Rural workers	*7 to 8*	31	—	*38 to 39*
Pensions	5	15	—	20
Health	2 to 3[c]	4	—	6 to 7
Family allowances	—	12	—	12
Occupational hazards	—	[d]	—	—
Life insurance	—	[f]	—	—
Domestic servants	*5*	15	—	*20*
Pensions	5	15	—	20
Occupational hazards	—	[d]	—	—

Sources: *Revista de Seguridad Social,* 4 (December 1971), p.
1126, and legislative information compiled by the author.

a. Employers of construction workers pay an additional 4 percent
for the unemployment fund.

b. Taxes: on government advertisements (10 percent) for journalists and printers; on government freight (2 percent) for merchant
marine; and on insurance premiums for insurance personnel.

c. Unmarried people pay the smallest percentage and those married the highest percentage.

d. Employers pay whole cost through direct provision of benefits
or insurance premiums which vary according to risk.

e. Employers pay whole cost of allowances directly to employees.

f. Premium paid by the employer.

g. The state employer contributes 27 percent of the salary of troops
and 36 percent of that of officials, and a proportion (ranging from 2
to 99 percent, according to years of service) of most pensions.

h. In the army, the maximum contribution of an insured married and
with three children or more is 1.55 percent.

i. This is the contribution in the navy; exact percentage contributions in the army and the air force are not available.

j. About 40 percent of the budget is paid by the state in the
navy; state subsidies in the army and the air force are not available.

Life insurance formerly covered civil servants, state railroad, public-utilities, and rural workers only; since 1974 it has been expanded to cover all workers in dependency relationship. It is financed by a minimum and equal premium paid by the employers. Unemployment insurance exists only for construction workers and is financed through the employer's contribution of 4 percent.

In 1970 the financing system of pensions was quite heterogenous, but, three years later, due to the unification process, it became homogeneous within the civil sector as table 5-8 shows. In 1970 the insured paid from 5 to 10 percent, with domestic service, rural, commerce, industry, printing, and banking paying the smallest percentage (5 percent); merchant marine, journalism, state railroad, public utilities, insurance, and armed forces paying 8 percent; civil service paying 9 percent; and self-employed workers, professionals, and entrepreneurs paying 10 percent. (The latter's contribution has remained unchanged; its high percentage is due to the lack of the employer's contribution.) If we exclude banking, therefore, the insured contribution appears as fairly progressive, the percentage increasing with the income of the subgroup. The employer's contribution ranged from 8 to 36 percent, with domestic service, rural, and journalism paying 8 percent; merchant marine, state railroad, public utilities, and insurance paying 12 percent; civil service, 14 percent; commerce, industry, printing, and banking, 15 percent; and armed forces paying 27 percent (for troops) and 36 percent (for officers). In general, the percentage contribution from employers increased with the income of the subgroup, hence playing a regressive role in income distribution.

In the period 1971–1973 the percentage contribution of the employees in dependency relationship in the civil group was gradually made uniform at 5 percent: the percentage of banking, commerce, industry, rural, and domestic employees (5 percent in 1970) remained unchanged; the percentage of insurance, public utilities, journalism, merchant marine, and railroad employees (8 percent in 1970) was reduced by 3 percentage points; and the percentage of civil servants (9 percent in 1970) was reduced by 4 percentage points. To compensate for the employee's percentage cut, the percentage contribution of the employer in this group was gradually regulated to 15 percent: the percentage of banking, commerce, and industrial employers (15 percent in 1970) continued unchanged; that of insurance, public utilities, merchant marine, and railroad employers (12 percent in 1970) was increased by 3 percentage points; and that of journalism, rural, and domestic service employers (8 percent in 1970) was increased by 7 percentage points. Although something positive was achieved in terms of simplicity and uniformity, the combined effect of these reductions and increases resulted in a financial system in 1973 that was probably more regressive than in 1970. The medium-income stratum (insurance, public-utilities, merchant-marine, railroad, and civil-service employees) perhaps benefited most from the change because of the substantial reduction in their contributions. The lower-income stratum (rural workers and domestic servants) did not experience any cut in their contributions although their employers' contributions increased dramatically. A very large segment of the insured (commercial and industrial employees) did not experience any change at all.

Now all the civilian insured in dependency relationship pay 5 percent and their employers 15 percent for pensions, while the self-employed continue to pay 10 percent personally. The percentage contributions of the armed forces remain unchanged with their employer's percentage being about twice as high as the rest of the system. In addition, state subsidies and taxes continue in operation (see table

5-8). Taxes on government-paid newspaper ads subsidize journalists and printers, taxes on government-paid freight subsidize merchant-marine personnel, and taxes on insurance premiums subsidize insurance personnel. In the armed forces, the state subsidizes pensions, paying from 2 to 99 percent of their cost. All these subsidies are granted to subgroups which have medium incomes and hence also have a regressive effect.

Table 5-9 presents a partial picture of the proportions of fund revenues actually contributed by the insured and the employer. Unfortunately the table has little use since it does not provide disaggregated data by subgroups, omits all data from the armed forces, and does not include information on revenue from taxes and subsidies.

Table 5-10 divides the total revenue received by each subgroup in 1961 by the number insured in that subgroup in the same year to obtain the corresponding revenue per capita (rpc). The lowest rpc was registered among self-employed workers, domestic servants, and rural workers, the same subgroups that were at the bottom of the income ladder in 1961. Conversely, the highest rpc was that of banking and insurance, the subgroup at the top of the medium-income stratum in that year. With few exceptions the rpc of each subgroup is directly correlated to its income, indicating that the social security system does not perform a progressive income redistribution function. Some of the few exceptions to this rule can be explained. For instance, professionals and entrepreneurs were at the top of the income ladder in 1961 but were right below industrial workers according to their rpc. There were two reasons for this discrepancy. First, the provincial pension system for professionals, developed long before the national one, had lower contributions and better benefits for the insured than the national fund which, therefore, became the receptacle of professionals who had been unable to enter the provincial system and who usually had low incomes. Second, the contribution of professionals and entrepreneurs is not proportionate to actual income but is based on a percentage scale of "payment categories" fixed by the law; most professionals and entrepreneurs adopted the minimum payment category periodically determined for each occupation by the executive branch.

An analysis of the financial situation of the national pension system in the period 1950–1972 including data for all the groups and subgroups, in constant (1960)

Table 5-9
Percentage Distribution of Social Security Fund Revenues by Financing Source and Occupational Group in Argentina: 1972

Occupational Group	Insured[a]	Employer[b]	State	Investment Returns	Others[c]	Total
Blue- and white-collars	26	68	—	—	6	100
Civil servants	30	64	—	—	6	100
Self-employed	87	—	—	—	13	100
Total	32	61	—	—	7	100

SOURCE: Ministerio de Bienestar Social, Subsecretaría de Seguridad Social, *Revista de Seguridad Social*, 4 (January–June 1973), p. 252.
a. Active, passive, and self-employed.
b. Includes the contribution of the state as employer.
c. Payments of debt, interests, fees, and fines.

Table 5-10
Revenue of Social Security Funds per Insured by Occupational Group in Argentina:
1961

Occupational Group	Revenue (in thousand pesos)	Number of Insured (in thousands)	Revenue Per Capita (in pesos)	Ratio[a]
Blue- and white-collars	*326,396.1*	*2,388*	*136.7*	*8.6*
Industry	123,012.0	975	126.2	8.0
Commerce	147,447.4	700	210.6	13.3
Rural workers	7,344.8	450	16.3	1.0
Merchant marine	13,102.8	93	140.9	8.9
Banking and insurance	27,803.3	78	356.5	22.6
Journalists and printers	7,006.0	49	142.9	9.0
Domestic servants	679.8	43	15.8	1.0
Civil servants	*177,859.8*	*1,163*	*152.9*	*9.7*
General	99,103.8	746	132.8	8.4
Railroads	51,239.5	225	227.7	14.4
Public utilities	27,516.5	192	143.3	9.1
Self-employed	*7,898.6*	*353*	*22.4*	*1.4*
Workers	2,610.1	199	13.1	0.8
Entrepreneurs	4,810.9	150	32.1	2.0
Professionals	477.6	4	119.4	7.6
Armed forces[b]	*25,660.9*	*127*	*202.0*	*12.8*

SOURCES: *Blue- and white-collars, civil servants,* and *self-employed* from data provided by the INPS to the Program for Social Security, Pan American Union, Department of Social Affairs, May 1963. *Armed forces* computed from Héctor L. Diéguez and Alberto Petrecolla, *Estudio estadistico del sistema previsional argentino en el periodo 1950–72* (versión preliminar)" (Buenos Aires: Instituto Torcuato Di Tella, Centro de Investigaciones Económicas, August 1974).

a. Ratio of revenue per capita in relation to domestic servants.

b. The figure was computed from data on revenue from Diéguez and Petrecolla. Their data on revenue from blue- and white-collars, civil servants, and self-employed tend to be lower than mine. Hence, an average of the difference between the two data sets was applied to the Diéguez-Petrecolla figure for the armed forces in order to make it comparable with my data.

pesos, shows five clear trends.

(1) The blue- and white-collar group had a consistent surplus during this period with an accumulated 2,575 billion new pesos. This was generated basically by three subgroups: banking-insurance, industry, and commerce (in that order). This surplus was large enough to compensate (and still leave a substantial net surplus) for the deficits (particularly in the 1960s) of the rest of the subgroups: merchant marine, domestic servants, journalists and printers, and rural workers (in that order).

(2) The group of civil servants has had a consistent deficit since 1959, for an accumulated deficit of 216 million pesos for the period. This was mainly caused by the deficits of railroad and public-utility subgroups throughout most of the period and the deficit of civil servants since 1964.

(3) The group of self-employed had a consistent surplus until 1970, thereafter having a deficit; for the whole period the group accumulated a surplus of 293 million pesos. The three self-employed subgroups generated surpluses (with the exception of self-employed workers during two years) until 1970; thereafter self-employed workers alone probably created the deficit.

(4) The group of the armed forces had a consistent deficit throughout the period for

an accumulated deficit of 634 million pesos. Within this group, the military subgroup had a consistent deficit, while the police subgroup began to have a deficit in 1957.

(5) In the whole period, the surplus generated by part of the system (banking-finance, industry, commerce, and all self-employed) offset the combined deficit of the rest (armed forces, civil servants, merchant marine, domestics, journalists-printers, and rural workers) and left a net surplus of 2 billion pesos. Nevertheless, since 1966, the surplus generated by the financially stable subgroups has not been large enough to offset the deficit created by the financially troubled subgroups and an accumulated net deficit of 35 million pesos resulted.[24]

The reasons for the different financial situations of the various groups are four: the social security revenue generated by the group, the relationship between benefits and financing, state debt, and employer/employee evasion. Subgroups that have—see table 5-10—a very high rpc (e.g., banking-insurance and commerce) are usually generators of surpluses, while those that have a very low rpc (e.g., domestic servants) are usually troubled with deficits. There are important exceptions to this rule; thus the armed forces have a relatively high rpc, but have systematically produced a deficit. The explanation for this phenomenon is that often the level of benefits paid to this subgroup is too high in relation to its revenue. A recent study has commented on this: "It is notoriously unfair that the subsystem 1 [blue- and white-collars] generates a surplus with a low average benefit while the subsystem 4 [armed forces] has chronically generated a deficit with a high average benefit."[25] Finally, the financial instability may have been created or aggravated by the failure of the state, employers, and/or employees to fulfill their obligations. In the 1960s, the capital of most funds was borrowed and invested by the state which promised to repay it with interest ranging from 4 to 8 percent. In 1966 the official estimate for the state debt was 3 billion (new) pesos for the civilian private sector—about 3,000 pesos per insured—and 1 billion pesos for the civilian public sector—about 1,000 pesos per insured.[26] (This combined 4 billion peso state debt is similar to the accumulated deficit generated by all pension funds from 1950 to 1972.) Most of this debt has not been and probably will never be repaid to the pension funds. In 1973, however, the government of General Perón repaid another state debt, 600 million pesos owed to pensioners under INSSPJP.[27] Evasion among private employers was also frequent in the 1960s, particularly in the rural sector as well as among the self-employed.[28] Moratoria granted in 1967 and 1970 helped reduce the problem and increase revenue if only temporarily.

Let us now return to the issue of transfers of revenue among groups and subgroups. The possibility for *actual* compensation (of deficits with surpluses) among subgroups was opened in the 1960s when the process of unification of the civil group began. (The armed-forces group has been excluded from the unification process and hence from any possibility of transfer of revenue with the civilian group.) A Common Fund for Compensation was created so that surpluses from some funds compensate for deficits from others. Although theoretically the merging of funds and compensation between surpluses and deficits is consistent with the solidarity principle, in practice it is unfair because in many cases surpluses from subgroups of low income are used to compensate deficits from subgroups of higher income.[29]

The merging of all revenues among subgroups *within a fund* means that surpluses of blue- and white-collar subgroups in the medium-income stratum are used to compensate for deficits of subgroups in the low-income stratum, with a progressive effect in terms of income redistribution. For example, there is a clear transfer from the top medium-income subgroup (banking-insurance) to the bottom low-income sub-groups (domestic servants and rural workers). In the same manner, the surpluses of entrepreneurs and professionals compensate for the possible deficit of self-employed workers. On the other hand, there are inequitable transfers within sub-groups in a similar income stratum, for example, from industry and commerce to merchant marine and journalists-printers. The merging of all revenues from the *three funds* creates additional regressive effects in terms of transfers. For instance, deficits of public utilities, railroad, and civil servants were partially compensated by surpluses from commerce, a subgroup in a lower income stratum than the other three.

The ECLA study of 1961 is the only attempt so far to measure the overall effect of social security on income distribution in Argentina, and it is incomplete because it used only data on pensions for the 1950s and 1961.[30] According to the ECLA study, the combined insured's and employer's contribution to pension funds had a regressive income-redistribution effect of 0.8 percent of family income. The redistribution effect of insured contributions was equivalent to a transfer of about 0.6 percent of disposable monetary income from the bottom 90 percent income group to the top 10 percent income group; the redistribution effect of employers' contributions was equivalent to 0.2 percent. The study also found, however, that the system of benefits (i.e., pensions) resulted in a progressive redistribution of income: a transfer of 2.5 percent of family income from the top 10 percent to the lower 90 percent. The net redistributive effect of the whole pension system was progressive: 1.7 percent was transferred from the top to the bottom.

The ECLA study has a serious deficiency. It measured income redistribution between the top 10 percent income group and the bottom 90 percent. It had to be expected that only a small proportion of the top income stratum would benefit from the social security system. It would have been more significant therefore to dis-aggregate the income redistribution effect within the bottom 90 percent, to measure if there was a transfer, for instance, between the bottom 30 percent of the population, which probably was either not protected at all or poorly protected, and the second, third, and fourth deciles that probably had good social security protection. In view of the trend towards unification of social security in the late 1960s and early 1970s, a thorough study of the current effect of the total social security system in income redistribution, particularly in the middle and bottom strata, is needed more than ever.

The cost of social security in Argentina increased slowly, with some variations, in the 1960s (see table 5-11). In 1960, expenditures on pensions of the main three pension funds (excluding their administrative expenditures and overall costs of military and police pensions) were 2.9 percent of GNP and 33.0 percent of government consumption expenditures. (In relation to revenue, the proportions were 3.6 percent of GNP and 37.4 percent of government consumption expenditures in 1960 which increased to 4.3 and 45.1 percent in 1970.) Separate data on expenditures in state health care, available for 1964 through 1969, show a tendency to increase, from 1.6 percent of GNP and 16.8 percent of government consumption expenditures in 1964 to 1.9 and 19.3 percent respectively in 1969.[31] When the expenditures in pensions and health are added for 1969, they represent 6.7 percent of GNP and 69.6 percent of government consumption expenditures. This excludes pensions for the armed forces, health care under mutual insurance funds and unions, family allowances, and other minor expenditures.

The rising costs of social security are mainly the result of new benefits granted by the law, rising administrative expenditures, and the expansion of social security coverage to new groups. The total number of pensions in Argentina rose from 744,708 in 1960 to 1,427,775 in 1971, although the rates of growth in pensions granted in the period 1950–1955 have not been reached again. In the decade 1960–1970 the labor force increased by 17 percent, but the number of "passive workers" (e.g., retired, pensioners) increased by 86 percent (see table 5-2). The average ratio of active vis-a-vis passive workers was 5.4 to 1 in 1960 and steadily declined to 3.1 to 1 in 1969. While in the first half of 1972, 87.6 percent of social security expenditures went to pensions, the proportion increased to about 94.2 percent in the first half of 1973.[32]

Expenditures in the administration of social security (mostly in the blue- and white-collar funds) increased systematically in the first half of the 1960s, but decreased from 1.8 percent of total social security expenditures in 1966 to 1.4 percent in 1968. This fact might be due to the partial unification of the social security system in 1967. In 1971–1972, however, there was an increase to 1.6 percent in administrative expenditures.[33]

The expansion of social security coverage to include new groups of low income has also contributed to the increase in costs. In the late 1960s and early 1970s, through government pressure and unionization, evasion among agricultural employers was substantially reduced. Finally in the late 1960s and early 1970s an increasing number of self-employed workers, entrepreneurs, and professionals, most with low incomes, entered the social security system. If the comprehensive social security program launched by the administration of former President Perón is implemented, a substantial increase in social security expenditures in the immediate future may be predicted.

Benefits

The regulations on benefits within the national system are the same throughout the territory of Argentina; there are differences, however, in the quantity and quality of hospital and medical services by region. The most significant inequalities in benefits are derived from the occupational structure as summarized in table 5-12 which includes the benefits enjoyed by the main occupational subgroups which are clustered into four main groups. A simple count of the boxes in the table allows us to rank the occupational groups by the number of benefits granted: (1) military and federal police with 26 benefits; (2) civil servants and practically all blue- and white-collars with 24 benefits; (3) seasonal rural workers with 20 benefits; (4) domestic servants with 18 benefits; and (5) self-employed with 10 benefits.

If we exclude the self-employed, the Argentinian system of benefits is fairly uniform; this is the result of the process of standardization initiated in the late 1960s. The armed forces still appears to be the group eligible for most benefits. Only militarymen and policemen are eligible for pensions due to seniority and partial permanent disability, and only their survivors are eligible for devolution of contributions if not for pensions. They, apparently, do not receive indemnification for layoff, but their social security laws are loose enough to allow a pension when they are permanently dismissed. For instance, militarymen can receive a pension "by causes other than those specifically regulated in the law," permitting those laid off in frequent political moves to retire if they have accumulated ten years of service. Federal policemen can be granted a definitive retirement if, after having been in a situation of temporary absence from their jobs (for several causes including "leave of absence for personal

Table 5-11
Cost of Social Security in Argentina: 1960–1970
(in millions of current new pesos and percentages)

Year	GNP	Government Consumption Expenditure	Social Security Revenue			Social Security Expenditure[a]		
			Total	Percent of GNP	Percent of Government Consumption Expenditure	Total	Percent of GNP	Percent of Government Consumption Expenditure
1960	9,806.9	863	323.0	3.6	37.4	284.7	2.9	33.0
1961	11,755.3	1,168	430.6	3.7	36.9	398.0	3.9	34.1
1962	14,766.7	1,559	500.4	3.4	32.1	483.0	3.3	31.0
1963	18,454.0	1,748	654.9	3.5	37.5	665.9	3.6	38.1
1964	25,655.4	2,411	1,008.5	3.9	41.8	912.3	3.6	37.8
1965	36,043.4	3,469	1,371.4	3.8	39.5	1,161.9	3.2	33.5
1966	44,900.0	4,806	1,699.7	3.8	35.4	1,764.3	3.9	36.7
1967	58,707.2	6,047	2,919.5	5.0	48.3	2,633.1	4.5	43.5
1968	68,314.9	6,579	3,170.4	4.6	48.2	3,310.9	4.8	50.3
1969	79,822.7	7,200	3,370.9	4.2	46.8	3,395.9	4.3	47.2
1970	94,640.6	8,910	4,059.3	4.3	45.6	4,022.0	4.2	45.1

SOURCES: *GNP, 1960–61* from Ramón Medina, *Estadística económica argentina* (Buenos Aires: Instituto Torcuato Di Tella, Centro de Investigaciones Económicas, 1965); *1962–1971* from OEA, Instituto Interamericano de Estadística, "Situación económica," *América en cifras 1972* (Washington, D.C.: OEA, 1973). *Social security revenue* and *expenditure 1960–1961* from *Boletín del Instituto Nacional de Previsión Social,* 6 (April 1962) and *1962–1970* from *Revista de Seguridad Social,* 4 (May 1971). *Total government expenditure* from U.N., *Yearbook of National Account Statistics 1966, 1969,* and *1972* (New York: U.N., 1967, 1970, and 1973), and *Monthly Bulletin of Statistics,* 28 (March 1974).
a. Includes only benefits for pensions in the main three funds; excludes administrative expenditures, family allowances, and health for such funds, plus all expenditures from the police and military funds.

reasons" and imprisonment), they cannot return to work later.

Next in line are those in the dependency relationship, that is, civil servants, and blue- and white-collar workers. (Surprisingly these workers are eligible for a pension if disabled due to nonoccupational hazards only in unique circumstances.) Within these two groups there are subgroups with privileged benefits and others deprived of the basic benefits available to most of the group. Thus construction workers are the only ones eligible for unemployment compensation. Through collective bargaining, electrical workers receive a bonus equivalent to three months of the salary that they had at the time of retirement, while workers in the plastics industry get a one-month salary bonus.[34] On the other hand, seasonal rural workers are paid neither subsidies for temporary disability caused by occupational hazards nor lump sums for layoff or life insurance. Domestic servants are not eligible for family allowances nor paid maternity leave.

The self-employed receive the fewest benefits. They are the only group not eligible for any type of "other cash benefits," family allowances, or rehabilitation in case of disability from occupational hazards.

To analyze more fully the varying conditions attached to a given benefit available to several groups or subgroups, four types of conditions will be discussed: (a) requirements to gain the right of the benefit, (b) basic salary used to compute the benefit, (c) the amount of the benefit, and (d) the compatibility of the pension with other pensions or salaried work. Once again, the standardization of conditions at-

Table 5-12
Social Security Benefits by Occupational Group in Argentina: 1973

Occupational Group	Pensions						Other Cash Benefits													Family Allowances								Health-Maternity								Total
	1	2	3a	4a	5	6b	7	8	9	10c	11	12	13	14	15	16c	17	18	19	20	21	22	23d	24	25	26	27	28	29	30	31	32	33	34	35	
Blue- and white-collars																																				
Industry	x	x	x	xe		x				x	x	x	x	g	x	x	x		x	x		x	x	x			x	x	x	x	x	x	x		x	24
Commerce	x	x	x	xe		x				x	x	x	x		x	x	x		x	x		x	x	x			x	x	x	x	x	x	x		x	24
Rural workers	x	x	x	xe		x				x	x	xh	x		xh	xh	x		x	xi		xi	xi	xi			xi	x	x	x	x	x	x		xh	24
Merchant marine	x	x	x	xe		x				x	x	xh	xi		x	x	x		xi	xi		xi	xi	xi			xi	x	x	x	x	x	x		x	24
Banking and insurance	x	x	x	xe		x				x	x	x	x		x	x	x		x	x		x	x	x			x	x	x	x	x	x	x		x	24
Journalists and printers	x	x	x	xe		x				x	x	x	x		x	x	x		x	x		x	x	x			x	x	x	x	x	x	x		x	24
Domestic servants	x	x	x	xe		x				x	x	x	x		x	x	x		x								x	x	x	x	x	x	x		x	18
Civil servants																																				
General	x	x	x	xe		x				x	x	x	x		x	x	x		x	x		x	x	x				x	x	x	x	x	x		x	24
Railroads	x	x	x	xe		x				x	x	x	x		x	x	x		x	x		x	x	x				x	x	x	x	x	x		x	24
Public utilities	x	x	x	xe		x				x	x	x	x		x	x	x		x	x		x	x	x				x	x	x	x	x	x		x	24
Self-employed																																				
Workers	x	x	xf	xf		x																						x	x	x	x	x	x		x	10
Entrepreneurs	x	x	xf	xf		x																						x	x	x	x	x	x		x	10
Professionals	x	x	xf	xf		x																						x	x	x	x	x	x		x	10
Armed forces																																				
Military	xj	x	x	x	xj	x				x	x	x				x	x	xk	x	x		x	x	x			x	x	x	x	x	x	x	xl	x	26
Federal police	x	x	x	x	xj	x				x	x	x				x	x	x	x	x		x	x	x			x	x	x	x	x	x	x	xl	x	26

Sources: *Seguridad Social*, 6 (December 1973) and legislative information compiled by the author.

Note: See code following table for definition of benefits here signified by numbers 1–35.

a. For total permanent disability only, with the exception of the armed forces.

b. All funds grant survivors' pensions to the widow and children as well as parents and sisters.

g. Available for construction workers only.

h. Available for those permanently employed only; seasonal and temporary workers are excluded.

c. There are two different and accumulative benefits, one paid by the employer for occupational hazards and another through compulsory life insurance.

d. Includes extra allowance for "large family," i.e., when there are three children or more.

e. Only available when the insured, after ten years of service, has ceased to work and the disability occurs in the next two years after his cessation.

f. The law is ambiguous; it apparently grants the disability pension for both occupational and non-occupational causes providing that the person is actively insured.

i. Merchant marine is protected through the industry fund; longshoremen through their own fund. Benefits are similar for both subgroups.

j. Although there are no concrete regulations for this type of retirement, this is possible under the broad regulations for compulsory retirement.

k. Instead of a lump sum, the contributions paid by the insured are returned to the survivor.

l. At reduced price, fluctuating from 30 to 50 percent; free in some cases.

Code for Social Security Benefits

Pensions:
1. Old-age.
2. Seniority.
3. Permanent disability (total or partial) caused by occupational hazards.
4. Permanent disability (total or partial) caused by nonoccupational hazards.
5. Unemployment/layoff.
6. Survivors'.

Other Cash Benefits:
7. Restitution of contributions.
8. Lump sum at retirement.
9. Bonus added to pension for work-years above the minimum required for retirement.
10. Lump sum for permanent disability (total or partial) caused by occupational hazards.
11. Subsidy for temporary disability caused by occupational hazards.
12. Subsidy for temporary disability caused by nonoccupational hazards.
13. Salary (or percentage thereof) paid for a period before and after childbirth.
14. Unemployment/layoff temporary subsidy.
15. Unemployment/layoff lump sum.
16. Life insurance, lump sum.
17. Funeral aid, lump sum.
18. Lump sum to survivors when no right to pension is granted.
19. Year-end bonus to retired and pensioners.

Family Allowances:
20. Marriage.
21. Pregnancy.
22. Childbirth.
23. Children.
24. Spouse.
25. Parents.
26. Child food (percentage of salary or in kind).
27. School aid (for insured or his/her children).

Health-Maternity Benefits:
28. Preventive medicine.
29. Curative medical care.
30. Rehabilitation and prosthesis in case of occupational hazards.
31. Maternity care.
32. Surgical treatment.
33. Hospitalization.
34. Medicines.
35. Dental care.

tached to benefits available to the two major groups of insured in Argentina (personnel in dependency relationship and self-employed) has substantially reduced this type of inequality. Still, noticeable differences remain between these two groups and the armed forces and between the standardized regulations applicable to the two groups as a whole and special privileges granted to subgroups within them.

In compulsory retirement, the required years of service are set at 10, while the age requirement declines as follows: 70 years for self-employed; 65 for civil servants and blue- and white-collars; and 45 to 55 for policemen. (There is a maximum age allowed for each police rank; retirement is mandatory if the insured is not promoted upon reaching that age.) For voluntary retirement, both age and years of service decrease as follows: 65 years of age for male (60 for female) and 30 years of service for self-employed; 60 years of age (55 for females) and 30 of service for civil servants and white- and blue-collars; 55 years of age (52 for females) and 30 of service for bus drivers and administrative personnel in police stations; 55 years of age (50 for females) and 30 of service (25–27 for females) for telephone-telegraph personnel and meat-processing and veterinary-control employees; and 52 years of age and 25 of service (regardless of sex) for teachers. In jobs labeled as risky, unhealthy, or strenuous, age and years of service are reduced; this is reasonable in the case of miners, railroad machinists, pilots, sailors, fishermen, longshoremen, and steel workers. However, other jobs included in this category (e.g., teachers, administrative personnel in police stations, telephone and telegraph personnel) are difficult to justify. Often, conditions attached to an obviously risky job are equal to those granted to jobs which are not seemingly risky or unhealthy, for example, fishing versus teaching or railroad machinist versus telephone operator.[35]

Seniority pensions are usually voluntary, with years of service declining as follows: 30 for diplomats; 20 for police officials, and 17 for low-ranking police personnel; and 10 for militarymen. (These are the minimum; normally, 25 years are required for officials and 20 for low-ranking personnel.)

Concerning the time counted for service, professionals in the armed forces can convert all years of university training into years of service, and each year spent by militarymen under frequent "emergency conditions" is counted twice. The latter privilege is also granted to diplomats for years of service abroad. Civil servants and blue- and white-collars may count towards time of service paid leave of absence for sickness, accident, and maternity, and compulsory military service and other time rendered to the armed forces and the police. They also receive credit for honorary service to the nation. These regulations do not apply to the self-employed.

The basic remuneration to compute the benefit is just the salary, wage, or income for all civilian workers, but, in the armed forces, several salary supplements and bonuses are included. In the computation, an average of the income for all years of service is used for the self-employed;[36] an average of the best three years in the last ten years of service for civil servants and blue- and white-collars; and the last month for Supreme Court judges and attorneys and those in the armed forces. Within the latter, in case of death or disability resulting from occupational hazards, the salary of the immediately higher rank is used as a base for computation. Former presidents of the nation receive a pension equivalent to the then-current salary of the president of the Supreme Court, while former vice-presidents receive three-fourths of such a salary.

The percentage applied to the basic remuneration to compute the benefit varies according to the type of pension. In old-age pensions (using 30 years of service in all cases because the percentage normally increases with years of service) the percentage rises as follows: 70 percent for civil servants, blue- and white-collars, and self-employed; 82 percent for merchant-marine officials, banking workers, and electricity personnel (through supplementary insurance granted by collective agreements); 85 percent for commercial pilots (also through supplementary insurance) and judicial employees; and 100 percent for policemen. In pensions for total permanent disability resulting from occupational hazards, the percentage is 70 percent for all civilian insured, but 115 percent for the armed forces. In survivors' pensions (regardless of the cause of death), the percentage is 75 percent for all civilian insured and policemen, but 100 or 115 percent for militarymen (depending on whether the cause of death is nonoccupational or occupational).

In case of temporary disability resulting from occupational hazards, a subsidy equivalent to 75 percent of the basic salary during the first month and 100 percent thereafter (with a limit of one year) is paid to civil servants, and blue- and white-collars. But the armed forces are paid 100 percent of their basic salary from the first day of disability for a period of up to two years.

The regulations for compatibility of pensions are very generous in Argentina. A pension can usually be accumulated with income from a job or another pension. For instance, pensioners who previously worked as civil servants or blue- or white-collars can become self-employed and, eventually, receive a second pension. Self-employed pensioners cannot take a civil service or blue- or white-collar job but are allowed to work in another self-employed job. Retired militarymen and policemen can work in civilian jobs (either in the public or private sector, in dependency relationship, or self-employment) and can accumulate several pensions. Perhaps the most lax rules apply to teachers; they can become "partially retired" from one teaching job and continue working in another teaching post; furthermore, they can "totally" retire from several teaching jobs and still maintain a job in higher education.

The discriminative analysis of differences in the conditions among groups and subgroups enforces the ranking made before, based on table 5-12, but widens the gap between the armed forces and civilian insured. In the 10 comparisons presented above, the armed forces (both militarymen and policemen) ranked first in 7 comparisons, while civil servants, blue- and white-collars, and self-employed ranked first in none. The self-employed ranked last in half of the comparisons. The comparison also reveals that in spite of the standardization, noticeable privileges within a given subgroup remain. For instance, Supreme Court judges and attorneys, the president and vice-president, diplomats, and teachers receive special privileges within the subgroup of civil servants. The same is true of electrical workers within public utilities and commercial pilots within merchant marine.

The unfair privileges of these categories of insured are compounded by the granting of gratuitous concessions (still in use in Argentina) which often favor former presidents, Supreme Court judges, and militarymen. The privileges enjoyed by the armed-forces group have stimulated powerful civilian subgroups to withdraw from their own funds and transfer to the armed-forces fund or, at least, to have the armed forces' privileged set of rules applied to their funds. Thus, personnel of the presidential office recently had their own regulations changed to those of the federal police.

The legal requisites for obtaining monetary benefits are nothing compared to the extraordinarily lengthy and cumbersome procedure necessary to collect benefits. In the late 1960s 80,000 applications for pensions had accumulated and the average time to complete an application was from 4 to 5 years (among the self-employed, delays of 10 years were not extraordinary). Legal requisites were extremely complex and divergent and were checked in a judicial type of procedure. In general, the smaller the subgroup of insured, the better organized its files, and the shorter the period to obtain the benefits and vice versa. Huge deficits and the lack of resources were additional causes for artificial delays in the granting of benefits. Delays in the procedure were longer among self-employed, rural workers, and civil servants. The process of unification and standardization and the partial use of computers has helped to reduce the accumulation of applications and their processing time. In 1969 delays of one year were still common and the goal quoted by some officials was to reduce the procedure to three months.[37] Powerful subgroups have exerted pressure to reduce the procedural time. Thus, in 1973, the Federation of Electricity Workers signed an agreement (with the Secretariat of Social Security) to help process benefits in order to cut the time required to ten days, assigning the benefit only one month after the application was filed.[38]

Table 5-13 compares average yearly pensions per capita among the various groups and subgroups in 1966. The first two columns refer, respectively, to old-age and survivors' pensions; the third column is an average of both. The last column provides a ratio of the overall average pension per capita of each subgroup and group in relation to that of domestic servants. The ranking of subgroups according to their pension per capita, highest to lowest, is as follows: armed forces, banking-insurance, journalists, public utilities, transportation (average of merchant marine and railroads), civil servants (general), entrepreneurs, commerce, industry, rural workers, domestic servants, self-employed workers, and professionals. This ranking is almost identical to that made by the 1961 ECLA study on income distribution. In the latter, data on the armed forces were missing; this group appears in table 5-13 at the top of the distribution. (The average per-capita pension of the armed forces was 5.2 times higher than that of domestic servants.) On the other hand, in the ECLA study, professionals and entrepreneurs were ranked at the top of the income distribution, while in table 5-13 professionals appear at the bottom and entrepreneurs at the center of the pension per-capita distribution. This is probably the result of a special contribution of these subgroups (not based on actual income but on a minimum payment within a scale) which, in turn, reduces the basis for computing the pension.[39] The conclusion to be drawn from table 5-13 is that the pension system reproduces income inequalities like a mirror; it does not perform any progressive income redistribution function.

It is not possible to make a sophisticated analysis of the differences in health facilities by occupational groups in Argentina. These facilities are clustered in sectors, most of which are unrelated to the main groups and subgroups identified in this nation. The major difficulty is the lack of data; the very scarce information available suffers from serious gaps and is often contradictory. Roughly one-third of the population (the poorest who are unable to afford better service) goes to public hospitals, another third to mutual insurance institutions, one-fourth to union clinics, and the rest to private clinics. The best hospital system is probably that of the military, with the army having the finest facilities. The largest number of hospital beds and physicians are concentrated in the public system. This system, the oldest in the country, has experienced physicians but obsolete facilities. An official report of the Public Health Secretariat said of it in 1969: "The state or public system has been gradually deteriorating in the last two or three decades in terms of installed capacity and attention to the public due to scarcity of financial resources and lack of paramedical person-

Table 5-13
Average Yearly Pensions by Occupational Group in
Argentina: 1966
(in current pesos per capita)

Occupational Group	Old-Age	Survivors'	Average	Ratio[a]
Blue- and white-collars	*1,352.4*	*958.8*	*1,022.4*	*1.4*
Industry	1,052.4	785.4	1,000.8	1.4
Commerce	1,138.8	820.2	1,052.4	1.5
Rural workers	857.4	632.4	820.8	1.2
Merchant marine	1,769.4	1,126.8	1,564.8	2.2
Banking and insurance	2,358.6	1,680.6	2,161.2	3.1
Journalists and printers	1,582.2	1,141.8	1,490.4	2.1
Domestic servants	709.2	525.6	707.4	1.0
Civil servants	*1,452.6*	*984.6*	*1,312.8*	*1.8*
General	1,540.8	972.6	1,374.6	1.9
Railroads	1,221.0	910.8	1,107.6	1.6
Public utilities	1,596.0	1,069.8	1,456.8	2.1
Self-employed	*875.4*	*635.4*	*801.0*	*1.1*
Workers	674.4	487.8	646.8	0.9
Entrepreneurs	1,273.8	901.8	1,145.4	1.6
Professionals	678.6	516.0	610.8	0.9
Armed forces	—	—	*3,314.6[b]*	*5.2*
Total	1,246.2	908.4	1,158.6	1.6

SOURCES: *Blue- and white-collars, civil servants,* and *self-employed*
from Ministerio de Bienestar Social, Secretaría de Estado de Seguridad Social, Comité Ejecutivo Censal *Censo de Beneficiarios de los
organismos nacionales de previsión social,* Buenos Aires, 1966.
Armed forces computed from Héctor L. Diéguez and Alberto Petrecolla, *Estudio estadístico del sistema previsional argentino en el
periodo 1950–72.*
    a. Ratios of average pension per capita (third column) in relation
to domestic servants.
    b. The figure was computed from data on benefits provided by
Diéguez and Petrecolla. Although their benefits were principally pensions, their benefit per capita for blue- and white-collars, civil servants, and self-employed tend to be higher than ours. Hence, an
average of the difference between the two data sets was applied
to the Diéguez-Petrecolla figure for the armed forces in order to make
it comparable with our data.

nel. This has resulted in a poor image of public medical care."[40] The same report
stated that the system of mutual insurance funds and unions was better than the public one especially in terms of equipment but that it was overcrowded and in a state of
crisis. Private and armed-forces hospitals are probably the best, in terms of beds,
physicians available per user, and quality of equipment and service.[41]

Table 5-15 shows the 1965 distribution of hospital beds and physicians by geographical region in Argentina. The Metropolitan region (Federal Capital) had the
highest ratio of hospital beds per 1,000 inhabitants, followed by Patagonia (mainly
due to the large number of hospital beds in Tierra del Fuego); then came Pampa,
Center, Northwest, and Comahue which had similar facilities, followed by Cuyo, and
ending with the Northeast region which had the lowest ratio. (The provinces best

Table 5-15
Health Facilities by Geographical Region in Argentina: 1965

Region	Total Population[a] (in thousands)	Hospital Beds	Beds per 1,000 Inhabitants[b]	Physicians	Physicians per 10,000 Inhabitants	Composite Weighted Index of Beds and Physicians
Metropolitan	2,966.6	30,259.3	10.2	13,617	45.9	33.1
Pampa	9,456.3	55,792.2	5.9	10,118	10.7	8.0
Center	2,056.3	11,720.9	5.7	2,961	14.4	10.0
Northeast	1,616.4	4,687.6	2.9	663	4.1	3.3
Patagonia	206.5	1,796.6	8.7	114	5.5	7.1
Cuyo	1,176.4	5,176.2	4.4	965	8.2	6.2
Comahue	461.9	2,309.5	5.0	300	6.5	5.5
Northwest	2,073.1	10,365.5	5.0	1,099	5.3	5.1
Total	20,013.5	122,107.8	6.1	29,837	14.9	10.5

SOURCES: Presidencia de la Nación, Consejo Nacional de Desarrollo, *Plan Nacional de Desarrollo 1965–1969* (Buenos Aires, 1965) and *Distribución de médicos en la República Argentina por provincias y departamentos* (Buenos Aires: Tema de Divulgación Interna, No. 43, 1964); and Fiat Delegación para la América Latina, Oficina de Estudios para la Colaboración Económica Internacional, *Argentina económica y financiera* (Buenos Aires: OECEI, 1966).
a. 1960 figures.
b. 1963 figures.

served in terms of hospital beds were Tierra del Fuego, Federal Capital, Buenos Aires, and Córdoba with a ratio of hospital beds well above the national average, while the provinces of Formosa, Misiones, and Chaco had a ratio well below that average.) Physicians were heavily concentrated in the Metropolitan region which had a ratio (physicians per 10,000 inhabitants) 3 times that of the Center, 4 times that of Pampa, 6 to 7 times that of Cuyo and Comahue, and 9 to 11 times that of Patagonia, Northwest, and Northeast. In 1965, the Federal Capital and the provinces of Buenos Aires, Córdoba and Santa Fé had the best supply of physicians (less than 700 inhabitants per physician), while the provinces of Formosa and Misiones had the worst (over 2,500 inhabitants per physician).[42]

The Inequality Effect of Social Security Stratification

The inequalities in Argentina's social security system can be seen in coverage, financing, and benefits. The most significant jump in the coverage of the economically active population (EAP) took place from 1944 to 1954 with the entrance of industrial, commercial, and rural workers, as well as the self-employed, into the insured population. Data collected for this study pertain to the 1960s when the majority of the EAP was already insured. Nevertheless, a significant expansion of coverage of the EAP is shown, from 55 percent in 1960 to 68 percent in 1970. Coverage of the total population also increased from 44 to 55 percent in the same period.

The percentages of the active insured in 1960 were as follows: blue- and white-collars 59 percent, civil servants 29 percent, self-employed 9 percent, and armed forces 3 percent. Ten years later, blue- and white-collars were still the largest group of insured although the proportion declined to 41 percent. Surprisingly, the group of self-employed came second, with an increasing proportion—37 percent. Civil servants had fallen to third place with 19 percent and the armed forces had declined slightly to 2.6 percent.

Using data on income distribution for 1960, the insured population can be clustered into three major strata, each one embracing various subgroups of insured: the high-income stratum (professionals and entrepreneurs); the medium-income stratum (banking-insurance, public utilities, transportation, civil servants, armed forces, journalists, commerce, industry, construction); and the low-income stratum (other services, agriculture, and domestic servants).

The degree of coverage among occupational subgroups varied greatly in 1960, the most recent year for which data disaggregated by occupation for both the overall population and the insured population are available. A clustering by "class of worker" showed that salaried workers and wage-earners (including blue- and white-collars, civil servants, and armed forces) were covered, as an average, by almost 70 percent (although with varying degrees of coverage by group and subgroup as will be seen later). Less than 23 percent of self-employed workers and professionals and less than 16 percent of entrepreneurs were covered. By 1970, however, coverage among the self-employed had increased dramatically, particularly among workers (who in that year represented 70 percent of all the self-employed insured).

A different clustering, by economic activity, makes it possible to disaggregate somewhat the huge category of salaried and wage-earners, giving an idea of the divergent degree of coverage within it. The subgroups with better coverage were public utilities, transportation, and communication (almost 97 percent) and banking-insurance, commerce, and services (85 percent). (The *services* group embraced, however, subgroups as different as civil servants and domestic servants, and it is not possible to estimate their respective degree of coverage.) At a considerable distance came manufacturing, mining, and construction (with a coverage of 57 percent) and agriculture and fishing (with 54 percent). Self-employed were at the bottom with 19 percent.

Evidence accumulated in this chapter suggests that the segment of the labor force with the best coverage is made up of salaried and wage personnel working in strategic trades, usually with a long history and high degree of unionization and ranked in the upper half of the medium-income stratum. This includes banking-insurance, public utilities, railroad, and merchant marine. Belonging to this segment, although generating most of their power from sources other than unionization, are the civil service and the armed forces. The next segment of the labor force in terms of coverage, is that in trades of rising significance, with lower degree of unionization and ranked in the lower half of the medium-income stratum. This is made up of industry, construction, and probably commerce. (Although the clustering by economic activity places commerce in the first segment, this is an average of subgroups with divergent coverage.) The poorest covered segment of the labor force is that employed in less strategic trades, which either became organized recently or are not unionized at all and ranked in the low-income stratum. Here we find rural workers, domestic servants, and self-employed workers.

The financing of the national social security system in Argentina was made more uniform in 1973 as the result of the unification and standardization process initiated by the military seven years before. Within the civil sector, all employees' and employers' contributions for various programs (pensions, health) are equal for all subgroups, with a minor exception. Some of the changes in contribution probably had a progressive effect in income redistribution (e.g., contributions from rural workers and domestic servants were not changed, but their employers experienced an increase of 7 percentage points), but most had a regressive effect (e.g., the contributions of insurance and public utilities personnel, journalists, railroad and merchant-marine workers, and civil servants were reduced and their employers' contributions increased by an average of 3 percentage points). The armed forces, excluded from the standardization process, continue with their old system of financing. Although the military currently pays 8 percent of its salary for pensions (versus 5 percent in the rest of the system), its employer—the state, from public revenues—contributes 27 or 36 percent (versus 15 percent in the rest) and, in addition, subsidizes from 2 to 99 percent of the cost of most pensions.

With few exceptions, the social security revenue per capita (rpc) of each subgroup is directly correlated to its income, indicating that the financing system does not perform a progressive income-distribution function. The highest rpc is that of banking-insurance, the subgroup at the top of the medium-income stratum, while the lowest rpc is that of self-employed workers, rural workers, and domestic servants, all subgroups in the low-income stratum. Professionals and entrepreneurs ranked in the high-income stratum have, however, a rpc more typical of the low-income stratum. This can be explained by their special system of coverage which results in actual coverage of medium- and low-income individuals and by their special financing which results in contributions not proportionate to their actual income.

The financial situation of the social security funds throughout the period 1950–1972 varied substantially. Usually the subgroups with a relatively high rpc, benefits congruent with their revenues, and good control of evasion had financially stable funds which generated surpluses (e.g., banking-insurance). There were some funds with a relatively high rpc but with deficits either because they had a system of benefits excessively generous (e.g., armed forces), or a serious problem of evasion or accumulated state debts (e.g., civil servants, public utilities, transportation), or both. Subgroups with a relatively low rpc were often plagued, in addition, with problems of evasion and suffered from deficits (e.g., rural workers, domestic servants).

In the late 1960s all revenues from civilian funds were pooled into a common fund which permits the compensation of deficits with surpluses within the system. (It should be noted that the only privileged group in terms of contribution, the armed forces, is excluded from this mechanism.) The compensatory mechanism creates two different effects in terms of income distribution. A progressive effect results when surpluses of some medium-income subgroups (banking-insurance, commerce, industry) are used to cover the deficits of the low-income subgroups (rural workers, domestic servants). Probably the surplus of the high-income subgroup of entrepreneurs compensates for the deficit of low-income, self-employed workers achieving a similar effect. Conversely, a regressive effect in income distribution is provoked when surpluses from lower–medium-income subgroups (commerce and industry) are used to offset deficits of upper–medium-income subgroups (public utilities, transportation, and civil servants).

Although the process of standardization in the Argentine social security system has eroded significant inequalities in benefits that prevailed prior to 1968, important differences still remain. A simple count of the number of social security benefits available to each occupational group allows us to rank them as follows: (1) armed forces with the highest number; (2) civil servants and practically all blue- and white-collar workers (part of the rural workers and all domestic servants are eligible for fewer benefits than those granted to their group but for more than the next group); and (3) self-employed.

The conditions for granting benefits (such as requirements to gain the right, basic salary to compute the benefit, the amount of the benefit, and the compatibility of the benefit) have also been standardized within the civil sector into two major and equal regulations: one for personnel in dependency relationship (that is, all blue- and white-collars and civil servants) and a second, less generous, for the self-employed. The exclusion of the armed forces from both uniform sets has resulted in a widened gap (in relation to conditions to grant benefits) between that group and the civilian insured. The standardization process has not eliminated some advantageous conditions granted to privileged individuals within subgroups. This is the case of Supreme Court judges and attorneys, the president and vice-president of the nation, diplomats and teachers, within the subgroup of civil servants; and electrical workers within the public utilities subgroup.

The ranking of subgroups according to their per-capita pension is similar to their ranking according to income: armed forces, banking-insurance employees, journalists, public-utilities personnel, transportation workers, civil servants, entrepreneurs, commerce employees, industrial workers, rural workers, domestic servants, self-employed workers, and professionals. The ratio of the armed forces pension per capita to that of rural workers is 4 to 1. A discrepancy between income and per-capita pension distributions is obvious in the cases of professionals and entrepreneurs; it results from their special system of coverage and financing explained above. In summary, the pension system does not perform a progressive function in income redistribution.

Differences in health facilities by occupational groups cannot be traced quantitatively in Argentina due to both the lack of adequate data and the fact that such facilities are clustered by sectors that do not necessarily correspond to the occupational structure. Scattered information suggests, nevertheless, that armed-forces and private hospitals (the latter used by high-income stratum) are probably the best in terms of physicians and beds per capita and in the quality of their equipment and service. Next follow the hospitals of mutual insurance funds and unions, which apparently serve the bulk of the civilian insured and are overcrowded and in financial crisis. At the bottom are the state hospitals, used by the noninsured and which have gradually deteriorated in the last two or three decades.

The various comparisons presented above allow us to rank the major groups and their subgroups, according to the excellency of their social security systems, as follows: (1) armed forces; (2) civil servants and blue- and white-collars (with a significant distance, within the latter, between the "labor aristocracy" made up of banking-insurance, public utilities, railroad, and merchant marine and the rest of the group made up of commerce and industry); (3) rural workers and domestic servants; and (4) self-employed in this order: entrepreneurs, professionals, and workers.

Social security inequalities among the eight geographic regions of Argentina were detected in the degree of coverage for pensions and availability of health facilities. These regions can be ranked, in terms of their development, using several indicators (i.e., degree of industrialization, contribution to GDP, production per capita, urban population, number of most populated cities, availability of natural resources) as follows: Metropolitan closely followed by Pampa; next, Center with Northwest and Cuyo lagging behind; finally Patagonia with Comahue and Northeast at the bottom.

Differences among provinces within a region are also significant. There are no data available on income distribution by regions or provinces. We assume that the regions rank in terms of income similar to that of development.

Coverage of the population in pension programs is higher in the most developed regions and lower in the least developed as follows: Metropolitan (52.9 percent), Pampa (19.8 percent), Center (11.3 percent), Northwest and Cuyo (7.9 percent), Patagonia (6.8 percent), Comahue (4.9 percent), and Northeast (3.5 percent). Coverage of the EAP in provinces follows, with few exceptions, the same pattern as among regions: the Metropolitan area and provinces in Pampa region have higher coverage than provinces in the Center, Northwest, and Cuyo; the latter, in turn, have higher coverage than provinces in Patagonia, Comahue, and Northeast. The range goes from total coverage in the Metropolitan area down to 6 percent in Formosa. Significant correlations were found between the degree of social security coverage in provinces, on the one hand, and both the size of the EAP in provinces (.82) and the urban percentage of the EAP in provinces (.65).

Data on the distribution of health facilities (combining both hospital beds per 1,000 inhabitants and physicians per 10,000 inhabitants) among regions largely duplicates the ranking by degree of coverage in pensions: Metropolitan (33.1), Center (10.0), Pampa (8.0), Patagonia (7.1), Cuyo (6.2), Comahue (5.5), Northwest (5.1), and Northeast (3.3). The high ranking of Patagonia is due to the great number of hospital beds in oil-rich Tierra del Fuego. The low ranking of Pampa is probably due to the fact that its population, being close to Buenos Aires, uses the latter's health facilities.

In summary, the most developed and urbanized regions/provinces have a concentration of vital economic activities (in transportation, public utilities, banking and insurance, commerce, manufacturing, government services) and probably strong unions and political activism. The most powerful pressure groups are concentrated in these regions/provinces which consequently received early social security protection and currently have the highest degree of coverage in pensions and the best health facilities. Conversely, the more backward, isolated regions/provinces are those with a labor force largely engaged in agriculture, controlled by landowners, and, probably, poorly unionized and politically passive. Lacking strong pressure groups, these regions/provinces were latecomers in social security and currently have the worst social security protection in coverage for pensions and health facilities.

The massification of privilege flourished in Argentina in the late 1950s and early 1960s until it was halted by the countermovement towards unification-standardization which began in 1967. Underprivileged subgroups such as rural workers and domestic servants made significant advances in obtaining benefits previously reserved for privileged groups. Today their standardized legal system is similar to those of other subgroups within their group. They also profit from the transfer of revenue from higher income subgroups through the compensatory mechanism also introduced in the late 1960s.

The process of expansion of coverage and massification of privilege, compounded with rising administrative expenditures, caused social security costs to rise steadily throughout the 1960s. Revenues from pension programs alone represented 3.6 percent of GNP in 1960 and 4.3 percent in 1970, while expenditures increased from 2.9 to 4.2 percent in the same period. When expenditures in pensions and health were combined for 1969, they represented 6.7 percent of GNP. From 1960 to 1970 the labor force increased by 17 percent, but the number of passive workers jumped by 86 percent. The average ratio of active vis-a-vis passive insured was 5.4 to 1 in 1960 and steadily declined to 3.1 to 1 in 1969.

From 1950 to 1965, the surplus generated by part of the social security system offset the combined deficit of the rest. Nevertheless, since 1966, the surplus has gradually decreased, becoming smaller than the deficit, resulting in an accumulated net deficit of 35 million pesos. The military achieved significant success from 1967 to 1973 in unifying and standardizing most of the system and providing some temporary financial relief for it, but excluded themselves from the unification process and failed to solve the financial crisis in the long run. The restoration of Peronism from 1973 to 1976 certainly did not contribute to the correction of the remaining problems of Argentina's social security system.

6 The Case of Mexico

Historical Evolution of Social Security in Mexico Since Independence

The Mexican war of independence which began in 1810 was largely a result of domestic problems which divided the society of New Spain.[1] One of the most crucial problems was the rampant inequality existing between the minority of white Spaniards and most creoles on the one hand, and the mass of the population made up of Indians, mestizos, and castes (mixes of Indians and blacks) on the other. The whites, mainly peninsulars, controlled land, wealth, and high posts in the government and church. The nonwhites were either confined to lowly jobs as hacienda peons, domestic servants, and workers in mines and artisan shops or were peasants in Indian communities. The problem was compounded by the almost total lack of social mobility: nonwhites were condemned to a life of illiteracy since education was essentially available only to the Spaniards and their offspring.

This volatile situation provoked, during the colonial period, several insurrections led by Indians and mestizos. In 1810 Miguel Hidalgo, a creole priest, decreed the abolition of slavery and servitude (*peonaje*) and annulled all tributes paid by Indians and castes. Hidalgo's successor in the insurgency movement was another priest, a mestizo, José María Morelos, who advocated the improvement of the bottom stratum of society, the reduction of inequality in wealth distribution, and the suppression of the hacienda system. Some of these principles were incorporated into the first political constitution, enacted in 1814.

1821–1924

Political independence from Spain was eventually attained in 1821 but led by a very different ideological group. Its leader was Agustín Iturbide, a conservative creole who had opposed Hidalgo and Morelos, and who took control in order to avoid both the radical change demanded by the dispossessed Mexican masses and the liberal currents emanating from Spain. In 1823 Iturbide was overthrown, and new liberal and conservative coalitions dominated Mexican politics, alternating in power, for three decades. In 1824 a conservative federal constitution was enacted which rhetorically proclaimed political equality for all citizens. Among the first laws enacted in the new republic was a decree in 1824 which replaced the old *montepío civil* with a compulsory mutual fund which granted retirement pensions to officials in the executive, judiciary, and treasury. (This system was subsequently expanded to include pensions for survivors—mothers of deceased officials—in 1832; disability pensions and extended coverage to diplomats in 1834; and a special pension for postal employees in 1856.) The *montepío militar*, however, continued for one century. Artisans, who received economic protection through customs barriers, remained associated in guilds and protected by *cofradías*, which soon began to decay. The low stratum of the population did not experience any significant improvement in its situation. Although tributes were abolished, the hacienda system survived and thus kept the peons in virtual servitude.

The ruling elite during this period (1821–1855) was unable or unwilling to develop a strong national state, power largely remained at the local level, and anarchy reigned. The predominant segment of the elite was conservative, made up of large landowners (*hacendados*), clergymen, and merchants in large establishments. An opposing liberal force—made up of professionals, medium landowners, small merchants, and owners of artisan shops—endorsed a secular, modern, national state. The equilibrium between the two forces was maintained by the army, thus increasing its power. During this period of increasingly conservative rule and military assumption of power, the situation of the masses deteriorated and by the mid-nineteenth century, social stratification in Mexico was probably more rigid than before.[2] In 1854 an insurgent movement broke out and made public a political document (the Ayutla Plan) which demanded separation of church and state, religious freedom, and nationalization of church property. The armed struggle spread throughout the country and overthrew the conservative military government.

A new liberal government coming to office at mid-century enacted in 1857 a constitution which represented the triumph of economic liberalism and political federalism in Mexico. Following the laissez-faire philosophy typical of the times, the constitution endorsed the free operation of market forces, called for the dissolution of corporate property, treated labor as merchandise, and proclaimed that the state would abstain from meddling in economic affairs. The constitution also empowered the Congress to grant gratuitous concessions. In 1858, Benito Juárez became president and soon enacted the Reform Laws which endorsed, among other things, the separation of church and state (an issue long disputed in Mexico) and the abolition of corporate forms of property.

The liberal measures would eventually result in a higher concentration of land in fewer hands, those of the *hacendados*, and in the deterioration of conditions for segments of the lower stratum. The church land was nationalized and bought at low prices by landowners, merchants, and bureaucrats (including some in the liberal government). Furthermore, the land of Indian communities and church missions was also nationalized and sold, forcing the peasants to become peons on the haciendas. The movement against the church and corporations also affected forms of social protection; thus Indian *cofradías* attached to the church missions and artisans' *cofradías* disappeared. The liberal philosophy applied to international trade resulted in the elimination of protectionist measures, hence increasing imports and hurting artisans, many of whom would eventually become workers in factories. The old guilds and *cofradías* were replaced by less successful mutual-aid societies and cooperatives, some of which nevertheless survived until the twentieth century.

The restoration of the republic in 1867 reentrenched the liberal-oligarchic state which lasted until the revolution. There was a serious contradiction between the theory and practice of this regime. It proclaimed itself in favor of a secular, democratic, egalitarian, laissez-faire state in which the market forces would operate freely in trade, labor, and agrarian relations. Hence the abolition of servitude, of corporations and communal property, of trade barriers both within and outside of the nation, as well as the facilities given to foreign investors in mines, railroads, banking, and industry. But the liberal laws strengthened the hacienda system and the liberals eventually became landowners themselves, joining the old *hacendados*. The power of the landed oligarchy blocked the implementation of most liberal ideals and hence the *peonaje* system, racial discrimination, and local *caudillismo* persisted. The liberal governments, however, supported the goal of a national, modern state against the regional and local interests represented in the Congress. Largely as a result of that fight, these governments were typified by a strong executive, no real autonomy of the Congress and judiciary, and weak power of the states. The governments gradually developed a national bureaucracy and army and often intervened in economic affairs; for example, they reintroduced protectionism, permitted commercial monopolies, and financed the construction of railroads. There were no true political parties. Most of the population was deprived of the right to vote and civil liberties were enjoyed only by a small segment of the population and for a short period of time, during the Juárez years.

After the death of Juárez in 1872, the opposing interests within the government broke into an open conflict, and from 1876 until 1910 General Porfirio Díaz either controlled the presidency or ruled as dictator. During the *Porfiriato,* a balance was maintained between the landed oligarchy and the growing national bourgeoisie. The federal bureaucracy grew increasingly technocratic (led by the *científicos*), sponsored the introduction of modern techniques in transportation (railroads), mining, public utilities, manufacturing, and agriculture (particularly sugar plantations and mills), and helped to consolidate national vis-a-vis regional power. Emphasis was given to economic development, facilitating the sharp increase in foreign investment without concern for distribution. These policies generated a phenomenal boom, doubling real GDP in about a decade.

In the midst of this prosperity the situation of the lower stratum hardly improved. The regime took a definite anti-Indian position. Peons received ridiculously low wages and became indebted for life to the hacienda stores (*tiendas de raya*) which gave them credit and charged extremely high prices for their merchandise. Peasant and Indian uprisings were common by the turn of the century. Labor continued to be treated as merchandise in the regulations of the Civil Code of 1870–1884 and the Commercial Code of 1889–1894. The gradual disappearance of the artisans and rapid industrialization generated a growing proletariat employed in factories under intolerable conditions. At the beginning, workers organized mutual aid societies copied from those developed by the artisans; soon, some of these societies began to defend the workers' interests against their employers. In 1872 a Círculo de Obreros de México was founded to protect the workers and improve labor conditions; in 1874 a Gran Círculo de Obreros added specific goals such as the regulation of working hours and wage rates; railroad brotherhoods and associations were organized in the 1890s. The first strikes occurred in 1865 and 1867, among textile workers, and in 1874 among miners. Although these strikes resulted in few concessions (e.g., wage increases, regulation of women's and children's labor), strikes did not become generalized until the first decade of the twentieth century as a result of rapid industrialization, harsh labor conditions, and the influence of Anarcho-Syndicalist and Utopian-Socialist ideas and American railroad strikes.

In 1906 in opposition to Díaz the Liberal Mexican party (of Anarcho-Syndicalist philosophy) was founded and publicized a program which addressed the problems of peasants and urban workers. The program advocated state distribution of uncultivated land, the creation of an agricultural credit bank, eight-hour industrial workday, prohibition of child labor in factories, the obligation of employers to indemnify for industrial occupational accidents, and the introduction of retirement pensions. The Liberal party later supported workers' demands and strikes and Díaz harshly suppressed its members.

Under the *Porfiriato* only the most dynamic economic activities such as textiles, mining, and railroads had called strikes. In 1906 the Gran Círculo de Obreros Libres de Orizaba (the cradle of the Mexican labor movement) was founded. An increasing number of strikes in copper mines and textile mills met with government repression. The two most industrialized states of Mexico reacted to this increasing labor activism by enacting laws making employers responsible for the indemnification of disability and death from occupational accidents: Mexico in 1904, and Nuevo León in 1906.

The already difficult social situation was aggravated by the international economic crisis of 1907–1908, coupled with severe stagflation in Mexico. Political stability was threatened by a confrontation between *científicos* and regional forces, and Díaz's plan to reelect himself once again in 1910. Two opposing parties (Democratic and Anti-Reelectionist) joined forces to nominate Francisco Madero (1911–1913), a liberal representative of regional forces, for the presidency. The Democratic party, in a manifesto made public in 1909, had requested the passage of legislation to protect workers from the effects of occupational accidents, while the Anti-Reelectionist party in its 1910 convention promised to take action to improve workers' conditions. Madero also pledged passage of legislation to grant disability and survivors' pensions in cases of occupational accidents in mining, industry, and agriculture. After fraudulent elections, Madero led a nationwide insurgency movement which forced Díaz to resign, and took office in mid-1911.

Madero's Constitutional Progressive party program advocated the introduction of a federal system of indemnifications and pensions for workers suffering occupational accidents. After a quarter century of deprivation and repression, workers took advantage of the new freedom, labor activism boomed, and labor demands and protests rapidly accelerated. Unions of textile and mining workers and a federation of printers were organized. In 1912, the first national labor organization was founded, led by Anarcho-Syndicalists who had been associated with the Liberal party: Casa del Obrero Mundial (COM). Waves of strikes were launched at the end of 1911 and throughout 1912 by textile, mining, railroad, and dock workers. Madero approached the volatile political situation with divergent techniques. On the one hand he tried to calm the workers by establishing a Department of Labor in the Ministry of Fomento to deal with labor conflicts through conciliation and arbitration and organized a commission to draft a law providing indemnification for occupational accidents. On the other hand, towards the end of his presidency, he disbanded workers' demonstrations, exiled or imprisoned some union leaders, criticized the COM, and encouraged the formation of a less militant labor organization. In 1913 Victoriano Huerta deposed Madero, but then was overthrown in 1914, leaving behind chaos and civil war.

General Venustiano Carranza ended the war by taking military control. In 1915 he enacted laws under which land might be distributed to peasants, abolished the *tiendas de raya,* and established minimum wages for all workers in the territory occupied by his army. COM upheld Carranza in exchange for freedom to organize workers and lobby for national labor legislation. When Carranza won support of part of the higher social stratum of the Mexican society, anxious to restore peace and order, he took a more compromising attitude: he pushed for some labor reform but within the capitalist framework. Carranza also established the basis for the politico-military bureaucracy that would run the country for several years.

Soon problems arose between the president and COM and a split had developed by the end of 1915. The following year COM launched a series of violent strikes and then a general strike against the government; and Carranza banned the COM. In 1918, a new labor confederation was organized (Confederación Regional Obrera Mexicana, CROM), led by Luis Morones, a leader of the electrical workers. CROM originally had Anarcho-Syndicalist tendencies but soon took a more compromising attitude and supported Presidents Alvaro Obregón and Plutarco Elias Calles, thus beginning the Mexican tradition of the labor movement's dependence on the government.

The most significant accomplishment of the Carranza administration was the enactment, in 1917, of a new constitution (still in force today with few amendments) which set the legal basis for the consolidation and stable development of the revolution. The constitution broke with the laissez-faire philosophy and introduced the principle of state regulation of labor conditions although within the framework of a market system; trade unions would be controlled by the state and have a reformist not revolutionary role. Article 123 of the constitution became the pioneer in the Latin American movement of constitutionalization of labor rights: equal wages for equal work, eight-hour workday, six-day workweek, a day of rest (Sunday), minimum wages, compensation for unjustified layoff, prohibition of child labor, and the right to strike. In the field of social security the constitution showed the spirit of compromise between social and private insurance: it clearly held employers responsible for payment of indemnification for death as well as for permanent and temporary disability of workers caused by occupational accidents.[3] But, elsewhere, it vaguely and timidly stated that the federal and state governments should promote funds of popular insurance (*cajas de seguro popular*) or mutual savings associations to be financed solely by workers to help them in case of death, disability, accidents, and layoff.[4] In the following years, fifteen states enacted laws implementing the constitutional mandate on occupational hazards, but there was no effective public action on mutual savings funds.

In 1920 CROM and the new Mexican Labor party supported General Alvaro Obregón (1920–1924) in his bid for the presidency. Obregón began agrarian reform, initiated the professionalization of the army, and took a strong pro-labor stand. The collaboration of CROM with the government alienated the Anarcho-Syndicalist group which in 1921 established a new federation (Confederación General de Trabajadores, CGT). In the same year, Obregón organized a commission which proposed a national social security system financed by a payroll tax paid solely by the employers, and granting workmen's compensation, old-age pensions, and life insurance. But the draft met opposition from employers and was dropped.

1925–1942

In 1924, General Plutarco Elías Calles (1924–1928) was elected president, also with the endorsement of the Labor party and CROM. But the first three modern social security systems he established did not include the average worker. In 1925 all federal civil servants became eligible for old-age, seniority, disability, and survivors' pensions, protection against occupational hazards, and funeral aid. In 1926 the military (who under Calles had been allocated as much as 44 percent of all federal expenditures) received a similar system of pensions and protection against occupational hazards. As an official publication states: "The laws enacted by President Calles certainly served to consolidate the revolutionary government which, having assured the loyalty of the armed forces and the efficiency of civil servants, could in subsequent years devote all its energies to fostering the development of the nation."[5] The third social security system created by Calles protected federal school teachers. The latter had begun to engage in mutual aid societies and associations in 1918 but these organizations, in the face of violations of the teachers' rights, were gradually transformed into unions. In 1922 teachers of the city of Veracruz led by Marxist leader Vicente Lombardo Toledano struck, demanding payment of salaries that were due them. Other teacher strikes were launched in 1925 and 1928. In 1928, Calles—a former teacher—established the Teachers' Federal Insurance granting them survivors' pensions and funeral aid.

The 1928 elections provoked a confrontation between the government and the Labor party and CROM marking the beginning of the latter's decline. CROM had its own candidate and opposed Calles' candidate, Obregón, who organized a supportive Social Security party (Partido de Previsión Social), one of whose goals was to implement the federal social security program envisioned in Obregón's draft. Obregón was elected but was assassinated before taking office, and Emilio Portes Gil became president. In 1928, Gil took a pro-labor stand and advocated a constitutional amendment entrusting the federal government with the enactment of separate labor and social security laws.[6] The amendment also endorsed a national compulsory social security program to cover workers in case of disability, death, unemployment, and occupational accidents and diseases. (Provision for old age was not contemplated.)

In 1929, the Revolutionary National party (Partido Nacional Revolucionario, PNR)—the first antecedent of PRI—was founded and accommodated groups of divergent philosophies and extraction. It would become a pivotal instrument in constructing a modern centralized state by gradually overcoming the fragmentation of power held by military heroes, local caudillos and caciques, and leaders of interest groups. One of the first actions of the PNR was to endorse the social security draft prepared by the late Obregón.

The federal labor law was finally approved in 1931, during the presidency of Pascual Ortiz Rubio (1930–1932), but, since social security had been excluded from its content, the law only regulated protection for occupational accidents and diseases. Several social security laws were proposed, but none passed.

The period 1929–1932 was one of the most difficult in recent Mexican history. Economically there was stagnation compounded by the world depression. Wages declined and the leadership grew increasingly conservative in social matters. Politically, the assassination of Obregón left a vacuum largely filled by Calles who, as "Maximum Chief of the Revolution," exerted significant influence if not open control of the presidency. Peasant uprisings, strikes, and a grave conflict with the church complicated the scenario. The PNR was in control from 1929 on and other parties were either dominated or, as in the case of the Communist party, declared illegal and their members repressed. Workers' discontent and activism increased significantly. In 1929, the Communist party established its own labor confederation (Confederación Sindical Unitaria, CSU). In 1933, Marxist labor leader Lombardo Toledano left CROM and founded another dissident labor confederation (Confederación General de Obreros y Campesinos de México, CGOCM).

General Lázaro Cárdenas (1934–1940), the candidate of Calles and the PNR, was elected president in 1934. Calles thought that he would be able to continue his dominance but Cárdenas resisted the pressure. The latter took a permissive attitude toward labor; in 1935 the number of strikes tripled and the number of strikers increased tenfold.[7] Calles bitterly complained about this situation and accused Cárdenas of leading the nation into chaos. In the power struggle between Cárdenas and Calles which ensued, the Marxist CGOCM, the Communist CSU, and powerful unions such as those of railroad and electrical workers joined forces in a National Committee of Proletarian Defense which backed Cárdenas (CROM and CGT refused to participate). Also supporting Cárdenas was a newly created (1935) national peasant confederation (Confederación Nacional Campesina, CNC). Cárdenas won the struggle and, in 1936, expelled Calles from Mexico. In that year, the Committee of Proletarian Defense convened the Congress for the Unification of Workers which gave birth to the Confederación de Trabajadores de México (CTM), still today the most powerful labor confederation in the nation. The CTM, led by Marxist Lombardo Toledano, advocated in its program: free health care, pensions for old age, disability, death, and unemployment, and full protection against occupational accidents and diseases. The rate of unionization increased dramatically under Cárdenas, reaching a record of 14.5 percent of the labor force in 1940.

Cárdenas adopted a progressive attitude and introduced important socioeconomic reforms: nationalizing oil, breaking the *hacendados'* power, speeding up land distribution and the organization of *ejidos,* and increasing labor's share in the national income. In 1938 the president reorganized the PNR into the Partido de la Revolución Mexicana (PRM), direct predecessor of the PRI. The PRM was divided into four sectors: agrarian (mostly *ejidatarios* represented by CNC), labor (represented by CTM), "popular" (civil servants, bureaucrats, professionals), and the military.This shrewd move guaranteed the future predominance of civilian over military forces: Cárdenas recognized the power of the military but institutionalized and regulated it, while balancing its power against that of the other three sectors within PRM. In spite of the labor movement's role in Cárdenas' victory over Calles, its partial unification into the CTM and its political institutionalization through PRM, the mass of urban workers did not receive any social security benefits from Cárdenas' administration.

The only social security laws enacted by Cárdenas were in favor of the military: one established a savings bank for officials of the armed forces (1936) and the other improved their pension system (1939). Also under Cárdenas, two powerful unions (petroleum and railroad workers) signed collective agreements which included significant social security benefits. In 1935 petroleum workers, organized into a powerful federation (Sindicato de Trabajadores Petroleros de la República Mexicana, STPRM), received pensions for old age, disability, and survivors, workmen's compensation, and health care. A year later, the crisis in the oil industry began and its workers heartily backed Cárdenas who nationalized the industry in 1938. Railroad workers had been the first to organize into unions in the 1890s and to launch strikes; they actively participated in the overthrow of Díaz, increased their strikes in the late 1920s and early 1930s, and, in 1933, founded one of the first union federations of the nation (Sindicato de Trabajadores Ferrocarrileros de la República Mexicana, STFRM) which backed Cárdenas in his struggle against Calles and was very active in the foundation of the CTM. In 1938 the STFRM signed a collective contract with the nationalized railroad enterprises, receiving a social security package similar to the one previously obtained by petroleum workers.

Civil servants considerably increased their power under Cárdenas. In 1932, they began to organize unions in federal agencies dealing with transportation, printing, public health, and financing. Calles had repressed these unions, but, under Cárdenas, they gained strength, joined first into an Alliance of State Workers and later founded a National Federation of State Workers, which became the Federación de Sindicatos de Trabajadores al Servicio del Estado, FSTSE. Cárdenas enacted a law protecting the rights of these workers (allowing them to organize unions in all government activities of the executive, legislative, and judicial branches, as well as in autonomous public agencies) and giving them some additional social security benefits. He also proposed the creation of a National Confederation of Popular Organizations (Confederación Nacional de Organizaciones Populares, CNOP) to represent the bureaucrats in the party's "popular" sector, but it did not become operative until 1943.

Cárdenas' six-year plan (1934–1939) proposed the enactment of the federal social security law to protect the mass of workers. The president promised several times to enact such a law (in 1935, 1938, and 1940), and new legal drafts were prepared by the presidency, the Departments of Labor and Public Health, and the Ministry of Economics. One of the most elaborated drafts was done in 1938, by Ignacio García Téllez at the request of Cárdenas; it included protection of all risks including unemployment. But like their predecessors, none of these drafts became law.

1943–1953

The new president, General Manuel Avila Camacho (1940–1946), consolidated the reforms introduced by Cárdenas, settled the oil dispute with the United States, reached a compromise with the church, protected private property, gave security and incentives to private and foreign investors, fostered industrial production (helped by the demand for domestic products during World War II), and presided over the Mexican economic takeoff. In large measure economic growth was the result of the governmental policy in favor of capital accumulation at the cost of distribution.[8] The structuralization of the party into sectors was now extremely useful in making the capital accumulation policy feasible, since popular mobilization had been channelled into organizations and party sectors controlled by the state. Soon after taking power Avila Camacho replaced Lombardo Toledano with the moderate Fidel Velázquez as Secretary General of the CTM (1941) and coopted other labor leaders. The rate of unionization declined sharply during his term and corruption among labor leaders became widespread. In June 1942, in the midst of the war, a Pact of Workers Unity was signed by the CTM, the CROM, and the CGOCM to minimize labor conflicts. And yet, waves of strikes occurred in 1943–1944, either controlled by the CTM or repressed by the government. The number of strikes sharply declined in 1945–1946; and the total number under Avila Camacho was less than that under Cárdenas.

Avila Camacho not only used repression vis-a-vis labor but also implemented the federal social security law, more than twenty years after the first draft had been prepared by Obregón. The president created the Ministry of Labor and Social Welfare and appointed García Téllez—the technician who had prepared Cárdenas' draft—as minister. The latter then organized a technical commission to study the social security draft. This commission, led by Manuel García Cruz, different from its predecessors in that it was made up of representatives from workers, employers, and the Congress. The final draft was presented to Congress and became law in early 1943.

Was the introduction of social security for the mass of urban blue- and white-collar workers in Mexico a direct consequence of union pressure or was it mainly due to government initiative? The wave of strikes of 1943–1944 began after the law had been approved and hence could not influence its inception. Reyna claims that this step was taken, precisely in 1943, to help urban workers who were the hardest hit by inflation.[9] There is evidence that some radical unions perceived the law as a government palliative or a substitute for wage increments and violently opposed it. García Cruz, the head of the technical commission which prepared the law, called the opposition's movement against it "a revolution without rifles." But, in fact, he described such opposition in rather violent tones: a good number of workers opposed the law with strikes and demonstrations, some unions joined employers' associations to request the law's annulment, and there was even an attempt to set the headquarters of the incipient social security administration on fire.[10] Avila Camacho, however, stood firmly behind the law and eventually received the endorsement of all the major federations that had signed the Pact of Unity.

The law created the Mexican Institute of Social Insurance (Instituto Mexicano del Seguro Social, IMSS) as a federal, autonomous agency in charge of the administration of the social security system, which would eventually embrace all blue- and white-collar workers, making them eligible for old-age, disability and survivors' pensions, workmen's compensation, and health-maternity care. Actual coverage, nevertheless, was rather limited for many years. Health services began in 1944, at first limited to the Federal District and slowly expanded to other major cities: Puebla and Monterrey, in 1945, and Guadalajara and other large cities in Jalisco in 1946. At the end of 1946 the IMSS covered only 2 percent of the population and 3 percent of the labor force.[11]

Other subgroups received social security benefits during Avila Camacho's term: electrical workers, IMSS employees, and the military. Electrical workers established their first union in 1914, organized in the 1920s one of the largest labor federations (Sindicato Nacional de Electricistas de la República Mexicana, SNERM), participated in the founding of the CTM in 1936, and signed a collective agreement in 1941 with both government (the Federal Commission of Electricity, CFE, founded in 1937) and privately-owned power enterprises, gaining a social security package similar to that previously given to petroleum and railroad workers. Employees of the IMSS negotiated, in 1943, for additional benefits. In 1940 Avila Camacho abolished the military sector as a separate party entity and fused it with the popular sector; six years later, emphasizing the maturity and stability of the revolution, he changed the title of the party to Partido Revolucionario Institucional (PRI). In 1946 the military received life insurance as well as other benefits under a newly established Bank of the Army and the Navy.

In the period 1946–1958 the policy of capital accumulation and economic growth was accentuated: more incentives were given to investors, the infrastructure was expanded, protectionism to industry climaxed, the wage freeze continued while the cost of living climbed, U.S. investment poured into Mexico and was coupled with high rates of domestic investment, and GNP rates of growth were steadily high. Under two civilian presidents, social security policy continued with gradual expansion of IMSS coverage and concession of additional social security benefits to selected groups. This policy was adopted partly in order to keep the social and labor peace.

In 1947, under Miguel Alemán (1946–1952), the powerful railroad federation dropped out of CTM and helped found a separate organization (Confederación Unica de Trabajadores, CUT). In 1948 the government signed a new collective agreement with railroad workers which included improved social security benefits. Significantly soon thereafter the railroad federation withdrew from CUT. (In 1946–1948, teachers and war veterans were incorporated into the civil servant fund, but with extra benefits.) In 1947, Lombardo Toledano—no longer Secretary General of the CTM—founded the Popular party (later Popular Socialist Party, PPS) and unsuccessfully tried to elicit the CTM's support. The year after he was expelled from the CTM and organized a new Marxist confederation (Unión General de Obreros y Campesinos de México, UGOCM) which received its main support from *ejidatarios*, landless peasants, and agricultural workers. The UGOCM took a radical stand vis-a-vis the official peasant confederation of the agrarian sector of PRI: Confederación Nacional Campesina. In 1949, those insured under IMSS received new health benefits, requisites for pensions were relaxed, and allowances for marriage and new-born children added. Sugar plantation workers, organized in a union, signed a collective contract and became the first group in agriculture to receive health and maternity care through a hospital built exclusively for this group after a violent strike in 1951. IMSS coverage was extended geographically to additional cities and to the most urbanized and developed states (Nuevo León, Jalisco, Veracruz, and México), and to those close to the Federal District (Puebla and Tlaxcala). Still, by 1952, IMSS coverage included only 4 percent of the population and 5 percent of the labor force.[12]

1954–1973

During the first decade of the IMSS (1943–1953), its coverage was limited to urban workers. In the meantime agricultural workers, particularly wage-earners, began to organize. In 1952, a radical new confederation including peasants was established: Confederación Revolucionaria de Obreros y Campesinos (CROC). President Ruiz Cortines faced a severe economic recession at the beginning of his term (1952–1953), a high rate of inflation, and an increase in the number of strikes in 1953–1954. In 1954 another radical labor confederation was established (Confederación Revolucionaria de Trabajadores, CRT). To oppose the more militant labor confederations, Ruiz Cortines encouraged a Block of United Workers (BUO) made up of the more moderate confederations (CTM, CROM, CGT, federal civil servants, railroad workers). In another move, in 1954–1955, the president extended IMSS coverage to permanent wage-earners, and small farmers and *ejidatarios* who were members of production cooperatives and/or credit associations.[13] Coverage began in the developed state of Sonora and by 1958 had expanded to ten states, practically all in the North and characterized by large plantations, relatively modern agriculture, and rapid economic development. The number of those insured in agriculture was still small in 1958: 27,886 or 3 percent of the total number of insured. In the same year, however, IMSS services to selected groups of urban workers had been expanded to all the states although with varying degrees of coverage. By 1958 IMSS coverage had increased to 7 percent of the population and 9 percent of the labor force. The slow geographical expansion of IMSS coverage was combined with the steady vertical accumulation of benefits by those already insured who, since 1956, had begun to receive additional benefits in education, sports, and recreation. Ruiz Cortines also passed various measures in favor of the military: in 1955 he regulated their pensions and created the Direction of Military Pensions; and, in 1956, the military officials' savings program was extended to the troops.

In 1958 the combination of economic growth, political stability, and labor peace maintained for two decades in Mexico began to crack. Economic growth slowed down and the per-capita GNP was stagnant in 1958–1959. In 1958 the number of strikes reached 740; two of the strikes, launched by railroad and telegraph workers, assumed grave proportions. Federal civil servants, led by FSTSE, had been involved since the early 1940s in a struggle to have their rights recognized in the constitution and they increased their efforts in the 1950s. The most powerful federation of civil servants, that of teachers (Sindicato Nacional de Trabajadores de la Educación, SNTE), also launched a violent strike in 1958. Various militant confederations and federations (CROC, CRT, sugar, electricity) founded the National Confederation of Workers (CNT) opposed to the moderate, progovernment BUO. Former President Cárdenas led several left-wing groups in organizing a National Liberation Movement in the early 1960s. Peasant uprisings took place in 1960–1961; a new radical peasant federation was founded, closed to the PPS, in 1961 (Central Campesina Independiente, CCI); and land invasions organized by the Marxist UGOCM and the Socialist-oriented CCI occurred in 1961 and 1962.

The new president, Adolfo López Mateos (1958–1964), faced these problems with the classic policy of the stick and the carrot. Three months after taking power, when his efforts to negotiate a peaceful settlement to the railroad strike proved futile, he crushed the strike using military troops and imprisoned the union's secretary general. The army was also used to halt the peasant rebellion and various agrarian leaders were jailed. On the other hand, the president—more progressive than his three predecessors—introduced profit-sharing for workers, granted wage increases (including substantial ones to the armed forces and civil servants), and gave renewed attention to land reform; thus labor's share in the national income began to increase. Social security concessions were instruments used to restore social peace among federal civil servants (including teachers) and agricultural workers.

López Mateos' actions in favor of the federal bureaucracy are significant in view of the fact that he was the first Mexican President from the postrevolutionary generation and a true career administrator. He advocated a constitutional amendment to regulate labor conditions, recognize the right to strike, and implement a social security system for civil servants of the three branches of the federal government and the Federal District. The latter resulted in a social security system for federal civil servants (1959) administered by a federal, autonomous agency: Instituto de Seguridad y Servicios Sociales para los Trabajadores al Servicio del Estado, ISSSTE. This system, the best in the nation, includes pensions for old age, disability, and survivors; protection against occupational hazards; health and maternity care for the insured and their dependents; life insurance and funeral aid; indemnification for layoff and other social benefits (education, day-care centers, sports and recreational facilities, stores with reduced prices, loans with low interest, and a housing program). Civil servants and school teachers employed by the states do not belong to ISSSTE but have special systems, different in each state.[14] Systems in the wealthier states offer benefits similar to those of ISSSTE or have signed agreements with the latter.

IMSS coverage in agriculture increased tenfold under López Mateos, from 27,886 in 1958 to 272,671 in 1964. In August of 1960, temporary and seasonal wage-earners employed by agricultural, livestock, and forestry enterprises, as well as in farms and *ejidos,* and members of production coops and credit societies gained coverage by IMSS. (The incorporation of farmers and *ejidatarios* not members of production cooperatives and credit societies was recommended but not implemented.) In 1963 sugar cane workers were included in IMSS. As a result of these measures, by the end of López Mateos' term, IMSS coverage had jumped to 17 percent of the population and 18 percent of the labor force.[15]

The administration of Gustavo Díaz Ordaz (1964–1970) did not pass any significant social security legislation. Nevertheless several powerful unions negotiated new collective contracts which improved their social security benefits: petroleum, railroad, electrical, and sugar workers, and IMSS employees. Coverage of IMSS, increased again, although at a slower pace than under López Mateos, to 25 percent of both the population and the labor force.

During the late 1960s and early 1970s, scattered student riots, electoral disturbances, labor conflicts, agrarian revolts, and guerrilla insurgency added to the political instability in Mexico. Facing these difficulties, President Luis Echeverría (1970–1976) developed a populist image and a policy emphasizing "democratic openness" and distribution vis-a-vis growth. In line with this shift, the president promised the expansion of IMSS coverage to the low-income stratum of the population and, indeed, some plantation workers have been covered, e.g., *henequen* workers (1971), tobacco growers (1973). Acknowledging that, in spite of the progress made in the past thirty years, only one-fourth of the population was covered by IMSS, that among the noninsured there were marginal groups in urgent need, and that despite steady national growth, income inequalities persisted, a 1973 law promised that IMSS would extend its coverage to all municipalities in the nation (in 1971, 78 percent of the municipalities still did not have any coverage) according to the particular socioeconomic conditions of the various regions. In addition, compulsory coverage by IMSS would be expanded to include domestic servants, home workers, the urban self-employed (artisans, small merchants, professionals, small entrepreneurs) and the remaining *ejidatarios* and small farmers (that is, those who were neither members of cooperatives nor of credit associations). The date of implementation and conditions of that extension, however, were left to future decrees, although elective insurance is now available to these subgroups. To the best of my knowledge, until the end of 1973 no decrees had been enacted to extend compulsory insurance, although insurance was regulated at least for one subgroup—domestic servants. Conversely the 1973 law immediately improved benefits to those already insured: the amount of several benefits was raised, some provisions were made for students, and the construction of urban day-care centers was prescribed. If the promised expansion of coverage is implemented in the immediate future, the 1970s will be a landmark in Mexican social security; otherwise the decade will pass into history without any significant imprint.

The evolution of social security in Mexico may be divided into four stages, in each of which a significant part of the system was established. (1) In the first century after independence (1821–1924), pensions for selected civil servants were introduced, numerous state laws regulating occupational hazards were enacted, and the Constitution of 1917 held employers responsible for the results of occupational hazards. (2) In the next two decades (1925–1942), federal laws were enacted granting pensions and other benefits to federal civil servants, the military, and teachers, and protection against occupational hazards for industrial workers; in addition, collective agreements signed by petroleum, railroad, and electrical workers made them eligi-

Table 6-1
Significant Social Security Legislation in Mexico: 1821–1973

Year	President	Type of Coverage	Group Protected
1824–1856	Victoria (m) and others	Pensions	Civil servants (executive, judiciary, treasury, diplomacy, post office)
1904–1928	State Governors	Occupational hazards, other protective measures[a]	Salaried industrial workers[b]
1925	Calles (m)	Pensions, occupational hazards, funeral aid	Civil servants (federal)
1926	Calles (m)	Pensions (including seniority), occupational hazards[c]	Military
1928	Calles (m)	Pensions (survivors'), funeral aid	Teachers (federal)
1931	Ortiz Rubio (c)	Occupational hazards	Blue- and white-collars
1935	Cárdenas (m)	Pensions, occupational hazards, health[d]	Petroleum
1936–1938	Cárdenas (m)	Pensions,[d] health	Railroad
1941	Avila Camacho (m)	Pensions, occupational hazards, health[d]	Electricity
1943	Avila Camacho (m)	Pensions, occupational hazards, health-maternity[e]	Blue- and white-collars[f]
1943	Avila Camacho (m)	Additional benefits[g]	Employees of IMSS
1946	Avila Camacho (m)	Life insurance	Military
1946–1948	Alemán (c)	Pensions, occupational hazards, funeral aid, and other benefits	Teachers, war veterans
1948	Alemán (c)	Pensions, occupational hazards, health-maternity[d]	Railroad
1951	Alemán (c)	Health-maternity[d]	Sugar
1954–1955	Ruiz Cortines (c)	Pensions, occupational hazards, health-maternity	Permanent rural wage-earners, and small farmers and ejidatarios that belong to production co-ops and credit associations
1959	López Mateos (c)	Pensions, occupational hazards, health-maternity, life insurance, and other benefits	Federal civil servants, teachers, police
1960	López Mateos (c)	Pensions, occupational hazards, health-maternity	Seasonal rural wage-earners, temporary urban workers
1963	López Mateos (c)	Pensions, occupational hazards, health-maternity[h]	Sugar
1966–1970	Díaz Ordaz (c)	Additional benefits[d]	Petroleum, railroad, electricity, IMSS employees, sugar
1970	Echeverría (c)	Pensions, occupational hazards, health-maternity	All workers in dependent relationship including those without contracts

Year	President	Type of Coverage	Group Protected
1971–1973	Echeverría (c)	Pensions, occupational hazards, health-maternity	Henequen, tobacco
1973	Echeverría (c)	Pensions, occupational hazards, health-maternity	Domestic servants, urban self-employed (artisans, small merchants, professionals, employers) and rural self-employed (remaining *ejidatarios* and small farmers)[i]

SOURCE: Information on legislation and collective agreements compiled by the author.

NOTE: (c) = civilian; (m) = military.

a. Usually occupational accidents and diseases, labor safety, etc. The first round of state laws was enacted from 1904 to 1916 prior to the Constitution of 1917; the second round implemented the constitution and covered more ground.

b. Salaried workers in manufacturing, transportation, mining, construction, and public utilities; rarely in agriculture and domestic service; none in commerce.

c. The original law has been modified in 1939, 1955, 1962, and 1970.

d. Not by law but through collective agreements which have been revised every two years often granting additional benefits.

e. The original law has been modified in 1947, 1948, 1956, 1959, 1965, 1970, and 1973, often granting additional benefits.

f. Although the law theoretically included the agricultural sector, its protection has been slow: in the mid-1950s small groups of rural permanent wage-earners, small farmers and *ejidatarios* both members of co-ops and credit associations began to be covered; in the early 1960s it was the turn of seasonal rural workers and sharecroppers; in 1963 sugar; in 1971–73 tobacco and henequen workers.

g. Covered by IMSS but with an additional system of benefits.

h. This sector has been incorporated into IMSS but keeps the additional benefits from its collective agreement and special laws.

i. Compulsory coverage will not be effective until the proper decrees are enacted; in the meantime voluntary coverage is open to all these subgroups.

ble for pensions, health care, and other benefits. (3) In the next decade (1943–1953), the core of the social security system (IMSS) was created, introducing pensions, health care, and other benefits for blue- and white-collar workers (mostly in urban areas); at the same time benefits were added for the military, railroad workers, teachers, IMSS employees, and sugar workers. (4) During the last twenty years (1954–1973) there has been a gradual expansion of social security coverage (basically of the IMSS) to include part of the agricultural workers, farmers, and *ejidatarios,* and part of the urban self-employed and domestic servants; there has also been a reorganization and significant improvement of the civil servants' social security system (through the ISSSTE), as well as the concession of additional benefits to military, petroleum, railroad, electrical, and sugar workers, and IMSS employees. (See table 6-1.)

The Role of Pressure Groups in Social Security Stratification

Four important pressure groups may be identified in Mexico: (1) the military, with the army, air force, and the navy as subgroups (policemen are partially protected by the civil servants' fund); (2) civil servants, with those in the federal government and the IMSS and federal school teachers as privileged subgroups, and state employees as a less privileged subgroup; (3) powerful unions in strategic trades such as petro-leum, railroads, electricity, and sugar; and (4) blue- and white-collar workers, mostly in urban areas.

The military has dominated two-thirds of Mexico's republican history. During the first century of the republic, the nation was ruled by military *caudillos* who alternated in the presidency, controlled puppet presidents, or openly ran a dictatorship. The social security system of the military was formalized at the apogee of their power. In 1926 General Calles replaced the obsolete *montepío militar* (established in 1761) with a modern pension fund, the second in the nation, probably to gain the loyalty of the armed forces and consolidate the revolution. Two other generals, Cárdenas and Avila Camacho, were instrumental in achieving the institutionalization of the revolu-tion, stability in political succession, the professionalization of the armed forces, and civilian predominance over the military. In this difficult transitional period they granted additional benefits to the military: a savings bank and life insurance. Since the 1940s, the Mexican military has become one of the tamest and least political in Latin America. The power of the military has obviously been reduced but not elimi-nated: they still play "residual political roles," such as preserving internal order through the control of labor, peasant, student, and electoral disturbances.[16] In the last three decades, no significant additions have been made by civilian governments to the social security system of the military. The limited power remaining to this group has been sufficient to upgrade their system, through periodic reorganization (1955, 1962, 1970), adjusting benefits to the level of all other groups, except perhaps federal civil servants.

Federal civil servants in Mexico are probably among the most powerful bureau-cracies in Latin America. Their main source of power is control of the public adminis-tration and integration into the political machinery, but they are also strongly unionized and active. As a powerful social security pressure group, they have won equal attention from both military and civilian governments. In 1925 General Calles replaced the *montepío civil,* dating from 1763, with a pension fund for civil servants, the first modern social security system instituted in Mexico. This was a shrewd move to secure the support of the government bureaucracy in Calles' struggle to consoli-date both his power and the revolution. Under General Cárdenas, civil servants grew stronger and organized the largest labor federation in Mexico (FSTSE), reaching a membership of half a million. The FSTSE fought in the 1940s and 1950s to have its rights recognized in the constitution. It finally succeeded in 1959, under the first president from the post-revolutionary generation and a career administrator, López Mateos, who reorganized and substantially improved their system, creating ISSSTE, the best social security institution in Mexico.

Federal teachers are among the most organized and militant civil servants. They founded their first union and repeatedly struck in the 1920s; received funeral aid from Calles in 1928; became incorporated into the civil-servant fund (with extra benefits) by Alemán in 1946; launched a violent strike in 1958; and were covered by the ISSSTE in 1959, preserving some of their extra benefits. The teachers' labor federa-tion (SNTE) reached 230,000 members in the 1960s and is the most important affiliate to FSTSE.[17] Both federations are independent from (although maintaining close links with) the CTM and are members of the CNOP which represents the "popular" (bureaucratic) sector of PRI. Civil servants and teachers employed by the states are not covered by ISSSTE but by special systems, different in each state. Finally, IMSS employees (more than 70,000 by 1970), the administrators of the largest social security system in Mexico, have obtained through unionization, strikes, and biannual collective agreements, benefits which generously supersede those available to the IMSS insured.

As in Uruguay and Argentina, and unlike Chile and Peru, there is no significant group distinction in the social security coverage of blue- and white-collar workers in Mexico. There are important differences, however, between the coverage of the labor aristocracy and that of the rest of this group. The labor aristocracy is made up of workers employed in strategic sectors of the economy and organized into large and politically influential federations (petroleum, railroads, electricity, sugar). Selected demands from these groups are often satisfied by the government in order to neutralize their activism and violence. Most of these groups are employed in enterprises which used to be foreign monopolies or oligopolies and later became totally or partially nationalized. These enterprises generate large profits and are highly capable of paying social security benefits. All of these labor groups became protected by social security (through collective bargaining) long before most blue- and white-collar workers.

Railroad workers were among the first to organize brotherhoods and associations and to strike at the end of the nineteenth century. They played a significant role in the 1910 revolution, struck frequently in the 1920s and 1930s, founded one of the first and most powerful labor federations in 1933 (STFRM, which reached a membership of 90,000 in the 1960s, the third largest federation in the country), helped Cárdenas win his struggle against Calles, were founders of the CTM in 1936, and signed a collective agreement with the nationalized railroad enterprises at the end of the 1930s. Since then, they have received periodic improvements in their social security system through collective bargaining occasionally preceded by violent strikes. The degree of unionization of transportation workers in 1964 was 57 percent, one of the highest in the country.[18]

Electricity is currently organized as an oligopoly made up of three enterprises. Their workers organized the first union in 1914, got a collective agreement with a foreign corporation in 1925, established a federation which supported Cárdenas, and founded the CTM in the 1930s. Since 1941, they have signed collective agreements with the state enterprises. There are now three electricity federations (SNERM, SME, and STERM) with a combined membership of 70,000 workers, the fourth largest labor group in Mexico. The degree of unionization of electrical, gas, and oil workers in 1964 was 89 percent, the highest in the country.

Petroleum workers are employed by a state monopoly (PEMEX). They signed their first collective agreement—which included social security benefits—in 1935, under Cárdenas, and later heartily supported the nationalization of foreign oil corporations. Their federation (STPRM) has the sixth largest membership, embracing 40,000 workers.

Sugar is the least powerful of these groups. Nevertheless, Mexico has been an important sugar producer and exporter since the *Porfiriato*. The sugar sector expanded rapidly in the 1940s and enjoyed high prices during World War II, the Korean War, and the mid-1950s. Sugar workers were quick to organize a national union (FNTA) which by the 1960s ranked fifth in membership with 52,000 workers. In 1951 they became the first agricultural group to obtain social security protection through collective bargaining and, in 1963, were incorporated into IMSS while retaining many of their privileges.

The mass of blue- and white-collar workers has been the latest to receive social security protection. The first legislation in favor of this group—protection against occupational hazards—was enacted by the states, in the critical period before and after Porfirio Díaz's downfall under pressure of increasing labor unionization and violence. The 1917 constitution consecrated the principle of employers' responsibility in occupational hazards, but rather than prescribing federal compulsory social security for the workers, timidly recommended voluntary savings associations. THe first draft for a social security law was elaborated in 1921, by Genearl Obregón, who had received the support of CROM. This draft, however, would be the first in a long parade of legal projects, presidential promises, political parties' proclamations, and six-year-plan mandates that did not materialize. The old dream did not come true even during the progressive administration of Cárdenas, who entrenched his power and institutionalized the revolution with labor support, fostered the foundation of the CTM, and made labor a sector of the official party. It took two decades to pass the social security law and when passage came, under the administration of General Avila Camacho, it was anticlimactic. Rather than a result of direct union pressure, IMSS was probably created by the president as compensation for declining real wages. This may explain the opposition to the law from radical labor.

In IMSS' first decade of operation, social security coverage was limited to a small proportion of the urban, unionized labor force, concentrated in the most industrialized cities and states. This was consistent with the government policy which emphasized economic growth over distribution. In the meantime, agricultural workers began to organize, helped to found more radical confederations, and launched demonstrations and land invasions. (Yet, in 1964, the degree of unionization among agricultural workers was 2 percent, still the lowest in the nation.) In 1954, Ruiz Cortines began the long, slow process of having the agricultural sector covered by IMSS. First came the strongest subgroups: permanent wage-earners, small farmers, *ejidatarios*—members of cooperatives and credit associations. Six years later the less powerful seasonal wage-earners received coverage. In the late 1960s and early 1970s violence and political instability increased and President Echeverría seemed to take a more positive attitude towards redistribution. In 1973 a new law promised that the remaining small farmers and *ejidatarios* would be covered, but thus far only elective insurance is available to them. The same situation prevails among other unorganized workers who lack bargaining power, such as the urban self-employed and domestic servants.

Studying the relationship between the welfare bureaucracy and clientele politics in the Mexican system of social security, Guy Poitras suggests the following conclusions: (a) social security is a consequence rather than a prime mover of socioeconomic improvement of the labor force; (b) by being sensitive and granting concessions to the politically powerful, the social security system has neutralized emerging groups and contributed to political stability; (c) in spite of its gradual expansion, social security still is mainly confined to the relatively small and privileged elite of urban unionized workers (who least need its services) and neglects the large mass of rural unorganized workers (who need the services more); and (d) by emphasizing the political goal, the system has overlooked the social goal of redistribution of wealth to the lower strata.[19]

Current Structure and Organization of the System

There is neither a single legislative body regulating the organization of social security in Mexico nor a public or even private compilation of all the laws, decrees, and regulations in force. The Federal Labor Law set only minimal national standards for occupational accident and disease protection. There is not an equivalent federal social security law; each group (and some subgroups) has its own legislation, often modified several times, regulating coverage, financing, and benefits. In addition, there are numerous state laws regulating various types of social security protection.

At the national level, within the civil sector, there are two major social security systems covering blue- and white-collars (IMSS) and federal civil servants (ISSSTE). In addition, there are a dozen systems (covering some 300,000 workers), some of which preceded the two major ones (e.g., petroleum, railroad, electricity). Most of these systems were created through collective bargaining with state monopolies. In some cases when a subgroup that previously had a law or collective agreement later became incorporated into a major system it retained some benefits above those available to the major system (e.g., sugar in IMSS, federal teachers in ISSSTE). In another case, a subgroup protected by a major system (IMSS employees) has signed a collective agreement with its administration to receive extra benefits.[20] There are also special agreements of groups incorporated into IMSS (e.g., telephone, tobacco, *henequen*). As complementary systems, there are compulsory public funds that cover subgroups (e.g., policemen of the Federal District), as well as numerous private voluntary mutual insurance associations. In the military sector there are two systems, one for the army and the air force and another for the navy. Some of the social security systems are public, decentralized, and autonomous institutions (e.g., IMSS, ISSSTE), but others are of a private nature (e.g., some generated by collective agreements). At the state level there are also separate social security systems for civil servants and policemen.

There is no overall agency for planning or coordinating this conglomeration. Economic planning in Mexico has assumed less importance than in other Latin American countries, particularly since 1970. Although there have been national six-year plans since Cárdenas' administration (1934–1940), these have been limited in scope and effectiveness. Social security has never been included in a plan, except in vague statements or principles. President Echeverría replaced, in 1970, all planning bodies with the Direction of Economic Studies whose objectives are the development of a national data bank and the analysis and solution of concrete economic problems. Of primary concern to the new Direction is the growing cost of social security to the federal government and how to cut such expenditures or find alternative sources of financing.[21]

There have been occasional attempts to unify at least part of the social security system. A Commission created in 1965 to plan and coordinate hospital facilities to avoid duplications in services and reduce costs had achieved nothing by 1971.[22] That same year President Echeverría announced a plan to reform ISSSTE in order to cover all civil servants from federal, state, and municipal governments under a single and uniform system, but, once again, no action has been taken.[23] Some specialists and employer representatives feel that it is necessary to unify and standardize, at least, the health-maternity services and the major groups (e.g., all civil servants, all blue- and white-collars) in order to avoid duplications, increase efficiency, and eliminate excessive privileges. But the feasibility of this move is questionable in view of the vested interests of the most privileged groups.[24]

Supervision of social security is not unified either; at least a dozen federal ministries and agencies perform this role. (See figure 6-1.) At the apex of the system is the president of the republic who appoints the top officials in some of the public, decentralized social security institutions (e.g., IMSS, ISSSTE) and supervises the functions

FIGURE 6-1

Administrative Structure of Social Security in Mexico: 1972

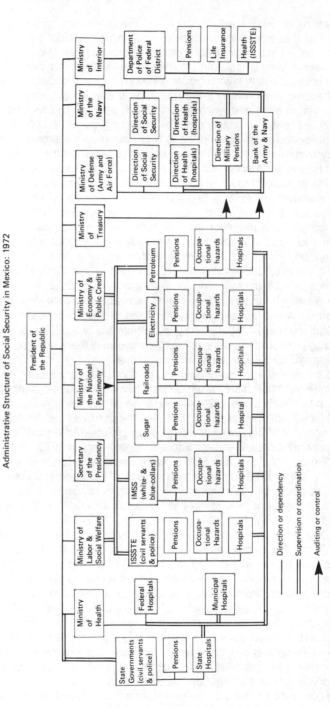

of the ministries. In the civilian sector, the secretary of the presidency is in charge of economic studies and programming investments for all the public, decentralized institutions (e.g., IMSS, ISSSTE, PEMEX—oil, railroads, CFE—electricity). The Ministry of Economy and Public Credit (Ministry of the Treasury for civil servants) collects and handles government contributions and supervises budgets. The Ministry of the National Patrimony (the General Comptroller) audits all public decentralized agencies. The Ministry of Labor and Social Welfare checks compliance with the Federal Labor Law in the matter of protection against occupational hazards and industrial safety (coverage against this risk may be provided directly through a social security institution or through a contract with commercial insurances). This ministry also registers collective agreements which may include social security clauses. The Ministry of Health controls all federal hospitals and coordinates (along with state governments) the state hospitals; it also supervises the health-maternity services of the public, decentralized social security institutions. In the military sector, the Ministry of National Defense controls its Directions of Social Security and Military Health, whereas the Ministry of the Navy controls similar but separate Directions of Social Security and Naval Health. In addition, there are two public, decentralized autonomous institutions which serve both military branches: the Direction of Military Pensions and the National Bank of the Army and the Navy (the latter audited by the National Banking Commission). These two institutions have some connections with the Ministries of Defense and the Army. The Ministry of the Treasury supervises part of the military sector.

The organization of the most important social security systems, grouped according to the pressure groups already identified, is explained below.

Armed Forces

The armed forces are divided into three subgroups: army/air force, navy, and police. The army/air force subgroup receives: funeral aid and other services through the Direction of Social Security of the Ministry of Defense; health care through the hospitals of the Direction of Military Health of the same ministry; pensions through the Direction of Military Pensions; and life insurance and other services (e.g., mortgages, personal loans, low-rental housing, consumer goods at reduced prices) through the National Bank of the Army and the Navy. The navy subgroup receives the same services through the corresponding Directions of the Ministry of the Navy, the Direction of Military Pensions, and the Bank. The subgroup of policemen is covered by civil-servant rather than by armed forces' institutions. There is no federal police corps in Mexico. Policemen in the Federal District are covered, for pensions and life insurance, by a special fund of the Department of Police and Traffic attached, in turn, to the Ministry of Interior; health care is provided by ISSSTE. Policemen of the states are covered, together with state civil servants, by the state social security systems.

Civil Servants

Civil servants are divided into four major subgroups: federal civil servants, state civil servants, IMSS employees, and employees of some autonomous agencies. ISSSTE is the most important fund; it covers civil servants in the federal government, the Federal District, the former Federal Territories (Quintana Roo and Baja California Sur which in the early 1970s became full-fledged states), the diplomat corps, federal schools, and a few autonomous academic institutions such as the Universidad Autónoma de México and El Colegio de México. Benefits include pensions, health-maternity care, life insurance, protection against occupational hazards, funeral aid, day-care centers, loan and housing programs, and consumer goods at reduced prices. Employees and workers of the 31 states and 2,391 municipal governments are protected by numerous independent funds, some of which have agreements with ISSSTE or IMSS for the provision of certain benefits.[25] Employees of IMSS are insured by this institution but, in addition, have a collective agreement (signed in 1943 and renegotiated every other year thereafter) granting them additional benefits. Employees of other autonomous institutions, such as the Banco de México, have independent funds.

Blue- and White-Collar Workers

The employees (both blue- and white-collars) of enterprises in strategic economic sectors such as railroads, petroleum, electricity—all three of them state monopolies—have privileged independent social security systems gained through collective agreements. These systems usually provide pensions, health-maternity care, funeral aid, and other benefits; protection against occupational hazards is the responsibility of the employer who often signs a contract with IMSS or is insured with commercial companies.

The bulk of blue- and white-collar workers of the private sector are covered by the IMSS for pensions, health-maternity care, funeral aid, and other benefits. Protection against occupational hazards is provided either by IMSS, commercial insurance, or by the employer. Many blue- and white-collar subgroups covered by IMSS have an additional collective agreement which grants them special benefits (e.g., telephone workers). Special agreements have been signed by agricultural subgroups such as sugar, coffee, *henequen,* tobacco, cotton, and strawberry workers.

The Noninsured

The majority of the labor force in Mexico is noninsured. Most noninsured are concentrated in agriculture, mainly independent peasants, small farmers, and *ejidatarios* not associated with cooperatives or credit associations. The other large group of noninsured is made up of the urban self-employed, domestic servants, professionals, small entrepreneurs, temporary workers, and unpaid family workers. Most of these groups have the option of elective insurance under IMSS, but only a small proportion have joined. Several laws (most recently in 1973) proposing to expand compulsory insurance to cover these groups have failed to be enacted.

For the noninsured high-income stratum of the population, protection is available from private insurance or clinics. For the low-income stratum, health-maternity is the only service partly available through the network of federal and state hospitals, the Red Cross and Green Cross hospitals, and emergency stations (municipally administered), and a few charitable hospitals. Attention by folk doctors is common in the rural areas and in the poorer sectors of the urban areas.

Inequalities of the System

As in all previous case studies, the inequalities in the Mexican social security system are most evident among the pressure groups and subgroups already identified. There are also inequalities among geographical regions. The available data on differences among occupational groups and geographical regions, mostly in terms of income, are considered below.

The most recent data available on personal income is provided by the 1970 population census.[26] These data refer to the average monthly income of members of the economically active population (EAP), classified by both major occupational groups and sectors of economic activity. Three strata can be identified in the classification by major occupational groups. The high-income stratum of the EAP is made up of entrepreneurs, professionals, technicians, top civil servants, and executive personnel. The medium-income stratum is made up of clerical (administrative) personnel, merchants, and salesmen. The low-income stratum is made up of nonagricultural and agricultural blue-collar workers. Members of the high-income stratum have average incomes which are from 5.8 to 8.5 times the average income of agricultural workers (1.0 at the bottom of the scale). In the medium-income stratum, average incomes range from 2.8 to 3.0 times that of the bottom. Finally, average incomes within the low-income stratum range from 2.1 to 1.0. This income classification is difficult to compare with our classification by social security pressure groups.

A more effective comparison can be made to the classification of average income by sectors of economic activity within the EAP. The following ranking presents a ratio of the average income of the workers in each sector in relation to the lowest income sector: petroleum (5.3); electricity (4.7); government—federal, state, and local (3.5); transportation (3.2); industry (2.9); commerce and services (2.7); construction (2.5); and agriculture and other extractive activities (1.0). Within agriculture, certain activities, such as sugar, have higher incomes than the overall sector average. This ranking broadly matches the pressure groups and their social security institutions: petroleum (covered by PEMEX social security system); electricity (mostly covered in the CFE social security system); government (with the federal subgroup covered by ISSSTE); transportation (partly covered by the railroad social security system and the IMSS); and the rest of the sectors—industry, commerce, services, construction, and agriculture (partly covered by the IMSS). It was not possible to obtain information on the income of the armed forces.

Mexico is often divided into five major geoeconomic regions: (1) North Pacific (states of Baja California Norte, Baja California Sur, Nayarit, Sinaloa, Sonora); (2) North (states of Chihuahua, Coahuila, Durango, Nuevo León, San Luis de Potosí, Tamaulipas, Zacatecas); (3) Central (Federal District and states of Aguascalientes, Guanajuato, Hidalgo, Jalisco, México, Michoacán, Morelos, Puebla, Querétaro, Tlaxcala); (4) Gulf of Mexico (states of Campeche, Quintana Roo, Tabasco, Veracruz, Yucatán); and (5) South Pacific (states of Chiapas, Colima, Guerrero, Oaxaca).[27]

The North Pacific region covers 21.1 percent of the national territory and has the smallest population (8 percent) of which 61.8 percent is urban.[28] The region has one of the most developed fishing industries in the nation, and also benefits from tourism and trade with the United States. The region ranks third in contribution to GDP (10.5 percent) and fourth in contribution to industrial product (5.3 percent), but first in per-capita production. It has three of the ten most populated cities in the nation: Mexicali, Culiacán, and Tijuana.

The North has the largest territory (40.7 percent of the total), but has only 19.8 percent of the population which is highly concentrated in the border states and largely urban (59.2 percent). There is an ample industrial nucleus located in Monterrey; oil wells in Tamaulipas; agriculture in the technologically advanced (usually irrigated) border states; and rich mineral resources supplying four-fifths of national mineral output (excluding oil). However, the north-central states (Durango, San Luis Potosí, and Zacatecas) are underdeveloped, their economy based on traditional agriculture. The region ranks second in contribution to GDP (20.3 percent) and industrial product (20 percent), as well as in per-capita production. Three of the nation's most populated cities are here: Monterrey, Ciudad Juárez, and Chihuahua.

The Central region covers 14.0 percent of the national territory and has 49.1 percent of the total population, 66.6 percent urban. Two great industrial nuclei are concentrated in this region, one in the Federal District and Mexico City and the other in Guadalajara. Most financing and government services of the nation are also concentrated in the Federal District. The rest of the region (excluding the states of México and Jalisco) is rather underdeveloped, with agriculture and stock-raising as the major activities. The Central region ranks first in its contribution both to GDP (55.3 percent) and industrial product (67.6 percent), but only fourth in per-capita production (due to low per-capita production of eight of its states). Four of the ten most populated cities of the nation are located in this region: Mexico City, Guadalajara, Puebla, and León.

The Gulf of Mexico region includes 12.1 percent of the national territory and has 11.3 percent of the total population, 48.2 percent urban. The core of the oil industry is located here; the fishing industry and the important port of Veracruz provide additional economic strength; and the tropical climate of the region allows the cultivation of diverse agricultural products. The region, however, is largely underdeveloped; about one-tenth of the state's population (one-half of the population in the Yucatán peninsula) is Indian. The region ranks fourth in contribution to GDP (9.7 percent) and third both in contribution to industrial product (5.9 percent) and in per-capita production. It has none of the ten most populated cities.

The South Pacific region comprises 12.1 percent of the national territory and 11.8 percent of the total population, 32 percent urban. Agriculture, mostly based on traditional techniques, is the most significant economic activity; tourism is important on the coast, particularly in Guerrero; and oil wells are now being exploited in Chiapas. About one-fourth of the population is Indian. The region ranks last (fifth) in contribution to GDP (4.2 percent), industrial product (1.2 percent), and per-capita production. It has none of the ten most populated cities.

An overall ranking of the five regions, as to their level of development (taking into account indicators such as contribution to GDP and industrial product, per-capita production, urbanization, number of most populated cities, and availability of natural resources), gives the following results: first come the Central, North, and North Pacific regions; then the Gulf of Mexico region; finally, at a considerable distance, the South Pacific region. (If the Federal District were considered a region by itself, the Central region would drop to some point between the Gulf of Mexico and South Pacific regions.)

There are no accurate data on income distribution by geographic region in Mexico. Ifigenia Navarrete has grouped the states into three income brackets (high, medium, and low), but she uses basically the per-capita product, not income, for this clustering.[29] This indirect approach cannot give a clear ranking of the regions as a whole. Another indirect approach is to assume that the larger the EAP of the region engaged in agriculture (the worst-paid economic activity), the lower the income of the region would be. This approach would result in a ranking of the regions similar to that given above.

Differences among states are even more significant than among regions. In 1965, per-capita production, measured in the most developed states in relation to the lowest per-capita production states (Tlaxcala and Oaxaca), was as follows: Federal District (10 times); Nuevo León (8 times); Baja California Norte and Sonora (6 times); Coahuila, Baja California Sur, and Tamaulipas (5 times); and Sinaloa (4 times). Per-capita production in Tlaxcala and Oaxaca was one-fourth of the national average per-capita production.[30]

Coverage

Table 6-2 presents a picture of the overall coverage of the Mexican social security system (in pensions and health care) in the 1960s. Data on the economically active population in the table seem overestimated; a lower EAP for 1970 (used in tables 6-4 and 6-5) was given by the latest population census. The total number of insured in the table excludes some subgroups, most significantly state civil servants and policemen. Therefore, proportions of insured in table 6-2 are probably underestimated by as much as two percentage points. According to the table, in the period 1960–1970, the number of active insured increased threefold and the percentage of the EAP insured increased twofold, from 12 to 24.7 percent. Similar increases were registered in the total number of insured, including active and passive (pensioners

Table 6-2
Insured Population in Relation to Total and Economically Active Population in Mexico: 1960–1970

Year	Total Population (in thousands) (1)	Economically Active Population (in thousands) (2)	Insured Population (in thousands)				Percent of EAP Insured (3)/(2)	Percent of Total Population Insured (6)/(1)	Ratio of Active to Passive (3)/(4)
			Active[c] (3)	Passive[d] (4)	Dependents[e] (5)	Total (6)			
0	36,046.0	11,332.0	1,360.2	58.2	2,459.7	3,878.1	12.0	10.8	23.4
1	37,268.0	11,721.5	1,595.0	67.8	2,947.8	4,610.6	13.6	12.4	23.5
2	38,543.0	12,125.7	1,785.7	80.2	3,478.6	5,344.5	14.8	13.9	22.3
3	39,871.0	12,544.8	1,928.7	88.2	3,845.0	5,861.9	15.4	14.7	21.9
4	41,253.0	12,978.5	2,311.9	103.4	4,653.5	7,068.8	17.9	17.2	22.4
5	42,689.0	13,427.0	2,601.3	118.1	5,701.9	8,421.3	19.4	19.8	22.0
6	44,145.0	13,890.4	2,753.5	135.2	5,593.4	8,482.1	19.9	19.3	20.4
7	45,671.0	14,368.4	2,960.8	158.8	6,042.7	9,162.3	20.6	20.1	18.6
8	47,267.0	14,861.2	3,178.1	183.9	6,441.5	9,803.5	21.4	20.8	17.3
9	48,933.0	15,366.5[b]	3,571.6	205.5	7,356.0	11,133.1	23.3	22.8	17.4
0	49,788.0[a]	15,888.9[b]	3,912.0	257.2	8,209.1	12,378.3	24.7	24.9	15.2

SOURCES: Total population, 1960–1969 from United Nations, Demographic Yearbook 1967 and 1969 (New York: ., 1968 and 1970) and 1970 from Secretaría de Industria y Comercio, Dirección General de Estadística, Censo eral de población 1970: Resumen general (México, D.F.: Talleres Gráficos de la Nación, 1970). Economically ve population from Secretaría de Industria y Comercio, Dirección General de Estadística, Anuario estadístico pendiado: 1968 (México, D.F.: Talleres Gráficos de la Nación, 1969). Active insured from table 6-3. Passive and endents from same sources as in table 6-3.

Census population (January 1970) plus 3 percent adjustment used by United Nations.

Extrapolation of series of Secretaría de Industria y Comercio, using their assumed annual rate of growth: 3.4 cent.

Includes IMSS, ISSSTE, and railroads in 1960–1970, plus armed forces in 1965–1970, plus petroleum in 1969.

Includes IMSS and ISSSTE in 1960–1970, plus petroleum in 1969 and railroads in 1970.

Includes IMSS and ISSSTE in 1960–1970, plus railroads in 1965–1970, plus all armed forces in 1970 (navy only 966–1969), plus petroleum in 1969.

Table 6-3
Occupational Groups Protected by Social Security in Mexico: 1960–1970

Occupational Group	Number Insured											Percentage Distribution in 1969
	1960	1961	1962	1963	1964	1965	1966	1967	1968	1969	1970	
Blue- and white-collars (IMSS)	1,200,708	1,419,030	1,594,315	1,703,402	2,069,480	2,209,915	2,315,103	2,447,398	2,633,054	2,915,261	3,221,363[b]	81.6
Civil servants (ISSSTE)	129,512	133,015	134,352	163,267	176,465	261,425	300,718	367,981	390,946	421,200	520,000[b]	11.8
Armed forces[a]	—	—	—	—	—	60,000	63,700	67,400	71,100	74,800	78,600	2.1
Railroads	30,000	43,000	57,000	62,000	66,000	70,000	74,000	78,000	83,000	89,000	92,000	2.5
Petroleum										71,367		2.0
Total	1,360,220	1,595,045	1,785,667	1,928,669	2,311,945	2,601,340	2,753,521	2,960,779	3,178,100	3,571,628	3,911,963	100.0

SOURCES: *Blue- and white-collars* from IMSS, *Memoria de labores de 1969. Datos estadísticos* (Mexico: Talleres Gráficos de la Nación, 1970). *Civil servants* from ISSSTE, *Anuario estadístico 1965 to 1968* (Mexico: ISSSTE, 1967–1970) and *Tendencias 1960–1979*, mimeographed, 1970. *Armed forces* based on data from Secretaría de la Defensa Nacional, Ejército Mexicano, Dirección General de Seguridad Social Militar (1965 and 1970), Armada (1965–1970) and interpolations. *Petroleum* from Ricardo Orozco Ferrera, *Seguridad social de Petróleos Mexicanos*, unpublished paper, 1970. *Railroads* from Ferrocarriles Nacionales de México, Departamento de Personal, March 15, 1971.

NOTE: Figures include only active insured, at the end of the year.
a. Army, air force and navy, police excluded.
b. Estimate.

and dependents, the latter covered only by health-care): 10.8 percent in 1960 to 24.9 percent in 1970. In spite of the remarkable acceleration of coverage in the 1960s, three-fourths of both the labor force and the total population of Mexico remained uninsured in 1970. If the promised expansion of coverage to urban and rural self-employed and domestic servants indeed materializes, another impressive jump in coverage should occur in the 1970s.

Coverage against occupational hazards is twice as large as that of pensions and health care. According to the 1970 population census, a total of 8,054,822 workers were covered by the Federal Labor Law or about half of the labor force.[31]

The total number of active workers insured is disaggregated by occupational groups in table 6-3. A few significant subgroups are included in the major groups (e.g., 98,215 sugar workers within IMSS in 1969); others are excluded from the table due to lack of accurate data (e.g., some 41,000 electricity workers insured c. 1969). The number of those excluded is relatively small and should not significantly alter the aggregate figures. The table shows that in 1969 more than four-fifths of the total number of insured were blue- and white-collars under IMSS; the second largest group was that of federal civil servants with almost 12 percent. The rest of the groups represented about 2 percent of the total insured each; sugar and electricity (not shown in the table) represented, respectively, 2.7 and 1.1 percent of the total insured. In 1960–1970 the group of insured that increased most was that of federal civil servants (a fourfold increase); this was the result of the creation of ISSSTE in 1959 and the rapid growth of Mexico City and the federal bureaucracy in the 1960s. Second in expansion were railroad workers (threefold increase), closely followed by blue- and white-collar workers (2.7 times increase). Expansion of IMSS coverage is associated with the incorporation of new municipalities, as well as of subgroups of agricultural workers and farmers and of seasonal urban workers.

A first attempt to measure the degree of social security coverage by occupational groups in 1969 is made in table 6-4. It contrasts the distribution of the labor force by type of worker with a clustering of active insured in major social security institutions. Insured salaried workers and wage-earners are disaggregated into urban and rural segments. The insured urban segment is a cluster of blue- and white-collar workers covered by IMSS, civil servants under ISSSTE, armed forces, petroleum, and railroad workers. The insured rural segment is made up of permanent and seasonal wage-earners and sugar growers covered by IMSS. Insured self-employed are mainly small landowners and *ejidatarios* also covered by IMSS. The table shows that 60 percent of urban salaried workers and wage-earners are covered but only 11 percent of their rural counterparts. (Self-employed are covered by less than one percent and the other categories are practically unprotected.) In 1971 only 11.8 percent of all active insured in IMSS were in rural areas, while 88.2 percent were in urban areas; this, however, was a significant improvement in relation to 1954 when only 0.5 percent of the insured lived in rural areas. Coverage among rural wage-earners in IMSS is concentrated in a few activities: 34 percent are permanent sugar workers and 57 percent are seasonal workers (of which one-half are in sugar plantations and one-fourth in cotton plantations).[32]

Table 6-5 gives a more precise idea of the inequalities in the degree of social security coverage within the occupational structure by using disaggregated data by sectors of economic activity. The computation of the table presented one serious difficulty: IMSS data referred to salaried workers and wage-earners who contribute to social security, hence excluding the self-employed, while the rest of the data em-

Table 6-4
Degree of Social Security Protection by Class of
Worker and Occupational Group in Mexico:
1969–1970

Class of Worker	Labor Force[a] (in thousands)	Insured[b] (in thousands)	Percent Insured
Salaried and wage-earners			
Urban	5,402	3,243[c]	60
Rural	2,667	294[d]	11
Self-employed and co-op members	3,278	27[e]	0.8
Employers	798	0[f]	0[f]
Unpaid family workers	849	0[f]	0[f]
Total	12,994	3,564	27.4

SOURCES: *Labor force* from *IX censo general de población y vivienda: 1970. Occupational groups insured* from table 6-3 and IMSS, *Memoria de labores de 1969. Datos estadísticos* (México, D.F., julio 1970).

a. January 28, 1970.

b. December 31, 1969.

c. Includes IMSS urban workers, ISSSTE civil servants, armed forces, petroleum, and railroad workers.

d. Includes IMSS permanent and seasonal wage-earners and sugar growers.

e. Includes IMSS small farmers and *ejidatarios*.

f. Some in this group may be covered by IMSS.

braced all the insured. Therefore degree of coverage in the agricultural sector, as well as in construction and services, is seriously underestimated. According to the table, the sector having the poorest protection was agriculture with only 1.4 percent coverage; however, if the self-employed covered by IMSS are added, coverage rises to 6.6 percent. Next come mining and construction with coverage at 7.4 and 8.4 percent of their workers. Coverage in services was twice as high with a rate of 15.7 percent. All these four sectors had a degree of coverage well below the national average of 23.7 percent. Commerce and manufacturing were well above the national average with coverage of 44.2 and 58.4 percent, respectively. The four best-protected sectors were transportation (including railroad, 67.7 percent), petroleum (83.5 percent), government (112.5 percent), and electricity and gas (113.2 percent). Overprotection in the last two sectors may be the result of definitional discrepancies between the two columns or moonlighting which resulted in duplication of insurance. The ranking of these sectors, in terms of degree of coverage, is almost identical to their ranking according to income. Thus the higher the income of the sector, the better its social security coverage. There is also a significant positive correlation between the degree of organization of the sector (measured by union membership and rate of unionization—see historical section) and their degree of social security coverage.

Inequalities in coverage by region are also evident. Until the mid-1940s, social security protection (except for occupational hazards) was practically limited to the Federal District (D.F.). In 1953, ten years after the creation of the IMSS, only the D.F.

Table 6-5
Degree of Social Security Protection by Sector of Economic Activity
in Mexico: 1969

Sector of Economic Activity	Labor Force (in thousands)	Insured[a] (in thousands)	Percent Insured
Agriculture, livestock, forestry, hunting, fishing	5,103	74[b]	1.4[b]
Mining	95	7	7.4
Petroleum, gas	85	71[c]	83.5
Manufacturing	2,169	1,267	58.4
Construction	571	48	8.4
Electricity, water	53	60[d]	113.2
Commerce	1,196	529	44.2
Transportation, communications	369	250[e]	67.7
Services	2,158	339	15.7
Government	407	421[f]	103.4
Not specified	747	0	0
Total	12,953	3,066[g]	23.7

SOURCES: *Labor force* from Secretaría de Industria y Comercio, *Anuario estadístico compendiado 1969* (México, D.F.: Talleres Gráficos de la Nación, 1970). *Insured* from IMSS, *Memoria de labores de 1969: Datos estadísticos* and table 6–3.

a. Insured by IMSS only, unless specified. IMSS statistics refer to salaried workers and wage-earners who pay contributions and exclude the self-employed.

b. If small farmers, *ejidatarios,* and other agricultural workers are included, the number of insured increases to 336,000 for 6.6 percent coverage.

c. Insured by petroleum fund.

d. Combined insurance by IMSS and collective contracts.

e. Combined insurance by IMSS and railroad fund.

f. Insured by ISSSTE; the latter also covers a group within services. Protection by armed forces may correspond to *services* or *not specified.*

g. This figure underestimates real coverage by some 400,000 insured due to exclusion of self-employed and armed forces.

and 7 states (out of 31) had some degree of coverage. With few exceptions, the first states and municipalities covered by IMSS were those geographically closer to the D.F., more populated, and wealthier. In 1958 the IMSS reached all the states, but in 1970, 78 percent of the municipalities (mostly rural ones) were still unprotected. Degree of coverage of municipalities within states seems to be positively correlated to level of development: in 1970, 100 percent of the municipalities in the relatively well-developed D.F. and the state of Baja California Norte were covered by IMSS; 50 to 65 percent of the municipalities in the relatively well-developed states of Coahuila, Sinaloa, and Tamaulipas were covered; but only 8 percent of the municipalities in the backward state of Yucatán and 4 percent of the municipalities in the least-developed state, Oaxaca, were covered.[33] Coverage by IMSS seems also to be directly correlated to city population: in 1969 all cities with more than 20,000 inhabitants were covered, but only 36 percent of those cities with 5,000 to 10,000 inhabitants were covered, and only 22 percent of those with less than 5,000 inhabitants were covered. In 1969 the concentration of the insured in the D.F. was shocking: 40 percent of those under IMSS, 57 percent of those under ISSSTE, and from 50 to 65 percent of those insured by the armed forces, electricity, petroleum, and railroads.[34]

Table 6-6
Degree of Social Security Protection of the Total Population by Geographic Region in Mexico: 1969

| | Total Population | | Insured Population | | | | | | |
| | | | IMSS | | ISSSTE | | Total | | |
Region	Thousands	Percent	Thousands	Percent	Thousands	Percent	Thousands	Percent	Percent of Total Population Insured
North Pacific[a]	3,907.7	8.1	340.6	11.7	20.7	5.3	361.3	10.9	9.2
North[b]	9,051.7	18.8	551.9	18.9	41.4	10.6	593.3	17.9	6.5
Center[c]	24,161.0	50.1	1,685.8	57.8	284.0	72.7	1,969.8	59.6	8.1
Gulf of Mexico[d]	5,681.8	11.8	245.6	8.4	21.9	5.6	267.5	8.1	4.7
South Pacific[e]	5,423.0	11.2	91.2	3.2	22.8	5.8	114.0	3.5	2.0
Total	48,225.2	100.0	2,915.2	100.0	390.9	100.0	3,305.9	100.0	6.8

SOURCES: *EAP* from *IX Censo general de población: 1970. IMSS* from *Memoria de labores de 1969: Datos estadísticos. ISSSTE* from *Anuario estadístico 1968*.

a. States of Baja California Norte, Baja California Sur, Nayarit, Sinaloa, and Sonora.
b. States of Chihuahua, Coahuila, Durango, Nuevo León, San Luis de Potosí, Tamaulipas, and Zacatecas.
c. Federal District and states of Aguascalientes, Guanajuato, Hidalgo, Jalisco, México, Michoacán, Morelos, Puebla, Querétaro, and Tlaxcala.
d. States of Campeche, Quintana Roo, Tabasco, Veracruz, and Yucatán.
e. States of Chiapas, Colima, Guerrero, and Oaxaca.

Table 6-6 presents percentage distributions of the population in each of the five geoeconomic regions of Mexico insured by both IMSS and ISSSTE. The most significant difference between the two distributions is the substantially higher percentage of ISSSTE insured in the Central region, an obvious result of the concentration of the federal bureaucracy in the D.F.[35] The last column of table 6-6 measures the degree of coverage (combining IMSS and ISSSTE) in each region. Social security protection is much better in the three most developed regions than in the two least developed regions: coverage in the North Pacific and Central regions is almost twice as high (and in the North 1.4 times as high) as in the Gulf of Mexico region, and coverage in the latter, in turn, is more than twice as high as in the South Pacific region.

As table 6-7 documents, inequalities in coverage are even more noticeable among states. Data on the table support the proposition, with few exceptions, that the D.F. and states in the North Pacific, North, and Central regions have better coverage than the states of the Gulf of Mexico and South Pacific regions. The eight states which have coverage above the national average of 25.5 percent (fluctuating from 63 percent in the D.F. to 27.5 percent in Tamaulipas) are all in the three most developed regions. Conversely all the states in the two least developed regions have a degree of coverage below the national average (fluctuating from 21.4 percent in Campeche down to 4.5 percent in Oaxaca).[36] These backward states also happen to have the highest proportion of Indians in their populations. A second proposition that can be tested with data in table 6-7 is that the larger the size of the EAP in a state, the higher its degree of social security coverage. The correlation between these two variables is significant at the 5 percent level: .72 (N = 32). A third proposition is that the higher the urban vis-a-vis rural proportion of the EAP in a state, the higher its social security coverage. The correlation between these two variables is also significant at the 5 percent level: .64 (N = 32). This is close to the correlation in Argentina and much higher than those in Peru and Chile; the reason is that civil servants are included in the Mexican distribution of insured. Had those insured in the armed forces, railraods, electricity, and other subgroups (e.g., special banking institutions) which are highly concentrated in cities been included in the Mexican distribution, the correlation would have been even higher.

If we compare Navarrete's ranking of the D.F. and states by "levels of income" (actually production per capita) with the ranking of states according to their social security coverage in table 6-7, the similarity is remarkable. Navarrete describes a "vicious circle" created because the most developed states are the most industrialized, attract most capital and skilled human resources, generate the highest rates of growth, capture the largest proportion of federal and state funds for economic and social developmental goals—are, in summary, the wealthier states and, hence, can provide more and better public services including social security. Conversely, the least developed states are the least industrialized, their labor force is mostly engaged in traditional agriculture, they are unable to attract sufficient capital and human resources, their rates of economic growth are either low or stagnant, they capture only a tiny fraction of federal and state funds for development, and are, in summary, the poorest states and, hence, lack the resources to provide the most basic public services, one of which is social security.[37]

In the late 1960s, González Casanova accumulated raw data to indicate that Mexico's rural population, the poorest in the nation: (1) had the lowest percentage of voters and opposition votes in national elections; and (2) presented the least opposition in such elections. From this he concluded that these groups/states were largely

Table 6-7
Degree of Social Security Protection of the Economically Active Population by States in Mexico: 1969

| | EAP[b] | | Insured[c] | | | | | |
| | | | IMSS | | ISSSTE | | Total | |
State[a]	Thousands	Urban Percent	Thousands	Percent[d]	Thousands	Percent[d]	Thousands	Perce
Federal District	2,189.5	97.5	1,157.9	52.9	222.3	10.1	1,380.3	63.
Baja California Norte	221.8	87.6	98.7	44.5	4.2	1.9	102.9	46.
Nuevo León	483.3	78.7	213.4	44.1	4.3	0.9	217.7	45.
Sonora	289.8	68.7	112.0	38.6	5.8	2.1	117.9	40.
Coahuila	283.3	70.8	87.3	30.8	7.7	2.7	95.0	33.
Morelos	166.2	76.0	49.6	29.8	3.9	2.4	53.5	32.
Sinaloa	343.9	52.9	105.2	30.6	4.9	1.4	110.0	32.
Tamaulipas	383.4	70.4	94.5	24.6	11.0	2.9	105.5	27.
Aguascalientes	86.3	66.3	18.7	21.7	2.7	3.1	21.4	24.
Baja California Sur	34.3	56.6	4.8	14.0	2.7	7.9	7.5	21.
Jalisco	888.4	71.5	184.1	20.7	8.4	1.0	192.5	21.
Campeche	71.7	67.2	12.7	17.7	2.6	3.7	15.3	21
Veracruz	1,004.8	52.7	192.2	19.1	11.5	1.2	203.6	20.
Colima	68.1	72.5	11.4	16.7	2.5	3.6	13.8	20
Chihuahua	416.9	67.7	69.7	16.7	6.8	1.6	76.4	18
Querétaro	127.2	40.0	19.6	15.4	3.0	2.4	22.6	17
Durango	227.2	46.9	33.8	14.9	3.4	1.4	37.1	16
Nayarit	144.9	56.5	19.8	13.7	3.1	2.1	22.9	15
Yucatán	207.5	69.2	28.2	13.6	4.0	1.9	32.1	15
Guanajuato	567.8	55.7	78.1	13.7	6.8	1.2	84.9	14
San Luis de Potosí	331.9	43.1	42.2	12.7	5.8	1.8	48.1	14
Puebla and Tlaxcala	781.2	57.2[e]	86.0	11.0	11.6	1.5	97.5	12
Guerrero	372.5	41.8	34.3	9.2	7.5	2.0	41.7	11
Hidalgo	307.8	35.9	22.9	7.4	4.8	1.6	27.7	9
Quintana Roo	25.3	42.3	1.1	4.6	1.1	4.3	2.2	8
Michoacán	552.8	43.6	40.3	7.3	7.4	1.3	47.6	8
Chiapas	413.3	32.9	27.4	6.6	5.6	1.4	33.0	8
Tabasco	200.2	39.7	11.4	5.7	2.7	1.4	14.2	7
Zacatecas	223.3	31.8	11.1	5.0	2.4	1.1	13.5	6
Oaxaca	568.4	37.3	18.2	3.2	7.3	1.3	25.6	4
México	965.6	67.8	28.6	3.0	13.2	1.3	41.9	4
Total	12,948.8	59.5	2,915.3	22.5	390.9	3.0	3,306.2	25

SOURCES: EAP from IX Censo general de población: 1970. IMSS from Memoria de labores de 1969: Datos estadísti ISSSTE from Anuario estadístico 1968. National urban percent from U.N. Demographic Yearbook 1970 (New Y 1971) and state percentages computed by the author based on the 1970 population census.
a. Ranked according to degree of coverage (last column).
b. According to 1970 census taken in January.
c. Active insured at the end of 1969 for IMSS and the end of 1968 for ISSSTE.
d. Percentage of EAP (first column).
e. Simple mean of the urban percentages of both states.

marginal in politics, assumed a passive political attitude, lacked or did not exercise their rights properly, and "did not have effective representation to exert pressure towards the solution of their problems."[38] In the early 1970s, Reyna conducted a sophisticated study which added substantial evidence to support most of González Casanova's assertions. He established a relationship between the "class structure" and the "level of development in the states" on the one hand, and voting patterns in national elections on the other. Within the class structure, the urban groups (of which the middle sector is a leader) support the system less and oppose it more often than the rural groups (particularly the peasantry and the Indians). The latter are concentrated in the most backward areas, are not highly politicized, are controlled through manipulation from the central political machinery, tend to support the system in elections and, hence, their bargaining power is low. Within the geographical setup, Reyna found a significant positive correlation between the level of development of the states (partly measured through their degree of urbanization) and opposition to the system manifested in elections. His data also showed that the least developed states tend to back the system and present less electoral opposition to it.[39]

The data discussed above allow us to conclude that developed, urbanized states in Mexico, which contain the most populated cities and have a large EAP engaged in strategic activities (i.e., government services, energy, railroad and port facilities, manufacturing, tourism and trade with the United States, modern agriculture, and fishing), also have generated high union and political power and, therefore, have been able to procure the earliest and highest social security coverage. Conversely, the backward states are usually less populated, overwhelmingly rural, have a large proportion of Indians and a labor force engaged in traditional agriculture; logically they are also weak in terms of unionization and political power and, hence, are late entrants and have the lowest social security coverage.

Financing

In the national system, the percentage of contributions over salaries/wages or income (and lump-sum contributions) are the same throughout the territory of Mexico; hence, differences in social security financing are limited to occupational groups and subgroups. (Most states and some municipalities have divergent financing in their own systems covering civil servants.) Table 6-8 shows differences in the contributions from the insured, employer, and the federal government by risk or program at the national level.

An analysis of the differences in both the overall and program percentage contribution among all groups is meaningless because, with the exception of blue- and white-collar workers (and some civil servants), the contribution cannot be presented in percentage form; the employer/federal government either totally finances the system or assumes its deficits. Therefore, the analysis will be made by program and, within each, by groups.

The insurance against occupational hazards is the most homogeneous in terms of financing, largely as a result of the standardized norms established by the Federal Labor Law. Employers either assume the whole cost of the program or pay a premium either to the social security institution or a commercial insurer. The premium paid to IMSS is the highest and varies according to risk; that of ISSSTE is smaller and constant (obviously resulting from the nature of bureaucratic jobs). There are no premiums in the remaining institutions: the employer/federal government assumes all costs.

The employer/federal government pays all life insurance costs in the petroleum and electricity funds. The insured pays a fixed premium (quite small and unrelated to risk) in the case of the armed forces and railroads, while the employer/federal government covers all remaining costs. Civil servants, blue- and white-collars, and sugar workers are not eligible for this benefit.

Table 6-8
Social Security Contributions from Employees, Employers, and State by
Occupational Group in Mexico: 1971
(in percentages of wages or income and pesos)

Occupational Group	Employees		Employer		State (percent)	Total (percent)
	Percent	Pesos	Percent	Pesos		
Blue- and white-collars[a]	3.8	—	11.2	—	1.9	16.9
Pensions	1.5	—	3.8	—	0.8	6.1
Health-maternity	2.3	—	5.6	—	1.1	9.0
Occupational hazards	—	—	1.8[b]	—	—	1.8
Civil servants	8.0	—	12.8	—	c	20.8
Pensions & others	2.0	—	6.0	—	—	8.0
Health-maternity	6.0	—	6.0	—	—	12.0
Occupational hazards	—	—	0.8	—	—	0.8
Armed forces						
Pensions	—	—	—	—	e	—
Health-maternity	—	—	—	—	e	—
Occupational hazards	—	—	—	—	e	—
Life insurance	—	1–16[d]	—	3–18[d]	c	—
Railroads	—	10[d]	—			
Pensions	—	—	f			
Health-maternlty	—	—	f			
Occupational hazards	—	—	f			
Life insurance	—	50[d]	f			
Petroleum						
Pensions	—	—	f			
Health-maternity	—	—	f			
Occupational hazards	—	—	f			
Life insurance	—	—	f			
Electricity						
Pensions	—	—	f			
Health-maternity	—	—	f			
Occupational hazards	—	—	f			
Life insurance	—	—	f			
Sugar						
Pensions	—	—	f	—	—	
Health-maternity	—	—	f	—	g	
Occupational hazards	—	—	f	—	—	

SOURCE: Information on legislation and collective agreements compiled by the author.

a. Employees of IMSS pay the same rates, but have generous extra benefits which are financed by their additional contribution of 1 percent while IMSS pays the rest. Members of cooperatives and small farmers and *ejidatarios* who belong to credit associations do not pay; their system is financed half by the federal government and half by the associations or co-ops.

b. Average premium; the actual premium ranges from 0.2 to 5.6 percent according to risk.

c. The federal government pays any resulting deficit.

d. In pesos, monthly (if there are different rates they are fixed according to rank).

e. All costs paid by the federal government.

f. All (or remaining) costs paid by the employer.

g. State contribution to main hospital.

Health-maternity is totally paid by the employer/federal government in the armed forces, petroleum, electricity, and railroads. In the case of sugar, the private employer pays most costs except for a share of the operation of their major hospital which is paid by the federal government. The insured contributes to this program only if he is a blue- or white-collar worker (2.3 percent) or civil servant (6 percent), with an additional contribution from his employer (5.6 and 6 percent respectively), and a contribution from the federal government: 1.1 percent in IMSS and the assumption of any resulting deficit in ISSSTE.

Pensions are totally financed by the employer/federal government in the armed forces, petroleum, electricity, and sugar. The insured pays a token lump sum in railroads and the employer takes care of all remaining costs. The insured makes a substantial contribution only if he is a blue- or white-collar worker (1.5 percent) or a civil servant (2 percent), with an additional contribution by his employer (3.8 and 6 percent respectively), and a contribution from the federal government: 0.8 percent in IMSS and any resulting deficit in ISSSTE. Small farmers and *ejidatario* members of coops or credit associations, compulsorily insured in IMSS, do not pay any contribution to a program; their system is financed half by their associations and half by the federal government.[40] The self-employed, voluntarily insured in IMSS, pay both the insured and employers' contributions.

The analysis of the financial system of Mexico's social security suggests that it plays a regressive role in income distribution. The insured, when part of groups that are at the top of the income distribution (petroleum, electricity, railroads, and, probably, armed forces), do not contribute at all to any of their programs or pay only a token, tiny sum. The employer, which happens to be the federal government, generally pays all costs or assumes the deficits resulting from all these programs. Civil servants, with an income at least twice as high as that of the average blue- and white-collar worker, pay an overall percentage contribution twice as high as the latter. But benefits available to civil servants are considerably superior, both in quantity and quality, to those available to blue- and white-collars. Furthermore, the employer pays an overall percentage contribution to ISSSTE higher than to IMSS; in terms of actual contribution, the difference should be even larger because of the higher average income of civil servants. Finally, the federal government contributes 1.9 percent to IMSS (a percentage which has been declining in the last decade), whereas it covers any resulting deficits from ISSSTE. These deficits have not occurred since the early 1960s, but when they did occur, they were substantial and were absorbed by the federal government.[41] Within the agricultural sector, sugar workers who have an income considerably higher than the sector's average do not pay any contribution to their system which is financed mostly by the employer and the federal government. The financing of low-income small farmers and *ejidatarios* who belong to coops and credit associations is probably one of the few to have a positive role in income distribution: the insured does not pay and the association and the state each pay half. And yet those small farmers and *ejidatarios* who do not belong to co-ops or associations (and who probably have a lower income than those who do belong) have to pay all the contributions by themselves.

Table 6-9 shows the proportions of the fund's revenue contributed by the insured, the employer, and the federal government but only in two institutions and for one year. The combined contribution of the employer and the federal government for blue- and white-collar workers was substantially higher (71.7 percent) than that of civil servants (50.1 percent), suggesting a positive effect in terms of income distribu-

Table 6-9
Percentage Distribution of Social Security Fund Revenues by Financing Source and
Occupational Group in Mexico: 1969

Occupational Group	Insured	Employers[a]	State[b]	Investment Returns	Others	Total
Blue- and white-collar	23.9	59.8	11.9	4.4	0	100.0
Civil servants	35.1	50.1	0	14.5	0.3	100.0
Total	26.6	57.4	9.1	6.8	0.1	100.0

SOURCES: *Blue- and white-collars* from IMSS, *Memoria de labores de 1969: Datos estadísticos. Civil servants* from ISSSTE, *Anuario estadístico 1969* (Mexico, D.F., 1971).
a. Private employers and government contribution as employer.
b. Direct contributions and subsidies.

tion between these two groups. However, if the year 1963—when a deficit in ISSSTE was absorbed by the federal government—had been chosen, the results would have been dramatically different. Data are not available from the remaining groups in which the employer/federal government pays practically all costs.

Table 6-10 also presents partial data on the revenue per capita (rpc) received by the two major social security institutions: IMSS and ISSSTE. The table shows that the rpc of civil servants is four times as high as that of blue- and white-collar workers. This is the result of both a higher overall percentage contribution and substantially higher incomes of civil servants vis-a-vis blue- and white-collar workers. (Nevertheless the gap of rpc between the two groups shrank during the 1960s.)[42] Once again, data on the rpc of the remaining institutions are not available, but figures in table 6-10 reinforce the hypothesis that social security does not perform a progressive income redistribution function.

In the 1960s the financial situation of IMSS rapidly deteriorated while that of ISSSTE steadily improved. The reasons for this were not only the higher rpc in ISSSTE than in IMSS but other serious administrative problems. In 1969, the IMSS health-maternity insurance branch had an accumulated accounting deficit of 6.8 billion pesos (and increasing). The IMSS occupational-hazards insurance branch had an accumulated deficit of 60 million pesos by the end of 1965, although an increase in premiums

Table 6-10
Revenue of Social Security Funds per Insured by Occupational
Group in Mexico: 1969

Occupational Group	Revenue (in thousand pesos)	Number of Insured	Revenue per Capita	Ratio[a]
Blue- and white-collars	6,978,888	2,915,261	2,394	1.0
Civil servants	4,104,527	421,200	9,745	4.0

SOURCES: *Blue- and white-collars* from IMSS, *Memoria de labores de 1969: Datos estadísticos. Civil servants* from ISSSTE, *Tendencias 1960–1970* and *Seis años de proyección nacional: 1965–1970* (México, D.F.: Editora de Periódicos S. C. L., 1970).
a. Revenue per capita of each fund divided by the revenue per capita of the smallest fund.

restored the balance and generated a small surplus in 1969. The IMSS pension fund was the only one to show a substantial surplus (about 10 billion pesos) in 1969, but its reserves had been seriously depleted to cover the deficits in health-maternity. The combined result was an accounting surplus of 3.2 billion pesos in 1969 which has since then gradually been reduced. The *actuarial* deficit of IMSS was calculated at 8 billion pesos in 1966 and was reportedly growing.[43] In 1963, ISSSTE had a deficit of 7 million pesos which was absorbed by the federal government, but in the rest of the decade it generated an increasing surplus which by 1970 had reached 1.4 billion pesos.[44] There are no figures available on the actuarial situation of ISSSTE. There are no financial data available on the other funds either, but, since their costs are almost totally paid either by the state or the employer, it is fair to assume that they do not face any serious financial crisis.

In summary, three-fourths of the Mexican population, who are not insured, indirectly contribute to the social security funds in existence either through federal taxes or higher consumer prices or both. Among those insured, 81 percent (blue- and white-collars) covered by IMSS indirectly contribute through the same channels to other more privileged social security institutions, each of which covers only 1 or 2 percent of the total insured (except for ISSSTE which covers 12 percent). Obviously the contribution of these small groups to the IMSS is smaller than what they receive in return. Those unprotected are mostly rural and urban self-employed and domestic servants who are at the bottom of the income ladder. Those protected by IMSS have, as an average, lower incomes than those protected by petroleum, electricity, civil-servant, railroad, and (probably) armed-forces social security institutions. The social security system, therefore, plays a regressive role in income redistribution, transferring resources from the lower-income stratum to the medium- and high-income strata of the population.

The cost of social security in Mexico has risen steadily since the mid-1940s and accelerated its increment in the 1960s. See table 6-11. Still such costs are relatively small when compared to those of Uruguay, Chile, and Argentina. Data on social security costs in the table are limited to the two major Mexican institutions (IMSS and ISSSTE) which cover about 93 percent of all insured. Data from other federal and state social security institutions as well as government direct expenditures on health are excluded. Actual total costs, therefore, are somewhat higher. Social security expenditures steadily increased (from 1961 to 1968) from 2 to 3 percent of GNP (social security revenue showed a similar increment from 2.3 to 3.2 percent of GNP). As a proportion of government consumption, social security expenditures increased from 37.2 percent in 1961 to 49.1 percent in 1966, but declined in 1967–1968. (In terms of social security revenue, the increase went from 44.2 percent in 1961 to 52.5 percent in 1967 with a decline in 1968.)[45]

Reasons for the rising cost of social security are many. First there is the gradual expansion of coverage to incorporate new segments of the labor force and municipalities which are usually poorer than those already covered; hence, their contributions are smaller while some of the benefits that they receive (e.g., health care) are constant. This problem is compounded by frequent evasions, delays, and fraud in contributions, both by employers and the insured. Second is the increase in benefits (both in amount and quality), the reduction of certain requirements to acquire such benefits, the fraud of insured in the use of medical services, and the introduction of new costly benefits. The epitome of the latter are the "social benefits," particularly granted by IMSS, which include luxurious vacation, recreational, cultural,

Table 6-11
Cost of Social Security in Mexico: 1961–1968
(in billions of current pesos and percentages)

			Social Security Revenue			Social Security Expenditure		
Year	GNP	Government Consumption Expenditure	Total	Percent of GNP	Percent of Government Consumption Expenditure	Total	Percent of GNP	Percent of Government Consumption Expenditure
1961	163.8	8.6	3.8	2.3	44.2	3.2	2.0	37.2
1962	177.5	9.6	4.4	2.5	45.8	3.8	2.1	39.6
1963	192.2	11.2	5.0	2.6	44.6	4.3	2.2	38.4
1964	224.6	12.5	6.0	2.7	48.0	5.7	2.5	45.6
1965	242.7	13.8	7.0	2.9	50.7	6.5	2.7	47.1
1966	272.1	16.1	8.2	3.0	50.9	7.9	2.9	49.1
1967	301.4	17.7	9.3	3.1	52.5	8.5	2.8	48.0
1968	334.3	25.9	10.8	3.2	41.7	9.9	3.0	38.2

SOURCES: *National income* from U.N. *Statistical Yearbook,* 1970 (New York: 1971). *Social security revenue* and *expenditure* 1961–1966 from International Labour Office, *The Cost of Social Security, Sixth and Seventh International Inquiries, 1961–1963 and 1964–1966* (Geneva: ILO, 1967 and 1972); 1967–1968 author's computations based on data from IMSS and ISSSTE and estimate of other revenues and expenditures. *GNP* and *Government consumption expenditure* from U.N. *Yearbook of National Account Statistics 1965* and *1970* (New York: 1966 and 1972).

sports, and training centers. Third is the dramatic increase in administrative expenditures, resulting mostly from the expansion of personnel and their remuneration but also from luxurious installations and costly equipment (often underutilized). ISSSTE administrative expenditures, as a percentage of revenue, ranged from 20 to 30 percent in the 1960s. IMSS administrative expenditures increased from 8.9 percent in 1945 to a peak of 20.6 percent in 1952 and then declined to 16–19 percent in the rest of the 1950s and throughout the 1960s.[46] The ISSSTE staff grew from 14,393 in 1965 to 20,640 in 1971, an increase of 43 percent in 6 years. In 1971 the new director of ISSSTE laid off 4,000 employees that "were not performing any function and were collecting 8 million pesos per month."[47] The IMSS staff grew from 19,027 in 1959 to 54,415 in 1965, an increase of 186 percent in 6 years.[48] The personnel of these institutions have also had substantial salary increases. From 1955 to 1965 IMSS employees received biannual increases gradually rising from 20 to 100 percent. The average annual increase in ISSSTE in the period 1965–1968 was 30 percent.[49] These increases were well above the rate of inflation and, when compared with the salary increases of the insured for the same periods, show that the social security personnel did considerably better, with a probable regressive effect on income redistribution. Poor investment policy, particularly in IMSS in the 1960s, has certainly not helped counteract increasing social security costs. (According to table 6-9, investment returns in IMSS represented 4.4 percent of revenue, while investment yields in ISSSTE accounted for 14.5 percent of revenue.) In some cases, investment was made in stocks which did not produce dividends for a long period of time; a good portion of investment funds went into mortgage loans and low-rental housing, often resulting in heavy losses; in summary, the average annual investment profit was usually well below the required legal minimum of 5 percent and yielded one-third to one-fourth the usual market profit.[50]

A few technical studies have been done on the financial problems of social security in Mexico. In 1966 a Commission of Study to Reform the IMSS was organized with representatives from the federal government, the insured, the employers, and IMSS employees. The commission recommended, among other things, the reform and better control of collection of contributions, a freeze or reduction in personnel (compensated with simplification of proceedings and increase in productivity), more frugal collective agreements with personnel, better control in the administration and use of health services, and a more solid investment policy.[51] In 1971 the Secretary of the Presidency, concerned with the growing domestic deficit and foreign debt, analyzed social security costs to the federal government, with the aim of reducing them and finding alternative sources of financing, particularly for ISSSTE.[52] To the best of my knowledge, however, few concrete reforms have been implemented to alleviate the problems discussed here.

Benefits

The regulations on benefits, within the national systems, are the same throughout Mexico. There are significant inequalities, however, between the federal system (covering civil servants and policemen) and those of the states. Usually, the wealthier and most politically powerful states (e.g., Sonora, México, Baja California Norte) have been able to develop the best system of benefits for their employees, some of them signing agreements with ISSSTE. In addition, there are important differences in the quantity and quality of hospital and medical facilities by region.

The inequalities in the type of benefits available to the main occupational groups and subgroups are summarized in table 6-12. The top section of the table includes the major social security institutions created by law, while the bottom section refers to social security systems developed through collective bargaining (sometimes the insured in the latter have coverage in a major institution and extra benefits in the agreement). The totals in the table reveal the following ranking: (1) civil servants with 24 benefits; (2) IMSS employees and petroleum with 23 benefits; (3) electricity with 22 benefits; (4) armed forces and railroads with 21 benefits; and (5) sugar and blue- and white-collar workers with 20 benefits.

Although the Mexican system of benefits appears fairly uniform, there are still some noticeable inequalities: seniority pensions are available to all groups and subgroups except for sugar workers and blue- and white-collar workers. Survivors' pensions are unavailable only to sugar and railroad workers whose survivors only receive an indemnification; survivors of petroleum workers receive a pension for two years and the widow is eligible for a job. Blue- and white-collars and civil servants are the only two groups not eligible for life insurance lump sums. In some cases the benefit is not available to a group due to the peculiarities of its trade, e.g., the armed forces are not eligible for maternity subsidies and unemployment lump sums.

Table 6-12 excludes, however, multiple benefits which do not strictly belong to the concept of social security as used in this study. For example, there are stores that sell cars, home appliances, clothing, and groceries at reduced prices (e.g., 40 percent below market prices in ISSSTE stores); mortgage loans at low interest rates (e.g., half the market rate to ISSSTE members, two-thirds of the market rate to the armed forces); subsidized houses for sale (free lot and homes sold at half the market price to the armed forces) and low-rental houses; funeral homes that provide free or very cheap services (e.g., coffins and cemetery plots at one-fourth the market price and, in addition, two-thirds of both paid by the armed forces); vacation centers,

Table 6-12
Social Security Benefits by Occupational Group in Mexico: 1971

Occupational Group	Pensions								Other Cash Benefits										Family Allowances							Health-Maternity[a]										Total
	1	2	3	4	5	6[b]	7	8	9	10	11	12	13	14	15	16	17	18	19	20	21	22	23	24	25	26	27	28	29	30	31	32	33	34	35	
Main Funds																																				
Blue- and white-collars	x	x	x	x	c	x				x	x	x	x		x		x			x						x[d]		x	x	x	x	x	x	x	x	20
Civil servants	x	x	x	x	c	x	x	x		x	x	x	x		x			x								x[d]	x	x	x	x	x	x	x	x	x	24
Armed forces	x	x	x	x		x	x[l]	x			x	x				x	x	x								x[e]	x	x	x	x	x	x	x	x	x	21
Collective Agreements																																				
IMSS employees	x	x	x	x	c	x				x	x	x	x	x	x	x	x			x						x		x	x	x	x	x	x	x	x	23
Railroad	x	x	x	x	c					x	x	x	x		x	x	x	x										x	x	x	x[f]	x	x	x	x	21
Petroleum	x	x	x	x				x		x	x	x	x		x	x	x	x									x	x	x	x	x	x	x	x	x	23
Electricity	x	x	x	x[k]		x				x[f]	x	x	x		x[i]	x	x	x									x	x	x	x	x	x	x	x	x	22
Sugar	x		x	x				x		x	x	x	x		x	x[g]	x[j]					x[h]					x	x	x	x	x	x	x	x	x	20

SOURCES: Information on legislation and collective agreements compiled by the author; Comité Permanente Interamericano de Seguridad Social, *Seguridad social y convenios colectivos* (México, D.F.: Mesa Redonda OIT-AISS-CISS, October 26–31, 1970); and comparative tables prepared by Ricardo Orozco Farrera.

NOTE: See code following table for definition of benefits here signified by numbers 1–35.

a. For the insured and his family, except in preventive medicine and rehabilitation and prosthesis; in some groups a small charge is made for services rendered to relatives.

b. All funds grant survivors' pension to the widow and children, as well as parents; in addition, the armed forces grant pensions to sisters.

c. Pension for layoff but for IMSS with 60 years of age and minimum contributions which makes it more like an old-age pension; for railroads only in a few exceptional cases.

d. Help for milk if mother is incapacitated.

e. In addition cash subsidy for food expenses for the whole family.

f. Also in case of nonoccupational hazards.

g. Only in case of occupational hazards.

h. Only in case of premature birth.

i. Also for workers' voluntary resignation.

j. Also for death of relatives.

k. Only a percentage of salary for about one-third of each year of disability (without limit).

l. Only of contributions to Bank of the Army and the Navy.

Code for Social Security Benefits

Pensions:
1. Old-age.
2. Seniority.
3. Permanent disability (total or partial) caused by occupational hazards.
4. Permanent disability (total or partial) caused by nonoccupational hazards.
5. Unemployment/layoff
6. Survivors'.

Other Cash Benefits:
7. Restitution of contributions.
8. Lump sum at retirement.
9. Bonus added to pension for work-years above the minimum required for retirement.
10. Lump sum for permanent disability (total or partial) caused by occupational hazards.
11. Subsidy for temporary disability caused by occupational hazards.
12. Subsidy for temporary disability caused by nonoccupational hazards.
13. Salary (or percentage thereof) paid for a period before and after childbirth.
14. Unemployment/layoff temporary subsidy.
15. Unemployment/layoff lump sum.
16. Life insurance, lump sum.
17. Funeral aid, lump sum.
18. Lump sum to survivors when no right to pension is granted.
19. Year-end bonus to retired and pensioners.

Family Allowances:
20. Marriage.
21. Pregnancy.
22. Childbirth.
23. Children.
24. Spouse.
25. Parents.
26. Child food (percentage of salary or in kind).
27. School aid (for insured or his/her children).

Health-Maternity Benefits:
28. Preventive medicine.
29. Curative medical care.
30. Rehabilitation and prosthesis in case of occupational hazards.
31. Maternity care.
32. Surgical treatment.
33. Hospitalization.
34. Medicines.
35. Dental care.

sports fields, day-care centers, arts and crafts and vocational training schools, and theaters. In terms of these benefits, ISSSTE and the armed forces are well ahead of the rest of the groups and subgroups.[53]

A more discriminating analysis of the varying conditions attached to a given benefit available to various groups and subgroups compares 6 types of conditions: (a) requirements to gain the right; (b) basic salary to compute the benefit; (c) the amount of the benefit; (d) the adjustment of pensions to the cost of living; (e) the speed of processing the benefit; and (f) the transfer of time of service from one institution to another and the compatibility of a pension with other pensions or salaried work.

In old-age pensions the minimum age required increases as follows: 45 to 55 years of age for military troops and minor officials in the armed forces (for compulsory retirement; age increases from 55 to 65 for higher officials); 55 years of age for civil servants, petroleum, and electrical workers; 60 years of age for IMSS employees, railroad, and sugar workers; and 65 years of age for blue- and white-collar workers. The years of service required, in addition, for retirement increase as follows: 10 years of service for IMSS employees and blue- and white-collars, 15 years for civil servants and railroad workers, 20 years for the armed forces, 25 years for petroleum, 30 years for electricity, and 35 years for sugar workers.

Seniority pensions are granted regardless of age with required years of service increasing as follows: 20 years of service for armed forces; 25 years for petroleum and female railroad workers; 30 years for civil servants, IMSS employees, and male railroad workers; and 35 years for electricity. Most retired militarymen are young officers who immediately take other jobs. Since the age for entrance into military schools is 16 or 17 and the time of instruction is counted as years of service for retirement purposes, those in the military often retire as young as 36. This is officially considered advantageous for several reasons: the retired militarymen bring the army virtues of discipline, courage, and patriotism to civilian life; a good number of positions are left vacant, facilitating promotions; and the budgets of the Ministries of Defense and the Army are relieved of a burden because payment of pensions is made through the budget of the Ministry of the Treasury.[54]

Pensions for permanent disability not caused by occupational hazards require the following minimum years of service: 3 years of service for both IMSS employees and blue- and white-collars; 10 years for both electricity and railroads; 15 years for civil servants; 20 years for armed forces; and 25 years for petroleum workers. There are no significant differences in the conditions attached to disability pensions for occupational hazards and only a few for survivors' pensions. These are available for widows, orphans, and parents, in that order; in the armed forces, sisters and brothers also have a right to pensions if there are no other surviving relatives. Orphans can collect the pension until they are 18 years old if they are the beneficiaries of civil servants or militarymen but only until 16 years of age if they are the beneficiaries of blue- and white-collar workers.

The basic remuneration for computing the benefit is the salary or wage, including overtime, compensation for special services, and merit awards for all groups except blue- and white-collar workers. As a base for the computation, the current salary of the immediately higher rank is used for the armed forces, the last month for IMSS employees and electrical workers, an average of the last year for petroleum and sugar workers, an average of the last two years for railroad workers, and an average of the last five years for civil servants and blue- and white-collars. Of course, the larger the period of time of service used for the computation, the smaller the average base will be.

The percentage applied to the basic remuneration to compute the pension varies according to the type of pension and the social security institution granting it. For seniority pensions it ranges from 70 to 100 percent; for old-age and occupational disability pensions, from 60 to 100 percent, while for nonoccupational disability pensions, from 40 to 100 percent; and for survivors' pensions, from 20 to 50 percent (to any given single survivor). In descending order of percentages applicable, the groups could be ranked as follows: railroad, electricity, sugar, petroleum, civil servants, armed forces, IMSS employees, and blue- and white-collars.

There are other significant inequalities concerning the fixed amount or percentage of the salary and length of other monetary benefits. Funeral aid is fixed at four months' salary for the armed forces; three months' salary (or wages) for petroleum, electricity, railroad, and sugar; two months' for civil servants and IMSS employees; and one month's for blue- and white-collar workers. The maternity-leave subsidy for insured female workers is fixed at 100 percent of the salary/wage for all the following groups but for a decreasing period of time: electricity (150 days); petroleum (100 days); civil servants and IMSS employees (90 days); and railroad (84 days). Blue- and white-collars receive only 60 percent of the wage for 84 days. The subsidy for nonoccupational illness is fixed at 100 percent of the salary for a period of: one year for civil servants, IMSS employees, and armed forces; 270 days for petroleum; and 150 days for electricity. It is fixed at an average of 70 percent of the wage for 145 days for railroads; 50 percent of the wage for 107 days for sugar workers; and 60 percent of the wage for 100 days (excluding the first 5 days) for blue- and white-collars.

During most of the last two decades, Mexico enjoyed an unusual financial stability with a low rate of inflation; therefore, the problem of adjusting pensions to the cost of living has not been a matter of concern until very recently. With increasing rates of inflation (12 percent in 1973 and 23 percent in 1974), however, those groups that are able to adjust their pensions more frequently are in a privileged position. The social security systems developed through collective bargaining (petroleum, electricity, railroads, IMSS employees, and sugar) usually introduce biannual adjustments to the cost of living. The law stipulates adjustments every 5 years for the armed forces and blue- and white-collars, and every 6 years for civil servants.[55]

Information on the time required for processing pensions is limited to the three major institutions and based on personal interviews; thus it should be taken cautiously. Data from other countries suggest that the smaller the group of insured, the faster the procedure to obtain the benefit. In Mexico, the average time to process pensions for civil servants and armed forces is 6 months; for blue- and white-collars, from 6 to 12 months in the Federal District, but from 2 to 4 years in the states. (One important reason for the delays in IMSS is that the Consejo Técnico has to approve each pension—some 1,500 monthly—as well as other benefits.)[56] An educated guess is that pensions in electricity, petroleum, and railraods are processed as fast or even faster than those in the armed forces and civil service.

Transfers of time of service from one social security institution to another (contributions are never transferred) is limited to one case: from public decentralized institutions (e.g., petroleum, railroad, electricity) to ISSSTE. Other transfers of time of service within the public sector (e.g., from ISSSTE to armed forces or vice versa) or between the public and the private sector are not possible. For instance, a teacher who has worked ten years in a private school (covered by IMSS) and moves to a federal school (covered by ISSSTE) loses the ten years of service and contributions accumulated in IMSS.

For those who are already retired, however, life is easier, particularly if they are insured in an institution which permits the accumulation of various pensions or of a pension with remunerated work. An armed forces pension can be accumulated with another pension from the private sector; and a former employee in the Direction of Military Pensions can accumulate as many as three pensions: from the armed forces, ISSSTE, and IMSS. A pension from ISSSTE can be accumulated with one from IMSS but neither with pensions from public decentralized institutions nor from the armed forces. A military pensioner can perform salaried work in any place outside the armed forces; even within the armed forces, he can work as a teacher in a military academy. A civil service pensioner can perform salaried work in the private sector but not in the federal government unless he is under annual contract for an honorarium. A pensioner from IMSS is allowed to work outside of the private sector, but the sum of his pension and his salary cannot exceed the salary that he received at the time of retirement.

An analysis of differences in the conditions to acquire benefits among groups and subgroups alters somewhat the ranking made before, based on table 6-12. In the 16 comparisons presented above, the armed forces ranked first in 10; while electricity, railroads, civil servants and IMSS ranked first in 4; and petroleum ranked first in 3. Conversely, blue- and white-collars ranked last in 11 of the 16 comparisons. The ranking resulting from these comparisons is as follows: (1) armed forces; (2) electricity, railroads, civil service, IMSS employees, and petroleum; and (3) sugar and blue- and white-collar workers.[57]

Table 6-13 compares average yearly per-capita pensions among some occupational groups and subgroups in 1969. Data on the armed forces are based on a gross estimate; information was lacking on electricity and sugar. The average pen-

Table 6-13
Average Yearly Pensions by Occupational Group in Mexico: 1969
(in current pesos per capita)

Occupational Group	Average Pensions	Ratio[a]
Blue- and white-collars	3,088	1.0
Civil servants	19,692	6.4
Armed forces	17,000[b]	5.5
Railroads	19,740	6.4

SOURCES: *Blue- and white-collars* from IMSS, *Memoria de labores de 1969: Datos estadísticos. Civil servants* from ISSSTE, *Anuario estadístico 1969. Armed forces* and *railroad* data gathered by the author in 1971 in personal interviews.

a. Ratio of average pension per capita in relation to the lowest average per capita, that of blue- and white-collars.

b. Gross estimate for 1968 based on expenditures of 340,145,300 pesos divided into an estimate of 20,000 pensioners (out of 71,000 active insured).

Table 6-14
Health Facilities and Expenditures by Occupational Group in Mexico: 1969–1970

Occupational Group	Number of Insured[a] (in thousands)	Expenditures[a] (in billion pesos)	Per Active Insured[a]	Hospital Beds[a]	Per 1,000 Active Insured[a]	Physicians[b]	Per 1,000 Active Insured[b]
Blue- and white-collars	2,915	4,076	1,398	15,976	5.5	11,740	3.6
Civil servants	421	1,056	2,508	1,940[c]	4.6[c]	3,693	7.1
Armed forces	75	164[d]	2,192	1,950[d]	26.1	970[d]	12.3
Railroads	89	141	1,589	1,288	14.5	469	5.1
Petroleum	71	241	3,376	842	11.8	774	10.8
Noninsured[e]	11,795	1,052	89	47,498[f]	4.0	16,680[g]	1.4
Total	15,366	6,730	438	69,494	4.5	34,326	2.2

SOURCES: *Expenditures* and *hospital beds* from Secretaria de Industria y Comercio, Dirección General de Estadistica, *Anuario estadistico compendiado, 1970* (México, D.F.: 1971). *Physicians* from ibid., *Anuario estadistico compendiado, 1971–1972* (México, D.F.: 1973). *Active insured* from table 6-3.

a. 1969.

b. 1970.

c. Includes only ISSSTE facilities, not those contracted with other institutions, hence ratios per insured are underestimated.

d. Secretary of Defense and Secretary of the Navy.

e. Covered by services from Secretary of Public Health and Assistance, Federal District, other government agencies and private institutions. Per-capita computations were made by dividing available facilities by the noninsured labor force.

f. Public, 26,333; private, 21,165.

g. Public, 7,374; private and others, 9,306.

sion presumably includes old-age, seniority, disability, and survivors' pensions; disaggregated data were not available. The table shows that civil servants, railroad workers, and the armed forces had an average per-capita pension about 6 times higher than that of blue- and white-collars. Gross estimates done by the author place petroleum average per-capita pensions at the top of the distribution: more than twice the pension received by civil servants and 13 times that of blue- and white-collars. The ranking of groups according to average pensions is very similar to their 1970 ranking according to income (by economic sector). Differential ratios in pensions, however, are considerably higher than those based on income, suggesting that the pension system expands income inequalities, playing a regressive role in income distribution.

A similar conclusion can be reached from table 6-14 which presents the inequalities in hospital and medical facilities by occupational groups. In terms of per-capita health expenditures, petroleum again comes first (in spite of the fact that the expenditures used were those for 1966, while the rest were for 1968) with twice as much as blue- and white-collars, which are at the bottom of the insured. Per-capita expenditures of the armed forces and civil servants are 1.5 and 1.2 times higher than those of the bottom. In comparisons of physicians and hospital beds, civil servants are not considered because their ratios are underestimated due to the exclusion of contracted services. Concerning physicians per 1,000 active insured, petroleum is also at the top, with 1.3 times more physicians (per insured) than the armed forces, 4 times more than railroads, and almost 5 times more than blue- and white-collar workers who are, again, at the bottom. Finally, with respect to hospital beds per 1,000 insured, the armed forces rises to the top with almost twice as many beds (per insured) as railroads and petroleum, and almost 5 times more than blue- and white-collars, again at the bottom.

Health care to the noninsured is provided both by public institutions (e.g., Ministry of Public Health, Federal District, states, municipalities) and private hospitals. Ratios of physicians and beds per noninsured are below those of blue- and white-collars (see table 6-14). However, the distribution of both physicians and hospital beds shows that the public sector embraces about 56–57 percent of the facilities and the private sector the remaining 43–44 percent. Since the public sector has to service the low-income, usually indigent, large masses of noninsured, while the private clinics serve a high- and middle-income, small segment of noninsured, the ratios of facilities per user should be much higher in the private sector than in the public sector.

The quantitative figures of table 6-14 require an additional qualitative evaluation of health and medical facilities in Mexico.[58] The facilities (physical plant, equipment, personnel) of the IMSS are the best in the country, although the quality of installations in the Federal District is superior to that in the states; the latter, however, are less crowded and therefore personal attention is better. The main IMSS hospital is the Centro Médico Nacional (CMN) located in the D.F.; it is not only the best in Mexico, but one of the finest hospitals in the world. This modern hospital covers all major specialties, including sophisticated services such as nuclear medicine; its center for rehabilitation is excellent. Rooms are well-equipped and usually have four beds. Medical personnel are highly qualified and well-paid. The serious problem of excess demand of available services is not visible in the CMN, but it is notorious in local hospitals, particularly in the D.F. In these, patients have to wait in line for as long as six hours; overscheduled physicians give minimal attention; appointments for specialties are difficult to obtain (often taking as much as two months). Many patients requiring surgery are told to wait and are given medical treatment only. There is a limited assortment of medicines available which reportedly expands with the contribution bracket of the insured, and there are complaints that the quality of attention is related to the personal appearance of the insured and his connections.

The second best facilities are probably those of ISSSTE. As in the case of IMSS, installations in the D.F. are superior to those in the states, but attention in the latter is better. The main hospital, in 1971, Hospital 20 de Noviembre (a larger one, Hospital López Mateos, was opened in 1973) is comparable to the CMN, except its staff is smaller. Its rooms have only two or four beds. The pressure of demand is more noticeable here than in the CMN, because ISSSTE has fewer state and local hospitals and many patients are transferred to the D.F. Beds are used at maximum capacity and there are problems of overcrowding (these may have been alleviated with the opening of the second major hospital in the D.F.).

The third-ranked hospital and medical facilities are those of the armed forces. The main hospital of the army/air force, in the D.F., is older and smaller than its IMSS and ISSSTE counterparts but has all the major specialties, good equipment and staff. Rooms are of three classes with 30 beds in a room for troopers, 6 beds for minor officials, 2 beds for major officials, and one bed with bath for generals. Demand for services is smaller, only three-fourths of the facilities are in use, and, hence, personal attention is better than in the other two groups. The D.F.'s main naval hospital is smaller, older, and has fewer specialties, staff, and beds than the army hospital.

Many of the naval patients are transferred to the army hospital where rooms have fewer beds (although also stratified according to rank) and only two-thirds of them are occupied.

The railroad hospital in the D.F. is similar to the army hospital (in terms of physical plant, equipment, specialties, and staff) and better than the naval hospital. Rooms have only one or two beds and attention is much more personal. Next in ranking are the main hospitals (in the D.F.) of petroleum, electricity, and sugar. The sugar hospital has the basic specialties and equipment, but its physical appearance is poor. It is overstaffed, one-fourth of the beds are not occupied, and personal attention is good. There are also special hospitals in the D.F. for subgroups such as bank employees, actors, and cinema employees.

Private clinics are of various kinds: *beneficencias* based on ethnic associations which are usually of high standards; commercial clinics which have varying standards; Red Cross hospitals of fair standards; and charity *beneficencias* which usually have low standards and are operated by religious orders. In the public network of hospitals, those federally operated in the D.F. and in coordination with the states (*coordinados*) provide good care; those operated independently by the states and municipalities are declining in importance and have low standards. In many rural, isolated areas, particularly those with high concentration of Indians, the only services available are those of the *curandero* or witch doctor.

Table 6-15 shows the 1969 distribution of health facilities by geographic regions in Mexico. In terms of both physicians per 10,000 inhabitants and hospital beds per 1,000 inhabitants, the Central region ranks first, closely followed by the North and North Pacific regions, and then by the Gulf of Mexico; the South Pacific region is at the bottom, well below the other regions and the national average. While the Central region has 1.7 beds per 1,000 inhabitants and 8.9 physicians per 10,000 inhabitants, the South Pacific region has ratios of 0.4 and 2.4 respectively. Availability of health facilities is, therefore, positively correlated to the region's level of development. The gap in health facilities increases considerably when comparisons are made among the states. In 1969, the ratio of beds per 1,000 inhabitants in the Federal District was 3.0 (about twice the rate of the Central region), but in the state of Oaxaca the ratio was only 0.3.[59]

Table 6-15
Health Facilities by Geographic Region in Mexico: 1970

Region	Total Population (in thousands)	Hospital Beds[a]	Beds per 1,000 Inhabitants	Physicians	Physicians per 10,000 Inhabitants	Composite Weighted Index of Beds and Physicians
North Pacific	3,908	5,375	1.4	2,483	6.3	4.1
North	9,052	13,086	1.4	5,818	6.4	3.8
Center	24,161	40,817	1.7	21,530	8.9	5.4
Gulf of Mexico	5,681	7,740	1.4	3,165	5.6	3.2
South Pacific	5,423	2,476	0.4	1,330	2.4	1.5
Total	48,225	69,494	1.4	34,326	7.1	4.2

SOURCES: *Beds* from Secretaría de Industria y Comercio, Dirección General de Estadística, *Anuario estadístico compendiado 1970. Physicians* from ibid., 1971–1972 (1973).
a. December 1969 figures.

The Inequality Effect of Social Security Stratification

Until the mid-1950s social security coverage in Mexico was limited to a tiny fraction of the population and the labor force. In the next decade, however, coverage increased almost 4 times (to embrace about one-fifth of the population and the EAP) as a result of the gradual entrance into IMSS of agricultural workers, small farmers, *ejidatarios,* and seasonal urban workers, as well as IMSS expansion to new municipalities and the creation of ISSSTE. By 1970 the social security system covered almost 25 percent of both the EAP and the total population.

The active insured were distributed among occupational groups, in 1969, as follows: blue- and white-collars, 81 percent; civil servants, 12 percent; armed forces, railroads, and petroleum, about 2 percent each; and electricity, about one percent (sugar, included in the first group, embraced 2 percent of the insured). The group of insured that expanded most in the 1960s was that of civil servants, followed by blue- and white-collars and railroad workers. Mexico has one of the largest proportions in Latin America of blue- and white-collar workers in the insured population.

Using data on income distribution for 1960, the income of the insured population can be ranked as follows: petroleum; electricity; government (mostly civil servants); transportation (part of which are railroad workers); industry, commerce, and service (the large majority of those insured in IMSS); sugar; and agriculture (insured in IMSS). Income data on the armed forces were not available, but tentatively we can rank them at the same income level as civil servants. The ratio between the highest and the lowest income strata was about 5 to 1.

In 1969, the degree of coverage among the urban salaried and wage-earners (clustering civil servants, armed forces, petroleum, railroad, and most of the IMSS insured) was 60 percent; among rural wage-earners (IMSS insured) 11 percent; and among self-employed (IMSS insured in agriculture) less than 1 percent. Coverage among employers and unpaid family workers was insignificant. This situation may change in the 1970s if the government's promise to expand coverage to most self-employed in urban and rural areas is kept.

A better picture of the degree of social security coverage, in 1969, is given when an EAP distribution by sectors of economic activity is used. The groups and sub-groups with better coverage were electricity and civil servants, and probably armed forces (more than 100 percent); petroleum (84 percent); and transport-railroads (68 percent). Coverage of industry, commerce, and service workers (the bulk of the IMSS insured) diminished from 58 to 16 percent; while coverage among agricultural wage-earners was 1 percent (7 percent if rural self-employed were added). The best-covered groups/subgroups are those working in strategic trades, with a high degree of unionization, and relatively high income. Conversely the worst-covered groups/subgroups are those engaged in nonstrategic activities, poorly unionized, and with low income.

The financing system of Mexico's social security system seems to play a regressive role in income distribution. Groups/subgroups at the top of the 1970 income distribution (petroleum, electricity, railroads, armed forces) do not contribute at all or pay a token sum to their systems which are essentially financed by the federal government. Most of these groups are employed in monopolies that can easily transfer price increases to the consumers. Civil servants with an average income twice as high as that of blue- and white-collars have a percentage contribution to their system twice as high as that of blue- and white-collar workers. And yet, ISSSTE benefits are remarkably superior to those available under IMSS. Besides, the combined percentage contribution of the employer/federal government to both systems is similar and, in terms of actual payments, the contribution should be higher to ISSSTE than to IMSS due to the difference in income between the two groups of insured. As a result, social security revenue per capita for civil servants is 4 times higher than that of blue- and white-collars, larger than the income inequalities between the two groups. Sugar workers who have an income higher than the average agricultural worker (insured in IMSS) do not contribute at all to their system which is mostly paid by the employer with some help from the federal government. Three-fourths of the EAP who are not insured contribute to the social security system of those insured (especially to those heavily financed by the federal government) through taxes and/or higher consumer prices.

The financial situation of the two major social security funds (the only ones on which data are available) is significantly different. IMSS faced an increasing accounting deficit in its health-maternity branch in the 1960s which had to be offset by heavily drawing from the reserves of its pension fund. In 1969 IMSS still generated an accounting cumulative surplus of 3 billion pesos (1,000 pesos per insured), but such surplus was declining; furthermore, IMSS' actuarial deficit was calculated at 8 billion pesos in 1966. ISSSTE had an accounting cumulative surplus of 1.4 billion in 1970 (3,325 pesos per insured); there was no information on its actuarial situation.

A simple count of the number of social security benefits available to each occupational group/subgroup results in the following ranking: (1) civil servants, (2) petroleum and IMSS employees, (3) electricity and railroads, (4) armed forces, and (5) sugar and blue- and white-collar workers. A more discriminating analysis of the varying conditions related to the acquisition and generosity of such benefits alters somewhat the previous distribution: the armed forces rises to first place; civil servants, IMSS employees, and petroleum move below electricity and railroads; sugar and blue- and white-collar workers remain at the bottom.

The ranking of subgroups according to their higher per-capita pension is similar to their ranking according to income: petroleum, civil servants, railroads, armed forces, and blue- and white-collars. (Data on electricity and sugar were not available.) The ratio of the petroleum workers' pension to that of the bottom (blue- and white-collars) was 13 to 1; the ratio of civil servants, railroads, and armed-forces pensions to the bottom pension was about 6 to 1. The pension system, therefore, probably expands existing income inequalities in the active labor force.

Inequalities in hospital and medical facilities follow a pattern similar to that of pensions. In three comparisons done in 1969 (health expenditures, number of physicians, and number of beds per insured), petroleum ranked first in 2, armed forces in 1 (and second in 2), and railroads and civil servants ranked always well above blue- and white-collars who systematically came last. Extreme differential ratios (of physicians and beds per insured between the top and the bottom) were of 5 to 1, thus duplicating the income differential ratios between similar sectors of economic activity in 1970. Health facilities available to the noninsured were the worst in overall averages, but the high- and middle-income noninsured who can afford private hospitals are probably better protected than the large mass of low-income noninsured who have access to public hospitals only.

The various comparisons presented above allow us to rank the major groups/subgroups, according to the excellence of their social security systems, as follows: (1) the political and military pressure groups, i.e., civil servants, closely followed by armed forces; (2) the labor aristocracy, that is, IMSS employees and electrical workers, closely followed by petroleum and then railroad workers; and (3) the mass of blue- and white-collar workers, with sugar slightly above the average and agriculture well below the average.

Social security inequalities among the five geographic regions in Mexico were detected in degree of coverage in pensions and health programs and availability of health facilities. These regions can be ranked, in terms of their development, using several indicators (i.e., contribution to GDP and industrial product, production per capita, urban population, number of most populated cities, availability of natural resources) as follows: Central region, closely followed by the North and North Pacific regions; next, Gulf of Mexico; and South Pacific last. Differences among the states (and Federal District) within a region are significant also. There are no accurate data on income distribution by regions/states; we assume that ranking of regions in terms of income is similar to that in development.

The degree of the population's coverage in pensions-health programs is higher in the three most-developed regions and lower in the two least-developed: North Pacific (9 percent), Center (8 percent), North (7 percent), Gulf of Mexico (5 percent), and South Pacific (2 percent). Coverage of the EAP in the Federal District and the states follows, with few exceptions, the same pattern as among regions: all the D.F. and the seven states that have a degree of coverage above the national average are in the three most-developed regions, while all the states in the two least-developed regions have a degree of coverage below the national average. The range of coverage goes from 63 percent in the D.F. down to 4.5 percent in Oaxaca. Significant correlations (at the 5 percent level) were found between the degree of social security coverage in the states, on the one hand, and both the size of the EAP in states (.72; $N = 32$) and the urban percentage of the EAP in provinces (.64; $N = 32$) on the other hand.

The ranking of the regions according to their health facilities (combining both hospital beds per 1,000 inhabitants and physicians per 10,000 inhabitants) is similar to the ranking of the provinces by their level of development: Central (5.4), North Pacific (4.1), North (3.8), Gulf of Mexico (3.2), and South Pacific (1.5). The range of hospital facilities goes from 3 beds per 1,000 inhabitants in the D.F. down to 0.3 beds per 1,000 inhabitants in Oaxaca.

In summary, the most developed and urbanized regions/states have a concentration of vital economic activities (government services, energy, transportation, industry, commerce, modern agriculture); they are also the strongest in political and union power. The most powerful pressure groups are concentrated in these regions/states which consequently received early social security protection and currently have the highest degree of coverage in pensions-health and the best health facilities. Conversely, the more backward, isolated regions/states are those with a labor force largely engaged in traditional agriculture and with a high proportion of Indians; they are poorly unionized and politically passive or controlled. Lacking strong pressure groups, these regions/states have been latecomers in social security, most of their municipalities are still unprotected by pensions-health, and those already protected have the lowest degree of coverage and the poorest health facilities.

The massification of social security privileges has taken place on a small scale in Mexico. The bulk of the system, that of IMSS, has been in operation for three decades but only recently began to cover a sizable proportion of the population. The vertical expansion of benefits (i.e., the addition and improvement of benefits to those already insured) has usually taken priority over the horizontal expansion of benefits (i.e., the incorporation of noninsured into the system). In spite of the gradual expansion of IMSS coverage to the rural sector, about 90 percent of this subgroup is still not protected. Other underprivileged groups such as the urban self-employed and domestic servants remain basically uninsured. Competition for the addition and improvement of benefits seems to take place mostly within the small segment of privileged insured groups such as civil servants, the armed forces, IMSS employees, and the labor aristocracy.

The gradual process of expansion of coverage and relative massification of privilege, compounded with the significant increase in administrative expenditures (mostly resulting from the rapidly growing social security staff and of its salaries) caused social security costs to rise in the 1960s. The cost of social security in Mexico is still small in comparison to other Latin American countries. Social security expenditures represented 3 percent of GNP in 1968 (rising from 2 percent in 1961) and about half of government consumption in 1966. In the decade of the 1960s, the labor force increased by 40 percent, but the number of passive workers (i.e., retired, pensioners) jumped by 340 percent. The average ratio of active vis-a-vis passive insured was 23.4 to 1 in 1960 and steadily declined to 15.2 to 1 in 1970; these ratios, however, are still very high compared with those of Uruguay, Chile, and Argentina. And yet if the 1960s trend continues in Mexico in the 1970s, ratios of 6 or 7 to 1 should be expected.

The possibility of unification and standardization of social security in Mexico seems quite remote today. Once in a while there are official statements in favor of the coordination of public health services and of the unification and standardization of the federal and state systems protecting civil servants. These partial processes of unification are the only realistic and feasible reforms that we may see in the near future. But the probability of the powerful groups/subgroups being forced to resign their privileges under the current situation is practically nil.

7 The Role of Pressure Groups and the Measurement of Social Security Inequality

This chapter summarizes and compares the major findings of the five case studies; tests the ideal typology of pressure groups and the set of hypotheses on the stratification of social security; and measures the inequality of the stratified social security system. After a summary of the role of pressure groups in the evolution and stratification of social security, I construct a set of indicators to measure social security inequality and analyze the effects of stratification on the historical appearance of the legislation, current coverage, financing, and benefits. Finally the indicators of inequalitiy are integrated to yield a ranking of the countries in terms of social security inequalities.

A Comparison of the Role of Pressure Groups

One of the main hypotheses of this study is that the power of a pressure group (as described in the ideal typology) is positively related to the excellence of its social security system: the more powerful the group, the earlier it gains protection, the higher its degree of coverage, the less it has to pay to finance its system, and the better the amount and quality as well as the less stringent its conditions to acquire benefits.

The power of the pressure groups has, admittedly, not been easy to measure. Mostly I have relied on loose indicators of power which pertain to the size of the group and its income. Additional indicators of power have been, in the case of the military group, the length of time it has controlled the governmental apparatus and, in the case of the union group, its level of activism as roughly measured by strikes. Although there are not enough quantitative data to allow systematic cross-country comparisons, the available statistics and qualitative information permit, at least, a ranking of the groups/subgroups in terms of their power.[1]

The military group appears to be the most powerful in the majority of the countries studied. Since the independence from Spain until the early 1970s, this group has directly controlled the government for more than a century in Peru and Mexico, and for about 60 years in Argentina, 40 years in Chile, and 35 years in Uruguay. No other single group with the rare exception of the politico-administrative group has possessed so much power for such a long period of time. The absolute size of the military forces (excluding the police) in all these countries is at least equivalent to the membership of the largest national union in the private sector. By the end of the 1960s, the proportion of militarymen in the labor force was: 1.8 percent in Argentina, 1.5 percent in Peru, 1.4 percent in Chile and Uruguay, and 0.5 percent in Mexico. This ranking roughly reflects the relative size of the military in the five countries. Data on income is, unfortunately, not available (or if available not accurate enough) to permit comparisons with other groups.

The politico-administrative group seems to be the second most powerful in most countries. (Mexico is probably an exception; this group is *currently* more powerful than the military.) According to available data, civil servants constitute the largest group in terms of membership in unions or associations. They compose more than 3 percent of the labor force in Chile and Mexico, countries ranked in Latin America among those with the largest government bureaucracies. In addition to the power derived from their control of the state administration, this group has occasionally resorted to political allegiances as well as associations or unions and strikes to achieve its goals. The scarce data available on income indicate that this group has well above the average income of the union group and, at least, matches that of white-collars in the economic group and the labor aristocracy in the union group.

The power of the economic or market group is probably the most difficult to measure. Professionals such as teachers make up the largest national unions after that of civil servants. Data for white-collar membership in unions or associations, available only in Chile, rank this subgroup as the largest after that of teachers. Bank employees in Argentina have a degree of unionization considerably above the national average. Income of the economic group is at least twice that of the unions.

The union group has to be divided, in terms of power, into the labor aristocracy, the remainder of the urban labor force, and the rural workers. (Domestic servants and the self-employed could be treated either as a special subgroup here or as a group by itself.) The labor aristocracy is made up of subgroups that were the earliest to become unionized, and currently are the largest in union membership, the highest in degree of unionization, and the most active. Electrical and petroleum workers are at the top, in most countries, in degree of unionization, followed by railroad, maritime (or fishing), and mining workers. Agricultural workers on large, modern plantations (e.g., sugar in Argentina, Mexico, and Peru) could be considered part of the labor aristocracy due to their high degree of unionization. Most of these subgroups became unionized at the end of the nineteenth century or early in the twentieth century and are in strategic sectors of the economy, have the power to paralyze the country or the production of a major product, are in monopolies or oligopolies which generate high profits, and have long histories of labor activism and strikes. The remaining segment of the labor force has a lower degree of unionization, with manufacturing more unionized than commerce. Finally, traditional agriculture has the lowest degree of unionization. The range is exemplified by electricity at the top (89 percent unionized in Mexico and 79 percent in Argentina) and agriculture at the bottom (respectively 2 and 5 percent unionized). Domestic servants and the self-employed are rarely unionized. The ranking in terms of unionization parallels that of income, the labor aristocracy making from three to five times the income of rural workers and domestic servants.

In evaluating the role of pressure groups in the inception and development of social security, the information available, particularly in relation to the bulk of the labor force (the union group), is often insufficient to develop clear-cut conclusions.[2] The summary presented below, should, therefore, be taken as a first approximation, subject to further empirical verification.

Pressure groups/subgroups may be classified in three categories in terms of their impact on the evolution of social security: (1) the military and politico-administrative groups, (2) the economic group and the labor-aristocracy subgroup from the union group, and (3) the remaining subgroups within the union group. The existing political system, whether patrimonial-oligarchic, liberal-pluralist, or authoritarian-corporatist, also conditions the role of pressure groups.

In the early nineteenth century, the newly proclaimed republics were fragmented by *caudillismo* and regionalism and had weak central governments usually controlled by the military (in coalition with oligarchs) and operated by a small group of civil servants. The political regime was usually patrimonial-oligarchic with authoritarian overtones. The nation had not yet been built and the embryonic state was largely controlled and administered by two small groups. The military granted itself and civil servants the first social security program, as an extension of the colonial *montepíos*. The consolidation of the central government and its expansion was completed by the end of the nineteenth or early twentieth century by the same groups, either through military dictatorships or fraudulent conservative civilian governments. At this point, the power of the government bureaucracy began to grow, and this group together with the military, obtained the first modern social security programs. In summary, as represented in Model 1, the military and the politico-administrative groups, operating within a patrimonial-oligarchic political regime, largely controlled the embryonic state and enacted social security for themselves:

Model 1

PG
$\updownarrow \rightarrow$ SS
S

In the development of the modern state, a high priority was placed by some countries (e.g., Uruguay, Argentina) on the expansion of education. Teachers were in high demand (particularly in the frontier) and to further strengthen its position this subgroup resorted to association and occasional strikes. Hence it logically followed that, by the end of the nineteenth century, teachers became the first economic subgroup to receive social security protection by the state. Industrialization combined with heavy immigration and imported ideologies and a conservative, elitist state which refused to make concessions to the labor force, produced: militant unions in strategic economic sectors (e.g., railroads, mining, public utilities, docks); an increasing number of strikes; and the organization of both reformist and revolutionary parties. This social ferment gained momentum and, in the first three decades of the twentieth century, climaxed with national crises in most countries.[3] The crises were temporarily solved through peaceful (electoral) means in Uruguay (1904), Argentina (1916), and Chile (1924). Actually, in Uruguay the crisis never reached serious proportions because the well-developed political parties served as channels for articulation and satisfaction of demands of the pressure groups; additionally, Batlle introduced timely political and social reforms. In Peru, the crisis was temporarily halted by Benavides' stick-and-carrot approach and a later compromise of the power elite and the opposition. In Mexico the crisis led to revolution. By one way or another, in the majority of these countries the government ceased to be the fief of the military-oligarch elite; it widened its scope to include the rising middle class and was led by populist leaders who appealed to the proletariat. In the context of a better delineated national state with a more liberal-pluralistic political system, well-organized pressure groups/subgroups in strategic activities (the labor aristocracy and white-collars, now part of the government coalition) naturally obtained social security protection. Because these groups/subgroups were willing to negotiate and make compromises, they set the example for the rest of the labor force with a subsequent decline of revolutionary unions. Populist political parties (either in power or, at least, influential), such as the Colorados in Uruguay, Democrats and Radicals in Chile, Radicals in Argentina, and Apristas in Peru, developed a strong relationship with these groups/subgroups and supported their demands. Notice, however, that neither the state nor the parties introduced social security (except protection against occupational accidents) for the bulk of the union group. Since a central, broad social security fund had not yet been established, the bureaucracy could not play a role in the expansion of social security. In summary, as represented in Model 2, the economic pressure group and the labor aristocracy subgroup, operating within a relatively liberal and pluralistic political system, gained social security protection by applying direct pressure upon the state, often with additional aid from political parties with which the group/subgroup had close ties:

Model 2

$$PG \rightarrow S \rightarrow SS$$

PP

The bulk of the union group did not receive social security protection until the second and third quarters of the twentieth century, after the other groups/subgroups.[4] Within the union group, urban blue-collars were covered first, then selected rural wage-earners on modern plantations, much later the bulk of agricultural workers (in some countries), and only recently domestic servants and the self-employed (in some countries). The inception of social security in favor of this group appears to be more a result of state initiative rather than direct pressure from the group. This group is not as well organized and cohesive as the other groups/subgroups: qualifications for membership are lower; trades are not related to strategic economic sectors; the group embraces a very large number of people and its coverage is costly to finance; finally, the group has immediate needs (e.g., minimum wages) which take priority over social security coverage. The urban segment of the group usually receives protection in a period of political instability and from a leader often populist and either of military background or supported by the military. The historical situations vary: the leader may have promised social security as part of a political platform and, in the midst of a national crisis, implements it to reestablish order (Alessandri in Chile); he may organize the workers into unions and grant them social security coverage (Perón in Argentina); or he may attempt to pacify the masses after a period of grave national strife and pass social security legislation as a palliative (Benavides in Peru); or social security may be given as a noninflationary concession to divert labor pressure from more immediate needs (Alia Camacho in Mexico). In summary, as represented in Model 3, in all the above cases, the state, through the executive and operating in an authoritarian rather than liberal-pluralistic milieu, enacted social security as an instrument to coopt most of the union group and generate political support and/or stability:

Model 3

In a pluralistic-liberal regime, the union group/subgroup may receive protection through a combination of factors: its own strength, political party influence, and the interests of the bureaucracy. In Uruguay, the union groups was covered in a gradual process, largely as a result of the initiative of political parties responding to group leverage in order to gain electoral support. In Peru, under Prado in 1961, the influence of a populist party combined with a well-organized and efficient lobbyist labor movement (both of which had reached a compromise with Prado) resulted in coverage for the union group. In Chile, political parties and the state were instrumental in organizing peasants and shantytown residents for political purposes and, eventually, these union subgroups (e.g., agricultural workers, domestic servants, self-employed) gained strength and were covered by the social security system. In Mexico, with a less liberal-pluralistic regime, part of the subgroup of peasants was organized by the opposition in the 1950s and 1960s, received political support from a powerful expresident (Cárdenas) established national federations, and created foci of political instability (through land invasions, demonstrations, rural uprisings). The government has tried to coopt this subgroup using, among other things, selective social security coverage. These four cases can be illustrated by slightly modified versions of the second and third models.[5]

A word about the social security bureaucracy as a potential factor in the evolution of social security. In those countries which have a large social security fund in charge of most of the system (e.g., IMSS in Mexico) or a central agency that supervises or coordinates most of the system (e.g., SSS in Chile, BPS in Uruguay), the bureaucracies in those funds or agencies may exert influence over the state by favoring the incorporation of the noninsured and less powerful groups/subgroups into the system. Reasons behind this attitude may be multiple: the vested interest of the bureaucrats for self-perpetuation and expansion, their reaction to political situations perceived by them as threatening to the status quo, direct pressure from the groups/subgroups, and/or executive incitement to build up national support in favor of the expansion of coverage. There is no evidence in this study to support this case since the focus of my research has been on pressure groups and to a lesser extent on the role of the state. Future research on the role of the bureaucracy may produce such evidence.

In summary, the first model is rarely operative today although some may argue that the third model is a modified version of the first. (In countries currently under military-autocratic rule, it may also be alleged that the exclusion of the military from a unification process and the preservation of military privileges in social security can be better described by the first model.) The second model is predominant in countries with a liberal-pluralistic tradition such as Uruguay and Chile (until the military takeover in the 1970s). This model also surfaces in short interregna of liberal-pluralist regimes in countries which have a more autocratic tradition; examples of these interregna are the Frondizi-Illia intervals in Argentina and the Prado interval in Peru.

The third model predominates in countries that have a less liberal-pluralistic tradition such as the one-party system of Mexico. It also operates in periods of authoritarian disruption of traditional liberal-pluralistic regimes, such as the first Ibáñez period in Chile. Today, the third model seems to predominate in all five countries due to recent takeovers by authoritarian military regimes, some with corporatist features, in Peru, Uruguay, Chile, and Argentina.

A Set of Indicators to Measure Social Security Inequality

In this section, the standardized statistical tables discussed for each of the five countries are compared and used to develop a set of indicators to measure the degree of inequality in their social security systems. Discussion of the tables is divided into four major sections in this book: (1) historical appearance of social security legislation, (2) current coverage, (3) financing, and (4) benefits. A list of all fifteen standardized tables, their availability (or absence) for each country, and the indicators generated from them is shown in table 7-1.

Table 7-1
Availability of Standardized Tables in the Five Countries and Their Generation of Indicators

Table Number	Table Title	Countries Where Table Is Missing	Indicator Number	Tables in Which Indicators Appear
1	Significant Social Security Legislation	—	1, 2	7-2, 7-3
2	Insured Population in Relation to Total and Economically Active Population (EAP)	—	3, 4	7-4
3	Occupational Groups Protected by Social Security	—	none	none
4	Degree of Social Security Protection of the EAP by Class of Worker	Uruguay	5	7-6
5	Degree of Social Security Protection of the EAP by Sectors of Economic Activity	Peru, Uruguay	6	7-7
6	Degree of Social Security Protection of the Total Population by Geographic Region	—	7	7-8
7	Degree of Social Security Protection of the EAP by State/Province	Uruguay	8	7-9
8	Social Security Contributions from Employees, Employers, and State by Occupational Group	—	9, 10	7-10, 7-11
9	Percentage Distribution of Social Security Fund Revenues by Financing Sources and Occupational Group	—	11, 12	7-12, 7-13
10	Revenue of Social Security Funds per Insured by Occupational Group	—	13	7-14
11	Cost of Social Security	—	none	none
12	Social Security Benefits by Occupational Group	—	14	7-16
13	Average Yearly Pensions by Occupational Group	—	15	7-17
14	Medical Facilities and Expenditures by Occupational Group	Argentina	16, 17	7-18
15	Health Facilities by Geographical Region	—	18, 19	7-19

NOTE: The number of the table is the same in each country but preceded by the number of the corresponding chapter, e.g., table 1, on Chile (chapter 2) is 2-1, while for Uruguay (chapter 3), it is 3-1. Table 2-10a, "Transfer of Social Security Costs among Occupational Groups," is not shown in the table because data for it were available only for Chile and hence a comparison with other countries was precluded.

Chile and Mexico are the only countries for which a complete set of tables is available; Argentina and Peru have only one table missing each; Uruguay is the worst in terms of the availability of data with three tables missing. Tables 3 and 11 for each of the chapters are employed here only for comparative purposes and analyses. The remaining tables are used in this chapter not only for comparisons, but also to compute nineteen indicators of inequality based on gini index, standard deviation, ratio, and percentage.

Historical Appearance

Tables 7-2 and 7-3 compress the data presented in table 1 for all five countries pertaining to the historical appearance of the most significant social security legislation (or similar compulsory measures) covering groups/subgroups of the population against specific risks. It should be remembered that data in those tables refer to the enactment and theoretical implementation of the law, not to practical enforcement. It was absolutely impossible to attempt an analysis of *actual* coverage through time because statistics were not available until the mid-twentieth century. Figures in the tables represent the age of the legislation measured in decades prior to 1980. Thus if a law was passed in 1970, it receives a score of 1 equivalent to one decade; if

Table 7-2
Time of Earliest Pension Legislation by Occupational Group:
1800–1973
(in decades prior to 1980)

Occupational Group	Argentina	Chile	Mexico	Peru	Uruguay
Blue-collars					
General	4[a]	6	4	4	6
Railroads[b]	7	7	5	4	7
Maritime[c]	5	6	4	5	6
Petroleum[d]	4	6	5	4	—
Rural workers	3	6	3	2	4
Domestic service	3	6	1	1	4
White-collars					
General	4[a]	6	4	4	6
Banking	6	6	4	4	6
Civil servants					
General	18	10	19	19	15
Public utilities	6	6	4	4	7
Armed forces					
Military	19	19	19	19	19
Police	4	6	6	—	9
Indicator of inequality[e]	5.6	3.8	6.0	6.4	4.7

SOURCES: Tables 2-1, 3-1, 4-1, 5-1, 6-1.

a. Includes industry and commerce only.

b. Except for Uruguay which embraces all transportation. The railroad is state owned (and therefore could go under civil servants) in Argentina and Mexico. This subgroup covers primarily blue-collar workers.

c. Includes merchant marine and longshoremen. In Argentina includes both blue- and white-collars.

d. Includes both blue- and white-collars.

e. Standard deviation. The higher the figure, the greater the inequality.

Table 7-3
Time of Earliest Health Care Legislation by Occupational Group:
1800–1973
(in decades prior to 1980)

Occupational Group	Argentina	Chile	Mexico	Peru	Uruguay
Blue-collars					
General	2[a]	6	4	5	2[a]
Railroads[b]	4	6	5	5	2
Maritime[c]	4	6	4	5	2
Petroleum[d]	2	6	5	5	—
Rural work	1	6	3	5	0
Domestic service	2	6	1	0	0
White-collars					
General	2	5	4	4	2[a]
Banking	3	5	4	4	2
Civil servants					
General	3	6	3	4	1[e]
Public utilities	3	6	4	4	1
Armed forces					
Military	5	7	6	3	8[f]
Police	3	5	3	—	2
Indicator of inequality[g]	1.3	0.6	1.3	1.6	0.9

SOURCES: Tables 2-1, 3-1, 4-1, 5-1, 6-1.

a. Includes industry and commerce only. In Uruguay only certain groups: wool and hides, metallurgy, textile, printing, garment, beverages, glass, restaurants, and night clubs.

b. Except for Uruguay which embraces all transportation. It is state owned (and therefore could go under civil servants) in Argentina and Mexico. This subgroup covers primarily blue-collar workers.

c. Includes merchant marine and longshoremen. In Argentina includes both blue- and white-collars.

d. Includes both blue- and white-collars.

e. Congress, state bank, and fuel institute became covered in the 1940s (4).

f. For the standard deviation this figure was treated as an outlier and deleted.

g. Standard deviation. The higher the figure, the greater the inequality.

passed in 1960, it receives a score of 2, etc. The higher the score, the older the legislation (and presumably legal coverage of the group/subgroup). Since there were neither enough data nor laws enacted to do a comparison for colonial times, the period encompassed in the tables is 1800–1973, that is, roughly from independence to the present time. Any law enacted prior to 1800 receives the maximum score of 19.

The two most important social security programs, pensions and health, have been selected for comparison and are presented in separate tables. This distinction is made because legislation on pensions is older and spread over a longer time period than health legislation; the latter is highly concentrated in the last thirty or forty years. If the two programs had been clustered, the lower scores of the health program would have offset the higher scores of the pension programs.[6]

In spite of the problems caused by standardization (explained in note 6), tables 7-2 and 7-3 are valuable for tracing the pattern of the historical inception of social security coverage which roughly parallels the power of pressure groups. For on pensions, the gap between the earliest and latest coverage is more than 200 years, the chronological order of coverage being as follows: (1) militarymen (mid-1700s to beginning of 1800s); (2) civil servants (mid-1700s to 1880); (3) teachers—not shown in the table (1880–1930); (4) police (1890–1940); (5) the labor aristocracy, made up of public utility, bank, petroleum, and maritime employees (1910–1940s); (6) the bulk of the urban labor force made up of blue- and white-collars (1920–1940s); (7) rural workers (1930–1950s); (8) domestic servants (1930–1970s); and (9) self-employed— not shown in the table (1950–1970s). The pattern of inception in health is somewhat different with the gap in coverage sharply reduced to seventy years, the military being covered first (1900–1950s); the bulk of the groups/subgroups in the middle (1920–1960s); and domestic servants and the self-employed last (1960–1970) or not covered at all.

The indicators of inequality were developed using standard deviation.[7] They measure the dispersion in historical coverage among the various groups/subgroups. Those countries in which the gap of coverage is wider are more unequal, while those countries in which the gap is narrower are more equal. Thus in Mexico and Peru, the gap in coverage between civil servants and domestic servants is eighteen decades, while in Chile the gap is reduced to four decades. The most significant indicator of inequality (shown at the bottom of table 7-2) is historical coverage in pensions. Based on this indicator the five countries discussed in this book can be ranked, in terms of their inequality as follows: Peru (6.4), Mexico (6.0), Argentina (5.6), Uruguay (4.7), and Chile (3.8). In health, the ranking is the same but the scores are lower: Peru (1.6), Mexico (1.3), Argentina (1.3), Uruguay (0.9), and Chile (0.6).[8] The indicator of inequality for pensions is about five times higher than that of health due to the significantly wider gap in coverage of the former.

Current Coverage

Tables 7-4 to 7-9 compare the various types of coverage by social security systems in the five countries and present six indicators of inequality developed from the data. This set of tables measures *actual* coverage in the decade of the 1960s, while tables 7-2 and 7-3 measure *legal* coverage throughout almost two centuries. Three types of coverage are analyzed here: first, overall coverage of the total population and the economically active population (separating the insured from the noninsured sector of the population); second, degree of coverage within the insured population by both type of worker and economic activity of the labor force; and, third, degree of coverage also within the insured population by region and state/province.

Table 7-4 presents a static comparison of population coverage in 1969 as well as coverage trends for the 1960s.[9] Coverage of the economically active population (EAP) is measured by the number of active workers insured by pensions. Uruguay covers almost the entire EAP (95 percent), followed by Chile (69 percent), Argentina (48 percent), Peru (35 percent), and Mexico (23 percent). The extension of coverage seems to be linked to the overall age of the social security system and, particularly, to the period of time for which the bulk of the labor force has been insured. This in turn seems to be the result of the degree of unionization and activism of the trade union group. For instance, pension coverage of most blue- and white-collars in Uruguay and Chile preceded by about two decades similar coverage in Mexico. Naturally, the average annual rate of increase of the EAP insured in the 1960s is higher in countries which have a smaller proportion of the EAP already covered, and sharply diminishes as coverage embraces most of the labor force.[10]

Table 7-4
Total and Economically Active Population Insured: 1969
(in percentages and ratios)

	Argentina	Chile	Mexico	Peru	Uruguay
Total population insured[a]	40.7	68.8	22.8	12.3	64.5
Average annual increase[b]	1.3	0.6	1.3	0.4	0.1
EAP insured[c]	48.4	69.0	23.3	35.6	95.0
Average annual increase[b]	1.2	0.2	1.3	1.3	−1.4
Ratio of active to passive insured	3.1	3.7	17.4	37.3	2.3
Average annual increase[b]	−0.7	−0.3	−0.7	−3.3	−0.2
Indicators of inequality[d]					
Total population uninsured	59.3	31.2	77.2	87.7	35.5
EAP uninsured	51.6	31.0	76.7	64.4	5.0

Sources: Tables 2-2, 3-2, 4-2, 5-2, 6-2.

a. Active plus passive plus dependent insured. The latter through the health maternity programs in all countries except in Argentina and Uruguay for which family-allowance coverage was used due to the lack of a national health insurance.

b. 1960–1969 inclusive except for Argentina, which covers 1960–1970, and Peru, which covers 1961–1969.

c. Active workers insured in pensions in all countries. In Chile, Mexico, and Peru coverage also includes health and/or maternity programs.

d. Percentage uninsured of total population and economically active population. The higher the figure, the greater the inequality.

The percentage of the total population insured (also shown in table 7-4) is substantially lower than that of the EAP because society places a higher priority on protecting its productive members than its nonproductive members. There are some changes in the ranking of countries by their total population insured as compared to that of the EAP insured: Chile moves up to the first place (69 percent), followed by Uruguay (64 percent), and Argentina (40 percent); Mexico moves up to the fourth place with a similar percentage of both the EAP and the total population insured (23 percent); and Peru falls to the fifth place (12 percent).[11] Except for Peru, the average annual rate of increase of the total population insured in 1960–1970 follows the same pattern as that of the EAP: it is higher in the countries that have a smaller coverage and lower in the countries that have a higher coverage.

Perhaps the most dramatic data shown in table 7-4 are the ratios of active to passive insured which might be called the *supportive ratio,* i.e., how many insured workers who are part of the labor force are supporting (as an average) pensioners (either retired, disabled, or survivor). Those countries with a small proportion of the EAP insured and relatively new pension programs have a high supportive ratio, e.g., Peru 37 to 1, Mexico 17 to 1. Where insurance coverage is greater and the pension program is older, the ratio diminishes, e.g., Chile 3.7 to 1, Argentina 3.1 to 1, Uruguay 2.3 to 1.[12] The supportive ratio indicates the the weight of the burden of the social security system on the labor force and, together with data on the overall cost of the system (see table 7-15), measures the degree of financial stress that social security imposes upon the economy of a developing nation. (Perhaps the current economic crisis of Uruguay is partially due to the fact that back in 1969 two active members of the labor force were supporting one pensioner.)

The two indicators of inequality shown at the bottom of table 7-4 are the single most important indicators in this study. Inequality is measured by the percentage of both the EAP and the total population which are not included in the system, that is, the noninsured. (The remaining indicators in the study measure inequality *within* the system, that is, among those insured.) The higher the proportion of noninsured, the more unequal the system and vice versa.[13] Inequality rankings for the noninsured EAP are: Mexico (77 percent), Peru (64 percent), Argentina (52 percent), Chile (31 percent), and Uruguay (5 percent). When the noninsured total population is ranked, slight changes occur: Peru (88 percent), Mexico (77 percent), Argentina (59 percent), Uruguay (36 percent), and Chile (31 percent).

Table 7-5 compares the percentage distribution of the active insured by major occupational groups in the five countries in 1967.[14] The proportions of blue-collar plus white-collar insured are as follows: Chile (85 percent), Mexico (83 percent), Uruguay (79 percent), Peru (77 percent), and Argentina (56 percent). The five countries could be ranked exactly in the opposite order in terms of their proportion of insured civil servants. The percentage distributions of armed forces and self-employed do not follow—at least at first glance—any specific pattern.

If Mexico is excluded, it appears that the older the social security system, the larger the proportion of blue-collars plus white-collars insured. The reason is that, historically, coverage is first granted to relatively small groups and subgroups (e.g., the armed forces, civil servants, teachers), next to a very small proportion of white-collars and skilled blue-collar workers (the labor aristocracy), and finally to the bulk of blue- and white-collars (first to urban workers and later to rural ones). Therefore, the two oldest systems (Chile and Uruguay) have the highest proportions of blue- plus white-collars insured, while a younger system (such as in Argentina) has a smaller proportion. Following this rationale, in countries that have older social security systems, the percentage of insured blue-collars should be substantially higher than that of white-collars. This seems to be confirmed by the data available (shown in table

Table 7-5
Percentage Distribution of Active Insured by
Occupational Group: 1967

Occupational Group	Argentina	Chile	Mexico	Peru	Uruguay
Blue collars		71.0		46.8	
White collars	55.5[a]	13.9	82.7[a]	30.1	79.0[a]
Civil servants	25.9	11.7	15.0	18.6	18.5
Armed forces	3.4	3.4[b]	2.3	2.2[c]	1.3
Self-employed	15.2	[d]	[e]	2.3	1.2
Total	100.0	100.0	100.0	100.0	100.0

SOURCES: Tables 2-3, 3-3, 4-3, 5-3, 6-3.

a. Includes blue- and white-collars.

b. Armed forces exclude policemen in all countries except in Chile; if policemen are excluded in Chile, the proportion declines to 2.0 percent.

c. Figures for the armed forces in Peru are grossly underestimated, probably the real proportion is close to 3 percent.

d. About 5 percent of the total insured were self-employed, covered mostly by the blue-collar fund and the rest by the white-collar fund.

e. Less than 1 percent of the total insured were self-employed covered by the blue- and white-collar fund.

7-5) from the two countries (Chile and Peru) which have disaggregated these two major groups.[15]

When adjustments are made in table 7-5 to make the proportions of the military personnel truly comparable,[16] the countries are ranked as follows: Argentina (3.4 percent), Peru (about 3 percent), Mexico (2.3 percent), Chile (2 percent), and Uruguay (1 percent). Since all militarymen are normally insured, the crucial variable here is the overall size of the armed forces in each of the countries. Notice that data refer to 1967 when the military were not in power in Chile, Peru, and Uruguay, but were in power in Argentina. Hence the proportion of insured militarymen roughly reflects both the historical trend in coverage (discussed above) and the size and power of the military corps in each country.

Trends on coverage of the self-employed are difficult to trace due to statistical problems. However, the older the social security system, the higher the number of self-employed insured and consequently its proportion of the total insured.

To accurately measure the degree of social security coverage, this study should have determined the proportion of the total members of the group/subgroup (within the EAP) that were insured. Unfortunately, it was impossible to obtain a comparable set of data for the five countries showing the distribution of the labor force by the occupational groups and subgroups that I have used in this book. As substitutes for the ideal comparison, two different distributions of the labor force (by class of worker and by economic activity) were contrasted with the number of insured in the corresponding category. The results are presented in tables 7-6 and 7-7.

Table 7-6 shows the degree of social security protection by class of worker.[17] It indicates that the degree of coverage of salaried workers and wage-earners is highest in Chile (90 percent), followed by Argentina (70 percent), and Peru (64 percent), with the lowest coverage in Mexico (44 percent).[18] The degree of coverage of self-employed in table 7-6 is substantially below that of salaried employees and wage-earners. The self-employed enjoy the highest degree of coverage in Argentina and Chile, with that of Peru and Mexico being considerably lower. All these rankings tend

Table 7-6
Degree of Social Security Protection by Class of Worker
(in percentages)

Class of Worker	Argentina (1960)	Chile (1964)	Mexico (1969)	Peru (1965)
Salaried and wage-earners	69.5	90.3	43.8	64.3
Self employed	22.8	13.7	0.8	1.6
Employers	15.9	a	a	a
Unpaid family workers and unspecified	a	a	a	a
Total	52.8	67.7	27.4	31.5
Indicator of inequality[b]	9.2	19.9	28.1	42.5

SOURCES: Tables 2-4, 4-4, 5-4, 6-4.

a. A small number may be included as insured in other categories.

b. Gini index. The higher the figure, the greater the inequality in the degree of coverage. Complete inequality = 100. Employers, unpaid family workers, and unspecified were excluded from the computations due to disparity of data among the four countries.

to reinforce the explanation given above, that social security coverage is mainly a function of the age of the system and of the power of the pressure groups. Normally, salaried workers and wage-earners have a higher degree of skills and unionization than the self-employed.

The indicator of inequality shown at the bottom of table 7-6 is based on a gini index. It shows the gap in coverage between salaried and wage-earners on the one hand and the self-employed on the other. Peru is ranked as the most unequal (42.5), followed by Mexico (28.1), in spite of lower degrees of coverage for both categories in the latter, with Chile (19.9) next, and Argentina (9.2) as the most equal system due to its relatively high degree of coverage of the self-employed. (However the value of this indicator is very low due to the problems explained in note 17.)

Table 7-7 shows the degree of social security protection by sectors of economic activity.[19] After a careful analysis of table 7-7 (and data from the case studies), a systematic pattern of coverage by economic sectors in the three countries becomes evident. The sector with the best coverage is that of petroleum, electricity, gas, water, other public utilities, and transportation. (Disaggregated data available in some countries indicate that electrical, gas, and water employees are fully covered, or even overcovered as a result of duplicate coverage, that petroleum employees are almost totally covered, but that only two-thirds of transportation workers are covered.) The second best covered sector is banking, insurance, commerce, and personal services. (Disaggregated data indicate that civil servants are fully covered or overcovered, while about one-half of commerce employees are covered, but only a very small proportion of personal services are covered.) The third best covered sector is mining, manufacturing, and construction. (Disaggregated data show signif-

Table 7-7
Degree of Social Security Protection by Sector of
Economic Activity
(in percentages)

Sector of Economic Activity	Argentina (1960)	Chile (1966)	Mexico (1969)
Agriculture, livestock, forestry, hunting, and fishing	54.5	54.8	1.5
Mining, manufacturing, and construction	56.8	93.1	46.6
Petroleum, electricity, water, other public utilities, and transportation	96.9	77.1	75.1
Government, banking, insurance, commerce, and personal services	85.1	66.4	34.3
Self-employed	19.4	—	—
Not specified	—	—	—
Total	52.6	73.3	23.7
Indicator of inequality[a]	11.9	11.2	46.1

SOURCES: Tables 2-5, 5-5, 6-5.

a. Gini index. The higher the figure, the greater the inequality in the degree of coverage. Complete inequality = 100. Self-employed and not specified were excluded from the computations due to disparity of data among three countries.

icant variations in coverage among countries; e.g., mining is overcovered in Chile— because of the strategic significance and union power of copper workers—but very poorly covered in Mexico, and the same is true of construction; manufacturing, however, has high coverage with few variations.) The economic sector with poorest coverage (outside of domestic service) is agriculture, livestock, and fishing. (Although there are no disaggregated data, table 7-7 shows that about half of the workers in this sector are covered in Argentina and Chile, countries in which either agriculture is a vital sector in the economy or the agricultural workers are fairly well unionized or both; in Mexico where those conditions do not exist, coverage of this sector is almost nil.)

The indicator of inequality at the bottom of table 7-7, based on a gini index, shows that the greatest inequality in coverage is in Mexico (46.1), followed by Argentina (11.9), and with Chile having the lowest score (11.2). This ranking, together with the differences in the degree of coverage by group/subgroup discussed above, suggests a strong relationship between the power of those groups/subgroups and their degree of coverage by the social security system. Not only did the most powerful groups/subgroups receive protection earlier, but currently they have the best coverage within the system. Conversely, the least powerful groups/subgroups were the latest to receive protection and currently either receive the poorest coverage by the system or are not covered at all.

Data on income distribution by occupational groups presented in the five case studies are, unfortunately, not comprehensive, accurate, or comparable enough to permit a statistical analysis of parallel patterns of income distribution and social security coverage (as variables similarly shaped by the power of pressure groups). However, the available information roughly indicates that the higher the income of the group/subgroup, the better its degree of social security coverage. The labor force of the five countries is crudely divided into three income strata: high, middle (subdivided into upper-middle and lower-middle), and low. The high-income stratum (made up of landowners, industrialists, financiers, wealthy professionals, and top-ranking politicians and militarymen) has an average income which fluctuates from 6 to 10 times the average income of the low-income stratum. The high-income stratum is mostly outside of the social security system but obviously provides for its own protection. Some politicians, professionals, and civil-servants in this stratum, however, have full social security protection in various countries (e.g., presidents, cabinet ministers, congressmen, Supreme Court judges, diplomats, notaries public). The upper-middle income stratum (made up of civil servants, most militarymen, and the labor aristocracy—employees in petroleum, public utilities, banking, and strategic sectors such as copper) has an average income from 3 to 5 times that of the low-income stratum, and it is fully covered by the social security system (often being insured by more than one fund). The lower-middle income stratum (made up of the bulk of urban blue- and white-collars in mining, manufacturing, transportation, commerce, and construction) has an average income of at least twice that of the low-income stratum and about two-thirds of it is covered by social security. The low-income stratum (composed of rural workers, artisans, domestic servants, the self-employed, and the unemployed) has both the lowest income and the poorest coverage of social security.

So far inequality in social security coverage has been discussed in terms of the insured and noninsured population and in regard to the divergent degree of coverage among the various groups/subgroups. When the geographical dimension is introduced, the place of residence of the potential insured bears great importance in terms of degree of coverage. (The two dimensions—occupational structure and geography—are actually closely interrelated, as will be discussed later.) Two geographical units have been chosen for the comparison: the region and the state or province, the former broader than the latter. The region embraces several states/ provinces which are in geographical proximity; regional boundaries are usually set by the level of socioeconomic development or planning objectives but also by topography and history. Due to divergent clustering criteria, the region's boundaries are not always the most rational. The state or province boundaries are normally determined by historical, administrative, and political considerations, but, due to its smaller size, the state/province unit is more suitable for comparative measurement of social security coverage.

Table 7-8 compares social security coverage of the regional population of all five countries and attempts to measure the degree of inequality of that coverage. Despite the serious statistical problems faced in table 7-8,[20] the comparisons in it are not useless. The table shows a ranking of the countries by the highest score in both extremes of the coverage range, which is similar to the ranking done on overall coverage of their populations (table 7-4). In Chile, the most poorly covered region has 13.7 percent insured, while the best-covered region has 20.1 insured; in Mexico, however, the range is 2.0 to 9.2 The interval of range is smallest in Chile (6.4) and largest in Argentina (23.6). The indicator of inequality based on a gini index ranks the countries as follows: Peru (35.8), Argentina (24.5), Mexico (15.4), Uruguay (9.9), and Chile (6.2).

Table 7-9 compares the differences in the degree of coverage of the EAP by state or province in four countries. By using more disaggregated and comparable data,

Table 7-8
Degree of Social Security Protection by Geographic Region

Geographical Region	Argentina (1960)	Chile (1966)	Mexico (1969)	Peru (1965)	Uruguay (1969)
Number	8	3	5	3	2
Range in coverage[a]	3.5–27.1[c]	13.7–20.1	2.0–9.2	2.2–16.9	29.4–43.8
Interval of range	23.6[c]	6.4	7.2	14.7	14.4
Indicator of inequality[b]	24.5[c]	6.2	15.4	35.8	9.9

SOURCES: Tables 2-6, 3-6, 4-6, 5-6, 6-6.

a. Range in the percentages of the total population insured by geographical regions. For Argentina, the insured population is an estimate based on the distribution of pensioners. For Uruguay, the population insured is an estimate based on the distribution of expenditures on family allowances.

b. Gini index. The higher the figure, the greater the inequality in the degree of coverage. Complete inequality = 100.

c. Argentina was the only country which included the Federal Capital as a (metropolitan) region and due to the very high coverage in the latter, the indicator of inequality was dramatically increased. To assure a more accurate comparison, the federal capital was clustered with the region where it is located—Pampa—and averages of both were used in the range, interval, and indicator of inequality. Deleting the Federal Capital would have resulted in a gini index of 23.1.

Table 7-9
Degree of Social Security Protection by State/Province

State or Province[a]	Argentina (1960)	Chile (1960)	Mexico (1969)	Peru (1961)
Number	24	25	32	24
Range in coverage[b]	6.4–63.3[d]	18.3–80.5	4.3–63.0	2.2–65.1
Interval of range	56.9[d]	62.2	58.7	62.9
Indicator of inequality[c]	22.7[d]	9.2	41.7	26.4

SOURCES: Tables 2-7, 4-7, 5-7, 6-7.

a. All states in Mexico; all provinces in Argentina and Chile; the most populated province in each of all departments in Peru.

b. Range in the percentage of the EAP insured by state/province. The lowest figure in the range is the percentage of coverage in the poorest covered state/province, while the highest figure in the range is the percentage of coverage in the best covered state/province.

c. Gini index. The higher the figure, the greater the inequality in the degree of coverage. Complete inequality = 100.

d. The actual highest coverage in the Argentinian range was 123.9 percent (Federal Capital), more than twice the next best covered province (Buenos Aires). It was adjusted to 63.3 percent to correct distortions caused by both the derivation of the active insured from the pensioners and the large number of insured in the Federal Capital receiving more than one pension. Deleting the Federal Capital would have resulted in a gini index of 23.1.

table 7-9 uncovers inequalities hidden in table 7-8 and hence provides a more accurate measurement.[21] Practically all scores in table 7-9 are higher than those in table 7-8 because of the disclosure of inequalities as well as the different population sets compared (EAP in table 7-9 versus total population in 7-8). The ranking of the countries by the highest score in both extremes of the coverage range is similar to that of table 7-8 but with substantially higher scores, e.g., in Chile the poorest-covered province has 18.3 percent insured and the best-covered, 80.5 percent; in Mexico the range is 4.3 to 63.0. The intervals of range are also substantially above those of table 7-8 but surprisingly close: the smallest in Argentina (56.9) and the highest in Peru (62.9). The indicator of inequality, based on a gini index (that is more accurate in this table than in the previous one because of a larger number of observations), ranks the countries as follows: Mexico (41.7), Peru (26.4), Argentina (22.7), Chile (9.2).

Which are the variables that have determined a better and more equal geographical coverage in the five countries? Tables 7-8 and 7-9 rank the five countries in a fashion similar to that of the tables on historical and actual coverage by occupational groups but, before discussing this further, let us turn to other variables which can be more adequately tested.

The degree of coverage of a state/province is positively correlated to the size of its EAP and to a lesser extent to its rate of urbanization. In other words, the larger and more urbanized the EAP of a state/province, the higher its degree of social security coverage. The results of running a correlation (based on tables 2-7, 4-7, 5-7, 6-7) between: (a) the *total* EAP and the insured in each province/state, and (b) the urban *EAP* and the insured in each province/state are shown below:

Correlation Coefficients	Argentina (1966)	Chile (1960)	Mexico (1969)	Peru (1961)
(a) Total EAP	.82 (N = 24)*	.99 (N = 25)	.72 (N = 31)	.98 (N = 24)*
(b) Urban EAP	.65 (N = 23)*	.24 (N = 25)	.64 (N = 31)	.40 (N = 24)

*Significant at the 5 percent level.

The correlation coefficients between *total* EAP and insured are significant in all cases and considerably higher in Chile and Peru. (In the latter, the most populated province in each department was used to run the correlation and probably this helped increase the coefficient.) The correlation coefficients between the *urban* EAP and the insured are significant in two cases: Argentina and Mexico. The low coefficients in Peru and particularly Chile have been explained in the corresponding chapters by the exclusion from the tables of insured from groups/subgroups which have a very high degree of coverage and are essentially urban. In Argentina and Mexico those groups/subgroups were included among the insured, thus raising the correlation coefficient significantly.[22]

Correlations in regions and states/provinces between degrees of coverage, on the one hand, and economic development, income, unionization, political mobilization, and lack of Indian concentration, on the other hand, could not be run due to lack of systematic data for all countries. Nevertheless, available information suggests positive relationships in all of them. Ranking of regions by their level of economic development (done in most countries using variables such as regional contribution to GDP, industrial product per capita, degree of urbanization, number of most populated cities, and concentration of natural resources) proved to be parallel to the ranking of the same regions by degree of social security coverage. Data on production per capita in Argentina, Chile, and Mexico, and income per capita in Peru, also discussed in the chapters, resulted in similar rankings of the states/provinces in terms of both development and social security coverage. Chilean data on percentage of the EAP unionized and on percentage of the total population registered to vote by regions indicates that the most unionized and politically active regions are the ones with the best social security coverage. Mexican data on the percentage of opposition votes in the states also suggest that the most politically rebellious states are the best covered by social security. Finally, scattered data on the geographical distribution of Indians show that Indians are concentrated in the regions with poorest social security coverage: the South in Chile, the South Pacific and Yucatán in Mexico, and the Sierra in Peru.

The connection between social security inequalities in coverage among occupational groups and among geographical regions and states/provinces is obvious. The best coverage is in the most populated, urbanized, developed, unionized, and politically active regions and states/provinces. These, in turn, concentrate most economic activities in government, security, banking, public utilities, energy, transportation, industry, and commerce. These activities are performed by occupational groups which are among the most powerful in society and have been able to obtain excellent social security coverage. Conversely, the poorest social security coverage is in the most depopulated, isolated, rural, Indian-concentrated, politically passive, and nonunionized regions and state/provinces whose basic economic activity is agriculture. The latter, in turn, is the economic sector or occupation that has the lowest degree of social security coverage in all countries. Lacking strong pressure groups, these regions have been unable to obtain adequate coverage. Within these poorly covered regions and states/provinces, there are often enclaves which show a fair or high degree of coverage; this is due to the strategic nature of the economy of the enclave which has served as a basis for strong unionization and pressure. Examples of these enclaves are oil in Magallanes, Chile; steel in Cerro de Pasco, Peru; mechanized plantation type of agriculture in the north of Mexico; and sugar in certain areas of Peru, Argentina, and Mexico.

Financing

The task of measuring social security inequality becomes increasingly complex when dealing with its financing system. In this section, tables 7-10 to 7-14 (and appendices A through E) compare various aspects of financing in the five countries and present five indicators of inequality. Two sets of data are analyzed: first, the percentage contribution established by law based on the insured salary (or wage) and due from employees and employers plus the state (tables 7-10 and 7-11, as well as appendices A and B); and, second, the sources of *actual* revenue (that is, the percentage of social security revenue paid by employees vis-a-vis employers-state) and total revenue per capita (tables 7-12 through 7-14, as well as appendices C through E).

The first set of data provides comprehensive information on the employee contribution for all groups but only partial data on the employer-state contribution: in the cases of the armed forces and civil service, the most significant contribution from the employer-state is difficult to quantify because it is not a percentage based on the insured salary but consists of the absorption of deficits (by the state) or the imposition of public taxes. Since the latter two forms of contribution are not comparable with salary percentages, a methodology is developed below to obtain a gross estimate. The second set of data, if comprehensive and accurate, would be the most appropriate to generate indicators of inequality. Unfortunately, as has been seen in the case studies, data on the armed forces and civil servants are usually unavailable or incomplete. These missing data cannot even be grossly estimated (as in the first set) and hence the second set of data is not too accurate and should be taken cautiously. Finally, both sets of data present a common problem: how to control the direction and impact of inequality. To cope with this problem, a methodology has been developed below to make the indicators truly reflective of the progressiveness or regressiveness of the financing system in terms of income distribution.

Table 7-10 shows the total percentage contributions (to all programs) due from employees in the four major groups.[23] To tackle the problem of direction of inequality, three assumptions were made: (1) that blue-collars have a lower income than the other three groups (an assumption supported by empirical evidence); (2) that the blue-collar percentage contribution should be lower than that of the other groups to allow for the possibility of a progressive system; and (3) that if the percentage contribution of blue-collars is higher than that of the other groups, a regressive effect would probably result. The next step was to compute the differences (in percentage points) between the blue-collar percentage contribution and that of the other three groups. If the blue-collar percentage was smaller than that of other groups, a positive sign (indicating progressiveness) was assigned to the difference. (For instance, in the case of Chile, the difference between the percentage contribution of blue-collars, 8.5 percent, and that of the armed forces, 15.5 percent, produced a positive dif-

Table 7-10
Social Security Percentage Contribution Due from Employees by
Occupational Group

Occupationl Group[a]	Argentina (1973)	Chile (1968)	Mexico (1971)	Peru (1973)	Uruguay (1969)
Blue-collars	7.0	8.5	3.8	5.0	25.5
White-collars	7.0	13.0	3.8	5.0	25.5
Civil servants	7.0	19.5	8.0	6.5	15.5
Armed forces	9.0	15.5	0.0	1.5	16.5
Indicator of inequality[b]	1.9	1.0	2.0	2.2	2.8

SOURCES: Tables 2-8, 3-8, 4-8, 5-8, 6-8.
NOTE: Total percentage contribution from all programs (basically pensions and health) based on the salary or wage of the employee (insured) and paid by him.
    a. Only major groups; the inclusion of subgroups would have made the computations extremely complex.
    b. Ratio of the countries related to the country which has the most equal (progressive) employee-contribution system which receives the value of 1.0. The higher the ratio, the greater the inequality. Ratio computations are shown in appendix B.

ference of +7.0.) Conversely if the blue-collar percentage contribution was higher than that of other groups, a negative sign (indicating regressiveness) was assigned to the difference. (Thus in the case of Mexico, the difference between the percentage contribution of blue-collars, 3.8 percent, and that of the armed forces, 0.0 percent, produced a negative difference: −3.8.) The three differences resulting from the computations in each country were then summed up and averaged, and the following scores obtained: Uruguay (−6.3), Peru (−1.2), Mexico (+0.1), Argentina (+0.6), and Chile (+7.5). Finally, ratios were computed using those scores by relating each country to the most progressive one (in this case Chile) which was considered the mean and received a value of 1.0.[24] (See computations in appendix B.) The ratios are shown at the bottom of table 7-10 as the indicators of inequality.

The employer-state contribution by occupational groups is shown in table 7-11. The most serious problem encountered was to estimate, in percentage terms, the portion of this contribution which assumed the form of a deficit absorption by the state in the cases of civil servants and the armed forces.[25] Assuming first, that the systems of benefits of civil servants and the armed forces were at least equal to that of white-collars (an assumption to be proved later); second, that the income of these three groups was roughly similar; and, third, that in order to finance the systems of civil servants and the armed forces it was necessary to have a *combined* employee and employer-state percentage contribution equal to that of the white-collar group,[26] the undetermined portion of the employer-state contribution for civil servants and the armed forces, that is, the contribution not fixed as a percentage of salary (denoted as X), was estimated as a residue. Denoting civil servants as CS, white-collars as WC, the employee percentage contribution as e, and the employer-state percentage contribution as rs, $X_{cs} = (WC_e + WC_{rs}) - (CS_e + CS_{rs})$. In the case of the armed forces, the same formula was used substituting AF for CS. The results of these estimates are shown in table 7-11.

The indicator of inequality was computed in a manner similar to that of table 7-10 but with one important difference: since the discussion in this case deals with the

Table 7-11
Social Security Percentage Contribution Due from Employers/State
by Occupational Group

Occupational Group[a]	Argentina (1973)	Chile (1968)	Mexico (1971)	Peru (1973)	Uruguay (1969)
Blue-collars	29.0	43.0	13.1	14.4	39.5
White-collars	29.0	52.3	13.1	11.5	39.5
Civil servants	29.0[c]	45.8[c]	12.8	10.0[c]	50.0[c]
Armed forces	38.5	47.8[c]	16.9[c]	15.0[c]	48.5[c]
Indicator of inequality[b]	3.5	4.5	2.5	1.0	5.0

SOURCES: Tables 2-8, 3-8, 4-8, 5-8, 6-8.
NOTE: Total percentage contribution from all programs (pensions, health, occupational hazards, family allowances, life insurance, and unemployment) in some cases based on the salary or wage of the employee and paid by the employer or state (but see c below).

a. Only major groups; the inclusion of subgroups would have made the computations extremely complex.

b. Ratio of the countries related to the country which has the most equal (progressive) employer-state contribution system which receives the value of 1.0. Ratio computations are shown in appendix C.

c. In this case a significant portion of the employer-state contribution was not fixed as a percentage of the employee salary but came as either a partial or total absorption of deficits or in the form of state taxes imposed upon the population. For comparative purposes, an estimate (in percentage) of that portion was made by the author and added to the percentage established upon salaries. The methodology used is explained in the text.

employer-state contribution, it follows that as the employer-state percentage contribution increases with the income of the groups, the system is probably regressive and vice versa (if the percentage contribution decreases with the income of the group, the system is probably regressive). Therefore it was assumed that: (1) blue-collars have a lower income than the other three groups; (2) the employer-state percentage contribution to the blue-collar fund should be higher than that of the other groups to open the possibility of a progressive effect; and (3) if the employer-state percentage contribution due to the blue-collar fund is smaller than that due to other groups, the system is probably regressive.

In computing the differences (in percentage points) between the employer-state contribution due to blue-collars (denoted as BC_{rs}) and that due to other groups, the signs were logically reversed. If $BC_{rs} < WC_{rs}$, for instance, a negative sign (indicating regressiveness) was assigned to the difference; thus in Chile: BC_{rs} (43.0) $-$ WC_{rs} (52.3) $=$ -9.3. Conversely, if $BC_{rs} > WC_{rs}$, a positive sign (indicating progressiveness) was assigned to the difference; thus in Peru: BC_{rs} (14.4) $-$ WC_{rs} (11.5) $=$ $+2.9$. The three differences resulting from the computations in each country were then summed up and averaged, and the following scores obtained: Uruguay (-6.5), Chile (-5.6), Argentina (-3.2), Mexico (-1.2), and Peru ($+2.2$). Finally, ratios were computed using these scores by relating each country to the most progressive one (in this case Peru) which was considered the mean and received a value of 1.0.[27] (See computations in appendix C.) The ratios are shown at the bottom of table 7-11 as the indicators of inequality.

The second set of data (tables 7-12 to 7-14 and appendices D to F) deal with the *actual* social security revenue. Table 7-12 contrasts the percentage distribution of active insured by major occupational group, and the percentage distribution of revenue generated by employees by the same occupational groups.[28] A mere visual inspection of table 7-12 reveals that in Chile, Mexico, and Argentina, the lowest-income group (i.e., blue-collars, in two cases merged with white-collars) has a percentage of the total insured larger than the corresponding percentage of total employee revenue paid by the group. As we move into groups with higher income, the situation is reversed, i.e., the percentage of insured is smaller than the corresponding percentage of revenue (with the exception of the armed forces in Chile). This indicates that in these three countries the employee contribution is probably progressive. Conversely, in Uruguay and Peru, the percentage of blue-collar insured (alone or merged with white-collars) is slightly smaller than the percentage of revenue paid by that group, while the percentage of civil servants in Mexico and the armed forces in Uruguay is slightly higher than their corresponding percentage of revenue. These differences are very small, however, and hence we may conclude that in these countries, the employee contribution appears to play a neutral or slightly regressive role.

In computing the indicators of inequality, problems arose since the gini coefficient does not rank groups according to their income and hence cannot detect progressiveness or regressiveness of the financial system in terms of income distribution.[29] To solve this problem I resorted to a technique similar to that used when computing the indicators for tables 7-10 and 7-11, making the same assumptions about income of the groups and role of employee contribution in income distribution. First, the employee revenue per capita (rpc) for each group was calculated; second, an index was done by dividing the rpc of each group by the blue-collar rpc which was assigned a value of 100; third, differences were obtained by comparing the blue-collar rpc with the rpc of the other three groups (white-collars, civil servants, and armed forces); fourth, the differences were summed up and averaged; and fifth, a ratio was calculated based on the average difference of each group (see calculations in appendix D). The resulting ratios became the indicators of inequality entered at the bottom of table 7-12 ranking the countries as follows: Peru 2.02, Uruguay 2.01, Argentina 1.99, Mexico 1.5, and Chile 1.0. This ranking is similar to the one made by visual inspection (and also to the one made in note 29 assigning plus and minus signs to the gini index).

Table 7-13 contrasts the percentage distribution of active insured by occupational groups with the percentage distribution of revenue generated by employers plus the state by the same groups.[30] The analysis of inequality of table 7-13 assumes that as the income of the group increases, the revenue received by the group from the employer-state should decrease (proportionally) to have a progressive effect; otherwise (if the revenue increases), there is a regressive effect. A visual inspection of the table reveals that in Mexico, Peru, and Argentina, the lowest income group (i.e., blue-collars, in two cases merged with white-collars) has a percentage of insured smaller than the percentage of revenue received by this group from the employer-state; conversely, the percentage of civil servants insured (merged in one case with white-collars) is larger than the percentage of revenue received by them from the employer-state; hence these three countries seem to have a progressive system. The opposite is true in Chile and Uruguay where, for example, blue-collars receive in relative terms less than militarymen, evidence of a regressive system.[31] The final indicators of inequality, shown at the bottom of table 7-13, were computed following the same technique as in table 7-12 (see computations in appendix E). The indicator

Table 7-12
Percentage Distribution of Active Insured and of Social Security Revenue from Employees by Occupational Group

Occupational Group	Argentina Insured (1970)	Argentina Revenue (1972)	Chile Insured (1965)	Chile Revenue (1965)	Mexico Insured (1969)	Mexico Revenue (1969)	Peru Insured (1967)	Peru Revenue (1967)	Uruguay Insured (1969)	Uruguay Revenue (1969)
Blue-collars	68.3b	66.3b	71.9	30.5	87.4b	53.7b	49.1	50.1	98.4b	98.6b
White-collars	31.7	33.7	13.7	43.3	12.6	46.3	50.9c	49.9c	n.a.	n.a.
Civil servants	n.a.	n.a.	10.6	23.4	n.a.	n.a.	n.a.	n.a.	1.6	1.4
Armed forces			3.8	2.8						
Total	100.0	100.0	100.0	100.0	100.0	100.0	100.0	100.0	100.0	100.0
Indicator of inequality[a]	2.0		1.0		1.5		2.0		2.0	

SOURCES: *Insured* from tables 2-3, 3-3, 4-3, 5-3, 6-3; *revenue* from tables 2-9, 3-9, 4-9, 5-9, 6-9.
NOTE: In Chile and Uruguay, subgroups were clustered under the corresponding major groups; in Argentina, Mexico, and Peru only major groups are included (therefore, the table excludes petroleum and railroad in Mexico, as well as taxi drivers in Peru). Self-employed are excluded.
a. Ratio of countries related to the country which has the most equal (progressive) employee revenue per capita system which receives the value of 1.0. The higher the ratio the greater the inequality. Ratio computations are shown in appendix D.
b. Includes blue- and white-collars.
c. Includes white-collars and civil servants.

Table 7-13
Percentage Distribution of Active Insured and Social Security Revenues from Employers plus State by Occupational Group

Occupational Group	Argentina		Chile		Mexico		Peru		Uruguay	
	Insured (1970)	Revenue (1972)	Insured (1965)	Revenue (1965)	Insured (1969)	Revenue (1969)	Insured (1967)	Revenue (1967)	Insured (1969)	Revenue (1969)
Blue-collars	68.3[b]	70.3[b]	71.9	47.7	87.4[b]	96.0[b]	49.1	54.0	98.4[b]	96.1[b]
White-collars	31.7	29.7	13.7	40.7	12.6	4.0	50.9[c]	46.0[c]	n.a.	n.a.
Civil servants	n.a.	n.a.	10.6	6.0	n.a.	n.a.	n.a.	n.a.	n.a.	n.a.
Armed forces	n.a.	n.a.	3.8	5.6	n.a.	n.a.	n.a.	n.a.	1.6	3.9
Total	100.0	100.0	100.0	100.0	100.0	100.0	100.0	100.0	100.0	100.0
Indicator of inequality[a]	1.9		14.5		1.0		1.5		4.1	

SOURCES: *Insured* from tables 2-3, 3-3, 4-3, 5-3, 6-3; *revenue* from tables 2-9, 3-9, 4-9, 5-9, 6-9.

NOTE: In Chile and Uruguay, subgroups were clustered under the corresponding major groups; in Argentina, Mexico, and Peru, only major groups are included (therefore, the table excludes petroleum and railroad in Mexico, as well as taxi drivers in Peru). Self-employed are excluded.

a. Ratio of countries related to the country which has the most equal (progressive) employer-state revenue per capita system which receives the value of 1.0. The higher the ratio, the greater the inequality. Ratio computations are shown in appendix E.

b. Includes blue- and white-collars.

c. Includes white-collars and civil servants.

produces a ranking of inequality similar to the visual one (and to the one in note 31 assigning signs to the ginis): Chile (14.5), Uruguay (4.1), Argentina (1.9), Peru (1.5), and Mexico (1.0).

Finally, table 7-14 contrasts the percentage distribution of insured by occupational groups with the percentage distribution of total revenue of the social security system (generated by employees, employers, the state, and other sources) by occupational groups. The indicator of inequality of total social security revenue per capita shown at the bottom of table 7-14 was computed in a manner similar to that of table 7-13 (see computations in appendix F). It produces the following ranking: Chile (21.3), Mexico (7.7), Uruguay (1.8), Peru (1.4), and Argentina (1.0).[32]

In summary, the overall effect of the financing system is probably regressive due to the higher weight and regressivity of the employer-state contribution over the employee contribution. The percentage contribution paid by the employer-state in all countries is roughly from 3 to 4 times higher than the percentage contribution paid by the employee. The employee percentage contribution is progressive in most countries, while the employer-state percentage contribution is regressive in most countries (an exception being the armed forces in most countries). The variation of inequality among countries is considerably lower in both the percentage contribution due from employees and the proportion of social security revenue paid by them than the variation in the percentage contribution due by and share of revenue paid by the employer-state.[33]

Further, the most powerful groups seem to pay proportionately less for their social security protection and receive more from the employer-state than the least powerful groups, thus reproducing (and even more, augmenting) overall income inequality. In comparison to what blue-collars pay (percentage contribution of employees) and receive (percentage contribution of employer-state), white-collars pay and receive approximately the same, but civil servants pay less and receive more than the previous two groups, and the armed forces pay the least and receive the most of all groups. The distribution of social security revenue per capita (rpc) among occupational groups shows the regressivity of the financing system: blue-collars have the lowest rpc; white-collars have the same rpc as blue-collars in three countries, but have a higher rpc in the other two (receiving as much as 5 times what blue-collars receive); civil servants have a higher rpc than blue-collars in all countries (receiving as much as 4 times more); and the armed forces are the group having the highest rpc in all countries (receiving as much as 8 times more than blue-collars). A comparison of data on social security rpc by major groups (and of scattered data on rpc by subgroups) with national income per capita clearly indicates, in four countries, at least, that social security revenue is more unequally distributed than national income, thereby expanding income inequality instead of correcting it.[34]

Moreover, in combining the findings summarized above and the indicators of inequality (especially the two most reliable ones in tables 7-10 and 7-11), it is obvious that Uruguay is the country with the most unequal (regressive) financing system. Chile has probably the second most unequal system because, although its employee contribution appears as the most progressive, it is outweighed by the second most regressive employer-state contribution and the most regressive rpc distribution. Furthermore, the indicators of inequality in Uruguay and Chile would certainly have been higher if all the subgroups had been included in the computations. The process of unification has tended to reduce inequality and regressiveness in the financing system. This is apparent in the case of Argentina, which still appears as the

Table 7-14
Percentage Distribution of Active Insured and of Total Social Security Revenue by Occupational Group

Occupational Group	Argentina		Chile		Mexico		Peru		Uruguay	
	Insured (1970)	Revenue (1970)	Insured (1965)	Revenue (1965)	Insured (1969)	Revenue (1969)	Insured (1965)	Revenue (1965)	Insured (1969)	Revenue (1969)
Blue-collars	65.6[b]	67.7[b]	71.9	42.8	87.4[b]	63.0[b]	59.2	53.1	72.8[b]	79.1[b]
White-collars	30.5	29.7	13.7	41.4	12.6	37.0	40.8[c]	46.9[c]	25.2	19.6
Civil servants	3.9	2.6	10.6	11.0	n.a.	n.a.	n.a.	n.a.	2.0	1.3
Armed forces			3.8	4.8	n.a.	n.a.	n.a.	n.a.		
Total	100.0	100.0	100.0	100.0	100.0	100.0	100.0	100.0	100.0	100.0
Indicator of inequality[a]		1.0		21.3		7.7		1.4		1.8

SOURCES: *Insured* from tables 2-10, 3-3, 4-3, 5-3, 6-3; *revenue* from tables 2-10, 3-10, 4-10, 5-10, 6-10.

NOTE: In Chile and Uruguay, subgroups were clustered under the corresponding major groups; in Argentina, Mexico, and Peru, only major groups are included (therefore, the table excludes petroleum and railroad in Mexico, as well as taxi drivers in Peru). Self-employed are excluded.

a. Ratio of countries related to the country which has the most equal (progressive) total social security revenue per capita system which receives the value of 1.0. The higher the ratio, the greater the inequality. Ratio computations are shown in appendix F.

b. Includes blue- and white-collars.

c. Includes white-collars and civil servants.

third most unequal system, and Peru (equality is impaired in these two countries mainly by exclusion of the armed forces from the unification process). Peru and Mexico are very close and ranked as the least unequal systems; in the case of Mexico this may be the result of its relatively small coverage, recent inception, and equal treatment of blue- and white-collars within a little-stratified system.

Finally, the burden of social security financing (measured by the size of the percentage contributions of both employees and employer-state) is heavier in those countries where the social security system is older, covers more people and risks, and provides more benefits, and lighter where social security is newer, covers fewer people and risks, and provides fewer benefits. A ranking of countries by this criterion is: (1) Uruguay (contributions ranging from 15 to 50 percent); (2) Chile (from 8 to 52 percent); (3) Argentina (from 7 to 39 percent); (4) Mexico (from 3.8 to 17 percent); and (5) Peru (1.5 to 15 percent). Notice that this is also the ranking of countries by the inequality or regressiveness of their financing system. In the section dealing with coverage, it was also noticed that, in terms of the supportive ratio (number of active insured per passive insured), the ranking of countries was similar: Uruguay had the lowest ratio (2.3 to 1), closely followed by Argentina and Chile (3.1 and 3.7 to 1 respectively), and far from Mexico (17.4 to 1) and Peru (37.3 to 1). The supportive ratio was considered a significant indicator of the financial burden of the system: the lower the ratio, the higher the financial burden.

Table 7-15 compares the cost of social security in relation to GNP. In 1965, the year for which there are data for all countries, social security expenditures were equivalent to the following proportions of GNP: 14.5 percent in Uruguay, 12.8 percent in Chile, 3.2 percent in Argentina, 2.9 percent in Peru, and 2.7 percent in Mexico. This ranking ratifies the other rankings based on percentage contributions and supportive ratios. It also suggests that in spite of its tremendous cost, social security in Uruguay and Chile has been unable to reduce income inequality. In conclusion, stratification is an important determinant of high social security costs, because the most powerful pressure groups are capable of impeding unification which obviously would bring about an increase in their contribution and a reduction in the contributions accrued to them by their employers and the state.

Benefits

Tables 7-16 to 7-19 (and appendix G) compare various aspects of social security benefits in the five countries and develop six indicators of inequality. Four aspects of the latter refer to occupational groups insured: number of benefits, average yearly pensions, hospital beds, and health expenditures. The other two indicators pertain to geographical regions: distribution of beds and physicians.

Table 7-16 summarizes the data of the number of benefits (from the standardized table which includes a total of 35 benefits) by major occupational groups.[35] Based on the table, the countries can be ranked by the number of benefits available as follows: Chile (28), Uruguay (27), Argentina (26), and Mexico and Peru (24). This ranking shows the degree of *vertical expansion* of the social security system; that is, how the insured has gradually received increasing coverage against risks as well as additional benefits. This is probably a function of both the age of the system and the power of the most privileged groups. Table 7-16 also shows that, with one exception (Uruguay), blue-collars are the group eligible for the least number of benefits. Civil servants, militarymen, and white-collars (in that order) are eligible for more benefits than blue-collars in four of the five countries.

Table 7-15
Cost of Social Security

Year	Argentina Revenue[a]	Argentina Expenditure[b]	Chile Revenue[a]	Chile Expenditure[b]	Mexico Revenue[a]	Mexico Expenditure[b]	Peru Revenue[a]	Peru Expenditure[b]	Uruguay Revenue[a]	Uruguay Expenditure[b]
1960	3.6	2.9	12.2[c]	8.2	—	—	—	—	—	—
1961	3.7	3.9	—	—	2.3	2.0	1.8	2.7	—	—
1962	3.4	3.3	—	—	2.5	2.1	2.2	2.9	—	—
1963	3.5	3.6	13.1	10.7	2.6	2.2	2.2	3.2	—	—
1964	3.9	3.6	13.4	11.0	2.7	2.5	2.2	3.3	—	—
1965	3.8	3.2	14.4	12.8	2.9	2.7	2.3	2.9	10.1	14.5
1966	3.8	3.9	14.4	12.4	3.0	2.9	2.2	—	9.4	13.0
1967	5.0	4.5	—	—	3.1	2.8	2.1	—	9.9	13.6
1968	4.6	4.8	14.7	—	3.2	3.0	2.0	—	9.0	11.8
1969	4.2	4.3	14.4	—	—	—	—	—	9.6	14.2
1970	4.3	4.2	15.8	—	—	—	—	—	—	—
Average annual change	0.1	0.1	0.4	0.6	0.1	0.1	0.03	0.05	-0.1	-0.07

SOURCES: Tables 2-11, 3-11, 4-11, 5-11, 6-11.
a. Percentage of social security revenue out of total GNP.
b. Percentage of social security expenditure out of total GNP.
c. 1959.

Table 7-16
Number of Social Security Benefits by
Occupational Groups

Occupational Group	Argentina (1973)	Chile (1970)	Mexico (1971)	Peru (1973)	Uruguay (1969)
Blue-collars	24	25	20	17	27
White-collars	24	28	20	19	27
Civil servants	24	28	24	24	25
Armed forces	26	27	21	24	25
Indicator of inequality[a]	1.0	1.4	1.9	3.6	1.2

SOURCES: Tables 2-12, 3-12, 4-12, 5-12, 6-12.
NOTE: Major occupational groups only. In Argentina and Uruguay, blue-collars are represented by industry and commerce funds; in Chile, blue-collars, white-collars and civil servants by the general funds. Self-employed are excluded.
a. Standard deviation of the distribution of benefits by groups. The higher the figure, the greater the inequality.

Additional information, not shown in table 7-16 but included in case studies, ratifies some of the findings discussed above but reveals important inequalities. Subgroups belonging to the labor aristocracy (e.g., banking, petroleum, electricity) occasionally enjoy the highest number of benefits in the system and usually match the number of benefits for which civil servants and the armed forces are eligible or, at least, have more benefits than white-collars. Conversely, the underprivileged subgroup of rural workers normally has fewer benefits than blue-collars; domestic servants, in turn, usually have fewer benefits than rural workers; finally the self-employed is the group/subgroup having the least benefits or no benefits at all.[36]

The number of benefits for which blue-collars are eligible could be used as an indicator of the degree of massification of privilege in the social security system: the higher the number, the more advanced the massification process. Using this criterion, the countries are then ranked almost equally in terms of the highest number of benefits available: Uruguay (27), Chile (25), Argentina (24), Mexico (20), and Peru (17). If we then obtain the difference between the number of benefits for which blue-collars are eligible and the highest number of benefits for any other group, we arrive at the following ranking: Uruguay (+2), Argentina (−2), Chile (−3), Mexico (−4), and Peru (−7). Notice that Uruguay is the only country in which blue-collars have the highest number of benefits; Argentina improves its ranking here due to the unification of benefits (outside of the armed forces) that took place in the early 1970s. The degree of massification is probably a function of the power of the trade union group to reduce the gap between the number of benefits for which it is eligible and the number of benefits enjoyed by the most privileged groups.

The indicator of inequality, shown at the bottom of table 7-16, has been computed using a standard deviation. According to this indicator, the countries can be ranked in terms of the inequality in the number of benefits available for the four major groups as follows: Peru (3.6), Mexico (1.9), Chile (1.4), Uruguay (1.2), and Argentina (1.0). If progressiveness of the system were to be taken into account, Uruguay would be the least unequal system, due to the unique advantages enjoyed by blue-collars. The

Table 7-17
Percentage Distribution of Passive Insured and of Expenditures in Pensions by Occupational Groups

Occupational Group	Argentina		Chile		Mexico		Peru		Uruguay	
	Insured (1966)	Pensions (1966)	Insured (1967)	Pensions (1967)	Insured (1969)	Pensions (1969)	Insured (1969)	Pensions (1969)	Insured (1969)	Pensions (1969)
Blue-collars	56.9b	48.7b	63.1	37.8	73.9b	31.8b	90.2	83.9	74.3b	66.1b
White-collars	37.5	37.2	10.2	18.8	17.1	46.8	9.8c	16.1c	21.3	27.1
Civil servants			12.9	15.6	9.0	21.4	n.a.	n.a.	4.4	6.8
Armed forces	5.6	14.1	13.8	27.8						
Total	100.0	100.0	100.0	100.0	100.0	100.0	100.0	100.0	100.0	100.0
Indicator of inequality[a]	11.5		27.8		42.6		6.3		8.6	

SOURCES: Tables 2-13, 3-13, 4-13, 5-13, 6-13.

NOTE: In Argentina, Chile, and Uruguay subgroups were clustered under the corresponding major group; in Mexico and Peru only major groups are included (therefore, the table excludes railroad in Mexico as well as taxi drivers in Peru). Self-employed are excluded.

a. Gini index. The higher the figure, the greater the inequality. Complete inequality = 100. For another technique to measure inequality in the distribution of pensions (ratio) see appendix F.

b. Includes blue- and white-collars.

c. Includes white-collars and civil servants.

above ranking once again shows the success of the unification process in Argentina; if the year 1971 had been used (instead of 1973), Argentina's inequality would have increased considerably, placing it between Chile and Mexico.

To have a complete picture of inequality as related to the number of benefits, it is necessary to discuss two additional aspects which are ignored in table 7-16: the divergent legal conditions pertaining to benefits and the different economic value of them. Table 7-16 equates benefits of the same nature which in law and practice are significantly different according to six criteria: (a) requirements for acquiring the right to the benefit; (b) basic salary used to compute the benefit; (c) amount of the benefit; (d) adjustment of the benefit (pensions) to the cost of living; (e) compatibility of the benefit (pensions) with similar benefits or/and remunerated work; and (f) length of time required to legally process and actually receive the benefit. Standardized tables on this type of inequality were not presented because of comparability problems: the six criteria on legal inequality could not be systematically applied to all the countries (due to lack of information), and the number of comparisons fluctuated from 5 in Uruguay to 25 in Peru. Nevertheless, these legal inequalities (all of which have economic implications) were grossly measured in all five case studies by ranking the major groups (and selected subgroups) in terms of their legal advantages/disadvantages with the following results: in all countries, the armed forces ranked first in 50 to 70 percent of the comparisons; in 4 countries, civil servants ranked first in 20 to 40 percent of the comparisons; in 2 countries, white-collars ranked first in 10 to 30 percent of the comparisons; and in all countries, blue-collars ranked *last* in *all* comparisons.

Also, in table 7-16, all the potential 35 benefits receive equal weight, although it is obvious that some of these benefits are considerably more valuable than others in financial terms. For instance, blue-collars are not usually eligible for seniority pensions, a benefit normally available to militarymen, civil servants, and white-collars. This benefit allows the insured to retire as young as 45 years of age in some countries and receive a pension for the rest of his/her life, in many cases allowing the pensioner to perform remunerated work. Obviously, a seniority pension is much more valuable than funeral aid, a benefit paid only once as a lump sum, and universally available to all groups. The problem here is how to assign weights to the various benefits. One possibility is to fix the weights according to the proportion of expenditures that a given benefit (or, at least, a cluster of benefits, e.g., all pensions) has out of the total expenditures of the system. Unfortunately that information was available for only two countries and precluded the use of weights. Another alternative is to take the two most important types of benefits, pensions and health care, and attempt to measure the inequality in their distribution (in monetary terms) among groups/subgroups. This is done in tables 7-17 and 7-18.

Table 7-17 contrasts the percentage distribution of passive insured (pensioners) with expenditures in pensions by major occupational groups.[37] A mere visual inspection of table 7-17 indicates that the distribution of pension expenditures is regressive in all countries. As in tables 7-10 to 7-14, it is assumed here that blue-collars are the group having the lowest income of the four. It is also assumed, in terms of income redistribution, that: (a) if the percentage of pension expenditures is equal to the percentage of pensioners in the four groups, the effect is neutral; (b) if the blue-collars' percentage of pension expenditures is higher than the blue-collars' corresponding percentage of pensioners (and vice versa in the other groups), the effect is progressive; and (c) if the blue-collars' percentage of pension expenditures is lower

Table 7-18
Health Facilities and Expenditures by Occupational Group

Occupational Group	Chile (1965) Beds (per 1,000)	Chile (1965) Expenditure (in ratios)[a]	Mexico (1969) Beds (per 1,000)	Mexico (1969) Expenditure (in ratios)[a]	Peru (1964) Beds (per 1,000)	Peru (1964) Expenditure (in ratios)[a]	Uruguay (1968) Beds (per 1,000)	Uruguay (1968) Expenditure (in ratios)[a]
Blue-collars	7.9	1.9	5.5[b]	1.0[b]	6.7	2.1	6.3[f]	1.2[f]
White-collars	8.4[c]	5.5	4.6[d]	1.8	6.8[c]	2.6[c]	—	—
Civil servants	3.2	3.6	26.1	1.6	2.6[e]	1.0	8.4	1.0
Armed forces	—	1.0	—	—	—	—	—	—
Total	7.6	—	5.3	—	2.9	—	6.2	—
Indicators of inequality[g]								
Beds	5.2	—	9.2	—	20.3	—	0.9	—
Expenditure	—	14.7	—	8.6	—	17.0	—	0.4

SOURCES: Tables 2-14, 3-14, 4-14, 6-14.

a. Per capita expenditure for each occupational group divided by that of the fund which has the smallest sum.

b. Includes blue- and white-collars.

c. Includes white-collars and civil servants.

d. Figures are underestimated because a substantial portion of services are under contract with other hospitals and not included in the total.

e. Figures are underestimated because the number of insured was grossly overestimated.

f. Health facilities in Uruguay are not clustered by occupational groups except for the armed forces. The figures are an average of beds available at and expenditures of public and mutualist facilities; private facilities are excluded.

g. Gini index. The higher the figure, the greater the inequality. Complete inequality = 100.

than the corresponding percentage of pensioners (and vice versa in the other groups), the effect is regressive. The latter is true for all five countries and all four groups with the single exception of civil servants in Argentina. It is interesting to notice that in all countries the armed forces enjoy a percentage of pension expenditure about twice their percentage as pensioners. In the case of Mexico, the privileged nature of civil servants is further demonstrated: their percentage of pension expenditures is three times their percentage as pensioners.

Since the direction of inequality is similar in all countries, the gini index can work accurately as an indicator of inequality reflecting the regressiveness of the distribution of pension expenditures. This indicator, shown at the bottom of table 7-17, produces the following ranking of inequality: Mexico (42.6), Chile (27.8), Argentina (11.5), Uruguay (6.8), and Peru (6.3).[38] The distribution of pensions suggests once again that social security reflects (or even aggravates) inequalities in income distribution. The ranking of the four major groups in terms of both income per capita and pensions per capita is roughly parallel in all countries: blue-collars have the lowest income and pension per capita; both income and pension per capita increase as we move into the other groups: white-collars, civil servants, and militarymen. Information on subgroups presented in the case studies indicates that subgroups of the labor aristocracy (e.g., banking) often have the highest pension per capita in the whole system, or at least, one higher than that of its corresponding groups. On the other hand, subgroups that are at the bottom of the income ladder (i.e., rural workers, domestic servants) have also the lowest pension per capita. When all data on pensions per capita (including subgroups) are analyzed, it appears that the extreme differential ratio (between the lowest and the highest pension per capita) is largest in Chile and Uruguay (1 to 8), followed by Mexico (1 to 6), Argentina (1 to 5), and Peru (1 to 2). Therefore, if all subgroups had been computed separately in table 7-17, the indicator of inequality for Uruguay and Chile would have been higher. Finally, a comparison between the distribution of social security revenue per capita and pension per capita indicates that inequalities in the latter are less salient than in the former.

Table 7-18 presents available data on health facilities by major occupational groups: beds per 1,000 insured and health expenditures per capita.[39] Granting that the statistical accuracy of table 7-18 is low, it shows that blue-collars have proportionately a lower number of hospital beds and expenditures per capita than white-collars and civil servants (the latter with one exception). The armed forces, however, have lower scores than blue-collars in most cases. The table includes only major groups and only in one country, Mexico, is there information on subgroups that have independent health facilities. These subgroups (e.g., petroleum, railroads) belong to the labor aristocracy and have scores, both in beds and expenditures, well above those of blue- and white-collars.

Two indicators of inequality are generated in table 7-18, both based on gini index and producing similar rankings.[40] The indicator of beds per 1,000 insured produces the following ranking of inequality: Peru (20.3), Mexico (9.2), Chile (5.2), and Uruguay (0.9). The indicator of expenditures per capita generates, in turn, the following ranking of inequality: Peru (17.0), Chile (14.7), Mexico (8.6), and Uruguay (0.4). The only difference in the rankings is that, in the second one, Chile becomes more unequal than Mexico; this is, in part, the result of Chile having 4 observations versus only 3 in Mexico. In both rankings Uruguay is favored by having only 2 observations.

Differences in the quality of hospital equipment and facilities were detected in evaluating the case studies. In Argentina and Uruguay (which do not have a national health system), the best quality was found in the armed-forces hospitals, followed by mutual-insurance and private hospitals. In Chile and Peru, the armed forces also had the best hospitals followed by those of civil servants and white-collars, and then those of blue-collars. In Mexico the ranking of quality was diverse; the best hospitals were those serving blue- and white-collars, followed by those of civil servants and then those of the armed forces. In all five countries, state and public-charity hospitals attending the noninsured were of the worst quality.

So far the discussion of inequalities in benefits has been limited to occupational groups. Table 7-19 presents two indicators that measure inequalities in the distribution of health facilities (beds and physicians) by geographical regions.[41] The ranking of countries according to the lowest national average of beds per 1,000, as well as to the lowest scores in both extremes of the range among regions is as follows: Mexico, Peru, Chile, Argentina, and Uruguay. In terms of physicians per 10,000 inhabitants the ranking changes somewhat: Peru, Chile, Mexico, Uruguay, and Argentina. In view of these two rankings, the indicators of inequality, based on gini index and shown at the bottom of table 7-19, are surprising. The indicator of inequality on regional distribution of beds ranks the countries as follows: Peru (23.5), Argentina (15.1), Mexico (11.7), Chile (10.2), and Uruguay (8.2). In turn, the indicator of inequality on regional distribution of physicians results in the following ranking: Argentina (38.4), Peru (36.0), Uruguay (32.0), Chile (20.7), and Mexico (15.3).[42] One interesting difference between the two indicators of inequality in table 7-19 is that the gini scores for physicians are about twice as high as the gini scores for beds suggesting a worse regional distribution of physicians than of beds.

Within each country, the distribution of beds and physicians is directly related to the degree of development of each region: the more developed the region, the higher the proportional number of beds and physicians that it has. A comparison of all countries shows that the most developed region has from 2 to 4 times the number of beds, and from 3 to 10 times the number of physicians, than the least developed region.

Combining the six indicators of inequality in benefits, the five countries can be ranked as follows: Peru has the most unequal system, followed by Mexico and Argentina which are very close, then comes Chile, and, finally, Uruguay. It should be recalled, however, that most indicators were computed in a way that concealed inequality in Chile and Uruguay, while the unification of benefits in Argentina was not taken into account in the indicators dated in the 1960s.

The above ranking and the discussion in this section suggest that in the countries that have the oldest social security systems and most powerful trade union groups (i.e., Uruguay and Chile) massification of privilege has reduced the inequality gap in benefits, although considerable stratification still remains. In the countries that combine a powerful labor movement with a unification of the social security system (i.e., Argentina), inequalities in benefits have also been reduced. Countries in which the trade union group has considerably less power vis-a-vis other groups, such as civil servants (Mexico) or the military (Peru), show the largest inequalities in benefits.

The four major occupational groups are ranked in terms of the excellence of their benefits in the same manner as in historical inception, degree of coverage, and financial advantages. The armed forces appear as the best, in all five countries, in terms of the generosity of legal conditions related to benefits, the size of the average

Table 7-19
Health Facilities by Geographic Region

Health Facility	Argentina (1965)	Chile (1964)	Mexico (1969)	Peru (1970)	Uruguay (a)
Number of regions[b]	8	3	5	3	2
Beds (per 1,000)					
National average	6.1	3.9	1.4	2.3	6.4
Range	2.9–10.2	2.7–4.5	0.4–1.7	1.3–3.5	5.4–7.6
Interval	7.3	1.8	1.3	2.2	2.2
Physicians (per 10,000)					
National average	14.9	5.0	7.1	4.8	11.5
Range	4.1–45.9	2.5–6.8	2.4–8.9	1.6–8.6	4.5–19.5
Interval	41.8	4.3	6.5	7.0	15.0
Indicators of inequality[c]					
Beds	15.1	10.2	11.7	23.5	8.2
Physicians	38.4	20.7	15.3	36.0	32.0

SOURCES: Tables 2-15, 3-15, 4-15, 5-15, 6-15.

a. Total population in 1970, number of beds in 1963. This probably reduced the national averages. We lack data to predict the effect on the indicators of inequality.

b. No summary data by region can be presented because of the incomparability among regions of the five countries.

c. Gini index. The higher the figure, the greater the degree of inequality in the distribution of health facilities by regions. Complete inequality = 100.

yearly pensions per capita, and the quality of their hospitals. (In two countries, the military also enjoyed the largest number of benefits in spite of the fact that due to the nature of their occupation, they were not eligible for some of those benefits.) Civil servants have the largest number of benefits in three countries, are second in terms of generosity of legal conditions and size of pensions, and, together with white-collars, are first in the number of beds and expenditures per capita. White-collars are ranked third, in most countries, in number of benefits, generosity of legal conditions, and size of pensions. Blue-collars, in most countries, have the smallest number of benefits, their legal conditions are the toughest, their pensions are the lowest, and their health facilities are usually the poorest. Subgroups of the labor aristocracy (e.g., banking) occasionally rank first in number, legal conditions, amount of pensions, and quality of benefits or, at least, are above the level of their corresponding group. Conversely, underprivileged subgroups (e.g., rural workers, domestic servants) are normally below the level of benefits of the blue-collars.

Benefits usually play a regressive role in income distribution. For instance, average pensions per capita in most countries appear as more unequally distributed than national income per capita, hence aggravating instead of reducing inequality. It should be recalled that the excellent benefits enjoyed by the most privileged groups are largely financed by employers' contributions and state subsidies, hence aggravating the magnitude of that inequality.

As was noted before, regional and occupational inequalities are closely related. The most developed regions are not only the first to receive social security protection and currently have the highest degree of coverage, but they also have the best health facilities. Conversely, the least developed regions received protection last, have the poorest degree of coverage, and the worst health facilities in all countries.

Ranking of Social Security Inequality

In this final section, the nineteen indicators of social security inequality are integrated, in order to measure the overall degree of inequality in all countries and to rank them accordingly.

Table 7-20 presents a summary of the scores of the nineteen indicators of inequality for the five countries, divided into four clusters: appearance of legislation, coverage, financing, and benefits, representing four dimensions of social security inequality. (An attempt was made to use both nonmetrical multidimensional scaling and factor analysis to empirically verify the dimensions, but they did not work optimally because of the nature of the data. The dimensions, however, are not necessary to measure and rank the indicators. See explanations in appendix H.) The appear-

Table 7-20
Indicators of Inequality in the Social Security Systems

Indicator by Cluster	Argentina	Chile	Mexico	Peru	Uruguay
Appearance of legislation					
1. Pensions[a]	5.6	3.8	6.0	6.4	4.7
2. Health[a]	1.3	0.6	1.3	1.6	0.9
Coverage					
3. Percentage of total population[b]	59.3	31.2	77.2	87.7	35.5
4. Percentage of economically active population[b]	51.6	31.0	76.7	64.4	5.0
5. By class of worker[c]	22.5	24.1	37.2	50.2	—
6. By sector of activity[c]	11.9	11.2	46.1	—	—
7. By regions[c]	24.5	6.2	15.4	35.8	9.9
8. By state/province[c]	22.7	9.2	41.7	26.4	—
Financing					
9. Percentage contribution of employee[d]	1.9	1.0	2.0	2.2	2.8
10. Percentage contribution of employer[d]	3.5	4.5	2.5	1.0	5.0
11. Revenue p/c from employee[d]	2.0	1.0	1.5	2.0	2.0
12. Revenue p/c from employer plus state[d]	1.9	14.5	1.0	1.5	4.1
13. Total revenue per capita[d]	1.0	21.3	7.7	1.4	1.8
Benefits					
14. Number of benefits[a]	1.0	1.4	1.9	3.6	1.2
15. Average yearly pensions[c]	11.5	27.8	42.6	6.3	8.6
16. Beds by occupational groups[c]	—	5.2	9.2	20.3	0.9
17. Health expenditures by occupational groups[c]	—	14.7	8.6	17.0	0.4
18. Beds by regions[c]	15.1	10.2	11.7	23.5	8.2
19. Physicians by regions[c]	38.4	20.7	15.3	36.0	32.0

SOURCES: *Indicator no. 1* from table 7-2; *no. 2* from 7-3; *nos. 3 and 4* from 7-4; *no. 5* from 7-6; *no. 6* from 7-7; *no. 7* from 7-8; *no. 8* from 7-9; *no. 9* from 7-10; *no. 10* from 7-11; *no. 11* from 7-12; *no. 12* from 7-13; *no. 13* from 7-14; *no. 14* from 7-16; *no. 15* from 7-17; *nos. 16 and 17* from 7-18; and *nos. 18 and 19* from 7-19.
NOTE: The higher the number, the greater the inequality.
a. Standard deviation.
b. Percentage.
c. Gini index.
d. Ratio of each country to least unequal which is given a value of 1.0.

ance of legislation is a dynamic dimension which measures inequality through time: from the beginning of the 1800s to the early 1970s. Conversely, coverage, financing, and benefits are static dimensions which measure inequality at a given point in time: a year either in the 1960s or in the early 1970s. The dimensions can be interpreted in a different manner by distinguishing: social security inequality in the society at large (insured versus noninsured), and inequality within a social security system, that is, among those insured. Under this approach, coverage becomes the most important single dimension because it measures the proportion of the labor force (and population) which is both inside and outside of the system.[43] Obviously, to be a subject of inequality within the system, one first has to be a part of that system. The other three dimensions measure inequality among the insured based on differences in historical coverage and current financing and benefits.

The scores of the nineteen indicators presented a problem for aggregation: they are the product of four diverse statistical techniques used in this study to measure social security inequality, i.e., percentages, ratios, standard deviations, and gini indices. Hence, standardized scores were computed based on a mean of zero and a standard deviation of one for each indicator. Results are shown in table 7-21. The standardized scores are positive and negative: the higher a positive score, the greater the inequality; the higher a negative score, the lower the inequality. At the bottom of each dimension, in table 7-21, the means of the standardized scores of that dimension are shown; those means are based on the total number of available indicator scores for each country. At the bottom of table 7-21, the means of all the nineteen standardized scores and both unweighted and weighted means of the four dimensions are presented. (I did not have sufficient theoretical and empirical bases for weighting each of the nineteen indicators, although I consider some of them, e.g., coverage, more important than others.) The standardized scores and means roughly indicate the relative degree of inequality among countries (but see discussion in appendix H about the "ordinal" versus "interval" properties of the data). For instance, in the dimension mean of "appearance," Chile has a mean of −1.41 (as the least unequal system) and Peru a mean of 1.12 (as the most unequal system); hence Peru is almost twice as unequal as Chile.

Using the data from table 7-21, the five countries are ranked in table 7-22. Countries are ranked among themselves in a five-point ordinal scale: the most unequal country is ranked as 5 and the least unequal as 1.[44] When two or more countries in table 7-21 had an identical score, they were given the same rank in table 7-22, but the tie was taken into account to assign the next rank order. For instance, in indicator 2, Argentina and Mexico had the same scores and were tied in third place (a rank of 3); Peru was next in ranking and received a rank of 5. When a score for an indicator was missing in a country, the country's mean for the corresponding dimension (and the resulting rank) was computed using the available scores only.[45]

Three different techniques were used to compute the composite or overall ranking of inequality of the five countries, all of which produced *identical* results in the rank order: (1) the unweighted means of all nineteen standardized scores (this served as a check to find out if the clustering of indicators into dimensions would alter the ranking); (2) the unweighted means of the four dimension means; and (3) the weighted means of the dimension means—assigning a weight of four to the coverage dimension and a weight of two to each of the other three dimensions and dividing the result by ten (this distribution of weights was done taking into account the two types of inequality explained above: between insured and noninsured and

Table 7-21
Standardized Scores and Means

Indicator by Cluster	Argentina	Chile	Mexico	Peru	Uruguay
Appearance					
1	0.29	−1.43	0.67	1.05	−0.57
2	0.41	−1.38	0.41	1.18	−0.61
Mean[a]	0.35	−1.41	0.54	1.12	−0.59
Coverage					
3	0.05	−1.08	0.76	1.19	−0.91
4	0.21	−0.52	1.09	0.66	−1.44
5	−0.85	−0.73	0.29	1.29	—
6	−0.56	−0.59	1.15	—	—
7	0.51	−1.02	−0.25	1.46	−0.71
8	−0.17	−1.18	1.25	0.10	—
Mean[a]	−0.14	−0.85	0.72	0.94	−1.02
Financing					
9	−0.12	−1.51	0.03	0.34	1.26
10	0.12	0.75	−0.50	−1.43	1.06
11	0.67	−1.57	−0.45	0.67	0.67
12	−0.48	1.75	−0.64	−0.55	−0.09
13	−0.65	1.70	0.12	−0.61	−0.56
Mean[a]	−0.09	0.22	−0.29	−0.32	0.47
Benefits					
14	−0.78	−0.40	0.08	1.70	−0.59
15	−0.51	0.54	1.50	−0.84	−0.69
16	—	−0.44	0.04	1.37	−0.96
17	—	0.61	−0.21	0.92	−1.32
18	0.23	−0.59	−0.34	1.62	−0.92
19	0.99	−0.78	−1.32	0.75	0.35
Mean[a]	−0.02	−0.18	−0.04	0.92	−0.84
Mean of all scores	−0.04	−0.41	0.19	0.60	−0.38
Unweighted mean of means	0.02	−0.56	0.23	0.67	−0.50
Weighted mean of means[a]	−0.01	−0.61	0.33	0.62	−0.60

SOURCE: Table 7-20.
NOTE: Standardized scores have a mean of zero and a standard deviation of one.
a. The coverage dimension received a weight of 4 and each of the other three dimensions a weight of 2.

among those insured). Although the results of the three techniques were equal in terms of rank order, the distance in inequality among countries varied. The second technique resulted in slightly increased scores for all countries expanding the distance among them (except in the case of Mexico which reduced its distance from Argentina). The third technique (probably the most accurate) increased even more the scores of Chile, Mexico, and Uruguay but reduced slightly the scores of Argentina and Peru; the net result was an approximation between Uruguay and Chile (almost a tie) but an expansion of the distance between these two countries and the others.

Let us now turn to the analysis of the rankings of countries in table 7-22. The rank

Table 7-22
Ranking of Countries According to the Inequality of Their Social
Security Systems

Indicator by Cluster	Argentina	Chile	Mexico	Peru	Uruguay
Appearance					
1	3	1	4	5	2
2	3	1	3	5	2
Rank	3	1	4	5	2
Coverage					
3	3	1	4	5	2
4	3	2	5	4	1
5	1	2	3	4	—
6	2	1	3	—	—
7	4	1	3	5	2
8	2	1	4	3	—
Rank	3	2	4	5	1
Financing					
9	2	1	3	4	5
10	3	4	2	1	5
11	3	1	2	3	3
12	3	5	1	2	4
13	1	5	4	2	3
Rank	3	4	2	1	5
Benefits					
14	1	3	4	5	2
15	3	4	5	1	2
16	—	2	3	4	1
17	—	3	2	4	1
18	4	2	3	5	1
19	5	2	1	4	3
Rank	4	2	3	5	1
Overall ranking[a]	3	1	4	5	2

SOURCE: Table 7-21.
NOTE: Ranking on a five-point ordinal scale based on scores and means from table
7-21. The most unequal country receives 5 and the least unequal 1.
a. Ranking is identical using any of the three means at the bottom of table 7-21.

orders in the dimensions of historical appearance and coverage are almost the
same. In appearance the rank is: (1) Chile, (2) Uruguay, (3) Argentina, (4) Mexico,
and (5) Peru. In coverage, Uruguay becomes first and Chile second and the rest of
the countries remain stationary. The change in order is mostly the result of missing
scores in Uruguay (in 3 out of 6 indicators) which gives more weight to the very low
inequality score in indicator 4 (coverage of the economically active population,
where Uruguay is considerably more equal than Chile). The similarity in the countries'
rankings in appearance and coverage is a logical one: the countries in which the
least powerful groups (which also embrace the highest proportion of the labor force)
received protection earlier are naturally those with the greatest proportion of their
labor force covered. The opposite is true in those countries in which the bulk of the
labor force became protected recently. Geographical equality in coverage is closely

related to the expansion of coverage of the social security system; the degree of geographical coverage is highly correlated to the degree of urbanization, and it has been shown that the most urbanized countries also have the highest percentage of the insured among blue-collars (the largest contingent within the labor force). The two indicators of degree of coverage among the insured (by class of worker and economic activity) are incomplete and not too accurate. The rankings that they generate, however, place Chile and Argentina close together as the least unequal systems, while placing Mexico and Peru close together as the most unequal.

Rankings in the dimension of benefits (table 7-22) are similar to those in the dimensions of historical appearance and coverage: (1) Uruguay, (2) Chile, (3) Mexico, (4) Argentina, and (5) Peru. The main difference here is that Mexico is less unequal than Argentina. This change in rank is, again, largely the result of statistical disparities rather than actual inequality.[46] When the statistical problems are taken into account, it becomes clear that countries with the most equal coverage also have the most equal system of benefits; this is the result of the massification of privilege. Once all major groups are covered, the groups focus their effort on improving their benefits, hence gradually reducing the gap with the most privileged groups. The unification process by standardizing benefits and its requisites has a positive impact in reducing inequality.

The ranking of countries in the dimension of financing are converse to those in the other three dimensions: (1) Peru, (2) Mexico, (3) Argentina, (4) Chile, and (5) Uruguay. It shows that the massification of privilege has not touched financing. Employers and the state, by subsidizing the most privileged groups, stand out as the main sources of inequality (and regressivity) in most countries. The groups at the apex of the social security pyramid may not oppose raising benefits of the groups at the base (unless they perceive that raise as a threat to their privileges), but they do oppose—and have the power to stop—substantial cuts in the financial subsidies that they receive as well as sharp increases in their dues. The unification process in Argentina and Peru (where powerful pressure groups have been subdued) has had a positive impact in equalizing their financing systems; in 1973 this had not yet happened in Uruguay, while in Chile the financing system remained highly stratified.

Finally, at the bottom of table 7-22 an overall ranking of the five countries is shown, combining the rankings of the four dimensions. No matter which of the three means at the bottom of table 7-21 is used, the resulting overall ranking is identical. Such a ranking evaluates in a global manner the social security systems of the five countries, placing them in a continuum which goes from the least unequal to the most unequal: (1) Chile, (2) Uruguay, (3) Argentina, (4) Mexico, and (5) Peru.[47]

The overall ranking is equal or similar to the rankings in the dimensions of appearance of legislation, coverage, and benefits but opposite that of financing. It appears that—except for financing—a system that covers a large proportion of the population is relatively equal internally, but one that covers a small proportion of the population is relatively unequal internally. Early and large coverage of the labor force has usually resulted in stratification but, in proper time, the massification of privilege has mollified disparities in benefits, while leaving undisturbed financial inequalities and regressiveness. The combination of extensive coverage, massification of privilege, and regressiveness in financing is a fatal one. It normally provokes skyrocketing social security costs and spiraling inflation. There is evidence that the latter is a mechanism for reintroducing old inequalities in benefits because the most powerful pressure groups get faster adjustment of their pensions to the cost of living than the less powerful groups. (The speed in processing benefits is another mechanism for reintroducing inequalities through the back door.) The stratification of social security is solidly entrenched in most countries and even under partial unification some groups find avenues to preserve their old privileges in spite of societal pressures.

Appendices

Notes

Index

Appendix A

Percentage Contribution Due from Employees and Employers/State by Program and Occupational Group

Program and Occupational Group	Argentina		Chile		Mexico		Peru		Uruguay	
	(1)	(2)	(1)	(2)	(1)	(2)	(1)	(2)	(1)	(2)
Pensions										
Blue-collar	5.0	15.0	6.5	12.5	1.5	4.6	2.0	4.0	17.0	19.0
White-collar	5.0	15.0	8.5	16.8	1.5	4.6	2.0	4.0	17.0	19.0
Civil servant	5.0	15.0	10.5	18.8	2.0	6.0[a]	2.0	4.0	15.0	20.0
Armed forces	8.0	36.0[a]	8.5	0.5[a]	0.0	[a]	1.5	3.5[a]	15.0	[a]
Health										
Blue-collar	2.0	2.0	0.0	5.5	2.3	6.7	3.0	8.0	7.0	5.0
White-collar	2.0	2.0	1.0	2.5	2.3	6.7	3.0	4.0	7.0	5.0
Civil servant	2.0	2.0	1.0	2.5	6.0	6.0[a]	2.5	3.5	—	—
Armed forces	2.0	2.5[a]	1.0	1.5[a]	0	[a]	0	[a]	1.5	[a]
Others[b]										
Blue-collar	0	12.0	2.0	25.0	0	1.8	0	2.4	1.5	15.5
White-collar	0	12.0	3.5	23.0	0	1.8	0	1.5	1.5	15.5
Civil servant	0	[a]	8.0	22.5[a]	0	0.8[a]	0	[a]	0	[a]
Armed forces	0	[a]	6.0	[a]	0	[a]	0	[a]	0	[a]
Total										
Blue-collar	7.0	29.0	8.5	43.0	3.8	13.1	5.0	14.4	25.5	39.5
White-collar	7.0	29.0	13.0	52.3	3.8	13.1	5.0	11.5	25.5	39.5
Civil servant	7.0	17.0[a]	19.5	43.8[a]	8.0	12.8[a]	6.5	7.0[a]	15.0	20.0[a]
Armed forces	9.0	38.5[a]	15.5	2.0[a]	0	[a]	1.5	3.5[a]	16.5	[a]

SOURCES: Tables 2-8, 3-8, 4-8, 5-8, 6-8.
NOTE: (1) Employees; (2) Employers-state.
a. The employer or state pays all costs or absorbs any deficit.
b. Others include occupational hazards, family allowances, unemployment, and life insurance.

Appendix B

Computation of Indicator of Inequality for Employee Percentage Contribution

	Computation of Differences[a]			Score		Indicator[d]
Country	$BC_e - WC_e$	$BC_e - CS_e$	$BC_e - CS_e$	Sum[b]	$\bar{x}$[c]	$\left(1 + \dfrac{\bar{x} - x_1}{\bar{x}}\right)$
Argentina	7.0−7.0 = 0	7.7−7.7 = 0	7.0−9.0 = +2.0	+ 2.0	+0.6	1.9
Chile	8.5−13.0 = +4.5	8.5−19.5 = +11.0	8.5−15.5 = +7.0	+22.5	+7.5	1.0
Mexico	3.8−3.8 = 0	3.8−8.0 = +4.2	3.8−0 = −3.8	0.4	+0.1	2.0
Peru	5.0−5.0 = 0	5.0−6.5 = +1.5	5.0−0 = −5.0	− 3.5	−1.2	2.2
Uruguay	25.5−25.5 = 0	25.0−15.0 = −10.0	25.5−16.5 = −9.0	−19.0	−6.3	2.8

SOURCES: Appendix A and explanations in chapter 7.

a. BC_e stands for percentage contribution of blue-collar employees; WC_e, of white-collar employees; CS_e, of civil servants; and AF_e, of armed-forces employees.

b. Sum of the differences resulting from the three subtractions.

c. Average difference. The higher the score (+), the more progressive the system; it means that the employee pays a higher percentage contribution as the income of the group increases. Conversely, the lower the score (−), the more regressive the system; it means that the employee pays a lower percentage contribution as the income of the group increases.

d. Indicators of inequality entered in table 7-10.

Appendix C

Computation of Indicator of Inequality for Employer-State Percentage Contribution

| Country | Computation of Differences[a] | | | Score | | Indicator[d] |
	$BC_{rs} - WC_{rs}$	$BC_{rs} - CS_{rs}$	$BC_{rs} - AF_{rs}$	Sum[b]	$\bar{x}$[c]	$(1 + \frac{\bar{x} - x_i}{\bar{x}})$
Argentina	$29.0 - 29.0 = 0$	$29.0 - 29.0 = 0$	$29.0 - 38.5 = -9.5$	-9.5	-3.2	3.5
Chile	$43.0 - 52.3 = -9.3$	$43.0 - 45.8 = -2.8$	$43.0 - 47.8 = -4.8$	-16.9	-5.6	4.5
Mexico	$13.1 - 13.1 = 0$	$13.1 - 12.8 = +0.3$	$13.1 - 16.9 = -3.8$	-3.5	-1.2	2.5
Peru	$14.4 - 11.5 = +2.9$	$14.4 - 10.0 = +4.4$	$14.4 - 15.0 = -0.6$	$+6.7$	$+2.2$	1.0
Uruguay	$39.5 - 39.5 = 0$	$39.5 - 50.0 = -10.5$	$39.5 - 48.5 = -9.0$	-19.5	-6.5	5.0

SOURCES: Appendix A and explanations in chapter 7.

a. BC_{rs} stands for percentage contribution of employer-state due to blue-collars; WC_{rs}, due to white-collar; CS_{rs}, due to civil servants; and AF_{rs} due to armed forces.

b. Sum of the differences resulting from the three subtractions.

c. Average difference. The higher the score (+), the more progressive the system; it means that the employer-state pays a lower percentage contribution as the income of the group increases. Conversely, the lower the score (−), the more regressive the system; it means that the employer-state pays a higher contribution percentage as the income of the group increases.

d. Indicators of inequality entered in table 7-11.

Appendix D

Computation of Indicator of Inequality for Employee Revenue per Capita

Country	Index of Employee Revenue per Capita[a]			
	Blue-Collar	White-Collar	Civil Servant	Armed Forces
Argentina	100.0	100.0	107.7	n.a.
Chile	100.0	745.6	468.6	530.2[b]
Mexico	100.0	100.0	597.8	n.a
Peru	100.0	95.8	95.8	n.a.
Uruguay	100.0	100.0	n.a.	86.8

a. Employee revenue per capita (rpc) of each group divided by the employee rpc of blue-collars.

b. Police only.

Country	Computation of Differences[a]			Score $\bar{X}$[b]	Indicator[c] $\left(1 + \dfrac{\bar{x} - x}{\bar{x}}\right)$
	$BC_{rpc} - WC_{rpc}$	$BC_{rpc} - CS_{rpc}$	$BC_{rpc} - AF_{rpc}$		
Argentina	0.0	+ 7.7	n.a.	+ 3.8	2.0
Chile	+645.6	+368.6	+430.2	+481.5	1.0
Mexico	0.0	+497.8	n.a.	+248.9	1.5
Peru	− 4.2	− 4.2	n.a.	− 4.2	2.0
Uruguay	0.0	n.a.	− 13.2	− 6.6	2.0

SOURCES: Same as in table 7-12.

a. Figures come from the index. BC_{rpc} stands for employee revenue per capita of blue-collars; WC_{rpc}, of white-collars; CS_{rpc}, of civil servants; and AF_{rpc}, of armed forces.

b. Average difference. The higher the score (+), the more progressive the system; it means that the employee rpc increases as the income of the group increases. Conversely, the lower the score (−), the more regressive the system; it means that the employee rpc decreases as the income of the group increases.

c. Indicators of inequality entered in table 7-12.

Appendix E

Computation of Indicator of Inequality for Employer-
State Revenue per Capita

	Index of Employer-State Revenue per Capita[a]			
Country	Blue-Collar	White-Collar	Civil Servant	Armed Forces
Argentina	100.0	100.0	91.0	n.a.
Chile	100.0	510.5	155.0	963.4
Mexico	100.0	100.0	29.2	n.a.
Peru	100.0	81.9	81.9	n.a.
Uruguay	100.0	100.0	n.a.	246.7

a. Employer-state rpc of each group divided by the employer-state
rpc of blue-collars.

	Computation of Differences[a]			Score	Indicator[c]
Country	$BC_{rpc} - WC_{rpc}$	$BC_{rpc} - CS_{rpc}$	$BC_{rpc} - AF_{rpc}$	$\bar{X}$[b]	$\left(1 + \dfrac{\bar{x} - x_i}{\bar{x}}\right)$
Argentina	0.0	+ 9.0	n.a.	+ 4.5	1.9
Chile	+410.5	−55.0	−863.4	−443.0	14.5
Mexico	0.0	+70.8	n.a.	+ 35.4	1.0
Peru	+ 18.1	+18.1	n.a.	+ 18.1	1.5
Uruguay	0.0	n.a.	−146.7	− 73.4	4.1

SOURCES: Same as in table 7-13.
a. Figures come from the index. BC_{rpc} stands for employer-state revenue per capita of
blue-collars; WC_{rpc}, of white-collars; CS_{rpc}, of civil servants; AF_{rpc}, of armed forces.
b. Average difference. The higher the score (+), the more progressive the system; it
means that the employer-state rpc decreases as the income of the group increases. Conversely, the lower the score (−), the more regressive the system; it means that the
employer-state rpc increases as the income of the group increases.
c. Indicator of inequality entered in table 7-13.

Appendix F

Computation of Indicator of Inequality for Total Revenue per Capita

	Index of Total Revenue per Capita[a]			
Country	Blue-Collar	White-Collar	Civil Servant	Armed Forces
Argentina	100.0	100.0	111.9	147.8
Chile	100.0	532.7	223.2	816.1
Mexico	100.0	100.0	407.1	n.a.
Peru	100.0	128.3	128.3	n.a.
Uruguay	100.0	100.0	139.6	167.7

a. Total revenue per capita (rpc) of each group divided by total rpc of blue-collars.

	Computation of Differences[a]			Score	Indicator[c]
Country	$BC_{rpc} - WC_{rpc}$	$BC_{rpc} - CS_{rpc}$	$BC_{rpc} - AF_{rpc}$	$\bar{X}$[b]	$\left(1 + \dfrac{\bar{X} - x_i}{\bar{X}}\right)$
Argentina	0.0	− 11.9	− 47.8	− 19.9	1.0
Chile	−432.7	−123.2	−716.1	−424.0	21.3
Mexico	0.0	−307.1	n.a.	−153.6	7.7
Peru	− 28.3	− 28.3	n.a.	− 28.3	1.4
Uruguay	0.0	− 39.6	− 67.7	− 35.8	1.8

Sources: Same as in table 7-14.

a. Figures come from the index. BC_{rpc} stands for total revenue per capita of blue-collars; WC_{rpc}, of white-collars; CS_{rpc}, of civil servants; and AF_{rpc}, of armed forces.

b. Average difference. The higher the score (+), the more progessive the system; it means that the total rpc decreases as the income of the group increases. Conversely, the lower the score (−), the more regressive the system; it means that the total rpc increases as the income of the group increases.

c. Indicator of inequality entered in table 7-14.

Appendix G

Computation of Ratio of Inequality for Average Yearly Pension per Capita

Country	Index of Pensions per Capita[a]			
	Blue-Collar	White-Collar	Civil Servant	Armed Forces
Argentina	100.0	100.0	116.1	295.1
Chile	100.0	306.9	203.6	336.4
Mexico	100.0	100.0	635.9	549.0
Peru	100.0	176.2	176.2	n.a.
Uruguay	100.0	100.0	143.5	175.1

a. Pension per capita of each group divided by pension per capita of blue-collars.

Country	Computation of Differences[a]			Score $\bar{X}$[b]	Indicator[c] $(1 + \dfrac{\bar{x} - x_i}{\bar{x}})$
	$BC_{pc} - WC_{pc}$	$BC_{pc} - CS_{pc}$	$BC_{pc} - AF_{pc}$		
Argentina	0.0	− 16.1	−195.1	−155.6	2.6
Chile	−206.9	−103.6	−236.4	−182.3	3.1
Mexico	0.0	−525.9	−449.0	−492.5	8.3
Peru	− 76.2	− 76.2	n.a.	− 76.2	1.3
Uruguay	0.0	− 43.5	− 75.1	− 59.5	1.0

SOURCES: Same as in table 7-17.

a. Figures come from the index. BC_{pc} stands for average yearly pensions per capita for blue-collars; WC_{pc}, for white-collars; CS_{pc}, for civil servants; and AF_{pc}, for armed forces.

b. Average difference. The lower the score (−), the more regressive the system; it means that the pension per capita increases as the income of the group increases.

c. Ratio of inequality in relation to the least regressive system which receives a value of 1.0.

Appendix H

Computation of Factor Analysis and Nonmetric Multidimensional Scaling

Originally I intended to utilize factor analysis to verify empirically the four dimensions used in this study and summarized in tables 7-20, 7-21, and 7-22. Through this technique, variables (indicators) which have a high correlation are clustered; the programs separate the variables that "define" a dimension from those which are less important for that particular dimension. In addition, factor-scoring can be used for weighting and aggregating the variables into a composite index for each dimension. The data set of this study, however, presented a problem that precluded a proper use of factor analysis: the data did not have "interval" properties, a *sine qua non* for factor analysis. Still the data could have been treated as "ordinal" and nonmetric multidimensional scaling used for developing the dimensions. Here I faced other problems with the data that also made this technique unsuccessful (and would have compounded the difficulties of applying factor analysis): missing data on many variables, considerably more variables than cases (countries), and a high correlation among many variables.

One major drawback of the factor analysis technique is that it assumes that the data are measured in "interval levels of measurement"; that is, that the data are continuous and normally distributed (among other things). At first glance the data in this study may appear to meet the interval assumptions since the data involved variables which are usually considered to be continuous and normally distributed (e.g., population, revenue, expenditures). In many cases, however, there was not sufficient raw data for the creation of an index which could be considered interval. For example, in some of the gini indices in this study, there were data for only two points. It could be argued, therefore, that if more data had been available (and thus more points on the Lorenz curve), the gini index might have varied substantially. (The same could be said of the aggregation of divergent groups of insured, for example, blue- and white-collars, white-collars and civil servants.) To avoid the problems related to the "interval" assumptions, the data can be considered at the "ordinal level of measurement" (i.e., the data do not have to be continuous or normally distributed or of equal variance, etc.). Ordinal data make it possible to rank order without knowing how large the intervals are between the ranks. Finally if data are treated as ordinal, possible shifts in the gini index that might occur if more data were available would have little or no impact. KYST, an improved version of Knuskal's MDSCAL, was applied assuming "ordinal" properties of the data, but additional difficulties made this technique unsuccessful.

Data were not available for one-fourth of the variables in 3 out of the 5 countries. In the coverage dimension 3 out of 6 variables have missing data on at least one country; in the benefit dimension 2 out of 6 variables have missing data on one country. This would not have been so serious if a large number of cases had been compared.

The matrix of the data set is 5 × 19, that is, almost four times more variables (19) than cases (5). Normally when there is a data set with many cases, it is rare to find that any one variable will turn out to be the product of a linear combination of two or more variables. But in this study, with only five cases (and variables which are highly correlated—see below), this is a distinct possibility. The problem with data such as this is that when the program encounters such a correlation matrix, it finds it impossible to invert the matrix.

In both KYST and factor analysis, the goal is to come up with dimensions which are independent and cluster the variables. In the data set of this study, many of the variables have a very high correlation coefficient. This normally would not be a problem if clusters of variables were highly correlated among themselves but had low correlations with the other variables in the data set. As it turns out, however, in the data set of this study, a fairly large number of the nineteen variables are not only correlated within a given cluster, but the clusters themselves are usually correlated with each other. In other words, the dimensions which underlie the data are not completely independent of each other but in fact are correlated with each other. Since many of the variables and most of the dimensions are so related, it makes it difficult for both the KYST and factor analysis to neatly separate the variables into unique dimensions. This, after all, is to be expected; I have pointed out the close relationship between dimensions, particularly historical appearance, coverage, and benefits (the financing dimension is also closely related, although inversely to the others).

The KYST program was applied to the data with fair results. The stress coefficient was considerably low (.052 for stress formula 1) indicating a good fit to the data. The clusters of appearance and coverage appeared fairly well defined; however, two variables in the benefit cluster, and two in the financing cluster did not fit into the expected clusters. The factor analysis technique produced slightly better results: the clusters of appearance, coverage, and benefit came out fairly well defined, but, again, the financing cluster grouped only three variables with another two forming a separate cluster. Since tables 7-21 and 7-22 produced less complex techniques of aggregation and proved that the overall rankings were identical with or without clustering of the variables, I decided not to use the KYST and factor analysis techniques and only summarize them in this technical note.

Notes

Chapter 1. Introduction

1. The term *social security* (*social insurances* in most of Latin America) is used in this study in a broad sense—including pensions (old-age, seniority, disability, survivors'), health-maternity care, workmen's compensation, family allowances, unemployment relief, and similar types of protection. Housing and savings and loan programs have been excluded. The proliferation of terms in Latin America makes the standardization task difficult. Multiple titles such as *cajas, institutos, fondos, seguros,* with the adjectives *seguridad social, seguro social, previsión social,* refer to the institution itself. The same sector of the population protected by a social security institution in various countries also receives a variety of names, which have been standardized in this study.

2. ECLA, "A Study of the Economic and Social Classification of the Latin American Countries," *Economic Bulletin for Latin America,* 27 (1972), pp. 26–97.

3. U.N. Research Institute for Social Development, *Contents and Measurement of Socio-Economic Development* (New York: Praeger, 1972), p. 10.

4. Synoptical tables of social security legislation from Latin America are included in the series of the U.S. Department of Health, Education, and Welfare, Social Security Administration, *Social Security Programs Throughout the World* (Washington, D.C.: Government Printing Office, various years), but the material is so condensed that it precludes any sophisticated comparison. The ILO (in *The Cost of Social Security,* Geneva, various years) includes financial data on selected Latin American countries, but the level of aggregation is very high and the data incomplete. The same is true of data on social security coverage published by the OAS (in *América en Cifras,* Washington, D.C., various years). In all three publications information on Latin America is limited to the major social security institutions, sometimes leaving out dozens of middle-sized and small institutions.

5. Vladimir Rys, "Comparative Studies of Social Security: Problems and Perspectives," *International Social Security Review,* 19 (July–August 1966), p. 264. Rys' recommendations on how to conduct multinational social security comparisons were very valuable in my research.

6. By a "stratified" social security system, I mean a system that is fragmented into superimposed layers or subsystems, with those above being substantially better than those below.

7. I originally considered including Brazil and Cuba in the case studies. When I was unsuccessful in attempts to obtain a visa to do research in Cuba, lack of statistics on Cuban social security made it impossible to include that country. I decided not to include Brazil because of the different historical and cultural background in relation to Spanish America. However, my colleague at the University of Pittsburgh, James Malloy, is currently involved in a thorough analysis of the Brazilian social security system. My study has also stimulated research on Colombia and Costa Rica.

8. A pioneering study on the extension of social security coverage by risk, geographic area, and population in Latin America is [Peter Thullen], "Gradual Extension of Social Insurance

Schemes in Latin American Countries," *International Labour Review,* 78 (September 1958), reprint. For historical developments see also [Thullen], "Papel de la seguridad social y del mejoramiento de las condiciones de vida en el progreso social y económico," *Octava Conferencia de los Estados de América Miembros de la OIT* (Ginebra: OIT, 1966), pp. 1–6.

9. This theoretical position has been developed in Latin America by jurists specializing in labor law and social security based on the preamble and regulations of the social security legislation, as well as on the writings of some of the creators of modern social security such as Sir William Beveridge.

10. See David Collier and Richard E. Messick, "Prerequisites Versus Diffusion: Testing Alternative Explanations of Social Security Adoption," *American Political Science Review,* 69 (December 1975), pp. 1299–1315.

11. Mark B. Rosenberg, a former student of mine (now at Florida International University), explains the inception of social security in Costa Rica as the personal decision of President Rafael Angel Calderón Guardia to avoid the kind of social strife that he had seen in other Latin American countries. See Rosenberg, "The Politics of Social Insurance Health Care Distribution in Costa Rica," Ph.D. dissertation, University of Pittsburgh, Department of Political Science, 1976.

12. Gaston Rimlinger has shown that Chancellor Bismarck used his trio of social security laws in Germany in the 1880s in an effort to control the industrial proletariat and maintain the status quo. See *Welfare Policy and Industrialization in Europe, America and Russia* (New York: John Wiley and Sons, 1971).

13. For a compilation of the most significant sociological positions on this subject, particularly Davis and Moore, see Celia S. Heller, ed., *Structural Social Inequality: A Reader in Comparative Social Stratification* (New York: Macmillan, 1968).

14. See Frank Parkin, *Class Inequality and Political Order: Social Stratification in Capitalist and Communist Societies* (New York: Praeger, 1971), pp. 13–47.

15. ECLA, "Social Security and Development: The Latin American Experience," *Economic Bulletin for Latin America,* 13 (November 1968), pp. 34, 38, 44. The ILO expert Alfredo Mallet has analyzed the phenomenon of "ultra diversification" of social security programs in Latin America, tracing its origins to the occupational structure, trade union power, bureaucratic influence, and administrative-geographical divisions. See "Diversification and Standardization: Two trends in Latin American Social Security," *International Labour Review,* 101 (January 1970), pp. 49–83.

16. Jorge I. Tapia, "The Bureaucratic Phenomenon in a Developing Country: The Case of the Chilean Social Security Administration," Ph.D. dissertation, University of Texas, Austin, 1968; and Charles J. Parrish and Jorge I. Tapia-Videla, "Welfare Policy and Administration in Chile," *Journal of Comparative Administration,* 1 (February 1970), pp. 455–76.

17. This and other graphic models in this book are part of a larger number developed at the SSRC-sponsored Inter-American Research Training Seminar "Social Security in Latin America: Pressure Groups, Stratification and Inequality," held in Mexico City in the summer of 1975 (hereinafter cited as SSRC Seminar 1975).

18. Julio Cotler, *La mecánica de la dominación interna y del cambio social en el Perú* (Lima: Instituto de Estudios Peruanos, 1967), pp. 38–42; Carlos A. Astiz, *Pressure Groups and Power Elites in Peruvian Politics* (Ithaca, N.Y.: Cornell University Press, 1969), pp. 67–69, 206–11. See also James Petras, *Politics and Social Forces in Chilean Development* (Berkeley: University of California Press, 1969), pp. 1–5, 256ff, 294–97.

19. The bureaucracy may also play a role in the decision as to whether social security will expand horizontally (coverage of new groups of the population) or vertically (addition of new benefits to those already insured). In a stratified social security system, bureaucrats may oppose unification because of their vested interest in keeping their own spheres of influence; conversely, in a largely unified social security system, the bureaucracy may impede stratification to keep its power centralized and untouched. The power of the bureaucracy, however, is difficult to measure. See Peter S. Cleaves, *Bureaucratic Politics and Administration in Chile* (Berkeley: University of California Press, 1974), pp. 33–35.

20. Milton I. Roemer, "Medical Care and Social Class in Latin America," *The Milbank Memorial Fund Quarterly,* 42 (July 1964), pp. 54–64.

21. Marshall Wolfe, "Social Security and Development: The Latin American Experience," in *The Role of Social Security in Economic Development,* Everett M. Kassalow, ed. (Washington, D.C.: Government Printing Office, 1968), pp. 65–175.

22. According to Felix Paukert, in developing countries social security benefits to civil servants represent about one-third of the nation's social security expenditures contrasted with about one-tenth in developed countries. See "Social Security and Income Redistribution: Comparative Experience," in *The Role of Social Security in Economic Development,* pp. 101–27, esp. p. 111.

23. Ernesto Aldo Isuani presented at the SSRC Seminar 1975 a more complex typology, reproduced below, based on the degree of control of organizations (pressure groups, political parties, etc.) over three kinds of resources: economical, political, and ideological. Eight basic types are derived through a combination of high or low control of the three resources.

Degree of Control
Resources   of Organizations Over Resources

Economic	High				Low			
Political	High		Low		High		Low	
Ideological	High	Low	High	Low	High	Low	High	Low
Types	I	II	III	IV	V	VI	VII	VIII

For more details see E. A. Isuani, "Nuevos enfoques para el estudio de la seguridad social en América Latina," *Latin American Research Review,* 1 (1977), pp. 159–65. Although this typology is more elaborate than the one I use in the book, the former presents far more problems in terms of collecting data and making comparisons and ranking than my own.

24. A word about the advantages and disadvantages of using standardized ideal types in this study. The typology, while it makes abstraction from reality and omits national peculiarities, is a very convenient and useful tool to classify the labor force systematically into groups and subgroups that can then be subjected to multinational comparisons both in terms of their role in social security stratification and of the inequality of their social security protection. A different approach, to include and treat *all* the groups/subgroups as they actually exist in each of the five countries, however, would have made the task of classification, comparison, and ranking extremely complex. Furthermore, such a limitation to five specific cases would have precluded the further application of this study to other countries in Latin America. I decided, therefore, that the advantages of using the typology were far greater than the disadvantages and that the problems generated by this approach could be dealt with in the concluding chapter. I appreciate the observations made by Richard Wilson, Ph.D. candidate in sociology, Yale University, which helped me to evaluate the pros and cons of the typology's approach.

25. The case of physicians is a special one; in some Latin American countries, physicians hired by public institutions have occasionally resorted to lobbying and strikes to improve their remuneration and social security protection, but also to oppose certain social security decisions such as the introduction of a national health system. Physicians, therefore, act as a pressure subgroup both to obtain satisfaction of their demands and to block the demands of other groups/subgroups that may impair their privileges. Rosenberg discussed at the SSRC Seminar 1975 how "anti-forces" resist the pressure of organized groups in aspects such as the creation, expansion, and massification of social security. Examples of anti-forces are: physicians (who struggle against national health insurance), actuaries (who are conservatives in financial matters), employers (who resist social security taxation), revolutionary unions (e.g., anarcho-syndicalists and Maoists who reject social security as a reformist palliative), conserva-

tive parties, and the privileged pressure groups (which fear unification and expansion of coverage to lower income groups).

26. See Richard N. Adams, "Political Power and Social Structure," in *Politics of Conformity in Latin America*, Claudio Veliz, ed. (London: Oxford University Press, 1965), pp. 15–42, and Adams, *The Second Sowing: Power and Secondary Development in Latin America* (San Francisco: Chandler Publishing Co., 1967). For a discussion of the problem in Chile, see Robert J. Alexander, *Labor Relations in Argentina, Brazil and Chile* (New York: McGraw Hill Co., 1962), pp. 245, 247, 269; James O. Morris, *Elites, Intellectuals and Consensus: A Study of the Social Question and the Industrial Relation System in Chile* (Ithaca, N.Y.: New York School of Industrial and Labor Relations, 1966), pp. 17–18; and Charles J. Parrish, "Social Structure and Political Reform in Chile," St. Antony's College, Oxford University, November 1967. For Peru, see James L. Payne, *Labor and Politics in Peru* (New Haven: Yale University Press, 1965), p. 163; and Astiz, pp. 204–05. For Mexico, see Stanley M. Davis, "Empleados and Obreros," in *Workers and Managers in Latin America*, S. M. Davis and Louis W. Goodman, eds. (Lexington, Mass.: D.C. Heath, 1972), pp. 31–34.

27. Payne, p. 163; and Luis Ratinoff, "The New Urban Groups: The Middle Classes," in *Elites in Latin America*, Seymour Martin Lipset and Aldo Solari, eds. (New York: Oxford University Press, 1967), pp. 84–88.

28. See Henry A. Landsberger, "The Labor Elite: Is it Revolutionary?" in *Elites in Latin America*, p. 260.

29. Recent empirical research on the behavior of inhabitants of squatter and lower-class settlements suggests that they employ rational adaptation to the political milieu in the pursuit of their economic and social goals. In general, the level of political activism of the group increases under populist sympathetic governments and decreases under authoritarian repressive regimes. The group establishes itself and reaches the peak of its cohesion, activism, militancy, and confrontation with authorities when it becomes involved in an illegal land invasion. Thereafter, the activity of the group is channeled through communal associations which act within the existing political order to achieve their goals. The group appears as highly susceptible to cooptation since it usually votes in favor of governments that satisfy its demands. For a review of the literature, see Alejandro Portes and John Walton, *Urban Latin America: The Political Conditions from Above and Below* (Austin: University of Texas Press, 1976), pp. 70–110. I gratefully acknowledge Portes' comments on the original passage of my book. A new pressure group that has become increasingly articulate and powerful is that of the students. University movements have always played a crucial political role in Latin America, but not until recently have students become more sophisticated in their rebellious activities, e.g., integrating urban guerrillas in Uruguay, organizing a threatening demonstration in 1968 in Mexico, and engaging in bank assaults, kidnapping of VIPs, etc. In November 1973, an Inter-American Roundtable on Social Security and the Youth in Mexico City was sponsored by the ILO, the International Association of Social Security (AISS), and the Inter-American Committee of Social Security (CISS), with participation of representatives from the OAS and labor and youth organizations. The roundtable examined the explosive situation of youth and proposed several measures to include them in the social security system and to develop services that would provide them with something constructive to do during their free time (e.g., sports, recreation, arts and crafts).

30. For details on these negative effects, see my book *Planificación de la seguridad social*, 2nd edition (La Habana: Editorial Librería Martí, 1960), pp. 35–43. See also Mallet, pp. 61–65.

31. See Lucila Leal de Araujo, "Los sistemas de seguridad social como mechanismos de redistribución del ingreso en los países en desarrollo," *Revista de Seguridad Social* (Buenos Aires), 5 (March 1972), pp. 207–08. See also CIES, "Política y administración de la seguridad social," Washington, D.C., Unión Panamericana, February 18, 1966, pp. 5–6.

32. This goes against the traditional, altruistic position which claims that social security helps to redistribute income from the rich to the poor. There is evidence that the social security systems of some developed countries (e.g., the United States, Great Britain) do not meet their redistribution goals as well as desired, but in Latin America social security appears to be an obviously regressive force. On this issue, see Norval D. Glenn, "Social Security and Income

Redistribution," *Social Forces,* 46 (June 1968), pp. 538–39; Phillips Cutright, "Reply to Glenn," ibid., pp. 539–40; and Paukert, pp. 101–27.

33. Paul Fisher, "Social Security and Development Planning: Some Issues," in *The Role of Social Security in Economic Development,* pp. 246–47; and Paukert, pp. 118, 120, 124–26.

34. In the late 1960s and early 1970s the AISS, the CISS, the ECLA, and the OAS supported these conclusions by stating that the groups better protected by social security in Latin America are those of higher and middle income; the state and employers' contributions to social security are in most cases a negative factor in income redistribution; and the overall role of social security in income redistribution is nil or negative. OAS and CISS, "Seminar on Social Security and National Planning," Mexico, D.F., November 13–18, 1967; Gonzalo Arroba, "Seguridad social y economía nacional: Informe presentado ante la V Conferencia Internacional de Actuarios y Estadígrafos de la Seguridad Social (AISS) realizada en Berna del 13 al 18 de septiembre de 1971," *Revista de Seguridad Social* (Buenos Aires), 4 (September 1971), pp. 837ff; ECLA, p. 37; and OAS, "El financiamiento de la seguridad social, su relación con la distribución de ingresos y con la política de impuestos en la región americana," Washington, D.C., January 25, 1973. See also Mallet, pp. 62–63; Paukert, p. 103; and Leal de Araujo, pp. 213–16. The Eighth Inter-American Regional Conference of the ILO adopted in 1966 *The Ottawa Programme of Social Security for the Americas* (Geneva: ILO, 1966) which recommended the reinforcement of social security as an instrument for redistribution of income and encouraged uniform protection and the elimination of inequalities through the expansion of coverage to noninsured groups, the revision of privileged systems disproportionate to the nation's economic possibilities and distorting social security principles, and national financing of the system in all necessary cases.

35. Henry Aaron has argued that the share of social security expenditures in national income is determined primarily by the length of time a country has had a social security system, not necessarily by its degree of development. See "Social Security: International Comparisons," in *Studies in the Economics of Income Maintenance,* Otto Eckstein, ed. (Washington, D.C.: Brookings Institution, 1967), pp. 13–48. Paukert (pp. 124–25) has attempted to prove that the share of social security expenditures is a result of the degree of development and the higher such share is, the better the redistribution function of the system. Paukert, however, neglects the peculiarities of social security evolution in Latin America; there are countries in the region which have a high percentage of GNP devoted to social security and which are not necessarily developed nor do their systems play a proper redistribution function.

36. República de Chile, "Mensaje del Presidente al Senado y la Cámara de Diputados," Santiago, May 1966.

37. In a seminar that I gave on this subject at the Latin American Center of the Free University of Berlin in December of 1971, Marxist students rejected my approach to the problem as inadequate. They claimed that the basic issue was to change the politico-economic structure of the nation and that the rest was marginal. They alleged that Cuba was the only country to thoroughly solve the social security problem because it had previously changed the politico-economic structure. (Even with the power of the revolution, it took Cuba four years to complete the unification of social security.) Although I disagreed with them, it was very difficult to oppose their argument due to the absence of examples of Latin American countries that have solved the social security problem without a radical transformation of their societies.

38. I do not pretend to open new ground in this historical period and field and, hence, have resorted to secondary sources to obtain the necessary information. Basic works in the field are: José M. Ots Capdequi, *Instituciones sociales de la América Española en el período colonial* (Buenos Aires: Ed. La Plata, 1934); Julia Herráez Sánchez de Escariche, *Beneficencia de España en Indias* (Sevilla: Escuela de Estudios Hispano-Americanos, 1949); Sergio Bagú, *Estructura social de la colonia* (Buenos Aires: Ed. Ateneo, 1952); Richard Konetzke, ed., *Colección de documentos para la formación social de Hispanoamérica, 1493–1810,* 2 vols. (Madrid: Consejo Superior de Investigaciones Científicas, 1953 and 1962). Josefina Muriel de la Torre, *Hospitales de la Nueva España,* 2 vols. (México: Publicaciones del Instituto de Historia, 1956 and 1960); Ricardo L. Moles, *Historia de la previsión social en Hispanoamérica* (Buenos

Aires: Ediciones Depalma, 1962); and Adolfo Lamas, *Seguridad social en la Nueva España* (México: Universidad Nacional Autónoma de México, 1964). See also Francisco Walker Linares, *Panorama del derecho social chileno* (Santiago: Editorial Jurídica de Chile, 1950); Hermes Ahumada Pacheco, *Seguridad social* (Santiago: Editorial Universitaria, S.A., 1961); M. Zúñiga Cisneros, *Seguridad social y su historia* (Caracas: Edime, 1963); and Milton E. Roemer, *Medical Care in Latin America* (Washington, D.C.: Pan American Union, 1963).

39. According to Magnus Mörner, there were two different ranks of races, one of them sanctioned by law, the other corresponding to social status. The legal rank was: (1) Spaniards, (2) Indians, (3) mestizos, (4) *libertos,* mulattoes, and *zamboes,* and (5) slaves. In the social-status ranking, peninsular Spaniards took precedence over *criollos,* while mulattoes and *zamboes* ranked over *libertos* and Indians fell from second to last place. See *Race Mixture in the History of Latin America* (Boston: Little, Brown and Company, 1967), pp. 60–61.

40. *Montepíos* should not be confused with the *montes de piedad*—called *montepíos* in some countries—credit institutions that began operation in the last quarter of the eighteenth century, giving small loans at low interest.

41. I realize that the term *inception* is vague and that it could have been refined into more concrete stages such as public recognition of the problem, definition, deliberation, resolution, and implementation. This approach was not feasible here due to the limitations imposed by the comparative nature of the study, the enormous task of research on disaggregated facets of inception, and my lack of formal training in political science and sociology. The five stages of social security inception mentioned above were presented by James Malloy at the SSRC Seminar 1975 in the context of the Brazilian case. Charles Parrish also discussed a similar approach adding a sixth stage, that of administration. Mark Rosenberg has systematically applied the five stages to the analysis of social security's inception in Costa Rica with productive results.

Chapter 2. The Case of Chile

1. Because of space limitations this section is a summary of my original work and footnotes are excluded. General bibliographical sources used were: Robert J. Alexander, *Labor Relations in Argentina, Brazil and Chile* (New York: McGraw-Hill, 1962); Aníbal Pinto Santa Cruz, *Chile, un caso de desarrollo frustrado* (Santiago: Editorial Universitaria, S.A., 1962) and *Chile: una economía difícil* (México, D.F.: Fondo de Cultura Económica, 1964); Jorge Barría Serón, *Trayectoria y estructura del movimiento sindical chileno: 1946–1962* (Santiago: INSORA, 1963); Milton I. Roemer, *Medical Care in Latin America* (Washington, D.C.: Pan American Union, 1963); Víctor Alba, *Historia del movimiento obrero en América Latina* (México, D.F.: Libreros Mexicanos Unidos, 1964); Kalman H. Silvert, *Chile, Yesterday and Today* (New York: Holt, Rinehart and Winston, Inc., 1965); James O. Morris, *Elites, Intellectuals and Consensus: A Study of the Social Question and the Industrial Relations System in Chile* (Ithaca, N.Y.: New York School of Industrial and Labor Relations, 1966); Federico G. Gil, *The Political System of Chile* (Boston: Houghton Mifflin, Co., 1966); Germán Urzúa Valenzuela, *Los partidos políticos chilenos: Las fuerzas políticas* (Santiago: Editorial Jurídica de Chile, 1968); James Petras, *Politics and Social Forces in Chilean Development* (Berkeley: University of California Press, 1969); Francisco José Moreno, *Legitimacy and Stability in Latin America: A Study of Chilean Political Culture* (New York: New York University Press, 1969); Charles J. Parrish and Jorge I. Tapia, "Clases sociales y la política de seguridad social," Santiago, 1969; Alain Joxe, *Las fuerzas armadas en el sistema político de Chile* (Santiago: Editorial Universitaria, S.A., 1970); and Alan Angell, *Politics and the Labour Movement in Chile* (London: Oxford University Press, 1972). Social security legislation comes from several compilations published in Santiago; for historical legal data and juridical interpretations I used: Ezequiel González Cortés, *Proyecto de modificación de la Ley 4054* (Santiago: Talleres Gráficos La Nación, 1928); Eduardo Cruz Coke, *Medicina preventiva* (Santiago: Editorial Nascimento, 1938); Julio Bustos Acevedo, *La seguridad social . . . bases técnicas para su reforma* (Santiago: Talleres Gráficos La Nación, 1942); Alfredo Gaete Berrios, *Manual de seguridad social* (Santiago: Artes y Letras Ltda., 1949)

and *El seguro social y el Servicio Nacional de Salud* (Santiago: Editorial Jurídica de Chile, 1952); Waldo Pereira A., *La seguridad social en Chile* (Santiago: Escuela Nacional de Artes Gráficas, 1950); Jorge Mardones Restat, *La reforma de la seguridad social de los obreros: Motivos de la Ley 10,383* (Santiago: Editorial Jurídica de Chile, 1952); Hermes Ahumada Pacheco, *Seguridad social* (Santiago: Editorial Universitaria, S.A., 1958); Organización Iberoamericana de Seguridad Social, *Los seguros sociales en Chile* (Madrid: OISS, 1961); Francisco Walker Linares, *Esquema del derecho del trabajo y de la seguridad social* (Santiago: Editorial Jurídica, 1965); and U.S. Department of Labor, Bureau of Labor Statistics, *Labor Law and Practice in Chile* (Washington, D.C.: Government Printing Office, 1969; hereinafter cited as *Labor Law*).

2. Comisión de Estudios de la Seguridad Social, *Informe sobre la reforma de la seguridad social chilena* (Santiago: Editorial Jurídica de Chile, vol. 1, 1964 and vol. 2, 1965). Another pioneering study, conducted under Ibáñez, was [Misión Klein], *El sistema de previsión social chileno: Informe de la Misión Klein y Saks* (Santiago: Editorial Universitaria, S.A., 1958).

3. República de Chile, "Mensaje del Presidente al Senado y la Cámara de Diputados," Santiago, May 1966.

4. Statistics on voting population, union membership, and strikes come from *Latin American Political Statistics*, K. Ruddle and P. Gillette, eds. (Los Angeles: UCLA Latin American Center, 1972), p. 106; Petras, pp. 83–84, 110; and *Labor Law*, pp. 32–34.

5. Ibid.

6. Background for this section comes from *Labor Law*, pp. 26–27; Gaete Berrios, pp. 139–201; OISS, pp. 8–33; Roemer, pp. 193–245; Parrish and Tapia, p. 10; Pereira, pp. 124–25; and Luis Orlandini, et al., *Basic Characteristics of Social Security in Chile* (Santiago: INSORA, 1965).

7. Excluded are the president of the republic, cabinet ministers, and employees of state enterprises. Some 63 groups have been incorporated into the general system, many with special regulations: among them are legal clerks, notaries public, archivists, and registrars; lawyers in the judiciary and those self-employed; congressmen and mayors; physicians, dentists, and pharmacists; professors of state universities and teachers in prisons and private schools; and employees of some public corporations (e.g., housing and airlines) and of most social security funds.

8. Petras, pp. 339–40; Gil, pp. 18–19, 23–27; *Labor Law*, pp. 8–9; and Joxe, p. 138.

9. Alexander, pp. 245–47, 269; and *Labor Law*, pp. 9, 16–17.

10. Walker Linares, pp. 43–53, 144; Pereira, pp. 128–30; and Petras, p. 260.

11. See Petras, pp. 16–17; CORFO, *Geografía económica de Chile* (Santiago: Talleres Editorial Universitaria, 1965), pp. 404–09; Pablo Trivelli Oyarzún, *Tendencia a la igualación de los salarios en Chile* (Santiago: ODEPLAN, 1970), tables 3 and 5; and Peter Gregory, *Industrial Wages in Chile* (Ithaca, N.Y.: Cornell University, 1967), pp. 93–94.

12. Isabel Heskia, "La distribución del ingreso en Chile," *Bienestar y Pobreza*, CEPLAN, ed. (Santiago: Ediciones Nueva Universidad, 1974), pp. 17–57.

13. See Benjamín Subercaseux, *Chile o una loca geografía* (Santiago: Ediciones Ercilla, 1944); CORFO, *Geografía económica de Chile;* and Gil, pp. 1–13.

14. *Labor Law*, pp. 52–53; and República de Chile, Servicio de Seguro Social (SSS), *Estadísticas 1961 to 1970*.

15. Armand Matherlart and Manuel A. Garretón, *Integración nacional y marginalidad: Un ensayo de regionalización social en Chile* (Santiago: Editorial del Pacífico, S.A., 1965), pp. 37–39. Data from ODEPLAN, *Indicadores regionales y nacionales* (Santiago: n.d.) for 1967 show similar results.

16. República de Chile, ODEPLAN, *Informe económico anual, 1971* (Santiago: Editorial Universitaria, 1972), p. 205.

17. *Boletín de Estadísticas de Seguridad Social*, no. 24 (March–April 1965), p. 5; Eduardo Miranda Salas, "Comentarios sobre la nueva ley de accidentes del trabajo y enfermedades profesionales en Chile," *Seguridad Social*, no. 98 (July 1968), pp. 11–12; and Carlos Briones et al., "Antecedentes básicos y análisis del estado actual de la seguridad social en Chile," ibid., p. 67.

18. Roemer, pp. 201–03. Two factors were responsible for such disparate estimates—the uncertainty of the ratio of dependents to insured in the SSS (ranging from 1.3 to 2.6 dependents per insured) and the unknown number of indigents attended in SNS hospitals. The number of insured covered by the SMNE at that time was easier to compute because only the insured and his wife had a right to medical and maternity care respectively.

19. This categorization, however, does not necessarily agree with the source of power of the pressure group. Journalists have been assimilated into white-collar groups although they belong to the CNEPP and their power is generated more by their influence over public opinion than by the scarcity of their skills. State-bank employees have been classified as civil servants rather than with their colleagues in the private-bank group. State-railroad workers would be better placed within the blue-collar sector by both the nature of their work and the source of their power.

20. Same sources as in note 17.

21. The two columns in the table are not strictly comparable. *Salaried workers* are roughly congruent with the sum of white-collar, civil-servant, and armed-forces personnel who are paid on a monthly basis. *Wage-earners* are roughly congruent with blue-collars (including domestic servants) who are paid on a weekly, daily, or hourly basis. The self-employed have been disaggregated from the SSS and to a lesser extent from the CPEP; they receive neither unemployment nor family allowances.

22. One-third of all unemployed and almost all unpaid family workers, both lacking income, were unprotected. The majority of the self-employed and many employers were small artisans, peddlers, farmers, and fishermen who often received an income lower than that of the insured. (A minority of noninsured employers and self-employed were large and middle-level industrialists, merchants, financiers, landowners, and landlords, as well as wealthy professionals who did not need protection.) Comisión de Estudios de la Seguridad Social, pp. 50–51; República de Chile, Dirección de Estadística y Censos, *Censos de Población 1960: Resumen país* (Santiago: Imprenta de la Dirección de Estadística y Censos, n.d.), and data from table 3; table 4; Manuel Requena Criado, "Análisis de la estructura de los institutos de previsión en Chile," Memoria, Facultad de Ciencias Económicas, Universidad de Chile, 1968, p. 4; ILO, *Yearbook of Labour Statistics 1972* (Geneva: ILO, 1972), pp. 70–71; and ODEPLAN, *Informe económico anual 1971,* pp. 205–06.

23. Eduardo Miranda Salas, "El sector agrícola en la seguridad social de Chile," *Boletín de Estadísticas de Seguridad Social,* no. 27–28 (September–December 1965), pp. 109–11.

24. The definitional problem results from the fact that probably part of those classified as miners actually performed jobs in manufacturing or services, and part of those listed under utilities actually performed service jobs. Based on data from *Censo de Población 1960* and preliminary results of 1970 census in República de Chile, Instituto Nacional de Estadísticas, *Compendio Estadístico 1971* (Santiago: Instituto de Estadísticas, n.d.).

25. For instance, the province of Santiago, in which the capital and largest city of Chile is located, has the second highest urban proportion of the EAP, but it is only ranked tenth in social security coverage. The government bureaucracy, most of the armed forces, the state-railroad central station, and most banks are concentrated in the city of Santiago, but their insured are not counted in the table. The same may be said of the province of Valparaíso in which the second largest city and most important port of the nation is located. Merchant-marine insured, the majority of which are registered at Valparaíso, as well as a good number of insured in the navy (armed forces), CNEPP, and banks are excluded from the table resulting in a similar downward bias in terms of social security coverage. The 1960 data on insured may be, in addition, inaccurate. In a different comparison, using the *total* population of the provinces in 1966 (EAP by province was not available) and similar groups of insured in 1966, Santiago moved from tenth to fifth place and Valparaíso from fourteenth to tenth place. This computation was based on data from SSS, *Estadísticas 1966,* p. 110; Caja de Previsión de Empleados Particulares, *Boletín de Estadística 1966* (Santiago: CPEP, 1967), p. 7; Caja de Previsión de Carabienros, *Boletín Estadístico,* no. 1 (December 1966); and Superintendencia de Seguridad Social, *Seguridad Social,* no. 98 (July 1968), p. 35.

26. Most of these taxes are imposed upon the consumer of goods or services to support the fund which covers workers employed in that activity (for example, on passenger fares and freight for merchant-marine fund or on bets for racetrack funds). In some cases, however, the tax is imposed upon the consumer in benefit of a group totally disconnected with that activity, such as taxes on racetrack bets and entertainment fees that benefit journalists.

27. Briones (p. 37) included the armed forces in the civil-servant group (and probably made different clusterings of subgroups) arriving at a different percentage distribution for the same year. Insured: civil servants (25 percent), blue-collars (31 percent), and white-collars (43 percent). State plus employer: civil servants (72 percent), blue-collars (64 percent), and white-collars (60 percent).

Comparisons in table 2-9 are based on a single year. An analysis of the trend of percentage distribution of revenue in the 1960s in the three most important funds shows that: (a) the insured's contributions increased slightly in SSS and in CPEP, but declined sharply in CNEPP; (b) the employers' contribution declined slightly in all three funds; and (c) the state contribution was stagnant in SSS and CPEP but increased sharply in CNEPP. (Data are based on Unión Panamericana, Departamento de Asuntos Sociales, Programa de Seguridad Social, Washington, D.C., 1962–1969; and CNEPP, Sub-Departamento de Estadísticas, Santiago, August 1, 1969.)

28. The accumulated state debt to SSS in the period 1964–1970 was approximately 240 million E° in spite of a substantial increase in the state contribution to 114 million E° in 1970 (based on the author's computations from the SSS, *Estadísticas 1964* to *1970,* comparing the state dues with the sum actually paid). The director of the SSS stated in 1965 that if in that year the state had paid the amount due, the SSS pension fund would have generated a surplus of 8 million E° instead of a deficit (SSS, *Estadísticas 1965,* p. 10).

29. Based on SSS, *Estadísticas 1970,* pp. 7–8.

30. Comisión de Estudios de la Seguridad Social, pp. 827–38.

31. José Francisco Pizarro Blancaire and Juan Gutiérrez Vistoso, "Bases para un sistema integrado de pensiones: Estudio del costo," Memoria, Universidad de Chile, Facultad de Ciencias Económicas, 1967.

32. Briones et al., pp. 95–103.

33. ODEPLAN, *Informe económico anual 1971,* p. 204.

34. Gil, p. 178; and Comisión de Estudios de la Seguridad Social, p. 821.

35. The first pension funds were created in 1924–1925 and the period of maturation (in terms of retirement) came in the mid-1960s.

36. República de Chile, Ministerio de Hacienda, "Mensaje [Presidencial] no. 6 [al] Senado y la Cámara de Diputados," Santiago, August 30, 1968, p. 5.

37. Salas, "El sector agrícola," p. 128; and Briones et al., pp. 74–78.

38. For these and other data, see Unión Panamericana, Programa de Seguridad Social; CNEPP, Sub-Departamento de Estadística; Caja de Previsión de Carabineros, *Boletín Estadístico,* no. 3 (December 1968); Comisión de Estudios de la Seguridad Social, p. 850; and Briones et al., p. 93. For a comparison with other countries see ILO, *The Cost of Social Security* (Geneva: ILO, 1968).

39. Comisión de Estudios de la Seguridad Social, pp. xx–xvi. In spite of the large bureaucracy, complaints on the long delays in processing benefits are common, particularly in SSS (e.g., the processing for retirement or survivor's pension takes a year or more). Applicants are forced to resort to politicians or highly paid intermediaries to expedite the processing of benefits. A foreign specialist observed that the smaller and more solvent funds have a faster benefit-processing than the larger, financially troubled funds. From this he deduced that the delays were a means of bringing the real level of benefits down to the level of resources because prompt action on applications would have meant immediate bankruptcy. See also Marshall Wolfe, "Social Security and Development: The Latin American Experience," in *The Role of Social Security in Economic Development,* Everett M. Kassalow, ed., (Washington, D.C.: Government Printing Office, 1968), p. 165 and Luis Santibáñez, "Social Security in Chile," School of Industrial Relations, Cornell University, 1965, pp. 31–32 (unpublished paper).

40. Data comes from same sources as table 2–14.

41. Tom E. Davies, "Dualism, Stagnation and Inequality: The Impact of Chilean Legislation on the Chilean Labor Market," *Industrial and Labor Relations Review,* 17 (April 1964), p. 398.

42. A former Superintendent of Social Security reported that in 1965 7,693 applications for pensions were turned down by SSS for not meeting all requirements; however, 6,500 of those pensions would have been approved under the CPEP and some civil-servant fund regulations (Orlandini, p. 40).

43. Due to lack of statistics on a national scale, the previous comparison could not include data on privileged workers within subgroups that had gained additional benefits through 50,000 collective agreements by 1965.

44. ODEPLAN, pp. 207–12.

45. Author's computations based on *Boletín de Estadísticas de Seguridad Social,* nos. 27–28 (September–December 1965), pp. 31–32, 54.

46. The author of the second estimate does not explain how he disaggregated the total amount spent for indigents' health care, a difficult task because blue-collars and indigents are attended in the same hospitals and, to the best of my knowledge, separate accounts of expenditures are not kept.

47. The reader should be advised that statistics on the total number of hospitals and hospital beds in Chile fluctuate considerably; thus we cannot expect a reliable disaggregation. For recent estimates besides those quoted in the sources of table 2-14, see República de Chile, *Compendio Estadístico 1971; Statistical Abstract of Latin America, 1971,* K. Ruddle and D. Oderman, eds. (Los Angeles: Latin American Center, UCLA, 1972), pp. 113–15; Gloria Abate and William McCullough, *Health and Social Welfare* (Washington, D.C.: Pan American Health Organization, 1971), p. 8; and Mario Livingstone and Dagmar Raczynski, "Análisis cuantitativo de la evolución de algunas variables de salud durante el período 1964-1972," *Estudios de Planificación* (Universidad Católica de Chile–CEPLAN), no. 40 (July 1974), pp. 43–44. A recent study on income distribution and public expenditures in health, although extremely valuable, does not disaggregate expenditures among the five groups of table 2-14 (only among SNS and SMNE) and lacks data on hospital beds and physicians. José Pablo Arrellano M., "El gasto público en salud y la distributión del ingreso," *Estudios de Planificación* (Universidad Católica de Chile–CEPLAN), no. 41 (October 1974).

48. Roemer, pp. 193–242.

49. Information provided by Professor Ron Penchansky, Medical Care Organization, School of Public Health, University of Michigan, June 1969.

50. Comisión de Estudios de la Seguridad Social, pp. viii–ix, 1402; and Roemer, p. 232.

51. Emanuel de Kadt, "Aspectos distributivos de la salud en Chile," *Bienestar y Pobreza,* pp. 120, 148. See also Matheriart and Garretón, pp. 38–39.

52. Kadt, p. 145. See also *Boletín de Estadísticas de Seguridad Social,* no. 24 (March–April 1965), p. 39.

Chapter 3. The Case of Uruguay

1. For general information on the economic history of Uruguay the author has consulted the following sources: Simon G. Hanson, *Utopia in Uruguay: Chapters in the Economic History of Uruguay* (New York: Oxford, 1938); Juan E. Pivel Devoto and Alcira R. de Pivel Devoto, *Historia de la República Oriental del Uruguay, 1830–1930* (Montevideo: Artagaveytia, 1945); Russell H. Fitzgibbon, *Uruguay: Portrait of a Democracy* (London: Allen & Unwin, 1956); Philip B. Taylor, Jr., *Government and Politics of Uruguay* (New Orleans: Tulane, 1960); Alfredo Traversoni, *Historia del Uruguay y de América,* 4th ed., 2 vols. (Montevideo: Medina, 1964); Aldo Solari, *Estudios sobre la sociedad uruguaya* (Montevideo: Arca, 1964) and *El desarrollo social del Uruguay en la postguerra* (Montevideo: Alfa, 1967); Hubert Herring, *A History of Latin America,* 3rd ed. (New York: Knopf, 1968), chapter 44; Instituto de Economía, *El proceso económico del Uruguay,* 2nd ed. (Montevideo: Universidad de la República, 1971); Thomas E. Weil, et al.,

Area Handbook for Uruguay (Washington, D.C.: U.S. Government Printing Office, 1971); and Roque Faraone, *El Uruguay en que vivimos, 1900–1972* (Montevideo: Arca, 1972).

2. See Rafael Gelós Togores, "La Previsión Social en las Fuerzas Armadas del Uruguay: Caja de Retirados y Pensionistas Militares," *Revista Iberoamericana de Seguridad Social,* 20 (January–February 1970), p. 23.

3. It should be pointed out, however, that the preceding characterization is not fully representative of the complex reality. (In fact there was a spectrum of interests and stands taken by each of the two parties.) Whatever differences existed at the beginning, they tended to disappear through time.

4. Gelós Togores, p. 24.

5. Fitzgibbon, p. 180; Hanson, p. 165.

6. Herring, p. 790.

7. Gelós Togores, p. 24; Traversoni, vol. II, p. 508.

8. Gelós Togores, p. 24.

9. For instance, "spheres of influence" were established within the country and provincial governorships split between the two parties according to a pre-election formula.

10. For more on Varela and the foundations of public education in Uruguay, see Fitzgibbon, pp. 200–12; Taylor, pp. 107–09; and Marvin Alisky, *Uruguay: A Contemporary Survey* (New York: Praeger, 1969), pp. 102–18.

11. Hanson, pp. 167–68.

12. See Pedro H. Alfonso, *Sindicalismo y revolución en el Uruguay* (Montevideo: Nuevo Mundo, 1970), p. 33. For more information on the development of labor unions in Uruguay, see Alfredo Errandonea and Daniel Costabile, *Sindicato y sociedad en el Uruguay* (Montevideo: Biblioteca de Cultura Universitaria, 1969); U.S. Department of Labor, *Labor Law and Practice in Uruguay* (Washington, D.C.: U.S. Government Printing Office, 1971), ch. 7; and Weil, ch. 20.

13. Alfonso, pp. 25–26.

14. For more on Batlle's upbringing and first presidency, see Milton I. Vanger, *José Batlle y Ordóñez of Uruguay: The Creator of His Times, 1902–1907* (Cambridge, Mass.: Harvard, 1963) and Enrique Rodríquez Fabregat, *Batlle y Ordóñez: El reformador* (Buenos Aires: Claridad, 1942).

15. Hanson, pp. 165–67; Traversoni, vol. II, p. 508.

16. Rodríguez Fabregat, pp. 584–85.

17. For a good discussion of Batlle's economic philosophy, see Hanson, ch. 2, and others.

18. Hanson, pp. 150–64. For the congressional discussions surrounding the approval of this bill, see Domingo Arena, *Batlle y los problemas sociales en el Uruguay* (Montevideo: García, n.d.), pp. 130–41.

19. For the text of this and other laws covering workers in commerce and industry, see the compilation by Ofelia Belistri de Mila and José P. Zubillaga, *Sistematización orgánica de leyes y decretos-leyes y de decretos y resoluciones del Poder Ejecutivo* (Montevideo: Caja de Jubilaciones y Pensiones de la Industria y Comercio, 1964), 4 vols. See also Hanson, pp. 169–73.

20. Hanson, p. 152; Errandonea and Costabile, p. 135.

21. These were administered by the Caja de Jubilaciones, Pensiones y Subsidios de los Empleados Permanentes del Jockey Club and by the Caja de Jubilaciones y Pensiones de los Empleados de las Instituciones Bancarias.

22. Hanson, p. 161.

23. Ibid., p. 171.

24. C. G. Harris, *Overseas Economic Surveys: Uruguay* (London: His Majesty's Stationary Office, 1950), p. 1.

25. Instituto de Economía, p. 163.

26. Alfonso, pp. 67–72.

27. For more on family allowances, see Ruben N. Caggiani, *Las asignaciones familiares* (Montevideo: Universidad de la República, 1969); and Elbio Fernández Capurro, "Uruguay: La importancia de los servicios sociales en el régimen de asignaciones familiares para la ac-

tividad privada," *Revista Iberoamericana de Seguridad Social,* 19 (September–October 1969), pp. 979–82. For a compilation of legislation on family allowances, unemployment-compensation funds, accident and disease insurance, and health-insurance funds, see Jorge Luiz Lanzaro and Mario del Rosario Pedemonte, eds., *Recopilación sistematizada de normas de Derecho del Trabajo y Seguridad Social,* 2 vols. (Montevideo: Fundación de Cultura Universitaria, 1969).

28. Caggiani, pp. 145–47, 409–12.

29. Errandonea and Costabile, p. 136.

30. Much of the work written before 1960 by the founder of the CGRCP, Mr. Paulino González, appears reprinted in Adela Paulina González, *Don Paulino: Escuchando y leyendo a mi padre* (Montevideo: CGRCP, 1960).

31. The most recent analysis of the Uruguayan economy during the 1960s appears in Arturo C. Porzecanski, "Uruguay's Continuing Dilemma," *Current History,* 66 (January 1974), pp. 28–30, 38–39.

32. However, the military and the police received attention at the military hospitals and some subgroups of civil servants, e.g., congressmen and state bank employees, had special health services.

33. Weil, p. 391.

34. See Ariel Gianola Martegani, "El Banco de Previsión Social en la República Oriental del Uruguay," *Revista Iberoamericana de Seguridad Social,* 20 (January–February 1971), pp. 53–101; and Américo Pla Rodríguez, "El Banco de Previsión Social," *Temas Jurídicos* (Montevideo), 1 (1968), pp. 55–110.

35. See Oficina Internacional del Trabajo, *Informe al Gobierno de la República Oriental del Uruguay sobre Seguridad Social* (Ginebra: OIT, 1964); and Comisión de Inversiones y Desarrollo Económico, *Plan Nacional de Desarrollo Económico y Social, 1965–1974* (Montevideo: CECEA, 1966). See also *Evaluation of the National Economic and Social Development Plan of the Republic of Uruguay, 1965–1974* (Washington, D.C.: Pan American Union, 1967), 2 vols.

36. See *Latin America* (London), (October 26, 1973), p. 343.

37. See Comisión de Inversiones y Desarrollo Económico, vol. 1, pp. 164–66.

38. These occupations were ranked conversely in their proportion included in the lowest-15-percent income bracket: rural wage-earners (33 percent); domestic servants (21 percent); blue-collars and small merchants and artisans (12 percent); white-collars (4 percent); technicians and owners and managers (2 percent each); and professionals (none in the lowest income bracket). Ibid.

39. Dirección General de Estadística y Censos, *Uruguay: Anuario Estadístico 1961–1963* (Montevideo: Ministerio de Hacienda, n.d.), pp. L7–L8.

40. Due to declining birth rates and increasing life expectancy, Uruguay has become an almost unique case in Latin America. See Solari, "El envejecimiento de la población en el Uruguay y sus consecuencias," *Estudios sobre la sociedad uruguaya,* pp. 55–64.

41. See Luis Vicario, *El crecimiento urbano de Montevideo* (Montevideo: Banda Oriental, 1970).

42. Although there is no time-series data on employment in domestic services with which to confirm this, it might be hypothesized that, due to Uruguay's economic recession, many who could previously afford full- or part-time maids discharged them in an economy move. Had this been the case, enrollment in Rural and Domestic would certainly have dwindled.

43. See the discussion under *Financing.*

44. Tax evasion is acute in small businesses and rural enterprises, where employees are said to often collude with their employers in failing to accurately declare the number of workers or their total earnings. This is particularly understandable where part-time, low-paid, seasonal, or marginal workers are involved because they are far more concerned with maximizing their net current pay than with taxing themselves for the sake of future benefits. Also, they know that social security obligations increase labor costs and thus encourage the dismissal of workers who are not productive enough. The problem of delayed payment of contributions is linked to Uruguay's inflationary experience. The fact is that employers find it profitable to postpone forwarding social security withholdings because existing legal penalties have tended to be

lower than the high nominal interest rates typically associated with high inflation. In addition, numerous moratoria laws have condoned penalties and extended payment of the debt over a long period. This allows the debtors to repay the principal debt plus interest at a small fraction of the initial debt due to the inflationary spiral. Thus, employers use social security contributions for investment purposes or to meet payroll obligations since, during inflationary times, borrowing funds is far costlier than paying fines.

45. From information supplied by the various pension funds.

46. It is tempting to speculate how Uruguay's generous and thus expensive structure of social security might be partly responsible for the country's recent economic record and its pattern of production. The stagnation in the livestock sector may be due to the fact that, given the high cost of both labor and (imported) capital inputs, land-intensive methods of production became the simplest, least risky, and most profitable ones. Uruguayan cattle ranchers' reliance upon land as their sole factor of production may thus have been a market-determined phenomenon and, to a great extent, the result of policies which granted social security benefits to the community at the cost of raising the price of labor. Montevideo's economic growth may have been accomplished despite high labor costs because import substituters never operated competitively and because the government, a major employer, never behaved as a profit-maximizer. The hypothesis is that Montevideo's small and medium-sized industry was established and survived thanks to protectionist policies and that, in turn, the absence of competitive conditions made it possible for Montevideo businessmen to hire many more workers than would otherwise have been hired. Also, the existence of a large civil service resulted from active government intervention in the Uruguayan economy following political objectives; furthermore, those political considerations made it imperative that many more workers be hired than would have been employed had cost-minimizing, economic criteria been applied.

47. I do not discuss here aspects which are treated in the other countries, such as the calculation methods for fixing the amount of the benefit, and the actual amount of minor benefits (e g , family allowances and funeral aid) because no significant differences are found in these matters in Uruguay. Finally, the Uruguayan legislation relating to compatibility among pensions or between pensions and salaried work has been modified so frequently during the past few years and the proper information is so difficult to obtain that, out of necessity, these aspects have been omitted from the discussion.

48. Oficina Internacional del Trabajo, pp. 39–45.

49. Calculated from information in Fernando Suescún Caicedo, "Informe sobre la organización de servicios de atención médica, seguridad social y seguros de salud de la República Oriental del Uruguay," unpublished report of a 1968 mission to Uruguay by the Panamerican Sanitary Bureau, p. 82.

50. Dirección General de Estadística y Censos, p. C18; and Vicario, p. 16.

Chapter 4. The Case of Peru

1. Because of space limitations this section is a summary of my original work and footnotes are excluded. General sources for the historical background of this section have been: OISS, *Los seguros sociales en el Perú* (Madrid: OISS, 1961); Robert J. Alexander, *Organized Labor in Latin America* (New York: Free Press, 1965); James L. Payne, *Labor and Politics in Peru* (New Haven: Yale University Press, 1965); Frederick B. Pike, *The Modern History of Peru* (New York: Praeger, 1967); Julio Cotler, *La mecánica de la dominación interna y del cambio social en el Perú* (Lima: Instituto de Estudios Peruanos, 1967); David Chaplin, "Industrialization and the Distribution of Wealth in Peru," *Studies in Comparative International Development,* 3 (1967), and *The Peruvian Industrial Labor Force* (Princeton: Princeton University Press, 1967); U.S. Department of Labor, Bureau of Labor Statistics, *Labor Law and Practice in Peru* (Washington, D.C.: Government Printing Office, 1968); Carlos A. Astiz, *Pressure Groups and Power Elites in Peruvian Politics* (Ithaca, N.Y.: Cornell University Press, 1969); Magali Sarfatti Larson and Arlene Eisen Bergman, *Social Stratification in Peru* (Berkeley: Institute of International Studies, University of California, 1969); François Bourricaud, *Power and Society in Peru* (New York:

Praeger, 1970); Grant Hilliker, *The Politics of Reform in Peru* (Baltimore: The Johns Hopkins Press, 1971); Richard H. Stephens, *Wealth and Power in Peru* (Metuchen, N.J.: Scarecrow Press, 1971); Vivian Trias, *Perú: fuerzas armadas y revolución* (Montevideo: Ediciones de la Banda Oriental, 1971); Victor Villanueva, *Cien años del ejército peruano: frustraciones y cambios* (Lima: Editorial Juan Mejia Baca, 1972); and Marvin Alisky, *Peruvian Political Perspective* (Tempe, Ariz.: Center for Latin American Studies, Arizona State University, 1972). Social security legislation comes from several private compilations published in Lima and Gustavo Bacacorzo, *Derecho de pensiones del Perú* (Arequipa: Editorial Universitaria, 1969).

2. Initially the law caused negative effects: employers began to dismiss senior employees and froze wage increases for employees close to retirement (because pensions were computed on the basis of the last salary). To correct the first problem, a law established that employees with 15 or 20 years of service (females and males respectively) could be dismissed only by violation of the labor contract and then only following legal procedures. Another law permitted the employer and the employee to agree voluntarily on dismissal through payment of compensation. But the problem of frozen wages was not solved until 1969 when the responsibility shifted from the employer to an institution (FEJEP). See Julio Cuadros Muñoz, "El régimen de jubilación de los empleados particulares en el Perú," *Revista de Derecho del Trabajo* (Lima), 2 (October–December 1966), pp. 335–44.

3. See Ricardo La Hoz Tirado, "La integración de las indemnizaciones sobre accidentes de trabajo a la seguridad social," *Revista de Derecho del Trabajo* (Lima), 4 (September–December 1968), pp. 193–213.

4. Two ILO missions were contracted by Odría to study a health program and pensions for white-collars, but their recommendations were not implemented. See "Informe preliminar sobre la seguridad social en el Perú [al] Ministerio de Salud Pública," Lima, April 1954; and Gonzalo Arroba, "Informe financiero sobre el seguro de invalidez, vejez y muerte de los empleados particulares del Perú" and "Proyecto de esquema," Lima, May 1952.

5. For a detailed study of these events, see Payne, pp. 81–85.

6. See note 4 above. A second ILO mission led by Antoine Zelenka prepared a report (not made available to me) in 1957. A third ILO report, prepared by George Heubeck, was "Peritaje sobre el proyectado seguro de pensiones y de vida de empleados particulares," Lima, May 1959.

7. Antoine Zelenka, "Aspectos financieros de los seguros sociales," Lima, May 1969.

8. See Francisco de Ipiña Gondra, "Estructura financiera," "Recursos económicos," "Equilibrio financiero," "Causas del desequilibrio financiero," and "Conclusiones y recomendaciones," Lima, 1962, and "Estudio actuarial sobre pensiones," Lima, January 1963; José D. Gómez Sánchez, "Ley de Jubilación Obrera primer informe técnico sobre su estructura financiero actuarial," Lima, January 1963; and Alfredo Pérez Armiñán, "Informe sobre la situación administrativa del seguro social del empleado del Perú," Lima, 1965. Another report prepared by Giovanni Tamburi and Peter Thullen in 1965 was not made available to me.

9. Ipiña, "Estudio actuarial," and Zelenka, "Participación del estado en el financiamiento del seguro social obligatorio," Lima, April 1969.

10. See Zelenka, "Aspectos financieros," and "Inversiones y su rendimiento en el seguro de pensiones," Lima, April–May 1969.

11. In 1973, Minister of Labor Pedro Sala Orozco acknowledged that the creation of FEJEP was "a grave mistake of the revolutionary government." See *El Peruano,* April 30, 1973, p. 3.

12. Information given by David Chaplin in letter of April 6, 1973.

13. Misión Española de Asistencia Técnica, "Seguridad social en el Perú" (submitted to Ministry of Labor, SSO and SSE), Lima, August–October 1970.

14. The CTP actually initiated the criticism mostly against the government; see Santiago Tamariz, et al., "Informe de los Delegados de la CTP ante el Consejo de Administración del Seguro Social Obrero," Lima, July 1970. The severe criticism against SSO and SSE was launched by CGTP and MOSICP and published in the government-controlled newspaper *El Expreso,* October–December 1970. I obtained additional information on this controversy in

interviews with Julio Cruzado, Secretary General of the CTP; Santiago Tamariz, CTP representative before SSO; and Félix Loli Cepero, Secretary General of the CSEPP and its representative before SSE, Lima, January 8 and 25, 1971.

15. *El Expreso,* December 8, 1972. Details of the legal drafts were provided by General Carlos López Mendoza, manager of SSO and president of its Commission of Reorganization, Lima, January 14, 1971.

16. Interview with Julio Chávez Ferrer, member of the Commission of Reorganization, Lima, January 12, 1971; and *El Peruano,* July 27, 1971.

17. MOSICP in *El Expreso,* October 6, 1970; also interview with Roberto Robles, Lima, January 23, 1971. CGTP in *El Expreso,* December 7, 1970.

18. CTP from interviews with Cruzado and Tamariz, 1971.

19. CSEPP from interview with Loli Cepero, 1971.

20. Interview with Guillermo Donayre Barrios, employer's representative before SSO and SSE in 1969–1970, Lima, January 19, 1971.

21. The 1967–1970 plan included a program on health but nothing on social security; see Instituto Nacional de Planificación, *Plan de Desarrollo Económico y Social, 1967–1970* (Lima: Documento Orientador, 1966). The same was true of the long-run development strategy prepared by the Instituto Nacional de Planificación: "Bases para un Programa de Desarrollo Nacional a Largo Plazo: Documento de trabajo," Lima, April 1969. For the new plan, see "Plan Nacional de Desarrollo para 1971–1975," vol. 1, Plan Global, chap. 15: "Plan de Salud" and chap. 16: "Política de Seguridad Social," *El Peruano,* November 22, 1971. Preliminary documents of this plan were Sistema Nacional de Planificación, "Lineamientos de política de seguridad social para mediano plazo (Informe de la Comisión Horizontal de Seguridad Social)," Lima, August 1970, and "Plan Nacional de Desarrollo para 1971–1975," Plan Global, vol. 2: "Síntesis de los Planes Sectoriales," Primera Parte, Lima, December 1970. I also gathered information in interviews with Pedro Chirino Valdivia, in charge of the social security sector at INP, and Juan León Polo, in charge of the health sector at INP, Lima, January 20, 1971.

22. This is an enigmatic point of the Plan that probably caused concern among the insured. Zelenka's 1969 report recommended that part of the funds of the FNSBS and all the state contribution to SSE be transferred to SSO in order to alleviate its financial troubles. Zelenka, as well as Ipiña, cautioned against the expansion of social security without providing adequate resources to alleviate the burden of the SSO. The Plan echoed their caution but raised doubts on its seriousness with a vague statement suggesting a shift of government support without making clear how it would affect the SSO.

23. In the draft of the biannual plan for 1973–1974, most of the objectives of the long-run plan of 1971–1975 were ratified and a few significant ones added: (1) establishment of social security for peasants starting in most of the Sierra departments in which peasants are heavily concentrated; (2) completion of social security coverage of domestic servants and expansion of coverage to incorporate university students, firemen, those in liberal professions, and workers in home-delivery of some consumer goods; (3) continuation of expansion of health-maternity coverage in the Jungle; and (4) culmination of social security unification. See Instituto Nacional de Planificación, "Plan Bienal 1973–1974: Proyecto para discusión," Lima: 12.72-DII. 1, pp. 311–25.

24. *El Peruano,* April 30, 1973, pp. 1–7.

25. Ibid., December 8, 1973, p. 1.

26. *Siete Días,* May 4, 1973, pp. 4–7.

27. See "Peru: Working Class Opposition," *Latin America,* June 22, 1973, pp. 198–99.

28. *El Peruano,* December 27, 1972, p. 8.

29. Payne, p. 130; and U.S. Department of Labor, pp. 62–64.

30. See Cotler, p. 43; and Astiz, p. 50.

31. I used: for civil servants, *Legislación peruana de empleados públicos,* Pedro Patrón Faura, ed. (Lima: 1970); for white-collars, *Estatuto del Seguro Social del Empleado,* S. Martínez G., ed. (Lima: 1969); and for blue-collars, *Los beneficios sociales del obrero,* F. Bonilla, ed.

(Lima: Editorial Mercurio, 1970). Recent legislation and other additional information were supplied by: José D. Gómez Sánchez, actuary of SSO; Martín Fajardo C., technician of SSO; Carlos Benavides, Director of Social Security, Ministry of Labor; César San Román, Director of FEJEP; and Julio Chávez Ferrer, Member of the Commission of Reorganization.

32. I was not able, in spite of multiple requests, to obtain a single interview with any of the administrators of the social security system of the armed forces. Neither could I obtain statistics nor visit any of its hospitals. The legislation is not compiled and whatever I could gather was on my own effort.

33. Based on Luis Aparicio Valdez, "Estudio sobre convenios colectivos y seguridad social en el Perú," Lima, n.d.

34. See Payne, p. 21; Cotler, pp. 25–58; and Astiz, pp. 48–81, 191–230. For other classifications see Larson and Bergman, pp. 370–78.

35. Based on Rómulo A. Ferrero and Arthur J. Altmeyer, *Estudio económico de la legislación social peruana y sugerencias para su mejoramiento* (Lima: Santiago Valverde, S.A., 1957), pp. 32–38. For income differentials in 1961 using another categorization, see Larson and Bergman, pp. 155–56, 370–78.

36. Gómez Sánchez, interview of 1971; and SSE, *Boletín Estadístico 1958–1968.* For other wage differentials, see Zelenka, "Participación del estado," pp. 7, 19; and U.S. Department of Labor, pp. 44–45.

37. Ferrero and Altmeyer, pp. 11–30.

38. Cotler, pp. 1–2; Larson and Bergman, pp. 88–92, and appendices; U.S. Department of Labor, pp. 2–3.

39. J. E. Loftus, *Latin America Defense Expenditures 1938–1965* (Santa Monica, Cal.: Rand Corporation, 1968), pp. 59, 88; and Irving Louis Horowitz, "The Military Elites," in *Elites in Latin America,* Seymour Martin Lipset and Aldo Solari, eds. (New York: Oxford University Press, 1967), p. 154.

40. It should be stressed, however, that the two columns of the table are not strictly comparable. *Salaried workers* are roughly congruent with the sum of white-collars, civil servants, and armed-forces personnel paid on a monthly basis. *Wage-earners* are roughly congruent with blue-collars paid on a weekly, daily, or hourly basis.

41. Lamas López, "El aspecto asistencial de la seguridad social peruana."

42. Legislation; and Carlos Benavides, Lima, January 13, 1971.

43. Zelenka, "Participación del estado."

44. Bacacorzo, p. 49.

45. Ministerio de Economía y Finanzas, *La situación económica del país* (Lima: 1971).

46. Ipiña (1962).

47. Aparicio Valdez (n.d.).

48. CNSS, *Decimaséptima memoria correspondiente al año 1958* (Lima: n.d.) and *Memoria años 1961–1967;* SSE, *Boletín Estadístico 1958–1968;* Manual Hubi Campos, et al., "Evaluación de la contribución del Seguro Social del Empleado a los programas docentes para la salud en el Perú," Segundo Congreso Americano de Medicine de la Seguridad Social, Bogotá, 1970; and U.N., *Statistical Yearbook 1970* (New York: 1971).

49. Zelenka, "Aspectos financieros"; Ipiña, 1962; Gómez Sánchez, interview, 1971; and SSE, *Boletín Estadístico 1958–1968.*

50. Ipiña (1962) qualified this as a regressive step in income redistribution.

51. Bacacorzo, pp. 87–88. Compulsory retirement for the armed forces was not included in the 1972 regulations that unified their pension system, but it may still be in force as part of the statutes of the armed forces. Voluntary retirement for old age has never been granted because seniority retirement is so generous.

52. Milton I. Roemer, *Medical Care in Latin America* (Washington, D.C.: Pan American Union, 1964).

53. Octavio Mongrut, "Población y salud," *Boletín Informativo del Centro de Estudios de Población y Desarrollo* (Lima), 4 (June 1970), pp. 2–7.

Chapter 5. The Case of Argentina

1. Because of space limitations, this section is a summary of my original work and footnotes are excluded. General bibliographical sources for this section were: Ricardo Levene, *A History of Argentina* (Chapel Hill: University of North Carolina Press, 1937); U.S. Department of Labor, *Labor Law and Practice in Argentina* (Washington, D.C.: Government Printing Office, n.d.); Robert J. Alexander, *Labor Relations in Argentina, Brazil and Chile* (New York: McGraw Hill, 1962); Antonio Cortese, *Historia económica argentina y americana* (Buenos Aires: Ediciones Macchi, 1962); Aldo Ferrer, *La economía argentina* (Mexico: F.C.E., 1963); George Pendle, *Argentina* (London: Oxford University Press, 1963); José Luis de Imaz, *Los que mandan* (Buenos Aires: EUDEBA, 1964); Arthur P. Whitaker, *Argentina* (Englewood Cliffs, N.J.: Prentice Hall, 1964) and *The Argentine Upheaval* (New York: Praeger, 1965); José Luis Romero, *Breve historia de la Argentina* (Buenos Aires: EUDEBA, 1965); Samuel L. Baily, *Labor, Nationalism and Politics in Argentina* (New Brunswick, N.J.: Rutgers University Press, 1967); and Carlos F. Díaz-Alejandro, *Essays on the Economic History of the Argentine Republic* (New Haven: Yale University Press, 1970). Social security legislation comes from the following compilations: Jerónomo Remorino, *La nueva legislación social argentina* (Buenos Aires: Ministerio de Relaciones Exteriores y Culto, 1953); Ministerio de Bienestar Social, Secretaría de Estado de Seguridad Social, *Seguridad Social: Recopilación de leyes, decretos y resoluciones dictados por el Gobierno de la Revolución Argentina Desde 28/6/66 hasta el 31/11/68* (Buenos Aires: Departamento de Asuntos Técnicos, 1967); *Leyes de jubilaciones y leyes del trabajo* (Buenos Aires: Editorial Bregna, 1973); and Ministerio de Bienestar Social, Secretaría de Seguridad Social, *Revista de Seguridad Social,* issues September 1968 to December 1973. Additional information and juridical interpretation from the following works: José M. Goñi Moreno, *Derecho de la Previsión Social* (Buenos Aires: Ediar S. A. Editores, 1956); Consejo Federal de Seguridad Social de la República Argentina, *Primer Informe Técnico* (Buenos Aires: Editorial Almafuerte, 1961); Humberto A. Podetti, *Las contingencias sociales protegidas en el orden jurídico argentino* (Buenos Aires: Bibliográfica Omeba, 1962); Juan José Etala, *Derecho de la Seguridad Social* (Buenos Aires: Ediar S.A. Editores, 1966); Miguel Angel Cordini, *Derecho de la Seguridad Social* (Buenos Aires: EUDEBA, 1966); Guillermo Cabanellas, *Compendio de Derecho Laboral,* vol. 2 (Buenos Aires: Bibliográfica Omeba, 1968); and José María Rivas, *Manual de Derecho del Trabajo* (Buenos Aires: Ediciones Macchi, 1970).

2. Otilio A. Boron, "El estudio de la movilización política en América Latina: La movilización electoral en la Argentina y Chile," *Desarrollo Económico,* 12 (July–September 1972), p. 236. Subsequent references in this chapter on proportion of votes received by political parties come from this source.

3. These were the first family allowance systems, but between 1939 and 1945 various laws had granted bonuses for children of bank and insurance employees, journalists, and railroad workers.

4. See Consejo Federal de Seguridad Social de la República Argentina, *Plan de Seguridad Social* (Buenos Aires: Olivieri y Domínguez, 1963); and Equipos PASS, *Programa Argentino de Seguridad Social* (Buenos Aires: Artes Gráficas, 1965) and *Anteproyecto de Código de Seguridad Social* (Buenos Aires: Imprenta del Congreso de la Nación, 1966).

5. See Presidencia de la Nación, Secretarías de CONADE y CONASE, *Plan Nacional de Desarrollo y Seguridad 1971–1975* (República Argentina: 1971), pp. 191–94.

6. "Bases para un sistema de seguridad social en la Argentina," mimeographed, n.p., *circa* 1966, pp. 1, 3.

7. See *La Nación,* December 3, 1973, p. 5.

8. Juan Carlos Torre, "La tasa de sindicalización en la Argentina," *Desarrollo Económico,* 12 (January–March 1973), pp. 909–10. Subsequent references on degree of unionization come from this source.

9. Consejo Federal de Seguridad Social de la República Argentina, *Primer Informe Técnico,* p. 87.

10. Ibid., pp. 47–66, for a detailed description of the provincial systems.

11. For a summary of the organization of the social security civil sector, see "La seguridad social en la Argentina," *Revista de Seguridad Social,* 6 (December 1973), pp. 887–906.

12. See ECLA, *Economic Development and Income Distribution in Argentina* (New York: United Nations, 1969), pp. 50–86. In an attempt to rank social security groups, relating them, as much as possible, to the ECLA ranking of income strata, four clarifications are necessary: (a) when an income stratum does not have a counterpart in a social security group/subgroup, it is omitted; (b) when an income stratum is only part of an existing social security group, it is so indicated; (c) when a social security group is split into various income strata, it is so indicated; and (d) two social security groups (armed forces and journalists-printers) do not appear in the ranking because there are no disaggregated income data on them.

13. See *La Nación,* April 8, 1974. The ratio was calculated by taking the simple mean of the 1974 range of salaries of the armed forces and dividing it into the minimum legal income for salaried employees and wage-earners in the same year.

14. See José M. Dagnino Pastore, et al., "Regional Development in Argentina: Administrative and Organizational Problems," *Multidisciplinary Aspects of Regional Development* (Paris: Development Centre of the OECD, 1969). Data in the text pertaining to economic conditions in the region mostly refer to 1960 and come from the magazine *Argentina,* Numbers 1 to 52 (Buenos Aires: Editorial Abril, 1972–1973): ECLA, *Economic Development;* and *Bases para el desarrollo regional argentina* (Buenos Aires: Consejo Federal de Inversiones, 1963).

15. ECLA, *Economic Development,* p. 88.

16. Ibid., pp. 86–99.

17. The 1960 population census gave an EAP different from that in the table. See República Argentina, Poder Ejecutivo Nacional, *Censo Nacional de Población 1960* (Buenos Aires: Secretaría de Estado de Hacienda, Dirección Nacional de Estadísticas y Censos, November 1963).

18. Dirección de Economía Sanitaria de la Secretaría de Estado de Salud Pública, "Problemas de financiamiento del sector salud," *Revista de Seguridad Social,* 2 (June 1969), pp. 461–70.

19. See *The Statesman Yearbook* issues 1961–1970, John Paxton, ed. (New York: St. Martin's Press, 1962–1971).

20. Information on *class of worker* data comes from República Argentina, *Censo Nacional de Población 1960.*

21. República Argentina, Presidencia de la Nación, *Plan Nacional de Desarrollo 1965–1969* (Buenos Aires: CONADE, 1965).

22. In 1966, the number of beneficiaries was highly concentrated in the Federal Capital and the province of Buenos Aires (74.9 percent). The highest percentages after this were registered in the provinces of Santa Fé (9.1 percent), Córdoba (5.2 percent), and Tucumán (2.2 percent). The smallest percentages were in the provinces of Misiones (0.22 percent) and Santa Cruz (0.048 percent). See "Bases para un sistema de seguridad social en la Argentina," p. 6.

23. Correlation excludes Tierra del Fuego, a statistical outlier.

24. The reader should be warned at this point that references to compensation of deficits with surpluses do not mean that such compensation has actually taken place in all cases throughout the period. Data was computed and compared by Héctor L. Diéguez and Alberto Petrecolla, "Estudio estadístico del sistema previsional argentino en el período 1950–1972 (Versón preliminar)," Buenos Aires, Instituto Torcuato Di Tella, Centro de Investigaciones Económicas, August 1974, pp. 12–16 and 45–50.

25. Ibid., p. 42, n. 41.

26. "Bases para un sistema," pp. 9, 12.

27. Secretaría de Estado de Seguridad Social, Ministerio de Bienestar Social, *Primera Semana Argentina de Seguridad Social* (Buenos Aires: n.p., November 26–30, 1973), pp. 15–16.

28. See note 26.

29. Juan José Etala, "El proceso de la reforma jubilatoria," *Legislación del Trabajo,* 15 (November 1967), pp. 885–86.

30. ECLA, *Economic Development,* pp. 262–64. Héctor L. Diéguez and A. Petrecolla have recently completed two significant research projects on related subjects. The first is a macroeconomic study which analyzes the participation of active and passive insured in the social security system, the trends in the real income of both groups, and the functional redistribution of income between the two ("La distribución functional del ingreso y el sistema previsional en Argentina," Buenos Aires, Instituto Torcuato Di Tella, Documento de Trabajo No. 71, February 1974). The second study involves a statistical analysis of both the financial situation and the average benefits of the whole pension system for the period 1950–1972, including disaggregated information for all groups and subgroups ("Estudio estadístico del sistema previsional argentino, 1950–1972"). These two studies do not directly attack the problem of the social security impact in income redistribution among occupational groups and subgroups although they do provide basic data extremely valuable for undertaking such a study.

31. República Argentina, *Plan Nacional de Desarrollo 1965–1969,* p. 99; and OEA, Instituto Interamericano de Estadística, "Situación Social," *América en Cifras 1970* (Washington, D.C.: OEA, 1971), p. 72.

32. *Revista de Seguridad Social,* 5 (September 1972) and 6 (January–June 1973).

33. Ibid., 2 (February 1969), 5 (April 1972), and 6 (January–June 1973).

34. Ricardo R. Moles, "Seguridad social y convenios colectivos de trabajo," *Revista de Seguridad Social,* 4 (May 1971), pp. 411–50.

35. See *Revista de Seguridad Social,* 6 (December 1973), p. 896.

36. Actually the monthly average of the "payment category" (within the legal scale) assigned to the insured, who usually chooses the minimum payment determined by the president.

37. Interviews held in Buenos Aires, in May–June 1969, with Antonio López de la Fuente (Ministry of Social Welfare), Félix Luis Moscarelli (blue- and white-collar fund), José Pereira Rey (civil-servant fund), and Liberato A. Musacchio (self-employed fund).

38. Secretaría de Estado de Seguridad Social, *Primera Semana Argentina,* p. 7.

39. Diéguez and Petrecolla have computed the average pension per capita received by all groups and subgroups throughout twenty years (varying from 1950 to 1972), obtaining results similar to those in table 5-13. One difference, however, is that professionals rank higher (above rural workers). They also disaggregate the military and the police and, while the former stays at the top of the distribution, the latter falls below banking and insurance. See "Estudio estadístico," p. 18.

40. Dirección de Economía Sanitaria, "Problemas de financiamiento del sector salud," pp. 165 67.

41. Interviews with various physicians, from different systems, in Buenos Aires, May–June 1969.

42. República Argentina, *Plan Nacional de Desarrollo 1965–1969.*

Chapter 6. The Case of Mexico

1. Because of space limitations, this section is a summary of my original work and most footnotes are excluded. Sources for the historical background of this section have been: Víctor Alba, *Las ideas sociales contemporáneas en Mexico* (México, D.F.: Ed. F.C.E., 1960); Roberto de la Cerda Silva, *El movimiento obrero en México* (México, D.F.: UNAM, 1961); Howard F. Cline, *Mexico: Revolution to Evolution, 1940–1960* (London: Oxford University Press, 1962); Bureau of Labor Statistics, U.S. Department of Labor, *Labor in Mexico* (hereafter cited by title) (Washington, D.C.: Government Printing Office, 1963); William P. Glade and Charles W. Anderson, *The Political Economy of Mexico* (Madison: University of Wisconsin Press, 1963); Frank Brandenburg, *The Making of Modern Mexico* (Englewood Cliffs, N.J.: Prentice-Hall, 1964); Robert E. Scott, *Mexican Government in Transition* (Urbana: University of Illinois Press, 1964); Robert J. Alexander, *Organized Labor in Latin America* (New York: The Free Press, 1965); Daniel Cosío Villegas, ed., *Historia moderna de México* (México: Editorial Hermes, 1965) and *El sistema político mexicano: Las posibilidades de cambio* (México, D.F.: Cuadernos de Joaquín Mortiz, 1972); L. Vincent Padgett, *The Mexican Political System* (Boston: Houghton Mifflin,

1966); Pablo González Casanova, *La democracia en México* (México, D.F.: Ediciones Era, 1967); James Wilkie, *The Mexican Revolution: Federal Expenditures and Social Change Since 1910* (Berkeley: University of California Press, 1967) and *Contemporary Mexico*, J.W. Wilkie, M.C. Meyer and E.M. Wilkie, eds. (Berkeley: University of California Press, 1975); Edwin Lieuwen, *Mexican Militarism 1910–1940* (Albuquerque: University of New Mexico Press, 1968); Diego G. López Rosado, *Historia y pensamiento económico de México* (México, D.F.: UNAM, 1969); Morris Singer, *Growth, Equality and the Mexican Experience* (Austin: University of Texas Press, 1969); Francisco A. Gómez Jara, *El movimiento campesino en México* (México: Editorial Campesino, 1970); Jorge A. Lozoya, *El ejército mexicano (1911–1965)* (México, D.F.: El Colegio de México, 1970); Clark W. Reynolds, *The Mexican Economy: Twentieth Century Structure and Growth* (New Haven: Yale University Press, 1970); Roger D. Hansen, *The Politics of Mexican Development* (Baltimore: The Johns Hopkins Press, 1971); Martin Needler, *Politics and Society in Mexico* (Albuquerque, N.M.: University of New Mexico Press, 1971); Bo Anderson and James D. Cockcroft, "Control and Cooptation in Mexican Politics," *Dependence and Underdevelopment: Latin America's Political Economy*, Cockcroft, et al. (Garden City, N.Y.: Doubleday, 1972); Marjorie Ruth Clark, *Organized Labor in Mexico* (New York: Russell and Russell, 1973); Samuel León, "Clase obrera y cardenismo," México, D.F., Centro de Estudios Latinoamericanos, UNAM, n.d.; Juan Felipe Leal, "El estado y el bloque del poder en México: 1867–1914" and "El estado mexicano: 1915–1973," México, D.F., Centro de Estudios Latinoamericanos, UNAM, n.d.; José Luis Reyna, "Crecimiento económico y clase obrera en México," México, D.F., El Colegio de México, 1974. Historical antecedents, legislation, and juridical interpretation on social security come from: Mario de la Cueva, *Derecho Mexicana del trabajo*, vol. 2 (México, D.F.: Editorial Porrúa, 1959); Francisco González Díaz Lombardo, *Cursillo de seguridad social mexicana* (Monterrey: Universidad Autónoma de Nuevo León, 1959); Rafael Gómez Corral, *Los seguros sociales en México* (Madrid: OISS, 1963); Benito Coquet, *La seguridad social en México: Doctrina, servicios, legislación, información estadística*, vol. 1 (México, D.F.: IMSS, 1964); Luis Chávez Orozco, "Orígenes de la política de seguridad social," *Historia mexicana*, 16 (October-December 1966), pp. 155–183; IMSS, *Antecedentes de la Ley del Seguro Social* and *Las prestaciones sociales: Ruta de la seguridad social* (México, D.F.: IMSS, 1970); and Miguel García Cruz, *La Seguridad social en México*, vol. 1, *1906–1958* and vol. 2, *1958–1964* (México, D.F.: B. Costa-Amic Editor, 1972 and 1973).

2. Torcuato S. Di Tella, "Las clases peligrosas a comienzos del siglo XIX en México," *Desarrollo Económico*, 12 (January–March 1973), pp. 761–91. Using data from Querétaro in 1844, Di Tella distinguishes five income strata in Mexico: (1) high (hacienda owners, urban lessors, clergymen, merchants, and professionals); (2) upper-medium (hacienda administrators, medium-size farm owners, government employees, and industrial owners); (3) lower-medium (*colonos*, commerce clerks, and artisans); (4) upper-low (workers in industries, artisan shops, mines, tobacco plantations, and haciendas); and (5) bottom-low (construction workers, peddlers, domestic servants, and hacienda peons).

3. Eight states had anticipated this constitutional mandate: México and Nuevo León, already mentioned; Chihuahua, Veracruz, Jalisco, and Coahuila in 1914; Hidalgo in 1915; and Zacatecas in 1916.

4. The original draft of the constitution reserved labor legislation to the federal government, but this clause was deleted in the final version.

5. IMSS, *Antecedentes de la Ley del Seguro Social*, p. 367.

6. The 1917 constitution had left the regulation of labor and social security to the states and, from 1918 to 1928, the proliferation of state laws created considerable confusion and inequality. Towards the end of 1928, a proposal to include social security in a uniform federal labor law failed, due to the opposition of the employers, who feared the heavy financial burden social security would entail for them. Another problem was that the constitutionally-prescribed voluntary mutual savings funds financed by workers were obviously not a solution to the problem.

7. Statistics on number of strikes and striking workers in 1920–1963 come mainly from González Casanova, pp. 183–84. Another source which does not agree with Casanova is Francisco Zapata, "Materiales para el análisis del sindicalismo en México," Centro de Estudios

Sociológicos, El Colegio de México 1974. Zapata apparently includes only legalized strikes, although in some years he seems to count all strikes. A third source is *Labor in Mexico*, p. 104.

8. In 1939–1943 the purchasing power of workers declined by 50 percent and in 1939–1946 labor's share in the national income went down from 30 to 21 percent.

9. Reyna, p. 31. For the offical point of view on the creation of IMSS, see *El seguro social en México* (México, D.F.: Talleres Gráficos de la Nación, 1943).

10. García Cruz, vol. 1, pp. 85, 111.

11. Statistics on number of insured come from IMSS, *Memoria estadística de 1971* (México, D.F.: IMSS, 1972), while data on both the population and labor force are from Dirección General de Estadística, *Anuario estadístico de los Estados Unidos Mexicanos* (various years).

12. For an appraisal of Alemán's accomplishment on social security, see Gustavo Arce Cano, *Alemán y el seguro social* (México, D.F.: Editorial Ruta, 1951).

13. According to Lucila Leal de Araujo, a top official at IMSS, the extension of social security coverage to rural areas in Mexico had been and still is blocked by the type of employment of this group (dispersion, lack of entrepreneurs, instability) and its low income. See Leal de Araujo, "Extension of Social Security to Rural Workers in Mexico," *International Labour Review,* 58 (August–September 1973), pp. 127–42.

14. Most of these systems were established in the 1950s and 1960s, although some laws date from the 1930s. Starting as early as 1932, several subgroups of civil servants were granted health care although with divergent coverage and benefits: federal school teachers and employees of legislative and judicial branches; Ministries of Public Works, Treasury, Health, and Education; and the Federal District.

15. For documents and ideas on social security under López Mateos, see *Ideario de la seguridad social* (México, D.F.: Editorial La Justicia, 1961) and *El seguro social en beneficio del campesino* (México, D.F.: Editorial La Justicia, n.d.).

16. David Rondfeldt, "The Mexican Army and the Political Order Since 1940," in Wilkie, *Contemporary Mexico.*

17. Statistics on membership of labor federations come mainly from *Labor in Mexico*.

18. Rates of unionization come from González Casanova, p. 253.

19. Guy E. Poitras, "Welfare Bureaucracy and Clientele Politics in Mexico," *Administrative Science Quarterly*, 18 (March 1973), pp. 18–26. See also Poitras and Charles F. Denton, "Bureaucratic Performance: Case Studies from Mexico and Costa Rica," *Journal of Comparative Administration,* 3 (August 1971), pp. 169–87.

20. For a comprehensive treatment of social security in collective contracts in Mexico, see Mesa Redonda OIT-AISS-CISS, *Seguridad social y convenios colectivos* (México, D.F.: Comité Permanente Interamericano de Seguridad Social, 26–31 Octubre 1970), pp. 31–115.

21. Information on planning was given by Lic. Alfredo Genel and Lic. Francisco de la Concha, Dirección de Estudios Económicos, Secretaría de la Presidencia, México, D.F., March 3, 1971.

22. See "Social Security Merge Urged," *The News* (Mexico City), March 5, 1971.

23. See *ISSSTE,* no. 1 (January 1971), p. 3.

24. Interviews in Mexico City with: Lic. Francisco Plancarte, representative of the Confederación de Cámaras Nacionales de Comercio a la Comisión de Vigilancia del IMSS, March 2, 1971; Lic. Humberto Escoto, Secretario Técnico de la Comisión de Seguridad Social de las Cámaras de Industrias, March 9, 1971; and Dr. Hugo Italo Morales, Profesor de Derecho del Trabajo y Seguridad Social, UNAM, March 16, 1971.

25. I have compiled comparative tables of the benefits available for civil servants under most social security state funds and their agreements with ISSSTE and IMSS using the excellent archives of Professor Héctor Fix Zamurio, Instituto de Investigaciones Jurídicas, UNAM. These tables are not included in this study to avoid excessive complexity.

26. Secretaría de Industria y Comercio, Dirección General de Estadísticas, *IX censo general de población y vivienda,* México D.F., 28 de enero de 1970.

27. For this and other geoeconomic divisions, see: Angel Bassols, *La división económica regional en México* (México, D.F.: UNAM, Instituto de Investigaciones Económicas, 1967);

Claude Bataillon, *Las regiones geográficas de México* (México, D.F.: Siglo XXI, 1969); Luis Unikel and Edmundo Victoria, "Medición de algunos aspectos del desarrollo socio-económico de las entidades federativas de México, 1940-1960," *Demografía y Economía,* 4, no. 3 (1970); and Ricardo Carrillo A., "Regiones geoeconómicas de México," *El mercado de valores,* NAFINSA, 32 (March 1972).

28. Data on regions pertain to 1965 (except population which are for 1970) and come from Secretaría de Industria y Comercio, Dirección General de Estadística, *Anuario estadístico 1964-1965* (México, D.F.: 1967); and Ifigenia M. de Navarrete, "La distribución del ingreso en México: Tendencias y perspectivas," *El perfil de México en 1980,* vol. 1 (México, D.F.: Siglo XXI, 1970), pp. 70-71. See also notes 26 and 27.

29. Navarrete, pp. 70-71.

30. Ibid. Similar comparisons result from 1969 data compiled by Carrillo.

31. Secretaría de Industria y Comercio, *IX censo general de población y vivienda.*

32. IMSS, *Memoria estadística de 1971.*

33. Ibid.

34. IMSS, *Memoria de labores de 1969. Datos estadísticos* (México, D.F.: julio 1970); ISSSTE, *Anuario estadístico 1969* (n/p, n/d); and data obtained by the author in personal interviews in Mexico City, February-April, 1971.

35. ISSSTE coverage is unusually high in Baja California Sur and Quintana Roo because these, until recently, were territories which depended on the federal government and, hence, their civil servants were insured by ISSSTE.

36. Coverage in the state of México is surprisingly low: 4.3 percent, at the bottom of table 6-7. A reason for this is that a good proportion of the EAP of that state works in the D.F. and, hence, is insured there.

37. Navarrete, pp. 33, 70-71.

38. González Casanova, pp. 118, 124.

39. José Luis Reyna, "An Empirical Analysis of Political Mobilization: The Case of Mexico," Cornell University, Latin American Studies Program, Dissertation Series, no. 26, September 1971. See especially his conclusions, pp. 184-95.

40. For recommendations on financing for agricultural insured, see Leal de Araujo.

41. Lic. José Vallejo Novelo, Jefe Asuntos Internacionales, ISSSTE, interview in Mexico City, February 23, 1971.

42. In 1962 and 1964 the ratio between rpc of civil servants and that of blue- and white-collars was 6 to 1. I have computed a series for the 1960s using the same sources as table 6-10.

43. *Informe sobre la situación financiera, actuarial, administrativa y médica del Instituto Mexicano del Seguro Social* (hereafter cited as *Informe sobre la situación financiera*) (México, D.F., February 1967), pp. 103-105; and IMSS, *Memoria de labores de 1969: Datos estadísticos.*

44. Departamento de Estadística y Vigencia de Derechos, *Tendencias 1960-1979* (México, D.F.: ISSSTE, 1970), table 1.

45. James W. Wilkie's series of Mexico's percentage of public capital investment in social welfare from 1925 to 1970 (which includes social security and public health) indicates a long-run increasing trend from about 5-6 percent to 28-30 percent. See his *Statistics and National Policy* (Los Angeles, Cal.: UCLA Latin American Center, 1974), p. 169.

46. ISSSTE, *Anuario estadístico 1965-1968;* and *Informe sobre la situación financiera,* pp. 183ff.

47. ISSSTE, *Anuario estadístico 1965* and *1968* and *Manual de organización,* 1971; Humberto Luis Valdivia, "ISSSTE: un ejemplo," *La Prensa,* February 25, 1971.

48. García Cruz, vol. 1, pp. 107, 148, 255 and vol. 2, p. 44; and *Informe sobre la situación financiera,* pp. 155-56.

49. Ibid.; and ISSSTE, *Anuario estadístico 1965-1968.*

50. *Informe sobre la situación financiera,* pp. 21, 104, 141-93.

51. Ibid., pp. 6-10, 199-230.

52. Interview with Lic. Alfredo Genel, Secretaría de la Presidencia, March 3, 1971.

53. Interviews with: Directorio en Pleno del Banco Nacional del Ejército y la Armada, March 8,

1971; General Joaquín Morales Solís, Director de Seguridad Social de la Secretaría de Defensa, March 15, 1971; and José Vallejo Novelo, ISSSTE, cited; also visits of the author to the installations.

54. Interview with General Rafael Vargas Machuca, Jefe del Departamento de Pensiones de la Dirección de Pensiones Militares, March 16, 1971.

55. In 1971 the armed forces were trying to change to a system of automatic adjustment related to the increase of salaries of active personnel. See note 54.

56. The Consejo also has to process thousands of claims from employers. In the 1960s the Consejo usually met once a week with the resulting pileup of *expedientes*. Delegation of these functions in order to hasten the procedures and gain time for the Consejo to concentrate on more important matters was recommended in 1967 by the Commission of Study to Reform IMSS. See its *Informe sobre la situación financiera*.

57. According to Al Wichtrich, Executive Secretary of the American Chamber of Commerce of Mexico, the low level of and tough requisites attached to most benefits granted by IMSS have induced a proliferation of pension and fringe benefits plans through collective bargaining. The larger and wealthier enterprises—asserts Wichtrich—have been able to afford the best plans. Interview in Mexico City, March 3, 1971.

58. I visited the most important hospitals in Mexico City and held numerous interviews there. Information on the rest of the country was gathered from statistical reports and a specialized report submitted to the OAS in 1963. Hospitals visited in 1971 were: Centro Médico Nacional (IMSS), Hospital 20 de Noviembre (ISSSTE), Hospital Militar and Hospital de la Armada (armed forces), Hospital Colonia (railroads), Hospital Central de Petróleos Mexicanos (petroleum), and Hospital Azucarero (sugar). In addition interviews were conducted with a good number of physicians and administrators and with some fifty patients selected at random. Additional information came from IMSS, *Anuario estadístico de servicios médicos y de recursos humanos y materiales 1971;* ISSSTE, *Anuario estadístico, 1969;* Ferrocarriles Nacionales de México, *Servicios médicos proporcionados durante el año 1968;* Ejército Mexicano, *Anuario estadístico del Hospital Central Militar, 1968* (México, D.F.: Comercial Arte, n.d.); and Milton I. Roemer, *Medical Care in Latin America* (Washington, D.C.: Organization of American States, 1963), "Hospital Care in Mexico," pp. 125-68.

59. Secretaría de Industria y Comercio, *Anuario estadístico compendiado 1970,* pp. 70-71.

Chapter 7. The Role of Pressure Groups and the Measurement of Social Security Inequality

1. Without sufficient training in political science and sociology, I found it difficult to develop sophisticated techniques for adequately measuring the power of pressure groups; obviously, there is ample ground here for future research. I believe that my principal contribution in this study is not in this area but in that of the analysis and measurement of inequality.

2. Research being conducted now by political scientists and sociologists focusing on the role of the state and the bureaucracy versus pressure groups, devoting considerable space to historical analysis, and using sophisticated frameworks include: James Malloy, University of Pittsburgh, on Brazil; Hernando Gómez Duendía, Fedesarrollo, on Colombia; Mark Rosenberg, Florida International University, on Costa Rica; and Rose Spalding, University of North Carolina, on Mexico.

3. The role of industrialization in generating social ferment and eventually an increase in social security stratification is crucial. In some Latin American countries in which the industrialization process took place after social security was well established in the region (e.g., Costa Rica), pressure groups played a minor role, if at all, in the inception of social security. The latter was born late but unified, often as an executive tool to try to avoid the social strife suffered by the sister republics.

4. In Chile, urban blue-collars received protection at the same time as white-collars and prior to most of the labor aristocracy. However, rural workers, domestic servants, and the self-employed were not covered until considerably later.

5. For instance, the cases of Uruguay and Peru can be adapted to the second model, in which the arrow of the political parties is solid instead of dotted. The case of Chile can be adapted to the third model by adding the political parties pointing to the state with a double-pointed dotted arrow. The case of Mexico can be adapted to the second model but with the opposition substituting for the political parties and exerting influence over the pressure groups rather than over the state.

6. The four major occupational groups (blue-collars, white-collars, civil servants, and armed forces) shown in tables 7-2 and 7-3 are standardized as follows. When two groups were actually clustered in a country (e.g., blue- and white-collars in Mexico), they were entered separately in the tables and given the same score for the sake of comparison. Further, when a subgroup was not a separate entity (at least originally) but part of a major group, the subgroup was given the score of the group. Some subgroups were excluded from the tables because of a disparate nature of data available. For instance, the subgroup of teachers appeared in one country (Uruguay) as a separate all-inclusive entity; in two other countries, data were available only in part (federal teachers in Mexico, public teachers in Argentina); and in the remaining two countries, teachers were fused with the group of civil servants (Chile and Peru). If the data on teachers had been included in table 7-2 and 7-3, their scores would have been close but below the scores of civil servants. A similar problem was encountered with the self-employed. If the scattered data had been included in tables 7-2 and 7-3, the self-employed would have been ranked as below domestic servants and would thus have been the latest to receive coverage.

Standardization of groups and subgroups created the illusion of reduced inequality as shown by indicators. For instance, in the case of Mexico the groups of blue- and white-collars are clustered in reality but entered separately in the tables and given the same score for comparative purposes; this artificially increased the number of observations with equal scores and thus slightly reduced the gini coefficient. The effect of standardization was probably greater in Chile, where the deletion of various subgroups (hence eliminating divergent scores and reducing apparent inequality) and the separate tabulation for other subgroups actually part of a major group (hence artificially increasing the number of observations with equal scores and reducing apparent inequality) lowered inequality indicators. The alternative, including *all* groups and subgroups as they actually were in each country, would obviously have resulted in more accurate indicators of inequality but would have made comparisons almost impossible, created theoretical complications with the typology used to explain the inception of the stratified social security system, and made it difficult to detect the direction of inequality.

For the sake of a standardized comparison, in tables 7-2 and 7-3 the group/subgroup is given a score when it first received coverage and even if only against one risk or in one program. Thus a group or subgroup may be given the same score in two countries but in one was only covered for a single risk (death) while in another it received coverage against all risks (old age, disability, and death). Or a group or subgroup may receive the same score in two countries while its scope of coverage is much larger in one country than another. In all these instances, standardization has the indeliberate effect of diminishing existing inequalities, hence, the resulting indicator is lower than if all the actual disparities in historical coverage had been included in the computation. An opposite effect (that is, increasing inequalities artificially) results when a group/subgroup which had not yet historically appeared is compared with one which was in existence. For instance, in the early nineteenth century there were militarymen in all of the five countries, but there were no railroad workers. The earliest the latter could have received coverage was by the mid-nineteenth century, for that reason the indicator of inequality is artificially increased.

7. The standard deviation is based on the mean of each country. Some consideration was given to using a mean for the whole table or a mean of the means of the five countries, but this technique was discarded because it seriously distorted the computation.

8. In the computation of the standard deviation for Uruguay, the score of the military was deleted. The reason was that in Uruguay, health coverage was provided early in the century through voluntary mutual insurance funds and, in some cases, affiliation to mutual funds paid by the employer through collective contracts. Information on this type of coverage is scarce,

dubious, and incomplete. Compulsory coverage did not come through until the 1960s, and this is shown in the table. In the case of the military, health coverage refers to the hospital built for this group at the beginning of the century. Since the terms of comparison were different and the military score heavily distorted the indicator, I decided to treat the military score as an outlier and eliminate it from the computation.

9. This type of data is shown for the first time here since that published by international and regional organizations (e.g., ILO, OAS) is limited to the major insured group (or two major groups) in the country (e.g., IMSS plus ISSSTE in Mexico). Furthermore, with the exception of Chile, the countries do not have easily accessible coverage data on other groups and sub-groups. Table 7-4, therefore, is the distillation of painstaking work in compiling, refining, filling gaps, and standardizing dispersed statistics from the five countries.

10. Uruguay shows a negative rate due to the process of unification which partly eliminated duplication in statistical coverage.

11. It should be noticed, however, that data on dependent insured in Peru are incomplete and hence actual coverage should be higher.

12. Low supportive ratios in the last three countries—particularly Uruguay—are also a function of the age structure of their populations which have a lower proportion of young people and a higher proportion of old people than the Mexican and Peruvian populations.

13. The indicator referring to the EAP is more accurate than that regarding the total population because the former is based on more comprehensive and comparable data than the latter.

14. Three types of statistical problems affect the comparison: first, the groups are not strictly comparable because of definitional discrepancies which result in different clustering of sub-groups into the major groups; second, blue- and white-collars are disaggregated only in Chile and Peru; and third, self-employed are fused with blue- and white-collars in Chile and Mexico, while in Argentina their high proportion distorts the whole percentage distribution for the country.

15. Another variable that may affect the distribution of insured is the level of development of the country in question which influences the overall size of the urban blue- and white-collar sector. The rankings of Chile, Uruguay, and Peru permit the possibility of a combination of both variables (age of the social security system and level of development), but the ranking of Argentina suggests that development has little impact in determining the proportion of blue- and white-collars within the insured. Mexico's high ranking, even though this country has the youngest social security system, may be explained by its developmental level combined with the fact that a very small proportion of the labor force is insured.

16. This is done by reducing the Chilean figure to 2 percent by excluding policemen and increasing the Peruvian figure to 3 percent to allow for underestimation.

17. The value of the table is greatly reduced because: first, there are no data for Uruguay; second, dates for the four countries vary from 1960 to 1969 and the more recent the data, the better the coverage should be and vice versa; and, third, the categories of salaried employees (white-collars and civil servants) and wage-earners (blue-collars) had to be aggregated for comparison.

18. Disaggregated data—not presented in the table—for salaried and wage-earners, available in Chile and Peru, do not show any significant difference between the two groups in Chile, but in Peru salaried employees are fully covered while less than half of the wage-earners are covered.

19. The table presents several problems: first, data are not available for Peru and Uruguay; second, dates for the three countries vary from 1960 to 1969; and third, in order to standardize the economic groups for comparative purposes, it was necessary to cluster subgroups (for which data occasionally were disaggregated). As a result of the clustering, differences in the degree of coverage among subgroups were reduced because they tend to compensate for each other. For instance, within the service group in developing countries, usually bank employees (who make up a small proportion of the labor force) are fully covered while domestic servants (who make up a sizable proportion of the labor force) have a very small degree, if any, of coverage. When these two subgroups are clustered, the resulting average is forced down,

hiding the substantial disparity of coverage between the two. Conversely, in other cases, the clustering of various subgroups results in a rise of the average for the overall group. In the case of Chile, copper workers (who constitute a substantial proportion of the labor force) are over-protected and, when they are clustered with manufacturing and construction (with only a fair degree of coverage), the average degree of coverage of the overall industrial group is raised dramatically.

20. The table presents three statistical problems. First, although the regional population was taken in all countries from census data or estimates made by census agencies, different techniques were used to calculate the number of insured. In Chile and Mexico the active insured is the sum of most insured under pension programs in all states/provinces. In Peru, however, the active insured is a sum of the insured in pension programs only in the most populated province of each department. In Argentina and Uruguay the active insured is an estimate based, respectively, on data on passive insured (pensioners) and expenditures in family allowances. (There are also differences in the dates used for the comparison—1960 to 1969—but these are not too important because the percentage of the total population covered in that period did not change substantially except in Mexico.) The second problem confronted in table 7-8 is that the number of regions fluctuates from two to eight in the five countries and, the more disaggregated the data (i.e., as more regions are distinguished), the more the actual geographical inequalities are revealed (e.g., in Argentina). Conversely when there are fewer and hence broader regions, differences in coverage tend to be compensated and inequality is hidden (e.g., in Chile and Uruguay). The way in which the region is formed is also important to reveal or hide inequality. For instance, Argentina is the only country in which the federal capital is included as a region and because its coverage is significantly higher than that of the rest of the country, it dramatically increases the national score of inequality. (To assure a better comparability, the federal capital in Argentina was clustered with the region in which it is located—Pampa.) Conversely, in Mexico, the Federal District (with the highest coverage in the nation) is clustered with states of the Central region (e.g., Mexico, Zacatecas, Puebla, Tlaxcala) which have the lowest degree of coverage, hence compensating for each other and artificially reducing the inequality scores. The third statistical problem is created by the disparities in the comprehensiveness of the data on the insured population. Because data on geographical distribution of active insured were not available for all funds, the proportion of insured used in the computations varies; for instance, civil servants were included in three countries, but partially excluded in Peru, and totally excluded in Chile.

21. This table eliminates or reduces some of the statistical problems of table 7-8. It adds one problem, however, the lack of data on Uruguay, and it cannot correct the difficulties resulting from the way that estimates of the Argentinian and Peruvian insured population were done. Dates for the four countries also vary in table 7-9, from 1960 to 1969, but less than in table 7-8. The variation in the number of observations is much less a problem here: there are 24 or 25 states/provinces in three countries and 32 states in Mexico. Also in table 7-9, we deal with more and smaller geographical units and hence the distortions caused by regional clustering are almost eliminated. For instance, the capital city or metropolitan area is included in all countries which thus eliminates this source of disparity. Technically there is no difference in the comprehensiveness of the data used in the two tables. However, in table 7-9 we compare two more related sets of data, that is, the EAP and the active insured, while in table 7-8, we compare the total population not with total insured (active plus passive plus dependent) but with the active insured alone.

22. In Argentina the civil service, banking, merchant marine, and railroad were included and only the armed forces were excluded. In Mexico the civil service was included, but armed forces, railroads, and part of banking were excluded. Conversely in Peru part of the civil servants and white-collars, and the armed forces were excluded. Finally, in Chile, all civil servants, railroads, merchant marine, armed forces, and most banks were excluded.

23. Appendix A summarizes the legal data on salary percentage contributions due from employees and employers plus state by programs (pensions, health, and "others") in the four major groups, and adds, at the bottom, the total percentage contribution to all programs. The

complexity of the table, even with partial information only, makes evident the impossibility of comparing data from all subgroups. It should be pointed out, however, that the exclusion of data from the subgroups favors those countries that have a very stratified system (such as Chile and Uruguay) because disparity among subgroups is hidden. Originally, I thought of using the range (the lowest and highest salary percentage contribution in any group within the system) and the resulting interval of range as a measure of inequality, i.e., the higher the interval, the higher the inequality. This technique proved to be inadequate because seldom did the lowest and highest percentages correspond systematically to the same group. Furthermore, the frequent lack of a percentage in the armed forces resulted, in some cases, in zero being the lowest percentage in the system. This technique actually measured the disparity among all legally determined percentages but not the inequality of the system. The key problem was how to detect the direction of inequality or the progressiveness/regressiveness of the system in terms of its impact upon income distribution. Obviously, if this problem were to be solved, some type of ranking of the groups according to their income was necessary.

24. The formula used for computing the ratios was

$$1 + \frac{\bar{X} - X_i}{\bar{X}},$$

in which $\bar{X}$ represents the most progressive course and X_i any other score.

25. In one case (armed forces in Mexico) this portion was equivalent to almost the total revenues of the entire system, since the employee paid only a nominal fee. In another case (armed forces in Uruguay), that portion represented the whole employer-state contribution. In most cases, the undetermined portion was to be added to a fixed percentage based on the employee salary and paid by the state. If the undetermined portion had been ignored in the comparison, the results would have been seriously distorted, e.g., the armed forces of Mexico and Uruguay would have appeared as having no percentage at all paid by the state.

26. If, instead of using the combined white-collar employee plus employer-state percentage as the basis for the estimate, the blue-collar combined percentage had been used, the results would have been slightly different: decreasing Chilean inequality and increasing Peruvian inequality.

27. The formula used is the one in note 24.

28. The table presents serious difficulties: (a) the revenue data comes from several years (1965–1972) and is confined to one single year while an average of various years would have been better; (b) data are missing on the armed forces in three countries and on civil servants in one country; (c) there are different clusters (e.g., blue-collars and white-collars, white-collars and civil servants) which cannot be disaggregated and hence impede a systematic comparison among groups; (d) in the cases of Chile and Uruguay, data on subgroups were clustered into the corresponding major group and averaged, hence hiding inequalities; and (e) in the cases of Argentina, Mexico, and Peru, only major groups were included because of lack of data on the subgroups, also hiding inequality but to a lesser extent than in Chile and Uruguay.

29. The gini technique compares two distributions (in this case insured and their payments) and shows the disparity ("inequality") between the two: as the two distributions become more equal, the gini index decreases (and vice versa); if the two distributions are exactly alike—perfect equality—the gini index is zero. Since the gini index does not rank groups according to their income, it cannot detect the progressiveness or regressiveness of the financial system in terms of income distribution. For instance, in table 7-12, it is obvious that Chile has the two most divergent distributions (insured and revenue), while Uruguay has the two most similar distributions; hence we should expect the gini index for Chile to be the highest and that for Uruguay the lowest and, indeed this is the case (gini indices are: Chile 44.6, Mexico 33.7, Argentina 2.0, Peru 1.1, and Uruguay 0.2). If we had used ginis, therefore, Chile would have appeared as the most unequal system of the five; but if we had taken income distribution into account, Chile would have been the least unequal system. One way to correct this problem would be to assign positive and negative signs to the gini coefficients—based on the visual inspection of the two distributions. When this is done, the gini index then reflects income inequality and a different

ranking is produced: Peru −1.1, Uruguay −0.2, Argentina +2.0, Mexico +33.7, and Chile +44.6. The problem is that this method is not reliable enough and, besides, ginis with signs create technical difficulties when used in factor analysis and similar techniques.

30. The table presents the same problems found in table 7-12 plus an additional one: not all the revenue paid by the employer and the state is accounted for. For instance, in most countries, revenue from taxes and state absorption of deficits is not included. In some cases (e.g., Chile) practically all revenue is accounted for, and hence the degree of inequality of the financing system is truly reflected, while in the others it is hidden. The value of this table is, therefore, greatly reduced.

31. The gini index (with signs attached) ratifies the visual rankings of inequality: Chile (−30.3), Uruguay (−2.3), Argentina (+2.0), Peru (+5.0), and Mexico (+8.6).

32. The gini index of inequality (with signs attached) does not rank the countries exactly as the indicator of table 7-14 does: Chile (−33.5), Mexico (−24.4), Peru (−6.1), Argentina (+2.5), and Uruguay (+6.4). In this gini ranking, Uruguay is the least unequal system, while, in the indicator-ranking, Uruguay is the third most unequal system. Indicators based on table 7-14 (like those of table 7-13) may distort reality, as inequality becomes largely a function of the availability of data. And yet, the unification process of social security in Argentina and Peru must have had a positive impact in reducing inequalities in the financial systems of these countries (excluding the military, of course).

33. The extreme differential ratios in employee financing were 2.8 (percentage contribution) and 2.0 (revenue per capita). The extreme differential ratios in employer-state financing jumped to 5.0 (percentage contribution) and 14.5 (revenue per capita). This shows relative uniformity among countries in their employee contribution but substantial disparity in their employer-state contribution.

34. Appendix F shows the index of total revenue per capita by major occupational groups that can be compared with the information on national income per capita for similar groups discussed elsewhere in this book. The country that allows the best comparison is Chile because it provides almost comprehensive data on social security revenue by groups. In terms of national income, white-collars in Chile receive an average of 2 to 4 times the income of blue-collars (which are in the lower-income stratum); in terms of social security revenue, the former receives 5 times the average of the latter. Civil servants and the armed forces are ranked in Chile in the upper-middle income stratum and receive from 6 to 8 times the income of blue-collars; in terms of social security revenue, civil servants receive more than twice the average revenue received by blue-collars, while the armed forces receive more than 8 times the revenue of blue-collars. (Data on subgroups from table 2-10 show that subgroups in the labor aristocracy, e.g., bank employees, receive almost 10 times the social security revenue of blue-collars.) Mexico provides another revealing example of parallel inequalities in national income per capita and social security revenue per capita. Mexican civil servants (clustering federal, state, and local) earn an average of 3.5 times the average income of blue-collar workers in agriculture; in terms of social security, federal civil servants receive 4 times the revenue accrued by the average blue-collar worker.

According to appendix F (confined to the major groups), extreme differential ratios in social security revenue per capita in Peru, Argentina, and Uruguay are 1 to 1.3, 1 to 1.5, and 1 to 1.7 respectively. These differences are considerably smaller than those in national income. However, disaggregated data on subgroups available from the chapters on Argentina (table 5-10) and Uruguay (table 3-10) unveil the true magnitude of inequality. In the case of Argentina (in 1961 prior to the partial unification of the social security system) the occupational subgroups at the bottom of both the national income and social security revenue per capita are domestic servants and rural workers. The middle-income bracket, which includes the bulk of industrial and commercial workers, makes from 2 to 5 times the income of the bottom; in terms of social security revenue, however, these subgroups made from 8 to 13 times the average revenue per capita of domestic servants and rural workers. Finally, the higher-income bracket, which includes top military officers, civil servants, and selected employees in the labor aristocracy (e.g., banking, railroads, public utilities) make from 6 to 10 times the income of the bottom subgroup;

in terms of social security revenue, however, these subgroups receive from 8 to 23 times the average social security revenue of the bottom. Data for Uruguay (in 1969 when social security unification had begun) are less accurate than for Argentina, but also show domestic servants and rural workers at the bottom of both the national income and social security revenue ladders. The bulk of industrial workers, commerce employees, and civil servants, included in the middle-income bracket, receives from 1.5 to 2 times the average social security revenue of domestic servants and rural workers. Selected officials of the armed forces and the labor aristocracy included in the high-income bracket, receive from 3 to 8 times the average social security revenue of the bottom.

35. The table presents several problems. First, the years in the comparison vary from 1969 to 1973; in the two countries that had data on 1973 (Argentina and Peru), the unification process had a significant impact in reducing inequality. Second, only the main funds in each group were included and practically all subgroups were excluded; this works in favor of highly stratified systems (such as Chile, Uruguay, and to a lesser extent Argentina) because inequalities are hidden. Third, the armed forces group is not eligible for certain benefits due to its nature, i.e., militarymen cannot receive maternity leave or unemployment relief. The same is true of the self-employed; they do not have an employer and, hence, are not eligible for benefits connected with occupational hazards and unemployment, and seldom qualify for family allowances. A better alternative to the technique used in this study was suggested by Richard Wilson in the SSRC seminar held in Mexico in the summer of 1975: to calculate a percentage of the number of benefits actually available for a group/subgroup from the maximum number of benefits for which such a group/subgroup *could naturally have been eligible*. This technique can take care of the problem of the ineligibility of militarymen and self-employed for certain benefits. Unfortunately it was not possible to use it here because at the time it was suggested all the basic computations for this study had been completed.

36. In Chile, employees in private banking have the highest number of benefits in the system: 31 compared with 28 for white-collars and civil servants. In Peru and Uruguay, bank employees have the same number of benefits as the armed forces and civil servants. In Mexico, petroleum employees enjoy more benefits than the armed forces (and electrical employees have the same number of benefits). In Peru, petroleum and electrical employees have more benefits than white-collars. Conversely, in Mexico and Peru, domestic servants and most self-employed did not have any benefits at all until the 1970s.

37. For the sake of comparison, only major groups were included in Mexico and Peru; in Argentina, Chile, and Uruguay subgroups were clustered under the corresponding major groups; and self-employed were excluded in all cases. The exclusion and merging of subgroups probably hides inequality, particularly in the most stratified systems like Chile and Uruguay. Even with this standardization, the table presents serious difficulties for an accurate comparison because blue-collars and white-collars are merged in Argentina, Mexico, and Uruguay, while white-collars and civil servants are merged in Peru, and the armed forces are excluded in Peru due to lack of data. The result of these statistical disparities is that inequality is most revealed in Chile where there are four observations because all the four major groups are included and disaggregated (hence possibly compensating for the hidden inequality due to the clustering of subgroups). Inequality is least revealed in Peru where there are only two observations because one group is missing and two are merged. Varying dates (1966–1969) are not significant enough to distort the comparison. However, if 1973 data had been used, inequality in Argentina would probably have been reduced since in the late 1960s the unification process had not begun.

38. In the financing section the gini technique did not work and a ratio technique was substituted. Appendix G shows the computations for the ratio of average pension per capita, done in a manner similar to that for appendices D through F. The ranking of inequality based on the ratios is similar to that based on the ginis, except that, in the former, Uruguay becomes the least unequal system: Mexico (8.3), Chile (3.1), Argentina (2.6), Peru (1.3), and Uruguay (1.0). I decided to use the gini over the ratio technique here since most indicators in the benefit section are based on ginis and it was convenient to have the same technique for the final aggregation

into the index of inequality. It should be noticed, however, that the ranking of Peru as the least unequal system is an illusion created by the data: if information on the armed forces and the old civil servant system had been included, it is obvious that the inequality indicator for Peru would have been considerably higher.

39. The accuracy of the table is questionable due to several statistical problems. First, Argentina and Uruguay do not have a national health insurance divided by major occupational groups as do the other three countries. Data on Argentina are not available, while that of Uruguay is not strictly comparable to the rest except for the armed forces. Second, figures for Chile are crude estimates whose accuracy is difficult to assess. Third, in some cases, data on civil servants and the armed forces are underestimated either due to statistical problems or because contracts with other hospitals are not accounted for.

40. The statistical deficiencies explained for the table are compounded in this indicator with two additional problems. First, the number of observations in the table is 3 in most cases but 5 in Chile and 2 in Uruguay, which tends to increase inequality in the former and reduce inequality in the latter. Second, the direction of inequality is not identical throughout the table: in 5 cases the armed forces have the lowest score in the system, while civil servants have the lowest score in 1 case.

41. Data by state/province were not available and, hence, the reader should recall the discussion in the section on coverage pertaining to the statistical problems which result from the use of regions as units of comparison. Some of these problems are clearly visible in table 7-19; for instance, the number of regions fluctuates from 8 in Argentina to 2 in Uruguay and the larger the number of regions, the more inequality is revealed. Another problem results from the inclusion of the federal capital or metropolitan area (as regions) in Argentina and Uruguay. Because of this inclusion, the range of beds in Argentina goes from 2.9 to 10.2, while the range in physicians goes from 4.1 to 45.9 (respective ranges in Uruguay are 5.4 to 7.6 and 4.5 to 19.5). When measuring inequality in coverage by region (table 7-8), the Argentinian federal capital was clustered with the Pampa region to avoid this problem. In that case, however, Uruguay was not included in the comparison, while the latter is included in table 7-19; since we only have Montevideo (the capital city) and the rest of the country in Uruguay, a cluster here is out of the question. (If we had clustered the federal capital with the Pampa region in Argentina, the gini index would have been reduced to 10.2 in beds and 19.5 in physicians. If we had deleted the federal capital altogether, ginis would have been further reduced to 8.2 in beds and 16.6 in physicians.)

42. The gini index for Argentina is artificially raised in both indicators due to the problems explained above (largest number of regions plus inclusion of the federal capital). In the case of Uruguay we have two different factors operating against each other: the lowest number of regions (which artificially reduces inequality) and the inclusion of the federal capital (which increases inequality).

43. The coverage dimension actually includes two indicators (5 and 6) which measure the degree of coverage among strata of insured, that is, inequality within the social security system.

44. Another alternative would have been to rank the countries not among themselves but related to an independent scale probably on deciles. This technique would have presented a problem in that the data in this study have ordinal rather than interval properties (for this reason factor-scoring was ruled out). Since there were only five countries in this study, I thought the technique selected would be more accurate, easier to understand, and have more visible impact.

45. To check the ranking resulting from this technique, two alternative techniques were used which produced *identical* rankings: (a) a country with a missing rank in an indicator was assigned an average rank based on that country's mean value of the available ranks of other indicators within the corresponding dimension; in this technique the ranks of the remaining countries were kept *unchanged;* (b) a missing rank was filled as in (a), and then the rank of countries that were in the same position or above the average rank assigned were *moved upward.* For example, in indicator 5, Uruguay's missing rank was filled in with that country's

average rank of the three indicators in the coverage dimension (i.e., 2). If the first alternative had been used, the rankings of the other four countries would have remained unchanged. Conversely, if the second alternative had been used, the rank of Argentina would have remained unchanged (at 1), and the ranks of the other countries would have moved upward: Chile (from 2 to 3), Mexico (from 3 to 4), and Peru (from 4 to 5). Since these two techniques involved statistical manipulation and did not generate any change in ranking, I decided not to use them.

46. Argentina receives higher rank values in regional distribution of health benefits than Mexico; the reason is that the federal capital (with the best facilities) is included as a region in Argentina (thus increasing the indicator of inequality), while in Mexico it is merged with regions that have poor facilities (hence hiding real inequality). In addition, the indicator of pensions per capita in Argentina is based on the year 1966, prior to the unification process which probably reduced inequality. Finally, data on Argentinian health facilities by occupational groups are not available and, as a result, this country's mean (in the benefit dimension) is boosted by its upwardly biased ranks in the regional indicators.

47. To further test the overall rankings, a selection was made of the two most accurate indicators within each dimension: 1 and 2 in appearance, 4 and 8 in coverage, 9 and 10 in financing, and 16 and 18 in benefits. Both the mean of the four dimension means and the mean of all eight indicators (averaged without clustering) resulted in the same overall ranking as that in table 7-22.

Index

strategic sectors, 32, 260. *See also* Labor, organization
Urban labor force, as pressure group, 12–13, 169–72, 259
Urbanization, 6, 46–48

Varela, José Pedro, 71
Vargas, Getulio, 13
Velasco Alvarado, Juan, 120
Velázquez, Fidel, 215
Venezuela, 13
Vigilance Committees, 121
Vives, Juan Luis, 18

War of the Pacific, 22, 114
Welfare bureaucracy. *See* Social security, bureaucracy
White-collars: social security protection for, 9–10, 163, 216, 228
—as pressure group: Arg., 168–72; Chile, 31–32; Mex., 222–24; Peru, 119, 125–26; Uru., 82–83
—organization and structure: Arg., 176–77; Chile, 36; Mex., 228; Peru, 130–31; Uru., 87
Williman, Claudio, 73
Wolfe, Marshall, 9

Yrigoyen, Hipólito, 161–63, 172